TELEGRAPH AND TRAVEL.

TELEGRAPH AND TRAVEL

A NARRATIVE OF THE FORMATION AND DEVELOPMENT
OF TELEGRAPHIC COMMUNICATION BETWEEN ENGLAND
AND INDIA, UNDER THE ORDERS OF HER MAJESTY'S
GOVERNMENT, WITH INCIDENTAL NOTICES OF THE
COUNTRIES TRAVERSED BY THE LINES.

BY

COLONEL SIR FREDERIC JOHN GOLDSMID, C.B., K.C.S.I.,

Late Chief Director of the Government Indo-European Telegraph; British Commissioner for settlement of the Perso-Beluch Frontier (1870-71), and Arbitrator in the Perso-Afghan Boundary Question (1872-73).

WITH MAPS AND NUMEROUS ILLUSTRATIONS.

London:
MACMILLAN AND CO.
1874.

[The Right of Translation and Reproduction is reserved.]

LONDON:
CLAY, SONS, AND TAYLOR, PRINTERS,
BREAD STREET HILL.

THIS VOLUME IS INSCRIBED,

WITH SENTIMENTS OF RESPECT AND REGARD,

TO

HIS EXCELLENCY THE

RIGHT HON. LORD LYONS, G.C.B., D.C.L.,

ETC., ETC.,

IN REMEMBRANCE OF HIS KIND AND VALUABLE AID

TO THE CAUSE OF THE INDO-EUROPEAN TELEGRAPH,

WHEN FULFILLING

THE HIGH OFFICE OF HER MAJESTY'S AMBASSADOR IN PARIS,

AND AT CONSTANTINOPLE.

PREFACE.

One word on the much-discussed question of spelling Oriental words in English. Calcutta, Cawnpore, and an occasional other Indian name have been left in conventional but convenient faultiness. In other respects, as a general rule, the system last adopted by the Indian Government has been followed: and the reader is requested to bear in mind that, under this system, "a" without an accent is short, although there are many instances in which the accent, once used, is not repeated, or is omitted because palpably understood; "e" is pronounced as in Fez: "i" is invariably like *ee*; "o" is an English *o*; and "u" is invariably *oo*. Aware that deviations from an established principle of phonetics applied to language are fairly chargeable to philological inconsistency or ignorance, the author has reserved a respectful argument or excuse for a few exceptional cases. Here and there, however, he admits a difficulty in the absence of any authentic native spelling, such as for certain fishing villages on the Arabian side of the Persian Gulf.

viii   PREFACE.

He has been purposely sparing of accents, using the simple long accent to denote a marked sound, or where the circumflex would be written in French. To take one vowel in illustration, its effect upon a would be to deepen, as in *âpre*; upon âi, âo, âu, to separate the two vowels, as in the Italian words *aveû* and Aosta, and the Italian pronunciation of Menelaus; while aí, aó, aú, would simply need the greater stress upon the second letter.

Another word on the photographs or original drawings which have been so carefully reproduced in Mr. Cooper's woodcuts. The views of Muskat and Masandam stations are from photographs by Messrs. Lindley and Warren, of Bombay; Astrakhan is from a Russian photograph obtained on the spot; and the "Kothal Pir Zan" is from an original coloured drawing by Major O. B. St. John, R.E.

Of the smaller illustrations or vignettes in the first book, the tailpiece of the introductory chapter, the Caxaquez Monument, Kaäaba Library, Zobeide's Tomb, and the Wall of Gwádar, are from photographs; the Kothal Dukhtar is Major St. John's; Khasab is by Lieutenant Hewitt, I.N.; the "Chasseur à Cheval" is by Mr. Gerard Thomas, M.A.; and Fâo is by some friend unknown. The remainder are from original coloured drawings by Major Bateman-Champain, R.E.

In the second book, the Zouave and Ezra's Tomb, in Chapter VI.; the Persians, in Chapters VII. and VIII.; all but the Bastinado, in Chapters IX. and X.; the Shah, and the Bridge at Ispahan, in Chapter XI.; and the Georgian Minstrels and Baluchis, in Chapter XII., are from photographs. The rest are from original drawings, of which the Bastinado and Travelling Chapar are by Captain W. H. Pierson, R.E., to whom is due also the design on the title-page; Demavend, Miān-Kotbal, and Besitun are by Major Bateman-Champain; and others are by kind friends, the omission of whose names will not lead them to suppose that their favours are unappreciated or forgotten.

Yet one word more; last in order, but not least important in any sense,—the author would express his great and heartfelt obligations to Major-General Sir William Baker, R.E., K.C.B., to Mr. William Thornton, C.E., and those authorities at the India Office who have afforded him the same steady aid and support in the matter of this book, as in that of his telegraph superintendence generally; a support which has comprehended the sacrifice of time and convenience, and the investigation of dry detail. And he gladly takes the present opportunity of warmly thanking his successor and late coadjutor, Major Bateman-Champain, R.E., and his late coadjutors and companions, Major Oliver St. John, and Captain William Henry Pierson, R.E., for their original and valuable drawings, and other assistance rendered to him in preparing his volume for the press. He is also much indebted, for a readily-given and efficient revision of parts of his book, to Major-General Sir Arnold Kemball, C.B., K.C.S.I., to Lieutenant Stiffe, I.N., and

PREFACE.

Mr. Alfred Brasher. What have been the services of the officers of Royal Engineers and other their fellow-labourers, towards perfecting the "Government Indo-European Telegraph," it will be his agreeable duty to render some account of in the following pages.

If a "second last word" be allowable, the undersigned would acknowledge, though by such acknowledgment he cannot discharge, a heavy debt of gratitude to Mr. George Grove for most patient, courteous, and real aid in passing this volume through the press.

F. J. G.

1, SOUTHWELL GARDENS,
    11th May, 1874.

CONTENTS.

PART I.
TELEGRAPH.

INTRODUCTORY 1

CHAPTER I.
MEMOIR OF COLONEL PATRICK STEWART 9

CHAPTER II.
PRELIMINARY ARRANGEMENTS IN ASIATIC TURKEY.—NEGOTIATIONS WITH THE OTTOMAN GOVERNMENT 60

CHAPTER III.
THE PERSIAN GULF CABLE.—MATERIAL AND MANUFACTURE.—HOW LAID.—SOME ACCOUNT OF THE CABLE STATIONS; AND OF THE PEOPLE, PORTS, OR PLACES OF ANCHORAGE IN ARABIA AND OPPOSITE COAST 112

CHAPTER IV.
PERSIAN LAND LINES.—COLONEL STEWART'S REPORT OF THE COUNTRY. —NEGOTIATIONS WITH THE SHAH.—THE FIRST LINE AND WIRE. TURCO-PERSIAN CONVENTION.—OPENING OF TELEGRAPHIC COMMUNICATION.—DEATH OF COLONEL STEWART 182

CHAPTER V.
POLITICAL AND OTHER DIFFICULTIES IN THE INDO-PERSIAN AND INDO-OTTOMAN TELEGRAPHS.—CONVENTION WITH PERSIA OF 23RD NOVEMBER, 1865, FOR SECOND WIRE.—SECOND CONVENTION PROPOSED, IN FOLLOWING YEAR, FOR EXTENDING LAND TELEGRAPH, AND PROVIDING AN ALTERNATIVE LINE TO THE CABLE BETWEEN GWÁDAR AND BUSHAHR ; PUT ASIDE IN THE SPRING, BUT REVIVED IN THE WINTER OF 1867, AND CONCLUDED IN GREATLY MODIFIED FORM IN 1869.—DIPLOMATIC ACTION THEREON.— FULFILMENT OF CONVENTION OF 1865.—REPORTS OF OFFICERS CONCERNED 249

CONTENTS

CHAPTER VI

ORIGIN AND PROGRESS OF THE INDO-PERSIAN LINES — MEASURES TAKEN GENERALLY TO IMPROVE TELEGRAPHIC COMMUNICATIONS WITH INDIA FROM FIRST INAUGURATION TO CONGRESS OF VIENNA, 1868. — LAYING ROUND CABLE BETWEEN JASK AND BUSHAHR — EXTENSION OF MAKRAN COAST LINE WESTWARD TO JASK: WITH SCHEME OF WORK BEYOND THE CONGRESS ... 345

PART II

TRAVEL

CHAPTER VII

BUSHAHR: HOW REACHED FROM THE PERSIAN GULF — BAGHDAD TO CONSTANTINOPLE VIA MOSUL AND MARDIN ...

CHAPTER VIII

BAGHDAD TO CONSTANTINOPLE — THE ROUTE CONTINUED THROUGH DIARBEKR, SIVAS, ANGORA, AND BY STEAMER FROM ISMID ... 434

CHAPTER IX

LONDON TO KARACHI VIA ST. PETERSBURG, MOSCOW, AND ACROSS THE STEPPES — IN SEARCH OF THE EASTERN CRIMEA ... 474

CHAPTER X

LONDON TO KARACHI — THE ROUTE CONTINUED FROM NIJNI NOVGOROD BY THE VOLGA TO ASTRAKHAN, AND THENCE BY THE CASPIAN TO TEHRAN ... 505

CHAPTER XI

TEHRAN — THE ROUTE TO KARACHI CONTINUED, THROUGH ISFAHAN AND YEZD TO KARMAN ... 541

CHAPTER XII

KARMAN TO CHAHBAR AND KARACHI — THENCE TO THE THREE INDIAN PRESIDENCIES AND SIMLA — SOMETHING ALSO ABOUT KARACHI TO GWADAR AND CHAHBAR: WITH A FINAL GLANCE AT THESE OVERLAND ROUTES AND CITIES FOUND IN THEM ... 582

APPENDIX ... 639

INDEX ... 661

LIST OF ILLUSTRATIONS.

STEEL ENGRAVING.

Colonel Patrick Stewart, C.B., engraved by Jeens . . . . . *Page* 9

WOOD ENGRAVINGS.

Masandam; with Telegraph Station on Elphinstone Island.	*Frontispiece*
The Common Nile Boat . . . . *Page*	8
Cawnpore Monument	35
Library, with Stewart Memorial Window, at Karachi	59
Baghdad; Tomb of Zobeide	77
Ma'l Fort and Flag-staff, Fão, Turkish Arabia	95
Khasab; near Entrance of Persian Gulf, Arabian Side	112
Saif Bin Salim, Wali of Gwádar, 1862-3	123
Maskat . . . . *To face*	144
Lingah, Persian Gulf	151
Kothal Pir Zan; between Shiraz and the Sea . . . . . *To face*	186
Yezdikhast; between Shiraz and Ispahan	226
Tomb of Esther and Mordecai, at Hamadan, Western Persia	248
Kothal Dukhtar; between Shiraz and the Sea	308
Chasseur à Cheval, Persia	324
Jask, Makran Coast	367
The *Tweed* paying out Persian Gulf Cable, in tow of Steamer	390
The Prophet Ezra's Tomb, on the Tigris	397
Altun Kiupri	419
Artillery Soldier, 1855-6	428

xiv   LIST OF ILLUSTRATIONS

	PAGE
Infantry Sentry, 1865-6	428
Turkish Infantry, 1869	429
Persian Servant: Tabrizi	433
Yuzgat	462
Persian Servant (Baghdadi)	473
Great Bell of Moscow	485
Astrakhan Fish Dog-cart	505
Kalmuck of the Steppes near Astrakhan	512
Astrakhan	To face 516
Hindu Pilgrim	525
The "Felek," or Bastinado	537
Tiflis Wine-seller	540
Demavend	546
Kurds, or Irregular Cavalry	553
The Shah	554
Bridge at Ispahan	560
Kashkai: Member of a large Iliat Tribe	576
Sentry	581
Baluch of Makran	589
Pashtun, one march east of Kirmanshah, Western Persia	598
Baluch Woman: Coast of Makran	617
Georgian Minstrels, from a Tiflis Photograph	625
"Chaparing"	627
Man Kasch?	659

MAPS.

A Map showing the Routes of Colonel Sir F. J. Goldsmid, in Asiatic Turkey, Persia, and Baluchistan	To face	1
A Map of the Telegraphs to India, 1874	To face	349
Diagram of the Diversion of the Persian Gulf Cable from Elphinstone Island to Henjam and Jask	To face	649

ERRATA.

Page 20, line 2, *for* "Ampta" *read* "Amtah."

Page 103, line 11, *for* "miles" *read* "inches."

Pages 193, 194, 196 passim, *for* "Khushki Zard" *read* "Kushk-i-zard."

Page 259, line 8, and pages 257, 258 passim, *for* "Whittenbacke" *read* "Whittenback."

Page 268, line 6 from bottom, *for* "Meilis" *read* "Mejlis."

Page 375, line 6, *for* "Izaac" *read* "Izaak."

Page 527, last three lines, *for* "; but neither Mr. Mounsey nor Sir Arthur Cunynghame include any such notices in their" *read* ". Mr. Mounsey's report is brief, and Sir Arthur Cunynghame does not include Baku in his."

In page 264 the faulty French is retained in stern accordance with the official record; but "conviennent," line 12, is clearly "surviennent," just as "feriez," line 10, should be "rendriez."

In the large coloured map, erase outer red lines in Persian Gulf and Caspian, transposing the years given to the inner lines; so also the westernmost line between Kazvin and the Caspian.

PART I.

TELEGRAPH.

"I go, I go; look how I go,
  Swifter than arrow from the Tartar's bow."
                                    SHAKESPEARE.

TELEGRAPH AND TRAVEL.

INTRODUCTORY.

It is exactly ten years ago, that the Persian Gulf cable, manufactured and laid at the cost of her Majesty's Government, was under process of final submersion between Karáchi, the most North-Westerly of Indian ports, and the Turkish Arabian station of Fáo, or Fáva. The link connecting Gwádar, then an obscure fishing village of Makran, and Fáo, a very molecule amid hamlets, was completed on the 8th April, 1864; and notwithstanding the successful establishment of a land line between Karáchi and Gwádar, it was thought prudent to connect these stations also by submarine cable, and so strengthen communications. This alternative section was wholly laid on the 15th May, 1864. But while the Turkish and Indian dominions were thus placed in instantaneous correspondence, the result was a realized fact for Asia only. Out of Asia the benefit of a Persian Gulf cable or land line was barely perceptible. And no wonder. There was an extent of some 1,800 miles to be traversed between the new station at Fáo and Constantinople, before the line stretching westward was fairly in Europe:

and there was a greater distance again between Constantinople and London. The first of these divisions was not declared open to traffic till February 1865, and the second was so wretchedly served in a telegraphic sense, that it seemed a reasonable question whether the ordinary Post or Foreign Office Messenger was not the surer and swifter means of communication between her Majesty's Government at home and her Majesty's Ambassador at the Sublime Porte.

This difficulty in completing connection, by telegraph, of two quarters of the globe daily becoming more and more significant the one for the other, was the less readily met, because the Cis-India land lines in Asia were beyond the immediate control of her Majesty's and the British Indian Governments; and those in Europe had formed, not unnaturally, a minor consideration to the original Indo-European scheme. Much attention had been given to the creation of new lines in Turkey and Persia, and more still to the construction and disposition of a Persian Gulf cable; but it had been little contemplated that existing European lines would have presented so formidable a barrier as they have since proved themselves to be, to rapid and regular *through* working. The fact is, that the demand for an electric link with India, generally of an urgent nature, had become, as it were, imperative to England since the sad and serious warning afforded by the Mutinies; and the thing required was to be supplied at any price and with as little delay as practicable. The want was no longer confined to commercial or political interests; it was eminently national.

With a view to put matters on a better footing, the main object of Government Officers employed on this particular work was clearly to effect the readiest and

safest junction that could be found, not between England
and India, as heretofore, but between England and a
cable station in the Persian Gulf. In Asia, Persian as
well as Turkish lines were formed and brought into requisition by British workers, either separate from or
supplementary to native lines already in existence. In
Europe, negotiations with Governments and Administrations were opened, conducted, and concluded; International Conferences were participated in; and every
measure was taken which appeared likely to promote the
scheme contemplated. From 1865 to 1870, or for more
than five years, attention was given to supply wants, to
remedy failings, and to remove obstacles.

Experiences in such matters may be useful in the
record. In any case, a full report of progress, when
sufficiently mature, is due to the State, and should be
satisfactory to the reporters themselves. Nor is the
necessity less obvious, in a public sense, that there should
be a reference showing the circumstances under which a
great work like the Telegraph to India was undertaken
at all; and what have been and what now are its value
and cost to the country from whose coffers it has been
carried out and carried on. Hence arose the suggestion
that a narrative of the institution and development of
Telegraphic Communication between England and India
under the orders of her Majesty's Government should be
prepared and submitted; and hence was it ruled by the
Secretary of State for India in Council, so far back as
September 1868, that such relation, when completed,
should be published in a quasi-popular form.

More, however, remains to be said on this head. It is
not always pleasant to call spades by their proper names;
but it is often essential to do so, and the present is an

instance where plain statements should not be misinterpreted. Before the establishment of the latest Red Sea cable to Bombay, and about the period of its inauguration, the Government Telegraph lines to India were assailed in the press and other influential quarters in no measured terms. Among other pungent propositions, public opinion was asked to "decide for itself whether public money is being applied with common sense or at the instigation of those interested, who up to this time have monopolized the confidence and attention of the Government?" Letters and leaders pursued the subject so determinedly that the Government Officers concerned, loth to avail themselves of the weapons used by their assailants, were nevertheless driven into newspaper controversy.

Per contra, in November 1865, the present writer, then Chief Director, had stated to the Bombay Government: "It cannot be supposed that the electric wire "can be conveyed for 5,000 miles by sea and land through "the whole of Europe and South-West Asia with the "same facility that its progress may be traced in pencil "on the map. . . . I am humbly of opinion, that unless "some unforeseen great accident, physical or political, "intervene, they"—that is the Indian public—"will, "ere long, possess, whatever the route, the means of sure "and speedy communication with the old country. . . ."

About twenty months later he had, through the same channel, shown cause for delays and failures, without relaxing effort or losing hope in then pending arrangements. And as late as January 1869, the Bombay Government published in the local press his renewed expressions of confidence in the lines impugned. These are the concluding words: "Judging from antecedents,

"my own opinion is in favour of eventual success; and by
"'success' I am not employing the ordinary acceptation
"of the term: past and present records will show this to
"have been long since attained by the Indo-European
"line. I mean that the 'within 24' and 'within 48'
"hour messages of the present day will habitually arrive
"within 12 hours: that regularity and correctness may
"before many months be the rule; and that the corre-
"spondence will be subject to even a lower rate of tariff
"than the present."

The last extract is from a letter just four years old. And what are the results to be quoted in evidence, now that ten years have passed since laying the cable in the Persian Gulf? Are they favourable to the arguments of the Government Officers, or of those who set them aside as unsupported by experience or sound reasoning? Fair and impartial judgment is invited on all sides. It is true that a Company has organized and established a Submarine Line to India, the success of which affects injuriously the revenues of the State; but the Directors of that line themselves would be the last to maintain that the older and much vilified telegraph, crossing lands as well as seas, was a rival to be lightly esteemed. Nor can it be a source of surprise, as it is really no secret, that they should seek to join fortunes in a common purse with their opponents, rather than continue a competition as unexpected as severe. At the present time, the columns of the daily papers furnish abundant proof of the successful working of what is called the Indo-European system. Day after day do its wires bring home the news of the hour: and at the very moment of writing these lines does the casually taken-up *Times* of the morning contain an urgent message, sadly headed

"The Bengal Famine," conveyed by Indo-European Telegraph "*via* Tehran," and addressed from Calcutta at 7.35 of the previous night.

Such direct and conclusive testimony might be considered sufficient answer to the augurers of ill; to say nothing of the marvellous instances of instantaneous working obtained from tests made, within the last four years, by the London Offices in communication with those of Persia and India. But it is no less common to ascribe to chance and good fortune the successful issues of mental and physical toil, than to censure and condemn ill-starred agents for mishaps and reverses due to adverse circumstances beyond all human foresight and control. And, as in the case of the Government Telegraph to India a full statement of proceedings was judged officially advisable, the requirement became still more urgent on general grounds. It was therefore no regrettable accident that the pressure of travel and other duties incidental to his appointment compelled the Chief Director to defer the looked-for report until giving over charge in 1870, preparatory to availing himself of one year's respite from work. That he was, afterwards, called away during the same year to political duty and employed until March 1873 in the settlement of boundary questions, must explain the further delay apparent in submitting the volume to the public. A few explanatory words, in conclusion, on the book itself.

Those who knew Colonel Patrick Stewart, personally or by repute, during his short but active career, will not need to be told why the opening chapter should be devoted to a sketch of his life. He it was who, during the conduct of Indian affairs by Sir Charles Wood (now Lord Halifax), was chosen to give practical effect to the wishes of her Majesty's Government that India should be joined to Great Britain by Telegraph wires; to advise on the matter, to regulate, to control, and to execute. The first entire section of his work, the Persian Gulf Cable, was a brilliant success, and has been proved a permanent one. He scarcely lived to complete more; but he had put others in the way of achieving what he had so well begun. Conscientious readers will not dispute his title to the place of honour in these pages.

The two parts, headed "Telegraph" and "Travel" respectively, are designed to divide strictly official narrative from personal observation and record. Should the first be found painfully practical and matter of fact, overburdened with official details and wanting in the zest which keeps the eye willingly open and the hand steady to the book, the writer may reasonably claim some kind of excuse in the necessarily monotonous nature of the subject. As for the second, he must accept personal responsibility, and trust to kindly critics for tolerant dealing with his shortcomings. It will, at least, possess the recommendation of treating of little-known countries, and, in the case of the two final chapters, going over ground untrodden, with rare exceptions, by other European travellers at all.

One inevitable consequence of an institution such as the British Telegraph in Persia, at least for those officers called away from Indian service to assist in its rise, progress, and maintenance, is the realization of something like genuine "Overland" communication between England and India. Those who return homeward from Tehran have the choice of two main routes; one by Russia, the other by Turkey. For those who proceed, on the other hand, to India from the Persian capital,

TELEGRAPH AND TRAVEL.

there is the Baghdad route, the Bushahr route, and the
complete land route by Karmán and Baluchistan. The
respective merits of all these will, it is hoped, be sufficiently exemplified in the course of this volume to
make present mention superfluous. Meanwhile, it may
be fitly remarked that the "Overland" there indicated
does not rest its titular claim on the transit of a narrow
isthmus, the very material of which was not long since
abstracted by M. Ferdinand de Lesseps; its integrity as
a means of land communication having been already
impaired, at the outset, by a water passage of some
hours on the Nile and Mahmudieh canal.

COMMON NILE BOAT.

CHAPTER I.

MEMOIR OF COLONEL PATRICK STEWART.

THE subject of the following brief sketch is one of those men to whom a single chapter of an ordinary volume can render but poor justice. It is therefore quite as much because Patrick Stewart, as originator of the first practical Telegraph to India, is entitled personally to the first place of consideration in a history of that Telegraph, as because he has left behind him a distinguished name and example, that the merest biographical outline is given to a character worthy of a full and carefully finished portrait. It is a character which merits imitation as well as study; and as it could not fail to influence those moving within its range during a short but busy life, so should a record of its existence be perpetuated for the advantage of new generations.

Patrick Stewart was the second son of James Stewart, Esquire, of Cairnsmore, in Kirkcudbrightshire. He was born at the family residence on the 28th of January, 1832, and at ten years of age was sent to the Grange, near Sunderland, in Durham, then kept by Dr. Cowan. Thence, having been there more than four years, he went for a time to Perry Hill, at Sydenham. On the close of the Midsummer vacation of 1848 he entered the East India Company's Military College at Addiscombe, when the late Sir Ephraim Stannus was Lieutenant-Governor.

Now that Addiscombe is among the things of the past, and as even half a score of years effect much towards the obliteration of a mere reminiscence, it may not be out of place to say a few words on an institution which has produced many remarkable men of more than Indian reputation. Two years' experience of the place in the capacity of Orderly Officer, though hardly equal to a cadet's probation for the same period, is, perhaps, a better warrant of comprehension of the subject than any amount of remote investigation; and it was for the last month or two of such experience that the present writer had the advantage of becoming acquainted with the bright, intelligent, fair-haired boy with whom in after manhood it was his fortune to be associated, and to whose career this chapter is devoted.

The old College at Addiscombe was formed by transfer of the East India Company's Military cadets from Marlow and Woolwich, in 1809, to the house and grounds near Croydon formerly belonging to Lord Liverpool. During the time of that distinguished statesman the place had been the resort of many great men of the period; and its associations are eminently interesting in connection with the social and political history of the reign of George the Third. It may not be generally known, that, after possession by the East India Company and during the Governorship of Major Carmichael Smythe of the Bengal Engineers, the late William Makepeace Thackeray, that officer's stepson, was an inmate of the mansion.[1] Though not in the most picturesque part

[1] Nor is it unnatural to infer that one, whose affectionate instincts were scarcely less remarkable than his intellectual powers, should have derived his

of one of the most picturesque counties of England, it is in a fine healthy locality, and in the immediate neighbourhood of very charming spots.

There were about 150 Cadets in the College, and these formed four distinct sections:—
1. Students in their fourth, or last half year of study distinguished as old cadets.
2. Those in their third term, or young cadets.
3. Those in their second term, or second half of the first year; and
4. Those undergoing the experience of the first half year;

the two last being not very elegantly styled "Browns" and "Greens" respectively.

At the close of each half year, whether June or December, the old cadets were draughted away to their respective destinations: those who had passed the highest ordeal, to Chatham as Engineers; the next in merit into the Artillery; and the least successful on examination, to the Infantry. A Cavalry commission was occasionally available, according to interest or inclination, essentially the former. It may be safely said that the faults or shortcomings of the institution were few in comparison with its use as a rearing-place of young military aspirants; and that those few mainly arose from defects of discipline in controlling unruly spirits. Among its Professors were many whose names live in the scientific world as well as in the memory of the Addiscombe cadet. Its Governors are thought of with affectionate regard by those who not only knew them as men, but could sym-

predilections for Indian scenes and Indian persons from this early family connection with a nursery of Indian celebrities, as from a yet more distant retrospect of India itself.

pathise with their responsibilities as discharging an important trust; and set in the balance with similar establishments at home and abroad, there is little doubt but that the Hon. Company's Military College at Addiscombe would put in a creditable appearance.

Patrick Stewart was not a boy to remain long unknown, or in a secondary position. At the end of his first term at Addiscombe he came out first of the "Greens" in Mathematics and Fortification, and his general character for ability and assiduity was such as to stamp him a student of unusual promise. Whether it is that the subject is not so popular, or that it has not possessed chroniclers of equal attraction, it may be hard to say; but the strictly military curriculum of study has never been so thoroughly and pleasantly known to the general reader as that of Rugby or Harrow. Yet there were many Tom Browns and Walters[1] at Addiscombe, as there must be in all large assemblies of English gentlemen's sons. Young Stewart possessed one of those natures for which honour and high principle were guiding stars, without, as it were, any outward evidence of their shining. Free from any semblance of pride or pedantry, he preferred study to idleness, and manly sport to boyish dissipation; and it is therefore with no surprise that we find him, during his first few months' residence at the school, glad to get to his books and escape certain recognized exhibitions which may be called of a modified music-hall character, and in which it was the special privilege of the "Greens" to display their powers for the amusement of the old cadets. Boxing and singing were conspicuous among these. Now, a spar may not be unwholesome exercise, nor a fight always unprofitable occupation, in a wide sense of

[1] See Mr. Farrar's "St. Winifred's; or, the World of School."

the words; but a sensible lad of sixteen does not invariably apprehend why he should make himself a public spectacle in either. Again, it is not always easy or convenient to exercise vocal accomplishments at the will and pleasure of bigger boys; and when to these compulsory representations the vice of drinking is added, it is surely better to see the power of resistance effectually applied than the hand extended in token of approval and sympathy. Before long, however, and by the kind and readily-offered aid of one or two true friends—for there is unmistakeable truth in the friendship of boys—Patrick Stewart made for himself a comfortable social position, and fell easily into the groove of a cadet's life, both as regards the goodwill and esteem of his companions and the tight stock and uniform so ominous of a future career of discipline. As for parades, there must have been something like fifteen in the twenty-four hours.

That he was not insensible to the want of relief from a strict attention to work and duty his companions of boyhood would bear ample testimony; and, irrespective of participation in football and the regulation school games, there is a record that, during his second term, one Monday afternoon in March, after a parade of two hours' duration, he and four companions started for a chalk-pit about $5\frac{1}{2}$ miles distant, on the Godstone road, he and one other only reaching the goal, and returning to declare the whole distance of 11 miles performed in one hour and three-quarters. A mile in six minutes was his practised running.

During his second year of Addiscombe life there is a marked period of disturbances, in which, however, Stewart seems to have had little concern. The disorderly element was exhibited at this time in a more prominent manner than usual, and recourse was had to stern and severe measures. Our cadet was made, in his fourth term, a Corporal, and in this capacity found himself in no very enviable position, having to exercise supervision and to find fault where such interference would not always be well received. But the necessity of schooling and practice, in enforcing as in enduring discipline, is sufficiently urgent in a military career to demand early attention; and the system of Corporal Cadets is no doubt as wholesome as it is useful. His progress in study can hardly be said to have been so rapid as that he continued to maintain the high position in his class and among his comrades which he had attained on first admission. Especially was it in mathematics and fortification that he became distinguished. Head of his term in mathematics at the end of his third half year as the first, we find him at the completion of the full period of two years carrying off the first Fortification and second Mathematical prize, together with the Sword and Pollock Medal, the former being a reward for conduct, the latter for progress in study.

As among the choicest of ordinary mundane returns of a toilsome career are the congratulations of old friends on a fairly achieved success, so among the fairest records of Patrick Stewart's biography would be those many spontaneous testimonials of his work contained in the congratulatory letters of his contemporaries in the service. A letter from a brother Engineer in Brompton Barracks addressed to Cairnsmore immediately followed the news of his Addiscombe successes. The writer has since nobly fallen in the service of his country. Had he been living, he would assuredly have pardoned these quotations:—

"One line to congratulate you on the well-deserved success of your dear Pat. He has indeed done bravely, and realized what his friends expected of him. I say 'expected,' for all who know him would expect from him what few others could even hope from those who are not Pats. I was quite horrified to see the hollows all over his body, and his bones sticking out. . . . I feel quite proud of him when I hear anybody speak of him, and to be able to say that we are great chums; and I look forward with no small pleasure to have him with me at Chatham."

It was the usual practice for Addiscombe cadets qualifying as Engineers to receive commissions as Ensigns at home, and remain for a year and a half at Chatham,[1] whence, and after which probation, they proceeded to India. The choice of Presidency was generally given to the most forward of the term; but the final distribution depended naturally on local exigencies and requirements. Stewart selected and obtained Bengal, the most popular Presidency among the cadets, and for excellent reasons: it basked in the special sunshine of the supreme Government, and it offered by far the greater number of good appointments. Bombay, partly from position, partly from a certain energy and impulsiveness which kept it more prominently before the eyes of the civilized world, was the second in consideration; and Madras was unmistakeably last on the list. Indeed, it may be questioned whether any but those influenced by family or friendly connections with the place would have chosen Madras at all as a field for action.

Ensign Stewart's entrance to Chatham life was accomplished in the orthodox manner. He had to fit up his

[1] In 1852 the period was extended from sixteen to nineteen months.

one room, dividing off the bed by a screen, and introducing the essential furniture. In the process, he became acquainted not only with his own chairs, tables, knives, forks, spoons, and table-linen, but with his own mops, brooms, pails, and cooking utensils. He had, then, to be initiated and practised in the daily pursuits, whether of duty, pleasure, or necessity: attendance at parades in the morning, surveys during the day, and mess in the evening, with, perhaps, what was called "extra work," such as French and journalising at night, formed a not uncommon order in the programme. A small yacht in the Medway afforded something of recreation; but of shooting, there is mention only, at the time, of one covey of partridges pursued by half the garrison till the birds were so wild there was no getting near them.

Not many months, however, had passed when architectural drawings, and projects for attack and demolition, engaged his attention; and these were succeeded by more special employment in reviewing a plan which had been put forward for the sea-coast defences of England. There is good reason to believe that the young officer's report on this last important matter was favourably received by the recognized authorities in military science.

The Exhibition of 1851, to which he was fortunate enough to gain admission prior to its formal opening, was an occasion to him of high gratification. The "splendid pieces of machinery," to use his own words, were well fitted to attract his particular notice, and awake enthusiasm in the course of description. The studies of this year were pleasantly relieved by an occasional visit to friends in London, inspection of monuments and objects of general or scientific interest in the metropolis, and a levee and presentation at St. James's Palace.

In 1852, there is recorded a civil engineering excursion from Chatham to some of the principal towns and notable places in England; the little expense and great advantage attending which method of combining amusement and instruction should be suggestive of frequent repetition. The party consisted of ten cadets and a superintending officer. From the Great Western terminus in London they went by express to Swindon, where they visited the large engine manufactory and ironworks. From Swindon they went to Bristol and Clifton, down the Avon, across the Severn, and up the Wye to Chepstow; where, landing with his comrades immediately below the new bridge, young Stewart had the great good fortune to be accompanied over the works by Brunel himself. From Chepstow they proceeded to Cardiff and its docks; thence to Merthyr Tydvil and its ironworks; thence to Liverpool, Birkenhead, Manchester, Birmingham, and London again. At the close of a pleasant and profitable fortnight they were back at Chatham.

This agreeable and practical lesson may be said to have terminated the preliminary or English course of engineering study. On the 30th June of the same year Patrick Stewart embarked at Gravesend for Calcutta. He had taken his passage, *viâ* the Cape, in the *Maidstone*, a sailing vessel. Some warm-hearted young companions made marked demonstration of their friendship by escorting him to the very side of the ship as she was in the act of weighing anchor.

A voyage to India round the Cape, however tedious

and unprofitable to some, may be productive of both enjoyment and benefit to many, especially to those who, with a keen sensibility to novelty and outward impressions, possess that happy facility of observation, with intent to apply, peculiar to certain constitutions. The recollection of three or four months passed at sea must necessarily be vague in after life, and the more so as a voyage is repeated; but the diary of such episodes is not a whit the less valuable on that account; and a record of such experience, whether in the shape of a small manuscript volume or home letters, may be safely recommended to every young adventurer who can handle a pen, whatever his station or employment. Stewart's ship letters, written with all the candour and genuineness of honest boyhood, give many signs of a reasoning intelligence and comprehensiveness of mind which belong essentially to the full-grown man. Portraits of fellow-passengers and the narrative of adventures and amusements of a voyage differing little from other voyages are thus agreeably varied with descriptions of scenery, people, and atmospheric phenomena. They made a passage of unusual rapidity, having left the English coast on the 4th July and taken in the pilot at Sagor on the 15th October, or less than three months, allowing for a ten days' detention at the Cape. At Table Bay they were visited by one of those strong north-westerly gales against which, notwithstanding their frequent occurrence, the shipping appears to have been but little protected. So unsafe indeed were they considered in that particular instance, that a life-boat and some of the largest trading-boats were despatched from the shore, to land the soldiers in the event of accident to the vessel in her exposed anchorage. Owing to detention for a day at Sāgar, a well-known island at the mouth of the Hugli, Stewart and a fellow-passenger landed, and penetrated the jungle. The young Engineer, intuitively a sportsman, did not fail to notice there the recent tracks of very large tigers.

Gazetted a Second Lieutenant of Engineers from the 16th October, 1852, Patrick Stewart did not long remain unemployed at Calcutta. However warm his reception and pleasant his sojourn at the hospitable mansion of Mr. John Colvin,[1] in Alipur, and however attractive the snipe-shooting excursions to Nil Ganj and the general novelty of outdoor and indoor Indian amusements, he readily availed himself of a friendly suggestion to apply for appointment to a vacancy in the Canal Department under Colonel Cautley. This officer being, however, absent some thousand miles up country, the application could not be answered at once; and in the meantime Colonel Garstin, Commanding Engineer at Calcutta, found work for his newly arrived subalterns in a survey within easy distance of the Presidency. There was some talk of sending young Engineer officers to Birmah, for annexation in that quarter was then imminent. But the prospect was not inviting, and the chance of active service seemed at the moment to have passed away.

In November he started for Bardwān, near which place he had been instructed to commence the survey. The "bands," or artificial banks of the Damuda, a river running into the Hugli, were to be carefully inspected; and the tract of country to be surveyed was stated to be from 12 to 15 miles in width and 70 in length, in addition to which numerous lines of levels

[1] Afterwards Lieutenant-Governor of the North-West Provinces.

were to be taken. Measuring from its north-westerly extremity to Ampta, opposite Calcutta, the "district," in technical phrase, may be said to have extended about 100 miles. Those who know the localities would readily recognize the scene of operations between the Damuda and a second river, the Rup Narain. The waters of both were kept within their natural banks by a common but costly contrivance; and the object of the survey was to ascertain whether no other and more economical method could be adopted. Lieutenant de Bourbel was associated with Lieutenant Stewart on this service; but their individual duties kept them, as a rule, many miles apart. The latter, though somewhat ailing on first reaching Bardwân, seems to have had sufficiently good general health to enjoy his tent life in the cold weather. During leisure hours, his dog, his gun, and a country abounding with large and small game, afforded him ample means of recreation.

But as the hot winds and hot season drew on, fever and its accompaniments made troublesome visitation. Attended by kind friends on these occasions, the kindly feelings of reciprocity engendered in his own breast were destined to receive a shock not uncommon in India. His description of the sad and sudden death, by cholera, of a young and amiable lady, the wife of an officer, in the "compound" or enclosure of whose house his tents were pitched, reveals a sensibility not unbecoming a brave and noble nature. The language of honest pathos and sympathy in which the calamity is detailed is appropriate to a narrative of which the bare reality has a thrilling interest.

Colonel Cautley had forwarded the application for Stewart's employment on the canals, and had offered him an appointment on the executive staff of the Ganges Canal Department, which he had not hesitated to accept. Other openings, however, presented themselves to him; and at the commencement of May, 1853, he writes that he has been gazetted to the office of Superintendent of Electric Telegraphs during the absence of Dr. O'Shaughnessy, then on special duty in Europe. His prolonged and tedious survey had been completed; and his proposal for a new bed to the Damuda, 10 miles in extent, though at first approved, was eventually countermanded on account of the expensive nature of the work.

The position now occupied was an important one, and the fact of its importance naturally enhanced the credit of the young man of one-and-twenty who had been selected as a fitting incumbent. His selection, moreover, appears to have been made by the Local Government on immediate experience of his merits, and without any solicitation or even expectation on his part. Mr. Siddons, the Chemical Examiner to Government, had been first appointed to act for Dr. O'Shaughnessy, but on the death of that gentleman, after a few hours' illness, by cholera, Stewart was immediately directed to officiate. In no country but India could the abilities of a young military officer be provided with the wide field for display suddenly exemplified in instances such as this. He found himself in charge of an office at the Presidency, with a large establishment of assistants, as head of a Department in direct communication with the Government, to all intents and purposes his own master. Confidential intelligence connected with State interests must necessarily pass through his hands: he would be brought constantly before the notice of the highest authorities of the land; no wonder that he felt gratified at the compliment paid to his talents and industry.

His early observations, on taking charge of the Telegraph in Bengal, are sufficiently relevant to the present work to call for passing record. He writes from Calcutta in May:—"The lightning has come into the offices several times lately, destroying parts of the instruments completely, and sounding all the alarms. I have now before me one of the coils of fine wire, the cardboard of which was burned to a cinder last night, and the wire itself melted by the lightning, without injuring seriously anyone in the office. On the lower parts of the line near the bay, there are immense numbers of wild buffaloes that continually come to rub themselves on the posts of the telegraph, and not unfrequently knock them down or break them. I hope to pay my respects to some of them this week. Great numbers of birds, such as crows, kites, fishing eagles, &c., have been killed while sitting on the iron rods, by flashes of lightning passing along them." About a fortnight later the writer reports fulfilment of his hopes of encountering the buffaloes, and that he is expecting two pairs of horns, which are to be sent home should they arrive in tolerably good condition.

Lieutenant Stewart, besides making tours of inspection, was employed in arranging for the transmission and distribution of stores and instruments for the whole line from Calcutta to Lahor, and from Agra to Indor, 1,700 miles of telegraph. Nor did the lines down the river escape his attention. Among his first acts was to lay down and put in working order a 10-mile line from the Diamond Harbour Station to a dangerous shoal in the Hugli, the progress of vessels over which it was important to report to Government. It was only in the first month of his incumbency that he received orders to send stores of every description for a line from Prom to Sandoway in Birmah. It is a remarkable circumstance, illustrative of the then fast growing suspicion of the actions and motives of their rulers on the part of the people of India, that the majority of the natives did not believe in the working of the telegraph lines at all, and in many cases maintained that we "were cheating them out of their money without being able to send a single message!"

In October, Stewart was appointed Aide-de-camp to the Lieutenant-Governor of the North-West Provinces, on Mr. Colvin's accession to that high office. But such proof of personal regard and friendliness could have but temporary effect. An officer of the scientific branch of the army, and of such high repute for so young a man, could not be spared for duties comparatively trivial; and the Aide-de-camp still continued to control the wires, on the understanding that relief from the departmental superintendence would restore him to more strictly military duty in superintending a fortified cantonment projected for Firuzpur. When, moreover, Mr. Colvin had his audience of leave of the Governor-General, Lord Dalhousie took the opportunity of the official attendance of the young Engineer, to address him by name, and thank him for the able assistance he had rendered Government since he had held charge of the Telegraph. Not long after this occurrence, Dr. O'Shaughnessy returned from England, and Lieutenant Stewart's connection with the Indian telegraphs ceased, at least for a time.

While on this subject, an article may be quoted from

the *Friend of India*, dated the 6th April, 1854. Contemporary opinion is always of value when obtained from a reliable source. In this case the high character of the paper needs no evidence; but there *is* further evidence than any contained in its columns to show that the published eulogium was merely an act of justice:

"There is one officer who has been concerned in the successful introduction of the Electric Telegraph, who has never received his due meed of appreciation from the public. To Mr. Stewart, while acting as Superintendent of the experimental line, is due the credit of making all those arrangements which are so essential to success, yet are so seldom appreciated. Partly from the absence of any tangible result, and partly perhaps from the impression that so very young an officer could lend no serious aid to the work in hand, his services have been overlooked by all except his superiors. Yet his task was by no means light. The line was to be extended at once to Lahor, a distance of 1,280 miles; Dr. O'Shaughnessy had expressed a wish that depôts should be established at seven different places, and Government and the public were alike known to be feverishly impatient for success. Meanwhile, each successive ship discharged in Calcutta a portion of the materials required. Forty artificers arrived. Then came tons of wire, and miles of wire insulated with gutta-percha, besides the machines for straightening the lines. Thousands, or we may say hundreds of thousands, of posts were to be fixed at equidistant places all along this immense line, part of which runs through a tract where bamboos are only known by name, and where timber is an almost unattainable luxury. Then all these posts were to be grooved.

"They were to be set up 'properly,' a phrase which will be readily comprehended by those who know what it is to instruct native artificers to act according to rule on a work of which they do not know the object or the reason. Lastly, all this was to be effected in a country where there is but one road and no railways,—where delay is a habit, and unconscious disobedience perpetual,—and by an officer with no authority over anyone except his signallers,—and so young, that his appointment was received with a feeling of surprise. Let our readers remember how impossible a large combined operation is in this country, how frequently the most explicit instructions are misunderstood, and how great a danger existed of wires, men, and machinery all turning up anywhere except in juxta-position, and they will appreciate the nature of the task. Mr. Stewart's energy, perseverance, and good temper accomplished this most annoying duty. By dint of endless correspondence, which included the Military Board and the executive Engineers, all was placed in train. The artificers were despatched by steamer to the depôts, and reached them. The wire was carried by steamer and bullock-carts to thirty-two different places between Calcutta and Benares alone, all at unequal distances, and all, therefore, requiring their special length of coil. The straightening machines did not arrive in time, and they were made at the Kidderpur iron-yard, under Mr. Stewart's immediate superintendence. Throughout the line there was not, we believe, a blunder, or a single day's delay, and when Dr. O'Shaughnessy arrived, he found himself able to drive on the work as rapidly as if he himself had been upon the spot. We think it just that, in meting out their praise for this great undertaking, the public should not forget the officer who so successfully performed a task, none the less irksome that it was from its nature unattended by publicity or credit.

"It may not be unnecessary to state that we are not indebted for any of our facts to Mr. Stewart."

Towards the close of the year 1853 an incident occurred which, though unconnected with official progress or proceedings, is too remarkable to be omitted from the present brief memoir. Narratives of perilous encounter and marvellous escape are common enough to students in the annals of Indian Shikar, but seldom has the hero of an adventure such as the following lived to tell his own tale.

Stewart had left the Lieutenant-Governor's camp at

Mirzapur on the night of the 25th November for a day's shooting, and intending to return on the night of the 26th. He had been especially cautioned not to venture into the jungles, with the chance of meeting a tiger when on foot; but an eager temperament and intense love of sport overcame caution. He fell in with three brother sportsmen living in a ruined fort in the jungle. They went out together, found and attacked the too probable enemy; and a tigress was wounded in the leg. A wounded tiger may become the scourge of a district: it was natural that English sportsmen should make every attempt to kill the beast rather than leave her slightly disabled close to several large native villages. They tracked her by the blood, still wet beneath their feet, up the face of a steep stony hill, to a mass of rocks where was a cave, the mouth of which was visible above them. The place was very dangerous. They knew that the object of pursuit was close at hand, and most probably in the cave. A council was held, and it was proposed to defer proceedings till the following morning, in order to get buffaloes to the place, and, by driving them among the rocks, make the tigress show herself. Stewart opposed the delay. He had left camp on the understanding that he was to return that night, and in his eagerness to lose no time went straight up to the mouth of the cave and looked in. Providentially, nothing was there. He then tracked the blood a little beyond the spot; but as darkness drew on, he yielded to the general wish, and agreed to await the morning for further operations. Having to pass the place on his return to camp, he reckoned that an hour up the hill, added to the night's absence, would not cause any serious detention.

The next morning there was delay in procuring buffaloes, and the party had to go to work without them. The blood of the wounded animal being, moreover, dry, it was difficult to ascertain her precise locality. Division of opinion as to her movements ensued, the trail became lost, and there was a partial separation of the guns. Stewart appears to have been hidden from his companions by intervening bushes, when, crouching in a comparatively open part of the jungle, the tigress saw him approach and unexpectedly dashed on him. Struck down to the ground, he remained motionless. From his own account, he had no inclination to call out; and well that it was so. A strange necessity is that of suppressing all signs of the life it is man's instinct as well as duty to preserve. His enemy passed him, but soon returned to seize him by the left calf, changing to the thigh in an attempt to carry him off. Thinking her victim dead, she dropped him from her mouth, then struck him with her closed paw and left him, not, however, till she had inflicted no less than thirteen indelible wounds. On being found by his companions, he helped them for the moment in binding up his own wounds, but soon sank into a kind of delirium. He was put upon a litter, taken into Chunar, and by care and skill enabled in a few weeks to resume his wonted occupations.

A letter from the highest authority in India expressed to a mutual friend how grieved he had been to learn the serious accident just related, and added a characteristic message for delivery to the sufferer, when recovered, that he deserved a "skelping, for exposing a life that we all expect to be a useful one."

Were this a biography instead of a brief memoir, many pages might be filled with Stewart's experiences of Shikar. His love for the pursuit of large game was exhibited in the first six months of his residence in India. No better example of this dominant feeling could be found than when, on one occasion, standing below a certain tree, he fired at and wounded two bears nibbling fruit among its branches. One he killed on its descent; the other he ran after single-handed till it took refuge in the jungle.

Stewart left the Lieutenant-Governor's personal staff in January, and proceeded to Firuzpur *via* Delhi and Ambālah. In any but the scientific branches of the Indian Army the bare mention of some of the appointments he filled, or of which he had the offer, would prove a rare versatility of talent, and that he was held in peculiar esteem by his superiors.

But it would be unfair to the distinguished corps to which he belonged to pass over the fact that its younger officers are not uncommonly called to posts such as hoary-headed veterans in military lore might consider it an honour to hold. Stewart himself notes casually the circumstance that he had been named to no less than seven appointments in six months, the first, it is believed, of his Indian service. For the years 1854, 1855, and the first half of 1856, his field of action was the Panjāb; but in stating that his principal charge was a division of the Grand Trunk road, a very faint idea is given of the usefulness of his presence in a country illustrating perhaps the most important and successful annexation accomplished by British India. During the period stated, he is found, independently of his road supervision, fulfilling the double duties of Garrison Engineer at Lahor and Superintendent of Civil Buildings at Anarkallee; he watches over the construction of models of Indian tombs for the Paris Exhibition of 1855; he is more or less engaged in constructing fortified cantonments for Firuzpur, in designing a college for Lahor; it is authoritatively proposed that he shall undertake, at Rurki, the re-organization of the Pontoon train; that he shall become Secretary to the Chief Engineer in the Panjáb (Colonel Napier, now General Lord Napier of Magdala).

The nature of his occupations on the roads may be readily imagined from a passage in one of his letters, dated August 1854. He then writes that he has five saddle-horses, and that he requires them all to get through his outdoor work. He hoped to carry out the whole programme within twelve weeks, but adds that there were still twenty bridges to complete! A previous letter had explained the extent of his charge to be nearly 200 miles; and a subsequent one reports completion of his bridges at the time intended, notwithstanding a sharp intervening attack of fever. In July, 1856, he was appointed for the second time to the Electric Telegraph, and on this occasion to an acting-superintendence on a large scale. The vacancy had been caused by the departure again to Europe of Dr. O'Shaughnessy and the death of Lieutenant Chauncey.

Stewart's health had not been unaffected by the climate, but he had suffered more severely from accidental injuries than those incidental to Indian service. To the wounds inflicted by the tigress in 1853 might be added a severe fall from his horse at the close of 1854, when riding at full gallop. He and a party were hawking and in chase of bustard, and the horse he rode, unconsciously plunging both forelegs into a concealed hole, rolled over, throwing his rider far beyond him on the hard ground. He fell on his temples, was carried away senseless and narrowly escaped brain fever. At the commencement of 1856 a racket-ball struck him so violently near the left eye as to knock him down and cut an artery, causing much loss of blood before surgical aid could be obtained. Indeed, about the time of this last occurrence he had acquired a great local reputation as the most unfortunate of beings in respect of hurts and tumbles.

From the date of re-appointment to the Telegraph, a more marked individuality may be traced in Stewart's career. Always a rising man, his rise was in a certain sense impeded by the extent and indefiniteness of the sphere in which he moved. It was not so much that he was doing an undefined work, but doing work which it was the property of many of his colleagues to do, and in which his short period of service must inevitably keep him in comparatively subordinate employ. In the Telegraph, as constituted in 1856, he was at once set on a pinnacle; and his proceedings were watched, not from friendly interest towards himself, but from the great public and State interests involved in his appointment, which could not therefore fail to attract the attention of practical statesmen. At the same time, there were other spheres in which he must have been equally distinguished. The bent of his mind was for work—practical, useful work; his genius was especially energetic and active; his restlessness was that of a man seeking appropriate fields of ambition. A very few months before nomination to act as Superintendent of Electric Telegraphs in India he had been sighing for a sight of the magnificent valleys north-east of Kashmir; not merely for sport, great as the temptation offered: he "would still try to make the same excursion, even if there were not an animal in the whole country." One of his brother officers had applied for and obtained an appointment in the Great Trigonometrical Survey of India, and had been then ordered to Kashmir, whence he would move towards Thibet. On this he writes: "It is likely to be a most interesting, though rather difficult undertaking. Many of the passes he must cross are 19,000 feet and upwards; elevations that look down considerably on Mr. Albert Smith and Mont Blanc." His enthusiasm was great in contemplating the work then in progress. It was one quite to his own heart; and though not himself destined to participate in it, few would have acknowledged more readily than he the admirable manner in which it has been performed, had he lived to see the results of the labours of Captain Montgomerie and his associates.

On taking up his appointment, Stewart contemplates a tour during the first six months, "from one end of India to the other—from Ceylon to Simla and Peshāwar, and from Prom to Bombay and Karāchi." As regards the extent of the telegraph branches, he notes the fact that "nearly 4,000 miles of line are now working, and about 3,000 more are ordered, and may probably be completed within a year;" adding, "it is interesting work, and of a nature likely to become more and more so every year from the progress made in the science." India was indeed making a gigantic effort to vie with the sister empires of Europe in this latest but not least important demand of civilization; and at a time when her progress and prosperity were threatened by a visitation which, if foreseen in its reality, might have been interpreted by the wisest of political seers as fraught with paralysis and death.

Owing to sickness and other causes, the intended tour was not commenced until the hot weather of 1857. On the 19th April of that year, the Acting-Superintendent arrived at Galle from Calcutta, and arrangements were soon made for inspecting the locality of a proposed line of telegraph through the island. Stewart hoped to see the work in progress during May, then to continue his tour to Bombay, and return in about two months later to Ceylon again. Before, however, leaving the island in the ordinary course of duty, the news of the Indian Mutiny hurried him down from Kandi to Galle, and he received an urgent order to repair again to Calcutta with the least possible delay. Landing at Madras on his upward way, he had a long interview with Lord Harris, and took charge of important telegrams for Lord Canning, which had arrived from the Panjáb and North West, the telegraph line from Agra to Calcutta having been cut off at Cawnpore. It is not to be wondered at that before re-embarking he gave orders, on his own responsibility, to commence at once a coast line of telegraph from Madras to Calcutta, with a view of placing the two Presidencies in direct intercommunication at an early date.

Although at Madras on the 9th June, he left Calcutta on the 18th for Benares, with the full confidence of the Governor-General that he would do his utmost for the restoration and maintenance of telegraphic communication at a time when its value was at the highest. A little later he found himself at Allahabad, the only Engineer Officer available for consultation in all matters, civil and military; with more work than sufficient for the day, and passing the night, when he could apply one to its natural purposes, in a palankeen carriage or the verandah of the garrison chapel. The difficulties in the way of any public operations were extraordinary, but happily so was the emergency which occasioned them. It was almost impossible to collect coolies in adequate number for the most trifling work. The march of a small body of troops towards Cawnpore, at a crisis of unparalleled emergency, was delayed for twelve hours from the want of lascars and dooly-bearers. Butchers to kill the meat had to be hunted for and coaxed into employment, as though the profession they followed were a learned or scientific one. Even the ready low-caste hangman was wanting when required. Colonel Neill had been working day and night with insufficient assistance, and had set an example of spirit and energy which has now become a matter of history.

It was reported that there were from 2,000 to 3,000 Mulvis collected at Mahgãon, distant 16 miles from Allahabad, and as Major Renaud's force was moving in that direction, Stewart thought the opportunity a good one for inspecting the line of telegraph and rendering general professional aid. He therefore proposed to accompany the detachment for the first day's march, retracing his steps on the day following, preparatory to starting for Benares. He had examined the railway buildings and workshops at Allahabad, and found the damage done by the rebels enormous. The locomotives, though repairable, were useless, since the appliances for putting them in order had been destroyed. He suggested to Colonel Neill that the next steamer passing Benares should be directed to take in tow a few country boats that were bringing up a complete new locomotive. It was calculated that these craft were near Mirzapur, and the engine, if brought up at once, must prove of immense value.

The last accounts then received of the telegraph lines to Cawnpore were somewhat discouraging. Stewart had not given full credit to the reports first circulated about them; but he had good reason to apprehend that wire might be wanting to enable him to open communication as General Havelock's force moved up. The river-boat with the first instalment on board could not arrive for a fortnight; and the small supply of wire available would not nearly meet the requirements, should the stories told of wholesale destruction prove true. He had persuaded the Commissioner to issue a proclamation that any person found in possession of telegraph wire or posts would be hanged, if the stores were not conveyed within two days to the nearest point of the road; and he could himself vouch that for seven miles along the line the measure had proved effective.

Accompanying Major Renaud's force as arranged, on the 9th July, he returned to Calcutta, to hurry on the new coast line of telegraph. But before leaving that memorable month of June and the few days intervening, an extract from one of his home letters will form an appropriate introduction. It is dated the 21st July, the eve of a new departure from the Presidency for the North-West:—

"I came down from the North-West Provinces without scratch or accident of any kind, though I must confess to one or two providential escapes. I was to have breakfasted with poor Moore of the Civil Service at Gopar-ganj on the morning of his murder; but, arriving a few hours earlier than I expected, thought it better to push on, without a halt, to Banares. He and his two friends were murdered when dressing for breakfast.

Within six hours of my arrival in Allahabad I obtained Col. Neill's permission to take command of a body of 200 Sikhs and a few Irregular Cavalry, with four European officers, and to take them across the Ganges at night to attack and destroy the stronghold of one of the principal marauders. The utter want of discipline among the Sikhs, and the fact that I had been obliged to leave behind three-fourths of the Irregular

CAWNPORE MONUMENT.

Cavalry, on account of the quicksands we had to cross, obliged me to postpone the business until the following night, that of the 25th, on which the place was completely destroyed and blown up. On my return on the 26th (I had been up for the whole of three successive nights), I was fearfully tired, and nearly worn out.... Nearly *all* my greatest friends are gone. Many ladies as well as officers, whom I had seen so recently in perfect health and confidence, have been killed, with every refinement of outrage and cruelty. .... I have not, nor have I ever had, a moment's doubt as to the termination of this storm of rebellion, but in the meantime no words can describe the fearful condition of many who have still to be relieved in small detached out-stations or in concealment in jungles. And yet, some four short months ago, no single European would have believed one breath of all this. .... I shall not unnecessarily expose myself; but believing, as I do, that it is the duty of every European who can give the *slightest* aid to be in the front in such times as these, *nothing* would induce me to remain in Calcutta."

During the six weeks or two months of this second expedition into the interior, he devoted himself to stem the tide of insurrection, applying his individual services in the cause to the best of his judgment and ability. A halt of General Havelock's force before he could join them, as he had hoped and intended, changed however his original plans. His chief work at this particular time, irrespective of the Telegraph, was the strong fortified position at Rāj Ghāt, commanding a passage of the Ganges by Benares. It is one that called forth high eulogium both from local authorities and the press. A friend bearing a well known Indian name, who met and dined with him while engaged on the construction, writes in rapture of his host, describing him as ubiquitous in spite of rheumatism, or, if stationary, unsparing of his exertions. Few of Stewart's own letters written at this time are extant; and this circumstance he afterwards explains. The unfortunate difficulties which in Lower Bengal followed the mutiny of the Dinapur regiments almost entirely closed all communication between the North-West, where he then was, and Calcutta. Several of his letters, including a very important one to Lord Canning about the Benares fortifications, were forwarded for safety by a circuitous route, but the precaution had not availed to secure them from loss.

The Rāj Ghāt fortification originated in a recommendation of Lieut. Stewart, to Lord Canning and Sir Patrick Grant, that this particular site should be chosen instead of one in the old Cantonments where intrenchments had been commenced. The quick eye of the young Engineer had noted the particular facilities of defence offered by the position, four years before the Mutiny, and his views were now supported by the professional experience of the senior officer directed to report on the proposal. The construction was sanctioned, and eventually undertaken by the originator himself, assisted by Lieut. Limond of his own corps, and several railway engineers. Controlling a host of workpeople, amounting sometimes to twelve thousand, they constructed in some six weeks, at a mere nominal cost, a fortified position of immense strength, capable of containing, if necessary, 5,000 men, but easily defensible with a force of 350. Heavy guns, stores, ammunition, and provisions were thrown in, and every preparation made for a siege. Stewart's opinion that the security of Benares was indirectly attributable to this work, is well supported by the argument that its exposed position towards Oude would have made it an irresistible temptation to an attacking army had there been a prospect of success.

Stewart returned to Calcutta on the 16th September to hurry on the opening of the great coast line of telegraph connecting Madras and Ceylon with Calcutta, so essential to the controlling authorities at that disturbed period. But before the end of the following month he was moving again towards the principal scene of insurrection. He accompanied General Windham for more than 300 miles, and then went on in advance to arrange for transport at a part of the road where the Commander-in-Chief himself had nearly been taken by the mutineers. These last, on crossing the road, had stolen the horses from the Dak Station. On the 2nd November he was again at Allahabad, reporting himself *en route*, at Lord Canning's request, to join army head-quarters and accompany Sir Colin Campbell to Lucknow. He had arrived at the cantonment just as the guns were fired which announced the Chief's departure; and he was to leave that evening for Cawnpore, in the hopes of meeting there the head-quarters staff. The occasion was one to him of the deepest interest. Lucknow was to be fully and effectually relieved; and he yearned to assist in the military engineering operations essential to the undertaking. He purposed, moreover, to establish, if possible, telegraphic communication from Cawnpore to the outpost of Alam-bagh. To his mind the relief of the Lucknow garrison, comprising so many of his personal friends, independently of its intrinsic importance, was, next to the capture of Delhi, the great desideratum of the war; or, in other words, "the one scene in this strange drama which he should the most prefer to witness." On the 3rd November, Stewart reached Cawnpore; on the 5th he had laid down a line of telegraph for 20 out of the 53 miles between Cawnpore and Lucknow.

The story of the several and more or less effectual reliefs of Lucknow, during a period of unparalleled difficulty and danger, is recent, and comparatively well known: but it should be borne in mind that there were three distinct operations on this behalf which are not to be confounded together. The first relief was that by the troops under General Havelock on the 25th September 1857, among the more prominent incidents of which are, to use the language of the Despatches, the "disinterested generosity" of the valorous Outram in ceding a prerogative of military command, and the death of the "prompt and self-reliant" Neill. The second relief was that of the 16th and 17th November under Sir Colin Campbell, rendered memorable by daring feats of arms such as the attack on the Sikandar-bagh and storming the position of the Shah Najif. The third relief was the actual re-capture and re-occupation of the city effected in March 1858.

It was to the second of these occasions that reference is now made. Attached to the head-quarters staff, Stewart had the great satisfaction of assisting in the operations which, however severe and attended with loss, obtained the rescue of the women and children, the sick and wounded, from their beleaguered and dangerous situation. In his Despatch of the 18th November to the Governor-General, the Commander-in-Chief, while calling special attention to the services of certain officers, does not fail to mention "Lieutenant Stewart, Bengal Engineers, Superintendent of the Electric Telegraph, who accompanied the force; and made himself particularly useful throughout." A few days later, he was one of five officers who rode in with Sir Colin Campbell to Cawnpore, while the firing there was still heavy. The General's reception was a complete ovation, and Stewart shared in the enthusiasm exhibited for a leader who had inspired him with confidence as well as admiration.

On the 6th December a decisive action occurred near Cawnpore; and he accompanied the horse artillery and cavalry in pursuit of the flying enemy to a distance of about 14 miles from camp, the Chief himself riding foremost of the party. On the 8th December he again returned to Calcutta, on urgent duty in connection with his important charge; not, however, without eliciting an expression of regret at the loss of his immediate services on the part of the highest military authorities.

The undertaking specially entrusted to him, independently of general professional services and usefulness, was to carry the line of telegraph into the Alum-bagh, the entrenched garden rendered historical by Outram and his followers. This he performed successfully; but no sooner did the opportunity offer than the rebels destroyed his work. He moreover repaired the Cawnpore line on return to that station, and opened an office at the head-quarters camp, a position perhaps nearer to an enemy's guns than had ever before been occupied by telegraph officials at work. A round shot came into the very tent of the Superintendent himself, providentially while the energetic young officer was absent on a, to him, not uncommon outdoor duty. The fact is, that, though nominally a telegraphist, he was at this time more often employed on military duties immediately connected with his own branch of the service. From the 16th to the 28th November, as may well be credited, there was no attempt whatever made at doing telegraph work, except in the case of a successful semaphore which had been planned to meet emergencies. Stewart's value and versatility were doubtless highly appreciated at this critical juncture. It is well authenticated that the Chief habitually prefaced his orders to him by the stern injunction not to get shot, if he could help it!'

A correspondent of the Bengal *Hurkaru*, who accompanied the camp, describes the Alam-bagh:

"It is a large garden enclosed by a brick wall about 10 feet high; has circular bastions surmounted by cupolas at each angle, and a Moorish-looking gateway in the centre of the northern face. . . . In the centre of the garden is a large, square, solid-looking building, of two storeys, with a terraced roof, on the top of which floats the meteor flag of Old England; and a semaphore, got up by Lieutenant Stewart of the Telegraph, rises thinly above the mass, the wooden arms of which, grotesque as their movements look, are speaking eloquent and cheering words to our beleaguered countrymen in Lucknow. Since our occupation of Alam-bagh its walls have been loopholed, earthen bastions thrown up in advance of the original ones, a *banquette* runs through the interior, a ditch and camp round the exterior, of the wall, and altogether the place is becoming a very defensible position."

These were doubtless times when there was great risk of life and limb; and though Stewart escaped unscathed, it was circumstantially reported that he had lost a leg by a round shot. The origin of this report he thought attributable to having been seen asleep on the ground on the night of the 16th September, when most of his dress below the waist was stained with blood. Thankful, however, as he had reason to be for immunity from the

---

[1] The Bengal *Hurkaru* states that permission to join the second Lucknow expedition was given to Lieutenant Stewart somewhat reluctantly, and was accompanied by a telegram from the Governor-General to the Commander-in-Chief that he "was, if possible, not to be killed!" The paper adds: "Sir Colin read the order, and looking up, saw his object quietly slipping out with his rifle to join a party of skirmishers who expected hot work. 'Come out of that!' shouted the Chief in a strong vernacular, 'not content with killing yourself, you must give me the discredit of it.'"

many accidents of desultory as well as active warfare, and assuming himself, that campaigning and its attendant hardships "did him all the good in the world," in fact, that while undergoing them he was "twice as well and strong as when he left Calcutta," he could not but acknowledge that the doctors were right in deciding that he should not await another hot season in India to revisit England; and it was arranged that he should proceed home by one of the steamers in April 1858.

Returning to Calcutta from Cawnpore, just after the Gwalior force had been defeated and driven from the district, he was enabled to give Lord Canning details of all the more recent operations before any written accounts had come to hand. His reception at Government House was commensurate with the deep interest evinced by its distinguished inmates in the intelligence brought them. The loss of his horse during the severe fighting at Lucknow had entailed the loss of his diary, which, with other papers, had been put into the holsters attached to the saddle. That diary was the only record he possessed of all that had struck him as noteworthy during the two years preceding. Valuable as it must have been in the light of a private reference, it was perhaps of yet more importance professionally considered. He had to supply the deficiency by the best means available. At Lord Canning's request he drew out, and completed, plans illustrative of all the operations at or near Lucknow. Five copies of the connected Despatches, with seven plans attached to each, were forwarded to London for the Palace, the Horse Guards, and members of Government. The non-official way in which they were prepared will account for the omission of the draughtsman's name.

On the 18th January, 1858, Sir William O'Shaughnessy, who had returned to Western India from Europe, addressed from Punah the following special telegram to the Secretary to Government in Calcutta:—

"I claim the privilege, as the head of the Telegraph Department, to place on record an expression of the admiration and gratitude with which I regard the services rendered to Government and the public, during my absence in Europe, by Lieutenant Patrick Stewart while officiating as Superintendent of Telegraphs in India. His indefatigable exertions, almost incessant movements, and the gallant and scientific performance of his duties under every difficulty and danger, have been witnessed by the Governor-General and by his Excellency the Commander-in-Chief. It would be presumptuous in me to offer any definite suggestions as to the requital of his Oude services, but I will add my earnest hope that some substantial reward may be conferred on Lieutenant Stewart, not only as an acknowledgment of his great merit, but as an encouragement to others to follow the brilliant example he has set."

But Stewart's experience of active service during the Indian Mutinies was not yet complete. The state of his health had hushed all reasonable expectation of moving from Calcutta until the departure of the English steamer in April, when a sudden call acted like magic upon his eager nature. Lord Canning was about to leave the Presidency for the North-West, and the special talents and usefulness of the young Engineer were wanted. Persuading himself, and those for whom he had to exercise persuasion, that his rest had been ample to admit of a new expedition up country, he was allowed to proceed to Allahabad, where he was for four days with the Governor-General considering an engineering project in which His Excellency was greatly interested. It was proposed to make Allahabad an immense military position by constructing a chain of defensive works across the country between the Ganges and Jamna, some four miles above the Fort. The origin of this project was a memorandum drawn up by Lieutenant Stewart for General Havelock, with reference to the defences of Benares, Allahabad, and Mirzapur. But the extensive nature of the work had caused it to be put aside at a time when but a very small military force was available in India. It was now revived, as more applicable to the changed state of affairs. From Allahabad Stewart again joined army head-quarters, and was temporarily attached to the Staff by Sir Colin Campbell.

Besides re-opening the telegraph to Alam-bagh, Stewart was entrusted with what he calls " a glorious piece of mischief." This was the destruction with gun-powder of the whole of the temples and buildings on the bank of the Ganges immediately above the entrenchments at Cawnpore. Acts of this nature, however much, in ordinary times, they may merit the charge of Vandalism, must be judged by the circumstances under which they are sanctioned. The Indian Mutiny was not a common occurrence, nor had the Indian mutineer shown himself amenable to the treatment recognized by an enlightened civilization for common offenders.

The author of the " Diary in India," to whom the public is indebted for two most interesting volumes, which will long live to tell the tale of these days of trial and danger, became associated about this period with Lieutenant Stewart. Under the auspices of the Governor-General's own introduction, they travelled together from Allahabad to Cawnpore, and there occupied adjacent tents in the camp. The fact is noted to draw the reader's attention to the book in question, especially to those passages bearing upon the subject of this memoir.

These will, at least, prove "Pat Stewart" to be no equivocal or second-rate hero:—

"Never since its discovery," writes the Correspondent of the *Times*, "has the electric telegraph played so important and daring a *rôle* as it now does in India. Without it the Commander-in-Chief would lose the effect of half his force. It has served him better than his right arm. By it he is enabled to direct the march of his battalions, the movements of his artillery and cavalry, to receive news of their successes, to survey, as it were, at any one time the whole position of his army and of its auxiliaries, to communicate with the Governor-General and with his subordinate generals, to sift the truth from the falsehood of native information, to learn what posts are likely to be threatened, where the enemy are in force, to spare his staff and his messengers, and yet to send messages with clearness and despatch. So much for its importance. As to the daring action of the telegraph, which includes of course those who direct it, I need only observe that in this war, for the first time, a telegraph wire has been carried along under fire and through the midst of a hostile country. *Pari passu*, from post to post it has moved on with our artillery, and scarcely has the Commander-in-Chief established his head-quarters at any spot where he intended to stay for a few days when the post and the wire were established also. The telegraph was brought into communication with the Governor-General at Allahabad, with Outram at the Alam-bagh, with Calcutta, Madras, Bombay, and the most remote districts over which the system is distributed. It is mainly to the zeal, energy, and ability of a young officer of the Bengal Engineers, Lieutenant Patrick Stewart, that these advantages are due. He is assisted, it is true, by a few men, but he it is who devises and superintends the execution and the extension of the line from place to place. At one time his men are chased for miles by the enemy's cavalry—at another time they are attacked by the Sowars, and they and the wires are cut to pieces—again, their electric batteries are smashed by the fire of a gun, or their cart knocked to pieces by a round shot; but still they work on, creep over arid plains, across watercourses, span rivers and pierce jungles, till one after another the rude poles raise aloft their slender burden, and the quick needle vibrates with its silent tongue amid the thunder of the artillery. While Sir C. Campbell was at Cawnpore he could learn from Sir James Outram the results of an attack before the enemy had disappeared from the field. As he advanced towards Lucknow, the line was carried with or soon after him; a tent was pitched near his, a hole was dug in the ground and filled with water, and down dropped the wire from the pole stuck up in haste, dived into the water otter-like, the simple magnet was arranged, the battery set in play, and at once the steel moved responsive to every touch. Owing to the extreme dryness of the atmosphere and the power of the sun, which at this season bakes the earth like a brick, the insulation of the current is nearly complete. The wire is thick, and is not protected by non-conductive coatings of any kind; it is twisted round the top of a rude pole, fifteen or sixteen feet high, and under ordinary states of the atmosphere, it is found to answer perfectly. We had not been very long in the Dilkusha ere we saw, in dim perspective, the line of posts advancing towards us, and soon the wire was slipped into one of the drawing-room windows, and now it is at full work, surrounded by all the shattered splendour of the palace, inquiring after the Ghoorkas, asking for more of something or other, exchanging ideas between Sir Colin and Lord Canning, or flurrying along a newspaper message to himself, amid the whistle of the bullet, the roar of the round shot, and all the feverish scenes of war."

To state a plain case practically, and from Stewart's own official data, the line of telegraph constructed from Cawnpore to Alam-bagh, in November, 1857, having been almost entirely destroyed, and the recovered portion of the wire applied to other purposes, its reconstruction a few weeks later was no easy matter. On the 17th February, 1858, during reconstruction, an office was opened at about 34 miles from Cawnpore for convenience of communication between the military camps. On the 19th, the line was completed, and a second office opened in General Outram's camp at Alam-bagh. On the following day, the first office having been closed, a new one was substituted at 26 miles from Cawnpore. On the 26th February, the last was closed and one opened near the Alam-bagh camp, which remained at work up to the 3rd March. On the 4th March, the native working party delayed progress by panic and flight, but on the 6th an office was opened in the advanced position of the Dilkusha at Lucknow. On the 8th, an expression of the Chief's wishes caused immediate construction of a double-armed semaphore for work on the spot, and despatch of a second to General Outram, Stewart himself preparing the code and proceeding to the latter General's camp to superintend arrangements. Though nothing was done with this semaphore, owing to circumstances arising during the progress of the general assault on Lucknow, the occupation of the Martinière pending organization enabled one of the telegraph officers to set up the line to that station with great rapidity. On the 10th, the line was carried to General Outram's headquarters, and a third office opened in the Lucknow camp on the day following. On the 12th the head-quarters office was removed from the Martinière to a tent, for the convenience of the Commander-in-Chief. The Alam-bagh office, which had been uninterruptedly at work since the 19th February, was closed on the 18th March.

In the report from which these details are gathered, the writer, while naturally diffident in speaking of the extent to which the electric telegraph manifestly aided the Lucknow operations, has no hesitation in declaring that the result of its application in this particular and very remarkable instance proves how extensively it may assist all military operations, especially those of an offensive character on a large scale. The few years which have elapsed since the third relief of Lucknow have sufficed to organize a special system of military telegraphy, and to test its successful use in European warfare. But it is questionable whether its appliances and discipline, if brought to bear upon the Oude campaigns, would have surpassed in effectiveness the rough and ready resources of Patrick Stewart and his energetic assistants. A strong will, a noble example, and a good cause, have a wonderful power of attaining adequacy, without the prescience to grasp at coming inventions. No modern science could enhance the glories of Thermopylæ.

Taking part in the third as well as second advance upon Lucknow, "Lieutenant P. Stewart of Engineers, Superintendent of Electric Telegraphs," was honourably named, with many gallant companions, in the Governor-General's order of the 5th April, 1858, recording that "from the 2nd to the 16th March, a series of masterly operations took place, by which the Commander-in-Chief, nobly supported in his well-laid plans of attack by the ability and skill of the general officers and men of all arms, drove the whole successfully from all their strongly fortified posts, till the whole fell into the possession of our troops." The thanks of the Chief for this new service had been already publicly tendered to him in his despatch to the Governor-General from the Martinière. Fuller but not more valued personal tributes are not wanting in the records of the day. A friend, writing to Scotland from Calcutta on the 18th March, reports that a telegram of the previous night had come in from

Lucknow certifying Pat Stewart's health: that the rebels were leaving the city in large numbers, pursued by cavalry and horse artillery, and, for the particular satisfaction of well-wishers, that "Pat" was tied down to his telegraphs and duties at head-quarters, and *could not* therefore follow them. The *Times* Correspondent, writing on the 20th March, or two days before date of the Martinière despatch, states:—

"Lieutenant P. Stewart, the indefatigable officer of the Bengal Engineers, who has had charge of our venturesome electric telegraphs, and their odd branches from the Martinière, Dilkusha, Banks'-house, and the Alam-bagh, to all over the world, is about to leave by next mail for England on account of ill-health."

And so indeed it was. On the 9th April, Stewart left India and returned to England. Still a young man, and comparatively of short service, his five to six years of an Indian career had been sufficiently active to count twice the time of an ordinary garrison life. He needed a change homeward, and certainly deserved it. He would leave work behind him; but there were soldiers more than enough for its accomplishment. The fires of the rebellion had not been wholly extinguished, but they were now rather scattered and smouldering than fierce and continuous. The great events of Delhi and Lucknow had passed into the pages of history. Such work as loomed in the prospect was of a less momentous character, and foreshadowed rather retribution and reparation than battle and resistance. The second chapter of the great Indian Mutiny was without the horrors or the struggles of the first.

The good opinion of Lieutenant Stewart, expressed both publicly and privately by the Governor-General and

Indian officials of rank and influence, secured him a warm reception from many high and notable personages at home. What with dinners, balls, receptions, conferences, and ceremonies, his time was tolerably well occupied for at least the London season. He found time, however, to run down to Plymouth and join the expedition proceeding thence, in June, 1858, to lay the Atlantic cable, as attested by a letter dated the eve of departure on board of H.M.S. *Agamemnon*.

At the close of the year his attention was specifically drawn to two questions on which information was required by the State. One was the applicability to Indian Telegraphy of certain instruments manufactured in Prussia; the other his own employment on the Turkish Asiatic land lines, which it was in contemplation to extend to the Persian Gulf. His professional experience and practical intelligence were brought to bear, without loss of time, on the first of these matters. Instruments, descriptions, and plans were reported on and despatched to India; and Stewart returned from his second official visit to Berlin on the 28th January, 1859, bearing letters to Windsor Castle which had preceded by a few hours only the telegram announcing the birth of the young Prince Frederick William. Complimented on delivering his despatches in thirty-eight hours after receipt, it is no reflection on professional or amateur messengers to say, that owing to unforeseen obstacles, Stewart had really performed a feat of couriership. Left behind by the express at Oberhausen, he had to make the best of his way across country to Aix to recover his place in it. In this he succeeded, but with the loss of his passport and Calais ticket, which forced him to turn off to Bruges and cross from Ostend. Eventually his letters were delivered two hours earlier than expected, and not a moment of delay was caused by his misadventures.

As regards the second question, so much will have to be said by and by about the Turkish Telegraph, it will suffice to state in this place that an officer of Her Majesty's service was then engaged in assisting the Imperial Ottoman Government in the construction of their Asiatic lines; that it was under consideration to send out a second officer for the furtherance of the same work; but that Major Stewart was not destined to take any active part in first organizing and establishing this particular section of the Indo-European Telegraph.

Stewart had been made a Brevet-Major, in acknowledgment of his Indian services, on the 25th August, 1858, the day after attaining his Captaincy. He had been fortunate in regimental promotion. Promoted from Second to First Lieutenant in less than two years after landing in India, he became a Captain in barely four years afterwards.

During the year 1859 he had a severe attack of sickness which necessitated correspondingly severe treatment. He had never seemed to recover wholly from the fall in the Panjáb in December, 1854, and to this he attributed much indirect subsequent suffering. Though restored to comparative health, under the best medical advice, his physical condition was not such as to relieve his friends from anxiety, and it became a matter of serious consideration whether India was not an unsuitable climate for him. His wonted energy soon, however, dispelled all doubts on future proceedings. Recovery from temporary depression brought with it new determination to exert usefulness whenever and wherever it found a field. No wonder, then, that he was authoritatively instructed while at home, both in 1859 and 1860, to undertake scientific inquiries of high public importance, among which was conspicuous an effectual means of electric intercommunication for the defensive works round the better known English harbours, a duty which involved a certain amount of healthful locomotion. He had also to report on the submarine cable prepared by Government for connecting Gibraltar with England direct; and to consider, in minute detail, a proposal for telegraphic communication at Malta.

In August, 1860, Stewart married, and in November left England, with his bride, for the East again. The outward overland journey was rendered more than usually interesting by a diversion through the valley of the Rhine and Geneva, to Marseilles, from which port they embarked on the 29th November. Before the dawn of the new year they had reached Calcutta.

It was the intention of Government at this time to lay a cable from India towards China, and Stewart, who had been selected to superintend operations, would await at Calcutta news of the despatch of the Singapore section, which he would then hasten to meet at Penang. But circumstances changed, and accidents occurred, and the scheme never ripened into fulfilment. Months passed in expectation of the promised expedition; but at last came a countermand, and Stewart was detained in Calcutta until after the rains on other duty. New Government offices were required at the Presidency, and he was entrusted with drawing out the plans. In September, he was appointed with four others to a special commission for ascertaining the cause of the great mortality from cholera. In the prosecution of this inquiry they visited Agra, Delhi, Ambalah, Amritsar, Lahor, Gwalior;

also Simla, and neighbouring hill stations; returning to send in their results in Jan. 1862. The report was of a comprehensive character, and had in view the means of improving the sanitary condition of the soldier in India.

Scarcely had this labour been completed when orders were received to depute Major Stewart to Persia on a particular mission connected with the construction of a proposed Telegraph in that country. As a separate chapter of this volume has been reserved for the history of the Persian lines, and as the remainder of the short but brilliant career of the above lamented officer was mainly devoted to the furtherance of Indo-European telegraphic communication, to which the said Persian lines would contribute a respectable quota, and the true history of which, so far as carried out under Government orders, is the main intent of this whole work, the interval between Stewart's final departure from Calcutta and his fatal illness at Constantinople will be rapidly sketched, to avoid repetition.

Leaving Calcutta in February, and Ceylon, after some two or three weeks' detention, in March, he proceeded *viâ* Bombay and Karáchi to the Persian Gulf, disembarking at Bushahr, and journeying to Tehran by land. Sickness drove him from Tehran on the 18th June, and he at once went home through Russia. After recruiting his health in England under the drawback of incessant official duty, and completing the arrangements for the Persian Gulf cable with which he was entrusted as the responsible head, he proceeded to Bombay in November 1863, laid the cable from Gwádar to Fáo, and returned from the Persian Gulf to Bombay, thence to establish temporary head-quarters at Constantinople. He arrived here in the summer of 1864. Thenceforward, except to make a brief excursion into the neighbourhood or to change air and scene at Therapia, he remained in Pera until the day of his decease. On the 16th January 1865 he expired at Misseri's Hotel.

It was the painful privilege of the writer of this memoir to be present with Patrick Stewart during his last illness; and it became his duty to report its result as a matter of public as well as private interest and sympathy. However feeble the language, the lapse of years has shown no cause to revise the sentiments expressed. No apology will therefore be needed for re-publishing a letter which appeared in the *Times* of the 27th January:—

"A sad event has just occurred at Constantinople. A young and highly-accomplished officer of the scientific branch of the army, whose name is familiar as a household word in India, and promised to be equally celebrated in Europe, Lieutenant Colonel Patrick Stewart of the Royal Engineers, has breathed his last after three weeks of almost continual suffering. He had left England at the close of 1863 for the purpose of laying the Indo-European sea cable along the coast of Baluchistan and Persia, had successfully escorted his important charge up to the head of the Persian Gulf at Fáo, reaching the shores of Turkish Arabia in a few weeks after leaving Kurachi, and then moved up to Baghdad to see what was the prospect of ensuring an efficient communication to and from that city. Unfortunately, though the Ottoman Government had agreed to bring their land line to the Persian Gulf at the mouth of the Shatt-el-Arab, in time to meet the Indian sea cable, it was found on the arrival of the latter that a gap of 170 miles of the Turkish section still remained unfinished between Baghdad and Basrah. Nor was there promise even of speedy completion. The Turks wished to put up the line; the Arabs would not let them. The matter would have been trivial to a Power like England; it was a long-standing obstacle in Turkish Asia. We should have subsidized the rebellious Montefiks into guardians of the line. The obstinacy of a Turkish Pasha made them his bitter enemies, and consequently hostile to the telegraph which he wished to erect. Under these circumstances Colonel Stewart returned to India from Baghdad in April 1864.

"After making his arrangements in Bombay he embarked for Egypt and Constantinople, landing at Galata in July. From that time to the hour of his sickness he has been constantly engaged in urging the Ottoman authorities to organize at least one thoroughly efficient wire for the Anglo-Indian telegraphic service. In the first instance his attention was given to certain amendments in their Asiatic lines, inspected and re-inspected by British officers; to placing a competent staff of clerks and signallers along that line sufficiently acquainted with English to prevent a recurrence of the absurd mistakes heretofore committed by the misuse of that language and incorrect translations; and to framing a full convention with the Turkish Government which would meet all future requirements on the subject of international telegraphic communication. It then appeared that, while perfecting the Asiatic system, there was danger of deterioration on the European side. Attention was consequently drawn to the Danubian and Adriatic lines of Turkey. But a Turkish office is not like an English one. Several cigarettes have to be smoked, and several formal visits have to be got through, before the actual entry into business can be attempted; and in nine cases out of ten, even after business has been fairly begun, nothing results except under strong pressure. The first stage of inertion got over, the next one is a question of personal interests. It is the last stage only which can be considered the truly successful one, where something like punishment and degradation is held out *in terrorem*.

"Colonel Stewart had an able assistant in Major Champain, a brother officer of Engineers. This gentleman has held charge of the Persian line of telegraph, which, branching off from the Turkish line at Baghdad, takes a long course to the Persian Gulf through Tehran, and joins the Indian Sea cable at Bushahr. The completion of this alternative line would render the failure between Baghdad and Basrah of comparatively little importance, for the correspondence would then have effect from

Constantinople to Baghdad, from Baghdad to Bushahr, and from Bushahr—by submarine cable—to Gwadar or Karachi, at either of which places is a terminus of the Indian system. The difficulties which the above-named officer has had to encounter with the Persian authorities in achieving his important work are simply indescribable; but he managed to carry his point, and this route has already been declared open. It is not too much to say that devotion to his young chief has been a great element of Major Champain's success in a work of as much moral as physical obstruction.

"Nine months ago Patrick Stewart had fervently hoped to have completed one of these two lines of Indian telegraphic communication. His own fair share of the work he had done was publicly acknowledged by admission to the Order of the Bath. He had brought Bright's wondrous sea cable himself to the head of the Persian Gulf, and joined it to the fragment of land line found at Fáo; as far back as 1862 he had surveyed the Persian land line from Bushahr to Tehran. The rest was a political battle, which the director of the Anglo-Indian Telegraph was hardly called upon to fight. That he did fight it in conjunction with our diplomatists is owing to the accurate knowledge that he possessed of all details of diplomatic difficulty connected with these questions, as well as to the winning intelligence which made him the desired companion and coadjutor of public men, whatever their rank or station.

"But in serving the State as a true and loyal soldier, at the desk as in the field, he overtaxed his energies. Sharp and severe Indian sicknesses, constant warnings of danger from fevers which pursued him to Europe, daily-increasing sensitiveness in matters of duty—here were reasons, not only for relaxation, but temporary cessation from labour. He had not been really well for many weeks, but he could not be persuaded to quit Constantinople, which he seemed to consider for the time the post of honour. It was, in fact, the central point for a joint European and Asiatic line on the eve of completion, and especially favourable for watching and correcting defects when once the working had begun. Besides, there is no disguising the fact that the mal-administration of Turkish telegraphs called for the closest observation and care in the early operations of the Indian line. But this was not all. He had at length made up his mind to leave the place, but must delay for one more interview at the Porte to obtain some further concessions, with a view to the future security of his undertaking. This interview, though a day had been fixed, never had effect. About Christmas he was seriously ill. On the 28th of December his malady assumed the form of cerebral affection. A pernicious intermittent fever supervened, followed by a complication of disorders. The medical officers pronounced the case a difficult one, owing to the previous condition of the patient. The strain upon the mental powers had been too great, and the physical powers were generally disorganized. The best advice procurable was obtained. Those persons who know Constantinople will readily remember the names of Zohrab, Millingen, Fauvel, and Dickson, all of whom attended in consultation on the case, Drs. Millingen and Fauvel being present at the more critical periods. All was in vain. It was the Almighty's will that the young soldier should die—not on the visible field of battle, but on one not wanting in glory. On the morning of the 16th of January he ceased to exist; and on the day following he was accompanied to his grave by more than one sincere mourner. A residence of some months at Constantinople had secured him many true friends here as elsewhere. He rests in Scutari, about fifty yards from the monument to the Crimean heroes—an honourable resting-place, which he himself had visited in health during the milder season. His age was thirty-two.

"It is not my intention to describe Colonel Stewart's Indian career. The task is worthy of fitter pens than mine. Mr. Russell's 'Diary in India' has already thrown a light upon the theme. I speak now of the last year of his life, in which close and intimate acquaintance has enabled me to know more of him than of most men. But I may say a word on his character now that he is no more among us. In a long experience of life in all its phases I have rarely, if ever, met so thoroughly and generally attractive a person. A brave and dashing soldier, as well as ardent, enthusiastic sportsman, he was tender, gentle, and conciliating to a degree. Possessed of a high order of intellect and varied acquirements, he was modest and retiring in urging any claims to personal benefit or advantage. His extraordinary zeal in the public service, while it led him sometimes into the natural error of believing all others with whom he had to do possessed of the same British energy and liberal-mindedness, never caused him to overtax those employed under him. In this respect his great consideration was a remarkable feature in so young a man. A high authority, writing since his death, will forgive me for using his most appropriate words:—'So much knowledge, intelligence, earnestness, kind-heartedness, and winning simplicity can rarely be united in the same person, and in him there was no other side of the picture.'

'Not many days ago the Persian minister at this Court received a telegram reporting the completion of the Persian line from Baghdad to Bushahr. Another report showed the Basrah line to be also just completed, thanks to the exertions of Colonel Kemball, our Consul-General. Immediate telegraphic communication with India may, therefore, be expected. These facts were communicated to Colonel Stewart, when his fate was still doubtful. But the lamp was nearly out; their importance, if appreciated at all, was not to him what it had been. The spirit was soaring to a less worldly region than that of human science or effort.'

The testimony to Stewart's public services of the distinguished nobleman who ruled India in her most critical period is not confined to public letters or orders. It might be superfluous to quote non-official records in support of this particular assertion; but there is among these an expression, bearing on private worth, the felicity of which will plead excuse for publication. The late Lord Canning, while foretelling a brilliant career to the young officer, adds: "and there is no one with such pleasant good manners, or more agreeable society, or more unspoiled."

He was "unspoiled" because he had a fixed purpose of being useful to his generation; and all steps in the ladder of his ambition were steps towards that end. Had he allowed himself to be swayed by self-conceit, to lose want of consideration for his fellows, to prefer self to duty; had he turned aside from his chosen path to seek a pastime in actual vice or a study in spurious virtue, he would have marred the one object in view, which was essentially Christian in its comprehensiveness. This quality of conscience, as much perhaps as rare energy and ability, made him not only what is called a rising man, but kept him "unspoiled" as he rose.

In lasting token of respect and regard, no less than three memorials have been raised to Patrick Stewart since his death. One is the tomb at Scutari, one a subscription window and bust in the telegraph library at Karáchi, and one a subscription window in the family church at Minnigaff, near Newton Stewart.

LIBRARY, WITH STEWART MEMORIAL WINDOW, AT KARÁCHI.

CHAPTER II.

PRELIMINARY ARRANGEMENTS IN ASIATIC TURKEY.
NEGOTIATIONS WITH THE OTTOMAN GOVERNMENT.

THE practical progress of the Electric Telegraph during the last thirty years illustrates, in a remarkable manner, the rapidity with which development follows an important discovery of science. A miniature line of land telegraph, set up on the four miles of Blackwall railway in 1840, however limited its operation, was so successful that, in 1845, roadside wires had lost their novelty in England; and while speculations in the American press foreshadowed the great event of the Atlantic cable, a proposal was actually submitted in the course of that year to the British prime minister of the day,[1] for a joint land and sea telegraph of more than one thousand times the extent of the Blackwall experiment. By such mixed telegraph, communication was to be established with India viâ France, Sardinia, Malta, and Alexandria.

No active measures immediately attended this early introduction of a topic which, to say the least, must have been, at the time, startling in its strangeness. Reference

---

[1] Sir Robert Peel: "Correspondence respecting the Establishment of Telegraphic Communications in the Mediterranean and with India," page 78, line 10.

to the Parliamentary Blue Books shows, however, that not ten years afterwards, or on the 28th Sept. 1854, Mr. Lionel Gisborne put forward the project of a submarine telegraph from Constantinople to Alexandria, as a preliminary step to a telegraph to India; that on the 12th December, 1854, the projector was invited by the Porte, through Lord Clarendon, to discuss the question at Constantinople; and that on the 23rd April, 1855, a concession[1] was granted to the same gentleman for the construction of a telegraph from the Dardanelles to Alexandria, the Porte binding itself to complete the link between the Dardanelles and Constantinople. In connection with this scheme, which fell through in its original design from adverse influences to which similar undertakings must, in a greater or less degree, be subject, arose the " European and Indian Junction Telegraph Company," whose prospectus was issued on the 19th July 1855; and, as a sequel to it, the " Red Sea Telegraph Company," officially announced on the 29th August 1857.

The argument of the present chapter involves abandonment of the general question in its detail. We have to trace the origin and progress of the negotiations opened by her Majesty's Government with the Sublime Porte for establishing a land telegraph throughout the length of the Sultan's Asiatic dominions, to unite England and India. To carry out this purpose many scattered Blue Books and many scattered printed and manuscript papers must be consulted. The story of the Submarine Cable will be told with equal minuteness, but its disentanglement from the records is a much simpler affair; nor need

---

[1] "Correspondence respecting the Establishment of Telegraphic Communications in the Mediterranean and with India," page 76, from top to line 14.

the chronicler of its formation and utilisation search for his data elsewhere than in the shelves of the India Office and tributary departments.

It is by no means strange that the first mention of international negotiation betwixt England and Turkey for a telegraph to India should be found recorded in the annals of 1856. The alliance cemented by the Crimean war, and the enhanced value resulting from that war to telegraphic communication as a State requirement, would alone have ensured favourable reception by British diplomatists of a scheme to render available the vast Ottoman territory between Belgrade and Basrah, for a line of posts and wires in connection with an Indian submarine cable. Later, however, causes arose to give fresh impetus to the demand for an Anglo-Indian telegraph; and the Indian Mutiny of 1857, and failure of the Red Sea Cable in 1859, made it more than ever urgent to investigate and determine the lines offering the best advantages to telegraphic communication between Western Europe and the Persian Gulf.

In August 1856, when cables, and companies for the construction and use of cables, were not so numerous as at present, the European and Indian Junction Telegraph Company applied to the then existing Court of Directors of the East India Company for a guarantee on an estimated expenditure of 200,000*l.* for a line of land telegraph from Seleucia, or Suadiah, on the Syrian coast, to Korna, at the junction of the Tigris and Euphrates.[1] The link, if successfully completed and worked, would have rendered comparatively facile a

---

[1] Mr. Andrew to the Secretary, East India Company, August 5, 1856 : "Correspondence respecting the Establishment of Telegraphic Communications in the Mediterranean and with India," page 128.

whole line of Indo-European communication. For, to join a port on the eastern shores of the Mediterranean with the French system at Marseilles or the Italian system at Brindisi, would have presented no special difficulty to submarine telegraphy; and a successfully working Persian Gulf cable has long since become an established fact. That this, if not the truest direct route to India, is nearer the mark than any which has been hitherto before the public, whether for telegraph or railway, cannot even now be doubted by any unprejudiced person who has taken the trouble to master the subject in detail; and that it will be found so, before the speculation and enterprise of the present age shall have given place to new characteristics of progressive civilization, there is ample ground for belief. The question for decision seems to be whether or no the mouth of the Orontes is the fittest starting-point for rail and wire intended to connect the Mediterranean with the Persian Gulf? And here we may well pause to reflect whether too little attention has not in this respect been bestowed on the Syrian ports below Seleucia, on the Palmyra desert, and on the desert post-track between Damascus and Baghdad?

The notion of an Indian telegraph through Asiatic Turkey had, at this time, been just interpreted, more or less comprehensively, to the East India Company by Dr. O'Shaughnessy, Superintendent of Indian Telegraphs.[1] This officer, arguing in favour of a direct line of telegraph to connect Karáchi with Constantinople, proposed to lay a cable from the former place to Korna, to continue thence subaqueous communication to Baghdad,

[1] "Correspondence respecting the Establishment of Telegraphic Communications in the Mediterranean and with India," pages 118 to 124.

and to construct a land line between Baghdad and Scutari *viâ* Mosul, Diarbekir, Sivas, Amasia, and Tokat. In a second letter he suggested a modification of no small importance. This was to substitute for the long land line through Asia Minor a series of subaqueous cables in the Euphrates, and a subterraneous telegraph between the Euphrates and Seleucia, connecting the latter port by submarine cable with the European system. The feasibility of the modified project never having been tested, it might be premature to condemn it unreservedly, but the most recent experience will hardly bring fresh arguments in favour of its revival.

To return to the European and Indian Junction Telegraph Company. The Court of Directors were not unwilling to join her Majesty's Government in subsidising and otherwise promoting the success of the proposed line, but diplomatic action was too hampered and fettered to be made availing to the accomplishment of the Telegraph Company's wishes. Doubtless, it is often easier for the astute diplomatist to conduct an intricate negotiation on behalf of that Government whose interests he represents, than to plead the ordinary case of a private company or individual by virtue of mere official position at the court from which some special assent is awaited. The objections of the Porte to make the concessions required were accompanied with an express resolve to undertake the work on its own account. Mr. Andrew, Chairman of the Telegraph Company, rightly estimating the public importance of the proposed scheme, but undervaluing the professions and resources of Turkey, pressed a renewal of negotiations, on the ground that the Firman he sought could alone ensure the existence of a satisfactory line of communication as regards construction, maintenance, and working.¹ Matters had indeed gone so far that Lieutenant Hawes, an officer of the Bengal army, had been specially deputed on a mission to Baghdad, to take measures on behalf of the company, for commencing the work which they had engaged to perform. And the official report to the Secretary of the Treasury of this gentleman's departure on his mission bears date the day previous to that on which Lord Stratford telegraphed home news of the rejection by the Ottoman Council of the Company's proposals.²

In September 1857, however, Lord Stratford de Redcliffe, while verifying the validity of the Porte's former decision, informed Lord Clarendon that a wire would be made over to the British Government, with liberty to appoint British agents, workmen, and directors.³ Thus the concession withheld from a private company meant no want of harmony with the enlightened objects of a friendly State; and as further token of good intentions, a formal application was made by the Turkish minister in the January following for the services of Lieutenant-Colonel Biddulph of the Royal Artillery.⁴ An expression of willingness before notified, to employ English engineers in carrying out the operations, was moreover repeated. Compliance in both cases on the part of her Majesty's Government was natural under the circumstances.

Great social and political changes have taken place, both in the East and West, since the Crimean war; and

¹ Mr. Andrew to Mr. Hammond, September 18, 1857: "Correspondence respecting the Establishment of Telegraphic Communications in the Mediterranean and with India," pages 193, 194.
² Ibid. pages 142 and 144.
³ Ibid. p. 194.
⁴ Mr. Musurus to Lord Clarendon: Ibid. pages 206, 207.

by these changes England has, in common with the states of Continental Europe, been sensibly affected. Without entering into an analysis of profit and loss during this interval, or looking beyond the narrow limits of a Telegraph history, it may be safely asserted that, externally, her relations with Oriental powers, such as Turkey and Persia, have been simplified; while, internally, an administrative spirit has arisen out of commercial activity, to stimulate, or, if it fail to stimulate, to complicate the routine-tied administration of established Government. After the peace of March 1856, the remainder of the year may be considered a period of comparative repose and reaction in Europe. To England, moreover, there flickered in the distance the flame of a little war just kindled in Persia, which, however pale when contrasted with the red fires of Sebastopol, revealed an incident of much political method and meaning. In Turkey, at least, matters were then much as they were and had been for years before the Crimean war. For the Ottoman Empire, the transition state, if indeed begun, had exercised no perceptible influence. Progress, in its accepted sense of fusion of East into West, was more a promise and a semblance than a plain, incontrovertible fact; it was yet unwise and unsafe to bridge over, by anticipation, a gap which precedent would not admit of traversing without the warrant of Time; and although in these more recent days a few months may do the work of years, yet those few months are all the more indispensable from fulness of significance. In plain words, Turkey was not so Europeanized in 1857–8 as she has become in 1870.[1]

[1] Had this volume been of a political character, allusion to later signs and results might have been appropriately added. As it is, the passage remains as written more than three years ago.

At such a time, then, few British officers but would feel the construction of a telegraph in Asia Minor and Mesopotamia, dependent on the aid and subject to the approval of the Ottoman Government, to be a task of no small responsibility and difficulty. Ready to allow liberally for the natural difference of character between European and Asiatic, and with the best intentions of discouraging and barring access to every dangerous impulse peculiar to the former, the most patient and conciliatory mind would still be sorely tried in an isolation with which there could be no authoritative sympathy. It must be borne in mind that, at the period to which reference is now made, the Telegraph was as strange amid the tumuli of Nineveh and plains around Babylon as in the ancient days of splendour and greatness acknowledged for those cities. It is only within the last very few years that the inhabitants of modern Assyria and Chaldæa have not only become reconciled to these practical posts and wires, but have learnt to look on them as familiar and every-day objects. The officer named for the particular duty in question commenced active work in August 1858. Prostrated by a malignant fever which attacked his whole small staff, and disappointed in obtaining the support from the Ottoman administration on which success mainly depended, he shortly resigned the two first sections of his charge, retaining only the lower portion below Baghdad; and in February, 1859, applied for leave of absence. This step was followed in the same year by total withdrawal from the Superintendence.

Colonel Biddulph's report[1] of breaking ground is on record. It shows the progress made up to October 1859

[1] To Sir H. Rawlinson, K.C.B., dated Constantinople, October 9, 1859.

to be 325 miles out of an assumed total of 1,500; it explains, moreover, the impediments to success already apparent, and the measures which should be taken to secure results worthy of the trouble and cost of the undertaking. That as much had been done as could reasonably have been expected, in a short time and amid serious difficulties, was the formally expressed opinion of high authority in submitting the case to the Secretary of State for India. The work was continued by Mr. Carthew and two brothers named MacCallum, all retired non-commissioned officers of Artillery, who had been members of the original party, a staff which did not, at any time, contain more than eleven Englishmen. To the first named was entrusted construction of the line between Mosul and Basrah, in fulfilment of which trust he arrived, with four assistants, at Baghdad in July 1859.[1] The other Superintendents were engaged in the prolongation of the line already commenced in Asia Minor, eastward to Sivas, and thence southward towards Diarbekir and Mosul.

In addition to the report above mentioned, a valuable paper by Colonel Biddulph, throwing light on the history of the Turkish Asiatic Telegraph, and attached by the author to an elaborate map illustrative of his subject, has been printed. Divesting the pamphlet of personal matter, the introduction of which was unavoidable under the circumstances, its perusal will amply repay the interested reader. The view taken of the future of the Turkish Asiatic lines, if perhaps a shade too dark and gloomy, has not proved so mistaken as to throw discredit on the writer's discri-

[1] Major Kemball to her Majesty's Secretary of State for Foreign Affairs, dated Baghdad, July 20, 1859.

mination and foresight; and the map boasts a character of usefulness and importance in marked contrast to the ordinary illustrative accompaniments to telegraph schemes of the day. Here it may be remarked, *en passant*, that the reckless manner in which Mercator's, or the village schoolboy's World, has been subjected to the vaguest tracings of imaginary telegraph lines, to suit the purposes of promoters and speculators, however indirectly it may have led inquirers to a heretofore neglected study of geography, cannot be said to have imparted the wanting knowledge by any teaching of its own.

As stated in the preceding chapter, there had been some intention of employing Major Stewart in the construction of this long line of telegraph. Independently of the question of individual fitness, it appears that the services of an officer then in India had been applied for to assist Colonel Biddulph; and that an objection to withdraw officers from Indian stations had caused attention to be directed to the discovery of an eligible substitute at home. Patrick Stewart's name naturally suggested itself to the authorities. His state of health was, however, a bar to unconditional acceptance of service in Asia, and as a loan to a foreign administration; and it was, perhaps, well for him that a reference on his account to Constantinople went the way of many similar missives, and became obsolete before obtaining the favour of a reply. Major Stewart did not go out at all, and Colonel Biddulph, as above shown, felt himself compelled to resign the work of telegraph construction in Asiatic Turkey at the very outset.

A later chapter in this volume will be given to the author's own experience of the country traversed by the

Indo-Ottoman telegraph; and as this experience will bear more upon general than departmental questions, the reader will understand the exclusion of the former under the present head. The object is now to place on record the causes which have produced the means of telegraphic communication up to this time existing in Asiatic Turkey; and to let the public judge who, if any one, is fairly responsible if such means have not proved sufficient or satisfactory.

For facility of geographical reference, the line from Scutari to Baghdad may be shown under three heads:—

1. Scutari to Sivas, or the Asia Minor section; about 500 miles.
2. Sivas to Jazireh, or the West of Euphrates and Upper Mesopotamia section, about 450 miles; so called because the Euphrates crosses the post road from the East 140 miles below Sivas, and, by running a parallel course with the Tigris some distance further down, helps to enclose a great portion of the Diarbekir pashalik, in which the line runs.
3. Jazireh to Baghdad, or the East of Tigris section; about 300 miles.

The first of these sections is difficult in its mountains, ravines and forests. The second is free from forests, but not being confined to the high table-land of Asia Minor, contains, together with its mountains, large tracts of plain country, and thus presents ascents and

---

Lieut.-Colonel Gabband to Lieut.-Colonel Patrick Stewart, dated Pera, August 30, 1864; copy inclosed in Letter to Secretary to Government, Bombay, No. 35, of 31 December, 1864.

descents of a formidable kind. The third section is, for the most part, in low land, or amid low ranges of hills studding or overhanging the valley of the Upper Tigris. While the first two sections were of a character to tax severely the judgment as well as perseverance of the constructing engineer, the third section was perhaps the one most likely to be interrupted after construction. It was more open and exposed, and more subject to the influence of storms and freshets.

We gather from the earlier reports on this interesting and difficult work, that the general direction of the line was determined upon "from a rough outline furnished by Omar Pacha to the Ottoman Telegraph administration, having straight lines drawn joining the towns of Scutari, Izmid, Angora, Yuzgat, Sivas, Diarbekir, Mosul, Baghdad, and Basrah together."[*] It was questioned whether, on fairly entering the interior of Asia Minor, it should not have rather followed the post road to Sivas, through Bolu and Amasia, than the less frequented road through Angora and Yuzgat. And indeed it will be seen that this line accords with Sir W. O'Shaughnessy's first proposal. But it is probable that, beyond the advantage, if any, of keeping the more ordinary of two lines of traffic, much would not have been gained by such modification of the Turkish plan. The criticisms on the Ottoman administration and executive in putting their plan into execution seem to point more truly to the actual source of evil. Among the higher officials there is no lack of cleverness, and an ability passing average may here and there be acknowledged; but a supervision wanting honesty, fearlessness, thoroughness and perseverance, loses usefulness and power, however

[*] Colonel Biddulph to Sir H. Rawlinson, October 9, 1859.

favoured with mental capability. Of the subordinates, an experience of the Turkish character commencing eighteen years ago leads the present writer to the belief that the Turk of 1858-9, whatever his faults, and whatever the drawbacks over which he had no control, possessed in an eminent degree those qualities of obedience and endurance so valuable in the artificer and workman.

Before treating the line from Constantinople to Baghdad as a perfected whole and by the light of two detailed inspections under British officers after completion, it will be well to turn to the official correspondence in 1859-60; while it was still in progress, and before any definite arrangements had been made for completing the lower section from Baghdad to Busrah, and thence to the Persian Gulf cable.

The view taken by the Home authorities of the telegraph to India, in respect of the long link through Asiatic Turkey, at the period of Colonel Biddulph's resignation, was naturally not hopeful, nor such as to warrant a hopeful despatch on the subject to the Government of India. Sir William O'Shaughnessy, then Superintendent of Telegraphs in India, not only advised the East India Company as already stated, but had been, two years before, in personal consultation with Lord Stratford on the subject, which was therefore familiar to him. He now put forward a suggestion, transmitted by the Supreme Government to the Secretary of State, that the Turkish Government might be induced to receive the required staff and signallers to carry on and carry out the work, as a loan from the Government of India, whose treasury would meet the expenses. The suggestion was so far supported by the Governor-General of India in Council, that Sir W. O'Shaughnessy's offer to direct the operations in person and supply a staff to complete them was recommended as well worthy the attention of her Majesty's Government; but payment of the cost by India was not pressed as a necessary part of the scheme. It was in this sense that the ambassador at Constantinople was eventually addressed, and instructed to communicate with the Porte.[1]

The presence at Constantinople of her Majesty's Envoy to the Court of Persia was made available on this occasion for a detailed discussion of the question with the Turkish Minister for Foreign Affairs.[2] Sir Henry Rawlinson's intimate knowledge of the country and people, of politics and prejudices, in Anatolia as in Afghanistan, enabled him readily to elicit from Fuad Pacha all the information required. The Turkish Government was most anxious to complete the telegraph line towards India, and would accept the assistance proffered from that country, carrying the cost to their own debit in account, but on the clear understanding that all parts of the line in Asiatic Turkey would, when completed, be under the management and control of the Ottoman Telegraph administration. The prolongation of the line from Baghdad to Basrah should, in the Turkish minister's opinion, be by subfluvial cable in the bed of the Tigris, and as the British Government proposed to lay a submarine telegraph from Karāchi to the Basrah river, so could they provide an additional amount of cable to be continued to Baghdad, the cost of which would be debited to Turkey.

Subsequent despatches, while confirming the above

[1] Government of India to Secretary of State for India, June 16, 1859, and accompaniment. Secretary of State for India to Government of India, September 30, 1859.

[2] Sir H. Rawlinson to Secretary of State for India, October 10, 1859.

expressed wishes and intentions of the Porte, modified the kind of assistance which they were prepared to accept from the Indian empire. It was shown that great progress had already been made in the construction of the aërial line from Scutari to Baghdad, and suggested that if a sum of money were advanced to defray the cost of making, transporting, and laying a subfluvial cable between Baghdad and the Persian Gulf, the Ottoman Government would accept that responsibility also. Special stress was laid upon the circumstance that no concession could be given to any foreign company for a subfluvial line penetrating the interior of the Ottoman dominions.

Her Majesty's Government were not indisposed to negotiate on this latter basis. The India Office was prepared to advance the funds required for the work, on the understanding that its details were to be subject to independent scrutiny and approval. It suggested that the cable should be provided from England and placed in the hands of British officers on the spot. A debtor and creditor account might, moreover, be opened between the two contracting Governments; but it was judged advisable, before settling preliminaries, to certify that the unfinished portion of the line between Scutari and Baghdad was really progressing, and the whole likely to be maintained in permanent working order.

A Draft Convention was eventually prepared by the Porte, and forwarded to the Home Government by Her Majesty's ambassador, for "a Telegraph between Constantinople, Basrah, and India." The India Office, after reciting the views which it entertained on the manufacture and laying of the subfluvial cable, and indispensableness of reliance on the aërial telegraph then under construction, pressed only the insertion of one new clause in the Draft, to the effect that a separate wire should be provided for Indian messages along the whole Turkish line from the Austrian frontier to below Basrah. It is worthy of special note that at this time the Red Sea cable had just been completed, and that, disappointed as were its promoters in first appearances, its doom of utter uselessness had not yet been sealed. In adverting to its existence, it was ruled that the policy to be pursued with regard to the telegraph through Turkey depended on the value to be attached to an alternative line between England and the East; and that great advantage would be gained by a double security to the maintenance of telegraphic communication with India.[1]

Her Majesty's ambassador at Constantinople again referred the matter to the Porte.[2] The clause granting a special wire to Indian messages was conceded, and her Majesty's Government asked to specify the point on the Austro-Turkish frontier whence this wire should run to Constantinople. As the capital, it was stated, could be reached by telegraph from Western Europe, through Belgrade, through Scutari in Albania or Bucharest, a choice of routes was offered. This question was, however, reserved for after consideration, and the amended Draft Convention approved, with a few verbal modifications tending to show the necessity of progress and efficiency on the lines in Asiatic Turkey. A subfluvial cable to connect Mosúl and Baghdad was talked of by the Ottoman Government; but the scheme collapsed

[1] Foreign Office Letter to India Office, February 21, 1860. India Office reply, March 30, 1860.

[2] Foreign Office Letter to India Office, May 28, 1860, with copy Sir H. Bulwer to Foreign Office, 16th ditto. India Office reply, June 2, 1860. Foreign Office to India Office, June 7, 1860, and reply, 16th ditto.

It does not appear, however, that any formal agreement on the subject of a joint telegraph was actually concluded until some months, or indeed two or three years, after the interchange of these communications.

BAGHDAD: TOMB OF ZOBEIDE.

And there is every reason to believe that the following is the true explanation of delay:—The Turkish Government had resolved upon the adoption of a subfluvial instead of aërial telegraph line below Baghdad; and to carry this particular measure into effect was the gist of the convention which Sir Henry Bulwer had brought to the verge of ratification. But it was by no means clear that due consideration had been given to the comparative merits of the two systems which were available for the object in view. The great cost of making and transporting, added to the physical difficulties in submerging and preserving, a suitable cable for the Tigris and Shatt-el-Arab, might perhaps be wisely avoided by the substitution of a comparatively inexpensive and easily constructed land line. In favour of the subfluvial cable the chief arguments used had been, 1st, Security from wilful injury committed by the neighbouring Arab tribes; and 2ndly, simplicity in establishing communication; but neither of these were convincing if in any degree plausible. The India Office referred the subject for opinion to Major Patrick Stewart, who gave sound reasons for preferring the aërial telegraph. If the question were one of cost, he estimated a cable to be twelve times more costly than a land line. Independently of cost, he considered that not only would the chances of injury, before submersion, be extremely great, but that sooner or later, after submersion, injury must ensue, and the work of repair would, under such circumstances, be unusually difficult. He strongly recommended that at least the first experiment made should be that of a land line.[1] It is but fair to add that other and contrary opinions have been officially recorded on this question. These will be hereafter noted in a discussion on results. Coupling Major Stewart's report with the failure, during the same year, of the Red Sea cable, it is not surprising that, in 1860, a pause should

[1] Colonel Stewart to Under Secretary of State for India, August 18, 1860.

intervene in the course of diplomatic negotiations between England and Turkey, for the establishment of that particular and much abused telegraph which has never held a better or more distinctive designation than "Indo-Ottoman."

Meanwhile, the brothers MacCallum and Mr. Carthew were not idle, but carried on their labours of telegraph construction with a vigour, skill, and determination which brought credit to themselves and their subordinates, confirmed the truth of Colonel Biddulph's high appreciation of their capabilities, and reflected honour on the administration they served. On the 10th June 1861, Sir Henry Rawlinson, speaking of these Superintendents, informs the Royal Geographical Society at Burlington House: "It is mainly owing to the untiring zeal, the temper, and the skill with which they have encountered difficulties and remedied defects as they arose, that the line is now in a working and efficient state the whole way from Constantinople to Baghdad."[1]

Her Majesty's Government had, however, before attainment of this desirable consummation, or towards the close of the year 1860, deputed Colonel, now Sir Arnold, Kemball, her Majesty's Consul-General and Political Agent at Baghdad, to examine and report upon the whole line.[2] This step was taken under express sanction of the Porte. Mr. Greener, a professional telegraphic engineer of experience and sound practical sense, accompanied the mission, and the reports of inspection were submitted to her Majesty's Embassy at Constantinople as well as to the India and Foreign Offices, so that all

[1] Notes on the Direct Overland Telegraph from Constantinople to Karáchi. Murray, 1861.
[2] Ibid.

points demanding immediate attention might at once be brought to notice at the fountain head of power. Colonel Kemball's narrative and observations present, in a plain, practical way, a statement of the line and its requirements, its capabilities, its good and weak points, and such remedies for palpable defects as suggested themselves to the writer. No apology will be needed in reverting to them in this place, or in reviewing *seriatim* papers of so much interest and importance.

Arriving at Constantinople on the 15th December 1860, Colonel Kemball at once obtained, in personal communication with the Ottoman Telegraph Department, such information on the condition of the telegraphic line under construction between Constantinople and Baghdad as would at least prove useful prior to personal inspection. He found that the cable which formerly connected Constantinople and Scutari, after three separate repairs, had been finally abandoned, and that telegrams from Europe to Asia and *vice versâ* could only be passed across the Bosphorus by boat. Faultiness in manufacture and damage done by anchors appeared the more likely causes of failure in the communication attempted by submarine cable. The Turkish engineers had suggested changing the locality to the mouth of the Straits or the Sea of Marmora; but as both the risk of interruption and the cost would be increased by this arrangement, Mr. Greener's proposal to try the narrowest part of the Bosphorus was considered worthy of support. A cable of three wires, like one then working between Hull and New Holland, was suggested for trial, the cost, inclusive of all charges, not to exceed 1,000*l*. Mr. Greener agreed with the Turkish engineers in doubting the practicability of success in suspending an aërial steel wire across the Straits, even at an elevation sufficient to admit the constant passage to and fro of ships of every description.

The question of establishments for the efficient working of the line was discussed; the number and duties of the *personnel* defined, and the necessity of thorough and competent supervision enjoined. Foreseeing the advantage of enlisting the sympathies in the cause of order of those who could the more immediately injure or protect from injury the whole work, Colonel Kemball urged association in the undertaking of Arab chieftains, relatives or influential adherents of the heads of tribes inhabiting certain tracts designated, as also the employment of Arab horsemen drawn from the same tribes as paid guards or watchmen. The names and classification of stations proposed for Asia Minor and the lower tracts, and a brief notice of the result of a visit to the Scutari Telegraph Office, will, moreover, be found recorded in this preliminary despatch, which concluded with a well-merited compliment to Dāwud Effendi, the Director-General of Telegraphs in Turkey.[1]

After further inquiries on more palpable shortcomings, and a report to her Majesty's Ambassador, expressing anxiety lest the want of serious organization and earnest effort should prove fatal to efficiency in Asia, and suggesting administrative reforms by which the Telegraph would become a distinct department of the State, Colonel Kemball set out on his long land journey. He left Scutari on the 9th January and reached Angora on the 26th, marching at the rate of about 18 miles per diem. At first the roads were heavy from rain and snow, but

[1] Political Agent in Turkish Arabia to Under Secretary of State for India, dated Constantinople, 22nd December, 1860.

they became harder as the party proceeded and frost supervened. The material and construction of the line on this section were reported excellent, but the course taken might, it was considered, be changed with advantage. The *personnel* was faulty in the absence of skilled inspection and supervision. There were hands but not heads available to carry on the work. The inference from this state of things is plain to those who have lived much in the East. A manipulator can illustrate in practice the objects of a science without necessarily knowing anything of causes; and where superintendents of offices are mere manipulators, not only are they unable to instruct their subordinates in the discovery and remedy of casual defects in line working, but they want that very essential power to enforce respect and discipline which is in no way the exclusive property of science. Many porcelain insulators were found broken, some were quite useless or had disappeared. In long spans across gullies and ravines, and elsewhere, the wire had been recklessly bound down to the iron bracket, and even to the pole itself.[1]

On the 11th February Colonel Kemball arrived at Sivas. The experience of the march from Yuzgat, the midway point between Angora and Sivas, shook that officer's confidence in the permanent efficiency of the line unless revision of some portion were effected. "It seems to have been constructed," he observes, "as if there was no such season as winter, or as if, once constructed, it would require no further care or attention."[2] He also saw much to confirm his formerly expressed views of the insufficient supervision exercised.

[1] Political Agent in Turkish Arabia to Mr. Baring, dated Angora, January 28, 1861. [2] Ibid, dated Sivas, February 14, 1861.

The next report, addressed from Diarbekir, the approximate half-way station between Scutari and Baghdad, was encouraging in tone. With the exception of white porcelain insulators too fragile for hard service, the materials of which the line was composed were pronounced excellent. Changes of direction, to facilitate repairs and like objects, were suggested, on the principle that economy of material was out-balanced by the risks and expense of future supervision; and the absolute necessity of competent inspection was again urged. The formation of store depôts was recommended, and, in answer to a prevalent but mistaken wish of the authorities, attention was drawn to the advantages gained in retaining the larger and rejecting the smaller size wires for future as well as present purposes. A careful detail of the modifications proposed, and reasons assigned for each, was added: also a separate memorandum on the subject under Mr. Greener's signature.

The result of the survey from Scutari to Diarbekir was, however, so far satisfactory as to elicit an emphatic statement of opinion that under competent supervision, and after certain changes in the course laid down, the utmost confidence might be reposed in the permanent efficiency of the line up to the point reached.[1] Especially gratifying was the recorded conviction, the soundness of which has been proved by subsequent experience, that the security of the telegraph ran no risk between Scutari and Diarbekir from the inhabitants of the country. The absence of roving tribes, and presence of a settled population amenable to established authority; the friendly feeling towards the telegraph, amounting to appreciation

[1] Political Agent in Turkish Arabia to Under Secretary of State for India, March 14, 1861.

of its value, in the towns possessing stations; the trivial nature of the damage wilfully done and ease with which its recurrence had been checked by fine and imprisonment; these were rightly considered wholesome signs, and indicated that little or no danger need be anticipated from religious or sectarian antipathy to the Ottoman line of telegraph advancing towards British India, for at least its first 750 miles on the Asiatic side of the Bosphorus.

On receipt of this last report the India Office addressed a letter to the Foreign Office expressing the hope that her Majesty's Ambassador at Constantinople might be instructed to use his influence with the Turkish authorities to cause the carrying into effect Colonel Kemball's detailed recommendation for the improvement of the line.

On the 5th April progress down the Tigris was reported as far as Mosul. The remarks contained in the Diarbekir despatch on the state of the line between that place and the Bosphorus were held to apply in an equal degree to the section more recently inspected. The latter showed perhaps greater signs of haste and carelessness in construction; and objections were raised in some instances to the small size of the wire, and weakness of the poplar poles used. Changes of direction were suggested as before, for facility of access and repair, and security from risks of weather; and the great want of efficient supervision was exemplified in many instances minutely given. The establishment of depôts for tools and materials was pointed out to be an urgent requisite. Poles should be especially stored up in a tract where timber was scarce, or procurable only from a considerable distance.

APPREHENSIONS FROM KURDS AND ARABS.

A second despatch, dated the 15th April from the same station, is interesting on account of two special subjects treated: one, the mode of dealing with the Arab or Kurdish tribes on the outskirts of Mesopotamia; the other, the best way of extending telegraphic communication below Baghdad.

As regards keeping the line in any way secure from wilful damage, the Resident at Bushahr in the Persian Gulf had some years before recorded a most unfavourable opinion. Replying to a reference on the extension of telegraphic communication from Karáchi westward by the Persian Gulf, and through Asia Minor to Constantinople, he had held the scheme impracticable, "owing to the antagonism of the tribes in all the tract through which the line must pass, and the absence of an effective administration."[1] He had expressed his conviction that no amount of payment would ensure protection for any length of time, and estimated that the cost of a sufficient number of troops to control the nomads would form a more serious item in the accounts than would be the outlay on a submarine line of telegraph. An officer of experience among Turks of Europe and Asia, Colonel Sankey, writing to Consul Skene of Aleppo on the same subject, had stated his opinion that every convention with the Arabs in the interest of railway or telegraph companies would be uncertain of execution on their part. He doubted not that every bit of wire within their reach would be stripped off the telegraph to make heel-ropes for their horses.[2] However probable that the latter estimate

[1] Commander Jones to the Commissioner in Sind, July 6, 1856. Inclosure in Mr. Hammond's Letter: "Correspondence respecting the Establishment of Telegraphic Communications in the Mediterranean and with India," page 125. [2] July 29, 1857. Ibid. page 145.

might have been intended to carry strict application only to the Arabs of the Euphrates, such restriction cannot be supposed in the other case.

Colonel Kemball, grappling with the difficulty on the spot, saw his way to a solution. From Kharput, in Armenia, having heard of the wilful destruction of a portion of the line between Mosul and Baghdad, he had written to her Majesty's Embassy inviting authority to concert measures with certain Pachas for subsidising or otherwise treating with the Arab and Kurdish chiefs below Diarbekir; and this authority had been communicated to him by telegram. He had made arrangements with the Shammer Bedouins, who overran the tract between the Khabur to the north and the greater Zab to the south of Mosul; and he now proposed to deal with four other tribes between the Great Zab and Baghdad.

Any but casual mention of tribes, Arab or Kurdish, or of places and individuals, must be reserved for a more appropriate chapter; but having already entered upon the question of the respective merits of aerial or subfluvial lines of telegraph, we may note in this place that Colonel Kemball, when at Mosul on his downward route of inspection, foresaw great advantages in the aerial over the subfluvial system, and gave in his full adherence to the former, with reference to the proposed extension of telegraphs in Lower Mesopotamia and towards the Persian Gulf.

The India Office reply to the Mosul despatches throws light on the cause of hesitation in signing the Convention to which allusion has been made, and which her Majesty's Ambassador at Constantinople was ready to conclude with the Porte in 1860. Colonel Kemball's proceedings were approved by the Secretary of State;

but he was informed that the Baghdad-Basrah line should not be commenced without further communication with the home authorities. Some desire had been expressed on the part of her Majesty's Government and the Persian Government to continue the Indo-Ottoman line of telegraph overland, that is, from Baghdad to the Turco-Persian frontier and through Persia; and of this the practical result might, it was stated, be the abandonment[1] of a measure which brought in question the respective merits of sea and river cables, and indeed of aërial or subaqueous lines of telegraph. The *Great Eastern* had not then played her part in Ocean Telegraphy; a part destined to exercise so great an influence on science and the share market.

From Kifri, on the 24th April, Colonel Kemball forwarded a summary of the arrangements proposed by the local Governor for subsidising the tribes within his jurisdiction. These he discussed in detail; adding a list of injuries already done to the wire, from the character of which he inferred that, as on the outskirts of Asia Minor, there existed no wide-spread antipathy to the telegraph likely to cause permanent danger to its well-being. Rather might the mischief done attest the working of petty malignity on the part of individuals or the set purpose of a particular class.

Colonel Kemball's final report from Baghdad bears date the 7th May, 1864, at which time the heat of the low country must have contrasted strangely to the travellers with the cold experienced by them in the early part of January, on leaving Scutari and passing over the high lands of Asia Minor. The line had been

[1] Under Secretary of State to Colonel Kemball, dated India Office, June 6, 1864.

completed and interruptions repaired; but the want of a proper staff of signallers caused suspension of communication with Constantinople.

These reports and proceedings will at least have made it clear, that the several projects for establishing telegraphic communication between England and India, which circumstances had concentrated on the Turkish route, had not failed in securing progress of some kind towards the desired end. And although there was no incorporated company to represent private interests, nor any ratified convention to support British diplomatic effort at the Sublime Porte, yet were there in full operation preliminary measures of a sufficiently practical character to satisfy the initiated that time was not wasted or opportunity neglected to the detriment of the cause, either in Europe or Western Asia.

Meanwhile, in the far East, interest on the subject had ripened into action. An Indian mutiny had proved the vital importance of an Anglo-Indian telegraph. A Persian war had proved the necessity of closer intercourse and acquaintance with the Asiatic regions west of India. The proof in both propositions was undeniable; yet the separate facts were not viewed by all Englishmen alike. In the first case, home sympathies and responsibilities were earnestly engaged to prevent recurrence of calamity; in the second case, demonstration was as little heeded in England as prevention. The Rev. Mr. Badger, formerly chaplain at Aden, one of those remarkable Oriental scholars whose lore was not confined to books, had put forward a proposal for constructing from Karáchi to Basrah an aërial line of telegraph which would obviate the necessity of having recourse to a submarine cable, then considered little reliable and full of risk. And while Colonel Kemball was on the eve of quitting Constantinople to inspect the telegraph lines of Turkish Asia, the Bombay Government was issuing a circular to the Commissioner in Sind and Political Agents at Kelat, Maskat, and Bashahr, calling for report on the practicability, or otherwise, of Mr. Badger's project.[1] Three out of the four replies were in its favour; and had the question been one of mere physical difficulty, it is probable that such difficulty would have been overcome, and the land line carried out in its entirety. But political obstacles intervened; and there was no scientific process by which these could be removed or their removal accelerated.

Upon the whole, the year 1861 was a busy one in respect of the Indian telegraph. Much official correspondence which had to be written, was written on the subject, both at home and abroad. We have seen what was done in Turkey. Corresponding activity was apparent on the Indian side. A survey of certain ports of the Makran coast in a Government steamer was undertaken by one officer in June;[2] another was commissioned, in December, to move with an escort of horse from Karáchi overland to Gwádar.[3] It was determined to break ground, as early and as far as practicable, in establishing a line of British telegraph posts and wires on the seaboard of Baluchistan.

At this period the joint vigorous action of the home

[1] Mr. Badger to Secretary to Government, Bombay, December 17, 1861; Circular Letter, Secretary to Government, Bombay, to Commissioner and Political Officers; No. 72, January 7, 1861.

[2] Colonel (now Sir) Henry Green, C.B., K.C.S.I., an officer of long experience on the Sind frontier, and of hard and varied active service in Europe as in India.

[3] For some account of this expedition see Chapter XII.

and local Governments of India was maintained by intercommunication without loss of independence. The desired end of both was self-evident: the question of means was open to discussion; and while orders of a general nature were issued from home, numerous and valuable data, with proposals based upon them, poured in from India homeward. The political features of the undertaking were, perhaps, plainer in an Eastern aspect. Arid and unexplored tracts, however vast, like those of Southern Baluchistan, could interest the Indian politician alone; and even he, without some personal knowledge or experience of Sind and its outer frontier, would read their meaning darkly.

But a few words should be said in explanation of the policy which it had been determined to pursue at home, when the instructions were despatched to Colonel Kemball to defer commencement of the Baghdad-Basrah telegraph. These instructions emanated from a correspondence carried on between the India and Foreign Offices and the Persian Ambassador in England; where the notion had obtained favour, that, in order to utilize the Turkish telegraphs for Anglo-Indian communications, it might be safer to divert the line landward, through Persia, than to prolong it seaward to meet a submarine cable below Basrah. And there was as much anxiety felt at home as in India to avoid committing the wires to the deep, which had not at the time been proved to be their sure or natural repository.[1]

In 1862 matters assumed a more definite shape. Patrick Stewart, the young and talented Bengal Engineer, whose career has been traced in the preceding

[1] Mr. Merivale to Lord Wodehouse, June 6, 1861: "Appendix to Report from the Select Committee on East India Communications," page 358.

chapter, now appeared upon the scene. The confidence in his ability and judgment, inspired by reputation, was increased by nearer and more personal communication. As he became better known to the several authorities presiding over, or eminently connected with, British interests in the East, he was pronounced competent to advise, to guide, to represent his Government. Nor was the process by which this confidence was won, exemplified, and justified, a long one. In two short years from the time of his summons to the work he had accomplished the main object required. The reins once committed to his hands, he disentangled them, and drove his enterprise to success.

Diplomatic action at Tehran having followed the home discussions on a telegraph in Persia, and her Majesty's Minister at the Persian Court thinking that negotiation with the Shah's Government would be facilitated by the presence of an officer capable of advising on the technical details of any proposed draft of convention, the Secretary of State suggested to the Government of India to depute Major Patrick Stewart, late Officiating Superintendent of Indian Telegraphs, to the headquarters of her Majesty's Legation in Persia, there to render such assistance as might be required. The suggestion was readily complied with, and Stewart, accompanied by a brother Officer of Engineers, proceeded to Bushahr, the port in the Persian Gulf whence travellers from India usually commence the land journey to the Persian capital.[1]

From Bushahr, Colonel Stewart reported progress to the Government of India. He had been to Bombay and Karachi on his upward way from Ceylon, and after

[1] Mr. Baring to Mr. Hammond, March 10, 1862: "Appendix to Report from the Select Committee on East India Communications," page 264.

conferring with the Commissioner in Sind and his assistant, the latter of whom had just returned from a minute land exploration of the Makran coast, he made arrangements to visit such of the places between Karachi and Gwādar, described to be the more difficult for telegraph purposes, as were comparatively easy of access from a sea-steamer. He and Lieutenant Champain satisfied themselves by personal examination that the difficulties were not insurmountable; but he thought it desirable that a qualified officer of the Telegraph Department should be sent to re-examine one portion of the tract to be traversed by the line, before taking final steps for its erection.

"Though I have no doubt," wrote Colonel Stewart, in reference to the section indicated, "about the possibility of constructing and keeping up a land line by either of the routes . . . . yet, should it turn out that intensity of heat, difficulty of procuring water, or other serious obstacles, are likely to make the work of patrolling this particular portion of the coast line extremely difficult and uncertain during the hot season, a short submarine cable, properly protected at its extremities, might be laid, with every reasonable prospect of permanency and success.

"The very peculiar nature of the friable sandstone formation, not only at Malan, but at every part of the coast between Karachi and Bushahr, which we have been able either to approach or to learn any particulars about, is such, that even when, as at Malan, the coast line is boldest, and apparently most unpromising for a cable, the bottom is, in reality, a perfectly even and clean bed of the finest sand, very gradually shelving into water of a moderate depth at most convenient distances from the shore.

"I know of no similar extent of coast which I should say presented so many advantages for a submarine cable, but I by no means advocate its adoption on this or any other portion of the line from Baghdad to Karáchi, unless all attempts to establish communication by land prove ineffectual."[1]

At Maskat, Colonel Stewart met the Political Resident, Major Malcolm Green, who had recently accompanied his brother, Colonel (now Sir) Henry Green, and Mr. Hubert Walton of the Indian Telegraph Department, in a trip of survey along the Arabian side of the Persian Gulf. It had been asked whether a series of short deep sea cables laid between certain islands to be selected for telegraph stations might not afford the simplest means of connecting Makran with Turkish Arabia. The above-named officers, sent to investigate the merits of this scheme, had declared in its favour; but, although presenting a fair aspect in its freedom from political complications, it did not commend itself to Colonel Stewart in supersession of the original proposal. While determining, however, that, apart from all political considerations, telegraphic communication might safely be secured by a land line constructed from Karáchi to Cape Jask, or for some 700 miles across the sea frontier of Sind and along the coast of Baluchistan, he had not made up his mind, when writing to the Government of India from Bushahr, on two material particulars. One was the exact point on the Makran coast to which the land line should be carried westward: the other, whether a submarine line would, or would not, be necessary to join Basrah to the terminal station of Makran? It has been

[1] Lieut.-Colonel P. Stewart to Secretary to Government of India, Foreign Department. No. 2, April 5, 1862.

shown that, in the then stage of science and scientific experiment, he was naturally mistrustful of using a deep sea cable at all.[1] But whatever the means resorted to for securing the much-needed telegraphic communication, he placed on record, in this early stage of proceedings, an opinion that it would ultimately be advisable to construct a duplicate, or second line, for a part if not the whole of the way from Europe to India.

It is almost superfluous to add that every day's experience since the date of the letters quoted confirms the truth and soundness of the views expressed in them. Precarious indeed would be telegraphic communication with the East if dependent on one line only, whether aërial, subaqueous, or subterranean. The chances of serious interruption of one line must always be great, while those of similar interruption simultaneously on two or more lines should be remote. And, so far as man's energy and skill are available, it should be provided that interests of such magnitude as those involved in the rapid interchange of intelligence with our Eastern possessions can only be endangered by the remotest contingencies.

Passing over for the moment Colonel Stewart's elaborate report on the route from Bushehr to Tehran,[2] and noting his return to England in ill health, after failure of negotiations at the Persian capital, we come to a concise practical proposal laid by him before the Secretary of State for India; a proposal which found ready acceptance with a Government bent upon a great undertaking.

---

[1] Lieut.-Colonel P. Stewart to Secretary to Government of India. No. 2, April 5, 1862, paragraph 5.

[2] To his Excellency Charles Alison, Esq., her Britannic Majesty's Minister at Tehran, June 17, 1862.

and seeking the wisest advisers and fittest agents in carrying it out.

It was recommended that a land line should be completed from Karáchi westward, at least as far as Gwádar, and that a series of submarine cables should be laid from the head of the Persian Gulf to meet this line on the Makran coast. The more recent experience in submarine telegraphy obtained in England had been confir-

MUD FORT AND FLAG-STAFF, FÃO, TURKISH ARABIA.

matory of the justness of this matured opinion. And Colonel Stewart further recommended that permission be asked from the Ottoman Porte for British officers to treat with and, if necessary, subsidise the Arab tribes between Baghdad and Basrah; or, failing such permission, to endeavour to secure the co-operation of the Turkish authorities in constructing and maintaining an aërial line of telegraph, for which stores should at once be procured and despatched. Finally, he recommended that negotiations be reopened with the Court of Persia for a land line from Baghdad to Tehran, Ispahan, Shiraz and Bushahr. This would prove a valuable alternative, in case of interruption, to the Turkish line to the sea and the sea prolongation to Bushahr.

In a second despatch, dated about a month later, reasons were given for preferring Fāo, at the mouth of the Shatt-el-Arab, to Koweit, further down the Arabian maritime coast, as the terminal point westward of the submarine cable. A suggestion was at the same time put in to lay a small section of sea cable between Gwādar and Karáchi, as an alternative to the land line, for greater security of communication.[1]

This scheme, then, sketched and matured in 1862, became the accepted basis of future operations; and orders were issued without delay to carry out the several details. We will now return to Turkey, and trace to within a few weeks of completion the line of telegraph in the Ottoman dominions in Asia, of which the link from Baghdad to the sea had become the main object of attention to her Majesty's Government and the India Office.

The Porte declined to entrust to the British Government the construction of the telegraph from Baghdad to the Persian Gulf, but agreed to undertake the work on receiving the assurance that the Indian cable would be ready at the point of junction. It was informed in reply, that fulfilment of the condition might be confidently expected at the end of the ensuing year, 1863; but the acceptance of British co-operation was still

[1] Lieut.-Colonel P. Stewart to the Under Secretary of State for India, August 14 and September 22, 1862.

pressed, and a suggestion made that Colonel Kemball be associated with a qualified Turkish functionary in arranging the details about to be considered.'

Joint action in this modified form was in full accordance with the principle already admitted, and was not likely to meet with opposition at the Porte. Indeed, the Political Agent in Turkish Arabia had already been in communication with the Governor-General of the Province on the precise route to be followed by the contemplated line, when Colonel Stewart's programme forwarded by the Government of Bombay reached him in January 1863.² Namik Pacha had fully agreed to a proposal of preliminary inspection made to him by Colonel Kemball, who, by acting in concert with the Turkish local officers on such occasions, was honoured with a confidence not commonly tendered by His Excellency to Europeans.

On the 7th February, Lieutenant Stiffe and Mr. Greener arrived at the Baghdad Residency from Basrah, whither they had been brought by the Indian steamer. The former had been deputed by Colonel Stewart in England, under sanction of the India Office, to make investigations and take soundings in the Persian Gulf preparatory to laying a submarine cable; the latter, who had accompanied Colonel Kemball on his overland journey from Constantinople in the winter of 1860–61, had been again sent out to render aid in the construction of the line below Baghdad. Colonel Kemball and staff proceeded on their new journey of inspection on the 12th March. Lieutenant Stiffe, able to take home a satisfactory account of his labours, and eager for

¹ Mr. Baring to Mr. Hammond, November 13, 1862.
² Colonel Kemball to Under Secretary of State for India, Jan. 21, 1863.

progress, had left a few days before for the Mediterranean *via* Diarbekir and Aleppo. Had the officers of the Indian Navy bequeathed no other record of their existence than those admirable surveys, which not only embrace the Indian Seas, the Red Sea, and the Persian Gulf, but the rivers of Central Asia, they would have earned an imperishable title to consideration; and Colonel Stewart's Marine Assistant, if he may be so called, was a worthy representative of this distinguished class.

Returning to Baghdad after a month's tour, the Political Agent reported as follows:—"In submitting an itinerary, with a sketch map of the route selected for the proposed line of telegraph to Basrah, I have the honour to state that, by common consent of the Engineers of my party, no obstacles of moment exist to the prosecution of the work; nor need recourse be had anywhere to a subfluvial cable or the subterranean wires originally proposed by the Turkish employés."[1]

He divided the route into five sections, averaging somewhat more than 60 miles each; leaving to the discretion of the Turkish executive a diversion which would increase the distance by about 12 miles. The tract to be traversed, exclusive of the diversion, was thus estimated at 313 miles; the whole, with the exception of 38 miles into Basrah, being on the left bank of the Euphrates, or, in literal parlance, in Mesopotamia. Lower than Basrah this particular survey did not extend.

The first section, from Baghdad to Hilleh, was a great thoroughfare for pilgrims, and occasionally subject to tribe incursion, otherwise devoid of population as of

[1] Colonel Kemball to Under Secretary of State for India, April 29, 1863.

cultivation. In the following two sections, or from Hilleh to Khidhr, lay the doubtful portion of the route. It was questionable whether a better line might not be obtained by crossing and recrossing the river, and following 123½ miles on the right bank in lieu of 112 on the left bank of the Euphrates between Hilleh and Khidhr; but the preference shown by the local Government to deal with the tribes on the left bank eventually decided the point in its favour. These sections would include the midway station of Dewaniyeh, up to which from Hilleh the route was described as "favourable throughout for telegraphic operations." From Dewaniyeh to Khidhr, though no difficulties were apparent or apprehended, a further partial survey by Mr. Vice-Consul Johnston and Lieutenant Bewsher, I.N., would be awaited. These gentlemen, who were about returning from Baghdad to Basrah, would take the opportunity of investigating the question further on their downward journey. The fourth section, from Khidhr to Humar, was remarkable as keeping the left bank when the right would appear, *primâ facie* and physically, the more convenient. Here also, however, the Pacha was desirous of avoiding the right bank Arabs. Colonel Kemball, while finding no material objection to adopt the desired course, did not, however, lose sight of the fact that Arabs cross and re-cross a river when it suits their purpose. The fifth or last section involved a crossing to the right bank at Korna, where the Euphrates joins the Tigris, and forms with that river the broad stream, which, under the name of the Shatt-el-Arab, conveys their united waters to the sea. From this point, which occurs at two-fifths of the distance to be traversed from Humar, the line would follow the right bank of the Shatt-el-Arab, skirting the outer edge of the belt of date plantations, by which it is bordered throughout its course, to Basrah, and so eventually to Fáo, the station of the Persian Gulf cable, at its mouth.

The physical difficulties of construction, such as they were, being those natural to a low country, in which a river was the prominent feature and along whose bank the course must in a great measure be chosen, presented themselves in the shape of marshy land, drains, canals, and watercourses. Extra time and care were required to surmount these, but there was clearly nothing in the way of success which could severely tax the practised telegraph engineer. Mr. Greener, in a letter to Colonel Stewart accompanying Colonel Kemball's above-quoted despatch, designates the work contemplated "a straightforward piece of business," and expresses an opinion that, with a little energy on the part of the native employés and assistants, the line might be ready, or nearly so, by the time that the proposed Indian cable reached the sea mouth of the Basrah river.[1]

A very few days after the date of his own despatch Colonel Kemball was enabled to add the report of the two officers commissioned to inspect minutely the small tract of undefined land between Devaniyeh and Khidhr.[2] It was concise but exhaustive. A road, in extent only four miles further than computed, had been found, which presented "no obstacles whatever to the erection of a

[1] Mr. Greener to Colonel Stewart, dated Baghdad, April 29, 1863.
[2] Colonel Kemball to Under Secretary of State for India, May 27, 1863, forwarding Report by Mr. Johnston, Vice-Consul at Basrah, and Survey Map by Lieut. Beecher, I.N. These two zealous and intelligent officers are now no more. Lieut. Beecher, worn out in body, came home, and died at Mentone in 1866. Mr. Johnston took leave in failing health in 1868, and when about to return to his duty in the following year, was wrecked in the *Carnatic* in September. He reached Basrah to die there in November.

telegraph line." Two actual courses were indicated, and reasons given for preferring one to the other. Mr. Johnston observed many villages and much cultivation in the country traversed, and at one time rode along a belt of high land "varying in breadth from 200 yards to two miles, between two lines of wheat and barley cultivation, bordering in both instances marsh and rice lands." At another time the ground was so thickly covered with high thorn-trees as to become obstructive to horses. The Euphrates was then said to be within nine miles of the highest level reached for some years preceding. The Arabs met with on the way furnished example, as usual, of that internecine tribe hostility to which perhaps the European traveller, however he may deplore its existence, may often owe his life. Plunder may be a normal occupation; but retaliation is rather the ruling passion; and in this condition, the non-partisan is an object of comparative indifference.

Shortly after these proceedings the Government of Bombay was officially advised that, under agreement with the Turkish Government, materials for the telegraph line below Baghdad, including iron posts for the whole distance, had been provided in England, the cost being advanced by the Government of India. Moreover, that three sailing vessels laden with the same had started for the port of Basrah; that a specially qualified inspector was about to proceed, *viâ* Beyrout, to Baghdad, where he would assist Mr. Greener in distributing the stores; and that two non-commissioned officers of the Royal Engineers had been selected to promote the work of construction in association with the Turkish working parties.[1]

[1] Secretary of State to Government of Bombay; No. 9, August 15, 1863.

Bearing precisely the same date and address, but a prior number, another despatch notified the appointment by the Secretary of State of Lieutenant Murdoch Smith of the Royal Engineers and officers of the Indian Telegraph Department, as Superintendents of sections of the Turco-Persian Telegraph, the construction of which, from Baghdad to Khanikin, and Khanikin to Tehran, had been negotiated with the Governments of Turkey and Persia respectively. It further stated, that two Telegraph Inspectors had been engaged for the same service, and that, in addition to all these, two Engineer Officers and two Inspectors would be required from India. By this despatch the local Government addressed was vested with the responsibility of the operations in the Persian Gulf and Mesopotamia, and on the coast of Makran, as though these were conducted within the limits of the Bombay Presidency.[1] The arrangement was in accordance with a suggestion of the Government of India, after experience of its nominal control in the Foreign Department over the telegraph operations already carried out in Makran.

There is little occasion to revert to or record the delays, or causes of delay, in conducting the written terms which are found in the protocol signed at Constantinople on the 20th October, 1863, by Mr. Erskine and Ali Pasha.

The following appear to be the more noteworthy points of this record, and those which were unaffected by after correspondence on the subject :—

I. The Ottoman Government to extend at their own cost their aerial telegraph lines from Baghdad, in one direction to the Persian frontier at Khanikin, in the

[1] Secretary of State to Government of Bombay; No. 5, August 15, 1863.

other to Basrah. The Indian Government to lay at its own cost a submarine cable, prolonged from Bushahr westward to Basrah, or some other more convenient point of junction with the Turkish land line.

II. The Indian Government to supply all materials, including iron poles, for both the aërial lines from Baghdad, repayment being made from the proceeds of telegraph messages, under a special arrangement reserved for after decision. Salaries of British engineers employed in construction to be paid by Indian Government.

III. Operations to be commenced by both contracting Governments as quickly as possible; but the Baghdad-Khanikin line to await completion of the other.[1]

The note of preparation had now been fairly sounded; and a stir had been effected in England and in India, in Turkey and in Persia, which promised to realize the best results. On the 26th November, 1863, Colonel Kemball forwarded to the India Office a copy of his despatch to her Majesty's Embassy at Constantinople reporting commencement of operations for the completion of the Ottoman line of telegraph to the head of the Persian Gulf.[2] But the Political Agent, in undertaking to look after the work, so far as British interests were concerned, had heaped upon himself a not inconsiderable amount of labour. Fortunately for the success of the cause, he was able and willing to take in hand all difficulties of minor detail, as those of sheer political character; and while infusing a spirit of earnestness into the local executive, and luring a loth

---

[1] Mr. Hammond to Mr. Merivale, October 24, 1863, and Sir H. Bulwer to Earl Russell, 20 ditto.
[2] Colonel Kemball to Under Secretary of State for India, Nov. 26, 1863.

Administration to conciliate instead of irritate the proud and turbulent Arabs, he did not neglect the smaller but very essential facts that bills of lading should correspond in number and description with articles received, and that a brand or incision on a case was a surer distinguishing mark than a piece of tin liable to removal by the accidents of transport. These and other practical remarks were forced from him by an experience which, to say the least, is trying. Especially to the point was the opinion in favour of the malleable iron insulator with cap detached, or a malleable iron arm with removeable wrought-iron cap, against that with cast-iron arm and cap run in one mould. In the latter case, after packing, fracture is common, and completely disables: in the former, the packing is facilitated by reduction of weight, and fracture rendered improbable. The despatch treating of these matters reported arrival of the *Athene* and *Khimji Oodeyji*, two of three store-ships expected. Lieutenant Murdoch Smith with a detachment of Royal Engineers also reached Busrah on the 15th November.

Certain special circumstances attending the construction of the line below Baghdad, and equally affecting the further prolongation of the Indo-Ottoman Telegraph to its sea terminus at Fao, together with the chronological relation of this particular section to the whole work performed, render it expedient to take leave of working parties in these parts, and reintroduce them at a later period. They will be revisited on the scene of their labours when the story of the Gulf cable and the Persian negotiations shall have made their position more intelligible. Enough has been written at least to convince the reader that the winter of 1863-64 was a busy season for the few Englishmen engaged in constructing a land telegraph in Lower Mesopotamia. It will also have become patent that the difficulties encountered were rather of a political than a physical character.

Meanwhile, Patrick Stewart was on his way from Karáchi with the cable. Bringing in his charge to a temporary land station at Fao, the embouchure of the Shatt-el-Arab, and selecting a site for a permanent Office, he moved up the river to Baghdad, arriving on the 19th April. The proverbial hospitalities of the Political Agency, or Residency as sometimes called, were illustrated on this occasion in the usual manner, notwithstanding that the mission which presented itself there was formidable in point of numbers. After a few days' sojourn in the City of the Caliphs, Colonel Stewart, Sir Charles Bright, and others of the party, returned to Bombay. One remained the full month; and he was detained for authority from Constantinople to inspect the line to the capital in an upward journey from Baghdad to the Bosphorus, going over again the ground which had been traversed three years before by Colonel Kemball. It was on the 19th May that Colonel Goldsmid proceeded on this particular duty, accompanied by the late Mr. Assistant-Superintendent Kersting of the Telegraph Department.

The Report of the last-noted inspection is dated from Pera, where the writer joined Colonel Stewart in August 1864, about six weeks after that officer had himself arrived from India. It comprised, besides a rough diary and other incidental enclosures, a review of the then existing condition of the line of telegraph, and a memorandum of changes which appeared requisite for its general improvement. A few of the more salient points may be cursorily stated. Transfer of the Telegraph Station at Mosul to the left bank of the Tigris was particularly urged, owing to the constant exposure of the line to interruption by crossing and recrossing the river with the mere view of reaching, in the heart of the town, an Office which would be quite as well placed outside and on the opposite bank. Many of the posts were weak, and insufficient to the work. For 750 miles above Baghdad poplars were generally procurable without material cost or difficulty; for 480 miles further, up to Gaiveh, fir poles were the rule; and for the next two stages to Izmid the wood was oak. To meet the requirements of 1276 miles of telegraph from Baghdad to Izmid, there were found 18 Bash Chaoshes, or inspectors, and 107 Chaoshes, or sub-inspectors. Of these it was roughly estimated that three-fourths were active, intelligent men, and well fitted to their work. The heads of stations were not generally unintelligent, but stood much in need of theoretical instruction. Of the porcelain insulators used, it was rare to find half a dozen whole. The straining insulator was too seldom seen. Little appeared to have been done since Colonel Kemball's visit to remedy the minor though important defects which the Political Agent had brought to notice. Yet the opinion was expressed withal that the condition of the line, though not quite satisfactory in detail, promised good results, if only a sufficient number of qualified inspectors were appointed, attention given to remedy the defective insulation, and the changes specified admitted to have effect. A brief supplementary report with a few practical memoranda by Mr. Kersting were among the papers put into Colonel Stewart's hands on completion of the journey.[1]

The latter officer, on leaving Baghdad in April, had returned to India, again embarking from Bombay, on return to Europe, at the end of May. Taking the usual Red Sea route to Egypt, he proceeded from Alexandria to Constantinople. Here he had been for some time engaged in the many preliminaries inseparable from an anxiously expected announcement that telegraphic communication was actually open between London and Karáchi, when joined by the Overland travellers. The question of improving the existing Asiatic lines was at once discussed by Colonels Stewart and Goldsmid, Mr. MacCallum the inspector in Ottoman pay, and Mr. Courtenay the British telegraph commissioner, or official agent of her Majesty's Government appointed to look after the interests of the telegraph at Constantinople. The change of certain stations, notably Mardin and Mosul, better insulation of the second or Indian wire, greater care in passing the wire through large towns such as Yuzgat, Sivas, and Diarbekir, and a more *judicious* division of inspectors' ranges—these and other details were pressed, and more or less investigated. Diplomatic interviews followed: official and ceremonial visits were paid; but the *homme d'affaires* has not the same type in all cities, albeit these be restricted to Europe; and while "business is business" may be a proverb universally acknowledged, the practical definition of what *is* business will be perhaps very generally dis-

---

[1] Lieut.-Colonel F. J. Goldsmid to Lieut.-Colonel P. Stewart, August 30, 1864. Mr. Kersting, a zealous and public-spirited officer, died at Maskat in March, 1866.

puted. In this respect the ways of the Levant are not the ways of London and Liverpool.

Colonel Stewart's presence, however, was not unproductive of good, and even early fruits; and the active assistance of her Majesty's Embassy enabled him to see completed and sent home in September 1864, a Convention with the Porte, in amplification of the protocol of the previous year. With a short statement of the purport of this mutual understanding and the means by which it was attained, we will conclude a chapter not intended quite to reach the exact period when one unbroken line of telegraph first united England to India.

Mr. Erskine had in the commencement of 1864 drafted the project of a "preliminary" Convention with the Porte in accordance with certain instructions received from the Foreign Office on the subject of the telegraph to India; but Ali Pacha, the Turkish Minister for Foreign Affairs, had preferred transferring some of its stipulations to a separate note or omitting them altogether. In this view a re-draft was proposed to her Majesty's *Chargé d'affaires*, which the latter, after much negotiating and alteration, consented to forward to Lord Russell. The Convention now proposed was one for three years, and not of the preliminary character which had been contemplated in pursuance, it is conceived, of Colonel Stewart's expressed wishes to that effect. The question was at once referred to the India Office. After a delay of some weeks, to give time for inquiry and deliberation, the draft was returned, with certain modifications as to the number of clerks to be employed at Fao, the stations to be provided, the exchange of coin, and the rates for messages in Asiatic Turkey. Should these be accepted, it was answered, the Secretary of State for India had no objection to ratification ensuing.

There was not much real difficulty in disposing of the points at issue. The very sufficient limit of 50 was assigned to the English *personnel* at Fáo; permanent Ottoman stations were expressly stipulated for Baghdad and Fáo, though not for Basrah and Khanikin; and the exchange and rates were modified agreeably to the India Office suggestion.

The ratified Convention may be summarised as follows:—

ARTICLE I. Prolongation, at the cost of Turkey, of its Scutari-Baghdad telegraphic line, from Baghdad to the mouth of the Shatt-el-Arab on one side, and the Persian frontier at Khanikin on the other.

ARTICLE II. Submarine cable from India, to Bushahr and mouth of Shatt-el-Arab, to be laid and maintained by Government of India.

ARTICLE III. Establishment of British Telegraph Office, with staff not exceeding 50 persons, at mouth of Shatt-el-Arab, under exclusive orders of British Station Master. All cost of Office and material used, defrayed by British Government.

ARTICLE IV. Aforesaid British Office to be in building occupied by Ottoman station; apparatus of each office to be in separate compartments, and unconnected, but in close proximity.

ARTICLE V. Active service of said British Office limited to receipt and delivery by hand to Ottoman Office of cable messages from India, and transmission of messages delivered to it by Ottoman Office; and superintendence and maintenance of submarine communication with India. Chief direction of mixed station to devolve on Ottoman administration, with no right of interference in internal administration of British Office.

ARTICLE VI. Ottoman Government to establish permanent service at Baghdad and Fao, as well as at majority of stations between Constantinople and Fao, appointing a competent staff. To establish office of transmission, exclusively for Indian messages, at Constantinople also; its Station Master and officers being selected from those Ottoman telegraph officials who are thoroughly conversant with the English language.

ARTICLE VII. One wire from Constantinople to Fao to be exclusively devoted to Indo-European messages, with proviso for use of other wire in case of disorder.

ARTICLE VIII. Mutual observance of Convention of Brussels of 30th June, 1858, in details, unless at variance with present Convention.

ARTICLES IX. to XIII. inclusive. Regulating rates, tariffs, value of currency, and adjustment and interchange of accounts.

ARTICLE XIV. Messages to or from India to be forwarded according to convenience of service, *via* Basrah or Khanikin.

ARTICLE XV. Account current and administrative relations to be direct between British Indian and Ottoman Governments in respect to all messages, whether sent *via* Fao or Khanikin; and the two Governments to have no direct account current or administrative relations with Persia, except as regards payment of those messages which traverse the Persian lines from Khanikin to Bushahr.

ARTICLE XVI. Operation of Convention to date from time when Submarine Cable placed in communication with land lines of Turkey and India, remaining in force for three years from ratification. Modification admissible if by common consent.

CHAPTER III.

THE PERSIAN GULF CABLE.—MATERIAL AND MANUFAC-
TURE.—HOW PAID.—SOME ACCOUNT OF THE CABLE
STATIONS; AND OF THE PEOPLE, PORTS, OR PLACES
OF ANCHORAGE IN ARABIA AND OPPOSITE COAST.

As shown in the preceding chapter, the information
gained by Colonel Stewart on his homeward way from
Calcutta in 1862, and in England subsequently to his
return, had satisfied him that telegraphic communication
with the East could only be surely and speedily obtained
by the aid of a submarine cable at least from Gwádar to
Fáo. The little knowledge possessed of the people and

politics in Makran gave a precariousness to the aërial telegraph in that country not encouraging to its extension westward of Gwādar. The vacillation and instability manifested by the authorities in Persia were unfavourable signs of accomplishing there also an undertaking whose success was dependent on determined as well as combined action. The lapse of years had, moreover, brought apprehension of the fact that the main causes of failure in the Red Sea cable were by no means incapable of disconnection from future attempts of a like nature. He had come to the conclusion that he would, at all events, submit a recommendation in accordance with the spirit of the times. Many months had not passed since the Submarine Telegraph Committee had promulgated the authoritative opinion that the failures of existing submarine lines might have been guarded against, had adequate preliminary investigation been made; together with the conviction that, if due regard were had to certain principles theretofore enunciated, the class of enterprise to which these cables belonged might prove as successful as it had been disastrous.[1]

Colonel Stewart's first detailed proposal, in pursuance of the above views, reports the measures requisite for the early construction of a submarine cable, to be laid in the Persian Gulf, and for the establishment of electric communication with the East by that route. It was accompanied by an approximate estimate of the time and cost of manufacture, transport, and submersion. The length of cable to be provided was 1,050 nautical miles, computed on the assumed distance between Fāo and the land line terminus at or near Gwādar in Makran.

[1] Report of Joint Committee appointed to inquire into the Construction of Submarine Telegraph Cables, presented to Parliament, April, 1861.

As regards the core or electrical conductor to be used, the opinion of eminently qualified engineers had been invited, and was awaited, on the more important details, such as weight, dimensions, material, mode of construction and standard of electrical efficiency. In the meanwhile, progress had been made in collecting information on the subject, procuring specimens of core of various kinds, and reading practical lessons for guidance in the reports supplied to the Treasury on the condition of the Malta and Alexandria cable. Great stress was laid on the necessity of applying frequent and careful tests pending manufacture.

Colonel Stewart reckoned that it would take five months to make the core, and another five months to cover it. He allowed delays for testing and other purposes, and named a probable date on which to commence the process of stowing on board ship. Estimating the steam freight required on the weight of ordinary cables, he suggested that early steps be taken to provide for shipping exigencies, and especially for coal and coaling stations. He drew attention to the seasons which experience of the Persian Gulf had indicated as favourable to work; and showed that while vessels might sail without steam from about the latitude of the Mauritius to Maskat during August and September, such freedom of action could not be depended on at a later date. There were reasons to expect that the land line from Karāchi to Gwādar would be completed in March 1863, and the Mesopotamian line in December. All necessary arrangements for selecting stations and providing accommodation for the Staff might also be concluded by the new year; and it was considered the more desirable that the submarine portion of the work should be ready at the same period.[1]

A separate letter entered into the question of stations. Strong reasons were given for selecting a site at the mouth of the Shatt-el-Arab, and for preferring Massandam in Arabia to Larek, a Persian island on the opposite side of the Gulf. But while himself giving a very sufficient basis for full inquiry and report, Colonel Stewart pointed out the necessity of commissioning an officer to obtain all the preliminary information requisite to ensure a wise decision.

Not many days later a further report submitted the measures considered to afford the best security for efficient execution of the important and arduous duties, on the due performance of which depended the success of the whole programme. In advocacy of the principle of continued and undivided responsibility in every part of the enterprise, so that those employed be brought to hold their professional reputations directly concerned in the permanence, as in the first success of the work undertaken; a proposal made by Messrs. Bright and Clark, the eminent Engineers, to assist in the general control of cable operations, was recommended for approval. The tender of personal service being combined with that of providing all the requisite staff from first to last, and other contingencies, such an arrangement would enable Colonel Stewart to apply himself to the general superintendence of an undertaking of which a submarine cable was very justly explained to be by no means the only portion demanding his attention.[2]

[1] Lieut. Colonel Patrick Stewart to the Under Secretary of State; No. 12, September 22, 1862.
[2] Ibid. September 29, 1862.

It was reckoned that not less than four steamers would be required for the conveyance of the cable to destination and submersion. Shore ends were to be laid at Fao, Bushahr, and the two stations nearer India; and the vessel carrying these was to precede the others by at least a month. As regards the engagements to be undertaken by Messrs. Bright and Clark, it was explained that the Staff supplied by these gentlemen would be for the supervision and control of the operations of laying, not the actual execution of the work. And in literal fulfilment of this agreement it was provided that the duties of mechanics employed in uncoiling, cleansing, watching breaks, jointing and so forth, would involve an extra charge, though small, upon the State.[1]

Consultation was held with Captains Constable and Jones of the Indian Navy on the best route for the cable, and other matters connected with its maintenance and security in the Persian Gulf, a locality which former experience had rendered familiar to both. It has already been stated that an officer was deputed to take the soundings. Lieutenant Stiffe's presence in England prior to despatch on that duty was a fortunate circumstance for Colonel Stewart, at a time when interchange of ideas and oral expression of views had a value unknown to official foolscap. The charts prepared by Captain Constable and Lieutenant Stiffe gave especial prominence to the head-land of Masandam, where it was proposed to find a spot suited to the requirements of a working telegraph, and the position of which was naturally suggestive of a store depôt and convenient

[1] Lieut.-Colonel Patrick Stewart to Under Secretary of State for India, October 8, 1862.

port of call for vessels navigating the neighbouring waters.[1]

The reports, on the reference officially made to them, of Professor Thomson, Messrs. Siemens and Halske, Messrs. Ford and Jenkin, Mr. Varley, Mr. Walker and Dr. Esselbach, enabled Colonel Stewart to recommend to the India Office the description of core required for the proposed cable. And in forwarding such recommendation he asked permission to take immediate steps for the manufacture of 880 nautical miles of the said core at a cost not exceeding 85*l*. per mile; as well as to obtain, by public competition, tenders for manufacture of the completed cable, the preparations of which had been provided for by detailed specification.[2]

Furthermore, specimens of the proposed cable having been lodged in the offices of the Engineers, and advertisements inviting tenders published in the daily papers, a correspondence was opened with certain well-known firms coming forward to negotiate the manufacture. The offer made by Messrs. Henley and Co. was recommended for acceptance.[3]

In due course Colonel Stewart submitted to the India Office his detailed report on the measures which appeared necessary to secure freight and steam power for the transport and submersion of the Persian Gulf cable. Opinions of much practical value and the result of much careful study were expressed in this able and comprehensive paper, a full perusal of which will repay those interested or engaged in similar proceedings. The question of employing steam or sailing-vessels was

[1] Lieut.-Colonel Patrick Stewart to Under Secretary of State for India, October 20, 1862.
[2] Ibid. November 25, 1862.   [3] Ibid. December 15, 1862.

argued with a show of advantage on either side, and eventually decided in favour of the latter, for the transport of far the greater part of the cable; but it was held advisable to reduce the heavy expenditure contemplated to a minimum. To this end the employment of vessels belonging to the Admiralty seemed to offer the most natural suggestion. But the experience of the Atlantic Cable Expedition, in which H.M. ship *Agamemnon* had been exposed to unusual and excessive straining, was against the renewal of like arrangements. The objection, however, applied strictly to commissioned ships of war, and had hardly the same force in respect of other Government craft. Colonel Stewart's proposal was therefore to utilise "vessels which, though moderately new and still in excellent preservation, have become 'out of date' from the recent rapid changes in the science of naval construction, and which are unlikely to be either 'converted', plated, or commissioned as sailing vessels of war." He stated his belief that such were to be found lying as hulks at Chatham, Sheerness, Portsmouth and Devonport; that they represented in their then condition but little money value, and were deteriorating at their moorings. The strength of their frames rendered them well qualified for the purposes under consideration; and names were given in illustration of the reasoning. He anticipated the consent of the authorities of the Admiralty to place four such vessels at the disposal of the Government of India for a limited period, on condition that it bore wholly the cost of repairing, equipping, and sailing. The proposal was, moreover, considered advantageous to both the great Departments concerned. It comprised the permanent transfer to the Government of India of two smaller vessels of war, to be repaired, fitted, and sailed on the same terms as the larger frigates required for the cable, and to be employed immediately for conveying stores, and eventually as light-ships off stations in the Persian Gulf, after primary occupation as offices on the submarine line.[1]

To the foregoing summary of the more important despatches which passed on this projected union of East and West may be added the general statement that the Government of India acquiesced in and approved the arrangements in progress. Nor did the year 1862 close without an expression of public satisfaction at the measures taken in so wise and resolute a spirit. A prominent article in the *Times* described the whole scheme with sufficient exactitude to cause regret that it was not resuscitated in reply to much misapprehension subsequently expressed in the columns of the same paper. It represented the Indian line as asking for no subscriptions and making no appeal to the public: as undertaken by the Indian Government, of themselves, under circumstances which amply justified the step. It set forth that the entire superintendence and control had been entrusted to a distinguished and experienced officer, who had chosen Sir Charles Bright and Mr. Latimer Clark, electrical engineers, for the undertaking, and for submerging the line. It traced the course of the main land line through Asiatic Turkey, and the alternative section branching off therefrom at Baghdad and rejoining at Bushahr. No word was said of a Russian junction with this line, a contingency not then contemplated. It described the course of the cable,

[1] Lieut. Colonel Patrick Stewart to Under Secretary of State for India, February 23, 1863.

its cost and composition, pronouncing it to be, so far "as depends on minute care and a wide scientific experience, likely to be as perfect as skill or ingenuity can make it."

Between seven and eight months later the same paper notified that the expedition to lay the cable was about to leave England, drawing attention especially to the careful and quiet manner in which the Government plans had been matured, a good omen of successful accomplishment of the object in view. The following extract from the article under reference, appropriate to this place, is valuable, not only in point of accurate detail, but as expressive of the strong public sympathy then acknowledged for the Government enterprise. It should be premised that, in addition to the three sections of cable to be laid between Fão and Gwadar, a fourth section had been sanctioned as an alternative to the land line, and for greater security to the communication between Karáchi and Gwádar.[2]

'The design and construction of the cable differ very materially from any line hitherto laid. Every operation in submarine telegraphy—even the great Atlantic line, has contributed its quota of valuable experience; for, though successfully laid by Sir Charles Bright and his assistant engineers in spite of its imperfect construction, it was destroyed by the injudicious electrical treatment it received after submersion. This fact is now so well established that the cause of the failure of the Atlantic cable may be considered as set at rest for ever. The insulation of that line was not very perfect, as may be imagined from the infancy of the science at that time, but yet the electrical power used was such as would infallibly break down even the most perfect cables manufactured at the present day.

[1] *The Times*, December 26, 1862.
[2] India Office to Colonel Stewart, June 24, 1863.

Of this our readers may judge when it is stated that the large induction coils first used in signalling between England and America were probably equal in electrical power to 2,000 battery cells, while now it is found inexpedient to use more than two or three cells in working the longest submarine lines in existence. Some of this great power was no doubt used in the vain hope of forcing signals through the line at a greater speed than the very slow and unremunerative rate at which it has alone been found possible to communicate through an unbroken length of 3,000 miles. The result was disastrous, but the experience, though dearly bought, has proved of great value. It has taught electricians the value of moderating the power used in working lines, and above all has pointed out the imperative necessity of having no single section of a submarine line of more than 600 miles in length. To lay long submarine cables in a continuous length without intermediate stations has been found to answer no other purpose than that of greatly diminishing the speed of working and multiplying every imaginable risk both of manufacture and submersion. The Indian Government, acting under the judicious counsel of their scientific advisers, have wisely determined to divide the Persian Gulf cable into three sections, though its total length will not exceed 1,500 statute miles.

"The faults which led to the destruction of the Red Sea line were of another character. Though it was manufactured and tested with a care greatly superior to that taken with the Atlantic cable, it was submerged in a way which rendered its ceasing to work a question of a few weeks more or less. Sheathed in a covering of small wires, quite unprotected from corrosion, it was laid without any allowance for 'slack' cable to fall into the irregularity of the bottom of the sea. It consequently lay strained across the points of the inequalities, with a tension of several thousand pounds. As the unprotected wires rusted away, and the suspended portions of the line became loaded with coral and barnacles, the whole line crumbled into hundreds of pieces by its own weight. This is no mere hypothetical opinion, but a fact, which was amply proved by the expedition to the Red Sea in 1861 under Mr. Latimer Clark. There can be little doubt that the same cause led to the temporary failure of the Malta and Alexandria line, as well as that laid for the French Government between Toulon and Algiers.

"To obviate this cause of danger, which in the above-mentioned lines has probably occasioned a loss of property to the value of over a million sterling, the Persian Gulf line is cased in 12 No. 7 gauge hard-drawn iron wires, thickly galvanized, so as effectually to prevent their corrosion. But, in order to secure more effectually the permanent stability of the line, the whole finished cable is thickly coated with two servings of tarred hemp yarn, overlaid with two coatings of a patent composition invented by Sir Charles Bright and Mr. Latimer Clark. The composition consists of mineral pitch or asphalt, Stockholm tar, and powdered silica, mixed in certain proportions, and laid on in a melted state. While yet warm it is passed between circular rollers, which give it a round, smooth surface. When quite cold, this forms a massive covering of great strength and perfect flexibility, totally impervious to water, and incapable of being destroyed by the minute animalculæ which exist in such abundance in warm latitudes, and which, when the cable is not protected against their attacks, eat every atom of the hemp, as in the case of the cable laid between Toulon and Algiers. Galvanizing the wire is in itself an almost perfect protection from rust—certainly for many years, as the good condition of the cable picked up off the Kooria Mooria Islands, a part of which was galvanized, showed, as far as the galvanizing was concerned. But, with the final protection both from rust and animalculæ which Bright and Clark's compound affords, there appears to be no reason why this cable, when once laid in shallow or deep waters, should not remain good for a hundred years to come. The copper conducting wire is composed of four segments, drawn into a hollow tube in such a manner as to appear like a solid wire. By this means all the advantages of a strand wire are combined with the condensed bulk and small surface of a solid one. The copper from which the wire is drawn is especially selected by the engineers for its high capacity for conducting electricity. It is, perhaps, not generally known that different samples of copper vary as much as 50 or 60 per cent. in this respect,—that is, some specimens of copper wire will conduct electricity with greater facility than other specimens of double the thickness, though physically there may not be the slightest difference by which you can distinguish one from the other. This wire, which is nearly one-eighth of an inch in diameter, is then covered by the Gutta-Percha Company with four distinct coats of gutta-percha, and four coats of Chatterton's compound laid on alternately. This 'core,' as it is termed, is then tested in cold water, at a temperature of 90 degrees, and then under a pressure of 600 lb. to the square inch. After passing through all these ordeals, the loss by leakage through the gutta-percha covering does not exceed one hundred-millionth part of the current of electricity passing through the conducting wire in every nautical mile. To such minute perfection has the system of testing adopted by the engineers been carried, that the loss of one thousand-millionth part of the current by leakage could be detected and estimated on the instruments. In the present state of the insulation of the cable, the loss by leakage in working each section of the line will not exceed one four-hundredth part of the electric current sent through the conductor—a condition of insulation which we believe has never been equalled by any cable hitherto manufactured.

"Before being sheathed at Mr. Henley's works the coils of gutta-percha core, which are in three-mile lengths, are again tested under water for insulation and for resistance of conductor, therefore if any injury should have occurred to the fragile gutta-percha covering of the wire during its transit from the Wharf-road to North Woolwich it is detected before the cable is made up, and then the process of sheathing them in their outer covering is commenced. The first coating outside the gutta-percha is 12 thick strands of wet hemp, and over these again come 12 solid No. 7 gauge wires, which have been most carefully galvanized by Mr. Henley. The outer covering of iron wire is generally the last which a cable receives, but in this instance, as the line is to be laid in comparatively shallow water, the wires themselves, though galvanized, are to be still farther protected from their most formidable enemy, rust, which is done by the coverings of Bright and Clark's composition already described.

"During the whole time the cable is at Mr. Henley's the current is kept always through it, so that the slightest possible defect in the wire can be detected. In addition to this, the very able electrical staff test every portion regularly twice a day for insulation and resistance of conductor. When everything has been done which the most jealous care and the most fastidious scientific skill can suggest, it is passed out on the river side of Mr. Henley's factory and coiled away in tanks filled with water; and even here perpetually watched and tested. There are upwards of 900 nautical miles of it thus manufactured lying at Mr. Henley's works—huge coils of thick black-looking rope, nearly 1½ in. in diameter, weighing nearly four tons to the mile, and 2½ tons in water, and costing as nearly as possible 200*l*. per mile—the cheapest, strongest and, electrically speaking, the most perfect cable that has ever yet been made."

And a still later article supplies interesting and appropriate extracts:—

"The last ships of the squadron appointed to convey this cable, which in a few months will connect England with the remotest provinces of our Indian empire, have either sailed this week or will leave now in a few days more. Unforeseen causes, stress of weather, difficulty in obtaining all the varied appliances and apparatus necessary for so remote and important an expedition, have delayed the starting of some of the ships beyond the time at first contemplated. The *Assaye* left Plymouth on Saturday, the *Tweed* dropped down the river on Monday last, the *Marian Moore* and *Kirkham* are well on their voyage out. Only one more cable ship, the *Cospatrick*, remains

¹ *The Times*, August 13, 1863.

to follow. As they are all rather behind time, they will touch at no intermediate ports, but at once make all sail for Bombay. The public is, therefore, not likely to hear much of them till the great labour is completed, and the first intimation of success will most probably appear in our own columns in the telegram that will announce the state of the Bombay and Calcutta markets of the previous evening. It is only a few weeks since we gave a very long account of the mode of manufacture of this cable at Mr. Henley's factory—of the careful way in which it was almost hourly tested for insulation and resistance till it finally passed out from all the machines sheathed with galvanized iron wire to protect it from rust, swathed in hemp and tar over this, and, finally, coated over all with a mixture of asphalt, tar, and silica, laid on in a melted state and allowed to cool into a coating having almost the hardness of flint, and the flexibility of rope. In this completed state, nearly 1½ in. in diameter, weighing nearly 4 tons to the mile, and 2½ tons in water, it has been shipped in huge black-looking coils on board the vessels we have mentioned. The *Marian Moore* has taken about 700 tons, or 174 miles of the cable; the *Kirkham*, 183 miles; the *Tweed*, 350 miles; the *Assaye*, 370 miles; and the *Cospatrick* will have 173 miles ; or, in all, 1,250 nautical miles of submarine wire. In addition, each ship takes out complete telegraph stores for one station in the Persian Gulf. The little steamer *Charente*, to be hereafter called the *Amber Witch*, and to be permanently employed between the stations in the Persian Gulf, will carry out some 30 or 40 miles of shore ends of great strength, and this completes the tale of the scientific expedition, than which a more perfectly equipped one never left this country. The whole responsibility of superintendence, from the moment the cable was begun, down to the proper fitment of every ship chosen to carry it, has devolved upon Colonel Patrick Stewart, R.E., as well known for his high military services in India as for his superintendence of the admirably worked land lines through that country. Sir Charles Bright and Mr. Latimer Clark have been electrical engineers under Colonel Stewart, and have undertaken the whole responsibility of laying it successfully, but the principal labour has fallen to Colonel Stewart's lot, and to him will be due the great merit of the success of this national achievement.

"Each ship, as we have said, has been most perfectly fitted out, and each, as far as equipment goes, forms a perfect expedition in itself—a complete link in the chain of stations which is to connect Bombay with the head of the Gulf. The *Assaye* and the *Tweed*, the vessels which have just started with the greatest lengths of cable, may be taken as fair samples of the whole squadron. These vessels are sister ships built of Malabar teak, and intended as frigates for the old India Company. Both are of great speed, and both are of such prodigious strength that there are probably no wooden vessels in Her Majesty's navy so strongly bound together. In each of these as in all the other ships of the expedition three massive wrought-iron tanks have been built from the bottom up to the main deck,— one forward, one amidships, and one aft. In these the cable is carefully stowed away in three coils, the beginning and the end of each coil being carried along the ships to the testing room, and the tanks are then filled with water by a small steam pump on deck. A member of Sir Charles Bright's electrical staff goes with each ship, and has sole charge of the cable, which he can thus test through while under water in the tanks daily, and in case of any leakage being discovered have time to watch and localize the fault in the insulation, if any should occur, long before the time for submerging arrives. Being thus able to watch the condition of the wire from day to day is of the utmost possible importance, though from various causes it has not been practicable till now to adopt the precaution. With each section of the cable are also sent all the appliances necessary for paying out and buoying, with a staff of skilled workmen for making joints and cutting out faulty places, if any such should be discovered in the voyage out, iron posts for land lines, grappling-irons for raising the wire, and most perfect and costly sets of instruments, some of the most delicate kind, which will be kept either at the stations or at the head-quarters at Karáchi, in case of any unforeseen difficulties in working.

As far, however, as the most anxious care and forethought can
guard against accidents none are likely to arise. In fact, the
same delicate system of testing adopted during the manufacture,
which could detect and record the loss of one thousand-
millionth part of the current by leakage, shows that, if possible,
the cable now in the tanks on board the *Assaye* is in even better
electrical condition than when it left Mr. Henley's works. The
Assaye was driven into Plymouth by desperately heavy weather,
yet so strong was the ship, and so well was the cable stowed,
that the last tests taken before the vessel sailed on Saturday
showed each section to be in a higher condition of insulation
than any submarine cable ever exhibited before. On board
each of the ships go a certain portion of the staff which is
hereafter to work the line from station to station along the Gulf.
At each station will be a superintendent and deputy-super-
intendent, with six clerks—the latter the best instrument hands
that could be procured; the former all gentlemen of from ten to
twelve years' experience at the large stations in England. At
some of the stations the staff will have but a dull time; at
Khasāb, the lonely point of rock off the Arabian coast, for
instance, where the hostility of the Arabs may possibly oblige
all to live on board a hulk moored at some little distance from
the rocky desolate shore.[1] A well-chosen library of about 2,000
volumes goes out with the expedition, and these will be
divided between the five Gulf stations. The *Amber Witch*,
which will ply between the stations, will bring letters and
papers, and none of the staff will be kept more than two or
three months at a time at one station, so that there will at least
be constant change, if there is not much variety. The five
stations will be from Karāchi to Gwādar, a distance of 250
miles, from Gwādar across the Gulf to the peninsula of Khasāb,
from Khasāb to Bushahr, and from Bushahr to a place called
Fāo, a small eastern township on the estuary at the mouth of
the Euphrates, where the submarine wire meets the land lines
which carry it to Baghdad, thence to Mosul (the ancient

[1] See sketch at the head of this chapter. Khasāb never was used as a
cable station.

Nineveh), thence to Diarbekir, and thence to Scutari, on the Bosphorus, where it joins a dozen European land routes. Dr. Esselbach, so well known among scientific men in this country for his high attainments, is to be chief superintendent in charge of the whole line, and at his disposal will be a regular staff of mechanicians, &c., at the head-quarters at Karachi. The reason for going to the great expense and trouble of making five breaks or stations in the Gulf, on a length of 1,200 miles of wire, is of course, the great difficulty which would otherwise be experienced in telegraphing through an unbroken circuit of 1,200 miles. It was for the same reason that the Malta and Alexandria line was laid in three sections. Electricians are sanguine in their hopes that, in the course of time, and with increased knowledge and experience in submarine cables, this great difficulty, or rather obstacle, may be mitigated. As far, however, as present knowledge goes, nothing appears more certain than that messages cannot be sent through long unbroken circuits of submarine wires with sufficient rapidity and distinctness to make such undertakings commercially profitable, even if there were no risk of loss while being laid across deep seas. Even with the short circuits in which the Persian Gulf line is being laid, Dr. Esselbach is taking out with him some beautiful instruments specially made by Professor Wheatstone, Professor Thomson, Mr. Jenken, and others, in order to mitigate with them the influence of the electric wave in the conductor, which, to a certain extent, will interfere with rapidity and clearness of telegraphing, even along the wire where the longest unbroken submarine stretch is only 400 miles.'

The article concluded with a hearty wish that Colonel Stewart and his able engineers might achieve that success to which their unwearied care so justly entitled them.

Early in December the heads of the expedition were in Bombay, awaiting the arrival of the whole cable and disposal of all preliminaries to consigning it to the deep.

' *The Times*, October 21, 1863.

But the Christmas of 1863 is a period to be long remembered in the annals of Western India for other matters than the Anglo-Indian Telegraph.¹ The allurements of speculation were at this time fast assuming the guise of mania; and at the Presidency the common talk of almost every table was the share-market. People who had lived half a century, content, in following the quiet professional walk which had distinguished and formed so many "old Indians," to remain ignorant of the very meaning of stocks, funds, consols and the like, now rushed wildly forward to buy shares without money, and anticipate, often to realize thousands, without a foundation even in units. "Back Bay" and "Land Reclamation" were the magic words acting as keys to men's hearts and interest; and those who rue the remembrance of them in these more sober days, will admit existence of the time when he who cared not to learn the current Shibboleth was regarded as a foreigner, if not positively tabooed. In happy contrast to this prevalence of mammon was a notable movement in the ecclesiastical world, usually so little prominent in Indian official life. The rare occurrence of three Bishops officiating together under one roof could not but afford a grateful spectacle to all true lovers of the Church; and at this particular season the Bishop of Calcutta had visited Bombay, in his capacity of Metropolitan in India, to meet the two minor Presidency Bishops. Little, however, could the attentive hearers of the first foresee that the learned and estimable prelate's new career of usefulness was so soon to be brought to a close.¹ Among other objects of special

¹ The sad and sudden termination to Dr. Cotton's life and labours is too recent an occurrence for more than passing allusion.

local interest may be incidentally mentioned disturbances on the North-West frontier,—to which quarter Bombay, perhaps on account of her rural dependency, was always ready to look with gravity—and the appointment of a new Governor-General.

Telegraphic communication between England and India was a question calculated to command attention, among the frequenters of the Bombay share market as elsewhere. As fever produced by brain excitement must always be affected by intelligence bearing on the original cause of malady, so would the Indian patient under the share mania feel deep interest in the creation of a medium by which he could communicate, to home partners or constituents, with a rapidity hitherto unknown, fluctuations or other technical signs of immense personal import. And although there were many in India, as in England, who felt honest sympathy with the Government in carrying out a great work of progressive civilization and national benefit, without any regard whatever to selfish objects or results, it cannot reasonably be expected that a measure of such practical bearing on commercial transactions as the Indo-European Telegraph should fail to attract the majority in a purely utilitarian sense. Upon the whole, then, notwithstanding the share mania and other powerful influences acting upon the public mind, the Persian Gulf Cable Expedition could boast a tolerable, if not an excessive amount of interest in Bombay and the West, as in other parts of India remoter from the actual scene of action.

An outline of the work to be done will make the case clear to all readers, and will be sufficiently brief to be pardoned by those who stand in no need of detailed description. Karáchi is the sea terminus of the Indian Telegraph system at the north-west corner of the great Peninsula. Fáo, at the head of the Persian Gulf, is the sea terminus of the Turkish Telegraph system connected with the systems of Continental Europe and, through them, with England. Karáchi is distant from Fáo about 1,250 miles, reckoning the mile by the sea knot. It was intended to join the two by submarine cable laid in four sections, in round numbers as follows:— Karáchi to Gwádar 300 miles; Gwádar to Masandam 400 miles; Masandam to Bushahr 400 miles; Bushahr to Fáo 150 miles. The first section, that from Karáchi to Gwádar, would be the last laid, as there was a land line already working between the two stations which could be trusted at least as a temporary link in through communication. The first section to be laid would therefore be that from Gwádar to Masandam; and the ships immediately engaged were to *rendezvous* on the 4th February at the former station, whence operations would commence.

On the 27th January Colonel Stewart embarked from Karáchi in the *Coromandel* steamer, which was placed at his disposal in directing proceedings. His brother, Captain Colvin Stewart, accompanied him as personal assistant; and in the same vessel were Sir Charles Bright, Colonel Goldsmid, Dr. Esselbach, Mr. A. P. Young and Dr. Ponsonby Adair; the last three being employed respectively as Chief Electrician and General Line Superintendent, Assistant Marine Surveyor, and Medical Officer specially attached to the expedition. Lieutenant Carew of the Indian Navy commanded the steamer, and proved himself an adept in the difficult art of combining the good of the public service with the comfort and convenience of his passengers. Gwádar was reached at an early hour on the 29th; and although the Political officer, Captain Ross, had no large agency in which to receive his guests, both he and his amiable partner could always give them a cordial welcome to an English home in Makran. Their abode, something between a Swiss chalet and Crimean hut, had the charm of a baronial hall to the wandering Englishman whom chance or duty led to its threshold, and its inner tidiness was redolent of hospitality.

The town, or rather village, of Gwádar is built on a sandy isthmus at the foot of an abrupt rocky range projecting far to seaward, rising above the waters to a height of 100 feet, and forming two bays, which afford good anchorage in depths of from four to six fathoms. Viewing the promontory in its connection with the mainland, the length of rock runs east and west, and presents a sea front like the head of a hammer, to which the isthmus supplies a handle. The bay to the east is well protected in the south-west monsoon, and may be considered the natural harbour of Gwádar; but the western bay is equally available in the event of a blow from eastward. Detailed account of the place and its inhabitants belongs to the chapter on Baluchistan and the Makran coast. It may now, however, be stated that the political obstacles to making it a station had been provided for in the Political department; that the Arab Wali, or Governor, worthily seconded his master the Sultan of Maskat in readiness to coöperate with the peaceful enterprise of H.M. Government; that an English working office and store-depôt had been organized and established at Gwádar under the *ægis* of a Political Agent, and that so far from apprehensions of molestation being entertained by the British residents, an English lady was actually living there with her husband as quietly as she might have done in Calcutta or London.

The steamers and cable ships of the Gwādar-Masandam section having met as arranged, and the heavy shore cable being duly landed and laid, the expedition started on the evening of the 4th February. The *Coromandel*, with Colonel Stewart and staff, piloted

SAIF BIN SALIM, WALI OF GWADAR, 1862-3.

the course. The steamer *Zenobia*, towing the *Kirkham*, followed. In the latter were Sir Charles Bright and staff, laying and testing the cable, which was paid out at the rate of about five miles an hour.

The steamer *Victoria* had left Gwādar the day before the other vessels, with instructions to ascertain and mark a point at sea where a sudden fall in the bottom made the course unsuitable to the line of cable. Before taking up her position to await the coming of her

ships from the eastward, and, without so much as one mile of intervening land, a second inlet, the "Elphinstone," was to answer a similar purpose on the west. Day was passed at the Jask anchorage, so that the Arabian coast might be reached in the morning.

Two hundred and sixty-eight miles of cable had been laid when the ships again started. Shortly after mid-day on the 9th the *Marian Moore* anchored at the appointed landing-place, having raised the figure to 357. On the 13th the shore end was landed. The day following, the *Marian Moore*, towed by the *Zenobia*, started for Bombay to bring up the *Tweed* and *Assaye*, which had arrived there with 730 miles of cable on the 6th and 13th February respectively. In the words of the paper giving publicity to the minuter of these data: "So far nothing could have been more successful; the cable when laid being in very far higher electrical condition than any other line yet submerged, and having been laid without the smallest drawback or embarrassment, either mechanical or electrical."[1]

The Gwādar-Masandam section of cable having been successfully disposed of, no further progress in actual laying could be made until arrival of the ships expected from Bombay. But this want of material was not the sole cause of delay. Political difficulties presented themselves on the Arabian coast, for the removal of which no adequate provision had been made. A question had arisen as to sovereign control over the isthmus and inlets now under utilisation in the Telegraph scheme. However peacefully traversed by the wires on a chart of Eastern seas, the reduction to actual practice of a Western hypothesis was quite another

[1] *The Times*, March 1864.

affair; and when the real scene of action was approached, the Arab fishermen and inhabitants concerned were reluctant to bestow their friendly offices on comparative strangers without, at least, the guarantee of some substantial return for a manifest privilege. More than a month was spent at Masandam; and the Arabs gave a good deal of trouble during that time and for some time afterwards. The writer having joined Colonel Stewart here from Makran on the 12th February, is able to speak on the subject from personal knowledge and observation.

The singular appearance of the Peninsula terminating, to the northward, the Arabian province of Oman, cannot fail to have struck everyone who has investigated Eastern geography and the charts of Eastern seas. On the map it shows a quaint, irregular figure, inclining to the eastward, with island and inlet, bay, creek, and isthmus, in more or less profusion. A long narrow neck which connects the whole with the continent presents no apparent difficulties, whether for traversing or severance; and as this particular point is reached by the directest and most convenient of theoretical lines indicating the passage of the Indian Telegraph cable from Karachi to Basrah, no wonder that it should have attracted the notice of the vanguard of survey preceding the head-quarters of the actual expedition. But this quaint, irregular figure, which on the map looks so easy of snipping with the scissors of science, is in truth a mass of high, hard rocks; and when these are considered leisurely and under the influence of their heat and sterility, it becomes doubtful whether it would not have been better to have avoided altogether the intricacies of Masandam by keeping entirely to the opposite coast. After experience has certainly passed an unmistakable decision against the original selection, though it has in no way impugned the wisdom and expediency which occasioned it under peculiar and urgent circumstances.

Colonel Disbrowe, Political Agent at Maskat, had on the 8th January 1864, in anticipation of Colonel Stewart's arrival with the cable, proceeded to the localities which he, intelligibly but in somewhat technical parlance, designated the "Masandam Districts," to make inquiries bearing on, and with a view to forward generally, the interests of the undertaking. The steamer *Victoria* had conveyed him to Malcolm's Inlet, and in company with her commander, Lieutenant Arnott, of the Indian Navy, and Lieutenants Pierson and St. John of the Bengal Engineers, he had visited the isthmus of Maklab, the spot marked out by Lieutenant Stiffe for temporarily interrupting the submarine cable by the intervention of a short land line. It had been proposed to substitute here, at a later date, an underground for an aërial telegraph; but the distance under consideration was less than half a mile, and no physical obstructions of consequence had presented themselves. After re-embarkation of the exploring party, the *Victoria* had re-landed Colonel Disbrowe in another part of the inlet, and leaving him there with a couple of small soldiers' tents, servants and horse, had steamed away, with her remaining passengers, to Bushahr and Basrah.

A brief account of this self-imposed but useful mission is procurable from existing data. The village chosen for preliminary inspection was Habalain, situated on the southern side of the inlet and at an easy distance from the recently visited isthmus. It was sunset when the Political Agent fairly reached his camping-ground. The villagers flocked to see their unexpected guest, stared at him to their hearts' content, and left him for the night. Habalain was about 150 paces from the tents, but offered few attractions to the European stranger or any of the outer world. Unless rain fell, its water was brackish and undrinkable. Even the thirsty horse rejected the supply first brought, although the Arab inhabitants gave testimony in its favour in continued personal experience. Fortunately there was rain that night, and no inconvenience resulted on the score of drought.

Colonel Disbrowe was visited, early on the following morning, by the Chief of Habalain, a stranger from Sohar, the Mulla of the village, and a group of followers. Accustomed to the indispensable local ceremonies of reception, he treated his visitors to coffee and compliments, and entered into conversation with them on ordinary topics. He was not prepossessed by the strange assemblage. Seldom had he beheld a more unsightly set. "Eyes small; noses elongated; teeth of all shapes, very bad and in no grown up person complete; ears protruding; faces grinning;" such is his own description, in hurried pencil notes, of the men of Habalain; and only two of the thirty-four counted had seen an Englishman before the opportunity then offered.

After vain attempts to discover a practicable pass for horse and rider across the rocky ranges to the western coast of the Peninsula, so as to reach Khasab, a village which it was proposed to constitute a main emporium for the necessaries of life to the dwellers on the Maklab isthmus, Colonel Disbrowe obtained, on the third day of his sojourn at Habalain, a boat; and in this he determined to commence operations by revisiting the isthmus itself. The name "Maklab" given to this narrowest strip of the Arabian rocks, on either side of which the waters of the Persian Gulf and Indian Ocean respectively roll at a distance of less than half a mile apart, is, translated literally, a 'place of turning.' In like manner "Maskat" is a 'place of falling.' Should either word bear special signification to its object, the analogy would be doubtless derived from volcanic and natural phenomena.

Reaching the landing-place in Malcolm's Inlet, the party proceeded to cross the isthmus. The Political Agent had shouldered his own saddle-bags, and his servants were, under instructions, each carrying something in accordance with his powers. Two English guns and a Baluch peon's sword were the weapons available in the event of need. About midway the inlet of the Persian Gulf burst in sight, and at this same point the corresponding inlet of the Indian Ocean was still visible behind. The isthmus was traversed in some fifteen or twenty minutes. First an ascent, then comparatively level ground, then a descent to the sea. The ground was not very rugged, save in the immediate vicinity of the landing-places. It was estimated that with fifty or sixty labourers a good broad path might be made across in a week. In the Elphinstone Inlet was observed a diminutive island; and on the mainland beyond that island had already been found building sites, and building stone in abundance.

Taking boat again on the further side of Maklab, Colonel Disbrowe proceeded down the narrow but romantic channel leading to the open sea, to Khasab, a distance of six to seven miles. This large village is situated in a broad curve of the promontory running out in a westerly direction from the Arabian Peninsula, below the mouth of the Elphinstone Inlet, and terminating in the cape called by the Arabs "Ras Shaikh Masáúd." The landing is an inconvenient process at low water, as there is a flat extending from high-water mark under the Fort walls for about three-quarters of a mile into the bay. Not only was it at this awkward period that Colonel Disbrowe arrived, but after sunset; so that it was with considerable difficulty he achieved his purpose, and brought up his incumbrances to the village. The house provided for his reception, however hospitably intended, would have been better fitted to lodge a mermaid visiting *terra firma* for the night, than an ordinary British landsman unconnected with amphibia. Its marine odours were overpowering, and drove him to resort to his tent readily pitched outside.

Some days passed before the Agent's return to Maskat. From the 14th to the 22nd January he was mainly occupied in the very essential question of finding water and provisions for a supposed Telegraph Station at Makláb. As regards both these necessaries he arrived, moreover, at practical results, and was able to report in tolerable detail.[1]

This preliminary exploration had not, however, availed to ensure a satisfactory reception to the cable ships and their passengers on the part of the Arabs in the vicinity of the isthmus. Colonel Stewart and other officers of the expedition had made a few presents on arrival to the chiefs, or pretended chiefs, who first showed themselves, but the cupidity of these orientals

[1] Colonel Disbrowe to Lieut.-Colonel Stewart. Semi-official letter dated Maskat, January 27, 1864.

was unlike that of their Indian brethren: it knew no bounds, no restraint whatever, and was as irrepressible as unlimited. There was clearly no honest work to be got for money and fair dealing from the inhabitants; and on the 13th February, when the young Director General of the Telegraph, eager for progress and impatient of irrelevant obstacles, was on shore with one or two shipmates, the jealousy, avarice, and discontent aroused by the well-meant liberality which had been exercised, culminated in a regular Irish row. It appeared that a number of persons from Fillam, a neighbouring village, attracted by the report of strange arrivals and in the hope of sharing in further largesses, had come over to Maklab to reconnoitre. This deputation had alarmed the Arabs of the more immediate neighbourhood, who had naturally been first in the field; and the Shaikhs of Mukāka, a village, like Habalain, within walking distance of the isthmus, came over intent on resisting any participation in a plunder the sweets of which they had already tasted. By misapprehension of identity the Fillamites were selected to form the first working party in British pay, and the selection excited the anger of their rivals to the highest pitch. Nor was the clamour appeased by correction of error committed. The well-meant counter-choice of Mukāka invoked the direst wrath of disappointed Fillam. All effort at conciliation was vain. Neither one nor the other side would listen to reason. Words produced blows, and some of these blows, inflicted with sticks, with which the disputants were freely armed, came down upon the victims with savage force and meaning. One man who had been singled out by Colonel Stewart as a builder, and apparently the only competent man for the duty, was furiously handled for entering into an arrangement irrespective of his avaricious comrades. It was evident that the expedition had become mixed up with a wild, turbulent lot, who preferred club law to any amount of reason, and that, unsupported by acknowledged authority, the Telegraph Officers would have a difficult game to play. Mere conciliation was out of the question. It was useless to attempt it under the circumstances. All that could be done at the moment was to trust to the shipping, and to work on shore with such few hands as could be spared for preliminary clearing and building, and for protecting the few stores which it was necessary to land. Covetous of everything the English intruder might possess, up to the shirt on his back, these unprepossessing natives were jealous of each other, in the matter of gifts, as dogs with a stray bone. The one privileged person in each village was the Shaikh, but one false Shaikh begat fifty, and every Shaikh had a host of relatives striving to profit by the consanguinity. The village of Mukâka presented a notable instance of this squabbling and cupidity; but then, Mukâka was the weak point, and what had been seen of Fillam did not lend to the supposition that its civilization was of a higher order.[1]

But there was a doubt as to the authority, if indeed any, acknowledged by these Masandam Arabs. Some openly disavowed subjection to the Sultan of Maskat, and admitted no chief but Sultan Bin Sagar, the old ex-pirate of Ras-el-Khaima. Others gave vague and

[1] While these pages are going through the press, the kindness of the Bombay Government has enabled me to supply Colonel Stewart's own account of proceedings on the day of our landing at Maklâb. This will be found in the Appendix to Chapter III.

uncertain answers, intimating that they enjoyed a *quasi* independence. Larek, Kana, Mukāka, Habalain and Fillam had made themselves known, at least by name, to the new comers. The last was on the east side of the fifteen miles of promontory stretching out from the Maklab isthmus towards the Persian coast. On the same side of the same promontory were the villages or settlements of Sibi, Shābus and Shisa. On the west were Ghassa, Ghubba, Ghanam, and Kumzar.[1] The coming of many more Shaikhs and pseudo-Shaikhs might thus reasonably be expected, and those who came would hardly fail to assert their claims to conciliatory presents. Then again, south of the isthmus was the whole Arabian Peninsula.

On the 15th February, Colonel Disbrowe, steaming in from Maskat, joined Colonel Stewart, who at once explained in writing the difficulties of his position.

---

[1] The following entry was made in my journal at Baghdad in 1864, after looking into the Rev. Charles Forster's *Historical Geography of Arabia*, which I casually took from the Political Agent's bookcase:—

"As I could have wished, when journeying and journalising in Makran, that Dr. Vincent had been present to prove or disprove his philological and archæological results and theories, so could I wish that Mr. Forster were deposited at Masandam, to make deductions on the names of places and ethnology of races found upon that singular Peninsula. I call the 'Peninsula' the whole of that rocky projection stretching N.E. from the isthmus of Maklab. His map of localities is more indefinite than he supposes. His 'Dedan' is written in large letters, but not even does the final *n* encroach upon my Peninsula, which he leaves a blank. Yet what would he say to the settlements actually upon it? Eastward of Kumzar are Shisa, Shābus, Fillam, Mukāka; to the West may be reckoned Ghanam, Ghubba, Ghassa and Sibi. Is not Shabus manifestly like Sheba, and Sibi almost Seba itself? Ghassa has something of Kush; and if we take the continental side of the isthmus we have at its very border Khasab, another word with the much sought-for sound, and Habalain, which is philologically Hawilain, or a dual form of Hawilah, Havilah, or Hawl. . . . . Now all this information is to be found on the small and seldom-noticed tip of the tongue of land intersected by the *Ebhitari montes*."

Desirous of taking advantage of the interval which must elapse before the return from Bombay of the steamers with the cable ships in tow, to visit the Gulf Stations of Bushahr and Fao, he could not leave the Masandam anchorage without the certain knowledge that some officer was left behind competent and authorized to act in any emergency that might arise in dealing with the Arabs. The brief but material experience of the locality gained since his first arrival had proved to him how necessary it was that every precaution should be taken against the petty collisions which were inevitable without the most careful and constant superintendence.[1] But unfortunately the Political Agent had brought with him from head-quarters no solution to the problem of local sovereignty. The rights of Mukáka, or other troublesome villages, to interfere in a Telegraph line or Station at Makhab, or any adjacent undefined spot of territory, were not necessarily dependent on the rule under which these were placed respectively; but their good behaviour and hospitality to strangers could be better guaranteed by a ruling power than by any single Shaikh whose normal condition was feud with his neighbour. Eventually it was decided that Colonels Disbrowe and Stewart should proceed together to Maskat, and either obtain from the Sultan the required authority, or sufficient data on which to act without it. Colonel Goldsmid would, in the meanwhile, with Mr. Isaac Walton, Mr. Hirz, and one or two members of the Telegraph staff, remain in tents on the isthmus.

On the 26th February the *Coromandel* returned from her mission to Maskat, bringing back Colonels Stewart and Disbrowe. The week which had elapsed since their

[1] Lieut.-Colonel Stewart to Colonel Disbrowe, February 15, 1864.

departure from Maklab had not been unproductive of good. On the one hand, the visit to the Sultan had enlisted his active interest in the cause of the expedition, although the authority obtained, and under which the refractory Arabs were to be treated, was not very distinct or conclusive. His Highness had confirmed his own previous professions of good-will and assistance, and was ready to exert his own influence to any extent on behalf of her Majesty's Government. On the other hand, the Arabs of Masandam had become more accustomed to the presence of Englishmen bent on a work which could not harm any of them, and might be the means of benefiting such of their number as were well-disposed enough to co-operate. The chiefs and their followers had been troublesome and intrusive, as anticipated; and it had been necessary to deprive at least one offensive Shaikh of the *entrée* to the Maklab encampment. A threatening letter had, moreover, succeeded the act, professedly sent by the hill Bedouins with a view to favour certain claimants to the land occupied, and perhaps to extort more presents, and the messenger was to return for an answer. But they understood the character and objects of their visitors all the better from these proceedings and their results; and this was just what was required for the success of the Telegraph cause.

Although the electric wire would find its way by means of an aërial line across the isthmus, it was resolved to make the Telegraph Station as far as practicable independent of the more inquisitive than inviting Arabs of the hills and villages. Accordingly the Elphinstone Island in the inlet of the same name was fixed upon as a fitting site for the offices and residence of *employés*. This spot, before alluded to, had already attracted attention. Notwithstanding its miniature size, it stood conveniently in the way between the Maklab place of landing and mouth of the inlet, and was only distant from the former about one-third of a mile.

Three weeks passed from the date of return of the *Coromandel* to Maklab and the renewal of cable operations. During this time much was accomplished in improving the position, politically and generally, and much in providing water, provisions and building materials, and towards the establishment of a standing bazar for the contemplated Masandam Station. One Músa of Maskat, filling with admirable tact and cleverness the respective offices of agent, interpreter, pedlar, contractor, or envoy, according to circumstances, was sedulously engaged in the last-named undertaking, and his endeavours promised to be crowned with success. Short notices of excursions, made at this time by the present writer to Mukáka, Filiam, and across the Gulf to Basiduh, may be here introduced in illustration of the places and people, without irrelevancy to the narrative of the cable.

In the north-east corner, then, of the irregularly shaped isthmus joining the still more irregularly shaped peninsula commonly known as Masandam to the Arabian continent, is the village of Mukáka. The bay in which it is situated is reached through one out of many indentations of rocky coast, and is part of a deep, broad, land-locked inlet called by the natives "Ghubbeh Ghazireh." This is our "Malcolm's Inlet;" whereas the "Elphinstone Inlet," on the opposite or western side of the isthmus, is known by the Arabs as "Khor-es-Shem." The village, like many others in this ungenial quarter, is built on the slope of a rocky hill. The houses are constructed of stone walls loosely thrown up, without plaster or cement, with flat roofs of planks surmounted by stones also. A small space is built out and levelled in front of each dwelling, but there are no long lines of streets, nor is there anything corresponding to the Indian "angan" or compound. Dr. Adair and Colonel Goldsmid visited the place on the 2nd March, starting at about 11 A.M. The walk was a long one, and the road very rough at times, now in the more fertile-looking hollows, now skirting the hills. The sea views were really beautiful; and the village as beheld from the height, and descended upon, as it were, over the tops of its houses, was far from wanting in picturesque interest. Saiyid Muhammad, the Baghdad Munshi, went forward to notify the approach of visitors to Abid, relative and *locum tenens* of the temporarily absent Shaikh, Suliman. But the inhabitants had already espied the strangers and invited them by signals and cries to draw near. The women were especially loud in exclaiming "tãal," or "come." Abid himself, a rather square-built, sombre, middle-aged man, shortly appeared, and led the way to his own hut. It was a small abode, about 14 feet long, the length corresponding with the sea-front, and 5 or 6 feet broad; and the walls being about 6 feet high. The furniture and decorations were of the rudest kind; the principal objects being British quart bottles with flaming labels, evidently procured from the recently arrived vessels. Seats were given to the visitors on a covered earthen daïs, or ledge of mud, the rest of the party sitting on a lower one at right angles to, or fronting it. Rain-water was brought in a common china bowl, and found acceptable. When the doctor's profession was announced and he was introduced as the "Tabib-ul-Kabir" or head physician, patients were forthcoming on the instant.

One was an old man with a weak chest who had before been to the camp at Maklab for medical advice. The prevalence of blindness was noted here as elsewhere in these parts; and it was professionally considered that the affliction could in many cases have been prevented by ordinary precautions.

After a brief stay with Abul, the party, at his earnest solicitation, adjourned to the house of the absent Suliman. They were cordially received by the ladies of the family and feasted on dates. Some of the better huts, though low and confined by the uniform flat, mud-covered roof, were divided into two apartments, of which one was occupied by women and children. The former had their faces partly screened in Egyptian fashion, but were not much discomposed by the presence of strangers. In the particular instance recorded the reception by the ladies could not but prove a welcome alternative for one by the Shaikh in person. This Suliman of Mukaka had rendered himself especially obnoxious to the settlers in Maklab. Recollection of the trouble which his presence occasioned traces to the imagination a *physique* not soon to be forgotten. A long, thin, curved strip of humanity; a thing of strong animal instinct, and little mental power that is not subservient and secondary; a personification of covetousness; ready for cunning, treachery, and cowardice; jealous, envious, passionate. The expression of his grey eye, peering stealthily below a shaggy eyebrow, amid a profusion of wrinkles and furrows, is that of his general character. If it were possible for a gift to soften his heart, it could never succeed in softening his manners: the usual effect of a gift upon him is to sharpen the cries of rapacity to an extent almost beyond the endurance of conciliation. Such is the retrospect of this man. When his village was now visited by strangers it was said that he had sailed across the Gulf to Bandar Abbas, where was the Lieutenant-Governor of the Sultan of Maskat. It was, however, thought equally probable that he had gone to consult with Sultan Bin Sagar of Ras-el-Khaima. And, as it afterwards became hinted that this aged chief had advised the Masandam Arabs to assist rather than impede the objects of the Telegraph Expedition, there was good ground for such supposition.

The day following the visit to Mukaka, several Arabs from Khasab, Mukaka, and Fillam came on board the ships and stayed for a considerable time. The political officers of the expedition talked of paying the last place a visit the next morning, provided the inhabitants would supply a boat. This they readily agreed to do, and an arrangement to such effect was duly concluded. The ships, it should be explained, were at the anchorage west of the isthmus, and it was to the landing-place on the east that a boat would arrive from Fillam. On the morning of the 4th March a Fillamite messenger swam across to the *Coromandel*, coming on board wet and shivering, to announce that water carriage was ready on the further side of Maklab. Colonel Goldsmid, accompanied by an Arab official of the Maskat Political Agency and his own Sindi servants, proceeded at once by ship's boat to the isthmus, walked across, and met the specially deputed crew. The Arab boat in waiting was a small one, and sailed or rowed according to circumstances; sufficiently manned for all ordinary purposes by three or four adults.

Fillam is situated in the bay of an inlet, "Ghubbeh

Shábus," separated from the Malcolm Inlet or "Ghubbeh Ghazireh," by projecting rocks terminating in a sea cape, Ras Dallain. The village, though at no great distance from Maklab by land and as the crow flies, is reached easily only by water, but then the water journey is one of several miles. Behind it is a mountain, the peak of which is estimated at 2,500 feet high. This height, however exceptional for the actual promontory of Masandam, is surpassed by the Arabian mountains immediately below the Maklab isthmus, one of which is recorded as 4,470, one as 5,800, and one as 6,750 feet; while on the opposite Persian coast, behind Bandar Abbas, one mountain rises to 7,690, one to 8,500, and one to 10,660 feet.

The course from Maklab was about S.S.E. till the rocks were reached east of the Malcolm Inlet, when the boat worked gradually round to the N.N.E., and entered the wide and sheltered inlet in which is the bay of Fillam, sighting the village on the low sandy ground at foot of the Sibi hill. To the westward, and almost opposite Fillam Bay, is the village of Mansul, the second or alternative season settlement of the Fillamites. Such is Shem to the inhabitants of Kána in the Elphinstone, and Habshín to Mukáka in the Malcolm Inlet. The boatmen were civil, but had no sooner rounded the point fairly shutting out the telegraph isthmus and anchorage, than they declared themselves to be subjects of Sultan Bin Sagar, and quite independent of the Sultan of Maskat. Whether the time for such assertion were chosen or not, it is impossible to determine; at all events it had never before been publicly made, and in so distinct a manner. They said that Mukáka, Kána, Shábus, and others were in the same condition as they themselves in this respect. The reception of the strangers at Fillam was peculiar. There was no crowd or *empressement*; but after a time, a rusty old dismounted gun was fired, and the Shaikhs or quasi-Shaikhs appeared. To his astonishment Colonel Goldsmid recognized acquaintances among his hosts, one a very conspicuous leader in the disturbances on the isthmus. This last, moreover, by name Abdullah, was pointed out as the head Shaikh, and to his care he consigned himself. He led the way to a covered outhouse by the village, where a mat was spread for the visitor, and where the ceremony of salutation, sitting and conversation, was held. After a time the Shaikh went to prayers, and others followed. The women and children remained, staring and commenting on their strange guest, few of whose countrymen had ever been seen before in that locality, and none perhaps sitting among them. Prayers seemed to last unusually long; but this circumstance might have been occasioned by the day being Friday, the Musalmān sabbath. Upon the whole, the visitor was not sorry to take leave: there was a constraint on the part of the Arabs which they knew not how to overcome: they were at a loss what to do to express their feelings, evidently sore with reference to recent events; and yet the general intentions appeared hospitable. The passage from Maklab lasted about two hours and a half; something less than an hour was spent at Fillam; and another two hours and a half may be added for the return. The scenery of the inlets is most interesting. The rocks to the east are bold and precipitous; and some of the clefts striking and picturesque. Six or seven hours under a hot sun are, however, sufficiently trying to a body in comparative repose to make the shelter of a cabin welcome relief even from the best of out-door scenery.

On the 12th March the *Zenobia* brought in the *Tweed*, with 352 miles of cable, to the Elphinstone Inlet; and leaving her important charge in the anchorage, again steamed off, under instructions, on active duty. She was to fill up with coal, as early as practicable, at Basiduh, the old naval depôt in the Persian Gulf. Commander Bradshaw, R.N., and a party of telegraph officials were on board, and they were now joined by Colonel Goldsmid. Early in the morning of the 13th they were off Lingah on the Persian coast, or about 90 miles N.N.W. of the Elphinstone Inlet, and about 25 miles in a westerly direction from Basiduh. Here is stationed a so-called British agent, usually a native of the country; but as he had not put in an appearance up to 11 A.M. and there was work to be done, and information to be acquired on shore, Colonel Goldsmid secured the services of a fishing-boat, hailed from the *Zenobia*. Into this he entered with one attendant, a Baghdad Arab. The wind was blowing freshly from the north-west, and there was a tolerably rough sea; the steamer was, moreover, lying out in the roadstead some four miles from the shore; but under favour of a tow to a starting-place before the wind, a good run was made, and the shore reached about mid-day. While the attendant was searching for the agent, the inhabitants of Lingah flocked round the European stranger. The scene was a curious one, for there were faces and forms of many kinds and from many quarters. There was the fair and almost Italian-looking Baghdadi; the smooth-cheeked Persian *sarbaz*; the Perso-Arab of Afghan aspect, with the thin, curled or plaited locks; the Hindustani Fakir, once a *sipahi*; the coast merchant, the coast fisherman, the man of money, the beggar, the man of business, the loafer. All of these were more or less to

be recognized in the ring of cross-questioners and listeners
gradually formed upon the beach. Persian was the
language used, and its easy, melodious vocabulary was
a delightful change from the jargon of Masandam.
Again, the behaviour of the people was not like that of
the uncouth semi-barbarians of the opposite coast, or
indeed the semi-civilized nondescripts of many parts of
India. Among other topics of conversation brought
forward, questions were asked on the American war;
and surprise was manifested at the telegraph scheme and
its success up to Khasab, as they called the Masandam
station. After a time the messenger returned, and the
scene changed to the interior of the house of the Shaikh
of Lingah. This official was a young Arab of apparently
five or six and-twenty, slim, and of middle height, with
a face which might have been well-looking had it not
been deeply and plentifully scarred with pock-marks. He
proffered the Kaliān in the Persian fashion; and two
or three whiffs of this were followed by cakes and excellent coffee. To the visitors the ceremony had an intrinsic value, as, on this particular occasion, biscuits had
served the purpose of the day's breakfast. After a few
words had been exchanged on the subject of boats and
boat hire, coals and coolies, the visit concluded. The
return trip to the steamer was over a heavy sea, and she
lay far off the shore. There was some difficulty in
boarding her, and still more difficulty for the fishermen
to clear her after transferring their passengers to her
decks. Soon after 4 P.M. however, the *Zenobia* was on
her way to Basidah and cast her anchor, as night set in,
about a mile off the usual anchorage at that station. Early
the next morning she took up her proper position.

Lingah, for many years, has had the reputation of

being one of the most considerable towns on the south coast of Persia. Its traffic in pearls, and exchange of native products of the interior with India, have familiarised its name to Bombay merchants; but there is good authority for supposing its main trade to have been confined to the maritime Arab ports, and it has the disadvantages of a dangerous roadstead and proximity to Bandar Abbas, which even the periodical visits of "British India" steamers cannot remove. Colonel Pelly, visiting the place in 1863, estimated, for the township, a population of 8,000 to 10,000, of whom the bulk were Africans. The wealthier class he represented to be Persianised Arabs, and some Persians attracted from the upper country for labour on the spot or as carriers into the interior. About twenty Hindus were said to reside in the place as agents for firms in Bombay or Karachi; and the number of native craft belonging to the inhabitants was set down at a hundred and fifty.[1]

Basaduh Point, usually but erroneously called Bassadore, is at the north-west of Kishm, known to the Arabs as Jazirat-el-Towilah, the "Long Island,"—a title not undeserved, as its length exceeds fifty miles, the breadth varying from thirty two to nine. The ruins of a town once flourishing under Portuguese auspices are here pointed out, but the principal objects which now attract the eye, are the buildings marking British occupation, and the residence of British officials in the nineteenth century. There is nothing indeed in the straggling native village worthy of notice. The houses are poor and primitive, and, even amid the vestiges of the past, there are really no signs

---

[1] Visit to Lingah, Kishm, and Bandar Abbas; by Colonel Pelly, Resident Persian Gulf ("Journal of Royal Geographical Society," Vol. 34. Paper No. xvii.)

of bygone grandeur or advanced civilization. A short distance from the old town, and near the sea-beach, is a square-looking mound of respectable height and dimensions, on the east and west sides of which is a tower, or the *débris* of a tower, erected probably by the townspeople after the departure of the Portuguese, as a means of defence against the pirates. The Point is a prolongation of generally level ground with stony surface, having a slope towards the sea, which washes it, some twenty feet or more below, on the north and west. Owing to the projecting sandy spits and shoal water near Basiduh anchorage, and the inconvenient necessity for many ships wishing to reach it, of entering the Clarence Straits, away from the main entrance to the Persian Gulf, the position is hardly a fitting one for a naval depôt or rendezvous. Such, however, it has long been, and as such will it long live in the records of the Indian navy.

Nearly four days were spent at Basiduh, in coaling and other matters connected with the progress of the Expedition. The contractors were good men of their sort, and accustomed to the wants and ways of Europeans: they knew that British pressure, however disagreeable, was accompanied by British payments which were always acceptable; and they were upon the whole well disposed to hurry on an urgent work. But labour was scarce and there were more obstacles. The first day's work had been little satisfactory. Captain Bradshaw and a fellow-passenger, coming on board at night, learned that one big laden boat had been suffered to return untouched. As it was doubtful whether more supplies would be despatched from shore till morning, a midnight visit was planned, and the ship's gunner and the passenger aforesaid started off accordingly. All was still at the landing-place; hard by was the apothecary's house; thither went the two emissaries. On hearing a knock at his door, the inmate appeared—a small, excitable man, evidently wroth at this unexpected intrusion, and in fitter condition for peaceful slumber, than to fulfil any requirements of wakefulness. Folding his arms across his chest he seemed resolved to anticipate mischief, and bar all forcible ingress to his apartment. The gunner raised his lantern and completed a tolerably effective picture. Explanation and inquiry followed, but neither proved successful. "My instructions are not to let any ships go out without an indent," or words to this effect, showed that not much aid or information was procurable in this quarter; so the gunner led the way to the contractor's house, where at least a promise of work before daybreak, commencing with the loaded boat, was obtained. With this result, and the gunner's opinion that the apothecary might have been "horrified," the deputation returned to the ship at 2.30 A.M. On the following day, some of the ship's passengers visited the contractors on shore. Most Persians above the lower orders can be socially agreeable, and Mulla Hussin and Haji Mahmud were no exceptions to the rule. But the question was one of business. Their contracts only bound them to ship 60 tons of coal *per diem*, and the number of men employed was with reference to that quantity. They could hardly be expected to double the labour without additional labourers. These were reported not forthcoming, and the paucity of male adults compared to women and children was too remarkable to escape notice at Basidah. They might have been brought over from Lingah by the hundred, but as Government, and not the contractors, would have had to pay them, it was judged inexpedient to make this extra charge on the public purse. Another matter discussed at Lingah had been more successful in practical result; it was the hiring boats, or "baglas," to carry supplies of coal for the steamers to be employed up the Gulf. The demand had been noised abroad, and many candidates now offered themselves for the service. The Shaikh's terms seemed rather high, but a standard rate of 4 annas or about sixpence a ton, accomplished the hire of three baglas, one at 90, one at 80, and one at 50 tons, on a guarantee of employment for at least fifteen days. On the 16th March, the *Dalhousie*, *Victoria*, and *Semiramis* arrived at Basiduh, all for coaling. The day after, the *Zenobia*, with a bagla in tow, left on her return to the Elphinstone Inlet.

The Persian Gulf has not a good reputation for climate. From May to September inclusive, the heat is that of a furnace, especially to the unfortunate residents on shore. But to those accustomed to an Indian March, that month at Basiduh would present a charming contrast. Of the pleasantest kind is the recollection of its shore reunions, in March 1864, when, the dinner over, a move was made from the social table to the still more social fireplace, and pipes and cigars gave zest to conversation over cheery, flaming logs or glowing charcoal. And on these occasions, the presence of an amiable hostess invested the home colours of the picture with a bright reality. Such episodes of repose in a career of wandering abroad can only be appreciated by those travellers to distant parts who have not the same facility of carrying their homes, as their knapsacks, with them.

158 TELEGRAPH AND TRAVEL. [CHAP.

It has been said that the *Tweed*, with her section of cable, had reached the Elphinstone Inlet, towed by the *Zenobia*. On the 13th March, the sister cable-ship *Assaye* had been brought in by the *Semiramis*; and the *Victoria* had arrived on the same day, towing the flat *Hyderabad*. This last was designed as a temporary floating station for Fão, the proposed terminus of the submarine line, at the head of the Persian Gulf. On the 14th, the *Dalhousie* had brought in the two hulks, *Euphrates* and *Constance*, with their decks roofed in and otherwise fitted up for moving and immediate use at the Masandam station. The three steamers aforesaid had then been despatched to Bazidah, the *Semiramis* taking out the *Assaye* from the anchorage at the inlet, and dropping her in the roadstead off Lingah, there to remain during the operation of coaling. The *Zenobia* then, on return to head-quarters, would find but one steamer, the *Coromandel*, to co-operate in immediate active proceedings.

During the days of unavoidable delay at Masandam, some members of the Expedition had found time for the natural diversion of boating and shooting. The first derived a special charm from the wild and novel beauties presented in the scenery of the inlets, and the many little explorations of which the panorama was suggestive. The clearness of the water, deep to the very point of laving the perpendicular cliff, or working a passage among the isolated boulders and penetrating into shady masses of overhanging rock, brought to view strange interesting objects in its corals, sea-eggs, and various specimens of submarine life and vegetation. Nor were the several landing-places void of attraction; for if at one time the excursionist returned to his floating home with but ordinary trophies in the shape of fine bleached coral, at another he could astonish his shipmates by the exhibition of a rarer prize. The monster skeleton of the "Husaini Machhi," as the Indians called the remains of something "very like a whale," if not a whale itself, discovered near Maklab, was indeed a curiosity worthy the shelter of a museum. It was quite work enough for two men to lift the huge head. The proboscis was pointed and hollow, the bones were simply immense. One lascar remembered having seen a similar creature in Bombay, at the shrouding and burial of which he had assisted. They looked on it as a Daria Pir, or sea saint! Of the sporting excursions the most notable was one to the Tumb Island, about sixty miles west of the anchorage. Fourteen antelope were killed in the day or two given to shooting. Half the number fell to one gun, that of Captain Colvin Stewart, an experienced shot.

Anxiety for the success of his Telegraph cable, and attention to the well-being of the new Telegraph station at Masandam, gave Patrick Stewart little time for recreation, though well known as an enthusiastic explorer and sportsman. But the state of his health, even at this period, was such as to cause his friends no small concern, and to need the constant care and vigilance of his medical attendant.

At this particular stage of the Expedition, the narrative will be best recorded in Colonel Stewart's own words. That officer thus wrote to the Government of Bombay:—

"During the first fortnight of March, strong north-westerly winds had occurred in the lower parts of the Gulf, with sufficient frequency to cause some uneasiness about the weather that might be experienced while laying the remaining portion of the cable. About the 16th, however, there was a return of the calms and light 'land and sea' breezes we had found so propitious while engaged with the first section outside the Gulf, and in order that full advantage might be taken of this more favourable weather, everything was now done to expedite the preparations for recommencing work immediately on the return of the *Zenobia*.

"At the station itself, arrangements of every kind had ere this time been brought into very tolerable order. The whole staff were securely located on the Island or in the hulks; our relations with the Arab inhabitants had improved in all respects. Lieut.-Colonel Disbrowe had consented to remain on the spot till my own return, and as the gunboat *Clyde* lay close to the station, there was no longer cause for uneasiness in withdrawing all the other sea-going ships from the Inlet.

"At noon on the 18th, the *Zenobia* returned from Basidub with a full supply of coal. During the same afternoon, the end of the cable was landed from the *Tweed* and joined up to the testing and speaking apparatus in the temporary office on the Island, and at sunset the work of submerging the second section of the cable from Elphinstone Inlet to Bushahr commenced.

"The general method adopted was precisely the same as before. Captain Carpendale and the officers of the *Zenobia* had become so thoroughly conversant with the system of night and day signalling between the towing steamer and the cable-ship, that the rate of paying out and other details could be regulated with the greatest nicety. The proposed course had been carefully marked out on the charts before starting, and during the whole period of paying out, the surveying officers, Captain Bradshaw, R.N., and Mr. A. P. Young, took so constant a series of observations, cross bearings, and soundings from the *Zenobia*, that the exact course of the cable is now defined with accuracy more than sufficient to ensure its prompt recovery at any point where future repairs may possibly be required.

"The alterations in depth along the course selected are gradual and uniform throughout, the sea-bed everywhere even, and the mingled sand and mud of which it is composed, so soft and yielding that the sounding-leads invariably sink deeply into the bottom. In no part of the whole line from Masandam to Bushahr is the depth greater than 55 fathoms, and the average of the whole may be taken at about 38 fathoms; the depths diminishing as the head of the Gulf is approached. On board the cable-ship, the arrangements and appliances of every kind were so perfect that the cable was passed out with the regularity of clockwork, only sufficient strain being applied to prevent the loss of unnecessary slack.

"On first starting, and throughout the night of the 18th, the cable was paid out at a uniform rate of from 5 to $5\frac{1}{2}$ miles per hour. At 6.30 A.M. on the 19th, the ships were abreast of great Tumb Island, and distant from it about 4 miles to the north; a slight *détour* having been made to avoid a place where the soundings were known to be somewhat irregular. At this period the *Assaye* was sighted in the distance as she lay at anchor off Lingah; and as some portion of the cable she carried was required to complete the connection with Bushahr, the *Coromandel* at once turned northwards to pick up and take her in tow, while a messenger was despatched in a native boat to Basiduh, with orders for the *Semiramis* to follow as soon as her coaling was complete.

"At about 2 P.M. a head wind from the W.N.W. sprang up, and freshened during the afternoon and evening of the 19th sufficiently to retard considerably the progress of the cable-ship, the rate of paying out being at one time reduced to about $2\frac{1}{2}$ miles per hour. With darkness, however, the breeze moderated, the former rate of progress was resumed, and at 11 A.M. on the 20th, when abreast of Shilwar, 177 miles of cable had been paid out, giving an average since starting of about $4\frac{1}{2}$ miles per hour for the whole distance traversed. From this time until the whole of the 352 miles on board the *Tweed* were expended, the weather continued most favourable, and operations progressed with perfect regularity and success, the cable passing out at about $5\frac{1}{2}$ miles per hour throughout. At 8 P.M. on the 21st, the vessels anchored some 35 miles south of Bushahr, off a point on the Persian Coast known as the 'Asses' Ears.' During the following day, the 22nd, the splice between the end of the cable just submerged from the *Tweed*, and that still on board the *Assaye*, was effected, while the artificers and stores were transferred from the former to the latter vessel. After everything was completed the ships lay at anchor till 2 A.M. on the 23rd, the recommencement of operations being thus postponed until an hour that ensured the arrival of the vessels off Bushahr by daylight.

"I should here explain that during the time the ships thus lay at anchor, as well as at intervals during the whole of the previous operations of submerging the cable, we could at any time communicate through it by telegraph with the stations in our rear. Intimation was in this manner received of the arrival at Masandam of the repairing steamer *Amberwitch*, and also of her immediate departure, in obedience to instructions, to join the expedition. It thus happened that we were enabled to calculate on the presence of this vessel on the 22nd, and at once intended on her arrival to make use of her in piloting the *Zenobia* and *Assaye* to their anchorage near Bushahr, the position of which Lieut. Stiffe's previous survey of the coast enabled him to take up with accuracy. As the *Semiramis* had not yet appeared from Basiduh, the *Coromandel* now towed the empty *Tweed* towards Bushahr, all the vessels starting together at about 2 A.M. on the 22nd, and reaching the anchorage within sight of the city at 9 A.M. on the 23rd. The position thus taken up by the vessels of the expedition was much to the south of the usual anchorage, being abreast of, and about 3 miles from, the point previously selected for landing the cable. The latter spot is fully 6 miles south of the city of Bushahr, and close to the northern angle of the old fort of Reshir, and here, close to the beach, Lieut.-Colonel Pelly, to whom I had previously written on the subject, had kindly prepared a small camp.

"During the 23rd, the coast line in the neighbourhood of the landing-place was carefully examined by Sir C. Bright and myself, the exact spot for the cable decided on, and arrangements completed, with Colonel Pelly's assistance, for cutting a trench from the beach along the face of the soft sand-stone rock, and into the interior of one of the tents, which in the meantime was converted into a temporary office, with all requisite testing and signalling apparatus. At the same time, orders were given and acted on with the greatest promptness for undertaking the various additions and alterations required for the provision of a permanent office, and for the accommodation of the staff in the city itself. A double land-line of telegraph, to connect the cable with the proposed permanent office, was commenced, and a masonry building, to serve as 'Junction House,' and testing house at Reshir, was designed, and the permission of the Persian Governor of the Province obtained for its immediate construction.

"In all that related to the permanent location of the office and staff, I was glad to adopt the ideas the resident's experience suggested. And I should add, that having explained to Colonel Pelly, on my first arrival, how important it was that no time should be lost in completing the short remaining section of the line, from Bushahr to Fão, during the continuance of the favourable weather we enjoyed, I was enabled, through the cordial assistance received from him, to complete the whole of the shore arrangements, both for the temporary and permanent offices, during the time necessarily occupied in bringing the extremity of the cable to land. It was mainly owing to this that so satisfactory a result was achieved as the departure of the Expedition, and the recommencement of operations on the third section of the line, within little more than three days of first arrival at Bushahr. To return, however, to the progress of the work: I should explain that the preparations for landing the end of the cable from the larger vessels, from which the deep-sea portion is laid, often demand a great deal of forethought and consideration. On this occasion it was most fortunate that the *Amberwitch*, thoroughly equipped as she was for all such operations, arrived in time to take part in the work. Her lighter draught of water enabled her to approach within a quarter of a mile of the landing-place, while the *Assaye*, as before explained, had to anchor some three miles out. During the 23rd and 24th, the total length of cable required to reach the shore, was transferred from the *Assaye*,

2½ miles being coiled down in the *Amberwitch*, thus using her special machinery for the first time, and proving by the ease and success with which the work was accomplished, that the time and trouble devoted to perfecting her equipment in England had not been expended in vain. Shortly after sunset, the cable was joined up to the instruments in the temporary office on shore; its condition was ascertained to be perfect, and I had the great satisfaction of being enabled to forward at once to Bombay a telegraphic report of the successful completion of another section of the line.

"On the 26th, no time was lost in repeating the operations of the previous day, by landing from the *Assaye* one end of the cable which was still on board that vessel, and part of which was now to be laid from Bushahr onwards to Fáo. Before proceeding, however, to recount the laying of the last section of the line, I should explain, that in approaching the head of the gulf, the shallower soundings I have before spoken of had been reached. On no part of the proposed course, from Bushahr to the mouth of the Shatt-el-Arab, is a deeper sounding than 30 fathoms to be found.[1] While for fifty miles to the southeast of Fáo, the depths (varying from twenty fathoms at that distance, to four fathoms at a few miles from land) are at most places small enough to give rise to risk of injury to the cable from anchors of native craft. It was clearly desirable, therefore, in approaching Fáo, to select a line that would give the cable the security of the greatest available depth of water.

"The careful examination thus required of this part of the sea-bed, was one of the main objects of Lieut. Stiffe's surveying mission to the Gulf, in the beginning of 1863. His instructions then were, 'to examine minutely the Khor Abdullah, and to trace to seaward, so far as they may prove to be clearly defined, each of the channels which seem from existing charts to run in a south-easterly direction, from that creek, and from

[1] The figure is unfortunately a blank in the printed copy of Col. Stewart's report; but I have examined the carefully prepared chart showing the position of the submarine cable between Bushahr and Fáo, and find 28 fathoms the greatest depth recorded by Captain Bradshaw.

the mouth of the Shatt-el-Arab.' He was also directed to ascertain the best practical method of marking off the exact course, with buoys or beacons, previous to laying the cable. Lieut. Stiffe's preliminary survey at once established the existence of a continuous channel leading downwards from the Khor Abdullah, through the shallower soundings already referred to. And now that the cable was ready to be submerged, it only remained to mark off this gut in such a way that the ships might make for the lower extremity and pass along the line of deeper soundings found in its somewhat tortuous channel.

"The *Amberwitch*, which would otherwise have been selected for duty of this kind, being required to land the second shore-end at Bushahr, the *Victoria*, with Lieut. Stiffe on board, was despatched on the 25th with instructions to proceed to the Khor Abdullah (after leaving the flat *Hydrokoni* at anchor within the bar), and then to work back along the channel before referred to, placing flag-buoys at the requisite intervals for clearly defining the course, and coming out to seaward either till meeting the cable ships or till reaching soundings of 17 fathoms. In the latter case, the *Victoria* was to anchor and await the cable ships, holding herself in readiness to weigh on their arrival, and to pilot them in along the course thus marked out, while the *Amberwitch* was to follow, picking up the flag-buoys when these were no longer required.

"All this was done, exactly as proposed. The second connection with the shore having been successfully completed on the 26th, the cable ships left the anchorage south of Bushahr at 3 P.M., and soon after dawn, on the following day, the *Victoria* was sighted lying at anchor some miles to the south-east of Fāo. The instructions above referred to had been most ably carried out by Lieutenants Stiffe and Arnott, the latter of whom was in command of the *Victoria*; and the cable was thus paid out the remainder of the distance, along a buoyed channel most admirably adapted for its reception, and affording a depth of water greater throughout (by from four to eight fathoms) than could otherwise have been obtained. At 9 P.M. on the 27th the vessels anchored in the Khor Abdullah, in five fathoms of water, due south of Fāo, the condition of the cable, as shown by the tests, being most excellent, and the communication with Gwādar and Karāchi perfect.

"It was not till the following day, that the difficulties still to be encountered in landing the shore-end and connecting the cable with the Turkish lines were fully appreciated. Daylight showed, at a distance of ten or twelve miles to the north, a line of shore so low as scarcely to be visible. This line consisted, as we afterwards found, partly of distant date-gardens seen through mirage, and partly of the different 'bands' or 'sads,' but for which, the whole of the low spit, on which the Arab huts and enclosures at Fāo have sprung up, would be liable to occasional inundation. On one side of this spit, is the tidal estuary of the Shatt-el-Arab, on the other, the extensive inlet known as the Khor Abdullah, and in which the ships of the Expedition then lay.

"So far as facility for first establishing the Telegraph was concerned, nothing would have been simpler than to have laid the cable across the bar, and up the Shatt-el-Arab to the terminus of the Turkish land lines at Fāo, which is easily accessible, and can be closely approached on that side by sea-going vessels. The cable, so laid, must, however, have been continually liable to accidental injury from the anchors of vessels navigating the Shatt-el-Arab. And it was in order to avoid this serious risk, that the safer, though much more difficult, approach by the Khor Abdullah was decided on.

"From the anchorage of the larger vessels it was soon ascertained that the *Amberwitch* might move in, some three or four miles towards Fāo, on the Khor Abdullah side; and that for perhaps two miles further, the cable might be laid from vessels or boats of still smaller draught of water, but for the remainder of the distance, it was evidently impossible to provide for the laying of the cable in any of the ordinary modes. In order to examine the ground to be traversed, Sir Charles Bright, Colonel Goldsmid, Captain Bradshaw, and myself started in the *Victoria* on the 28th, and passing round to the bar at the entrance of the river, steamed up the Shatt-el-Arab to Fāo, where we found the river steamer *Comet* at anchor, with Mr. Johnstone, Vice-Consul at Basrah, on board.

"It was here that we first learned the true state of the case regarding progress made on the Turkish land-line from Fāo to Baghdad. This line had been completed from Fāo, along the right or western bank of the river to Kurna, a distance of 100 miles, when the complications with the Montefik Arabs put a stop to all further progress from the south. In a tent close to the edge of the river at Fāo, a temporary office had been established at the terminus of this line; and at the time of our arrival, this office was in communication with Basrah.

"Our first object, of course, was to bring the cable from the Khor Abdullah, across the intervening tracts of water, shoal, and mud, to this temporary office, and the requisite preliminary survey was at once commenced. The result went to prove that the difficulties to be encountered were of no ordinary character. To make this clear, however, I must explain that in calm weather, and with any ordinary tide, some three or four miles of the almost perfectly level mud to the south of Fāo (towards the Khor Abdullah), is uncovered at high water, and a further extent of 1½ or 2 miles at low water, while the bottom slopes so gradually that not even small boats can at any time approach within less than half a mile of the uncovered portion.

"Strong wind from the south-east, however, is always sufficient to bring the sea at high water, over the whole extent, up even to the date gardens at Fāo itself. And the result of this is, to reduce to a soft, greasy mud, in which one sinks deep at every step, the whole of the surface that may previously have been dried and hardened by the sun. Bad as the portions thus become that are only occasionally flooded, they are as nothing compared to the wretched and almost impassable tract lying between ordinary high-water mark, and the point where boats first ground when coming in towards the shore. In parts of this, those who were employed in landing the cable, sank so deeply, when standing upright, that they were compelled, as the only practicable mode of progression, to throw themselves down, and to crawl like turtle over the half liquid mud.

"When this tract was first crossed, by Sir C. Bright and myself, a few days only before the cable was actually brought in, there was comparatively little difficulty in landing, but a strong south-easterly wind, occurring in the interval, had flooded the flats to an unusual extent, and increased all the difficulties most seriously.

"The method ultimately adopted for landing the cable was this:—A sufficient length to extend from the point where the *Amberwitch* was compelled to anchor in approaching the shore, to a point perhaps a quarter of a mile above the mean high-water mark, was coiled away in the paddle-box boats of the *Zenobia*, and paid out in the direction of the shore. On reaching their own draught of water, these boats were still pushed on, as far as possible, over the softer parts of partially flooded mud; and the cable ultimately left in them, was then turned over in a bight, and carried or dragged by manual labour, until extended in a straight line as far in shore as it would reach. The *Amberwitch* with several miles of cable on board (forming part of the same length thus landed from the boats), afterwards steamed out to where the *Assaye* lay, paying out the cable as she went and joining the extremity to that of the Bushahr cable which had previously been buoyed and shipped from the *Assaye*.

"The operation thus described, did not, however, take place until the 5th April, nor until the work of completing the remaining portion of the line through the long stretch of mud flats leading up to Fao, had also been provided for in the following manner:—

"About 4 miles of cable were transferred on the 31st March from the *Assaye* to the river steamer *Comet*, and conveyed in her from the Khor Abdullah to a point near the right bank of the Shatt-el-Arab, about a mile to the south of Fão, where it was cut into lengths, and landed piecemeal, each length weighing about five tons and measuring more than a mile.

"These lengths were then successively carried or dragged, by manual labour, across the flats to that part of the line where each portion was required.

/ INDIA LINKED WITH TURKEY.

"At first examining the ground on the 28th March, I had arranged, with the Vice-Consul's assistance, that all the available Arab population of the neighbourhood, numbering some 500 men, should be got together and employed daily till the completion of the work. As a first operation these men were set to work to dig a trench 2½ feet deep for the cable, which was to extend through the mud flats from Fāo for upwards of 3½ miles to the proposed landing place in the Khor Abdullah. Colonel Goldsmid . . . volunteered to direct this work, and at once took up his quarters in a tent on the mud flats. On the 30th March, Captain Bradshaw joined him and undertook the control of the working parties employed in dragging across the flat the several short sections of cable, as each was landed from the *Comet*.

"In this way the total length required for the shore connections, weighing no less than 16 tons in all, was at last brought into position, the several lengths carefully joined and spliced, and the whole covered in, in the bottom of the wet trench above referred to.

"On the 8th April the connection between the Submarine Cable and the temporary office at Fāo was completed; and the pledge long before entered into by the British Government, to connect the Indian with the Turkish Lines, was at length fulfilled."[1]

The diary of one of the officers named in the above extracts will form an appropriate supplement to the narrative of proceedings at Fāo.

"*March* 28.—Invitation to go on board the *Victoria* this morning, for a trip to Fāo, landing on the river side. Start off with Captain S. accordingly, and after some difficulty occasioned by the unsteady and unceremonious movements of the steamer, we manage to board her. Meet Colonel S., B., and Sir C. B. Reach our new anchorage early in the

[1] Lieut.-Colonel P. Stewart to Secretary to Government, Bombay, dated Bombay, June 11, 1864.

shrouded tent-pole. In the afternoon observed a move from the shipping, and the *Comet* soon approached the shore. In due time she anchored, and lowered her boats. Figures were seen to enter, and they pushed off. Went out to meet the new comers, and had the happiness of recognising among those who appeared, like the old man of the sea, B., and Sir C. B., with Colonel S. A few words in very deep mud were exchanged: our work was explained and approved, and we separated, I securing B. for residence on shore. S. and Sir C. B. returned to their boat and reached the *Comet* again with some difficulty: B.'s servant and kit were obtained, and he and I made for the Flat and dinner. Tired and somewhat done by heat and fasting; but the presence of a cheery companion more beneficial than Philippe's best dishes. Mutton to-day, which is a decided improvement; but biscuit still answers the purpose of a fork. Before leaving the trench, Arabs favoured us with a war-dance, a truly characteristic wind-up to their day's work. We agreed that a regiment of such fellows, especially if organized, drilled and disciplined, would be no mean opponents on a battle-field. Get on famously with them; though they are very different from our Muslim and Hindu subjects in India.

"*March* 31.—On shore early; B. and I walking down to the tent-pole, after a hurried cup of coffee, biscuit, and so forth, in the Flat. Find the men assembled in fair numbers, and at work as before. . . . These Arabs are strange fellows. One man who calls himself my comrade (*rafik*), but whose friendship I am not over disposed to reciprocate, asked me for some arsenic (*süm*). 'Süm-ul-farr?' said I, to identify the actual poison.[1] 'Yes,' said he. I questioned him on what he wanted to do with it. 'It is not for myself,' he replied; 'but for a friend who needs it greatly: he wishes to die.' I endeavoured to impress upon him that such a notion was wrong, and the sooner his friend got over it the better. 'Ah but,' he continued with a smile, not in the least murderous or even malicious, '*I* wish him to die.' Something that I said in answer to this last astonishing remark was misapprehended, but brought out what

[1] *Süm*, poison ; *süm-ul-farr*, poison of rats, or arsenic.

appeared to be the truth. 'He has a beautiful wife: I want her. Oh, she is so charming; and I am so fond of her.' Could it be that I understood aright, and that here was a man wishing me to aid him in getting rid of a fellow-creature, that he might become possessed of his wife? And yet he looked a mere clown, and his face bore no clear sign of vice. I expressed repugnance at the notion, and would have no more to say to him. He tried to renew the conversation, and asked for a little gunpowder. This I refused in a manner to show that its application was mistrusted. He over and over again assured me that it was required merely for shooting birds, but to no avail. I asked this man's name in order to note him. War-dance this evening. Endeavoured to keep the Arabs of the right bank from those of the Persian side of the river, as flags were hoisted by either party, and a row threatened.

"*April* 1.—Visited by J. and A. at our encampment this morning. Our night in the tent was tolerable, but the smell of rank seaweed, or something similar, and a strong wind near my bed kept me wakeful. The wind setting in from the S.E. causes us to strike the tent in the afternoon, and remove to the Fort. Had some idea of selecting ground outside the walls, but the overflow from the river, as also a wish to prove the Fort as a dwelling-place, overrule it. B. continues his survey, and the trench goes on merrily and well. We dine on board the *Comet*, and *Assne*'s boat takes us back at night to the shore. In endeavouring to get a 'back' on to the jetty, both B. and I are plunged into the deep mud alongside. Manage to find our way to the tent in the Fort. This said Fort is an old tumble-down mud building,[1] rising from a swamp, used as a burial-ground, and not for that alone. We select the driest, most wholesome, and most convenient-looking spot for pitching in. Beside us is a huge flagstaff recently erected by our own people. It is not, however, deeply imbedded, and a strong north-wester might send it in our direction.

"*April* 2.—Come down early this morning to the *Comet*'s anchorage, to see about landing a mile and a half of cable

[1] See Illustration, page 95.

from that vessel. Delay took place, annoyance ensued, and to aggravate the position, some two or three hundred Arabs, dodging me about for orders, were only too ready to idle away their pay in war-dances. After some consultation, asked B. to take his steamer to a point a little lower down the river, more appropriate for landing the cable and carrying it across to the trench, and dismissed the Arabs to their usual occupation of digging or clearing.

"*April 3.*—B. and I slept last night on board the *Comet* to be ready this morning for what we had to do. This cable-landing is an intricate affair. A mile may be reckoned to weigh $3\frac{3}{4}$ tons, the mile and a half $5\frac{5}{8}$ths tons = 12,600 lbs. We had to land this much on a bank for which the word 'muddy' is no description. It was a swamp, and at this season constantly under water. The cable was drawn out of the *Comet* over an apparatus called a 'Fairweather,' and coiled by the Arabs on the bank. One coil of three-quarters of a mile completed, a second was commenced, and a bight left between the two. When the whole was landed, it had to be dragged out to the open beach where was the trench; but to get at this open space was not so easy, for it had to be passed up a shallow creek and a kind of lane, between a long mound and a farmhouse, and over a big boat and mud embankments. And now as regards the Arabs. Muhammad, on coming on board, informed me that the Doāsir men, or those living near at hand, refused to work without the promise of double pay, as cable-dragging was very different from ordinary labour; but that the Fāo men had nothing to say on the subject. The rejection of this claim was of little avail; for scarcely had we got the cable uncoiled from the banks when the labourers, as a body, gave up and vowed they could not undertake the job. Vain were shouts, vain were protests: order and discipline could not thus be restored. A consultation with B. resulted in a promise to give double wages, that is, two shillings per man, if the cable were carried to its destination by the evening. This promise had the desired effect, and the men returned to the charge. But day closed, and the cable was far from its proposed bed.

The top, and nearest part of the trench, was perhaps little short of two miles from the *Comet*; and the cable had to be stretched a mile and a half to seaward.

April 4.—Ailing last night and slept on board. On shore after breakfast, and find that E. has worked well in bringing up the narrow bight of the cable up the creek, and getting its extreme left toward the sea. Set to work with W., and by dint of encouragement in various forms manage to get in about a quarter of a mile from the head of the trench before striking work, but not to imbed it altogether; Mr. N., engineer of the *Comet*, and the three Europeans, all lending a hand with efficiency. They thought I allowed the Arabs to knock off work too soon; but my ideas differ from theirs on the subject. These men must be humoured for an emergency, and the present work is emergent. We cannot treat emergencies as every-day occurrences; nor do we as a rule. They were paid their rupee, and told that the double wages should not be given to-morrow, if the whole cable were not imbedded. Directed for to-morrow the labourers to be divided in three parties; one to the right under E., the foreman, who was to superintend laying the cable in the trench as it came up; one in the centre under W.; and one to the left under the foreman's two assistants. Endeavoured to dissuade these honest Europeans from risking health and life by working in light forage caps under a burning sun. Number of labourers entered at 229, one more than yesterday. We must hasten our work, for the south-easters are setting in and bring up the water to a great extent. This sand wind has caused my legs to smart considerably, and I have scarcely a shoe left to stand in. A pair of prettily-worked slippers had sunk so deep in the mud last Saturday, that they were recovered only for presentation to a Mosuli sailor.

April 5.—H.M.S. *Vigilant* arrived in the river to-day; also the *Coromandel*. Dined on board the latter. The day's work had been well, smartly, and quickly done. I think it was about 1 P.M., when we had progressed towards completion, that what had appeared to be two black chests floating in the mirage, proved to be the boats of the *Amberwitch* actually landing the cable from the *Assaye* to join our mile and a half about being imbedded. We had just finished laying the whole of our piece and disposing of a superfluous length, for which there was no room in the trench, when we descried the occupants of the boats trying to land their burden. The sight was curious. They got into the water, perhaps up to the middle; but the footing was so uncertain that they were compelled, after a time, to crawl. Such figures as they eventually appeared baffle description. There were S., Sir C. B., W., and others. Having brought in the cable to a certain point, they left it with the splicers, and with an intimation that two rupees (four shillings) would be given to those men who would bring the two ends together—that is, the sea-end to the shore-end. The distance was not great, but the work was by no means easy. I gave the signal, passed the word for double wages, and down came the Arabs like a volley of grape. Into the water they plunged, and at last seized the looked-for cable. They slipped —they floundered—but kept bravely at work; till a heavy thunderstorm came on, which seemed to shake them in their resolution. The lightning flashed vividly, though in broad day; the rain fell in immense drops; at length the struggling Arabs gave way and abandoned the cable, at, perhaps, three hundred yards short of the mark of junction!

"*April 6.*—Go down with Sir C. B. in the morning to the sea-shore—he to make his way to the *Amberwitch*, I to dispose of the workmen. No Arabs collected at the tents where I had arranged to meet them with the previous day's wages; nor had they gone down to the scene of the unfinished work of the evening. The whole party were found just where they were not required, in the middle of the trench, busily engaged in the easy occupation of throwing earth over the imbedded cable. . . . Never had I a much more difficult piece of diplomacy to execute than now. It was quite a scene. I ordered them down to their work at the sea, promising that, if they brought in the cable at once, *and continued the burying operation for the rest of the day*, they should receive a rupee extra to the pay of the day before. Some would; some would not. I grew angry; feigning perhaps a certain excess of indignation, in urging that they had blackened my face, while on my part I had been doing all to oblige *them!* One or two came up to speak to me. I turned away and walked further off. They sat down in whispering or sullen groups. One party went off a little way and danced a war-dance.' 'So,' said I, 'this is the way you behave, because you have not had your money of yesterday. I will send for the rupees at once. They are in my tent. But this is not what I had hoped to see.' Sent for the money to the tent in the Fort; but still they were sulky. Moving away from the Persian *clique*, who professed to be disobedient on compulsion only, not daring to act without the consent of the Arabs, I addressed myself at length to the latter. The great difficulty seemed to be the continuance of work when once they had got in the cable. The matter was very urgent; the splicers had come down with their tools, men available for the work were drawn together on the spot: I agreed to give the rupees *on completion of this particular duty*. Instantly a marvellous activity was evident in the crowd. They stripped themselves half naked, sprang rather than ran their mile or more to the well-known spot, regardless of mud and waves, quickly found the cable's end, and brought in their charge with a war-dance. I handed it to the splicers, and thus was Turkish Arabia linked to Bombay!"

There was yet more cable to be buried in the inner line of ditch which had been continued towards the Fort; and a small section would thence be required to unite it to the land-line; and although the final touches to the work would not need the same close and active superintendence as at the outset, the two original superintendents would have to pass a night or two more in the small tent within the low walls. The journal may, however, be closed with one brief additional extract:—

"*April* 7.—An Arab whom I made an A.D.C. was talking

strange things a day or two ago. He was most anxious to know about our relations with Turkey as regards telegraph expenditure and profits. One of his questions was quaint: 'They do say that there is no such person as the Sultan of Roum (Turkey); that is, there *was* such a person, but he was carried away by the English. Is it so?' I explained to him the story of the Crimean War, in refutation of so extravagant a fable. He smiled, and said that this was what some people had told him; he was ignorant and wanted information. He said, moreover, that he had understood France was a greater nation than England. Meeting the argument as applying to territorial space, I pointed out to him that England was rich in outlying possessions, and instanced Hindustan as an undeniable argument in favour of her power and greatness."

The number of labourers presenting themselves for employment kept steadily on the increase. On the 5th April there were 242; on the 6th, 287; on the 7th, 306, and on the 8th, 352. The next day may be said to have terminated the special nature of the work. When the superintending officers returned to their tent in the afternoon, they found half-a-dozen of champagne, a huge joint of wild hog, and the following letter in pencil:—

"COROMANDEL, *April 9th.*

"MY DEAR G.,

"I send a very solid piece of wild boar and some champagne for you and B., to drink good luck to the cable with, as you cannot be here. We are going to have a salute and dress ships at noon. Hurrah!!!

"Yours sincerely,

"C. B."

The writer of these pages has much of pleasant remembrance in the days passed on the monotonous seashore and amid the dilapidated outbuildings of Fāo, or Fava, a place barely existing but for the Indo-European Telegraph Station. Swamps, flats, ditches, here and there a dwarf tree or shrub; men and things disturbed and exaggerated by a marvellous mirage: such was indeed the scene at the mouth of the Shatt-el-Arab and Khor Abdullah. The inhabitants, however, are the prominent feature, especially the Arab and Persian-Arab workmen, accustomed, during the busy day, to obey the varied expressions "Imshi,"[1] "Zor bakash,"[2] "Come along, Jack," uttered by stranger lips; and evening after evening to form in cheerful rings, each man to receive his day's wages. Men in physical strength and build, children in mind and morale, with notions which must be strange, and, in certain cases, repugnant to civilization, they would soon make admirable soldiers, if not quite trustworthy men. But in this latter respect much might be said on their behalf, in excuse for the present, and in hope for the future. If the remarkable grouping and precision of the war-dance tell a tale of habitual feud and feudal organization, the fact that this same war-dance affords an outlet to exuberance of temper, and may be resorted to in such sense, when calmer deliberation would result in violence, is evidence of a more satisfactory kind. The enemies of ordinary life in the civilized world would perhaps find a safer vent to their bitterness by dancing off incipient animosities, than in resorting to the more common yet scarcely more dignified way of cherishing them by libel and misrepresentation.

Before concluding the present chapter it will be well to record the discovery and correction of an early flaw in the cable. This became apparent in the short section between Fáo and Bushahr on the second day after the arrival of the vessels in the Khor Abdullah. It was explained by Colonel Stewart as follows:—

[1] Arabic, "Get on."   [2] Persian, "Pull hard."

"The copper conductor adopted in the Persian Gulf cable differs considerably from any previously used. Though apparently a single solid wire, it is in reality composed of four different longitudinal pieces, arranged within and exactly fitting an outer cylindrical tube. These different component parts are fitted together in the manufactory, so as to form a short, thick rod, which is afterwards lengthened out into wire while being rolled or drawn down to the required diameter.

"The manufacture of wire such as this, on a large scale, was entirely novel; more than one important improvement was introduced soon after commencing the work, and tended, by increasing the toughness of the wire, to reduce the probability of fracture in the conductor; but in that part of the cable which was first manufactured (and which was ultimately included in the length laid from Bushahr to Fáo), these improvements were wanting. It now appears that in the earlier processes of manufacturing the cable, and probably before the core left the works of the Gutta-percha Company, the conductor must at one point in this section have been broken across accidentally. But as the broken ends remained in contact, the electrical continuity of the conductor was unaffected, until when the cable was submerged, the reduction of temperature, gradually affecting and contracting the copper wire, sufficed to separate the broken ends, and thus prevent entirely the passage of electrical currents."[1]

Mr. F. C. Webb, the senior of Sir C. Bright's engineering staff, proceeded with Mr. Laws, in charge of the electrical tests, to the spot where the latter had ascertained by observations that the conductor had parted, and effected a repair of the defect with a rapidity and certainty which Colonel Stewart justly considered "a most conclusive proof of the thorough efficiency with which the duties of the officers, responsible for different

[1] Lieut.-Colonel Patrick Stewart to Secretary to Government, Bombay, June 11, 1864.

parts of the work, had been performed." He added, "The position of the fault was calculated and laid down with a nicety which has never been surpassed. The course of the cable was so accurately defined by the surveying officers, and the vessels sent on the repairing trip so skilfully navigated, that the buoy intended to show the presumed position of the fault was actually laid down by the *Zenobia* within less than a quarter of a mile of its true position.

"But for the occurrence of this accidental defect, no practical demonstration of the unceasing care with which every part of the work was performed by the officers I refer to would have been afforded; and it is with the greatest pleasure that I now invite the special attention of Government to the only occurrence during the whole of the operations that might at first sight have suggested doubts as to the permanency or efficiency of the Submarine line."

In the clear and concise narration submitted for Colonel Stewart's information, and which accompanied his first quoted report to Government, Mr. Webb remarks that the rapidity with which the repairs were executed was due to the accuracy of the tests taken by Mr. Laws, the manner in which the position of the cable had been laid down by Captain Bradshaw and Mr. Young, the accuracy of the position taken up by Captain Stiffe (as also other assistance rendered by that officer), and the hard work and zeal of the foremen and men employed under exceptionally trying circumstances. He might further have attributed much of the result to his own skill and management, without departure from the strictest veracity.

It now remains only to be stated that the section of

cable between Gwádar and Karáchi, alternative to the land line connecting these stations, was successfully laid by Mr. Webb and his able assistants out of the *Assaye* and *Cospatrick*, aided by the steamers *Zenobia*, *Amberwitch*, and *Sind*, between the 28th April and 16th May of this same year 1864.

LINGAH, PERSIAN GULF. (*See page* 152.)

CHAPTER IV.

PERSIAN LAND LINES.—COLONEL STEWART'S REPORT OF
THE COUNTRY.—NEGOTIATIONS WITH THE SHAH.—THE
FIRST LINE AND WIRE.—TURCO-PERSIAN CONVENTION.—
OPENING OF TELEGRAPHIC COMMUNICATION.—DEATH OF
COLONEL STEWART.

IT behoves us to revert to a period more than two years antecedent to that marking the completion of the first cable communication between India and Turkey. Mention has been made in a previous chapter that Colonel Patrick Stewart had arrived at Bushahr in progress to the Persian capital, when he reported on the respective merits of a land and sea line of telegraph, to connect our Eastern Empire with the more western States of Asia. After a stay of six days in that ungenial port, he started for his inland journey on the 6th April, accompanied by his assistant, Lieut. John Underwood Champain, R.E., an officer who had rendered his country much hard and honourable service during the Indian Mutiny, and was in every way qualified by nature and habit to be what is aptly called a "right-hand man" to his young chief.

A review of the report to H. B. M. Minister at Tehran, allusion to which was made in the second chapter, will now be useful and appropriate; and time and experience having been afforded for judgment upon the recommendations put forward by one visiting Persia for the first time, but keenly alive to the merits of the case on the best evidence procurable, the test of soundness or otherwise may be readily applied.

The question to be solved on commencement of operations was, how to connect Bushahr by telegraph with Shiraz, the first important town on the road to the capital? There were two routes, one by Kāzarun to the west, of 165 miles, and one by Firuzabad to the east, of 222 miles. Colonel Stewart considered the former "beyond all doubt preferable." It was more frequented, and consequently more safe. The Firuzabad route was represented as better for the transport of artillery and for wheeled conveyances (of which none, however, were seen by the travellers from the coast up to Tehran), and might be so even for heavily-laden camels; but the poor supply of water, timber, and forage, as well as the greater distance, were on the other hand valid objections. Colonel Stewart himself proceeded accordingly by Kāzarun, arriving at Shiraz on the 18th April.

"Immediately on leaving Bushahr," to quote Stewart's own words, in describing this section of his route, "a circuit is made to the S.E. to avoid the arm of the sea lying between the Bushahr promontory and the mainland. Here there is an extensive tract of salt marsh which continues about fifteen miles to the desolate village of Chāhgodak. From this point to Dāliki, nearly sixty miles from Bushahr, the road passes over a tolerably fertile and undulating plain, dotted with several large plantations of date-trees, and with flourishing villages here and there. Near Dāliki, as the mountains are approached, the ground becomes broken by strong water-courses and ravines. The village, which lies at the foot of the bare western face of the first chain of hills, is an inconsiderable place, and remarkable only for the sulphurous streams and the springs of naphtha in its neighbourhood. It is very probable that the abundant produce of these springs might be turned to most valuable account, here and elsewhere, in preparing timber and protecting it both from natural decay and the ravages of insects. Naphtha is nowhere else so plentiful as here, but it is found in many parts of the route about to be described, and is everywhere collected and used by the Persians, solely as an external remedy for sores or wounds on cattle and horses. From its position we were not surprised to hear that the heat at Dāliki in the summer is almost unbearable.[1]

"Shortly after leaving this place the road turns to the right through a narrow gorge in the hills, which are here composed principally of sandstone and clay slate, and almost devoid of vegetation. After some mile or two of very steep and rocky ground, the Dāliki, a rapid, brackish river, has to be crossed by a ford,[2] soon after which commences the first pass, the Kothal Malu. The

---

[1] I had rather a painful experience of this heat when suffering from a sudden sickness with which I was attacked after the first day's march from Bushahr. The heat at Barazjūn, and some sixteen miles further beyond the village of Dāliki, was indeed something to be remembered. With reference to the latter traveller, I take an extract from my diary of June 1, 1874:—
"The sound of rushing waters among the rocks and ravines was pleasant; but oh, que diable de la chaleur! Under the half shadows of that bridge we experienced the hot winds in very earnest, and I shall not soon forget the experience. It was much that of Sukkarpur and Sukur, and of the hot parts of India, but without the relief of punka-wallahs or the full benefit of mess-servants and mess-stores. Our camp was pitched for a great part of the time in the water itself. My head was continually bound in freshly-wetted or soaked handkerchiefs; and S. and L., younger men, and perhaps in better health, actually lay down in the stream with their clothes on, letting them dry afterwards in the heated atmosphere. . . . This is certainly not the country to travel through in hot weather. The thermometer was at 112° in our encamping place."

[2] The new bridge called "Pul-i Mushir" was under completion in 1874. It is about a quarter of a mile higher up the stream than the old one, of which an arch yet remains; and there are said to be the ruins of a third bridge three-quarters of a mile above the new one. Mr. Scott Waring, who was here in 1802, says nothing of these ruins or of a bridge at all, but notices a stone building which he was informed had been the residence of a European whose occupation was to forward packets from Shiraz to the sea-coast. ("Tour to Shiraz, &c.," London, 1807.)

narrow pathway, more like the bed of a torrent than a road, leads up the face of a mountain to a height about 1,200 feet among huge stones and rocks which render the ascent far from easy, but present no formidable obstacle to the establishment of a telegraphic line. On reaching the top of the pass the fertile and well-cultivated plain of Khisht opens out. It boasts of several villages and plantations of date-trees. For about six miles the road lies across this plain, then for a mile or two over broken ground to the left bank of the Khisht river, which it follows closely for a short distance, and then turns abruptly to the right, to the foot of the second pass, or Kothal Kamārij. The path ascends this by a series of short, abrupt zigzags, and on the face of the otherwise inaccessible mountain with a deep and dangerous ravine on the right. These hills are almost all of limestone, and their formation is most extraordinary. In many cases the strata are nearly vertical, and the outlines excessively grand and sublime. This pass, though not so long as the first, is perhaps more dangerous, notwithstanding the slight attempts which have been made to smooth the track, and the small parapets which have been built here and there on the brink of the precipices. From the summit of this pass a slight descent leads into the plain of Kamārij, which is about six miles in length by three in breadth, and extends nearly north-west and south-east. It is beautifully green and level, and well supplied with water, and is surrounded by mountains. Date-groves are now no longer seen, and timber is very scarce. At the northern extremity of this basin the road passes through a rocky defile in the hills . . . and again descends into an angle of the extensive plain or valley of Kāzarun, near its north-western extremity, and not far from the bed of the Shābur river, a principal tributary of the Khisht. Shābur is also the name of the first village reached after entering this plain. It lies close to the extremity of an almost impassable range of mountains, to turn which has been the main object of the general *détour* to the north. From this point (which is consequently the most northern of the whole route to Shiraz), the road turns to the south-east and leads over a fine level tract of well-watered corn-fields to the considerable town of Kázarún, distant 108 miles from Bushahr. The range of mountains above spoken of, which bounds this valley on the south-west, is on this side pretty thickly covered with low wood; but it is not of a kind that could readily be utilized for a telegraphic line. Near the town a few date and poplar-trees are found within the garden enclosures, but the valley itself is otherwise quite destitute of timber. From Kázarún, the road continues for about seven miles along the plain; it then crosses by a causeway over the marshy estuary of a stream flowing into a brackish lake, turns to the left,[1] and approaches the foot of the third pass, or 'Kothal Dukhtar.' This pass, though not extensive, is very steep, and zigzags abruptly up the face of a mountain, about 800 feet high. Some trouble has been taken, however, to prevent accidents to travellers by smoothing the road itself to a certain extent and by building parapet walls. Soon after reaching the top, the road descends into the beautiful valley of Abdui, which is covered with Persian oaks of moderate size."

Another pass of considerable height now presents itself; it is called that of the "Pír Zan," or Old Woman, in contradistinction probably to the one immediately preceding, for "Dukhtar" means maiden or virgin. Stewart describes it as "the longest and easiest of all;" but the ascent to the midway caravans rai, reckoned at 5,730 feet above the sea, is steep and stony, nor is the second half to be readily surmounted with indifferent cattle. The summit is estimated at 7,150 feet. A mule, or the native "yabu," is better perhaps than the best horse for the work required. The report says:—

"The hills here are covered with low trees and bushes, and the climate for the greater part of the year must be excessively cold. After crowning a ridge, the highest point of the whole

[1] This point is marked by a carving in the rock, of modern date, called the "Nakhshah-i-Taimur."

NAHHAL, THE ZAX, BETWEEN CHERA AND THE SEA.

route, one descends into the swampy plain of Dastarjin.[1] For six miles the road traverses this plain, keeping near its northern side to avoid an extensive lake which occupies the lower end of the valley. After leaving the plain there is another slight ascent and a series of windings amongst low hills to the bed of a stream flowing towards Shiraz. This stream must occasionally be formidable, but was easily forded at the time we saw it. The country is quite open from this to the caravanserai at Khan-i-Zanian, situated on a tributary to the above-mentioned stream, and about thirty miles from Shiraz. The road onwards has a slight gradual descent through the undulating and open country, and finally leads into a small valley which opens out into the plain of Shiraz, about eight miles from that city."

Descending from the high mountainous country to the plain of Dastarjin, the stranger will be struck with the numbers of dwarf oak-trees observable on either side. These, though somewhat sparse to be considered forest, are yet sufficiently compact to give shelter to wild beasts, and the lion is no unfrequent attendant upon the passing traveller. In the spring of 1867 one of the officers of Royal Engineers[2] connected with the Persian telegraph narrowly escaped serious injury from the onslaught of this formidable foe. He was riding in the neighbourhood in question slightly off the beaten track, with no protective weapons but a pocket-pistol, and unprepared for aggressive man or beast, when he observed something like a lion in front of him. The intruder showed inclination to come to close quarters, and, as each drew nearer to each, kept his attention upon the horse, hovering about the startled animal, and finally assaulting him from behind. The horse reared: its rider leapt to the ground, and took occasion to fire his two weak barrels in

---

[1] I am told on good authority that this is Dasht-i-arjin, the "plain of the wild almond."   [2] Major Oliver St. John, R.E.

the direction of his antagonist, rather to scare than wound him. But the lion preferred a quadruped to a man in conflict; and renewed his attack upon the horse by a second spring, using his claws with effect to maintain his position. Away went horse and lion too, and back went the officer to a village in the Dastarjin plain, in which direction the assailant and assailed had disappeared from sight. Night ensued; the villagers could not be persuaded to light their torches and go in quest of the lion; but his coveted prey was descried the next morning at large in the plain, and recovered, though sorely disabled. In 1874 I was riding along this particular road, and the scene of this adventure was pointed out to me; also a tree from which a Persian Ghulam had shot a lion. Many of the tombstones at the village of Dastarjin bear rude and eccentric sculptures of the king of beasts.

Colonel Stewart, considering the feasibility of erecting a line of telegraph on the route traversed up to Shiraz, arrived at the conclusion that the passes presented no formidable barrier to the undertaking. Care and judgment would be requisite in selecting the position of posts and supports, which should be accessible from the road amid winter snows as at ordinary seasons. But the line once constructed with due forethought and precaution, he was of opinion there were "few natural agencies to be dreaded as likely to interfere with its permanence." Regarding materials for construction, he found the conditions for masonry so favourable as to make him recommend the occasional use of built supports; but date-poles were readily procurable at a low price between Bushahr and Kāzarun, and poplars could be brought from Shiraz to supply the deficiency of naturally grown timber elsewhere. The working season he regulated according to locality and nature of occupation; for the climate showed marked variations in this particular section, and actual construction needed allowances not applicable to mere conveyance and distribution of stores. He discussed the cost, capabilities, and available supply of mules, which, as the most approved beast of burden in those parts, appeared to represent the fittest means of transport for telegraph purposes. His calculation was that each mule would carry from 370 to 400 lbs., and make the journey from the coast to Shiraz in 12 days, but that the rate of payment would fluctuate between 9 and 22 rupees for 700 lbs, or nine shillings, and twenty-two shillings per mule. "Two months' notice," he said, "would suffice for the collection of from 5,000 to 8,000 mules, a number more than ample for all probable requirements. Camels and asses might be used, but are not so well suited as mules for so rocky and mountainous a road as this."

At Shiraz the travellers were busily engaged in making inquiries about the routes between that city and the sea: and the direct route to Bandar Abbas was one which more particularly demanded their attention.[1] It is in fact

---

[1] The supposed best route for the telegraph is recorded by Colonel Stewart as follows:—

Maharlu	9 Farsakhs	
Sarvistan	8 "	
Tangi Karun	9 "	
Shash Deh	9 "	
Mahadwan	6 "	Altogether 87 Farsakhs; or, at 3½ miles the Farsakh, 305 miles; or at 3¾ = 325 miles.
Deh Khair	6 "	
Rustak	6 "	
Furg	3 "	
Tajhat	6 "	
Sondatabad	6 "	
Kohtak	4 "	
Kezwan	6 "	
Bandar Abbas	9 "	

a question well worthy of close consideration whether any additional wire now supplied to existing communication, or even any future third wire between Shiraz and Bushahr, would not be best provided for by a wholly new line from Shiraz to Bandar Abbas? Bushahr, having long been the usual port of traffic with the interior of Persia for British Indian vessels, has reaped the honours and advantages of a recognized line of communication, but this state of things could never have originated in geographical position or natural superiority; it is one of those chance contingencies that take root in the East, irrespective of British interests and British advisers. As regards India, Bandar Abbas is, by sea, 425 miles nearer to Bombay than Bushahr, and the land distance from the former port to Shiraz is only 130 miles more than from the latter; and while it is 1,330 miles from Bombay to Shiraz *viâ* Bandar Abbas, it is 1,625 *viâ* Bushahr.[1] Colonel Stewart expressed himself well pleased with the attention of the British Agent, the Nawab Agha Muhammad Hasan Khan, who rendered him valuable assistance in the collection of essential data.

We continue to quote the route report for the second section, or from Shiraz to Ispahan :

'The road quits the plain by a narrow defile, and, after ascending considerably, turns the western flank of a rocky range looking down on the city. From this point it crosses a series of two ridges and flat-bottomed valleys for some six or eight miles. These are all completely bare of timber and quite uncultivated. The road then emerges into the valley of Zargun, an offshoot from

---

[1] These distances are as estimated by the British India Steam Navigation Company. The argument is not affected by the circuit made in touching at different ports, for the course from Bandar Abbas to Bushahr is tolerably direct, and it is this distance alone which is material.

the great marshy plains watered by the Bandamir, at the opposite or northern side of which stand the ruins of Persepolis.[1]

[1] In reference to these remarkable monuments, which I think deserve to be classed as *the* lions, *par excellence*, of Persia, and among the choicest relics of the whole classical world, the following extracts of a diary kept in 1871 may have some interest, however slender the information afforded :—

"*June* 17.—At the base of the line of rocky hills N.E. of Kinárah (fourteen miles from Zargun), and approached across a plain well covered with low but ripe crops of wheat, is a plateau or platform ascended by wide stone steps to a height of some thirty feet, the solid stone wall of which may be a quarter of a mile in frontage. Riding up the steps to our left—for the mules move with wonderful precision where a horse would waver and possibly fall—we come first upon the remains of a large gateway, exhibiting on either side the colossal figure of a bull. Passing through these we come upon two pillars, one on the right and one on the left, and find a corresponding gateway to the first, with large winged bulls, and a front to the hills. We return and take a course midway between the gateways and to the right of our original advance, and find ourselves among many pillars in better or worse preservation, fluted, and of marble semblance, the remains, as it were, of a vast temple or palace, and raised on a base ornamented with bas-reliefs of skilful execution. Continuing our course in the same direction, we reach a more compact building, with doors and recesses; and within the doorways and upon the walls are gigantic figures with beard and back hair, some plunging swords into lions or tigers, some marching in state with one or more attendants. Cuneiform writings abound, as also the more modern inscriptions of visiting travellers, among whom the irrepressible Briton takes the prominent place. Right and left are remains of other edifices. Retracing our steps for some little distance from the further end, or proper left of the plateau, we turn towards the hill, and pass through what must have been a temple or court of vast dimensions, judging from the space between the now-standing columns; and next make a new ascent of the rock itself. Here we find a high scarp buried between two huge projecting scarps, and ornamented by fine gigantic bas-reliefs, the upper one representing, it would seem, a priest, bow in one hand, reaching towards an altar whence issue flames of fire. Above his head, and between him and the fire, is a device like a cross, placed horizontally.

"*June* 18.—Some three or four miles west of Persepolis, or the 'Takht-i-Jamshid,' as called by all Persians, are situated the rock caves bearing the designation of 'Nakhshab-i Rustam.' Between the two runs the post-road, and a little way on, to the left of the traveller pursuing that road upward towards Ispahan, is a high rock with remarkable scarp. He should halt here before entering the pass, and go a little out of his way west, to see the caves, as he may probably have deviated east to see the temple remains. We visited Nakhshah-i Rustam from the village of Shamsabad, whither we moved yesterday evening in pursuance of a kind invitation from the 'Malik-i-Tajjar,' or Head of the Merchants, an intelligent Shirazi, who placed a house

"From this place there are two roads for caravans towards Ispahan, separating, not far from the ancient ruins, at a point some thirty miles from Shiraz, and meeting again at Yezdikhast, some eighty-four miles short of Ispahan. The more direct of these is the one invariably used by travellers and caravans, except for three months of winter, during which it is generally impassable by snow. The distance from Shiraz to Ispahan by this route is 269 miles.¹ The other road, which lies more to the eastward, and passes through the town of Murghab, is throughout on a lower level, and can be kept open when the other road is impracticable. It is consequently exclusively used during the winter months, though the distance by it is somewhat greater. The first is known as the 'Sarhad,' or cold route; the second as the 'Garmsir,' or warm route."

The travellers proceeded by the former, but Colonel Stewart eventually decided that the telegraph line should

at our disposal. It is much the same distance from Shamsabad to the Nakhshah-i-Rustam as from Kinarah to Takht-i-Jamshid; and Shamsabad is perhaps three miles nearer our stage of to-morrow than Kinarah. We skirted the flat village of Zangiabad, and approached, through cultivation, the rock to be visited. First we came upon quaint bas-reliefs of large size— two monarchs about to engage in play or fight. The Greek inscription was not very clear, and well above our heads. I ascended to it: a stiff climb. I followed, but soon came down again. The narrowness of the ledge was an incentive to dizziness. There are other rock tombs here; and a little further up to the proper right, a broken column above and others below—that is, they seem to be so from their square shape and fittings. But moving to the rear side, we perceive three caves high up in the rock, surmounted by the bas-relief of the colossal priest, the fire, the sun, and the cross seen yesterday. I climb, with the aid of men and ropes, the third of these; so do also S., L., and E. In the first place, we clear some fifteen feet of rugged rock, and land on a smooth platform cut from the stone; secondly, a stiff scarp of some twenty feet to the ledge leading to the actual cave. We enter the presumed burial-place of kings. The visit repays the journey and the special effort; but there is little to describe in the dark interior and sombre sarcophagi. How appropriate the Psalms of to-day, xc. 4 :—'A thousand years in Thy sight are but as yesterday; seeing that is past as a watch in the night.'"

¹ I made it 266, but inclusive of a short *détour* to visit Persepolis; so that our estimates appear much the same.—F. J. G.

follow the latter road; and no doubt he was fully justified in his decision. It is the road of the Government "Chapar," or post, and free from the dangers of interruption to which the higher one is liable in the winter season:

"Turning then to the westward from Persepolis, we passed along the left bank of the Bandamir for about twenty-five miles. Our route then entered a valley in the hills which had hitherto bounded the plain on the right, and, following the valley almost to its source, past the villages Maiyin and Imamzādah Ismail, led us to a very steep and strong pass, from the summit of which we again descended (but in a less degree) to the dreary plains of Ujain. The nature of this pass and of the cliffs that overhang it is certainly such that heavy snow might at any time make it impassable, unless artificially kept open; and it is quite possible that in such a pass all precautions might be rendered futile by a single avalanche at the very time of year when repairs must be most tedious and difficult of execution. On the plain of Ujain, and in all the level tracts of high land on the Sarhad route, snow of three or four feet in depth often lies for two months or more, but it is perhaps only in the pass just spoken of that any very serious difficulties would be experienced. The valley of Ujain itself is probably fifty miles in length by six to ten in width, and, like all the larger valleys in this part of the country, has a general north-westerly direction. Traversing this plain obliquely, the road crosses a low pass in the next range, by an easy ascent from the village of Asapas. It then skirts the north-eastern base of part of the same range, as far as the ruined caravanserai of Khushki Zard, passing along the edge of another extensive plain. This has a somewhat higher level than the plain of Ujain, but is equally destitute of timber, and more so of cultivation. Abundant pasture is, however, found; and the valley, when we passed (May 4th), was tenanted by a large number of Iliats, who had probably not less than sixty small camps in the neighbourhood. From Khushki Zard to a point five miles beyond the village of Deh Girdu there is some slight increase of elevation. The road then passes for about ten miles through an undulating and very barren country, to a nick leading through a chain of hills on the right, but from this point there is a decided and continuous fall to the plain on which stands the town of Yezdikhast. In the whole distance from Asapas to Yezdikhast not one single tree was observed far or near. The wretched village of Deh Girdu and a small mud fort near Khushki Zard (said to be occupied) were the only human habitations visible, except the black tents of the Iliats, and these were entirely confined to the particular tract above referred to, which had been selected by a tribe as their summer quarters, and at which they had recently arrived. At Yezdikhast, as before mentioned, the Sarhad and Garmsir roads reunite."

The Sarhad route has no doubt great advantages for travellers in the warm weather. Even in June the climate on the higher levels is delightful; and a few "ghulams" from Shiraz, and letters to the chief authorities of the wandering tribes whose tents may be pitched on or near the line of route, should ensure, combined with ordinary precautions, safe travelling and hospitable treatment. And there are charming spots to be visited without straying from the direct way. Maiyin, with its long row of trees and gardens, is at the commencement of the narrow road foreshowing the ascent of the high tablelands; except at the south, it is almost shut in by mountains. Twelve miles beyond, over a stony road rising in its second half, is Imamzādah Ismail, conspicuous from the shrine which gives its name to the few houses there: a tall building, shaped much as the typical pear, or design of the poplar in Persian paintings and embroideries. From this point the pass commences in earnest; and the direct ascent is a tolerably steep one of about six miles in length. The comparatively short descent is perhaps even more difficult, so that, altogether, the Imamzādah Kothal supplies a stiff bit of marching; although a Persian official of rank, the Saham-ul-Mulk, or Sword of the State, has been expending money upon improving it. The new plains next reached are part of the high table-land of the Sarhad districts; and the fine pure air and green meadows have an invigorating effect on the spirits, after a depressing experience of a Persian summer on the low lands. Here, with a thermometer rising little above 80°, and on an elevation of 7,500 feet,[1] a tent is enjoyable enough in June; and if to such accommodation the hospitality of the Ilkhāni, the prince of the wandering tribes, or of his Ilbegi, or vice-gerent, be added, the stranger, whoever he be, will have no reason to complain. Hence to Asapas the road is, with few exceptions, good, over the Ujain plains; and there are many villages, or clusters of huts, whence in some cases rises the large mud square fort, the most conspicuous of surrounding objects. As regards a day's encampment it is better to suffer the slight inconveniences of insufficient shade and persecuting flies under the Asapas willows near the strong and running stream, than to have recourse to an uncertain interior.[2] The road now leads

[1] The air was so cold on the night of the 23rd of June, when the tent had been abandoned at Riza Abad, that I actually turned in, clothes and all, under two coverlets, a red blanket and Scotch plaid!

[2] The officers of the Sistan Mission were at Asapas in June 1871, on their return to Tehran from Makran, and had made their bivouac below the trees, and beside the stream here mentioned. Facing them was a line of rocky hills, skirted by a well-defined road, into which they were to proceed at the commencement of the morrow's march. Their attention was drawn, towards evening, to a few armed men moving along this road, followed by numerous goats, sheep, cattle, and a large concourse of people, armed or unarmed, mostly mounted on donkeys or horses. The spectacle was explained to be Kashkāis, or members of the most important of Iliat tribes, returning from a retaliating raid upon other tribesmen, necessitated by a previous raid com-

to a high but gradual ascent, and another pass surmounted, new plains are crossed to the ruined caravanserai of Khushki Zard. More hills and plains succeed on the way to Deh Girdu, but the villages and cultivation begin to fail; and the next thirty-two miles' march to Yezdikhast is a dreary one indeed. The latter place has a singular appearance from its high, many-storied houses, looking still higher from the perpendicular cliff out of which they rise. It is not unlike a section, or three upper stories of houses in the old town of Edinburgh, only the windows are scarcely so regular and substantial. Below the cliff, and in the bed, as it were, of a ravine, are a post-house and a caravanserai.

From Ujain to Sao, a postal station north of Ispahan, Colonel Stewart prepared a road survey. He had found the information on the country traversed so inaccurately recorded, that the measure was deemed likely to be one of future utility. To resume his report:—

"From Yezdikhast onwards the country requires no minute description. As far as Kumishah (fifty miles from Ispahan), the road passes through a broad stony valley bounded by desolate, rocky, limestone hills. At first utterly barren, the country improves towards Kumishah, where, as well as at several villages near it, there are a considerable number of gardens and enclosures from which there would be no difficulty in procuring a certain

mitted upon them and attended with loss of life. It was said that some two or more had been killed or wounded on this occasion; and as for the cattle, flocks, and herds taken, there may well have been between one and two thousand! The tribe authorities still shut their eyes to these scenes, and probably find the mode of settlement adopted upon the whole the most convenient; and, in truth, there may be more rude honour at work in the conclusion of the many than there would be principle of any kind in the judgment of a single chief. On the day following, the large cavalcade was again sighted by the officers, drawn up and disposed like a regular military force. At night a member of the Mission was robbed, but there was no reason to suppose the thief to have come from the Kashkai marauders.

amount of timber. At Māya too, seventeen miles further on, are a few similar enclosures, but thence to Ispahan the country is quite desolate, the only feature worth notice being a defile through which the road passes eleven miles from Māya, and from which it descends by a short and unnecessarily steep pass to the level country beyond."

Ispahan is described in another part of this volume. Colonel Stewart says little or nothing of the place itself, but keeping the telegraph in view, he rejoices to find that poplar-trees, "admirably adapted for telegraph posts," might be procured at the very low rate of three to four krans each, or from 2s. 6d. to 3s. 4d. We go on to the third, or last section of his report, the route from Ispahan to the capital:—

"On the 15th of May we left Ispahan for Tehran. On getting clear of the cultivated land which extends for several miles to the north of the former, an open and level but very barren country is traversed for some fifty miles, only one small patch of cultivation occurring to break the monotony of the arid, stony plain. The road then gradually ascends in approaching the outskirts of a considerable mountain range which here crosses its general direction obliquely: the range lying nearly N.W. and S.E.

"At the valley of Sāo, fifty-seven miles from Ispahan, a small stream issues from these hills, irrigating a narrow strip of land in its course, and here a few gardens and enclosures, with the usual proportion of poplar-trees, are met with. The road ascends the valley of this stream for two or three miles, and then after gradually rising for nine or ten more through low hills and between spurs of the main range, it crosses the watershed at the course of the valley of Kohrud, and about seven miles above the beautiful village of that name. This pass is the highest point reached between Shiraz and Tehran. When we crossed in the middle of May, the snow, though not actually on the path, was lying unmelted on slopes to the left of it, at a level considerably below that attained by the road itself. A steep but not difficult descent leads to the village of Kohrud, embosomed in trees and orchards, and shut in by mountains of granite and limestone.[1] This place is sufficiently elevated to have a very cold climate all through summer; and for the same reason some difficulty must be anticipated, especially in the narrower parts of the valley, from snow-drifts in winter. We were informed that travellers are occasionally thus delayed for several days; but as the route from the capital to Ispahan is never permitted to remain closed, we may fairly conclude that the difficulties cannot be so serious as to cause any doubt about the possibility of patrolling a line of telegraphs in this, the only part of the whole route where such difficulties can be anticipated.

"After leaving the village of Kohrud the road continues to descend the ravine, the sides of which in some parts become very bold and precipitous. This descent is prolonged for about twelve miles, for the greater part of which distance some care and skill would be necessary in laying out the exact course of a line of telegraph. Leaving the valley the road emerges from the hills in view of a great desert tract which extends from the neighbourhood of this range to Khurasan, and turns again to the left down a long but gentle slope towards the town of Kashan, which is visible to the north at a distance of eleven miles.

"About Kashan, villages and gardens are plentiful. From this place to Sin-sin the ground is level and bare. At Sin-sin another chain of bare and rugged sand hills (an offshoot of the main Kohrud range along the north-east base of which the road has hitherto wound) is crossed; after which the road is again almost level as far as the town of Kūm.

"Both Kūm and Kashan are important places; certainly much more so than any others, except Shiraz and Ispahan, on

---

[1] Kohrud is one of many mountain-villages which in Persia and Asia Minor make the traveller forget the heat of the plains and the rough ascents and descents of the low country. They seem to possess a family resemblance in the briskness of their running streams, the freshness of their vegetation, the happy selection of their sites, and the modesty of their small, uncemented stone houses. As for Kohrud, its bright green trees, bursting upon the view after miles of dust and drab, are very grateful and refreshing.

the entire route from Bushahr. At the former is a shrine of great sanctity, much resorted to by pilgrims, who visit it in large bodies. It is therefore possible that, in the event of the telegraphic line being constructed along this route, and separate wires being allotted to local and through traffic, intermediate offices in connection with the former might be established with advantage at each of the places referred to.[1]

"From Kūm to Kināraħ Gird, twenty-five miles short of Tehran, the track lies alternately over dreary strips of the salt desert and sandy ravines. The heat for part of the year is intense, and drinking-water not procurable, except where (as at Hauz-i-Sultan) it is stored in tanks for use. A more miserable and deserted tract of country can hardly be conceived than the seventy miles here alluded to.[2]

"At Kināraħ Gird there are a few villages and fields: after which another low ridge of naked hills is passed, and Tehran itself appears in sight at a distance of about fifteen miles."

Colonel Stewart concluded his report by discussing the various details suggested by the object of his journey.

---

[1] Kūm is a place of great note in Persia, from possessing the shrine of the much-regarded Fatima; and to be buried there is a privilege still in high estimation, as may be certified by the numerous coffins borne into its precincts from without. It is a long, straggling, semi-ruined town, liberally endowed with sepulchral monuments surmounted by quasi-minarets certainly deficient in architectural beauty. There was nothing to which I could liken these, as seen in the distance, better than Jean Marie Farina's conventional basket Eau-de-Cologne bottles. This city is quaintly described by Sir Thomas Herbert, who says that "it was in ages past cald Guriana, and afore that Arbacta, perhaps built by Arbaces." ("Description of the Persian Monarchy:" London, 1634.)

[2] Melancholy, indeed: and the Persians have given to its worst part the name of the "Plain of the Angel of Death." When I was last at Hauz-i-Sultan, or just after the famine of 1871 had culminated, the people at the post-house begged me to represent their sorry plight to the authorities at Tehran. There was want of water, want of provisions, barrenness in every sense. Even the large and handsome caravanserai looked untenanted and falling to decay. I was informed that a "Bakāl," or petty dealer, and one other man, probably the custodian of the building, were the sole occupants, and that water was brought from a distance often miles to the westward.

Physically considered, the nature of the country seemed to offer extraordinary facilities for telegraphic communication. Timber was more or less artificially produced, but was nevertheless procurable in sufficient quantity. There was no obstacle to be apprehended in rivers. There might be danger to the line in some places from falling rocks, especially owing to the prevalence of earthquakes; but discretion would be used in selecting positions for supports, and the probability of accidents would thus be reduced to a minimum. As regards climate, "a point of no small importance where Europeans are concerned," he wrote—

"The whole of the route may be said to have immense advantages as compared with any part of India. From the Kothal Dukhtar to Tehran ... probably no part of the whole route is at a lower level than 3,200 feet; and though the elevation is not sufficient to prevent the heat of July and August from becoming excessive in the more barren and desert positions, the heat even there is of short duration; and everywhere tracts of sufficient elevation to give a delightful cool climate are of comparatively easy access. In travelling from Bushahr to Tehran between the 6th April and 20th May, we never experienced any inconvenience worth speaking of, from heat, although we never travelled by night, and were frequently exposed to the sun the whole day long. At the numerous places where no other cleanly accommodation was procurable we used a small, single-roofed tent of the lightest and thinnest description, and very rarely felt the want of any better protection from the sun."

Had our travellers been two months later, they would, perhaps, have felt some inconvenience from the hot winds and hot atmosphere of the low marshy country near Bushahr, as well as the more inland plains, until the actual rise to the high table-lands. But there is, no doubt, very much to be said on behalf of the Persian climate of the highlands, and many European residents or travellers will readily endorse the favourable opinion here generally expressed.

The questions of construction, and employment of natives under European superintendence were next adverted to. A separate sketch-estimate of cost was forwarded; and as the line might perhaps be treated in the first instance as purely experimental, this would be, with proper management, extremely small. Judging, however, from the practical results of an existing line between Tabriz and the capital, and other data, Stewart thought that a much larger expenditure might be afterwards found warrantable. The estimate, as first prepared, made the cost per mile £42 10s. or within £50,000 for a complete telegraph line from the Turkish frontier to Tehran, thence to Shiraz, and thence passing to the sea both at Bushahr and Bandar Abbas, roughly 1,407 miles. This estimate contemplated two wires, each of No. 5, B. W. G. best galvanized; the strongest pattern of Siemens' patent cast-iron and porcelain insulators; and the common poplar poles of the country. Colonel Stewart need not now be followed into his figures, whether for receipts of line or disbursements on account of maintenance and working. Circumstances have so completely changed within the last few years, both in respect of extraneous competition and our own relations with the Persian authorities, that all interest in such calculations must be obsolete. Suffice it to say that he based his conjectures on the existence of two properly-insulated wires along the whole line, one being exclusively used for "through," the other ordinarily for "local" traffic, supplemented at Bushahr by the submarine cable to Karáchi.

In reviewing the probabilities of wanton injury to the line from predatory tribes, stray robbers, or ill-disposed and mischievous persons, he expressed belief that the accounts of general lawlessness and contempt of authority, so commonly circulated in reference to Persia, would be found in practice greatly exaggerated. There is something very sensible and practical in the following remarks:—

"The fact of the wire being galvanized not only detracts very much from its value for all purposes involving the welding or working up of the metal, but also provides a certain means of identifying it at a glance if found in the possession of anyone. Considering the mode of life of the hill tribes, I can think of no way in which the wire could be readily utilized by them, excepting, perhaps, as matchlock ramrods; and some such simple measure as obtaining from the Persian Government an order making the possession of such galvanized wire penal, would probably be amply sufficient to deter those to whom it would occur so to use it from making the experiment. A similar mode of dealing with the insulators, &c., might be advantageous, but I doubt whether such articles present the smallest temptation, or could possibly be used in any other than the legitimate way. It is true that wooden posts might occasionally be coveted as fuel, but it is a fact worth recording that in the mountainous tracts, where the inhabitants have the credit of being least scrupulous in matters of *meum* and *tuum*, natural fuel is found in the form of scrub jungle in quantities sufficient to reduce considerably the comparative value of a wooden post."[1]

---

[1] Upon the whole, the experience of after years amply proves that, with the goodwill of the local governors, telegraph posts and wires may be kept in Persia as secure from wilful injury as in civilized Europe. Insulators have not certainly presented the temptations to pilferers which Col. Stewart rightly considered improbable; but both in Persia and Asiatic Turkey they have too frequently and effectively tempted reckless or mischievous wayfarers to use them as marks for matchlock balls or stones. There has been a tendency to steal wire shown on more than one instance, and once I remember the amount missing was large, and that some Saïyids, or descendants of the

Colonel Stewart reports well of the treatment personally experienced on his journey from the natives of the country:—

"From Bushahr to Tehran we did not meet with anything approaching to incivility, nor did we or our servants lose a single article either on the march or during halts. It is true that a decided disinclination to meddle with European travellers, and a wholesome dislike of rifles and revolvers, might to a certain extent account for this; but it in no way explains the fact that we also utterly failed in all our attempts to ascertain the details or locality of any recent robbery or act of violence. On the contrary, if an allowance be made for the anxiety of muleteers to exaggerate risks, with a view to enhancing the value of their own services, and of the heads of villages to secure the trifling advantage of being allowed to provide an escort of Tufangchis (matchlock-men), and to profit by their gains, the result of our inquiries invariably went to prove that the whole route was surprisingly secure, and that on the rare occasions when violence may possibly be attempted, the sole object must be that of plundering, from selfish motives, some small and entirely unprotected party, and not in any way that of causing wanton annoyance to the Government or its agents.

"Even in the case of our own personal effects ample opportunity for unresisted robbery was allowed. Our order of march was invariably as follows: The heavy baggage and servants, with some twelve or fourteen mules, led the way, making each march during the night. In the mountain tracts between Bushahr and Shiraz we were at first prevailed on to pay for a small guard of five to six ragged matchlock-men, whose arms were probably dangerous to none but their owners, but who as a matter of form accompanied this baggage detachment. This was entirely given up on our departure from Shiraz, when the

---

Prophet, were concerned in the participation of the stolen goods. But when the authorities punish such offences with promptitude and vigour, letting it be thoroughly understood they are in earnest, the temptations to pilfer are so combined with fear of chastisement and humiliation, that they lose their power, and soon cease to exist.

absurdity of the proceeding had become clear. We ourselves, retaining only our bedding and personal necessaries, always halted till daybreak, and then made the march entirely without guards, leaving the main road for very considerable distances whenever our doing so promised to reward us by a better view of the country from some neighbouring range, and taking every opportunity of visiting any villages or encampments of black tents we might approach. On all such occasions we were invariably treated with the greatest hospitality; any little delicacies the people might possess being at once placed at our disposal. Two mules with our bedding and appurtenances brought up the rear, and these were always unprotected and never accompanied us on the march.

"Of course, when Europeans or natives of importance are concerned, there must be some truth in what we were occasionally told; namely, that any loss sustained by them is certain to be represented and to attract attention, and that all interference with the property of such persons is to be avoided for this reason as well as from dread of resistance; but whatever weight this may have, the same considerations would apply still more forcibly in the case of wanton injury to a line of telegraph, the occurrence of which must instantly become known at the nearest station, and thus facilitate measures of detection or retribution, while the materials of the line can, as before explained, offer in themselves little or no temptation.

"It is now nearly two years since the occurrence of almost the only authenticated case we could hear of on this route of interference with any individual ever so indirectly connected with the Government. In this case a mounted Ghulam, taking amongst other property English letters and papers towards Bushahr, was, after leaving Shiraz, robbed not far from Khan-i-Zanian. This neighbourhood has the credit of being more insecure than any other on the whole route, or in other words, the authority of the Government is supposed to be less here than elsewhere. However, an order was sent from Shiraz threatening all persons in whose possession any of the missing property might be found, and before long the whole was quietly deposited in a public mosque in that city, and then recovered. From the plains of Bushahr to the highland midway between Shiraz and Ispahan, the whole of the country traversed is at one season or another of the year occupied almost exclusively by tribes of Iliats, who migrate north and south in search of pasture for their flocks in the spring and autumn respectively, and who move during these migrations by slow marches along the regular road. It may be well worth consideration whether the undoubted influence and control exercised over these tribes by their chief (the Ilkhāni, resident in Shiraz) might not be used by the Government with advantage, in securing the goodwill of these people and possibly in enlisting some of them permanently as guards."

We have now completed our extracts; but before taking leave of the Report, a word may be said on the quotations last recorded. They are given *in extenso*, because relating to a state of things interesting at the present day, when Persia has suddenly, as it were, made a *début* on the European diplomatic stage, and been brought into the share-market as a field for investment. There is much truth, and sense, and keen foresight in the sketch of the country here attempted, or supposed: but the colour of the picture is perhaps a little too roseate. Hospitality and fair treatment of strangers are common to a degree; a statement verified by Europeans in Persia Proper, and in the north, south, east, west, and centre of the kingdom. But life and property, however secure, must not be thought wholly dependent on the adventitious fact of particular nationality or *status*. The advantages of being a European, or a person of distinction, may in this respect be over-rated. A highwayman, from the dashing Bakhtiari to the mere footpad, is not invariably more scrupulous in Asia than in Europe, when in the way of professional temptation; nor is he invariably acquainted with the social position of the traveller thrown in his way. Since the wires were set up in 1864-5, instances might be given of aggravated assault on the open road, attended in some cases with fatal results, on British officers holding both high and responsible posts in the Telegraph Department, as well as on their fellow-labourers of inferior rank ; nor have robberies in camp or quarters been by any means unknown among the English *employés* generally. It is but fair to the Persian Government to say that such occurrences are at least the cause of distress to the ministers chiefly responsible ; and that if they have not in all cases shown by their acts a full determination to make severe examples of offenders, they have roused themselves now and then to vigorous action in some sense, as might reasonably be expected. It is just also to make allowances for something exceptional in the mere fact of Englishmen moving continually to and fro in parts of Persia where marauding is a normal condition ; and the passage of a European at all was, ten years ago, a novelty. Still, the truth remains, that even those who now traverse the country with a sense of comparative security, and take few special precautions for personal safety or protection of luggage, cannot deny the existence of seasons and circumstances when, or of localities where, molestation on the highway would be no improbable contingency.

Colonel Stewart reached Tehran on the 20th May, preceding his assistant Lieutenant Champain by two days, owing to the use of post-horses after leaving Ispahan. Thus, agreeably to orders, an officer had been selected by the Governor-General of India in Council " to proceed to Tehran and remain there attached to the

British Mission during the continuance of the negotiations for the formation of a line of telegraph through Persia."[1] This officer was now on the spot; all required was that the negotiations contemplated should commence. Submitting his report of journey through the interior of the country, working with his staff at "conditions for a Telegraph Treaty," and endeavouring by diplomatic or other legitimate agency to set the business ball going, he found his own estimate of time to be quite different from that of Persian officials. Progress, if such it could be called, was slow and unpromising. Stewart's health soon failed him, and he left Tehran for England, *via* Resht and the Caspian, on the 19th June, just one month after arrival. Lieutenant Champain remained in Persia, but his duties were not at this time very defined. To render general service at the Mission, and acquire personal knowledge and experience of a country known generally to the educated world by books, would best, perhaps, describe the nature of his employment. On the 12th October he quitted the capital for Hamadan and Karmanshah, thence crossing the frontier and continuing his journey to Baghdad, where he arrived on the 8th November. Were it not that our subject recalls us to the Persian negotiations, we might here add a summary of his valuable Route-Report on this occasion.

We must again go back for a year or two before narrating subsequent proceedings at Tehran. It had been proposed by Her Majesty's Secretary of State for India, early in 1861, to construct a line of telegraph from the Turco-Persian frontier through Persia, to

---

[1] Earl Russell to Mr. Alison, March 12, 1862, No. 18, page 11, in Printed Correspondence respecting the Construction of a Telegraph line through Persia.

Bandar Abbas, to form a component part of a longer line from England to India; and on the 17th May Sir Charles Wood forwarded a memorandum to Mirza Jiafar Khan, the Persian ambassador in London, offering as general terms of agreement:

1st. That the line should commence at Baghdad, proceed thence to Tehran, and from that city *viâ* Ispahan and Shiraz, to Bandar Abbas.

2nd. That the expense of the construction should be shared equally by the two countries.

3rd. That the line should be executed under the superintendence of British officers, to be selected by the Secretary of State for India.

4th. That it should consist of two wires, one for the exclusive use of the Persian, and one of the British Government.

The next three provisions were: for dividing expenses of working and maintenance, repayment to each Government being regulated by the value of the messages sent by them respectively under certain prescribed rates of tariff; for repayment of sums advanced by the British Government for construction, out of value of messages sent by them, above portion required for share of working and maintenance; and for repayment of sums last named by Government of Persia under other conditions, if such a course should be rendered necessary by acts of Persian subjects. The Mirza's reply was to the effect that a telegraph line like that contemplated was not actually essential to the Persian Government; but that the Shah might be induced to consider the question in the hope of securing the friendship and good feeling of the English Government. He thought that sanction might be obtained for constructing a line from Baghdad towards

Karáchi through Persia, by granting to his Government the privilege of transmitting a certain number of words daily, free of expense, and transferring to them, after a specified term of years, the whole line and its revenues. Or the proposal might be made to construct a line from the Baghdad frontier to Bandar Abbas, at the joint expense of the two Governments; the arrangement being qualified by a handsome bonus from the British Government, such as a gratuitous supply of wire or money, independently of any debtor and creditor accounts.

Sir Charles Wood acknowledged this letter by a counter-proposition. If the Shah preferred that the line contemplated should be altogether constructed and worked by British officers, her Majesty's Government would not object, on condition that it should remain in the hands of the Indian Government for a period of years, say twenty-five; all expenses being paid and all receipts retained by the latter. After that period it should be transferred wholly to Persia, on her undertaking to keep it in perfect working order, and to convey the messages of the British and Indian Governments at a rate mutually agreeable.

This correspondence having been communicated to the Foreign Office, was passed on for the information of her Majesty's Minister at Tehran, with a hint that, as Mirza Jiafar Khan was on his way back to Persia, his arrival be waited before coming to any decision on the proposals.

On the 4th September her Majesty's Minister wrote from Tehran, enclosing copy of a letter he had received from the ex-ambassador, who had arrived at Tabriz. In the true spirit of Persian diplomacy the latter excused himself for unlooked-for and compulsory delay, when he had pledged himself to Sir Charles Wood to return as soon as possible; and suggested that Mr. Alison, without waiting his uncertain arrival, should at once open discussion of the telegraph question with Mirza Saiyid Khan, the Minister for Foreign Affairs; though this high official was prepared to notify the Shah's objection to Mirza Jiafar's own proposal made in England.

Mr. Alison naturally asked that a gentleman conversant with the subject of telegraphic communication in all its details be attached to the mission for the impending negotiations; but before Colonel Patrick Stewart's appearance on the scene in compliance with this request, an important but disappointing phase in the question had supervened.

On the 6th November, 1861, a memorandum was put into Mr. Alison's hands from the Persian Foreign Minister, containing eleven Articles of an Agreement which the Shah was ready to subscribe to without delay. The first six, it was stated, had already been put forward, and it is presumed in England.

I. Expenses of construction were to be wholly defrayed by England.

II. The British Government would work the line and take the profits for twenty-five years.

III. Certain messages, under certain limitations, were to be sent free of charge for the Persian Government.

IV. Materials procurable in Persia were to be sold at the rate of the day.

V. The Persian Government would protect the line to the best of its power.

VI. The Persian Government would pay expenses incurred by English Government, if the line were stopped by contingencies of war, at the instance of a foreign power.

VII. Expenses of protecting the line would be paid by British Government.

VIII. The British Government would engage that whatever power and authority and proprietary right the Persian Government, from former times to the present day, possessed, from near Bandar Abbas to the Sind frontier, remain *in statu quo*.

IX. Also that if Persia desired to increase its power in those territories, the British Government would in no way oppose such action.

X. Also that if Persia should be in a condition to protect the line in those territories, such expense of protection would be defrayed by the British Government.

XI. If the Persian Government thought fit to reimburse the British for the expenses of the line from Khanikin throughout, then, on certain conditions, it would come into its full possession.

In less than a fortnight after communicating this proposal to the Foreign Office, Mr. Alison made a further report on the subject. He had received a visit from Farukh Khan, the envoy who had negotiated the Peace Treaty in Paris, and this nobleman was most urgent in enlisting the British Minister's support for the new Draft Articles. The Foreign Minister, moreover, sent a message to His Excellency with evidently a like intent.

On the 18th February, 1862, Earl Russell informed Mr. Alison that her Majesty's Government saw no objection to the letter of the sixth Article, admitting an undoubted liability; but could not suppose that Persia would act in so unfriendly a manner as stated in the hypothesis. Article VII. could not be accepted; but her Majesty's Government would undertake payment of half expenses of protection on certain conditions. With regard to the three next articles, her Majesty's Government would agree that no territorial claims of Persia should be affected by any arrangement made on account of the telegraph; but they declined to enter into any prospective engagements as to the protection of the line through the tracts indicated. There was no difficulty in the way of accepting the last article. To those accustomed to the routine between the two Government Offices concerned, it need hardly be explained that the Foreign Office letter to Mr. Alison was almost a verbatim copy of that addressed to it by the India Office. That no allusion was made to the first five articles of the Persian Memorandum, was perhaps tantamount to a tacit admission that they had been, as inferred, originally agreed to in England, and needed only the Shah's approval. Indeed the "new articles" are said to commence from that numbered VI. in the paper.[1]

It would really seem that there were not only no insuperable obstacles now in the way of a satisfactory conclusion, but that the question had resolved itself into a diplomatic nutshell. Persian politics, however, are clouded and tangled; and the lapse of time does not always serve to clear or unravel them. Mr. Alison's reply to Earl Russell, dated 25th April, pointing out that the Shah refused to consent to any alteration of his conditions, made no allusion whatever to renewal of

[1] In correction, apparently, of the Persian statement which would make it VII.

discussion, and wound up with the following curt paragraph:—"The subject of the telegraph may be considered to be completely disposed of for the present." At this time Colonel Stewart and Lieutenant Champain had passed Shiraz on their way to Tehran; and it cannot be said that a cheerful political aspect would greet them on arrival at the latter city.[1]

Throughout the whole of the summer months there seems to have been utter stagnation in the diplomatic "correspondence respecting the construction of a telegraph line through Persia," and, from the date of its resumption,[2] it may be inferred that the first batch of renewed communications on the subject only reached Tehran after Lieutenant Champain's departure. Indeed renewal at all was caused by receipt of Colonel Stewart's report sent home by Mr. Alison. The Foreign Office wished to be informed what were the views of the Secretary of State for India on the subject?

But Colonel Stewart himself had ere this returned to England, and was in active communication with the authorities. His letter of the 24th August, inclosing copies of much that he had written when absent, submitted a summary of his own opinions on the course to be pursued in furtherance of the telegraph project, "as affected by the failure of the recent negotiations with the Court of Persia." The main proposal was to construct a series of submarine cables extending from the head of the Persian Gulf to Gwādar or other point on the Makran coast,

[1] See letters referred to in printed Correspondence before noted, pages 7 to 10 inclusive.
[2] Mr. Merivale's letter to Mr. Hammond, dated Sept. 10, 1862, No. 21 in published printed Correspondence just noted. This letter would take about a month in reaching, and as there is but one mail in the month to Persia, could hardly have been despatched on the date it bears.

connected with Karáchi, and reach, if possible, the head of the Persian Gulf from the west by Turkish aërial line; but in any case to reopen discussion with the Persian Government, and come to an understanding as to the terms on which a line from Baghdad to "Tehran and Bushahr" might at once be constructed. Hence the reply to Earl Russell's question represented that "it would be very desirable to have a second line from Baghdad through Persia, to a suitable place on the coast, where it might be joined to the line through the Persian Gulf;" and Earl Russell transmitted a copy to Mr. Alison with instructions "to re-open negotiations with the Persian Government, with the view of carrying out the wishes of her Majesty's Government, as set forth in the India Office letter." In a month or so, this despatch was followed by a second, intimating the determination of effecting "telegraphic communication with India, in the first instance, by means of a cable to be laid down the Persian Gulf," and the intention of establishing "a station at Bushahr, and also, if necessary, at or near Bandar Abbas." The necessary permission was to be obtained from the Persian Government.[1]

Mr. Alison's despatch of the 4th November reported having recommended the subject of the telegraph from Baghdad to Tehran and the Persian Gulf to the Shah's favourable consideration, and having directed Mr. Thomson to communicate more fully on the "matter with the Persian Ministers." His Excellency took the opportunity of acquainting Earl Russell that the Shah was actually arranging for a line of telegraph to meet a Turkish line at the frontier near Baghdad, the cost "to be defrayed out of the Government treasury," and that a company

[1] Nos. 22 and 24, page 12, Printed Correspondence.

was "being formed to lay down a telegraphic wire from the capital to Shiraz." Of the composition or nationality of this company not a word was said. "It must be always borne in mind," was the characteristic conclusion of the despatch, "that telegraphic lines in Persia are always getting out of order."[1] Mr. Alison left for England on or about the date of this report.

There was a show of vacillation in the negotiations between Persia and the Porte; but it is impossible to determine what were the plain facts of the case. Several months had passed since the subject had been first mooted by the two Governments, and in January 1862, the Shah had expressed to the Ottoman Minister the great desire that he felt for the establishment of telegraphic communication between Tehran and Baghdad. On the 30th May, a few days after Colonel Stewart's arrival in the capital, Mr. Alison further reported to Earl Russell the abrupt termination of this affair also. The Turkish Minister had informed him that "having received full powers from the Porte to conclude a convention for the establishment of the telegraphic line between Baghdad and Tehran, in pursuance of a strong desire expressed on the part of the king, ... he lost no time in communicating with the Persian Government on the subject. Haidar Efendi," Mr. Alison added, "was not a little surprised at being informed, in reply, that the king had changed his mind, and now meditated establishing a telegraphic line between Resht and Tehran. I learn that it is the intention of the Russian Government to complete this telegraphic line to Tiflis, and to extend it, if possible, to Tabriz."[2]

[1] No. 25, page 13, Printed Correspondence.
[2] No. 20, page 11, ditto.

Mr. Eastwick became Chargé d'Affaires on Mr. Alison's departure; but as he was absent on duty at Mashhad at the period of his accession, the conduct of the telegraphic discussion remained for a time in Mr. Thomson's hands. On the 3rd December this gentleman reported that he had had frequent interviews with the Persian Ministers, in the cause of the projected telegraph. In illustration of the general result, it will suffice for our purpose to state that the Shah expressed his determination to construct, at his own expense, a line of telegraph from Khanikin on the Baghdad frontier to Bushahr, through Tehran, Ispahan and Shiraz, intended to be in connection with the proposed telegraph to India through the Persian Gulf. On the 9th December, Mr. Eastwick returned to Tehran, and ten days afterwards forwarded to the Foreign Office the draft of a convention, acceptance of which the India Office considered should at once be notified by telegram to Her Majesty's Chargé d'Affaires in Persia. This agreement was of six short Articles, as follow :—

I. Persia to construct a line of telegraph from Khanikin to Tehran and Bushahr, which the British Government might use on payment.
II. Persia to assign the sum sufficient for construction and materials.
III. Persia to purchase European materials from England at reasonable rates.
IV. Line to be superintended by an English Engineer officer under certain local restrictions, and paid by his own Government, Persia fixing the period of his employment.

No. 26, page 13, Printed Correspondence.

V. English superintendent empowered to make requisitions for necessary materials, under specified conditions.

VI. British Government to convey to Persian frontier materials purchased from them, with approval of Persian Minister in London, payment being made by five instalments, in five years.[1]

There is no doubt that, whatever imperfections and want of detail may be exhibited in this paper, viewed as a convention between two Governments on a question essentially practical and full of technicalities, its use as a preliminary to work is undeniable; and the ready and legitimate mode in which it was obtained may be cited as an example of how much may be done by determination, combined with ability. In the expression of such opinion it is not in the least intended to reflect on those who failed to secure for the telegraph in Persia the fair start which it required; nor to compare the public acts of one high official with those of another. Everyone who knows the Oriental character in diplomacy knows how much depends on happy moments and happy occasions; and if it be a merit to take advantage of these, as they present themselves, it is also no demerit to live through the season when they never arise at all. Judgments should, at least, be suspended on these things until much of every description of evidence has been thoroughly weighed. Nor would the question be alluded to in this volume at all, were it not the duty of the writer, in his position as an official chronicler, to acknowledge obligations of so marked a kind as those to the framer of the first practical paper with Persia on the subject of a telegraph, be it designated an agreement, an engagement, or

[1] No. 27, page 15, Printed Correspondence.

a convention. The Anglo-Persian Telegraph would, no doubt, have had substance of some kind, whether given to it by one Minister or another, but it is to Mr. Eastwick that its existence, such as we have seen and experienced it, is, without question, mainly due.

The subsequent communications were on details. Colonel Stewart submitted at once a programme for immediate operations, which was accepted, and forwarded through the usual channels to Persia. It was February when the telegram was despatched approving Mr. Eastwick's convention; so that stores, wires and insulators could not reach Bushahr till August. But work was at once to be "commenced by procuring and distributing strong timber posts along the whole line, which should everywhere follow the regular road." And the stores would be procured and sent as required; first for a single wire, but with a view to a second at some future period. English superintendence was to be continued for five years. Colonel Stewart's engagements detaining him with the Persian Gulf cable, Lieutenant Champain, who had been summoned home from Baghdad, would be sent with a staff to superintend the construction of the line in Persia. The charge for messages from Baghdad to Bushahr was fixed, in anticipation of satisfactory completion, at 10s. 6d. per twenty words, with prospect of eventual reduction.[1]

On the 14th February, Mr. Eastwick left Tehran, and Mr. Ronald Thomson was the Chargé d'Affaires in Mr. Alison's absence. This gentleman pushed on preparation of preliminaries by the Persian Executive, in compliance with his instructions; but a new difficulty had to be surmounted, in the division of messages between

[1] No. 29, page 18, Printed Correspondence.

Baghdad and Bushahr. If there were to be alternative lines between these two points, one through Asiatic Turkey and the sea cable, and one through Persia, which was to receive the bulk of the traffic? or was there to be no distinction? The Secretary of State for India, who had been in personal communication with the Persian Minister in London on this rather knotty question, agreed to despatch one-fourth of the messages through Persia so long as there was but one wire in that country, and one-half of the messages when there were two wires to meet the traffic. But to this arrangement Persia was indifferent, and Turkey demurred. The former displayed perfect confidence in the superiority of her embryo lines, as well as disbelief in any junction of the wires at all between Baghdad and the Gulf by Basrah. The latter seemed to dislike the intervention of Persia in the matter of Indian communications, and it needed some forcible arguments to keep her from withdrawing from the prosecution of the lines to Basrah and the coming cable.[1] Finally there was a kind of compromise, or drawn battle; and Article XIV. of the India-Ottoman convention provided for forwarding messages to or from India *viâ* Basrah or Khanikin with simple respect to convenience of service.[2]

His Majesty the Shah[3] objected to discuss the proposal of a second wire until the experience of the first should have established its necessity; and a formal engagement to place the telegraph under English officers was also distasteful to the Persian Government, although they did not deny their willingness to retain them until

---

[1] See Chapter II., *ante.*

[2] Printed Correspondence, No. 33, page 20 to end, *passim.*

[3] Mr. Thomson to Earl Russell, July 4, 1863, Printed Correspondence, No. 48, page 29.

the line had become thoroughly efficient. In other respects matters looked favourably for progress in this novel and important enterprise. On the 13th August the India Office reported to the Foreign Office that the European staff and stores for the telegraph had been despatched; and on the same date Earl Russell transmitted to Mr. Alison a detailed memorandum on the subject from Colonel Stewart. This enclosure represented the distance between Khanikin and Bushahr to be 1,102 miles, but that materials had been provided for a single wire of 1,200 miles. As a rule there would be twenty-one ordinary and three stretching insulators per mile, but exceptions would be made where rendered advisable by the nature of the ground. The greater portion of the stores would be landed at Bushahr for transport on mules towards Tehran; a small proportion would be sent *viâ* Basrah and the Tigris to Baghdad. One vessel might be expected at Basrah early in October, another one about the middle or before the end of that month at Bushahr. Two gentlemen, Messrs. Man and Walton, leaving England with a line inspector on the 8th August, would give all necessary information and assistance until Lieutenant Champain's arrival. The latter officer would proceed to Bushahr, soon after reaching Tehran, to meet the vessels and stores. Two Engineer officers had been applied for from India, and a third was to leave England about the end of August with ten trained non-commissioned[1] officers and men of the Royal Engineers. There would be five divisions of the line from Khanikin to Bushahr; each division having its superintendent, inspector, and two assistant-inspectors, the direction of the

---

[1] The number was increased to twelve, and two inspectors, who left England on the 27th August.

whole being in the hands of Lieutenant Champain, with head-quarters at Tehran. The pay of each grade was estimated, and the whole monthly expenditure stated in round numbers. Colonels Pelly and Kemball, the respective Residents at Bushahr and Baghdad, had been communicated with in respect to the landing and protection of stores in Persia and Turkish Arabia.[1]

Lieutenant Champain left London for Persia, *via* the Danube and Tiflis, on the 12th September; found two of his most active assistants, Messrs. Hoeltzer and Walton, hard at work at Tehran on arrival there, the 20th October; quitted Tehran the 3rd November; and, riding post for the greater part of the way, reached Bushahr on the 17th idem. Here he met Captain Murdoch Smith and the non-commissioned officers of Royal Engineers, with whom he returned to the capital, leaving Bushahr on the 7th December and reaching Tehran on the 28th January, 1864. Those acquainted with the local geography, and knowing something of the kind of country to be traversed, and means of traversing it by *chapar* or *charwadar*,[2] will acknowledge that this was rather severe travelling; and the more so when a journey from Tehran to Baghdad, Baghdad to Alexandretta, (*via* Aleppo,) and Alexandretta to London, had been performed by the same officer in the previous year; and a tour of inspection from Tehran to Baghdad, thence to Bushahr and back to Tehran, added to a further journey from Tehran to Baghdad, and Baghdad to Samsun, Constantinople and London, were to mark for him the first half of the years 1864 and 1865 respectively. That the intervals were not always intervals of repose may be readily admitted from the following

---

[1] Colonel Patrick Stewart's Memo., dated August 7, 1863. Printed Correspondence, pages 31 to 34. [2] *I.e.* Post or Caravan.

summary of the official accounts of setting up the posts and first Persian wire on the lines.

On the 13th October, 1864, Major [1] Champain reported for the information of the Bombay Government, completion of the line of telegraph from Baghdad, through Tehran, to Bushahr. At the same time he entered fully into explanations why the work had not been accomplished at an earlier date. No reasons for delay would have been asked had the matter been simply considered in its moral or physical aspect; but a period for construction had been specified, and in the true spirit of military exactitude, it was well to show why the estimated days had been exceeded.

We will briefly review this officer's proceedings, as related in his official report. Of the five gentlemen appointed to serve as superintendents, Major Champain had found Messrs. Man and Walton already in Persia, on his return thither in October, 1863. The former he then despatched to Ispahan, to see to the necessary collection and distribution of poles; the latter he sent to Baghdad, with instructions to expedite the looked-for wire and insulators to the Turco-Persian frontier, and thence distribute it along the line to Tehran. One of his inspectors, Mr. Ernest Hoeltzer, he left at Tehran to instruct young Persians in the use of the Morse instrument. He himself rode on to Bushahr, where, finding that much material had arrived, he at once set about sending it along the line on mules supplied by the Governor of the town. Some three weeks passed in this occupation; when, detailing two non-commissioned officers to continue the work until Lieutenant St. John,

[1] This officer is henceforth designated by the local rank which was accorded to him in Persia.

one of the Engineer officers awaited from India, should arrive, he again turned towards Tehran, but accompanied on this occasion by Captain Smith (who had recently returned from Basrah), one inspector, and four sergeants. After making arrangements at Shiraz for the despatch of stores expected from Bushahr to points further up the line; dropping two sergeants at Ispahan; ascertaining that some of the material had actually reached that city, moreover, that Mr. Man had already set up there two or three miles of posts and insulators, he repaired to his head-quarters at the capital. Here he remained a month, unsuccessfully endeavouring to obtain poles for his superintendent, so that work might be begun in the Tehran district. Then, thinking the locality the most likely to meet the exigencies of the occasion, he sent Captain Smith and his party to the city of Kum, a main station within his range of superintendence.

The five divisions were apportioned as follows. Major Champain had hoped to meet at Bushahr, Lieutenants Pierson and St. John, the officers appointed by the Government of India; but their arrival there from Bombay had been delayed:

For the line from Tehran west, or joining the Persian with the Turkish and European systems.

1st. Lieut. Pierson, R.E., from Baghdad to Kangawar.
2nd. Mr. H. V. Walton ,, Kangawar to Tehran.

For the line from Tehran south, or joining the Persian Land lines to the Indian Submarine Telegraph.

3rd. Captain Smith, R.E., from Tehran to Kohrud.
4th. Mr. H. Man, ,, Kohrud to Murghab.
5th. Lieut. St. John, R.E., ,, Murghab to Bushahr.[1]

[1] Giving, on an average, about 220 miles to each superintendent.

The Director, with the intention of reinspecting the whole course of the line, and assisting each superior officer in overcoming the difficulties presenting themselves, soon quitted Tehran and moved towards Baghdad. Mr. Man's serious illness caused him some anxiety; and he had to employ the services of Captain Gastaiger, an Austrian officer of Engineers in the Shah's pay, temporarily to supply the want of a superintendent. Major Champain speaks well of the manner in which this duty was performed. Captain Gastaiger, "placing himself under Mr. Man's orders, assumed charge of the working party, which that officer was too ill to direct. The operations were then being carried on some sixty miles north of Ispahan with great difficulties and delays. Labour and carriage for material were but scantily supplied by the Persians, and the intense cold at the time rendered the wire so brittle that it was almost impossible to join or strain it. Working for weeks together while the snow was lying waist-deep on the ground, and in the miserable villages scattered at long intervals from one another along the road, Captain Gastaiger and the two non-commissioned officers, Corporals Macdonald and Norman, could make but slow progress; but they deserve great credit for their indomitable perseverance, and for the cheerfulness with which they bore the very serious hardships to which they were exposed."

On his way to Baghdad,[1] Major Champain found that Lieutenant Pierson and Mr. Walton, whose divisions touched, had joined at the town of Karmanshah. The Prince Governor of the district had shown himself well

---

[1] There was much snow on the ground, and the cold was very severe though late in the season. Lieutenant Pierson had reached Karmanshah on the 9th March.

disposed to the cause; but an order from Tehran, notifying the appointment of a Persian telegraph officer responsible in respect of money and materials, seems to have disturbed his equanimity; and in spite of his expressed willingness to continue to help the British officers, it was with difficulty he could be persuaded, by the supply of two working parties, to enable the superintendents above named to work separately. Passing on to Baghdad, and proceeding thence by river to the anchorage of the sea steamer, Major Champain reached Bushahr again from the sea-side.[1] Here he met Lieutenant St. John, who had already, with his energetic assistants, completed seventy miles of inland telegraph, in addition to a short ten miles' line in connection with the submarine cable. But rapid progress depended on extraneous aid, and this was not always procurable. "The Governor of Bushahr," we are told, "had assisted Lieutenant St. John, but as soon as the line had passed through his territory into that of the Governor of Shiraz, the change was speedily felt. The labourers, no longer paid or fed, rapidly deserted: no representations to the Governor of Shiraz had any effect;" and when the Director came up with the working party, he found that it only numbered ten men out of sixty at first engaged. At Shiraz he tried three times to see the Governor, but was always refused admittance; and the Persian responsible telegraph official accounted for the failings on his own part by saying he could get no money for mules, and was completely powerless. The promise, from the higher authority, of men and mules was all that could be obtained, and with

[1] The *Zenobia*, in which he was a passenger, had, however, stopped midway from Basrah, at the anchorage of the ships conveying Colonel Patrick Stewart and the officers of the Cable Expedition. He bid adieu to his old friend for the last time on the 13th April, 1864.

this Major Champain was forced to be satisfied, and continued his way to Ispahan. Here, on the representations of Mr. Hoeltzer, who had taken charge from Mr. Man, he took the bold but essential step of authorizing his superintendents, by circular, to expend, from funds at their disposal, such sums for labour and material as they could honestly certify were indispensable calls, owing to

YEZDIKHAST : BETWEEN SHIRAZ AND ISPAHAN.

failure of Persian co-operation. In reverting to this circumstance at the conclusion of his work, he felt no hesitation in acquainting Government that had not the English superintending officers availed themselves freely of this permission, the only two divisions then completed would have been "the first and fifth, those furthest from Tehran." It might have been supposed that matters would have been better managed at the capital, where there was not only a Government to assert its authority in the person of the Shah and his Ministers, but her

Britannic Majesty's Legation to push all legitimate demands on behalf of British subjects and British interests. The result, however, showed how little ground existed for such suppositions. One Governor, basking in the very light of the royal presence, would supply no poles; another, but little removed from such lustrous propinquity, would not permit the English officer to work within the limits of his jurisdiction. Forty miles of telegraph were set up in the division of which Tehran was the northern terminus; but Major Champain, on return to that city, the 19th May, saw that unless vigorous measures were at once adopted, his work would be fairly paralysed. His report may here be quoted, though it rather under-estimates than represents his real difficulties. "After inexplicable delay the poles were gradually laid out about the end of August, and work proceeded. All this time the most stringent orders had been continually sent by the Persian Ministers and the Shah himself to the Governor of Tehran, who for three months would take no notice whatever of the firmans. An officer of the king's was quartered in the Governor's house to ensure obedience, but without effect. . . . . Nothing would induce the Persian authorities at Tehran to give us either mules or men for the work. Two of my officers and their subordinates had been idle for weeks, when at last the poles were laid out, and I thought it advisable to expend the comparatively small sum that would be required for labour, and to complete the line at our own cost."[1]

It would be needless to dwell on the failure of transport arrangements, so far as left to promise and per-

[1] Major Champain to Secretary to Government, Bombay. No. 119 of the 13th October, 1864.

formance on the part of the Persian executive; or on the causes of inefficiency of the native officers appointed to co-operate with the British superintendents. It was not simply that orders for money were dishonoured and disregarded; or that labour without wages was not procurable in Persia any more than in England. The miserable system of intervention acknowledged in the former country, by which the master does not deal directly with the menial nor the proprietor with the peasant, was at work, and the mediating agency, unless vivified by peculation without limit, was cold and lifeless. Sanction to pilfer is too much to solicit from honourable guardians of the public interests; for however bitter to many Englishmen the pill of conformity to national customs may have been on previous occasions, it could never have been made a universal state medicine if such had been a declared ingredient. Nothing that could in honour be accorded to the customs, or even prejudices of the country was to be withheld. Pride, temper, repugnance, all these sentiments were to be restrained to the utmost. But patience may lose her balance at times in the best-regulated minds; and if she had done so during early telegraphic operations in Persia, there would have been no cause of amazement. As it was, Major Champain, on reporting completion of the first wire of communication, pronounced the conduct of the officers and men to have been "admirable," adding that it was "to their intense perseverance and patience, notwithstanding the most harassing and vexatious treatment," that he attributed success, so far as it had been obtained, in the undertaking with which he had been entrusted.[1]

[1] Major Champain to Secretary to Government, Bombay. No. 119 of the 13th October, 1864.

Lieutenant Pierson had worked "most indefatigably and successfully" in the first division, passing "through perhaps the wildest parts of Persia;" and to his personal influence with the Prince Governor of Karmanshah and Kurdish chief of those parts, a tribute of well-earned praise was recorded. Dr. Baker had rendered him valuable professional and general assistance, and Mr. Inspector Willis and Corporal Whittenbacke, Royal Engineers, had "exerted themselves unweariedly." In the second division the "untiring zeal and activity" of Mr. Henry Valentine Walton were specially noticed; and instances were cited in illustration of the assertion that "notwithstanding disheartening difficulties, bad climate and ill health," he had "worked most cheerfully and ably on all occasions." Mr. Inspector Sharrat and Corporal Graves, Royal Engineers, had led a trying life during nine months. "Exposed at first to excessive cold and afterwards to intense heat, and encamped for many weeks at a time in deserts without water," their behaviour throughout was highly commended. The labours of Captain Murdoch Smith, Royal Engineers, who, in charge of the third division, had been "perhaps more annoyed by the Persians than any other superintendent," had resulted in a "beautifully laid out and finished line," a reward of the "most untiring patience and unconquerable determination." Inspector Signor Barbara, Sergeant Bower and Corporal Barry, Royal Engineers, had been spoken of by Captain Smith in the warmest terms for services rendered. In the fourth division the "great exertions" of Mr. Hoeltzer, and the "indefatigable way in which Corporals Macdonald and Norman, Royal Engineers, had carried on their duties," as well as their general conduct, were the theme of laudatory report; nor was the useful zeal of Mr. Stephen Agamor, the Armenian British Agent, forgotten. Finally, Lieutenant St. John, in charge of the fifth division, whose late arrival in the country prevented him from breaking ground until the 15th March, had not only finished his own division, but a part of the fourth also "with remarkable rapidity." In exactly five months that officer "joined up his wire with Mr. Hoeltzer's, 335 miles from Bushahr, after carrying it over by far the most difficult passes, and through the only really wooded country that the line traverses." He had displayed "most wonderful energy and peculiar tact in dealing with the Persians," and deserved the cordial thanks of his Director for his "great activity and perseverance." Mr. Inspector Daniell, Sergeant Isaacson, and Corporal Hamilton, Royal Engineers, and the Nawab Hasan Ali Khan were at the same time spoken of in high terms for services rendered in this division.[1]

But before dismissing the report, it will be well to glance at its enclosures, or the separate reports of the Superintendents themselves.[2]

One of Captain Pierson's main difficulties had been of a purely political nature. The Turkish and Persian Governments had been at issue in respect to the precise line of frontier dividing their particular territories; and if the lines of telegraph belonging to the two states respectively were to be united at all, some understanding on the point of junction was simply imperative. Now the village of Kasr-i-Shirin, or more strictly the post of

---

[1] Major Champain to Government Secretary, Bombay, No. 119 of the 19th October, 1864, paragraphs 16 to 21.

[2] A brief sketch of the services of these officers will be found in the Appendix to this chapter.

"Kalah-i-Sabz," was just the point from which, on the Persian side, to Khanikin, in acknowledged Turkish jurisdiction, lay the bone of contention, a space of about seventeen miles. Consequently from Kalah-i-Sabz to the westward, or towards Baghdad, Lieutenant Pierson could not carry on the construction of his line of telegraph without special authorization. Much valuable time had already been lost owing to this state of things, when the newly-appointed Persian Envoy Extraordinary to the Porte passed along the disputed tract *en route* from Tehran to Constantinople, *viâ* Baghdad. The presence at the last-named city of so distinguished an official might, it was reasonably inferred, be turned to account for removing the impediment existing to progress. Mirza Husain Khan was the man of all others to face the emergency. Active in mind and body, intelligent, ambitious, fond of Europeans, and experienced in Europe and its diplomacy, he readily took up the case, and proposed to Namik Pasha, Governor of Baghdad, a temporary equal division of disputed soil. The latter, with much the same opportunities as the Persian, was a man of different stamp. His interests were ultra-conservative; his sympathies were with Asiatic bigotry, rather than European civilization; and though he did credit to his diplomatic training by fluent and well-accented French and a perfectly courteous address, yet his thin and wiry form, sharp face with bluish grey eye, grey eyebrows and aquiline nose, and general exterior, were little suggestive of social *rapprochement*. The two diplomatists, at all events, came to an amicable understanding on the Mirza's proposal, which was accepted as a temporary expedient; and a paper was drawn out for Lieutenant Pierson's guidance, which would enable him to return to his duty and resume operations. But while the Persian statesman left all details to the young English officer, the Turkish Pasha named his own agent—in this case, however, also an Englishman—to carry out the settlement. Pierson joined up the wires at the point agreed, and worked back to Karmanshah, the head-quarters of his division. His own words describe the sequel:—

"When at Kirind the Governor of Karmanshah wrote to me . . . to return to the frontier, and pull up part of the Turkish line, substituting Persian posts and wire . . . subsequently modified to desiring me to cut the wire at the junction. In answer I . . . asserted that as my duty was confined to taking measures for erecting and maintaining the line, . . if he wished . . to destroy it for political reasons, he must send his own agents to do so. He accordingly caused the wire to be cut at the point of junction, in which state it still remains."

It appears that the Shah had not consented to the compromise made at Baghdad as to the junction of the lines, a result explained by the existence at Tehran of influences hostile to his envoy.[1] Hence the lesson that if Oriental jealousy has a special end to attain and the power to attain it, that jealousy must be satisfied and that power appeased, however clearly the pleasure of the individual operate to the prejudice of the mass. On the other hand money may be scattered wholesale; labour expended; life sacrificed in a cause, failure of which would affect thousands of persons, or even millions; all these considerations are as nothing with the other in the reasoning scale. But the temper and patience of the English superintendents was taxed in more than official

[1] That these influences have pursued Mirza Husain Khan, more or less, throughout his career, see an article in the *Pall Mall Gazette* of September 18, 1873, headed "The Persian ex-Prime Minister."

experiences. The internal condition of their own camps presented sometimes anything but quiet and good order. A Kurdi Farash in Lieutenant Pierson's service, on one occasion, savagely attacked and nearly killed with his sword two of his fellow-servants, grooms. Pierson, when first appearing on the ground, had seen the wounded men covered with blood; and his own life was threatened by their assailant. The soldiers of the working party actually aided in the assault, and refused to obey Lieutenant Pierson's order to capture the head offender. Moreover the Khan of the village of Kasr-i-Shirin would not arrest the man, though requested to do so, and though he was a notoriously bad character. As for the Governor of Kirind, who had originally recommended the latter to Lieutenant Pierson for employment, he coolly wrote to that officer, requesting him to return his Farash's sword and dagger, naturally retained by the offender's master after the affray.[1]

Mr. Henry Walton, one of the two superintendents first on the spot, had undertaken the construction of the line from Karmanshah to Kangavar, as well as that from Kangavar to Tehran. His difficulties, independently of those of distance and country, consisted mainly in want of poles and local assistance, and in the desertion of workmen.

Captain Smith's report is so characteristic of the occasion, and so faithfully descriptive of the troubles a British officer can manage to surmount, when resolved to fulfil his instructions, and when placed in exceptional and quasi-unprofessional positions, that more than one extract may be found interesting.

[1] Major Champain to H.B.M. Minister at Tehran. No. 58 of the 8th June, 1864.

He had left Tehran on the 26th February, and reached Kum, a distance of eighty-five miles, on the day following.

"On my arrival I was astonished to find that neither wire, insulators, nor tools had come from Ispahan, although the Persian authorities there had been instructed . . . as early as the beginning of January, to forward them without delay. I at once sent a courier to Ispahan, on whose return I learnt that some had been sent to Kashan notwithstanding . . . instructions to the Persian officers at Ispahan to despatch all the stores for Kum, before sending any of them anywhere else. I therefore sent the Mirza . . . to Kashan with a letter to the Governor, requesting him to send on all the tools and a specified quantity of wire and insulators to Kum. On the 13th March I received wire and insulators, but no tools. These I long afterwards found had been purposely kept back by the Persian Yawar at Ispahan, . . . with the object of preventing work in my division until he himself should join it after completion of the line from Ispahan to Kohrud. There was, moreover, no Persian officer appointed to attend to my requisitions for workmen, transport and materials."

He applied to the Governor of Kum to get some tools made in the bazaar, and was told that orders to this effect were wanting from Tehran. When with great difficulty a supply of some kind had been obtained, he applied for workmen. First came a few old men and boys; but after repeated remonstrances he got a working party of thirty labourers.

"As these men were either very badly paid or not paid at all, they naturally enough ran away, and others quite new to the work had to be found. I at length prevailed on the Governor to . . . pay them 16 shahis (about 7½d.) per day, in my presence, but it was not till the 25th March that this concession was made, and mules enough provided to enable me to move out of the town, form a camp, and fairly begin work."

WANT OF CARRIAGE.

The Governor had introduced in his correspondence with Captain Smith a form of address marking his own superiority, which, if not a covert insult, at least was likely to be so interpreted in a country where worth is measured by position, and humility is another word for disgrace. For this a written apology was exacted and reluctantly given; but the ruler of Kum had other failings than vanity.

"Seeing a number of good poles (about 600) lying near the *Chapar Khānah*,[1] I asked the Governor how they happened to be there, if, as he assured me, there were more than enough laid out along the road within his territory? He replied that those I saw were the first that had been brought, but as he did not consider them good enough, he had rejected them, and sent the others now lying scattered along the road, which were much longer and better in every way. This, I afterwards found, was utterly untrue, as the poles on the road were deficient in number, most of them much too small, and none of them suitable for stretching-posts. I was therefore obliged, after nearly a month's delay at Kum, when the poles at the *Chapar Khānah* might have been distributed, to carry all the stretching-posts required, and many of the ordinary ones, from the town, along the line as far as the boundary of the district of Tehran, a distance of forty-five miles."

Captain Smith had barely a sufficient number of mules for the carriage of wires, insulators and similar materials; yet had he to make his own arrangements, not only for the conveyance of poles, but for a supply of bread to the workmen. "In short," he wrote, "the Governor did almost nothing that I required, and I was only too thankful when left uninterrupted to do as best I could without his assistance."

[1] Posthouse.

On the 29th March arrived a Shahzadah, or Royal Prince, attached by the Persian Government to Captain Smith's division, to provide working parties and comply generally with the superintendent's requisitions. The Governor, in reporting the occurrence, took occasion to remark that his own connection with the telegraph had ceased, and that as he had presumed to allow the work to begin before the arrival of the specially-appointed officer, the Minister of Science had held him personally liable for all expenses incurred on its account.

Under the new *régime* matters could scarcely be said to have mended. After two days' delay, Captain Smith arranged with his Persian assistant that the men should be paid at the same rate and in the same manner as before. Work was then recommenced, but progress was slow, owing to the continued interruptions caused by want of money, want of bread, and want of poles. A Government letter was shown, giving fifty of the king's mules for the service of the telegraph. But only thirty were actually forthcoming; and of these, four were riding-mules for the use of muleteers, and out of the balance of twenty-six seldom more than twenty were available at a time. Twenty mules of the fifty were altogether mythical; for of them no account could be rendered. And with respect to two artillery carriages and eighteen horses, also reported at the disposal of the telegraph, their existence was not more real, for the service specified, than that of the twenty mules.

On the 5th April, the Persian agent, coming to the telegraph camp, reported he could no longer pay the workmen, and proposed to revert to the system of forced labour. The superintendent refused consent to such procedure; but the Prince said he could get no money from the Governor; there was no way to get unpaid work but by the use of the stick; and he could not prevent desertions.

Captain Smith explains his position in the following manner:—

"The officer to whom alone I could give my requisitions had himself no power to fulfil them, without applying to another who refused to give the necessary supplies; so that if I addressed myself to the Governor, he said he had nothing to do with me, and if to Abul Fath Mirza, the reply was that the Governor would give him nothing. The result was another stoppage of the work, and the breaking up of the working party which had been collected and partially instructed with great difficulty, and no resource was left me but an appeal to Tehran."

The appeal was made to her Majesty's Legation, whither Captain Smith at once repaired, riding in post to Tehran. He proposed that since the Persian Government required the attendance of one of their own officers in each telegraph division, the respective Governors of towns within his range of superintendence should be instructed to comply with his requisitions made through the native agent, and to have the workmen daily paid in his presence. After a delay of ten days the necessary orders were procured.

We resume the quotations:—

"The tedious work of collecting and drilling a new lot of workmen had again to be gone through. In this I received no assistance from the Persian officers. Notwithstanding repeated applications, not a single man was sent either by the Governor or Abul Fath Mirza, so that, at a distance of fourteen miles from the nearest town or village, we had to get our workmen as we best could ourselves. All my requisitions were neglected in the same way, although there was now no excuse to offer, of want of orders. The artillery horses and carriages remained, as a rule, in Kum, only occasionally bringing out a load of stretching-poles, and I could not obtain a single mule besides those belonging to the king, notwithstanding a special clause regarding them in the orders I had brought from Tehran. I applied repeatedly for tents for the workmen, but none were given, so that before we reached the inundation near Hauz-i-Sultan, they had to walk daily a distance to and from their work of eighteen miles. With a camp pitched near the work, and mules enough to supply it with bread and water, nearly half of each day would have been saved. . . . I never succeeded in getting more than thirty-five men . . . and from want of mules half of them had always to be employed in carrying poles."

Circumstances occurred to change the plan of operations. It had been intended to complete the line from Kum to Tehran; but it became necessary to stop about midway, and return to the former city, thence to work back to Kashan and Kohrud. Here again the old difficulties were revived; and the newly-appointed Governor of Kashan refused to lend any assistance whatever to the construction of the telegraph, as he had no orders from his Government. Moreover, in full accordance with the verbal asseveration of this functionary, when the working parties from Kum reached the Kashan boundary, none were there to replace them, and these being withdrawn, operations were suspended for six days. In this interval, orders appear to have been received from Tehran, and the Governor was in a position to comply with the requisitions of the British superintendent.

From the 2nd to the 10th June, some thirty-six miles had been completed in the new direction. A brief delay was caused by the intervention of the Muharam festival; but before the end of the month the boundary of

Nathenz had been reached, and the goodwill of the local authorities in that district enabled Captain Smith to join his line, through a long, rocky gorge, and in spite of physical obstacles unknown in the tracts he had lately quitted, to the line brought by his fellow-superintendent from Ispahan.

Returning to Hauz-i-Sultan, he laboured at completing the line thence to the capital; but as this part of his work has already been treated of in quotations from Major Champain's own report, we will take leave of Captain Smith with an extract from his concluding paragraph. He is speaking of the Persian agent in his camp, who had complained to him bitterly that his method of conducting business had "blighted his hopes of making what the Persians, by a quaint euphemism, call Mudākhil, or Income." Perhaps it would be better translated as "perquisites," for that is the generally-understood meaning of the word. "I had some difficulty in making him comprehend that Mudākhil in English went by a much harder name. From the highest official down to the meanest labourer, I found that all were actuated by the same principle. When they thought it possible to make Mudākhil, they were all activity, but when their income was interfered with by the system I adopted of seeing everything paid in my presence, and warning the villagers on no account to give 'presents' to anyone, they relapsed into their usual state of obstinate indifference."

The habit here spoken of has indeed become second nature. It appears to be engrained in the Persian child rather than generated by education. There is one doubt, however, of which it may be well to let the nation have the benefit. Englishmen, speaking of Persians, judge them mainly, though often unwittingly, by their conduct towards themselves, and it is highly probable that the Mudākhil principle is exercised more freely in dealings with Europeans than among co-religionists and fellow-countrymen.

Lieutenant St. John's report of setting up the line in his division is a plain, straightforward statement. He does not enlarge on his difficulties in detail, but cannot conceal that he had to contend with "delays, excuses and evasions;" and gives more than one instance where he himself, or an assistant, suffered from the mismanagement and spirit of peculation common to the native authorities. One working party refused to proceed with their duties, saying " that they were tired of the work," and " this appeared a good and sufficient reason to the Persians," who dismissed them.

He commenced operations at Chahgodak, fifteen miles from Bushahr, on the 16th March, but returned in a few days to Bushahr, at the desire of Colonel Stewart, who had arrived there with the cable from Gwadar. Then, before resuming the more inland progress of his line, left temporarily under charge of Mr. Inspector Daniell, he erected, with Sergeant Jameson's aid, a double line of wire from Bushahr to the landing-place of the cable, and connected Chahgodak, his original starting-point, with Bushahr. Owing to the passage of a tract of marshy ground called "Mashilah," in the neighbourhood of the latter place, the use of iron posts was considered a necessary precaution; but from the small number at his disposal, he could only place them over five miles, a space insufficient to include the whole extent of swamp.

Lieutenant St. John estimates that altogether, in his division, 350 miles of wire, or about 7,000 posts, in round numbers, were erected in five months and two days. Taking into consideration the numerous disadvantages under which he and his party had laboured; the frequent delays; the laziness, dulness, and dishonesty of those from whom he was forced to procure help; the great natural difficulties; and that the work had been carried on at the most unfavourable season of the year, the line had, in his opinion, been erected with a fair amount of solidity, and in a reasonable time. "In a few places," he adds, "improvements, suggested by our more perfect knowledge of the road, may be advisable, and I anticipate some trouble from the green poles, which have been, *faute de mieux*, put up on some parts of the line; but altogether I trust and believe that interruptions will not be more frequent in this division than elsewhere."

This officer's favourable mention of two or three of his Persian assistants forms a gratifying exception to the reports of his colleagues. One of them, whom we need not designate by name, displayed conspicuous energy and activity. The speedy completion of one part of the line was considered due "to his unwearied efforts." And a hope was expressed that his "services might be brought to the notice of the Government of his Majesty the Shah."[1] Lieutenant St. John acknowledges further having experienced the greatest politeness, and readiness to comply with requests, from the Wazir of Shiraz and Governor of Bushahr, and an "unvarying willingness" to carry out his requisitions "to the utmost of his ability" from

[1] The recommendation appears to have resulted ill. I learn that this unfortunate gentleman was turned out of the Persian service, receiving a severe bastinado, shortly after his return to Tehran! The pretext for such treatment was peculation, of which he was assuredly guilty, but not more so than the rest of those who were similarly tempted.

the Persian superintendent of telegraphs in the province of Fars.

The illness and departure of Mr. Man, the officer originally appointed to the fourth division, has already been mentioned. That gentleman died immediately after his return to England. No separate report of the division under his charge accompanied Major Champain's general letter to the Bombay Government; but the Director bore flattering testimony to the manner in which Mr. Hoeltzer had taken up and completed the work of the deceased superintendent.

Such, then, is the narrative of the construction of the new Persian line of telegraph, and setting up the first wire under Mr. Eastwick's convention, and in connection with the whole scheme of telegraphic communication with India, as approved by her Majesty's Government and eventually carried into execution by the officers employed. In reviewing the several reports submitted on the subject, we have shown that the Turco-Persian frontier between Baghdad and Karmanshah presented a political obstacle which, if not removed, might be wholly fatal to the use of the Persian telegraph as an alternative to the Indo-Ottoman lines to the Gulf. Prevention, it may be said, is better than cure; and the mischief should have been foreseen and obviated. But what better prevention could there be for the contingency, than a separate treaty for the Baghdad-Tehran line between the Persians and Turks themselves? And such a treaty had been formally agreed upon between the Sublime Porte and the Shah of Persia on the 28th November, 1863, about six months before the fiat went forth to sever the connection of the two lines effected by British officers: a fiat which was literally carried out.

Doubtless, the Porte was not well pleased that a Persian alternative line should partake of the profits of an Indo-Ottoman line of telegraph, constructed under agreement with her Majesty's Government; and the correspondence printed for Parliament shows that it had required some persuasion and much despatch writing to gain its acquiescence in the India Office views hereon. Ali Pasha, the Turkish Foreign Minister, had eventually, however, yielded to the urgency of the occasion, and consented to the British proposals put before him under conditions stated in a protocol signed by himself and Mr. Erskine, in the absence of the English Ambassador, Sir Henry Bulwer. Having already summarised the purport of this document, we shall now only refer to the 9th Article, which may be appropriately quoted *in extenso*:

"All the despatches addressed to, or coming from India, shall be equally divided between the line from Baghdad to Basrah on the one hand, and that of Khanikin on the other.

"To avoid all difficulty of execution, the application of this system of division shall be as follows:

"All despatches coming from India shall pass by the line from Khanikin. On the other hand, all those for India shall be sent by the line from Baghdad to Basrah."

The protocol was subsequently modified, at Sir Charles Wood's suggestion, to the extent of leaving messages to be forwarded indifferently from Baghdad, or *vice versâ* from Bushahr, by either Turkish or Persian line. And in little more than a month after signature, it was succeeded by the Turco-Persian Convention of 12 Articles, now summarised.

ARTICLE I. Persia promised extension of its lines of telegraph to a spot situated on the Ottoman frontiers;

and Turkey engaged to establish a branch from some point of its telegraph line between Scutari and Baghdad, to the same spot.[1]

ARTICLE II. Khanikin had been the point of junction mutually determined. Eventually, however, lines might be made to meet also at other points.

ARTICLE III. Regulated the transmission, without hindrance, of stated international despatches.

ARTICLE IV. Engaged to use the Morse apparatus and conform to the Convention of Brussels.

ARTICLE V. Classified despatches: 1st. Persian and Ottoman; 2ndly. Despatches of Foreign Governments.

ARTICLES VI. and VII. Regulated charges.

ARTICLE VIII. Divided " despatches leaving Europe by the Ottoman telegraph lines, addressed to countries of Asia situated beyond the Persian dominions, and those transmitted from these countries to the European continent, into two equal parts," of which one would pass by the lines of Khanikin and Persia, and the other by Baghdad and Basrah.

ARTICLE IX. Ruled that the telegraphic correspondence between the contracting states should be conducted in Turkish, Persian, French, and English.

ARTICLE X. Noted the value of certain currencies.

ARTICLE XI. Provided that the Convention be put in operation at the end of four months, and sooner if pos-

---

[1] I brought to the notice of the Bombay Government, in June 1867, that it would have been a far simpler matter at first to have joined Khanikin direct with Kifri, a station about 140 miles above Baghdad, than to have connected Baghdad itself with the main system. And even after the link to Baghdad had been completed, the continued inundations to which the country between Kifri and that city was subject made it a matter of importance to effect the double junction.

sible; continuing in force for ten years from day of exchange of ratifications.

ARTICLE XII. Provided for ratification within three months.

Article II. may well provoke a smile in its prospective arrangements, as may the two last articles, for the confident manner in which they notify the conclusion of a satisfactory agreement. We have just shown that six months after date the lines could not, from political reasons, be joined at *any one point*, and that not only the Turco-Persian, but the Anglo-Persian arrangements for telegraphic communication ran a risk of serious obstructions because there was no acknowledged line of frontier at all. As regards Article VIII. the Ottoman Government must have either forgotten, or held of minor importance, the division of messages therein expressed. For a reference to the Indo-Ottoman Convention, of which a summary is given in our second chapter, will show that according to its Article XIV. messages to or from India were to be forwarded *viâ* Basrah or Khanikin, "according to convenience of service," nothing being said at all of one route for India-going messages, and another for those received from the Indian cable.

That the difficulties were removed, and the line eventually opened to a short-lived traffic, at one time spasmodic, at another desultory, will be shown in the next chapter. Let us glance again for a moment at the purely Turkish lines, or those intended to work direct, and without Persian intervention, with the Gulf cable of British India.

We took leave of the working parties below Baghdad in November 1863. On the 18th of that month Colonel

Kemball reported his proceedings in anticipation of orders afterwards received, and on an understanding between himself and Namik Pasha. Mr. Inspector Joyce Perceval, with whom was associated Yuzbashi Omar Faizi Efendi, had commenced the first section to Hilleh. Particular duties were assigned to Mr. Carthew, Mr. Greener, and the non-commissioned officers from Persia; and the political agent proposed proceeding himself to the quarter "where alone any serious difficulties might be apprehended," accompanied by a duly authorized Turkish officer.[1]

Mr. Joyce Perceval had experienced some trouble in reaching his destination. He had followed the Damascus route, through the Syrian desert to Baghdad, and in reporting his arrival at the latter city he described how he had been robbed by the Bedouins of his property, and even stripped of personal clothing save "shoes, drawers, flannel shirt, and Turkish cap." As regards his after dealings with the Arabs he has himself published an account, placing on record useful data connected with his professional work.[2]

The distribution of material arriving from Liverpool was a matter, in some cases, of considerable embarrassment. Disturbances arose among the Arab tribes whereby the stores were wantonly subjected to loss, detention, and injury; but the lives of those engaged in distributing them, as in the work of construction generally, were exposed to serious risk. Had such a state of things been exceptional the contingency might have been met by provisional measures; but continuous as well as

[1] Col. Kemball to H.E. the Right Hon. Sir H. L. Bulwer, G.C.B., H.M. Ambassador at Constantinople.

[2] *Leisure Hour*; also *Telegraphic Journal*, September 1863.

stringent precautions became imperative, owing to the certainty, or at least extreme likelihood, of repeated agitation. Thus, for a time, action was necessarily suspended; and the great heats of summer had supervened before operations could be fairly resumed. The interval was, however, turned to good account in establishing telegraph stations and otherwise maturing preparations for the contemplated through traffic; and on the return of autumn, so soon as order had been sufficiently restored, the working parties were again in the field, and eventually, from a point near Kurna, where the two great rivers meet, a telegram despatched to England on one side and Bombay on the other, announced completion of the line.

This was on the 27th January, 1865. An important period had undoubtedly been reached in the annals of the Indo-European telegraph, and an important event announced to the world at large. But let us examine why the twofold telegram could not be said to sound a note of practical completion of the work contemplated. When the year 1864 came to a close, the cable had been brought successfully from the Indian side to the mouth of the Basrah river, and was in good working order from Karāchi to Fāo. The Persian land-line had been completed from Baghdad to Bushahr. Colonel Stewart, prostrated by severe sickness, was at Constantinople, in daily expectation of hearing that Baghdad had joined the Persian lines on one side, and Basrah on the other. The new year had but just commenced, when Patrick Stewart sank under his attack. Before the month of January had passed away, or in the early days of February, a few messages had struggled through the lines from India to Europe; notably one from the Duke of Brabant, then an illustrious traveller in the East. But there was no decisive success achieved wherewith to signalize the particular period. So long as five days was considered a respectable time for Calcutta to communicate with London, and that few messages traversed the distance so speedily as this, so long was it necessary to suspend the shout of victory or cheer of congratulation. Telegrams brought good news from below Baghdad, and brilliant promises from Persia, but hitches would occur somewhere, and the line was too long and the working of too novel and promiscuous a character for speedy repairs and corrections. In fine, the opening of communications was comparatively lame and unattended with *éclat*, and the science and energy which were available to make light of physical hindrance, were sorely taxed in dealing with national jealousies and the caprice of individuals.

TOMB OF ESTHER AND MORDECAI AT HAMADAN, WESTERN PERSIA.

CHAPTER V.

POLITICAL AND OTHER DIFFICULTIES IN THE INDO-PERSIAN AND INDO-OTTOMAN TELEGRAPHS.—CONVENTION WITH PERSIA OF 23RD NOVEMBER, 1865, FOR SECOND WIRE. —SECOND CONVENTION PROPOSED, IN FOLLOWING YEAR, FOR EXTENDING LAND TELEGRAPH, AND PROVIDING AN ALTERNATIVE LINE TO THE CABLE BETWEEN GWADAR AND BUSHAHR; PUT ASIDE IN THE SPRING, BUT REVIVED IN THE WINTER OF 1867, AND CONCLUDED IN GREATLY MODIFIED FORM IN 1869.—DIPLOMATIC ACTION THEREON.—FULFILMENT OF CONVENTION OF 1865.—REPORTS OF OFFICERS CONCERNED.

At the period of Colonel Stewart's demise, Major Champain was at Tehran, doing his utmost to turn the lines under his charge to immediate account. But the task was of no common difficulty. He had reported completion of the line from Baghdad to Bushahr on the 13th October, 1864, and that it would " in all probability be open to the public in a few days." On the 31st of the same month it became his duty to explain that very unsatisfactory relations existed with the local authorities; and until matters were mended in this respect it would be impossible for the British officers to remain at their posts in Persia. The following statement will require no comment in illustration of the position:—Tehran must be looked upon as an apex from which two lines of telegraph are drawn to the southward and westward respectively. When the first and longer line to Bushahr was inaugurated at the end of September, by some inadvertence a land-line instrument had not been made over to that station, so that messages had to be forwarded thence to Shiraz direct from the cable office. Accordingly, the needed article was supplied by Major Champain's orders a few days later; but the Persian clerks were not sufficiently expert to be trusted with its working. The Minister of Public Works at Tehran, hearing of these arrangements, sent instructions to a Persian clerk at Shiraz to prevent the English from talking with Bushahr by disconnecting their instrument; and these instructions were arbitrarily carried out under protest of the English Inspector. Major Champain was made acquainted with the circumstances, and appealed to the Persian officials concerned, urging that unless orders of the kind were communicated through him, or at least with his cognizance, his authority would become invalidated, to the detriment of the public service. From this action resulted a further order to cut the wire, and the execution of that order. The Director then considered he had no course open but to remove his instruments from Shiraz and Ispahan, and disconnect those at Tehran; and, having so proceeded, laid his case before her Majesty's minister. The complaint was rendered graver still by the conduct of the Persian authorities at Ispahan, where they had attempted forcible seizure of the instruments, and where the English superintendent had forbidden those of his countrymen under his orders to enter the city or Persian Telegraph Office.

It was only on the 7th December that Major Champain was enabled to report a better state of things, and the probability of soon re-opening communication between Baghdad and Bushahr. The Persian Government had agreed to give the English staff control of the telegraph offices, and working the line for five months from the date of renewing correspondence with India. The Minister of Public Works was to be acknowledged head of all telegraphs in Persia; but would issue no orders on the lines from Tehran to Khanikin or Bushahr, without the cognizance and consent of the British Director, whose suggestions should be carefully respected. After five months the English were to leave the country, making over the entire line to the Persians; but it was proposed to retain one Engineer officer and two assistants at Tehran, in a consultative capacity, for a further period of ten months. A formal and satisfactory apology had been offered for the behaviour of the Governor's retainers at Ispahan. These were the salient points of the statement submitted to the Bombay Government. The question of rates, though discussed in the same letter, has too little interest in its minutiæ to be here considered. Suffice it to mention that the result was expressed in a subsequent communication of the 13th December, reporting the determination of a fourteen-shilling tariff for a through message by Persia. But this last-noted letter gave official currency to a disheartening rumour, proved since to be too true, that "great damage had been done to the wire between Shiraz and the sea;" consequently that some fifteen or twenty days might elapse before communication could be renewed with India. With regard to the Turkish frontier, Major Champain understood that "the Shah had consented to the demands of the Porte," and believed that reply to a despatch forwarded some weeks before to Constantinople was only waited "to join up the wire near Khanikin and open throughout."

The facts were these. Colonel Kemball, the British Resident and Consul-General at Baghdad, after proposing every possible combination that seemed likely to reconcile or allay conflicting claims, hit upon the happy expedient of turning to account the telegraph poles used by the litigants respectively, to represent the national interests involved: that is to say, as the Turks used iron, and the Persians wooden posts for their respective lines, it was considered that alternate iron and wooden posts over the disputed tract would illustrate a mutual understanding, or perhaps rather the recognition of a misunderstanding, in a manner at once politically safe and socially unobjectionable. This arrangement, fortified by the inevitable exchange of *statu quo* declarations, was finally accepted by both parties, and is believed to be in force at the present day.

On the 20th January, 1865, Major Champain wrote from Tehran,[1] little knowing that his report of progress would no longer interest him to whom they were usually addressed, giving a more cheery account of his charge. "We are now open," he said, "and working with Karmanshah since the 24th December (to say nothing of one break, which was mended in a day); with Ispahan since the 2nd of January, and now, again, with Shiraz. The line is all right to Baghdad, but the Turks refuse to receive our messages."

His account of the interruption beyond Shiraz made

[1] To Col. Patrick Stewart, the news of whose death, on the 16th January, did not reach him there until the 24th idem.

it a very serious matter; and so, indeed, it was. But the case may now be stated by the light of after inquiry and corroboration.

When the wires were authoritatively cut between Shiraz and the sea-coast, the British cable office at Bushahr was debarred communication with the interior; and before traffic was resumed very severe damage had been done to the *matériel* by villagers, travellers, and especially Iliats, or nomads, migrating from their hilly summer quarters to the lower and warmer seaboard. Lieut. St. John, about the time of the Tehran difficulty, had been driven to sea by a severe attack of fever; and on return to Shiraz in December, verified the extent of mischief, and found that for twenty miles along the tract taken by the Iliats from the capital of Fars to the Kothal Dukhtar the line had been almost totally destroyed. The long spans, which had cost so much time and labour to erect, had been cut down; out of 600 consecutive insulators only twenty remained unbroken; and the wire was severed in pieces and lying on the ground, or confusedly festooned round the poles, many of which had been used for firewood. Fortunately Lieut. St. John was enabled to trace one main offender, whose position as a clan chief of the powerful Kashkai tribe made his punishment politically important. He had caused the fall of the large span across the Kothal Pir Zan, by smashing a lower supporting insulator with a bullet from his gun. By this time affairs had been amicably settled in Tehran, and the Persians generally were desirous to see the new telegraph working in their country, so that the reports of occurrences on the Shiraz-Bushahr line were doubly distasteful and untimely. To repair the harm done, a month was estimated necessary.

Mr. Alison represented the case to the Shah, who was pleased to issue stringent orders for the seizure and punishment of the culprits. Mirza Jiafar Khan, second in rank among Persian telegraph magnates, was ordered to proceed at once by *chapar* to Shiraz, with a royal executioner, to cut off any heads Lieut. St. John might indicate. Ali Khan Beg, the offending Kashkai chief, was to be sent in chains to Tehran, and a fine of a thousand tomans (400*l.*) was to be levied from the Ilkhāni, or head of the nomad tribes—a chief sufficiently powerful in Southern Persia to boast he can bring into the field in ten days a force of 20,000 horse and 30,000 foot. This programme was carried out with an approach to completeness rare in Oriental states. The Sarhang, minus, however, the executioner, posted down to Shiraz, found and seized Ali Khan Beg, whose existence was at first positively denied by the Governor of Shiraz, squeezed the prescribed fine from the Ilkhāni, plus a second thousand for his chief in Tehran, and 500 tomans for himself, and plundered the village of Dastiarjan, where he had been insulted by the villagers. But whatever the actual details by which the movement was followed, the spirit of the king's message was unmistakeable. The royal anger was aroused and made itself felt; and the despatch of a special envoy with full instructions and power to act, together with the decisive action resulting from his mission, changed the state of affairs as regards the telegraph from danger to security.[1] As to the *contretemps* by which the

[1] Major St. John, to whom I am indebted for this correction of official reports, written necessarily on imperfect information, states that during the nine years that have elapsed from the period in question, less wilful damage has been done to the telegraph in Fars, the most turbulent province of Persia, than in any other part of the line. He adds that Ali Khan Beg, after remaining

Baghdad line, though complete, was rendered inoperative, her Majesty's Minister despatched one of the Second Secretaries of Legation to make the necessary inquiry and report, and endeavour to arrange matters.

These particulars form the subject of an official communication of two days later date, addressed to the Government of Bombay. The despatch concluded with the statement that on the 21st of January the Shah had paid a visit of some two hours' duration to the telegraph office, conversing there, through the wires, with the Governors of Shiraz, Ispahan, Kashan, Kum, Hamadan and Karmanshah. "His Majesty," it was observed, "was very much pleased with the arrangements, and is impatient to be able to communicate with Europe and India."[1]

Subsequent correspondence tends to prove that the mischief done between Shiraz and Bushahr was too great, and the interest expressed by Persian officials in atoning for it much too artificial, for speedy restoration of through communication. Before the arrival on the scene of disaster of the telegraph Sarhang above-mentioned, the damage done to the wire, on the first burst of violence, had been nearly doubled. The chief of Chahkutah, a village twenty miles from Bushahr, destroyed the line up to five miles from that town; and in other places much additional mischief was wrought. Spans of exceptionally great length had been cut down, and the labour of setting up the wires over very difficult

in durance vile for two months, was at his (St. John's) request excused a journey to Tehran which might have had most disagreeable results, and set at liberty—an act of policy which has had the happy effect of securing the friendship of the Kashkai chiefs to the English Telegraph officers.

[1] Major Champain to Secretary to Government, Bombay. No. 153 of January 22, 1865.

ground had to be repeated. To say the least, such work was disheartening, for there was no sufficient guarantee of its permanence. It was a question of time; and on the 20th of February, when Major Champain reported that, owing to his nomination from the Secretary of State to perform the late Colonel Stewart's duties in the telegraph, he was about leaving Tehran for Constantinople, the Persian line was only working well between Shiraz and Baghdad. Below Shiraz, communication had not been fully restored.

Captain Murdoch Smith, R.E., assumed charge of the Anglo-Persian telegraph on Major Champain's departure. Although ripened acquaintance with the character of the people among whom he was thrown scarcely warranted the belief that his official duties would be plain sailing, the new Director undertook them with a strong wish as well as natural power to conciliate; and had already proved himself in his Persian career well deserving the "perfect confidence" reposed in him by his predecessor. There is no doubt, however, that the year's experience gained by our officers in Persia, and by the Persians of our officers, had been productive of good; and had not the general behaviour of the non-commissioned officers and men from Chatham been of an exemplary kind, operations could never have continued with such comparative smoothness for so long a period in the mere matter of individual complaints. The second year of employment of a British telegraph staff in Persia had much of brightness and good augury in its dawn. The Shah had evinced his personal interest in the cause they represented; the Governors of provinces had shown a liking for, as well as courtesy towards the officers with whom they had become acquainted; and one or more of the most rigid and influential opponents of the original scheme actually expressed anxiety for the prolongation of English superintendence.

The line between Shiraz and the sea was again put into working order, and the Persian alternative lines were at last fairly turned to account. But on the Turco-Persian frontier all arrangements had the semblance of political patching, of compromise, of temporary expedients. Actual honest work was clearly at a discount. Major Champain reached Baghdad on the 5th March, having carefully scrutinised the line defects apparent on the road, and sending a through message to India from the Persian frontier post of Kasr-i-Shirin. The Karmanshah office he had found in good order, and signals were constantly received there from Khanikin on the Turkish side; but Khanikin would or could make nothing of the Persian replies.

"I therefore set out," he tells Mr. Alison, "and, with Corporal Whittingbacke and a small instrument, marched leisurely along the line as far as Kasr-i-Shirin. There I made up a weak battery of seven cells, and found, as I anticipated, that I could talk well both with Karmanshah, 110 miles in my rear, and with Khanikin, 20 miles to my front. There was then nothing to do but to ride at once to the latter office. I galloped on as hard as I could go, and walked straight into the room. No one was there. Presently, however, in walked a listless Turkish signaller, and told me that the head of the office was in the 'Hamām.' When he heard who I was, he was very civil, and went to call his chief. I asked him if he could get Karmanshah, and he said "No!" I replied that was absurd, as I had just been working well with all Persia from this side of Kasr-i-Shirin. I met Whittingbacke, set to work, and by adjusting the magnets of the relay got Karmanshah in no time. When S. appeared, I asked for permission to take his apparatus to pieces and examine it, but proposed doing so late in the evening, so as not to interfere with traffic. He was evidently a little reluctant, and talked about his having been twenty years in the service, and being sure that no fault lay in his office. However, at 8 P.M. I went back, and before the Kaim Makam and the other Turkish officials, Whittingbacke and I took the whole thing to pieces and cleaned the various screws, &c., then found that the instrument worked well with Baghdad, the Persian offices at that hour being closed. I could find no fault, and it was useless my staying at the place. I allow that the Turkish officials seemed most anxious to open communication, but it is very strange that when once an Englishman is there the line works well, and directly our backs are turned all goes wrong. . . . I came into Baghdad, and found that the thing had broken again."

The case was stated to Namik Pasha, who directed Monsieur Oudit, a French inspector in the Turkish service, to proceed to Khanikin without delay. He was to test the iron posts in case the defects were not discovered in the office, regulating future proceedings by the result of his inspection. A European sergeant would also take a battery and instrument to Kasr-i-Shirin, there to open a testing office, so as to determine at once whether the fault was in Persia or Turkey.

That the line was open on the 12th March, by the Persian as Indo-Ottoman lines, is clear from Major Champain's Baghdad telegram of that date to Captain Smith at Tehran, notifying the willingness of the Turkish Telegraph Administration to send half the Indian messages by the Persian route, but their complaint at the same time of the slow working, and impossibility to communicate direct with Bushahr. The number of messages was reported to be very great. But as Major Champain was at this time only passing through Baghdad *en route* to Constantinople, we will change the scene to the latter city, and see what was the condition of the telegraph there on that officer's arrival. It was the 12th April when he came to Misseri's Hotel, somewhat ailing and very sunburnt, after sixteen days' hard posting over 1,400 miles to Samsun; from which port to the Golden Horn a three days' passage in the Austrian steamer was a pleasant relief.

Colonel Goldsmid, of the Madras Staff Corps, was, it has been shown, at Constantinople at the period of Colonel Stewart's fatal illness. Although his presence there, in the previous August, had been in immediate connection with the work of the telegraph, and consequent on his inspection of the Turkish-Asiatic lines between Baghdad and Izmid, his official associations with the young Chief Director had virtually ceased before the close of the year. He had proceeded home with the Telegraph Treaty in September, but was suddenly sent out again with a view of continuing his journey from Constantinople to Tehran. At Constantinople, the particular news which had caused his deputation being found erroneous, he was further delayed under orders from England; and eventually he received new instructions for a special service. It was while preparing to start for Poti by the Russian steamer, that his friend's serious illness caused him to hesitate in his movements, and to defer embarkation from week to week. Colonel Stewart died on the 16th January, under circumstances already stated. After making certain necessary arrangements and reports consequent on this sad event, Colonel Goldsmid was again about proceeding on his distinct duties, when the receipt of new instructions kept him yet longer in European Turkey. These were afterwards supplemented by authority to consummate, so far as practicable, what had been contemplated by Colonel Stewart relative to telegraphic requirements in the Ottoman dominions. On the 25th January a telegram from Colonel Kemball announced that completion of the Baghdad-Basrah line was expected on the day following; but that the Persian line showed signs of breakage. This intelligence was despatched at once by the wires from Constantinople towards London. But the lines connecting the Turkish capital with the capitals of northern and western Europe were so untrustworthy that it was hard to say when a Sublime Porte message would reach Downing Street. In fact, at the period of his illness and demise, Colonel Stewart was seeking to impress upon the Ottoman authorities that two great desiderata for securing efficiency in the Indo-European telegraph were: 1st, the establishment of two special wires for the service in Europe and Turkey; and 2nd, the instruction of *employés* on the European-Turkish lines, who were better acquainted with the English tongue than those then entertained. And as for the lines in Asiatic Turkey, even when completed, if a telegram reached Constantinople in five days from Karáchi, the fact was considered something of a feat. This, too, as late as the 10th February, very shortly after which date interruptions were reported on the last finished section, or that between Baghdad, Basrah, and the sea.

It may be interesting, in these days of rapid telegraphic communications east and west; when a girdle of electricity may, without any exaggeration, be put around the earth in " forty minutes," and Puck's boast to Oberon thus become a matter of easy fulfilment by mortals;

it may be interesting to revert to the first working of the wires between Turkey and India. The results of the months of February and March are shown to be as follows; but it must be borne in mind that the line was not fairly open during a greater part of the former month:—

In February: 10 messages were despatched from Constantinople to Karáchi, whereof the average time in transit was two days and eleven hours, the longest time taken being seven days and the shortest six hours. On the other hand, 52 were received from Karáchi, whereof the average time in transit was eight hours and twenty minutes, the longest time being fifteen days and four hours, and the shortest five hours.

In March: 324 messages were despatched from Constantinople, whereof the average time in transit was two hours and four minutes, the longest time taken being six days, and the shortest six hours. From Karáchi 262 telegrams were received in an average time of two days and eight hours, the longest time being six days and an hour, and the shortest six hours. Perhaps the most cheering sign of improvement was that, of the total of the above messages, 22 reached Karáchi and 30 Constantinople within twelve hours, and 41 and 61 the same places respectively within twenty-four hours.

This account, it will be observed, makes no allowance for the time taken up between London and Constantinople, which was usually considerable.

Mr. Courtenay, the zealous and experienced officer who, with the title of "Commissioner for the Government Indo-European Telegraph," was settled in Pera for purposes of international account and general reference; and which presence was equally useful in departmental relations with the Ottoman Administration and in supplying data or any technical information to her Majesty's Embassy; gave Colonel Goldsmid the benefit of his personal knowledge of details, and association with his Ottoman colleagues, in replying to a series of written questions on the precise condition of the several Turkish lines in respect of material and *personnel*. Although the information contained in these replies was mostly known to the questioner from verbal inquiries, its embodiment in a record rendered it a useful groundwork for decisive action. It gave the Commissioner's statement of routes available in Europe and Asia, the number and description of wires on each, the insulators used or proposed for use, the mode in which the stations were manned, the system of inspection, and his opinion on the best routes and usual causes of interruption in communications. As to the report on the Asiatic lines, officially submitted by Colonel Goldsmid in the previous year, Mr. Courtenay was able to say that copies of the proposals accompanying it had been "furnished to each inspector" for guidance as far as his districts were concerned, "with instructions to report thereon, to carry on the minor recommendations at once, and to leave the larger alterations till the summer."¹

Early in March Colonel Goldsmid prepared and submitted a memorandum on the failures in working the lines, and means of preventing them in future; and was placed by her Majesty's *chargé d'affaires* in communication with an Armenian gentleman of ability, one of the secretaries of the Foreign Minister, Ali Pasha. The case was referred from the Foreign to the Telegraph

¹ Mr. Courtenay to Colonel Goldsmid, March 4, 1865.

Department, which sent in its replies; and a *précis* of the whole was promised for the consideration and orders of the Minister himself. At all events, the Secretary assured Colonel Goldsmid some days afterwards that he had spoken upon the subject to his Highness, who wished existing arrangements to hold good until a new line, sanctioned by the Porte for traffic to western Europe and more especially for Indo-European messages, had been constructed and tried. In the midst of much disappointment and vexation it was something satisfactory to find that on the 24th March a telegram reached Scutari from Bombay in something like seven hours. Flashes of really good working were now occasional.

The Armenian Secretary having been called to London on the perpetually recurring question of Ottoman finance, the official control of foreign telegraph arrangements, under the Minister, became vested in the "Mustashir," a Turkish authority of considerable influence. But although more influential than his Christian colleague, who was rather a "*Chef de correspondance*" than a responsible adviser, the capacity for business was clearly on the side of the latter, who was a thorough adept in the ways and workings of the *bureaux* of western Europe. In either case it was pleasant to deal with men untrammelled by any departmental *etiquette* in respect of telegraphy; and to whose office the Director-General for the time being was necessarily subordinate in all questions of international discussion. At the particular season referred to, the same chance which took from his post at head-quarters the Foreign Under-Secretary, Abru Efendi, had removed temporarily Agathon Efendi, the very courteous, intelligent, and obliging head of the Ottoman telegraphs, whose duties had devolved upon a Turkish assistant, Faizi Bey. An extract from one of many appeals to the officials concerned will not be inappropriate, and will serve at the same time to show some of the subjects which had been on the *tapis* in the view of improving communications. It was a kind of *dernier ressort* resulting from a disheartening visit to the Pera telegraph office on the 30th March.

"Vous nous feriez un grand service avant votre départ d'adresser instamment quelques mots de conseil au Bureau de l'Administration des Télégraphes, au sujet des délais qui conviennent de jour en jour dans les correspondances Indo-Européennes. J'ai appris hier que quatre-vingt-six dépêches arrivées du côté de l'Europe, ne purent être expédiées aux Indes; et que soixante dépêches arrivées des Indes à Diarbekir, ne purent être reçues à Constantinople, à cause de l'occupation de la ligne par la correspondance locale. Selon l'Article VI. de la Convention, on doit nous donner un fil spécial affecté au seul service Indo-Européen en Asie. Il y a deux fils de Scutari à Baghdad, et on ajoute, à ce qu'on nous dit, un troisième fil jusqu'à Diarbekir. Cependant, quand il arrive un mélange, on fait attendre notre correspondance pour quelques heures: on ne trouve pas où est la faute; et en attendant qu'elle soit découverte et réparée, on ne fonctionne qu'avec un seul fil, quoiqu'il existe un second. Du moins doit on désigner un fil pour notre service en Asie. J'entendais qu'on avait arrangé de nous spécialiser le fil supérieur jusqu' à ce que le second fil fût mis dans une isolation plus parfaite. Et quant à ces mélanges, permettez que j'observe que le manque d'un nombre suffisant d'inspecteurs est cause non seulement que ces fautes ne se découvrent point pour des semaines entières, mais que quand même on les découvre, elles ne sont pas réparées à l'instant."

The permanent appointment of a successor to the late

Colonel Stewart had been referred for disposal to the Government of India. Meanwhile Major Champain was holding temporary charge of the whole Indo-European line, so far as the control or responsibility of the British Government was concerned; and his arrival at Constantinople has been mentioned. After a stay of three days in that city, during which the state of affairs was then discussed with Colonel Goldsmid, Major Champain continued his journey to London, reaching it by the Danube route on the 20th April, or within a month after quitting Baghdad, inclusive of halts. A month later Colonel Goldsmid was on his way home in obedience to a telegraphic summons from the Secretary of State. He had been appointed, in general orders by the Government of India, to the chief direction of the Government Indo-European telegraphs, and would be required, if taking up the appointment, to proceed almost immediately to Persia, to assist her Majesty's Minister in Tehran in carrying out a more full and particular convention than that then in force. The following extracts of an official report [1] written by this officer a few days before leaving Constantinople will explain how slowly the work had progressed in Turkey at that particular time, for the more than three months since the line had opened:—

"The imperial 'Iradeh' for the new special line to Nissa, has some days since been issued, and one of the clerks to be employed in the Turkish offices has arrived from England. But I regret much to state that the manner in which the correspondence is conducted throughout the Turkish dominions, especially in Asia, is far from satisfactory. Delays are frequent; despatches

[1] Dated May 11, 1865, to the Under-Secretary of State for India.

are irregularly transmitted; and though promises are profuse, I do not find that the improvement which we had a right to expect from two months' practice has become manifest. I hear it urged that one of the drawbacks to present efficiency is the absence in England of Agathon Efendi, the Director-General, but the excuse appears to me far from valid or sufficient.

'I have called . . attention . . to the apparent neglect of orders on the part of the Ottoman *employés* in Asia, whether as regards fulfilment of the provisions in the Brussels Convention, or the ordinary duties of the service. The time taken up in transmission, irregularity in mode of despatch, the indifferent orthography of the telegrams—all these subjects have been more or less dwelt on in my letter to the acting Director General. Allusion has also been made to his own verbally expressed intentions to increase the *personnel* of the Asiatic line, and his admission to myself that the Indian work is greater than he had expected. I have, moreover, urged the necessity of keeping pace in Asia with the improvements about to be introduced into European telegraphic correspondence under the late Paris Convention, such as direct communication, by large wires, with principal towns like Baghdad; and have again warned him of probable diminution of traffic owing to the defects of the service.

'At the same time I cannot disclaim the hopes expressed at the conclusion of my letter of the 5th ult. Doubtless very great delays occur in India, nay, in Europe out of Turkish territory, which are erroneously attributed to the Ottoman Administration. Indeed there are data to establish the truth of this supposition; and I therefore feel reluctant without further information to press too closely the question of delay in the more recent telegrams. Perhaps the surest and safest way to obtain a satisfactorily working line would be to supplement the present convention with certain clauses admitting a joint control, on our part at least, on the Asiatic side; and having Anglo-Turkish stations such as Fáo . . at Baghdad, Diarbekir and Sivas, or Angora. With these new *personnels*, might be associated one or two qualified inspectors. We require in Asia a staff of men working in a different spirit from ordinary Oriental *employés*, and evincing active interest and zeal at all times as well as for particular occasions. There is no doubt that such a proposal would not be entertained without the use of many and plausible arguments for a contrary course, and I should not feel warranted in suggesting it here without special orders. Under any circumstances, however, the first and most natural proceeding would be to submit to the Ottoman Government the complaints which now present themselves; and on bringing the subject of the enclosed letter to the acting Director General of Ottoman Telegraphs to the consideration of the higher authorities at the Porte, I shall be simply continuing the line of conduct authorized by the original instructions of the Right Hon. the Secretary of State."

With the letter above quoted was submitted the draft of a communication addressed in the French language to the Turkish official alluded to; and an original letter from Mr. Courtenay supplying certain data from the records of his department. Among the anomalies exhibited in the Commissioner's analysis of work done, the following are not the least curious:—

I. On the 23rd February, Constantinople received a Karāchi message of the 8th, three of the 9th, and two of the 13th idem; and on the 24th February, thirteen messages of the 9th, two of the 10th, three of the 11th, and two of the 13th. Again on the 25th February arrived an ill-starred message of the 10th. As Mr. Courtenay naturally asks: Why were the messages of the 13th received here before those of the 9th, 10th, and 11th; and where was the message of the 10th, received on the 25th, all this time?

II. Several Karāchi telegrams of the 28th February reached Constantinople on the 3rd March, whereas several of the 1st March reached on the 2nd idem.

III. Of the messages sent from Constantinople on the 5th March, some reached Karachi *viâ* Fao in 31, and some in 136 hours!

Yet with all this irregularity and uncertainty, the traffic returns of April had been financially promising. Some 2,180 messages had been exchanged against 1,447 of the previous month, the main increase being in the telegrams *to* India from Europe.

Any detailed account of negotiations such as these, or of the financial and promiscuous kind with which Pera is especially familiar, can have no great public interest. A whole winter and a month or so of summer, autumn, and spring—making, inclusive of breaks, a more than six months' residence there in the years 1864–65, chiefly at Misseri's Hotel, but partly on the Bosphorus—would not be unpleasant under certain circumstances. But regarded in an official point of view, the retrospect is not sufficiently bright to dwell upon in a narrative of early telegraph operations. The history would be rather that of an inner individual existence than of an agent of progress, and would tell more of anxiety and doubt, of hope and disappointment, than of practical measures and ready execution, or of combination and co-operation of two Administrations to accomplish a mutually desirable end. And for these reasons the record may reasonably pass away like the smoke of the many cigarettes which invariably open, prolong, and conclude every sort of mixed *meilis* at the Sublime Porte.

When Colonel Goldsmid, some five weeks after his return home from Turkey, left London in June 1865 for Persia, Major Champain remained in England on duty, receiving such references as were intended for the Chief

Director, and where practicable, disposing of them. The great length of the Indo-European line, the number of Administrations concerned in its working, and the necessity of giving as much attention to the European section, which was in foreign hands, as to the Asiatic lines, which were partly those of the British Government, partly those of the contracting States, gave more than the colour of expediency to such a measure; rather did it seem an essential to successful organization at the commencement of proceedings. Thus it became the practice, during the early years of this telegraph, that while the Chief Director's duties called him to Persia or India, his assistant should remain at the European end of the line, and *vice versâ*: and in reviewing the results of this arrangement, which met with the sanction of the Home Government, it cannot be considered other than sound and judicious. On his return from Tehran and Baghdad in April, Major Champain had availed himself of the opportunity to place the fruits of his Persian experience personally before the Secretary of State and India Office Committee of Public Works and Telegraphs; and a Draft Treaty on a basis sketched out by Colonel Stewart, and referred to his assistant at Tehran shortly before his death, was in readiness for the new Chief Director to take out to Mr. Alison, a very few days after his arrival.

At St. Petersburg, Colonel Goldsmid placed on record his views and impressions on the question of tariffs, in the event of competition. However willing the Turks had been to meet the wishes of her Majesty's Government in securing telegraphic communication with India, they had failed to render it so speedy and effective as to merit the confidence of the public. A four months' experience was not without value in forming a judgment on the shortcomings of the line. The frequent complaints of irregularity and delay which had been made by persons using the wires had been formally brought to the notice of the Ottoman Administration. Remedies had been proposed, such as increased establishment, improved inspection, and the like; and there was reason to believe that some had, at least, been applied. Still was it apprehended that a public, free to use its own means of communication, would avail itself readily of an alternative to the Ottoman line, or any part of it, should one offer of a more reliable and less costly nature.

The Russian lines of the Caucasus having been extended to Julfa on the Araxes, or Persian frontier, and the Persian line completed from Julfa to Tehran, it was clear that telegraphic communications between England and India, *viâ* St. Petersburg and Persia, might be carried out at once quite independently of the Ottoman lines. It was only a few days before, that one of the telegraph companies had transferred its whole messages to this route; and although circumstances had induced a speedy return to the original way, such an occurrence was of itself sufficient to point out the danger incurred by inattention to remedy the defects of the Ottoman telegraph in a reasonable time. Inefficient as the staff of the Russian lines might be found for the Indian service, it was clear that, under pressure, a very short period would suffice to supply the want, as also to turn to account the Persian line from Julfa to Tehran.

Supposing even the two lines working equally well, and to be equally worthy the confidence of the public, the tariff of the Russo-Persian line was so much lower than that acknowledged in Turkey that fair competition would be quite out of the question. Here was a difficulty which could only be met by an understanding with Russia. Should it be proposed to utilize her lines effectually for Indian communications, increased outlay would demand, no doubt, a revision of tariff. Otherwise it could scarcely be held a reasonable request that she should raise her charges to suit the Ottoman rates. The regulation of such a tariff might however be proposed as would enable the Turks, if necessary, to reduce their own charges; and not only so, but to remove the anomaly of a double rate of messages which Persia had adopted with reference to Russia and England respectively.[1]

Finally, a communication might be addressed to the Ottoman Government on the subject, pointing out that their own interests as well as those of the public were concerned in the reconsideration of rates and belief in possible competition; and that any arrangements made with the Russian Government, with reference to telegraphic communications to and from India through Russian territory, must be understood with intent to regulate, on a clear basis, the question of through rates by that line, and not in any way to draw off the traffic from the Turkish route, should that route succeed in giving satisfaction to the public.

Much to this effect was put into writing and despatched for consideration of the home authorities. And though action may not have been taken upon the suggestions conveyed, it would have been blindness on the writer's part to have ignored, as it would have been culpable to conceal, a state of things the bearing of which

---

[1] Russia, by Convention with Persia, had fixed a certain tariff on *all messages* passing between her frontier and Bushahr. England, by a separate Convention, had laid down a tariff equally high, or higher, for about two-thirds of the same distance.

on the prospective interests of Indo-European telegraphy was so manifestly important.¹

The Assistant Director, imbued with similar ideas, and beset on all sides by complaints against the working of the Turkish lines both in Europe and Asia, lost no time in studying the question in detail; and by virtue of his official position in London, submitted to Government a proposal for practical improvement of the defective communications which, though, from intelligible motives, not warmly received at the outset, will be considered in a subsequent chapter, in its relation to the existing Russo-Persian line to India.

Colonel Goldsmid reached Tehran on the 1st August, but it was not until the 4th December that he was enabled to quit the Persian capital with the satisfactory consciousness that a Convention had been concluded of a sufficiently binding nature to secure a two-wired line of telegraph available for Anglo-Indian correspondence, at least for a period of five years from date of completion. One of the two wires was to be exclusively under the direction of an English engineer officer and assistants,

---

¹ In my diary, under date Astrakhan, July 18, 1865, is this entry :—

"The more I consider the question of our Indo-European Telegraphic correspondence, the more does success seem to me to rest on *two great lines*:

"1st. The Indo-Ottoman, which seems to have become an acknowledged name for the line through Baghdad and Basrah;

"2nd. The Russo-Persian, or the line through Moscow and Tiflis to Tabriz and Bushahr.

"If these premises be admitted, our plan would be to enter into certain terms for the use of one, as we have done with the other; and then for both to remain open to the public to choose which proves the best. To avoid all preponderating influence on one side, Russia might arrange with the Persians for the communication between Julfa and Tehran *as we do* from Tehran to Bushahr. The connecting link between Baghdad and Tehran need, *as a rule*, be used only for Turco-Persian internal communication, and all dispute on division of messages would cease.

the whole number of British Government *employés* not exceeding fifty. Under sufferance the staff had already numbered thirty-eight, inclusive of the medical officer;[1] but henceforward the limits would be authoritatively enlarged.

How this Convention was produced at all out of the draft taken to Persia, or how it differed so materially from the latter as to cause relationship to be barely recognised, was of course officially explained: but the history of the whole procedure would perhaps be tedious, and little relevant in this place, and is rather illustrative of national characteristics than any particular stage in the development of telegraphic communications with the East.

The Persian Government, whatever disposed to sanction in practice, from friendly or political motives, was loth to commit to paper, and especially in the form of Treaty or Convention, to be read and commented on by other Powers, anything which might be construed into admission of need, whether of material, men, and money, or whether of moral supervision and administrative

---

[1] Shortly after arrival I found the number of *employés* to be:—

1 director and 3 superintendents	4
At Tehran, 1 traffic manager, 1 non-commissioned officer, and 5 clerks	7
At Ispahan, 1 inspector and 3 clerks	4
At Shiraz, 1 non-commissioned officer in charge and 2 clerks	3
At Bushahr, 1 inspector and 4 clerks	5
At Hamadan, 1 clerk	1
At Karmanshah, 1 head clerk, 2 clerks	3
On line-duty generally	10
Total	37

exclusive of Dr. Baker, in medical charge. The superintendents had been reduced from five to three, and were Lieutenants St. John and Pierson, R.E., and Mr. H. V. Walton.

control. Guided by this principle, it made a determined stand on conceding without accepting, and in confining its concessions to as narrow limits as possible. No better exponent of such a policy or stricter guardian of its integrity could be found than the Foreign Minister of the day; and as even the most inefficient attempt to sap his position required an unusual exercise of patience and perseverance, it may well be understood that success was not achieved without time and labour. The task was, in short, one of delicacy and difficulty; and the more so, because all former agreements on telegraph matters with England had been but provisional, and knotty points reserved for a regular Convention.

It may be further generally stated, without entering into the minutiæ of discussion, that Persia, at the outset, strongly insisted on paying for all constructive objects out of her own treasury, and setting up the required second wire herself. According to the argument used, the Government was solvent; Persian telegraphers were becoming expert; with the aid of the English officers for another three months, they would be able to carry on the work very well; at all events, at the expiration of three months, what was to be further done could be deliberated and determined. The Turks worked their own lines; why should not the Persians likewise? They had too much sense of shame (*khajálat*) to undertake what they could not perform. As regards the cost of working the line for Anglo-Indian messages, let Persia receive a fixed sum of money, say £10,000 a year, and the whole thing be left in her hands. To this last proposal the reply was naturally a counter-question on the receipts of messages; but as an answer showing their intended disposal had not been prepared, the matter dropped. With regard to the non-employment of English officers, Colonel Goldsmid felt it his duty to combat such a notion in the most positive manner, and submitted to her Majesty's Minister his views on the subject in a memorandum to the following effect :—

"The experience of the last two years has shown the impracticability of working the Persian lines of telegraph in any way but under a system of organization such as acknowledged in Europe. To this end it has been proposed that a Convention be concluded with the Government of his Majesty the Shah, by which a second wire should be given to the existing line, exclusively for Indian correspondence, under the superintendence of the engineer officers now engaged in working the single wire for twelve out of twenty-four hours. These officers and their establishment would, according to this convention, be retained for a fixed term, at the end of which it would be endeavoured to perfect the native telegraphers in their profession so as to act without extraneous aid. Should these terms not be accepted, it is not seen of what use would be any convention whatever, as the Persian line could not be looked upon as a sure link for Anglo-Indian communication. The undersigned would rather propose, in such case, that measures be at once taken to construct a second and alternative line in Asiatic Turkey, and to lay down a second cable to meet it."

Shortly after the occasion which called for this memorandum, one interview had a more than usually unfavourable aspect. A position had been taken up wholly opposed to our monied interests in the telegraph. Little enough had been asked, and a great deal conceded in that respect, but the Minister was not satisfied. We had wished to buy, and lay out a lump sum: they were adverse to any arrangement taking the line of telegraph out of their own hands. We had proposed to treat on the basis of a wire of our own: the Persians would not hear of such a thing. The wire must be theirs, and all expense of attaching it theirs; consequently, although we supplied the working establishment, the revenue was to be theirs equally. The premises being changed, all subsequent action changed also. As for paying the establishment for their trouble, that was our affair; because the measure was ours, and only admissible at our request! It might appear easy to reply that they could not work the line to advantage without us; but they said they could. Again, they would only have us for eighteen months, a period not worth the trouble of a Convention. Altogether issue had been joined on three important heads: traffic receipts, character of working establishment, limitation of period of agreement; and these were quite independent of less-defined controversy. One thing, moreover, had been omitted in the progress of negotiations. The golden key which opened all hard locks was disallowed. There was no "clinking" music, as in Malcolm's days, to charm the Asiatic serpent of jealousy; immediate, solid, substantial, tangible benefit was nowhere; and in an atmosphere where promise was too frequently followed by evasion, the tone of British policy seemed to have changed, and not for the better.

More than three months had passed, and the English officers had grown despondent at the slow progress made. Colonel Goldsmid had been twice with her Majesty's Minister to the King's presence; had had business interviews with the Minister of Foreign Affairs, alone or accompanied by the Oriental Secretary of Legation, and had endeavoured, not apparently without fruit, to enlist the sympathy and support of influential European or native official residents in the cause advocated; but negotiations seemed to hang fire. Suddenly there was a great commotion in the diplomatic world at Tehran about seats at the racecourse; and little as the telegraph could have to do with the matter, strangely enough, the matter seemed to have a direct affinity with the telegraph. For so it was, that while striving to appease the naturally aroused wrath of her Majesty's Minister at an offensive act laid to the charge of a high Persian dignitary, the responsible authorities took occasion to consider favourably certain references which had heretofore been put aside. Among these was the draft Persian Telegraph Convention, which, having been argued into definite shape and substance, only required the Shah's assent and the signatures of the respective Plenipotentiaries to be forwarded home for ratification.

The Convention was of nineteen Articles, of which the four first were as follows. The Persian Government agreed to attach a second wire to the poles before erected between Bushahr and Khanikin; the work to be done under the direction of an English officer and staff; the wire, 200 new posts, insulators, and instruments to be supplied by the British Government at a reasonable cost, recoverable in five years. The Persian Government further agreed that an English telegraph officer and staff, not exceeding fifty persons, exclusive of families, should be engaged for five years from opening communications through second wire, in organizing the line and giving instruction in telegraphy. At the conclusion of the specified period his connection with the work would cease, and the line be made over to the Persians.

The Fifth Article defined the control of the English Director, in especial relation to that of the Minister of Science, who was " to be considered the head and absolute chief of all the Persian Government telegraphs," and who would appoint officers, responsible to himself, for the protection of the line. The Sixth Article provided that " in filling up vacancies among the signallers, preference should be given by the English officer to natives of Persia," if held qualified to perform the duties required. The Seventh Article pledged the Persian Government to "build a new office adjoining the existing one" wherever there were not "separate rooms." The Eighth provided for the use of the first wire in case of injury to the second, and *vice versâ*. The Ninth regulated the rate between Khanikin and Bushair at fourteen shillings, with proportionate rates for the intervening towns. The Tenth credited the yearly receipts to Persia up to 30,000 tomans (12,000*l*.), any surplus to be "made over to the officers of the English Government for the cost of their establishment." The Eleventh gave all Indian messages to the second wire. The Twelfth secured the use of the first wire in the event of excessive traffic on the first. Of the remaining Articles, the Sixteenth accepted the terms of the Paris Telegraph Congress of 1865, "so far as not opposed to the terms" then agreed on, or to " the institutions of Persia;" and the Eighteenth limited the period of the Convention to five years from the date of despatch of first telegram by the second wire. The remainder call for no separate notice.

On completion of the telegraph negotiations at Tehran, the Chief Director saw no reason to remain any longer in Persia. Major Champain would attend to the due despatch of all materials required from home for the second wire, and engineer officers would be in waiting to receive them, commencing and completing their work as early as possible. He himself would proceed to India, reporting proceedings to the Bombay Government, under whose orders the telegraph was immediately placed, subject to a general supervision of the Supreme Government. After visiting the Presidency towns and conferring with the respective Chambers of Commerce, he would be guided by circumstances as to further movements. A congratulatory telegram from Sir Bartle Frere had contained instructions to Colonel Goldsmid to use his own discretion as to route in coming to Bombay, especially if he could do anything to promote branch line of telegraph to meet the already constructed English line in Makran; and the receipt of this authority was immediately acknowledged in the following terms :— "Major Smith[1] and I start for Ispahan on Saturday. Thence we propose to go together to Karman, which we may reach about New Year. Should all be well there, Smith takes Bandar Abbas, and I the Bampur route to Gwádar ... We hope to reach Bombay in March, Major Smith awaiting stores there for new Persian wire. Lieutenant St. John remains in charge of Persian line during Smith's absence, taking all urgent reports intended for me till my arrival at Gwádar notified."

The fact is, that the question of a whole land-line, that is, a line uniting Ispahan with Gwádar by Yezd, Karman, Bandar Abbas and the coast; perhaps by Yezd, Karman, Bampur, and the valleys or river beds leading seaward; had been broached at Tehran, and was under consideration, at least of the authorities in India. The Persian Minister of Foreign Affairs had not encouraged

[1] Local rank, as Major, was granted to Captain Smith, when director of the telegraph in Persia, vice Major Champain, whose services were required elsewhere.

the idea of practicability, or of the Shah's consent to the scheme; but the necessary passports and papers were readily given to enable the travellers to go on their way; and his Majesty, while kindly expressing to Colonel Goldsmid his opinion that he was going on a rough journey and among a rough people, never threw out a hint that there was any objection to the route being selected, except on the score of personal inconvenience and danger. Her Majesty's Minister having further placed on official record his approval of the project,¹ Colonel Goldsmid and Major Smith started on their expedition under fair auspices.

The programme was carried out much in the order laid down. The two officers parted a few stages east of Karman, and after three weeks' separate wandering, met again at the fishing village of Charbar, whence they steamed along the coast to Gwadar, and continued by sea to Karachi. The narrative of this journey belongs to another place, as do the subsequent rapid movements to Bombay, Baqar, Madras, Calcutta, Simla, Multan; Karachi, and Bombay again. But the results in relation to the telegraph should be recorded in the present chapter.

The Chief Director, in submitting to the Bombay Government his own and Major Murdoch Smith's report on the country they had traversed, thus expressed his views of the feasibility of constructing the line contemplated, according to the state of each separate section:

¹ In a letter, dated December 2, 1865: "I think it advisable that you should follow and examine the line of country between this and Gwadar best adapted for the construction of a new Persian land-line. . . . I do not believe that there is any danger in this journey, if you appear openly in your character of British officer."

"From Ispahan to Karman, a distance of 434 miles, there is nothing which can be held physically obstructive to setting up telegraph posts. The measure would be costly, because there is no wood available on this line; and it would be necessary to obtain the co-operation of the executive, as well as the consent of the head-quarter Government of Persia. But with funds available and authority to treat, I should have little doubt of the removal of other difficulties. . . Politically, it could not be otherwise than a mutual benefit to her Majesty's Government and the Shah, to admit the merchants of Eastern Persia to an intercommunication, the frequency and rapidity of which must serve to develop trade and strengthen the bands of friendship.

"There are at this moment about 4,500 Parsis at Yezd and Karman, and at Yezd 1,500 Jews. The Hindus of Shikarpur, although few in number, have a nucleus at either place sufficient to become a notable element of trade if duly fostered. At present, Jews, Parsis, and Hindus are labouring under the disadvantages which more or less attend all such persons in Muhammadan countries. I do not pretend to say that the telegraph would be a direct means of amelioration of their state; that it would make the Muslim debtor more punctual in the discharge of his debts, or the Muslim ruler more chary of imposing the Capitation Tax. But it is a wedge, and applied in the right direction.

"The Muhammadans themselves, in these parts, have already benefited by their proximity to British India. Those who have travelled thither, are men of much apparent intelligence and freedom from prejudice. The mercantile class is not a small one, and is very influential; but although they in some degree appreciate the advantages which would accrue to them from the telegraph, they are unable to come openly forward in its favour so long as the priests and officials of Government are not with them. My advice to the Masalman merchants was to address the Shah by petition . . . .

"From Karman to the sea, there are physical obstacles to be overcome, of which we know sufficiently to make it premature to fix at this moment the precise direction for a line. At the same time, I have no doubt whatever, that if Government be willing to press the measure a junction could be effected at Bandar Abbas, by a route more favourable to its erection and maintenance, than that taken by Major Smith under the auspices of the Wakil-ul-Mulk. This route is the one frequented in winter. That used by the káfilas in summer is shorter, if not otherwise preferable.

"Reports on the feasibility of erecting a coast line of telegraph between Bandar Abbas and Gwádar have already, it is believed, been laid before Government; and I have never heard that any difficulties had presented themselves to the scheme. Mr. Johnston has now reported on his and Major Smith's route from Jask to Surat near the Sadich river. From the Tenk river to Charbar I myself came near enough to the coast to estimate its general features. I was at Gwattar more than two years ago, and on that occasion sailed, close in to the shore, from Charbar to Gwádar. Still, it is true that even now there has been no complete survey, as in the case of the Gwádar and Karáchi line. I do not, however, think that more is necessary to be done in this respect. No part of the section can be regarded as a *terra incognita*. Physical obstacles alone intervening, we might commence operations without delay.

"The upper route from Kermán, by Bam and Bampúr, to the coast at Gwádar, though shorter and more direct than by Bandar Abbas, is objectionable from two causes: 1st. The extensive tract covered by barren rocks, and intersected by mountain streams, for the last half of the road between Regán and Bampúr; and the passes into Makrán, which present long difficult lines of access to the sea-shore, are physical obstacles which it would be well to avoid. 2nd. The want of water and shelter, especially in the hot, dry season, for distances which could scarcely be accomplished in a single day.

"But the difficulties are not insuperable, or indeed so formidable as those which have already been overcome in Eastern Makrán. And rather than not see carried out the alternative land-line, I would propose adoption of the road taken by myself as far as Kalanzao, and thence the caravan track direct to the

ROUTES FROM KARMAN TO SEA-COAST.

Fanoch pass, meeting my road again, and keeping it to Charbar

Were the question a purely political one, the proper course would be to take the line up the Kej district of Kalat to Sarbaz, where it would fall into Persian territory more immediately under the surveillance of Bampur, than any part of the coast. As our dealings in the matter must chiefly be with Persia, our greater security would naturally be found in those parts, where her Government is more settled and less affected by local revolutions."

Major Murdoch Smith, in recording his opinion, that between Ispahan and Karman "there would be no difficulty whatever" in setting up a line of telegraph, added:

"From Karman to Bandar Abbas, *via* Jiruft, the construction and maintenance of a line would be much more difficult. The mountain passes of Deh Bakri and Navargu offer many obstacles, and the difficulty of maintaining a line in the sparsely-populated plains would be considerable, especially in the summer, when the heat is excessive. Another objection to this road is, that although at present tranquil and safe under the strong rule of the Wakil-ul-Mulk, it might not continue to be so under his successor, the majority of the population between Jiruft and the lower plains being Baluchis. The distance too, 380 miles, is great. These difficulties are probably not insuperable, but I think, that in the event of the project of a line of telegraph being entertained, the other and more direct road from Bandar Abbas to Karman should be examined. Although the mountains near Karman were impassable on account of snow when I came by Jiruft, I was told that the length of road thus blocked up was not greater than 15 or 20 miles. If, therefore, this road should prove preferable in other respects, I think the difficulty of the snow might be got over by making that portion of the line of very strong steel wire slightly stretched on short, stout posts. The signals would pass perfectly well as long as the wire was unbroken, even if it should be buried in the snow.

"But there is still another road, and one that would most naturally suggest itself to any one simply looking at the map, viz., the direct route from Bandar Abbas to Shiraz. The objections to this route are, that part of the intervening country is said to be half independent and generally in a disturbed state, and secondly that the Persian Government would not care to have a line that only added so insignificant a place as Bandar Abbas to the towns in Persia already in telegraphic communication with the capital. This road, however, should also, I think, be examined before a decision is come to as to the precise route to be followed.

"At present, I am inclined to believe that the best of the three is the direct road from Bandar Abbas to Karman, especially as it must be 80 or 100 miles shorter than the other by Jiruft. And if proper measures were taken for guarding and patrolling the line, I believe there would be no physical difficulty in the way that could not be overcome."

Mr. Johnston's brief but interesting report was chiefly of a political nature, or with reference to the inhabitants of the Makran coast; but he brought to notice no physical difficulties of any consequence to the construction of a telegraph line there.

At Simla the Chief Director had the honour of personally stating his views to their Excellencies the Viceroy and the Commander-in-Chief, and to other members of Government. Returning to Bombay, he wrote a brief report of proceedings, and addressed a letter to the Secretariat urging prosecution of the scheme to connect Gwadar with Ispahan by an alternative land line. Not many days later he re-embarked for Europe, and soon after arrival in London, was called upon to report upon a communication addressed to her Majesty's Secretary of State for India by the Viceroy in Council.

The despatch in question adverted to a memorandum

submitted by Colonel Goldsmid in Simla, in anticipation of more detailed reports and proposals. The narrative of the recently-performed journey had not at this particular time been received from Bombay, and Major Smith's original and carefully-prepared map of the country traversed had been stolen, if not accidentally lost, somewhere between Delhi and Ambala; so that it had been imperative to put a case more or less from simple memory as to data. The Government of India had expressed an opinion that good reasons had been advanced

"For believing that an alternative line of telegraph connecting Gwadar and Ispahan (or Shiraz) would be of great value. At present," they continued, "the security of the Indo-European communication depends solely on the single line of submarine cable between Gwadar and Bushahr. If that cable gives way or is seriously damaged (and it is very liable to such damage), communication with Europe by telegraph must cease for a time, as was the case in 1865. The subject is one in which the English commercial public, and the Indian commercial public, and the two countries generally, have an equal and deep interest. . . . On the whole, the recommendations seem . . to be deserving of support, and we would suggest that the proposal be taken into . . early consideration, in the view to the opening of negotiations with the Persian Government, and the attainment of the assent of her Majesty's Government to share the expense of the proposed operations."

The reply to this reference contained a short *résumé* of events which had led up to the then posture of affairs, telegraphically and politically, on the Makran coast. A bulky appendix accompanied in illustration. Attention was called to the circumstance that the Bombay Government had written as favourably of the Director's proposals as the Supreme Government; and the two penultimate paragraphs may be quoted in full:

"As regards the advisability of taking the line from Bandar Abbas to Ispahan in lieu of Shiraz or (by the coast) to Bushahr, late letters from Persia give me more forcible arguments than any hitherto adduced. The experience of one severe winter has shown that in that country alternative lines to the coast are of material importance to maintain unbroken communications. The last paper in the appendix contains copies and extracts of letters from Lieutenant St. John, R.E., to which attention is respectfully invited. It is not that recent failure in the working of the Persian lines has in any way shaken the confidence entertained in their ultimate efficiency under the new Convention, but that there are occasions arising from the climate and natural features of a country which should render every available precaution especially necessary.

"It might be premature in this place to enter more minutely into the details of the proposed Convention and cost of the line to the British Government. But should the Right Honourable the Secretary of State take the same view of the case as the Governments of India and Bombay, and authorize the submission of draft articles and terms *in extenso*, I would do myself the honour of drawing up a detailed paper on the subject, with a view to early negotiations at the Court of Tehran."[1]

On receiving a copy of the letter last quoted, and in transmitting it to the Supreme Government, the Governor of Bombay in Council was pleased[2] to express his entire concurrence in the view therein expressed. Meanwhile the Secretary of State had received from Colonel Goldsmid in London the heads of a proposed Convention with the Persian Government, and sent them to the Foreign Office with a suggestion that, if her Majesty's Foreign Secretary approved, the Envoy at Tehran "should be

---

[1] To the Under Secretary of State, No. 126 of 1866; copy forwarded to Government of Bombay with Col. Goldsmid's memorandum, No. 134, dated August 9.

[2] Government Resolution; No. 259, of October 1, 1866.

instructed to open negotiations in the sense indicated."[1] A sum of 400,000*l.* had been stated as a maximum of outlay for constructing a line of 1,300 miles, whereof 800 miles would be provided for in a debtor and creditor account with Persia as between Khanikin and Bushahr; the remainder being a coast line paid for and worked by the British Government, who would reserve its receipts. The cost of subsidies to chiefs and for protection, added to English establishments between Gwādar and Bandar Abbas, was estimated at 600*l.* per annum.[2] The Foreign Office, acting on the India Office suggestion, addressed their Minister in Persia on the subject, and all requisite preliminaries having been disposed of, Colonel Goldsmid received his final instructions and left London on his second mission to Tehran about the middle of October, 1866.

He had at first proposed a rapid journey to his destination; but delays occurred between London and Constantinople. Major Champain had joined him in Paris, and proceeded thence direct to Berlin, while he himself took the lower route to Vienna. The purport of visiting these cities at this period will be clearer when we summarize the proceedings to improve telegraphic communications generally on the European lines used for ordinary Indian correspondence. Vienna was, it is true, strictly on the shortest route to Constantinople; but what with business interviews and official correspondence, five days were occupied, where one day would have amply sufficed in the mere course of travel. At Constantinople the work to be done, principally arising out of the five days at Vienna, kept the Chief Director nearly two months. It

---

[1] September 6, 1866.
[2] No. 144, of August 29, 1866.

was indeed most disheartening to find that nearly two years had passed since the Indo-Ottoman Telegraph had been opened, and yet messages were being despatched from the Pera offices to India which had been "more than ten days on their way from London!" Upwards of 25,000 messages had passed through the said office during the nine months of 1866, for which a computation had been made showing an average of nearly 2,800 per mensem, and not very far from 100 per diem. Moderate as this amount would seem, the figures must have been far higher, had the working been more rapid and regular. The irregularity was perhaps a worse feature than the slowness. For, in a statement of seven months' intercommunication, it was shown that only during one month (February) a message had failed to come "directly," that is with a mere flash, from Karáchi to Constantinople, and not a single month had passed without illustration of like instantaneous working, for messages going *from* Constantinople to Karáchi; and the average of this seven months was one day and nine hours for telegrams reaching Constantinople from Karáchi, and not twenty hours the other way.

We shall soon have to revert to the Constantinople correspondence at this period, and until the new year dawned; explaining as it does, the continuous or chronic phases of perplexity through which the Government telegraph to India passed while following the material route first indicated by policy and the crow's flight. For the present it will be well to resume the thread of the Persian story, till an exit from its mazes be obtained. But in no part of our narrative of telegraphic operations in 1866-67, where mention is made of negotiations with the Ottoman Government, however minor their character under so high-sounding a classification, would it be out of place to recall the continued interest evinced in, and invariable support given to the cause by the British ambassador at the Porte. The instances which might be cited in testimony of this assertion would not, perhaps, be surprising to those who know the Levant and its foreign diplomatists; but, as many readers of these pages may not possess that acquaintance, and merely look upon the representatives of her Majesty as distinguished officers fulfilling important functions in a certain conventional manner, there can be no violation of propriety in stating, on the best authority, that to Lord Lyons the public is indebted for active and practical aid in the advancement of telegraphic communication with India, which could not but bear fruit, and which did have a highly beneficial result.[1]

Colonel Goldsmid embarked at Constantinople on the 5th of January, and landing at Poti, pursued his journey to the Russian frontier through Tiflis and Erivan. He was accompanied by Mr. Charles Wills, a young medical practitioner of ability, and passed M.B., who was content, on far from lucrative terms, to try his fortunes in the new but limited sphere which had opened out, under Government, amongst the English telegraphers in Persia. Posting from the Arras, and halting for two or three days at Tabriz, they reached Tehran on the 12th of February, 1867.

To say that the negotiations for the alternative line between Ispahan and Gwādar, a sketch of which was

---

[1] The writer cannot miss this opportunity of expressing his deep obligations to the Honourable William Stuart, now her Majesty's Minister at Athens, for kind, ready, and constant aid given to the late Colonel Patrick Stewart and himself during the earlier negotiations at Constantinople.

submitted to and approved by the Indian and Home Governments, were unsuccessful at the Court of Persia, is hardly to give a true representation of the case, much less to do justice to those who were the main instruments in endeavouring to bring about a realization of the scheme contemplated. The three months' ventilation of the measure during the Chief Director's stay were not by any means thrown away, and proved nothing more or less than the prelude to negotiations re-opened by her Majesty's Minister a few months after Colonel Goldsmid's departure, which terminated in a Convention for the land line from Gwádar to Jask, and laying a second, or alternative cable, between Jask and Bushahr. But the whole affair looked unpromising from the moment of Colonel Goldsmid's arrival at Tehran and throughout his sojourn there. The Persian Minister of Foreign Affairs would venture nothing in the way of examining details, fearing to commit himself to acceptance of a basis of any kind: the British Legation had little to say on a matter exceptional and extraneous, as it were, in its bearings and interest, and to a great extent in its origin and growth: friends, well capable of giving sound opinions and prophesying prospective good results, augured unfavourably of immediate success; and the Shah was about proceeding on a, to him, novel and important pilgrimage to Mashhad, an event which of itself would at once postpone consideration of all diplomatic questions whatever.

On the 16th April Mr. Alison officially notified to Colonel Goldsmid that after repeatedly pressing the new proposals respecting the telegraph on the attention of the Persian Government, he had just received the Shah's final answer that he could not at present entertain them; and that, owing to his Majesty's early departure for

Mashhad, he did not consider anything further could then be done in the matter. This result had been anticipated more than a month before, and a report on the subject addressed to the Bombay Government on the 11th March.

With that report was submitted the copy of written communications made by Colonel Goldsmid to her Majesty's Minister since last arrival in Tehran, and the Director's proposals for future procedure:

"Though it were useless to conceal," he wrote, "the disappointment experienced at this indefinite postponement of a project which, however extensive, was, I am convinced, practical and possible, I would yet respectfully invite the attention of Government to the advisability of pressing a revival of the question at a more convenient opportunity. . . . I confess to miss my way to a practical measure for strengthening the Gulf section of the telegraph as effectual as that of utilizing the barren coast of Makran for a land-line up to Jask, or a more convenient point in the vicinity."

Illustration of the position, politically, geographically, and as it affected the telegraph, was then given, and the said extension to Jask, or a point some 400 miles west of Gwādar, mainly dwelt on.

In a memorandum of interview held with the Persian Foreign Minister on the 4th March, forming one of the enclosures noted, it was shown that no real cause had been assigned to the writer for refusing to negotiate the proposal on the Makran coast-line; while the counter-statement, of the trouble and cost of keeping up a long line through Eastern Persia, was undoubtedly without foundation in reliable data.

His Excellency the Governor of Bombay recorded a minute [1] on these papers, expressing his own opinion that

[1] Dated May 4, 1867.

while the result of the Tehran negotiations was to be regretted, on account of the importance of securing improved communications with Europe, attention should rather be given to securing an entirely separate line by the Red Sea, than to a coast extension of lines to the westward of Gwādar into Persian territory: and, referring to interviews he had had with the Pasha of Egypt, as with Nubar and Rashid Pashas, he suggested that such a telegraph was quite feasible, and might be considered in respect of cost by both the Indian and home Governments. A generally concurring minute by Mr. Ellis was at the same time in favour of continued exertions to secure an alternative land-line. The matter was eventually referred to the Government of India, who ruled, that if the Government of Bombay were "in favour of the extension of a land-line from Gwādar along the coast, as suggested by Colonel Goldsmid, and its continuance by another submarine cable to Bushahr, the probable cost of such a line, including payments to the local chiefs through whose territories the line would pass, should be ascertained."[1]

Having entered the phase of figures, the modified scheme may be said to have attained an advanced stage of progress; but out of India it was making way more rapidly still, as will be directly made apparent.

Fulfilment of the Chief Director's home instructions to continue his journey to Baluchistan, and negotiate with the chiefs there, on completion of the proposed Convention, had met with a determined, however temporary check; so he had contemplated returning to head-quarters in London, and awaiting the close of the hot weather to

[1] Secretary to the Government of India to Secretary to Government of Bombay: No. 2,614 of July 22, 1867.

proceed to India, trusting to the intervening time to put things on a better footing. But owing to a call by telegram from Bombay, he was obliged to change his plans and turn his face at once towards the far East. A sharp ride post, for eight successive days, brought him to Baghdad, whence the river steamer conveyed him to the sea steamer, and after a fair passage for the little propitious season, he reached Bombay, and shortly afterwards Punah, the last in about a month from leaving Tehran.

After personal conference with Sir Seymour Fitzgerald on the state and prospects of the lines under his charge, Colonel Goldsmid took occasion of this earlier than intended visit to the Western Presidency, to submit a written account of his later proceedings, in continuation of one dated Tehran, about nineteen months before. Allusion to both these reports will be made hereafter: for the present, it need only be stated that the writer re-embarked at Bombay, on 9th July, to steam through a monsoon-stirred sea to Socotra; thence to reach London again on the 5th of August. On the 19th idem, he submitted to the Indian Secretary of State a memorandum on the subject of the land-line telegraph extension along the coast in the Persian Gulf; and a few days later Sir Stafford Northcote transmitted a copy to the Foreign Secretary, expressing his concurrence in the views set forth, and requesting that, with Lord Stanley's approval, Mr. Alison might be instructed to renew negotiations on the Shah's return from Mashhad.[1] Colonel Goldsmid, it was added, would be in readiness to proceed to Bombay and the Makran coast, should a favourable reply be

[1] Dated August 30, 1867. Mr. Melvill to Under Secretary of State for Foreign Affairs.

received from Persia. Lord Stanley, without delay, instructed her Majesty's Minister at Tehran to the desired effect.[1] Three months had not elapsed, when the India Office were informed by the Foreign Office that the Persian Government had re-opened negotiations on the matter of the coast telegraph, and a question of detail was put, clearly proving the whole case to be under actual discussion. Early in April, after exchange of many telegrams between London and Tehran, and numerous transaulic references south of Downing Street, the conclusion of a brief Convention in the following terms was notified by telegraph:—

"1. In order to provide against any accident to the Persian Gulf cable, it is agreed that the British Government shall make arrangements in regard to the construction and efficient working of a line of telegraph between Gwádar and a point between Jask and Bandar Abbas.

"2. The Persian Government will employ its good offices and authority for facilitating its construction, maintenance, and protection; and the English Government will pay annually to the Persian Government the sum of 3,000 tomans, for leave to lay down a line of telegraph on those parts of coasts and places which are under the sovereignty of Persia the payment of the above sum being made from the day upon which the work of laying the wire is commenced.

"3. The present Convention to remain in force for twenty years."

The memorandum which had been forwarded by the India Office as a basis for the renewal of negotiations at Tehran had recited the proceedings of the Bombay Government on the receipt of Colonel Goldsmid's report of the 11th March; but dwelt mainly on the political considerations therein comprised. With reference to these,

[1] Sept. 3; Mr. Hammond to Under Secretary of State, India Office.

it had been suggested to put into the Envoy's hands a proposition which, if acceptable to Persia, might obviate the necessity of adopting any course affecting, or supposed to affect, her interests, without her consent and participation. The proposition was thus expressed:—

"We pay now, according to official statement for the year 1866, the sum of Rs. 42,371 per annum, for maintenance of our land-line of telegraph from Karāchi to Gwādar. Of this 21,000 is subsidy to chiefs.

"It might be reckoned that at least a similar sum would be required, were we to construct a land-line, as proposed, from Gwādar westward to a point between Jask and Bandar Abbas.

"At the present exchange, 10,000 tomans is the equivalent of Rs. 40,000. Half of this might be set aside for Persian territory, and half for territory in which Persia has no acknowledged jurisdiction.

"A sum of 3,000 tomans (Rs. 12,000) yearly to Persia, to allow us to treat with the Shaikh of Bandar Abbas, and any other chiefs on the coast of Baluchistan over whom she may assert control, would, it is believed, be acceptable; and while we, on our part, give a guarantee of non-interference with political pretensions, we might reasonably expect a similar guarantee, in return, of non-interference in telegraph arrangements, so far as the whole line is concerned."

The division of Rs. 40,000 was then roughly shown:

Subsidy to Kalat and Makran chiefs	Rs. 10,000
For actual maintenance and repairs	10,000
Proposed yearly payment to Persia for Bandar Abbas, &c. &c.	12,000
For actual maintenance and repairs	8,000
Total Rs.	40,000

And, in order to give a margin for contingencies, it was proposed to limit the yearly sum to Rs. 50,000.

As might not unnaturally be expected, some modification was found necessary in practice.

After attending the International Telegraphic Conference at Vienna in 1868, Colonel Goldsmid again set out for India, and entered upon the task of subsidizing the chiefs. His proceedings may be briefly narrated. The mission with which, on this occasion, he was charged was twofold. He had to prepare the way, politically, for the coming posts and wires along the barren and little-known coast between Gwādar and Jask; and to make a searching examination of telegraph expenditure, with a view to reduction and systematizing.

Leaving London with the night mail of the 16th October, and embarking at Marseilles early on the 18th, he landed at Bombay on the 7th November. A few days at the Presidency were passed in preliminary arrangements and general official work; but by the end of the month, Karāchi, Gwādar, Charbar, Sadich (a point near the old Perso-Kalat boundary), Jask and Maskat had been visited, and he was back at the first of these places on return to Bombay. December was little less peripatetic than the month preceding, for in it he journeyed *viâ* Nagpur to Calcutta, returning to Bombay at Christmas. In the former city he had the honour of personally reporting to the going Viceroy; in the latter, of paying his respects to the coming Viceroy.

The month of January was busily spent in Bombay. On the 1st February he again embarked for Karāchi; on the 8th idem, he re-embarked in Karāchi in the telegraph steamer *Amberwitch*, for Gwādar. From Gwādar he moved by land to Charbar, in company with Captain Ross, Political Agent on the coast, performing this short but somewhat eventful journey in eight marches and nine days. Returning to the telegraph steamer at Charbar, they landed at Jask to negotiate on the 24th February. Here Captain Ross remained behind; and Colonel Goldsmid, with Lieutenant Stiffe, I.N., proceeded to inspect the neighbouring island of Henjām, returning for Captain Ross on the 3rd March. The next day they anchored off Charbar, where a Darbar was held and much work done, and on the 6th March they returned to Gwādar. On the 7th Colonel Goldsmid, separating from Captain Ross, steamed back to Karāchi; and on the 12th idem he was again in Bombay. From that date until embarkation for Suez on the 1st May, he remained at the Presidency, engaged in unravelling the knotty question of telegraph accounts and summarizing, under instructions, the political history of the Makran coast. To assist in the former work, Mr. Kellner, the well-known accountant, now Military Accountant-General in India, had been specially deputed from Calcutta to Bombay; Captain Pierson, R.E., had been despatched from Tehran; and the Accountant-General in Bombay had been, moreover, associated with Colonel Goldsmid and his colleagues, in the capacity of President of Committee. The other business was of urgent nature, and the case demanded study and appreciation, not alone with reference to the future security of the telegraph, but for the guidance of our political relations generally in the regions through which the lines might be required to pass.

Instead of dwelling, in this part of the narrative, upon the negotiations with the Baluch or other chiefs on the coast, or showing how each agreement was signed and brought about, it may be simply stated that a resolution of the Bombay Government of the 8th June, 1869, conveyed the entire approval of his Excellency in Council to all Colonel Goldsmid's proceedings. The latter officer, on completing his work in Bombay, returned home, accompanied to Constantinople by Captain Pierson and Mr. Kellner.

But in connection with the land-line proposals, a really important operation was successfully carried out at the beginning of this year, which must not be passed over in silence. For a long time the trying climate and isolated position of the station at Masandam had attracted the attention of the telegraph authorities; and after a lengthened correspondence with Government,[1] and many references on the political as well as sanitary aspects of the question, it was resolved to transfer the cable from the Arabian side of the Gulf to Jask, and open out a new station in the island of Henjām. For the quiet and ready manner in which this change was effected, great credit is due to Mr. Walton's general superintendence, and Lieutenant Stiffe's careful and skilful execution.

The report of the Director, Makran Coast and Submarine Telegraph, to the Chief Director, describing these proceedings and his own arrangements for the proposed new stations at Charbar and Jask, is dated the 19th December, 1868. That all was not *couleur de rose* may be inferred from the following extracts :—

"Owing to prevalence of fever at Gwādar, I had already used that station as one of observation only, thus throwing all the work on Masandam, and causing some delay in the transmission

---

[1] 1865–69. Major Champain had reached Bombay on the 26th November, 1867, with instructions to carry out the transfer of the cable to Henjām, and establish a station there; but the measure was delayed with a view to the further discussion of preliminaries, the disposal of which was, politically, essential. More than a year had elapsed from the above date when the work was actually completed.

of messages. Finding that the health of the station did not improve, I left the Assistant Superintendent and two clerks only, intending to remove them also if they succumbed to the fever. I was obliged to remove the apothecary, as he was too ill to attend to his duties. This state of affairs rendered it important that a station should be opened at Jask at the earliest moment. . . . .

"The village of Jask is some five or six miles from the landing place, and I did not see the Naib. . .His brother, and others whom he sent to me, reiterated the assurance that we shall have every assistance from them; that they had been instructed from Maskat we were coming, and that we should choose our sites for building on. As usual, these people assured me that camels could be obtained to any number, that sheep and fowls were always procurable, and that we had only to ask for whatever we wanted and it would be supplied. The truth is that not a camel, sheep, or fowl is procurable at Jask, but it seems to be the customary etiquette all along the coast to assure one that the country abounds with every requisite for travelling, whereas it is just the contrary; and, except for a very few animals at a time, even water and fodder are not obtainable."[1]

The Director's letter may be further quoted:—

"Meeting Lieutenant Stiffe at Jask, the shore ends were landed, and the deep-sea cables on both circuits were joined on to them; and so efficiently was this duty conducted by that officer, that an interruption of only nine and a half hours resulted from the operation. An arrangement was, at the same time, made for the abandonment of the Masandam station and the removal of the clerks to Jask, simultaneously with the cutting out of the old cable, and the joining up the diversion by way of Henjām."

---

[1] The remedy, if still required, is very simple, but needs official authorization. We should open friendly communications with Anguran, the capital of Bashakird, and the interior, through the legitimate channels. The annexation to Persia of the province of Bashakird was formally notified in the *Tehran Gazette* of May 29, 1862.

Mr. Walton took the teak wood-house which had been in use at Masandam across to the island of Henjām, where it was to be re-erected on a stone plinth, constructed under the orders of the Government Engineer Officers detached for the occasion. The *Amberwitch* arrived with the cable true to her time, and such temporary arrangements as could be made for working the line, pending the opening of a regular station, were at once carried out. We continue the Director's own account:—

"Having arranged with Lieutenant Stiffe the time at which he would cut the Masandam Station out of circuit on the Bushahr side near Tūmb Island; and also when he could join over the new cable near Kuhi Mubārak, thus bringing Jask and Bushahr into communication by way of Henjām, I left for Masandam, and at once began to dismantle the place, and ship everything belonging to us that was on the island, so as to be ready to start for Jask as soon as we found that the *Amberwitch* had grappled the cable off the great Tūmb. This occurred on the evening of the 9th instant; and by noon of the 11th, Jask was in good communication with Bushahr through the new diversion, and I had landed sufficient clerks and requisites of every description to enable Jask to begin work at once as the central repeating station on the line.

"I consider that very great credit is due to Lieutenant Stiffe and Mr. Hirz, for the precision and exactitude with which the arrangements for picking up the old cable, and joining on the new, were carried out. I believe that no similar operation has ever been done in so short a time. It involved the grappling for and picking up and joining on the Masandam cable in some forty fathoms of water, under-running it for several miles, and then picking up and joining on the new cable in the same depth. A similar operation was necessary off Kuhi Mubārak, a distance of nearly 120 miles from the former position off Tūmb Island, and yet it caused a delay to the traffic of only forty-five hours. I must also thank Captain Tolputt for the manner in which he enabled me to move about so rapidly, and so to carry out my arrangements, as to ensure the Masandam station being abandoned, and the Jask station fully established, while the diversion on the cable was being brought into circuit."[1]

Mr. Walton also commended Captain Carpendale, I.N., for services rendered in command of the *Lord Elphinstone* steamer. The Chief Director, in forwarding the papers to the Secretariat,[2] took "the opportunity of submitting to the notice of his Excellency the Governor in Council that the diversion of the cable from 'through Masandam' to 'through Henjām,' and transfer of the telegraph station to Jask," were matters which had "long occupied the time and attention of Government," and that the successful accomplishment of both objects was "a step of considerable importance." He moreover stated: "I have informed the Director of my unqualified concurrence in the opinion expressed by him of the services rendered by Lieutenant Stiffe, I.N., Mr. Hirz, and the other officers he has named; and would respectfully add that Mr. Walton's own arrangements appear to have been highly judicious, and carried out with the same zeal and energy which have characterized his former labours in connection with the efficient maintenance of the line under his direction."[3]

In parting company, a few pages back, with Major Murdoch Smith, R.E., we purposed reverting, in chrono-

[1] The report of Lieut. Stiffe, the zealous and able engineer of the Persian Gulf cable, will be found, with forwarding letter, in the Appendix. Mr. Hirz was the electrician, a scientific and valuable assistant to the Director.

[2] No. 5 of January 4, 1869, to the Secretary to Government, Bombay; acknowledged in Government Resolution of 14th idem.

[3] Lieut. Carpendale had already been favourably mentioned for services rendered to the Persian Gulf cable. His name, and that of Dr. Adair, are both included in the long roll of death casualties among the participators in the Government Telegraph operations of 1864. See Chapter III. pages 131, 147, 160, &c. &c.

logical order, to his proceedings in the matter of setting up the second Persian wire, under the Convention concluded in November 1865; and although in tracing the Chief Director's own progress, the period has long been passed when this task was completed, it would have been inconvenient to have earlier dropped the thread of narration in respect of the coast-line extension, negotiations on which had originated almost simultaneously with those for strengthening the lines in Persia proper.

On the 4th September, 1866, Major Murdoch Smith reported to the Government of Bombay "the arrangements made for the erection and maintenance of the second wire of the Persian telegraph, from Bushahr, *viâ* Tehran, to the Turkish frontier, according to the Convention of the 23rd November." He had, immediately after his arrival at Tehran from India, explained verbally to the Persian Minister of Public Works, the measures that he hoped to see adopted by his Government, following up the statement by a written memorandum. The want of any response to this procedure caused him to address Mr. Alison, who, failing to get satisfactory notice taken of the subject in the Foreign Department, desired Major Smith to call on the Foreign Minister with his Oriental Secretary. Assurances that all necessary orders would be issued were made after the custom of the country; but it oozed out, in a separate channel, that funds from the royal or state revenues had been denied; and, as a natural consequence, the English Director was eventually requested to advance the requisite sums himself, recovering the amount expended from the future receipts of the traffic. The request was a strange one, considered in reference to the Persian arguments used when the Convention was under discussion; but it was judged expedient to humour it, and home sanction was solicited and obtained. So that, before Persia could move a step towards carrying out her self-imposed pledge to put up a second wire for the British Government, a kind of abnormal article passed virtually though impalpably into the text of the treaty, whereby the expense and transport of materials and erection of the wire was to be "defrayed by her Majesty's Government in the first instance, the amount thus expended being recognized as a debt by the Persian Government to be paid in instalments or otherwise from the receipts of the International Traffic."[1]

The *Hastings*, with stores for the second wire, had arrived at Bushahr two days before the date of Major Smith's last quoted despatch. On the 5th September he wrote:—

"Every effort will be made to open communication on the double line as soon as possible, but I fear we shall be unable to complete the work before next spring. Owing to the ravages of white ants, a large proportion of the existing poles must be changed. New ones in many places have not been provided by the Persian authorities, and delay may take place before we are able to obtain them ourselves. Wood fit for posts is very scarce in Persia, the distances are great, and wheel carriage is unknown. Upwards of 3,000 mule loads of material from England must be despatched from Bushahr, some of them to a distance of more than 1,000 miles. The distribution, under the most favourable circumstances, cannot, therefore, be completed before the end of November or beginning of December, soon after which time the weather, if like last year, may become so severe as to stop all attempts to continue the work. If the weather, on the other hand, be mild, the operations may be carried on almost without intermission."

---

[1] Major R. M. Smith, R.E., to Secretary to Government, Bombay; No. 392 of September 4, 1866.

On the 7th January, 1867, Major Smith reported progress. The report was, on the whole, satisfactory, but he was beset with difficulties. Dry-rot and white ants had proved formidable foes; and a large number of poles had already been replaced: for a great part of the line every pole had to be taken out and examined. There was great difficulty in getting beasts of burden, and in the province of Fars there had just been an epidemic among the mules. As "no amount of pressure could induce" the Persians to replace the decayed or useless poles, he congratulated himself that the cost of moving was placed in his own hands. "When the work is completed," he writes in conclusion, "and the 2,000 iron poles added, which I understand are being sent out by her Majesty's Government, I am very sanguine of a satisfactory result."

On the 1st August, 1867, the Director forwarded to the Government of Bombay reports of his assistants, Lieutenants St. John and Pierson, regarding the completion of the double line of telegraph from Bushahr to Tehran, and from Tehran to Karmanshah, respectively. It was explained that a short distance still remained to be done between Karmanshah and the Turkish frontier: otherwise the work was over.

Lieutenant St. John's report is dated 7th June, 1867. We commence quoting it, from his allusion in the second paragraph to the Convention of 1865:—

"The day that the news of its signature was transmitted to Mr. Walton and myself, working parties were sent on all sections of the line to complete the necessary repairs before the setting in of winter, and the line was made as secure as possible without the reserve of poles, the necessity for which had been so often impressed upon the Persian authorities. But the temporary repairs thus effected proved ineffectual against the snow and wind of the severest winter remembered in Persia. From December till March the most strenuous exertions failed to keep the line open for traffic, and it was not until the end of the latter month that regular working parties could be got together to repair effectually the damage wrought by the severity of the season.

"Immediately on the signature of the Convention, an estimate of new poles required had been submitted to the Persian Government, and orders sent to the local authorities to furnish them without delay.

"In Shiraz I succeeded in persuading the Governor . . to give me the purchase-money for the 700 oak poles required about Kāzarūn, and they were accordingly cut and brought on the line during the winter. Five hundred chinār poles I obtained in the same way at Shiraz, early in spring; but the rest of the poles, about 4,000 in number, were grudgingly supplied in tens and twenties during the summer, and on arrival of the *Hastings*, with the stores for the second wire, not a thousand had been collected, in addition to those above mentioned, over the whole distance from Bushahr to Tehran. This was the state of affairs when the arrangement was concluded with the Persian Government placing the whole of the expenditure in our hands. I immediately purchased 700 chinār poles to complete the number required at Shiraz, and arranged . . . for the immediate supply of poplar poles at Abadeh, Ispahan, Kashan, and Kūm."

The story of setting up the second wire in his division is told by Lieutenant St. John so briefly as regards unattractive technicalities, and so graphically as regards the little known localities traversed, that excuse would rather be needed for abbreviation or omission than literal extract. We have therefore freely adopted the latter course:—

"On the 2nd September the *Hastings* anchored at Bushahr. On the 7th, I reached the same place from Shiraz, and made immediate arrangements for the disembarkation of the wire and other material which was completed by the end of the month. I had obtained in Shiraz, from H.R.H. the Hisam-u-Saltaneh, firmans authorizing me to collect mules for the transport of the stores up country, by coercion or any other means I chose. With great trouble—caused first by the fear of the muleteers being forced to carry the telegraph stores as usual at a mere nominal hire, afterwards by an influx of imported goods to Bushahr which caused the merchants to raise the hire and use every possible means to prevent my obtaining mules—the whole of the wire and stores were despatched from Bushahr before the end of the year. By the middle of January, none of the stores for the second and first divisions remained in Shiraz.

"Early in November, two working parties were started from Shiraz to prepare the old line for the reception of the second wire. This was done by digging up all the poles that appeared in any way unsound, replacing them, if unfit to be replanted, by new ones; by attaching the insulators for the second wire to the poles, and by a careful examination and repair of the old wire.

"The first party, under Colour-Sergeant Bower, R.E., worked from Shiraz to Murghab, and completed their task by the end of the year. The second, under Corporal Norman, R.E., prepared the line for the reception of the second wire from Murghab to Abadeh, and arrived at that place early in January.

"About the end of November, Corporals Graves and Hamilton were similarly employed between Ispahan and Abadeh, while Mr. Hoeltzer worked from Ispahan to Kashan, and Sergeant Isaacson from that place to Tehran, which last section you¹ had kindly taken charge of.

"By the middle of January, the old line from Shiraz to Tehran was thoroughly repaired, and prepared for the erection of the second.

"Leaving Mr. Hoeltzer and Corporal Graves to stretch the second wire in their respective sections, and starting Corporal Hamilton to carry out the same work from Shiraz to Abadeh, I commenced operations with Colour-Sergeant Bower and Corporal Norman on the most troublesome part of the line, that from

¹ Major Smith, R.E., to whom the report is addressed.

Bushahr to Shiraz. An account of the difficulties of this section is given in a subsequent paragraph of this report. By the end of April, all parties in the third division had finished work, and the second line was complete.

"Lieutenant Lovett, R.E., had taken charge of the second division from the 1st of February, and the work of straining the second wire therein was carried out under his superintendence.

"A few remarks descriptive of the line in the division under my charge may possibly be of interest. Leaving the town of Bushahr opposite the British Residency, the line is carried, on 500 iron standards of the 'Siemens' pattern, across the 'Mashilah' to the village Chahgodak. From this, 250 'Hamilton' poles carry the wires to near Khushab, a point 27½ miles from Bushahr. Thence to the foot of the hills at Daliki the line is on the old poles, the first wire supported on insulators, the second simply nailed to the poles. This part of the line will be supported on the new standards of the 'Siemens' pattern now on their way from England.

"At Daliki the line enters the hills which form the barrier between the plateau of Iran and the low plain bordering the sea, and here are the most formidable difficulties we have had to encounter. The original line from Daliki to the river of the same name, eight miles distant, was carried from ridge to ridge at a considerable distance from the road.

"This course, though presenting fewer engineering difficulties, was found inconvenient from the impossibility of getting the line guards to inspect it; and I therefore changed it for one in view of the road, a most tedious and difficult work. From the Daliki river the line was carried up the Kothal Malu, a steep pass 1,500 feet in height, to the plain of Konartakhtah, 1,800 feet above the sea. A similar ascent leads to the valley of Kamārij, 1,200 feet higher. Thence a rugged defile, the 'Tang-i-Tarkū,' brings the line to the plain of Kāzarūn, in the town of which name is the first telegraph station, 100 miles from Bushahr, and 2,700 feet above the sea. Part of the iron 'Siemens' poles will be used in this and the Konartakhtah and Kamārij plains. Seven miles from Kazarun the line begins an ascent of 1,500 feet to the wooded plain of Dasht-i-Ber, culminating in the steep pass of Kothal Dokhtar, which is ascended by a single span 2,100 feet in horizontal, and 620 in perpendicular distance. Crossing the Dasht-i-Ber the line ascends the oak-clad heights of the Kothal Pir-i-zan in a succession of long spans, rising 3,000 feet in five miles. The longest of these, which crosses a ravine opposite the

KOTHAL DOKHTER, BETWEEN SHIRAZ AND THE SEA.

Miān Kothal caravanserai, is 2,950 feet long and 610 high; the most considerable, I believe, on the line. It is of steel wire, and has never given way, although the tension, from the unequal height of the supports, is as great as that of a span of 2,000 yards with a dip of 200. Crossing the summit of the Kothal Pir-i-zan, 7,250 feet above the sea, the line descends to the valley of Dasht-i-arjen, 1,000 feet lower, whence a pass of no great elevation brings the line to the Kāragach river, at which point the mountains cease, and an easy descent, first over low hills and then over plain, leads to Shiraz, 175 miles from Bushahr, and 4,750 feet high. Throughout the hills from Daliki to Dasht-i-arjan, the poles are of gall-nut oak, which, though unsightly in appearance, are of more durable quality than any other wood I have seen in Persia. It is to be regretted that they are found in so limited a region only.

"The bulk of the poles from Dasht-i-arjan to Shiraz are of Oriental plane (chinār), which is superior in every respect to the poplar generally used. I have chinār poles now seasoning at Shiraz to replace the few poplar poles remaining in this part of the line; and by November of this year there will not be a single poplar pole between Bushahr and Murghab, a guarantee of security for five years at least.

"Crossing the plain of Mardasht from the river Bandamir, past the ruins of Persepolis and Istakhr, the line ascends to the narrow valley of Polvar, from which it merges close to the tomb of Cyrus and the ruins of Pasargadae, on the plains of Murghab. It then ascends by easy slopes the lofty plateau of Dehbid, 8,000 feet above the sea, which, though without engineering difficulties, is one of the most troublesome portions of the line, from its intense cold in winter. A gradual descent of 80 miles long brings the line to Abadeh, the boundary of the second and third divisions, 355 miles from Bushahr, and 5,800 feet above the sea.

"The wire and insulators supplied from England have proved admirable. No difficulty has occurred in making the twisted joints in the coldest weather, and the equal size of the coils has saved much trouble in distribution.

"The tools, with some exceptions, notably the spanners, are of fair quality; the blocks particularly are excellent.

"The office stores are, with the exception of the insulated wire, which is execrable, superior to those first supplied. The protosulphate of mercury, however, was so carelessly wrapped up in paper parcels, that much of it was spoilt or lost by mixing with the straw and sawdust in which the stores in the same case were packed. Not a case was injured by sea-water, either on board ship or in landing.

"Comparatively little trouble has been experienced during the past year in guarding the line. One district alone, that of Borazjūn, near Bushahr, has until the last two months been a source of constant annoyance, from the inveterate habit of insulator-breaking indulged in by its inhabitants, the most lawless tribe between Tehran and the sea. Remonstrances, warnings, and fines being of no avail, H.R.H. the Governor of Fars has at last been compelled to occupy the village with troops as a guarantee for future good behaviour.

"Now that the line is placed in a thoroughly efficient state, and that the line-guards are entirely under our control, nothing is wanted to complete its security but the establishment of European signallers at each intermediate station. . . . At Kāzarūn an English signaller is already permanently stationed, and one will be shortly sent to Abadeh, and I hope that signallers may soon be spared for Dehbid and Kūmishah, Kūm, and Kashan.

"Great credit is due to H.R.H. the Hisam-u-Saltaneh for the admirable manner in which he has carried out the orders of the Government of Tehran regarding the repair and fitting up of the Bushahr and Shiraz offices. At Bushahr the two offices, Persian and English, are separated by a wide courtyard, are raised at least twenty feet from the ground, and open to the prevailing winds. The English office has, moreover, a broad verandah on each side. It contains instrument office and signaller's room, besides large storerooms and accommodation for the inspector in charge of the section.

"The Shiraz office is fixed in one of the historic buildings of Shiraz, the Diwan Khānah of Karim Khan. Two-thirds of this fine building had fallen into ruins, the rest having been used as a joint office for the last year and a half. I succeeded in inducing H.R.H. the Hisam-u-Saltaneh to put the whole in thorough repair, and have thus not only secured the best telegraph office in Persia, but had the satisfaction of arresting the decay of a building of historic interest. Not its least recommendation, in so turbulent a city as Shiraz, is its impregnability to assault in case of an *émeute*, an event always to be expected.

"While on this subject, I may mention that I experienced the greatest difficulty in finding suitable quarters for the telegraph staff in Shiraz, without scattering them over the town at inconvenient distances from the office and from each other in case of a riot. With great trouble, and by paying exorbitant rents, I have obtained sufficient quarters in one parish to accommodate the whole staff for the present year, after which, either by owners refusing to repair, or raising their rents, I shall probably have to begin a search for quarters anew.

"H.R.H. the Hisam-u-Saltaneh, on my mentioning the subject to him, offered me a piece of waste ground close to the telegraph office, to build quarters for the whole staff, adding that it would be matter of great satisfaction to him to know that we were thus in safety in case of an *émeute* in the city. Such a building would cost 50,000 rupees at least, and could not be designed, estimated, and sanctioned before next winter, during which building operations are impossible . . . ."

Lieutenant St. John, remarking on the admirable conduct of the staff under his orders, and the necessity forced upon him of throwing upon his inspectors an unusual individual responsibility, in matters of construction, organization and account, brought prominently forward the services of Mr. Ernest Hoeltzer, appointed an assistant-superintendent, commending his zeal, activity, and thorough knowledge of the particular tracts in which he was engaged. Colour-Sergeant David Bower had been, "as always, most indefatigable." The value of his services had been especially enhanced by "his skill in construction and talent for organization." Corporals Norman, Graves, Hamilton, MacDonald, MacGowan and Lapham, all of the Royal Engineers, were also lauded for good work and efficient aid; and the names of Messrs.

Thompson, Pack, and Rushton, in charge of offices, Mr. Constantine, superintending the despatch of stores, Corporal Kelly, R.E., in the account department, and Mirza Husain Ali Khan, the British agent at Shiraz, were mentioned with particular favour. Lieutenant St. John concluded with an expression of his best thanks "to H.R.H. the Husam-u-Saltaneh, Governor-General of Fars, for his unvarying courtesy and kindness on all occasions, and his anxiety to do all in his power to facilitate his work; and his obligations to Colonel Lewis Pelly, H.M. Resident at Bushahr, for his constant kindness and support."

Lieutenant Pierson's report is dated 20th July, 1867. In his division the second wire from Tehran to Hamadan had been completed and opened for traffic on the 28th May; and from Hamadan to Karmanshah on the 15th June. He had himself been on a mission to Tiflis in the previous year, only returning to Tehran on the 25th September, or some three weeks after arrival of the stores at Bushahr. One month later he had quitted the capital to commence active operations. The first object to be attained was the renewal of all defective posts; the second, to get and properly distribute his materials, which had been sent up from Bushahr to Ispahan, and were thence despatched by the main road to Tehran or by cross road to Hamadan and Karmanshah. The mere difference of time taken up in the transport of stores from Bushahr would go far to account for the completion of the work in this division some five weeks later than in the other, though the distance is considerably less.

The report of progress is no less interesting than that of the longer division, and copious extracts may be here appropriately given, with little exception, *verbatim*:—

"I entrusted the charge of the work from Tehran to Zerra, a section about 150 miles in length, to Corporal Hockey, R.E., and gave him as assistant Corporal Peattie, R.E., lately arrived in the country. They commenced work on the 28th February, by which time all the insulators required for this section had reached Tehran, and had been distributed along the road. Starting from Tehran they put the line into thorough repair, replacing 222 poles by new ones, and preparing it for the reception of the new wire by fixing the second insulator on each post. About 28 miles in all of the course of the line were altered, as experience had shown that certain parts of it became inaccessible in winter. Returning on the 8th May, Corporal Hockey strained up the second wire, and completed his portion of the work on the 28th May. He deserves great credit for the satisfactory manner in which he accomplished his task.

"From Zerra to Karmanshah, a section of 150 miles, was in the charge of Corporal Fowles, R.E. He commenced work at Hamadan on the 1st March, and completed the erection of the second wire as far as Zerra, about 50 miles, on the 17th. The posts of the first 8 miles from Hamadan had to be entirely removed, and the course of the line altered, as it originally ran through a series of vineyards and gardens that baffled all attempts at efficient inspection and maintenance. 175 new poles had been provided for this 50 miles, but were found insufficient. The work was not delayed on this account, but Corporal Fowles has lately returned to this portion, and is now engaged in renewing about 200 of the remaining posts. On the 19th March, starting again from Hamadan, he commenced working in the Karmanshah direction. The first 4 miles of this piece had also to be moved out of the vineyards, and on the 5th April he had brought the second wire to the top of Asadabad Pass, 24 miles from Hamadan, having renewed 70 of the old posts. Unfortunately Corporal Fowles at this time fell seriously ill, in consequence of his unremitting exertions while constantly exposed to the exceptionally bad weather he had met with during these operations.

"On hearing of the stoppage of the work caused by the illness of Corporal Fowles, I sent Colour-Sergeant Chattin, R.E., to relieve him. This non-commissioned officer had come out in charge of the last detachment of Royal Engineers, and was consequently new to the country; but the satisfactory manner in which he surmounted the difficulties incident to his slight knowledge of the Persian language and customs, more than justified me in the choice I had made of him. With him was Corporal Empson, also recently joined, who had been Corporal Fowler' assistant as well. On the 9th April they resumed work from the top of the pass, whence to Karmanshah is a distance of about 70 miles. No less than 600 new poles were used to repair this portion of the line; all the old poles were taken up for examination, and reset when long enough after the decayed ends had been cut off. Wherever the line passed unavoidably through marshy ground, the posts were coated with bitumen from the foot to some height above the surface of the ground. While the work was in progress opposite the village of Asadabad, the inhabitants of that place, from some unaccountable motive, wantonly destroyed upwards of 100 of the insulators that had just been put up. I am glad to say that measures have been taken by the Persian Government for severely punishing the culprits. In the Sahna district again, the inhabitants of a small village near the road offered considerable opposition to the construction of the telegraph. It had been found necessary to alter the course of the line at this particular place, and as the new direction adopted seemed objectionable to the villagers, they repeatedly destroyed at night all that had been done in the day. This practice was continued until the ringleaders were caught and punished. At another time, a Persian Prince, requiring some mules to enable him to go on a hunting expedition, seized those that were employed in bringing up poles and wire for the working party, and several days elapsed before he could be made to give them up again. These and other causes of delay prevented Colour-Sergeant Chattin from reaching Karmanshah until the 2nd of June, and even then he found himself short of insulators, so many having been willfully destroyed during his progress from Hamadan. The last few miles of the wire could not, therefore, be put up until several loads of insulators had been sent for and received from other parts of the country, and it was not until the 15th June that the second wire could be reported completed from Hamadan to Karmanshah.

This working-party had met with several misadventures, but the climax had yet to be reached. On their way back to Hamadán, from which place most of the labourers employed had been brought, they found half a mile of the line, at a pass called Bediswik, completely destroyed. While engaged in reconstructing it, a party of Kúrds came down upon them, and after maltreating them, left them stripped and bound under the telegraph, carrying off everything they possessed—tools, clothes, and all their hard-earned gains of the last three months, which they had just been paid, and were taking home to their families. Fortunately for the Englishmen, they were not present at the time, or they would have met with the same treatment.

"The work over the remaining section of my division, from Karmansháh to the Turkish frontier, a distance of 140 miles, I placed in the charge of Corporal Whittingback, R.E. The smallest number of new poles necessary to enable him to put this part of the line into good order was estimated at 1,500. As timber of any kind fit for telegraph purposes is very scarce and dear in that part of Kurdistan, I entered into an agreement with a Persian Shahzádah, the owner of extensive plantations in a remote district called Tusirkan, some 80 miles from Karmansháh. The trees, of a specified size, were to be cut down at once, it being the beginning of December, and left to season, until the approach of spring enabled them to be transported to Karmansháh. According to the custom of the country, the price agreed upon had to be paid in advance. Unfortunately I could spare none of the English staff to remain and watch the felling of the trees, the consequence of which was that, out of the 1,500 poles presented in the spring in the fulfilment of the contract, only about 400 could be accepted as coming up to the standard. The Shahzádah insisted that he had carried out his part of the agreement, and for a long time would not consent either to refund the price of the 1,100 rejected poles, or to supply others in their place. It was only after reporting him to the Persian Government at Tehran, who sent a Sarhang armed with special orders, that the Shahzádah was at length obliged to consent to replace the rejected poles by good ones. It was now May; and in June, when these new poles were supplied, I could only accept some 150 of them as at all fit for telegraph purposes. Then, fairly wearied out, I refused to lose any more time in endeavouring to obtain proper poles from the Shahzâdah in fulfilment of his contract, and have since remained engaged in attempting to recover the balance due to me of the money advanced to him. The above is but a bare outline of an episode that is a characteristic example of business procedures in Persia, and of the kind of minor difficulties with which the construction of a telegraph in this country is beset. During these transactions the Shahzâdah once so far forgot himself as to have the telegraph mūnshi, whom I had sent to him with a message, severely beaten by his servants, who took advantage of the occasion also to rifle the mūnshi's pockets. On after-reflection the Shahzâdah became frightened at what he had done; and this helped matters to some sort of a conclusion.

"In the meantime the work between Karmanshah and the frontier could not be commenced for want of poles. When I received information, however, that iron poles were on their way out from England, of which 800 were allotted to my division for use in the frontier section, there was no longer any reason for delaying the erection of the second wire over that portion of the line which would eventually be reconstructed with the iron posts, as the existing poles would support the double line sufficiently well during the approaching summer. I accordingly, on the 7th March, directed Corporal Whittingback to put up the second wire from the frontier to Kirind, a distance of 76 miles. He commenced work at once, and had completed the portion in question by the end of March, but not without considerable difficulty, as the poles were so affected with rot at the foot that but few would support the ladder necessarily placed against them to enable the workmen to fix on the second insulator. There now only remained the 64 miles from Kirind to Karmanshah to complete. As soon as it became doubtful whether the Shahzâdah at Tusirkan would ever supply the poles he had engaged to deliver, and on which I had been obliged hitherto to rely, I began taking measures to procure them from other quarters, chiefly from villages near Hamadan, and to send them to Karmanshah as fast as carriage could be obtained. In June a sufficient number of poles had reached Karmanshah to enable Corporal Whittingback to recommence work, and, under favourable conditions, a fortnight would have enabled him to fill up the gap of 64 miles that remained. The heat, however, had become so great that one batch of labourers after another deserted him, and could not be induced to remain on the work even by greatly increased rates of pay. It is worthy of remark that a Persian labourer, however poverty-stricken, refuses to be tempted, by any consideration, to work either in the great heats of summer or in the severe cold of winter. Added to this, the Kūrds at this time discovered that the iron hooks of the new insulators could be turned to several useful purposes, and began a course of systematic breakage in order to supply themselves with these coveted prizes. The work consequently came to a practical standstill after some 20 miles had been put up, and, although there only remain 40 miles to be done, no date can be fixed for its completion with any approximation to certainty. As soon as the iron posts arrive, the part from the frontier to Kirind will be reconstructed with them; as autumn will then have set in, but little time will be consumed in this. . . . I cannot conclude my notice of this section without bringing prominently before you the zeal and energy that Corporal Whittingback has displayed under these peculiarly trying circumstances."

Lieutenant Pierson further commended his men and materials. The British agents at Karmanshah and Hamadan had shown readiness to aid; the wire was of excellent quality, and the insulators, though too heavy and of objectionable form, were very good. The tools were also good, but many were obtainable in the country " of shapes more adapted for the use of the natives." He concluded his report with a few practical remarks on the necessity of supplying the wanting means for future maintenance of the line, which could not be safely entrusted to purely Persian vigilance and provision; with pointing out the advantage of establishing a central office at the Turkish frontier; and with an expression of his obligations to Sir Arnold Kemball, Political Agent at Baghdad, for help and support freely afforded "in all matters connected with the telegraph."

In forwarding the reports, of which the substance has been for the most part recorded in the words of the writers themselves, Major Smith expatiated on the difficulties that had been overcome; while on the subject of maintenance, dwelt upon by Lieutenant Pierson, he has himself much of interest to say:—

"It has to be borne in mind that the conditions of a line of 1,200 miles in a country like this, bear little resemblance to those of a line of similar extent in more civilized countries. The stations are necessarily far apart, with intervening tracts of pure desert. The climate, except in spring and autumn, is excessive, intense cold and heavy snow in winter, and great heat in summer. Throughout its extent the line is exposed to wilful damage by passengers and wandering tribes, and even by the resident population, who not unfrequently cut the wire near a neighbouring village with whose inhabitants they happen to be at feud. The natives are utterly untrustworthy in the performance of even the most trivial duties. Lastly, the power of the Central Government, despotic as it is, is extremely limited in the provinces, where the Governors act, while in office, very much as they please, and a system of police is quite unknown.

"Under such circumstances the difficulties of guarding, maintenance, and repair, are of course very great, especially with the small European staff in the country, most of whom are necessarily employed as clerks in the principal offices. The following is the system now in force, which has been adopted as the most practicable. Each of the three divisions is subdivided into three sections, in charge of as many non-commissioned officers of the first detachment of Royal Engineers who act as inspectors. Their duty is to go over their sections once in both directions every month, making such repairs as the line may require, and paying and looking after the horsemen stationed at each office for restoring communication in every case of interruption. Besides the principal stations, Bushahr, Shiraz, Ispahan, Tehran, Hamadan, and Karmanshah, intermediate ones have been established at Kāzarūn, between Bushahr and Shiraz; Dehbid (in progress), Abadeh and Kūmishah, between Shiraz and Ispahan; Kashan and Kūm, between Ispahan and Tehran; Nobaran, between Tehran and Hamadan; and Kirind, between Karmanshah and the Turkish frontier. These, with the principal stations, divide the whole distance into fourteen sections, of an average length of nearly ninety miles. At each intermediate and principal station, at least four horsemen, paid by the English inspectors, are kept in readiness to ride out in the direction of a break, and repair it as rapidly as possible. A daily patrol would be more satisfactory, but is quite impossible in this country. We have found by experience that no Persian can be entrusted with the duty of patrolling, even when regularly and liberally paid. First, unless there is someone to see him, he never goes under the wire, but simply along the road. Secondly, he thinks of nothing but plunder, and not unfrequently cuts the wire himself, in order, by accusing some unfortunate passenger, to extort money through his fears. For these and other reasons we had to give up all hope of ever establishing an efficient patrol, and to content ourselves with the present system of *repairing*. And even this plan, simple as it may appear, is not without its difficulties."

We quote the concluding paragraphs:—

"I beg to express my hearty acknowledgment of the invaluable services of Lieutenants St. John and Pierson, whose discretion, knowledge of the country and personal influence with the local authorities have been of perhaps even more importance than their professional zeal and ability. I quite concur in the credit given by them to the various members of the staff mentioned in their reports, and have much pleasure in testifying to the skill and perseverance of Sergeant Isaacson, R.E., who was employed more directly under myself in the section nearest Tehran.

"My best thanks are due to Colonel Sir Arnold Kemball and Lieutenant-Colonel Pelly, for their invariable kindness and assistance in every way that lay in their power."[1]

The roaming duties of the Chief Director had prevented him from supplementing these reports, when originally submitted, with a forwarding letter of his own; but when able to supply the deficiency, he readily did so. We shall bring the present chapter to an end by one or two extracts from his official communication on the subject addressed to Bombay from London, and the Government resolutions in reply; premising that the story of the Russo-Persian line will be told in the chapter immediately succeeding:—

"The correspondence respecting the construction of a telegraph line through Persia (1861-63) printed in 1864, as a Parliamentary Record, affords full information on the means by which was obtained from the Shah's Government an alternative to the section of the Indo-European telegraph between Baghdad and Bushahr. After-events and experience have shown that this particular section must, by the force of circumstances, be considered important rather in its capability of securing a general alternative to the whole European line, than as applied to the few hundred miles in and near the Persian Gulf; that is to say, of the whole distance from Khanikin to Bushahr, the two-fifths leading from Khanikin to Tehran may be considered out of the main Russo-Persian line, whose junction with the Indian and Indo-Persian system is effected at Tehran. It is to the three-fifths, or distance between Tehran and Bushahr, that attention must be given to make the Russian route in any way efficient, if not actually available.

"At the same time, the link between the two great alterna-

[1] Major R. M. Smith to Secretary to Government, Bombay; No. 570 of August 1, 1867, forwarding Reports of Lieuts. St. John and Pierson, R.E.

tive lines could not be ignored in any new arrangement made by the Indian Government with either Turkey or Persia. And though the section of telegraph joining Tehran to Baghdad did not promise to be one of frequent use, the cause was to be attributed more to petty jealousies and old national antipathies, than to any failure of its own to perform the functions required. Therefore, on the proposal of the late Lieutenant-Colonel Patrick Stewart to secure a whole wire to the British Government on the Persian lines, in place of a share in the one wire obtained by the earlier negotiations, the arrangement was to have effect for the full distance from Khanikin to Bushahr, and not to be confined to a single section.

"In June 1865 I proceeded to Persia, under the instructions of the Right Hon. the Secretary of State for India, to assist her Majesty's Minister at Tehran in negotiating with the local Government for a wire on the then existing line of telegraph, to be reserved entirely for Indo-European messages, and worked entirely by British officials in the pay of her Majesty's Government. I need not here recite the process by which the desired end was attained, the difficulties in the way of attainment, or the modifications in Colonel Stewart's original proposals which it became necessary to admit into the ratified Convention. On my departure from Tehran in December of the aforesaid year, the necessary stores and materials had been telegraphed for, and preparations had already been made for renovating and strengthening the posts on which the second wire was to be set up."

Accounting for the delay through which the whole of 1866 and half of 1867 passed away before the terms of the Anglo-Persian Convention had been literally fulfilled by erection of the second wire, the writer does not hesitate to arrive at a conclusion absolving the British staff of officers and men from all responsibility for tardy execution, and at the same time highly favourable to their character for zeal and industry. He adds:—

"The completion of the work at all, in eighteen months, must afford abundant proof how much has been achieved by the untiring energy and perseverance of the English superintendents and their assistants, on whom the onus of labour fell."[1]

The five next paragraphs refer to questions of detail more or less foreign to the general narrative. The next is confirmatory, from personal acquaintance, of the high character given by Major Smith and his assistants to many of the individuals named in their reports. The remaining paragraphs are quoted either wholly or in part.

"The non-commissioned officers from Chatham have not only had to perform duties demanding scientific or mechanical ability; their work demands, moreover, an exercise of responsibility, and withal temper and discretion, which would tax the training of commissioned officers of Indian repute. If they have occasionally erred in this respect, it cannot but be borne in mind how constantly and steadily the majority have succeeded; and success of this nature implies indirectly the spread of wholesome English influence in a quarter of no small interest.

"Lieutenant St. John places on record the acknowledgments which he considers due to the Hissam-u-Saltaneh, or Prince-Governor of Fars, for unvarying kindness and courtesy, and assistance generally, to his work of superintendence. Much credit is also due to Lieutenant St. John himself for securing the good offices and friendship of his Royal Highness, who is one of the most distinguished and influential men in Persia."

"As regards the services of Major R. Murdoch Smith, for more than two years Acting Director of the Persian telegraphs, and his immediate assistants—notably Lieutenants St. John and Pierson, whose reports are submitted to Government—I am convinced

---

[1] Lieut.-Colonel Goldsmid, C.B., to Secretary to Government; No. 128 of 21st October, 1867.

that it would be difficult to find officers better adapted for the delicate and often arduous and trying duties which they are called upon to fulfil in Persia. I can certify from personal experience that Major Smith's testimony to the character of his assistants is no other than the expression of an impartial and unbiassed judgment. And I can further certify, that the encomiums which he has passed upon these officers would be no less deserved if applied to his own case.

"While expressing thus publicly my obligations to the officers employed in setting up the second wire of the Persian telegraph, and submitting this expression of opinion to the favourable consideration of Government, I should fail to do justice to the occasion were I to omit the name of Major Champain, R.E. This officer accompanied the late Colonel Patrick Stewart to Persia in 1862, and was afterwards appointed Director of Telegraphs in that country. He assisted her Majesty's Minister in the early negotiations for the line, and superintended its original construction. The task was not an easy one. The field was comparatively new. Opposition was rife in every quarter. Major Champain, with his assistants, Captain Smith, Lieutenants St. John and Pierson, and Mr. Walton, overcame all obstacles, and the 1,100 miles of telegraph from Khanikin to Bushahr were opened in March 1865. Subsequent events called Major Champain to England, and for the last two years his sphere of usefulness has been confined to Europe. The services which he has rendered will, it is hoped, ere long be apparent in the thorough organization of Indo-European traffic by alternative routes, a desideratum which only constant experience and vigilance can enable its superintendents to achieve in so long a line as that connecting London with Calcutta and the other Indian Presidencies."

In conclusion, Lieutenant-Colonel Goldsmid respectfully invited attention to the acknowledgments recorded in Major Smith's report and accompaniments to Lieutenant-Colonel Pelly, the Resident at Bushahr, who had "on more than one occasion rendered special service to the telegraph officers, as during the late disturbance at Shiraz;" and to Colonel Sir Arnold Kemball, her Majesty's Consul-General in Turkish Arabia, to whom so much was due, "not only in respect of general improvements to Turkish Asiatic telegraph communication, but for the actual construction, maintenance, and efficient working of the line below Baghdad."

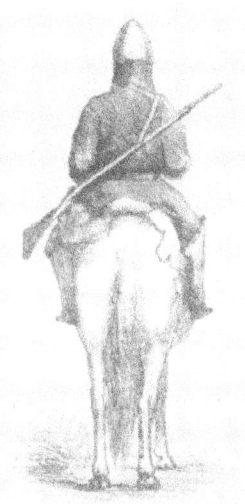

CHASSEUR A CHEVAL PERSIA.

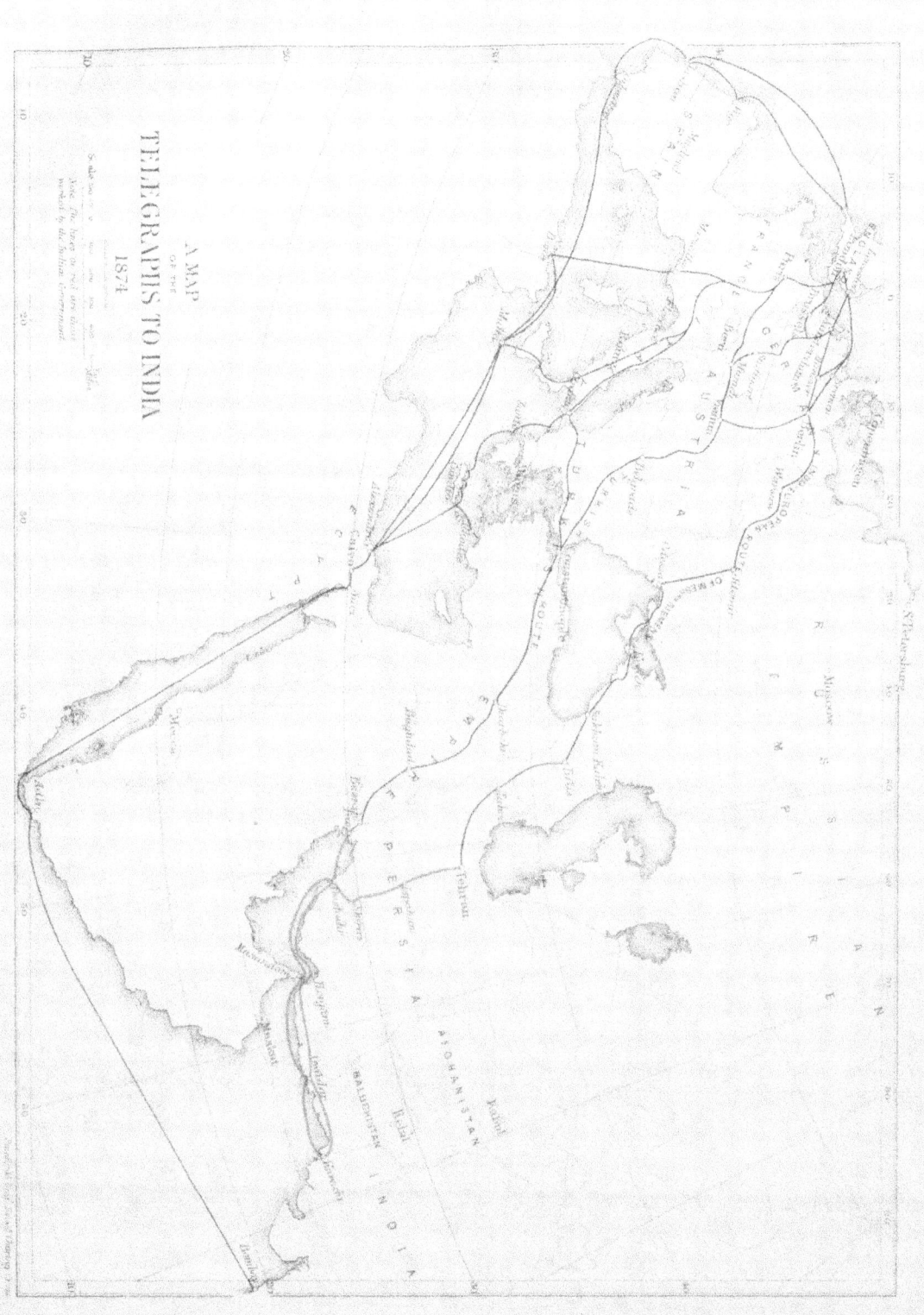

CHAPTER VI.

ORIGIN AND PROGRESS OF THE RUSSO-PERSIAN LINES.—MEASURES TAKEN GENERALLY TO IMPROVE TELEGRAPHIC COMMUNICATIONS WITH INDIA FROM FIRST ORGANIZATION TO CONGRESS OF VIENNA, 1868.—LAYING SECOND CABLE BETWEEN JASK AND BUSHAHR.—EXTENSION OF MAKRAN COAST-LINE WESTWARD TO JASK; WITH SUMMARY OF MORE RECENT PROCEEDINGS.

IT has been shown that on Colonel Goldsmid's departure for Persia, in June 1865, Major Champain's attention was drawn to the palpable advantages to Indo-European telegraphic communications obtainable from the institution of an alternative line through Russia to the Persian capital, and thence to Bushahr, where it would meet the Government cable. He had, indeed, written a short memorandum on the subject, which Colonel Goldsmid took with him to St. Petersburg, and re-transmitted to London from that city with his own comments. Russia was well disposed to assist the cause, and Dr. Siemens, head of a well-known firm in London, and himself a gentleman of high scientific attainments, and special ability as a practical telegraph engineer,[1] had

[1] Charles William Siemens, Esq., F.R.S. D.C.L., has too deservedly wide a reputation to need more than mention by name in a work of this nature.

expressed willingness to help any scheme of through communications from St. Petersburg to the Persian frontier, provided only he held further control of the Persian line from the frontier to Tehran, where English work began. It was not that Indian messages were shut out of the Russo-Persian line then existing; some were sent by that route; but in practice it was found less trustworthy than the Indo-Ottoman, and nothing had been done to put in order or organize a complete traffic, *via* Russia and Persia, to India. There were lines of some kind in Russia from the Baltic or the northern Prussian frontier, more or less, to Tiflis and the Persian frontier, and there was a kind of a line from Julfa, on the frontier, to Tehran; moreover, long before the conclusion of our own 1865 Convention with Persia, there had been signed by that State a treaty with Russia, consisting of articles regulating international telegraphic correspondence, as though such correspondence was a recognised institution. But all was crude, very crude. The Indian mercantile community, and others interested in telegraphs to India, made long and loud complaints against Turkey; but at this period it had no cause to be more satisfied with Russia. The first year that England interchanged messages by wire with India was not a successful one anywhere in steady telegraphic working; but those whose duty it was to watch causes and results, were more sanguine of eventual success than those who looked to results only, and were indifferent to reasons.

On the 31st August, 1865, while the Chief Director was endeavouring to advance negotiations in Tehran, Major Champain submitted a memorandum in favour of an alternative land-line, *via* St. Petersburg, Tiflis, and Tehran, " which would, in case of failure of the Baghdad line, take the whole of the Anglo-Indian traffic, or under any circumstances, tend to keep up a healthy spirit of rivalry in the management of the opposition or Turkish line." He considered in it the propositions to be made to the Russian and Persian Governments respectively in furtherance of the scheme, and the questions of rates on either line; but as his forwarding letter showed that objection existed to promote, by diplomatic intervention, any alternative measure detrimental to a power with which we had so recently signed a Telegraph Convention, there was little hope that authority would be given for immediate or effectual action. And so it was in reality. There was no course but constant watching, and continual pressure; the first, a matter-of-fact, business-like procedure, in connection with posts and wires; the second, a silent and ungracious task, in connection with dignitaries and officials. In October 1865, Colonel Goldsmid addressed to the Assistant Director a letter from Tehran, suggesting that his presence might be useful on the continent of Europe in improving the still highly defective state of communications between the Persian Gulf cable and western Europe; and in February 1866 Major Champain had removed to Constantinople. His report from that city in the April following, and the Chief Director's of the previous November from Tehran, are specially referred to in the report of the Select Committee on East India communications, sitting in London at the date just mentioned, as affording material information on the whole question.[1] In evidence given before that committee, it is stated that "Major Champain was sent out to Constantinople with the intention of going along the line and reporting on it; but he found

[1] See page 10, par. 37; and Appendix, pages 436 to 441, and 619 to 625.

that such an improvement had taken place during the last two or three months, that he has not thought it necessary to do so."[1] Later in the year, Colonel Goldsmid, on return from Persia, was personally examined; and, among other questions of detail, gave evidence on the then state of the Russo-Persian line. He was of opinion that the imperfect communication between Tehran and Tabriz was one of the chief causes of its failure.[2]

We have already mentioned that Major Champain had joined Colonel Goldsmid in Paris, in October 1866, when the latter officer was *en route* again to Persia, which country he had only left some nine months before. His report to the Under Secretary of State, dated the 27th idem, revives the proposal of an improved line through Russia:—

"Colonel Goldsmid," he writes, "on leaving England had intended to proceed to Berlin, in order to meet Mr. Wilson of the Electric and International Company, and in concert with him to endeavour to get a special wire through Prussia and Austria. Departure from London had however been considerably delayed, and it seemed very doubtful whether he could get to Berlin and meet Mr. Wilson, and then proceed to Vienna and arrive in time to catch the last boat of the season down the Danube for Constantinople. I therefore undertook the Berlin negotiations myself, and left Paris on Tuesday morning. At 7 A.M. on Wednesday I reached Berlin, met Mr. Wilson, and at once waited on the British Ambassador, to present a letter of introduction given by Lord Stanley to Colonel Goldsmid, and to explain why I had come in place of the latter officer. His Excellency... was good enough to introduce me at once to Colonel Von Chauvin, the

---

[1] Proceedings, May 15, 1866, page 145.

[2] *Vide* Report from the Select Committee on East India Communications pages 197, 199, especially queries 3493-7, 3520 and 3521.

Prussian Director-General, who received Mr. Wilson and myself most cordially. After stating our wishes, Colonel Von Chauvin said he was very desirous to further our views, and that, as far as he was concerned, he would be glad to give us a special wire through Prussia in any direction we might choose, provided of course that the same could be continued onwards. . . . Colonel Von Chauvin offered to lay us a thoroughly good special wire from the Dutch frontier to Thorn, on the Prusso-Russian boundary, near Warsaw, and said that, from what he knew of the Russian Director-General's views, he would answer for it that the special wire should be continued to meet our lines in Persia. . . . He was sure that Russia would give us a special wire from Thorn through Warsaw to Odessa, and thence to the Russian frontier of Bessarabia, near Tulcha. From Tulcha to Constantinople the Turks have already a line of telegraph; and if they could be induced to attach a special wire for our and their own benefit, the through special line would then be completed. The Russians would also give a special wire, if we wished, from Odessa to the Caucasus, Tiflis, and Persia, in case of the Turkish lines breaking down."

Major Champain then put schemes of alternative lines for adoption; but as the inquiry into these has now become of obsolete interest, we need not re-open their discussion. He solicited a speedy reply for communication to the Chief Director while at Constantinople, as his presence there might be useful in carrying out any arrangement preferred. Not many days after receipt of this letter, the Under Secretary of State, India Office, addressed the Under Secretary of State in the Foreign Office, very plainly setting forth what were the views entertained by Lord Cranborne on this question.

Reference had been made by the Foreign Office to the India Office for an expression of opinion "as to the steps to be taken on a suggestion of the East India and China Association of Liverpool, that representations should be made to the Turkish and other continental Governments with a view to the improvement of telegraphic communication with India." The India Office considered that the action taken by Lord Lyons was just what was required in Turkey. He had backed up the telegraph officers in their proposals for special wires for the particular service required, and he had warned the authorities at the Porte that unless attention were given to these and similar measures, Indian correspondence " would take a different route, from which it would be difficult subsequently to divert it."

As regards arrangements with the Governments of European States west of Turkey, for distant wires for Indo-European messages, Lord Lyons' opinion of the importance of these was fully concurred in; and the unofficial action taken already in the matter by Colonel Goldsmid and Major Champain had met with a satisfactory result. Should the Foreign Office think fit to further the cause by intimating to the several Governments concerned how much interest was taken by her Majesty's Government in the matter, it might be well to correct an erroneous impression on the part of some of the continental Administrations, that the Indian Administration had a preference for any particular line, and to notify to them that the Indian public were " perfectly at liberty to send telegrams either by the Turkish or Russo-Persian branch of the Indo-European telegraph, whichever they might at any time consider most suitable for their purposes."[1]

About three or four months later, Major Champain submitted, in more detail than before, a proposal from Messrs. Siemens and Co., of a simple and practical

Mr. J. Cosmo Melvill to the Right Hon. E. Hammond, Feb. 21, 1867.

nature, giving it his own earnest support, and basing his recommendation upon very plausible and at the same time reasonable grounds.

They offered to construct an independent double line of telegraph from London to Tehran, provided that her Majesty's Government would grant certain advantages, characterised as "indirect," namely:—

1st. To put their line on the same footing as any other respecting transmission of messages, leaving the public free to select in the matter.

2nd. To give diplomatic aid and countenance to the line in Persia and elsewhere.

3rd. To provide additional means for the transmission of messages between Tehran and India, in case the existing lines should prove insufficient.

4th. To give the public the benefit of a reduced tariff between Tehran and India, when, in consequence of a well-established scheme between London and Tehran, a large increase in the number of messages should take place.

The Russian and Prussian Governments had expressed their readiness to facilitate the realization of the project, and had permitted the firm to construct and work the entire line, charging a moderate royalty on all messages to effect reimbursement.[1]

One year and a half had passed since the Messrs. Siemens' original proposal had been mooted and set aside; and though the Indo-Ottoman lines had shown occasional signs of improvement, it could not be said that a means of communication by telegraph with India was available such as the public interested had been led to expect.

[1] Letter to Major Champain, dated February 7, 1867.

"If you will refer to the Constantinople traffic-returns," said Major Champain, writing to the India Office on the 12th February, 1867, "you will see that at no period since the opening of the Indo-European telegraph has the condition of the Turkish lines, both European and Asiatic, been more deplorable than during the past few months. The irregularity in the transmission of despatches is perhaps as vexatious as the general slowness; and the want of accuracy in the through signalling has given rise to very many complaints. . . . . For a month or two all may go well, but just as the public begins to realise the improved state of affairs, a break-down takes place, and the general confidence is once more thoroughly uprooted . . . . . The truth is that to ensure rapidity of transmission we *must* have wires extending from end to end of the line exclusively set apart for the through traffic. Until this is done our Indian messages will be constantly detained, and occasionally almost lost sight of, in the press of local traffic at some of the many continental stations on the line. Special wires would also very materially reduce the number of inaccuracies which now disfigure our through telegrams. Under the present system of working it surprises me that a message should ever reach England from India without mistakes. When it is remembered that the telegram is originally expressed in crammed or abbreviated language to avoid expense, and is then received and retransmitted twelve or fourteen times by Armenian, Greek, Turkish, German, French or Italian signallers, who probably possess an excessively faint knowledge of English, it must at once be seen how difficult it is to avoid the introduction of errors, which are exaggerated and give rise to others at every repetition. This would be the case if the work to be performed were the simple copying and recopying of ordinary handwriting; but the use of the Morse code of telegraph signals, simple though it is, at once introduces a new element of uncertainty, and greatly increases the chance of error. Thus, as in ordinary handwriting, two consecutive *n*'s might easily be mistaken for a variety of combinations of the letters *m*, *n*, *u*, or *i*; so in the Morse alphabet almost every letter can be mistaken for combinations of others. An *i* is the same as two *e*'s, an *h* the same as two *i*'s, and so on. In good signalling, as in good handwriting, errors need not of course occur, but where from frequent repetition many clerks are employed in the manipulation of each message, and on account of their ignorance of the language in which it is couched, assistance cannot be obtained from the context, it is clear that perfect accuracy is not to be looked for."

He dwelt especially on the complaints of the merchants and others to whom the telegraph was becoming a necessity, and urged that not only was confidence failing in the line as then available, but traffic was diminishing. He admitted that the Russo-Persian was no better than the Indo-Ottoman line, but maintained that the difficulties of improving the former were not of the description which had been proved to exist for the latter. He then proceeded to illustrate his argument by an exposition of the project he so strongly approved ; nor did he see any difficulty in recommending that her Majesty's Government should agree to the moderate conditions asked for by the gentlemen representing the firm whose proposals had been submitted. This letter was followed up by a statement of all that had been done to secure special wires on the Turkish route since Colonel Goldsmid's departure from Constantinople. The latter officer was at Tehran when a report of the revival of the project of a new line through Russia and Prussia reached him. Lest any doubt should exist on his own views of the propriety or otherwise of the purposed scheme, he addressed the Under Secretary of State with reference to the Assistant Director's letter submitting it.

"The Russian Minister at Tehran," he wrote, "is very much in favour of availing himself of such assistance for the line from Julfa to Tehran, without regard to any arrangements made by the Russian Government for the traffic in Europe. As I believe that his Excellency has so expressed himself in communication with his own Government, and as her Majesty's Minister in Persia saw no objection to my discussion of the question with M. de Giers, it is my opinion that at least this part of Messrs. Siemens' proposal should meet with every encouragement. I am not prepared to say that the management of the entire line could be better conducted by a private firm than by the departmental officers of continental Governments. But this is a matter which naturally depends so much on the pleasure of those Governments, that any further discussion of the point appears needless. Major Champain has placed before the Right Honourable the Secretary of State a full and comprehensive report, leaving little to be desired in the way of elucidation. But I may be pardoned for repeating my assurances, that, supported by the diplomatic agency proposed in the memorandum submitted[1] to her Majesty's Ambassador at Constantinople in January last, we should infinitely improve telegraphic communication in Europe, so far as regards the transit of Indian telegrams; and in all probability secure the special wires generally admitted to be the great desideratum. And the argument would hold equally good whether the Russian wires were in private or in Government hands, for it is too much to anticipate a continuous monopoly for one particular line.

The very careful and elaborate paper addressed at this period by Colonel Von Chauvin, the zealous and able Director of the Prussian Telegraph Department, to Major Champain, not only exhibiting a thorough knowledge of the subject, but a keen sympathy with the object contemplated, concluded with an intimation that the writer had been authorised by his Government to negotiate the whole matter with the Russian Government at St. Petersburg, where he would be joined by Dr. Werner Siemens, of the firm of Siemens and Halske,

[1] See Appendix to this chapter.
[2] No. 46 of the 15th March, 1867.

and Mr. Schütz Wilson, of the Electric and International Telegraph Company. And this intimation was accompanied by an invitation to Major Champain to attend the conference proposed as delegate of Great Britain, or perhaps rather as accredited representative of her Majesty's Indian Government.

About a month after receipt of this communication, Major Champain arrived at St. Petersburg, empowered to act discretionally in supporting the interests he served, but without authority to sign agreements or treaties, or commit his Government in any way by pledge or guarantee. On the 1st of May, the fourth day after arrival, he telegraphed to Colonel Goldsmid, who had returned on that date from Hamadan to Tehran: "*Affaire Siemens arrangée.*"

No time had been lost. He reached the Russian capital on Saturday, and commenced business on Monday, in consultation with the Russian and Prussian Telegraph Directors General. On the Tuesday, discussion was renewed at the quarters of the Minister of Posts and Telegraphs. The question, at first treated as one of rigid State requirement, involving political compensation for services rendered, eventually resolved itself into commercial considerations; and these, having been well digested beforehand by the more earnest of the Executives concerned, were neither obstructive nor obscure. Two or three more meetings ensued, and finally a Russo-Prussian agreement was concluded and signed, for the establishment of an international telegraph line between England and India.

Whatever opinions may be passed upon this simple and practical proceeding, it cannot be denied that a good stroke of business had been done for the mercantile world, and those to whom an efficient and a reliable telegraph between Western Europe and India was one of the exigencies of professional life. It may be said that the Red Sea cable, and the submarine adjuncts, superseded the necessity for this line; but the deep-sea lines had not been planned when the Siemens remedy was found for the Turkish shortcomings; and it was in mistrust of *all* then existing land telegraph communications that the scheme was matured and recommended to the public. The written instruments obtained by Messrs. Siemens Brothers, of London, and Siemens and Halske, of Berlin, were of a comprehensive kind. That of the Russian Government, confirmed by his Majesty the Czar on the 1st of September, 1867, granted to them an exclusive concession for erecting and working a direct telegraphic communication between London and India, "that is to say, between Europe and India," within the frontiers of the Russian empire. It was of twenty-three articles, of which the general tendency was to secure freedom of action and Government support for the work to be carried out. Of the conditions or reservations, the most important of all were those contained in the seventeenth clause, limiting the terms of agreement to twenty-five years. Independently of these it was natural that a royalty should be demanded, and five francs upon twenty words was no great consideration. It was also natural that the route selected for the contemplated line should be determined under sanction of the local Government. On the expiration of the term specified, the article provides that "the privileges are to cease, and the concessionaires must in due time come to an agreement with Government as to the further working of the Anglo-Indian telegraph line. Should no such agreement be come to, the entire undertaking, as it is carried out under the conditions of the present concession, is to pass over into the hands of the Government without compensation and in good condition."

That of the Prussian Government, dated Berlin, August 26th, 1867, granted "a concession for the construction and working of telegraph lines from London to the North German coast, so far as concerns Prussian territory (corresponding to the concessions demanded from the Imperial Russian and Persian Governments, for the purpose of erecting and working a direct telegraph between London and Tehran, that is to say London and India)," under seventeen conditions.

The first four of these bound the concessionaires as to materials and time in the construction of a land-line and cable from London to the Prussian North Sea coast. The fifth undertook, on the part of the Prussian Government, to construct and keep in good and efficient working condition during the term of the concession, from the landing-points of the cables to the Prusso-Russian frontier, two special wires of good material and large size, to be reserved exclusively for Anglo-Indian correspondence. The next twelve articles need no specification, but were, upon the whole, liberal to the concessionaires. The seventeenth and last article limited the term of the concession in this case also to twenty-five years, giving the concessionaires the right, on its expiration, should no agreement on this head be renewed, "to employ their submarine lines between the German and English coasts for the transmission of international correspondence."

That of the Persian Government, sanctioned by his Majesty the Shah on the 11th January, 1868, granted "an exclusive concession for erecting and working a line of telegraph between the Russian frontier (Julfa) and Tehran," in continuation of a direct line from London to Julfa, and for the transmission only of messages between India and Europe. As in the case of the two concessions already noted, the term was limited to twenty-five years; at the expiration of which, failing a new understanding, the line was to be handed over to Persia, without indemnity and in good condition. There were sixteen articles, of which the ninth seems to demand separate notice. By this the concessionaires renounced the right of participating in the receipts on international telegrams passing between Julfa and Tehran, and *vice versâ*, until expiry of the Anglo-Persian Convention of November 1865, on condition that then existing rates along that section were not raised. But on the expiry of the said Convention, unless a new one were made with the British Government, the Tehran-Bushahr line should be handed over to the concessionaires under certain rules and reservations. If a new Anglo-Persian Convention on the other hand were substituted for that of 1865, the concessionaires would then become entitled to one-third of the charge fixed upon for telegrams between Julfa and Bushahr, warranted not to exceed 10½ francs. And it was further stated, that "should the tariffs on the other lines be modified," the concessionaires would pay to the Persian Government integrally 2 francs for each telegram, the latter reserving the right of claiming 2 francs per telegram of twenty words, or a fixed annual sum of 12,000 tomans — about 4,000*l.*

To review the measures taken generally to improve Indo-European telegraphic communication from first organization, we must return for a while to Constantinople.

It has been shown that at the very outset of working from Europe to India through Turkey, the difficulty to be surmounted was not merely that of setting up and utilizing a line through semi-barbarous regions, but of interchanging telegrams regularly, rapidly, and surely, with Constantinople itself.

A Convention had been signed and sealed before Colonel Stewart's death, providing for the traffic east of the Turkish capital; but it was only during his actual residence in Turkey, and close upon the period of his last illness, that he became painfully and practically aware that out of five or more lines of telegraph between London and the Bosphorus, not one was reliable. And it is not unreasonable to believe that the disappointment occasioned in his mind by the little zeal and unsympathetic support of the Turkish authorities in promoting the cause he had at heart served to aggravate his physical complaint. Men differently constituted would have accepted the position as not only inevitable, but in the natural order of things. To him, an obstacle was apparent which it was his duty to remove, to clear the way to a great end. He saw how to do it, but was not permitted to raise an arm. He might advise, recommend, and await results; but action upon his advice and recommendation was in the hands of others; and their mode of working, as their tone of thought, was other than his own. After his death, an attempt was made by those who succeeded him to follow the course he had indicated and begun. Colonel Goldsmid's proceedings during the remainder of his stay at Constantinople in 1865, and Major Champain's at the commencement of the following year, have been already noticed: but we have yet to render an account of official results when the former officer revisited the city of the Sultan in 1866 *en route* to Persia.

He had passed through Persia and Vienna, and from Vienna he had reported progress. The letter is freely quoted:—[1]

"In August last I met Sir James Carmichael, Chairman of the Submarine Telegraph Company, in Paris, to confer with M. de Vougy, Director-General of French Telegraphs, on the possibility of procuring a special wire for our Indian messages traversing France. The Director-General saw no difficulty in giving us what we required, provided that our telegraph companies improved the existing means of communication between London and Paris, and that we could make satisfactory arrangements for our Indian traffic between Vienna and Constantinople. He promised, however, to do his best for us, if I would write him semi-officially on the subject."

A letter was accordingly written and authoritatively approved. The report then refers to an interview held between Colonel Goldsmid and Major Champain on the one side, and the French Director-General on the other, in October:—

"M. de Vougy told us plainly he was ready to meet our wishes, but that it was unclear to arrange simply for a special wire through France unless Austria would do her part as well. I had certainly been under the impression at our former interview that the French Director-General would undertake to make the necessary arrangements up to Vienna itself, in communication with the Administrations concerned; and I referred to what had before passed between us. M. de Vougy said I might tell M. Brunner, the Austrian Director, from him, that he was quite willing to give us a wire in France on the Paris and Vienna route, if the Austrians would act in like manner. . . . My de-

---

[1] *To the Under Secretary of State*; No. 185, of the 29th October, 1866.

parture from London had been unavoidably delayed for a few days, and M. de Vougy's absence from Paris had kept me two days longer there. To economise time, I resolved to proceed to Vienna direct, leaving Major Champain to be my substitute in Berlin."

From the last-named city he received, at Vienna, a telegram from Mr. Wilson, of the Electric and International Company, as follows:—"Special arrangements between us and you impossible. Other arrangements pending, *viâ* Odessa."

At Vienna he saw Count Mensdorff, Minister of Foreign Affairs, M. Wullersdorff, Minister of Commerce, and eventually, M. Brunner.

"A long conference held with him resulted in a proposal on his part to summon a meeting of specially-deputed telegraph officials from Austria, Servia, and Turkey, to arrange for two lines of communication between Vienna and Constantinople, one of which might always be available for Anglo-Indian traffic. This meeting would be convened by Austria or Turkey, and I (or any other authorized officer) would attend on the part of the Government of India. Without such arrangement, by which each contracting party could be bound, by *procès verbal*, to provide particular wires on particular lines for Indian as well as, if necessary, other correspondence, M. Brunner was of opinion that he could attain no satisfactory conclusion. He fully admitted that the grand defect was between Vienna and Constantinople, and I assured him that our Asiatic lines were becoming comparatively trustworthy and efficient. He considered that any arrangement for special wires between Paris (or Berlin) and Vienna was quite a secondary affair, for there were sufficient wires for every purpose on both lines. The Electric and International could work perfectly well with Vienna by Holland and Berlin, and the Submarine by Paris and Basle, without making any such provision. . . . . I subsequently saw his Majesty's *Chargé d'affaires*. . . It was his belief that the Austrian authorities would gladly render us such assistance in facilitating our telegraphic correspondence with India as could reasonably be expected.... I see no reason why there should not be a line, viâ Odessa, independent of Austria (as well as those viâ St. Petersburg and Tiflis, and Paris and Turin), if really obtainable, for the Indo-European traffic. But I think we should first give attention rather to the perfection of one or two of the whole number of existing lines than to increasing the number of lines generally. And as regards the proposed arrangements with Turkey, M. Brunner has shown me that very little is wanting to complete two efficient lines of traffic; one through Servia by Belgrade and Nissa, as promised long ago for Indian messages by the Ottoman Administration; and one through Agram and Bosni Serai already constructed by the Austrian and Turkish Administrations to their respective frontiers, but not yet utilized, because the Turks on their part have failed to put up a second wire for international correspondence. I would respectfully submit my recommendation that—unless some, to me, unknown advantages have been offered in an entirely new channel, which render advisable the comparative abandonment of the hitherto acknowledged best routes—an officer on the part of the Indian Government may be authorized to attend any such conference as that proposed by the Austrian Director. If held at Constantinople within the month, my presence there could so far be secured without detriment to the service, as I have every prospect of detention in quarantine for ten days, in addition to the time to be occupied in travelling, and settling with Mr. Courtenay, those questions of account and organization now awaiting my arrival."

In reply, the Chief Director was authorized to attend the meeting alluded to in his letter, if held within a convenient time, and without hindrance to the special duties with which he was charged; but his presence was to be merely in the capacity of an adviser, and his action should not go beyond pointing out the advantages which might be "expected to accrue to the countries represented, from the formation of improved lines of telegraphic communication with India, and testifying to the interest which the Indian Government take in the matter."[1]

On the 12th December, Colonel Goldsmid submitted, from Constantinople, to the India Office, the copy of a letter which had been addressed by him to her Majesty's Ambassador at the Porte at his Excellency's request,[2] together with accompaniments. The letter contained the following passages, and gave cover to a memorandum reprinted *in extenso*:—

"I do myself the honour of bringing to notice that the working of the Indian telegraph in the Ottoman dominions is still most unsatisfactory, and to a great extent nullifies the objects for which the Convention of the 3rd September, 1864,[3] was concluded.

"In that Convention, if no mention was made of the Turkish European lines, it must have been that full confidence was placed in the superior advantages of the European system, and that provisions rendered necessary for introducing, as it were, an important innovation through a comparatively uncivilized country, would be out of place west of Constantinople; but in practice it has been found that, as a rule, the Asiatic works better than the European line. . . . . With the sanction of her Majesty's Secretary of State for India, and under the impression that a line of telegraphic communication between England and India cannot be held restricted in usefulness to the terminal stations only, but must more or less command the interest of intervening continental States, I recently put the question of giving a special wire to this service to the French and Austrian Administrations. The result promises to be successful in obtaining due attention to our requirements from these and other

---

[1] Under Secretary of State to Colonel Goldsmid, November 22, 1866.
[2] Dated Pera, December 5, 1866.
[3] *Vide* p. 169, 10, 11, *ante*.

authorities concerned, provided we can secure a regular and rapid communication between Constantinople and Vienna.' This last is, no doubt, the one section of our whole line which at present requires the greatest attention, and the operation of the Convention of 1864 is so affected by its condition, at least within the limits of European Turkey, that it is quite as much for the interest of the Ottoman Government as our own to have it constructed and organized on the most efficient footing."

The brief summary of proceedings which followed may here be omitted, and the concluding paragraph of the letter alone quoted, in addition to the memorandum:—

"Owing to the very great importance to the Government and public that no opportunity should be lost of perfecting the Indian communication as much as possible, I would respectfully submit to your Lordship's consideration a memorandum and accompaniments, which it might be deemed advisable to refer to his Highness the Minister for Foreign Affairs, either before or after my departure for Persia.

"MEMORANDUM.

"The Indo-Ottoman Convention of the 3rd September, 1864, though not providing for any special line or wire for the passage of Indian telegrams through European Turkey, would be manifestly useless for the purpose contemplated if the arrangements in that respect were not perfected in accordance with the European system.

"Yet at the outset of telegraphic operations under the convention aforesaid, it was found that considerable delays occurred, owing to the faulty condition of the lines north and west of Constantinople.

"In reply to a remonstrance addressed by Lieut.-Col. Goldsmid to the Ottoman Telegraph Department at this particular period, Faizi Bey, then Acting Director-General in the absence of Agathon Efendi, wrote as follows, under date the 1st April, 1865:—

"'Je peux vous assurer, M. le Colonel, qu'ainsi qu'un fil spécial a été affecté en Asie à la correspondance télégraphique Indo-Européenne, de même deux fils ont été désignés en Europe pour la sus dite correspondance. L'un de ces deux fils est celui qui va de Constantinople vers la frontière Turco-Italienne de Valona, et l'autre de Constantinople à la frontière Turco-Serbe de Belgrade.'

"A glance at the accompanying map will explain, that had this intention of giving two wires, each on a separate line, been efficiently carried out, we might reasonably have anticipated regular communication with Italy and Austria, or at least one of the two in the event of accident. But experience has proved that no dependence can be placed on either. The official records of the last six months alone show that the condition of both is very bad.

"Two courses have now been suggested for more effectual communication. . . .

"1st. That a conference of delegates from the respective Telegraph Departments of Austria, Servia, and Turkey, should investigate and ascertain the causes of defective working, binding themselves, in writing, to provide the remedy.

"2nd. That the Ottoman Telegraphic Administration should address the Austrian Administration to the effect that direct communication be at once regularly established between Constantinople and Vienna.

"The first course was urged by Lieutenant-Colonel Goldsmid, Superintendent of the Indo-European line, on the part of the Government of India, and might readily embrace inquiry into the two lines to Vienna, one through Servia, and one through Bosnia, which have recently formed the subject of discussion in connection with international telegraphy. It appears to be the more practical one, because it is difficult to see how the second course can be carried out without an inquiry into the present state of the line, so that the blame may be fixed and the remedy applied in the proper quarter. But if the second be preferred by the Director-General in Constantinople, it is clear that the line to Nissa, on the Servian frontier, which he proposes to use for the direct transmission of Indian messages to Vienna through the Ottoman dominions, must at once be looked to, both as regards construction and maintenance. That the inspector has been wanting in his duty, or the line itself comparatively ill-constructed, may be inferred from the fact that the bad working of the eighth wire, declared to be special for Indian messages, has been reported to have lasted for five days in June last, eight in July, nine in August, eighteen in September, twenty in October, and twenty-three in November last. Messages supposed to be in transit are thus shelved for days in the Pera office.

"As regards the promised wire to Valona, a like course should be pursued, for the bad working with Salonica is notorious, and this as a general rule; a state of things which may be certified on inquiry. A summary of Mr Courtenay's previous reports on the subject is attached.

"The great improvement during the past year on the Turkish-Asiatic lines may be cited as a proof of the good results of a careful system of inspection and unusual energy on the part of the *employés* generally. Should this improvement continue, and the system of direct working for long distances be kept up, as promised, the Turkish lines from Scutari to Fao bid fair to attain a working condition superior to that of many older lines in Europe. There appears no reason why, with improved organization, the Turkish-European lines should not keep pace with the wires on the other side of the Bosphorus."

The remaining accompaniments to the letter consisted of:—

1st. Copy of a draft letter from Colonel Goldsmid to the Director-General of Ottoman telegraphs, a French translation of which was forwarded under date the 20th November, 1866, urging the propriety of holding a conference of delegates as already proposed, to provide for a better telegraphic communication between Vienna and Constantinople; or of obtaining a similar result by an alternative measure proposed by the Turkish Director and Servian *Chargé d'affaires*.

2nd. Copy of a letter from Colonel Goldsmid to her Majesty's *Chargé d'affaires* at Vienna, under date the 23rd November, explaining that the Director-General of Ottoman telegraphs and Servian *Chargé d'affaires* were averse to the scheme of a conference, because "the means were at their disposal to remedy the defects between Belgrade and Constantinople, and time would be saved by their at once availing themselves of them."

3rd. Copy of a letter from Colonel Goldsmid to the Director-General of telegraphs in Austria, making intimation to a similar effect, and expressing a hope that, although the writer himself was debarred from direct action in the matter, he hoped the Director-General would not cease, if necessary, to press the question of a conference.[1]

4th. Copy of a letter from the Director-General of Ottoman telegraphs to Colonel Goldsmid, dated 28th November, 1866, replying to his letter of the 20th idem: and representing that the condition of the Turkish lines in Europe was abnormal, that the Asiatic-Turkish lines had greatly improved, and that he proposed, in communication with the Austrian and Servian authorities, to set apart a special wire for direct and permanent traffic

---

[1] "Ne formant pas un parti intégral de la conférence en question, je me suis abstenu de trop l'activer ; mais j'espère, M. le Directeur-Général, que si les mesures qu'on se propose de prendre, et lesquelles nous seront soumises par l'Administration Ottomane, n'aboutissent pas d'une manière satisfaisante, vous aurez la bonté, dans l'intérêt de toutes les Administrations y concernées, de revenir sur la question d'une conférence, laquelle me paraît encore le meilleur moyen pour réussir. Quoique mon absence en Perse me privera de l'avantage d'y assister, ou mon collègue, le Major Champain, ou bien Monsieur Courtenay, notre délégué à Constantinople, se ferait un grand plaisir d'y être présent."

between Vienna and Constantinople. The letter concluded with anticipations of a happy result to such prospective arrangement.[1]

The mission on which Colonel Goldsmid was, at this time, more especially engaged, compelled him to leave Constantinople for Persia with as little delay as possible. He had been already detained two months, when embarking for Poti on the first weekly Russian steamer of the new year. The day before embarkation he addressed the following letter to her Majesty's Ambassador, in continuation of that of the 5th December:—

"JANUARY 4th, 1867.

". . . I have the honour to report that, with every reason to believe in the good-will and exertions of the Director-General of Ottoman telegraphs, I am still without satisfactory proof that the line from Constantinople to Vienna will be put into that efficient working state to enable a direct communication to be regularly carried on from capital to capital, as contemplated by Agathon Efendi in the following passages of his official letter to my address, of the 28th November last.[2]

"As regards the memorandum which your Lordship has referred to his Highness the Minister of Foreign Affairs, I under-

---

[1] "À la suite des avantages que j'essayerais de faire ressortir, auprès de ces deux Administrations, ayant déjà, de votre côté, préparé M. Brunner à une telle combinaison, et avec l'appui qui nous a été promis par M. l'Agent de Serbie à Constantinople, auprès de son Administration, j'ose espérer que ma proposition sera prise en sérieuse considération et agréée par les parties intéressées. Après l'affectation de ce fil aux communications directes entre Constantinople et Vienne, les dépêches de l'Angleterre à destination des Indes arrivant en quelques heures à Vienne, comme vous le dites, ne mettraient pas plus de temps pour parvenir à Constantinople ; et transmises avec la même célérité de Constantinople aux lignes Asiatiques, parviendraient à leur destination en quelques heures seulement, au lieu d'occuper des journées entières."

[2] Part of the extract here alluded to has been already given. The remainder may be omitted as unimportant.

stand that Agathon Efendi has been required to report to his Government, but presume that he is awaiting the reply from Vienna to do so.

"Had it not been that my presence in Persia appears necessary to the disposal of more than one question connected with our telegraph service in that country and the Persian Gulf, and that the approaching Ramazan is an unfavourable season for work in the departmental offices of the Ottoman Government, I should have suggested the propriety of my remaining here until completion of the present negotiations. As it is, I would bring to your Lordship's notice the fact that the written assurance of Faizi Bey, Acting Director of the Ottoman telegraphs in Agathon's absence, that he had given us a special wire on the Nissa and Belgrade line for Vienna, and another on that of Valona for Italy, has never been verified according to the spirit of the agreement entered into between us for securing efficient work. Had we had reliable wires, one on each of these lines, we should have had little cause of complaint against European Turkey. But though a wire was allotted us on the road to Nissa, its material and construction have failed to give it efficiency. Indeed, data in proof of the late defective working of every wire on the Turkish lines are all available, and may be obtained at any time from Mr. Courtenay's office.

"I regret to add, moreover, that for the last fortnight, and up to date, the telegraph in Asia has failed to keep up its improved character."

After the Chief Director's departure from Constantinople, her Majesty's Ambassador continued to press the question of improved working with Vienna, in communication with Mr. Courtenay, and received a formal assurance from Fuad Pasha that the Director-General of Ottoman telegraphs had taken the necessary steps to secure two special wires on a special line of posts both for international and Indo-European correspondence. The copy of a "Projet d'Arrangement," of Ten Articles between the respective Administrations of Austria, Servia, and Turkey, was, moreover, forwarded for Lord Lyons' information. The third article provided that one of the two wires noted should be used for the despatch of international and Indo-European telegrams, and the other for their receipt.¹

Under instructions from home, Mr. Courtenay submitted that the exclusive use of one wire between Vienna and Constantinople would be preferred to the partial use of two wires in the interests of British India; but objection still offering to this arrangement, a compromise was eventually reached. The Telegraph Commissioner afterwards notified that the Foreign Office had authorized Lord Lyons to accept two special direct wires between Vienna and Constantinople, one *viâ* Bosnia, the other *viâ* Servia, with absolute priority for Indo-European messages on whichever was best for the time being.²

The next step in importance, and according to the chronological order of events, was the admission of British India into the community of European States, which, under an article of the Paris Telegraph Convention of May 1865, were to meet at Vienna to revise the rules

---

¹ The Minister wrote:—" L'Administration Télégraphique n'aurait aucune objection à élever contre la proposition d'affecter un fil spécial à la correspondance Indo-Européenne, si elle prévoyait un avantage dans sa mise à exécution. Au contraire, et dans l'intérêt même de cette correspondance, notre Administration, au lieu de lui approprier un fil spécial, elle en affecte deux, tant à la correspondance internationale qu'à celle des Indes, qu'elles pourront emprunter indifféremment, et dans toutes les circonstances de mélange et d'interruption qui pourraient convenir à l'un et à l'autre de ces deux fils." The article specified "Un de ces deux fils spéciaux servirait pour la transmission de la correspondance Internationale et Indo-Européenne, et l'autre pour la reception de ces mêmes correspondances, afin d'éviter le retard toujours occasionné par le changement d'ordre de transmission."

² Mr. Courtenay's letter to Lieut.-Colonel Goldsmid; No. 208 of May 28, 1867.

subscribed to at the French capital. The congress was not actually held until June 1868; but arrangements for the participation in it of British Indian representatives were in active progress in the autumn of 1867. Colonel Goldsmid returned from India in August of that year, and proceeding in the same month to Paris, at once opened negotiations to the required effect with the French Administration. There was something singular and at first sight anomalous in the position. England, as England, having no telegraphs belonging to her home Government, but having connected her Indian Government lines with those of the continent of Europe, was led by the force of circumstances to seek representation of her Indian interests at the European Telegraph Congress. The inauguration meeting of delegates had been held in Paris, and as no second re-union had superseded its immediate influences, it was to the French ex-President and Secretary that applications to join a new gathering would naturally be addressed. Colonel Robinson, Director-General of telegraphs in India, was associated with the Chief Director and Assistant Chief Director of the Government Indo-European line in some of the interviews necessitated by the case. After three or four visits to Paris, and much correspondence, in which her Majesty's Ambassador at the French Imperial Court took part as readily as he had done two years before under similar circumstances at Constantinople, the preliminaries were settled.[1] The main difficulties in the way to a satisfactory understanding had been the mysterious mercantile cypher and the high rate charged for Persian Gulf cable messages; nor was the tariff on the Indian telegraphs of

[1] Mr. Merivale to the Under Secretary of State for Foreign Affairs, of Feb. 1, 1868.

a sufficiently liberal character to please the foreign Administrations, all of whom, without exception, had been aiming at a cheap as well as efficient international system. The Declaration of Adhesion was accordingly signed in due form by the Secretary of State for Foreign Affairs on behalf of her Majesty's Government. The next formal step was to join the re-union of European States. Colonels Goldsmid and Glover were appointed the delegates of Great Britain, one for her Indo-European, and one for her Indian local telegraphs, and proceeded on their respective duties. The conference was opened at Vienna on the 12th June, and work was completed on the 22nd July, 1868. There were present twenty-nine representatives, their position at the board being arranged, more or less, according to alphabetical order. Austria, however, as the State in whose limits the meeting was held, occupied the presidential chair, with Hungary on the left, and an Imperial Commissioner on the right. A Secretary-General was appointed by the same Government, but the French supplied the working Secretary and reporter of the proceedings. Baron de Beust attended in person to open the discussion. In one paragraph of his address allusion was thus prominently made to the adhesion of British India:—

"Since the institution by the Paris Convention of this great association of telegraph departments, its numbers have been recruited by new members. As its organ, I would express all the pleasure we feel in seeing here the representatives of the British Administrations, and I trust that the Imperial and Royal Government will be approved in having anticipated the consent of the assembly by welcoming proposals which introduce into the telegraphic system the electric wires uniting India with the West. The European character of our association should not suffer us to forget that the civilizing mission of which Europe has ever boasted would lead her to extend and not to restrain her sphere of action."[1]

As the work performed by this assembly is no sealed record, but forms a printed volume of proceedings and results, in the French language, or of results only, in its English dress,[2] no attempt will be made to render it comprehensible in detail. Its more immediate action upon British Indian communications will be apparent from the following extracts of an official paper on the subject:—

"From the 1st January next, the maximum rate of a message of twenty words from London to Calcutta and *vice versâ* will be 2*l*. 1*s*. 7*d*. This tariff will apply to eight routes, as follows:—

"Five 'Indo-Ottoman,' *i.e.* entering or leaving the cable at Fáo:

    1. By Holland, Austro-Germanic Union, Turkey.
    2. By Belgium,   "   "   "
    3. By France,   "   "   "
    4. By France, Switzerland, Austria, Servia, Turkey.
    5. By France, Italy, Turkey.

"Three 'Russo-Persian,' *i.e.* entering or leaving the cable at Bushahr:—

    6. By Northern Germany, Russia, Prussia.
    7. By Holland, Germanic Union, Russia, Persia.
    8. By Belgium, Northern Germany,   "   "

"The fourth of the above routes will be specially utilized for Indian correspondence by a Convention between the States concerned, of which a copy has been submitted to the India Office; and the sixth is the promised line of Messrs. Siemens Brothers. Under these circumstances, I do not think that the popular objection that telegraphic communication with India

---

[1] Report of the delegates of her Majesty's Indian Government on the International Telegraphic Conference held at Vienna, submitted to the Secretary of State for India, August 19, 1868.

[2] Conférence Télégraphique Internationale de Vienne. Révision de la Convention de Paris.

will be in the hands of one or two European powers, can be considered valid.

"I have further submitted for the ratification of the home Government a separate agreement drawn up and signed by myself, in concert with the delegates, at the recent conference of Russia, Persia,[1] and Turkey, by which the Indo-Ottoman will act as the alternative to the Russo-Persian lines in Asia, and vice versâ, in the event of interruption; by which the anomalies of tariff hitherto found in the ruling of conflicting Conventions will be removed; and by which the equal division of messages heretofore stipulated between Turkey and Persia will give way to the free use of either line according to the requirements of the public."[2]

In the course of discussion the question of delays in the passage of Indo-European telegrams through Europe was brought before the meeting, and the dissatisfaction of the commercial world on the general state of the communications represented. It was, moreover, stated that petitions had been submitted to H.M. Government for the establishment of a line wholly independent of the continent of Europe. The French delegate supported with considerable warmth a proposal to the Conference to move in the matter, and joining the protestations of his own country to those of England against an evil, the existence of which was undeniable, he suggested that a declaration should be formally made in the interests of the particular service alluded to, and with a view to amelioration. The suggestion was unanimously adopted, and a declaration in the sense contemplated placed upon the record. No doubt ample grounds for decisive action existed. There

[1] General Lüders, the Director-General of Imperial Russian Telegraphs, represented Persia, as well as his own Government, on this occasion.

[2] Colonel Goldsmid to Secretary to Government, Bombay; No. 125 of August 7, 1868.

had been great cause for discontent at the overland telegraph through Turkey and Persia. But something also was to be said on the other side. The Chief Director had replied to the complaints urged at a public meeting in the Mansion House and a long article in an influential weekly paper, by a pamphlet explanatory of the whole case. He showed that, whatever the shortcomings of the telegraph to India had been, there was well-grounded hope of improvement, if not by the Turkish, then by the Russo-Persian lines: but more time and more patience were required. He showed that the recommendations of the Select Committee had been attended to, and that the most important of them were being carried into actual practice. One charge had been that the latest telegraphic communication from Abyssinia was twenty days old. This, he represented, was to be attributed to an interruption on the Malta and Alexandria cable, a contingency from which no cable made or guaranteed by Government could be exempt. Other charges, such as the existence of a monopoly on the Turkish lines, the long period for which the line had been working without improvement, the precarious course taken by the wires, and the like, he was able to refute in mere point of fact. And with reference to the assumed general verdict of failure, "in the common acceptation of the term," it was argued that, so far from such being the case, the Indo-Ottoman line had, during the preceding month (February 1868), "transmitted by far the greater number of the 3,000 messages which passed between Europe and India, the remainder having gone by the Russo-Persian route."[1]

[1] "State and Prospects of the existing Indo-European Telegraph." Stanford, 1868.

As pertinent to the case, we may cite two further passages contained in a postscript to the pamphlet quoted. The one maintained that, although "the question of a line through Russia, as an alternative to that through Turkey, had engaged the attention of the Directors of the Government Indo-European telegraph so far back as 1865 (the first year of working), the practical project of Messrs. Siemens Brothers took no definite shape until May 1867." Its full realization was promised at the end of 1869; but its partial effect on intercommunications by telegraph with India had already been favourably felt. The other pointed to the coming Congress at Vienna for a natural remedy to "spasmodic and irregular working, unintelligible rendering, and the thousand and one defects more or less apparent in the existing line to India, irrespective of physical causes." And the likelihood of benefit was considered all the greater, because Turkey, an original member of the telegraph Congress for her European dominions, had just notified her adhesion to its rules on behalf of her Asiatic possessions.

That the hopes expressed in favour of the Siemens line have been unwarranted, or that the recognition of British India as entitled to the privileges of a European international telegraph code was a superfluous act, no evidence of disproof is surely required beyond the telegraph statistics of 1870 to 1873 inclusive.

Before taking leave of the Vienna Congress, it is impossible to omit mention of the splendid hospitalities exercised towards the various telegraph delegates assembled in the Austrian capital. Among the many particular acts which might be mentioned in illustration, the following are noteworthy. The Ministers of Commerce, both at Vienna and Pesth, respectively invited the foreign visitors to special banquets in honour of the occasion. M. de Beust, at the time Chancellor of the Empire, was the distinguished *cicerone* to accompany them, on a kind of railway picnic, through the magnificent scenery of the near mountains, to the Semmering; and the Emperor himself entertained them at dinner at the palace of Schönbrunn, conversing with each representative separately before sitting down, with those immediately on his right and left hand at table, and with many again separately after the repast, and preparatory to the dispersion of the guests. One of the delegates at the inaugural meeting had expressed, on behalf of the whole number, a desire to be permitted to wait on his Imperial Majesty before commencing practical business; and the reply was a general invitation to dine at the palace. Nothing could exceed the accomplished politeness of the whole design, and its execution was as easy and successful as the response to the regal courtesy was unanimous.

The conference at Vienna concluded, the next important operation in strengthening the Indo-European telegraphic link was to carry out the alternate or second line of communication, from Gwādar to Jask by land, and from Jask to Bushahr by sea. The diplomatic part of the work has been already reviewed; so that reference is now made to mechanical or practical progress.

Before leaving London for Vienna in 1868, Colonel Goldsmid had for long been in constant communication with the India Office and the telegraph Engineers regarding the choice of material for a second cable, to be laid between the proposed station of Jask and

Bushahr. On the 25th May he reported[1] fully his programme of work for the ensuing cold season; and this necessarily included a decision on the above question, as well as a detailed process for laying the new cable, and diverting a section of the old one from the Gwadar-Masandam course to a Gwadar-Jask-Henjam course to Bushahr. The opportunity appeared to him a desirable one for trying India-rubber in lieu of gutta-percha. Mr. Latimer Clark and Lieutenant Stiffe were referred to for opinions, and supported this view by their written replies. His own reasons for recommending the change will, however, be more clearly seen in the following extracts of his letter to the Secretary of State:—

"But I have not confined investigation to these sources.[2] I have sought and obtained evidence elsewhere; and the general result enables me to place on record an opinion in favour of procuring a core which offers peculiar advantages in a hot climate. Were the measure no more than experimental, the time for experiment would be opportune, because communication is alternated by, not dependent on, the proposed line. But I look upon any proof of non-inferiority required for our purpose, to affect chiefly the question of 'durability,' in which gutta-percha has a high repute; and it will be observed that even in this respect Mr. Clark's evidence is not inconclusive.

"A strong and undoubtedly plausible argument on behalf of gutta-percha has been found in the manifest convenience of having one material for the two cables. But I would deferentially remark that, in a progressive age like the present, a rule of the kind might operate injuriously on submarine telegraphy, where

---

[1] No. 100A of May 25, 1868; of which copy forwarded to Secretary to Government, Bombay, with 108 of June 2, 1868.

[2] Reference is here made to the reports of Mr. Latimer Clark and Lieut. Stiffe.

there are alternate cables at work. The one would naturally fail before the other—especially when laid down at an interval of years—and yet renewal in such case should hardly be restricted to renewal of the same material, irrespective of new inventions of science. Nor should the renewal be made unnecessarily costly, upon the principle that the introduction of a new and improved material must be simultaneously effected upon the two cables.

"That a cable with gutta-percha core can safely be joined to one with Hooper's material, Lieutenant Stiffe appears satisfied. But notwithstanding the satisfactory results of an experiment recently made to this effect, I am bound to state that the evidence obtained is not such as to warrant conviction of full security combined with feasibility. Time alone, and experience of the vicissitudes to which a Persian Gulf cable is subject, can decide the question conclusively. The point merits attention, because it might be found useful to introduce India-rubber into the shore end, even where the main core is of gutta-percha, in cases where intense heat renders exposure dangerous.

"If the suggestion be approved and adopted, I should recommend that measures be immediately taken by the Store Department to procure 525 miles of Hooper's core according to Mr. Clark's specification; that is, having a conductor weighing the same as the Persian Gulf cable, with sufficient India-rubber to give it the same electric capacity or working speed; the whole being covered to the same dimensions. The sheathing (and outer covering) might be similar to the pattern before adopted. Mr. Hooper would, it is concluded, be invited to make his new core, provided the requisite amount could be completed in three months, or in time for shipment and arrival in the Gulf by February, and tenders would be sought for the other portions of the work. But it should be clearly understood that it is the intention of Government to have the cable laid down before the end of the next working season."

The Bombay Government, to whom the question was referred in detail, approved generally the arrangements proposed for laying a new cable and modifying the course of the old one, and were content to place reliance on the Chief Director with regard to the material selected.

Major Champain had left England in November 1867, to superintend the transfer of stations from Masandam to Jask and Henjám, as also the diversion of the cable from the first to the other two places; but failing to carry out the work contemplated, from causes beyond his control,[1] he converted his mission into one of inspection of cable stations, and the Persian land-line between Bushahr and Tehran. Arrived at the capital, he was enabled to do further good service in aiding and advising her Majesty's Minister on certain questions pending with the Persian Government. He returned to London in time to give his professional knowledge and experience to the details of the Hooper's cable scheme; and during the Chief Director's absence in Vienna, his presence at head-quarters was especially opportune. Later in the year, and when Colonel Goldsmid had again proceeded to India, the whole management of the cable expedition was in his hands. The diversion to Henjám had become, by the force of circumstances, an entirely distinct affair, left to the management of the local officers, who had performed, as has been stated, their task with success.

It had been hoped to complete the shipping of the new cable early in November, so that the work of laying might be accomplished before the hot weather had set in; and the Chief Director had reckoned that his own arrival in India would be soon followed by that of the cable ships. He had already made two journeys from Bombay in the two exactly opposite directions of Calcutta and the Makran coast, and had returned from

[1] See ante, page 298, and footnote.

each respectively, when a telegram reached him, dated the 1st January, 1869, stating that heavy gales and failure in contractors' engagements had delayed departure of the vessels, which could not under the circumstances be expected before the end of April. A second telegram reached him near the end of the same month, reporting that the *Calcutta* and *Tweed*, two ships taken up for the service, would sail, one on the 25th January, the other a week later. The ship with the Makran landline stores had, on the other hand, arrived at Karāchi, and the material was being shipped to the coast with all due despatch.

But a sad calamity befell the first-named of the cable ships. Colonel Goldsmid was in Makran. He and the political officer, Captain Ross, had sent on their small stock of baggage ahead, and had themselves just started from Gwādar, *en route* to Charbar, a port about a hundred miles or so further west, and along the dreary desert coast, when a telegram was brought to the former. It was from Major Champain, dated the previous day in London, and ran thus:—

"*Calcutta* came into collision off Lizard; captain and thirty men lost. Vessel abandoned, but brought into Plymouth by the *Terrible* in a sinking state. Seventy miles cable had been thrown overboard to lighten ship. We have the *Calcutta* in dock and 200 miles of cable safe: hope to pick up the seventy. We expect *Calcutta* will start afresh in April. We think

---

[1] "I could almost have wished," said Colonel Goldsmid, in addressing the Bombay Government hereon, "that the despatch of the cable had been deferred till June, so that it might have reached Bombay at a better season; but under the circumstances, and considering the character of the vessels engaged, it is to be hoped that, however late, it may arrive in time to be laid at latest in the early part of June."

Tweed's cable should be laid and buoyed immediately, and *Calcutta's* cable laid after monsoon."

On the 19th February, the following account of the disaster was addressed to the Chief Director[1]:—

"The *Calcutta*, a fine iron ship of 2,083 tons, owned by Messrs. Mackay, Son, and Co., and commanded by Captain Owen, an experienced and highly esteemed officer, left Gravesend on Friday, the 29th January, with 273 miles of cable for Bombay and the Persian Gulf.

"The extraordinary persistence of south-westerly winds that have lasted with but slight intermission since November, led me, at the earnest request of the owners, to recommend that the ship should be towed clear of the Land's End to get a fair start for her long voyage.

"Severe gales kept the tug and the *Calcutta* for some days at the Nore, but on Friday, the 8th February, the two vessels parted company, and the *Calcutta* set sail in the best possible condition.

"On Saturday night she came into collision with a Russian barque, which immediately sank, four only of her crew of eleven men being saved.

"Such serious injuries were sustained by the *Calcutta* that after paying out and buoying all the cable in the fore tank (which contained seventy miles), and seeing that the vessel was apparently in a sinking state, the captain and crew decided to abandon her, and endeavour to escape in the ship's boats.

"Captain Owen and a considerable number of men were drowned in the attempt. We know at present that of the officers, crew, and cable hands on board, thirty-three escaped, twelve were undoubtedly lost, and twenty-one who formed the crew of the ship's lifeboat are missing. Hopes are entertained that the last-mentioned number were picked up by some outward-bound vessel, as their boat was washed ashore, and had evidently never been capsized.

---

[1] Major Champain to Colonel Goldsmid.

"On hearing of this calamity by a telegram from the crew of the first boat that reached land, I at once applied to the Admiralty for assistance. It appeared that the *Calcutta*, though abandoned, was still afloat, and we thought it possible that she might still be brought in.

"The frigate *Terrible* was immediately ordered to put to sea in search, and the result was that on Wednesday the derelict *Calcutta* was brought in and moored under shelter of Plymouth breakwater.

"I started by night train for Plymouth, and after application to Admiral Drummond, the Superintendent of the Devonport Dockyard, permission was granted to bring the *Calcutta* into one of the basins at Keyham for repair; and the services of two Government tugs were rendered available for the purpose. The appearance of the unfortunate vessel was most deplorable. Her figure-head was wanting, and her foremast was hanging over the port side. Much of her rigging seemed carried away or dismantled, and she had more than twenty feet of water in her hold, which of course brought her down by the head in an extraordinary manner.

"Nothing but the strength of the bulkhead of the fore compartment, and the precautionary measure of paying out the seventy miles of cable, prevented the complete loss of the ship, and as it was, her sinking was a mere question of time. We are now about to unship the cable still on board, so as to allow of the vessel being placed in dry dock and safety; and we may reasonably expect to see her once more ready for sea in the course of two or three months.

"Steps have been taken to recover the seventy miles which were 'jetsomed,' and Mr. Henley's steamer the *Caroline* will leave Plymouth with that object as soon as the violence of the gales shall have somewhat abated."

With regard to the sailing of the *Tweed*, it was resolved, on mature consideration, to pay a specified rate of demurrage on that vessel, and detain her until her sister ship should be ready; rather than start her singly, and thus cause a double expedition in the Gulf. The Secretary of State approved this decision, and notified the circumstances to the Bombay Government on the 29th of April.

Eventually the *Calcutta*, refitted and repaired, left Plymouth with her charge on the 27th June, and three days later the *Tweed* left Gravesend. Colonel Goldsmid and Major Champain had both been on board the former a short time prior to departure; and Mr. Webb, on parting company from her four miles south of the Eddystone, reported she had "a fair wind, all hands on board, and the steam launch¹ safely stowed." The shipping surveyor to the India Office wrote, moreover, of the *Tweed*, from the scene of her weighing anchor, that she had "just left in fine trim, in tow of two steamers."

The *Calcutta* and *Tweed*, indeed, made on this occasion a successful start, and the remainder of their voyage may be considered to have been accomplished in accordance with these fair auspices. But the whole expedition was not equally bright and felicitous. The serious injury done to the *Calcutta* was but the precursor of another fatal and unlooked-for incident. Major Champain, Mr. Latimer Clark, and the directing staff were on their way to join the cable ships overland, and had left Suez for Bombay in the P. and O. Company's steamer *Carnatic*. On the 17th September Colonel Goldsmid received the following telegram from Major Champain, dated the day before at Suez:—

"*Carnatic* utterly wrecked; all telegraph party saved; all mails and baggage lost."

---

¹ A purchase sanctioned for auxiliary duties connected with the Gulf cable and coast line.

So indeed it was; and the case must be fresh in the memory of many readers of these pages. The vessel had left Suez on the morning of Sunday, the 12th of September. On Monday morning, at one o'clock, she struck on a coral reef off Shadwan island and remained bumping till daylight. Fruitless endeavours were made during the day to extricate her; and on Monday night it was understood that passengers and mails would be landed on the island, which was distant about five miles. During the night water was reported in the engine-room, and passengers were ordered on the forecastle. Tuesday, the vessel, by parting midships, or sinking with the coral reef beneath her, went down with a crash, and the consequences may be imagined. The visible reef was reached by any means available, but not less than twenty-eight souls, fourteen Europeans and fourteen natives, perished. Eventually the survivors, after much endurance, were landed on Shadwan, where their position might have become more than precarious, had they not been rescued by the steamer *Sumatra* on her way from Bombay to Suez. Major Champain's conduct at this trying time was just what might have been expected of him. He was not only ready and eager to assist, but strong and capable to carry out his wishes. A sound adviser, a smart executive, a cheering comrade, his active usefulness amid the sufferers from the wreck will not soon be forgotten by those who could bear personal testimony to its exercise. And he himself has given ready witness to the noble exertions of the chief officer and others of his companions, whose names do not need this humble chronicle to make them eminent.

After taking to Suez the crew and passengers of the *Carnatic* rescued from the reef, the *Sumatra* returned to Bombay; and Major Champain, Mr. Latimer Clark,[1] and the other members of the Gulf expedition, availed themselves of the opportunity to resume their outward voyage. Bombay was reached by them in safety on the 1st October; and they found there in harbour both the *Tweed* and *Calcutta*, which had arrived on the same day, the 21st September, after making excellent passages.

As regards time, only one week had been lost by the accident of the wreck; but in other respects more serious damage had ensued. The telegraph officers had been compelled to resort to the wires at Suez to procure from London essential instruments and papers, as nothing in the shape of luggage had been saved. They were, however, enabled to leave Bombay on the 19th October, or in less than three weeks after arrival there. Major Champain, with Mr. Latimer Clark and staff, started at 9 A.M. on board the *Dacca* steamship of the British India Company, having in tow the *Tweed* and her share of cable. To tow the *Calcutta*, similarly freighted, the *Earl Canning* was engaged, and had taken precedence by three hours. The first of the steamers mentioned was of 1,700 tons and 350 horse-power, and had been chartered to tow first the *Tweed* to Jask, and then the vessel actually paying out cable. The second was of 150 horse-power only, but this provision was held sufficient to tow the *Calcutta* to Lingah, within the entrance of the Persian Gulf, besides which duty she had only to render general assistance to the ships on their return. We give Major Champain's own account of the operations:—

---

[1] This gentleman met with a severe fracture on the occasion of the wreck.

"Early on the 25th, the *Tweed*, in tow of the *Dacca*, reached Jask. The *Earl Canning* and *Calcutta* passed the next day on their way to Lingah, the port nearest to the spot where the *Tweed's* stock of cable would be expended. The *Amberwitch*, from Karáchi, with Lieutenant Stiffe, Mr. Hirz, and a staff of signallers from the Persian Gulf telegraph establishment to assist in the operations, anchored close to our ships on the evening of the 26th. The *Amberwitch* towed up from Karáchi a steam barge for laying the shore ends, and for tranship-

JASK, MAKRAN COAST.

ment of stores and other service. The Jask telegraph office is built on a tongue of land stretching out in a south-westerly direction to sea, and is about 500 yards from the spot selected for landing the shore end. A trench had been dug, according to instructions previously given, from the office to the sea-shore, in readiness to receive the end of our cable.

"The *Tweed* being anchored as near the land as her draught of water would permit, the steam barge was brought alongside on the morning of the 27th, and sufficient shore end was coiled on board to reach from the ship to the beach and from the beach to the office, altogether about 1,000 yards. The barge then steamed direct to the landing-place, paying out cable as she proceeded. A large party of workmen . . . was lent by Lieutenant Morgan, R.E. to drag the end of the cable from the barge, and to lay it in the trench, so that by about 3 P.M. the cable ship *Tweed* was in direct communication with the Jask office.

In the meantime Lieutenant Stiffe had started in the *Amberwitch*, and laid down two buoys to mark the direction which Captain Day of the *Dacca* was to follow. The *Amberwitch* had then gone out to a point about thirty miles along our course, where delicate steering was required in order to avoid overlaying the old cable, and was to burn blue lights so soon as the paying-out ships hove in sight. At 5 P.M. on the 27th October, the *Dacca* with the *Tweed* in tow left Jask, and steered the course laid down by Lieutenant Stiffe, the *Tweed* paying out her cable smoothly and well at from three to four knots per hour. Nothing could have worked better than the machinery employed, and the uncoiling apparatus answered admirably.

"Very great credit for these arrangements is due to Mr. F. C. Webb, who was Mr. Clark's assistant from the commencement of the cable manufacture in the summer of 1868 until a few days before we left England in September 1869, when he unfortunately found himself unable to accompany the expedition. His place has been well filled by Mr. Preece, who, under Mr. Clark's direction, superintended the fitting of the machinery, and most ably carried on Mr. Webb's designs. About 10 P.M. we distinguished the lights of the *Amberwitch*, and, five miles farther on, those of a little steam cutter which had been sent forward to act as a second beacon. Lieutenant Stiffe then boarded the *Dacca* and assisted Captain Day in towing our paying-out vessel, the *Tweed*, on her proper course. The weather, fortunately, was calm; the cable came up from the tanks easily and well; the machinery worked faultlessly, and we found it practicable to let the cable run out at a pace which at one time was nearly seven knots per hour. At 11 P.M. Friday the 29th, we had completed the *Tweed's* section of $240\frac{1}{2}$ miles, which brought us to a point nearly south of Gais Island. After sealing and buoying the end we started for our *rendezvous* at Lingah, which we reached at 8 the following morning.

"The greater part of the day was occupied in removing staff, baggage, and apparatus from the *Tweed* to the *Calcutta*. . . . Before sunset the *Earl Canning* left for Bombay with the empty *Tweed*, while Lieut. Stiffe in the *Amberwitch* pushed on in advance for our buoy off Gais.

"Next morning, the 31st, the *Calcutta* and *Dacca* left Lingah, and reached the buoy, with the *Amberwitch* alongside, about 4 P.M. Lieut. Stiffe had picked up the cable end, and, passing to him the end of that on board the *Calcutta*, we steamed slowly off, paying out cable in the direction of Bushahr and leaving Lieut. Stiffe to complete the joint, and catch us up during the night. By 1 A.M. of Monday, the 1st November, he was again on board the *Dacca*; and all went well until we had paid out 300 miles from Jask.

"Here for a time our good fortune deserted us. At 9 P.M. a terrific squall from the north west caught us unprepared, and brought up the *Dacca* and *Calcutta* as if they had run dead on to a wall. For a few minutes confusion prevailed. The awnings and windsails were flapping about. The vessels began to go astern, and the rapidity with which a heavy sea got up was amazing. Finding that our cable was being paid out to leeward of our course, and knowing that we had none to spare, we at last reluctantly decided to cut and buoy, which was safely done when the tempest was at its highest. By this time, the *Dacca*, which, happily for us, proved herself a magnificently powerful vessel, had got up more steam; and our hawsers holding, she succeeded in bringing our heads to the wind, and steered for the lee of the Persian shore. The steam barge which had been towing alongside the *Dacca* cut herself adrift, and great fears were entertained for her safety and that of her crew. Marvellous to relate, she was able to keep her head to sea, and though nearly swamped was picked up next morning by the *Amberwitch*. The little steam cutter was less lucky: her painter, while being passed astern the *Amberwitch*, was fouled by the vessel's propeller, and the boat capsized and had to be cut adrift. Happily the three men on board were all saved.

"By 3 A.M. of the 2nd November, the gale had subsided, and by 6, the sea calming as suddenly as it rose, was nearly smooth. We returned to our buoy, and the operation of splicing was again carried out on board the *Amberwitch*. Leaving her to complete her task, we once more commenced paying out in the direction of Bushahr. At 4 P.M. we encountered a second violent gale, almost as violent as that of the previous night. For this we were, however, prepared, and the *Bocca*, with full steam up, succeeded in towing our huge ship in the very teeth of the wind, at from one to two knots an hour.

"A more awful thunderstorm than that through which we passed can scarcely be pictured. The lightning struck our vessel, but did no damage; and by 7 or 8 P.M. the immediate fury of the tempest was over. The wind, however, continued excessively high, and at 9 o'clock a third squall, less violent than its predecessors, prevented the waves subsiding for many hours. The pitching of the *Calcutta* of course brought a fearfully heavy strain to bear upon our cable, and our anxiety on this account during the gale was great. Not an accident of any kind occurred. Had our hawsers parted, or had we been in tow of a less powerful ship than the *Bocca*, the loss of cable and loss of time would have been most serious.

"Before sunset on the 3rd November we buoyed the end of our cable off Bushahr, having paid out 490½ miles since starting from Jask, and leaving about twelve miles to Bushahr to be covered by shore end and tapers. The *Amberwitch* with the steam barge came up to our anchorage soon after dark, and the next three days we were busily engaged submerging the shore end, which had to be carefully laid clear of the original line."

"On the evening of the 6th November," adds the writer, naturally pleased at so successful a result of anxious labour, "everything was complete, and Bushahr in full communication with Jask by the new as well as by the old cable.[1] We left Bushahr for Bombay at half-past 10 in the morning of Sunday, the 7th instant."

To this detailed narrative of operations was added a favourable report of the India-rubber cable, which, according to Mr. Latimer Clark, gave the most wonderful insulation, and had been laid without the smallest indication of a fault.

Acknowledgment was made, in conclusion, of the services rendered by the officers connected with the cable expedition. Mr. Latimer Clark's widely recognized energy and abilities had been evidenced by the success that had attended his plans; and his very cordial co-operation with the Assistant Director was in like manner prominently noticed. Mr. George Preece and Mr. Her-

---

[1] Telegraphic reports of this important but little-noised operation were received in England. On the 27th a telegram from Tehran announced that the *Calcutta*, *Amberwitch*, and other vessels, had reached Jask the day previous, and that the operation of paying out cable would commence on the day following. It added, "Cable perfect; weather magnificent; all in good health." Other telegrams may be recorded agreeably to dates:—

"*October* 28; 2.5 P.M.—*Tweed* off Masandan Thursday morning, 9; sixty-seven miles cable submerged; tests perfect; all well.

"*October* 29; 9 A.M.—*Tweed* off Tumb Island; one hundred and sixty miles cable payed out; all well.

"*Same date*—Friday, midnight.—Off Gais Island. First half of cable laid and buoyed. Tests perfect. Commence second half on Monday. *Tweed* leaves for Bombay immediately. All well.

"*October* 31; 6.30 P.M.—Just spliced to first section, and paying out towards Bushahr.

"*November* 1, Noon.—Three hundred and twenty miles cable submerged; tests excellent; all well.

"*November* 12; 5 P.M.—Three hundred and sixty miles submerged 9 last night. Storm necessitated cutting and buoying. All well. Cable uninjured.

"*Same date*, 3 P.M.—Spliced at 2; at 4 encountered a heavy gale; now slightly moderated; four hundred miles payed out. All well.

"*November* 5; 4 p.m.—Off Bushahr; main cable completed; shore end to-morrow. Tests perfect.

"*November* 6; 10 P.M.—Cable complete and perfect throughout. Tests excellent. *Dacca* and *Calcutta* leave for Bombay to-morrow."

bert Taylor, of Mr. Clark's staff, had also rendered good service, the first by his foresight and admirable management, the second by his care and attention to testing.

The skill and activity of Lieutenant Stiffe, I.N., had been conspicuous throughout; the greatest credit was due to him for the course laid down, and for the efficient manner in which the cable ends were packed up, and joints made on board the *Amberwitch*. Captains Day of the *Dacca*, Tolputt of the *Earl Canning*, Smart of the *Tweed*, and Maxwell of the *Calcutta*, had rendered willing aid on all occasions; and Mr. Hirz, electrician, Mr. Mance and Captain Gabler, superintendents, and Mr. Possman, together with the staff of signallers engaged, as well as Mr. Melhuish, a volunteer from the Indian telegraphs, and Mr. Aspinall, the secretary and accountant, had all merited favourable mention.

To Captain Robinson, Superintendent of Bombay Marine, Major Champain expressed his sense of obligation for "ready and zealous aid rendered from first to last by himself and the department under his control."

We have already shown that the second wire of the land-line in Persia had been more or less completed in June 1867. To strengthen the communications in that country, and meet the probable increase of traffic from the Russian side, a third wire was then further projected, extending from Tehran to Bushahr, but the proposal remained for some time under consideration. The landline from Gwádar to Jask had been completed on the 15th August, 1869, or from two to three months before the cable was laid; and the successful accomplishment of the latest operation supplied a double line of communication for the whole way between Karáchi to Bushahr; from which port to London, and *vice versâ*, were two grand alternative lines, one *viâ* Tehran and Russia, the other *viâ* Baghdad and Constantinople.

Little has been said of the Makran coast land-lines. Yet their construction was a matter involving mental anxiety and powers of organization, with physical labour and endurance of no common kind. To Mr. H. Isaac Walton and his able and energetic assistants belongs the main credit of carrying out the line from Karáchi to Gwádar, under the protective arrangements made with the local chiefs in 1861-62 by Major Goldsmid, and confirmed by the Indian Government.[1] This work was commenced in 1862, and continued, under extraordinary physical and political difficulties, until completion in May 1863. One great feature in the line is the passage of the wires over the Malan cliff, regarding which section, Colonel Stewart thought it might be advisable to resort to a short sea cable, but which Mr. Walton resolved to surmount by a long and bold span. This plan had already suggested itself to Mr. Ryland, who accompanied Major Goldsmid, but the latter officer had inclined to the submarine alternative.[2] Mr. Walton has described this and other parts of his laborious task in official and non-official form. We quote from a letter already printed, but which may have escaped the notice of some readers of these pages:—

"You can imagine the work it has been, getting tons of iron posts and wire up the Malan, over 2,000 measured feet in height

---

[1] See Part II. Chapter XII.

[2] "One mode of overcoming the difficulty seems to me to run a short submarine line from the Hab hill to Pitok, on the easterly sea point of Malan, a distance of about fifteen miles. . . . Mr. Ryland has been struck with the flatness of the top of Malan; but it appears to me too high, and little accessible for communication with a line of wire on the beach below." (Major Goldsmid's Report on his Mission to Makran, printed by Bombay Government, 1862, page 8.)

... I found a valley called the Shum ... my best route, bearing in mind my settled determination to span the eastern face. Over a mile and a half of most difficult hills between the Shum valley and Malan Bay, the line runs along to the foot of the eastern precipice. The exact height of the drop here is 1,620 feet, and it is taken over the level plain at the top, to the back of the Khor Bat valley. Up the rock at this point I cut a road, over which material was brought by manual labour—no easy job, considering each post weighs over 2 cwt. and each mile of double wire 12 cwt. at least. Then—down the Khor Bat valley and along the sea-side to Manhaji, which is spanned by masts close to its mouth. Thence in a north-west direction, in order to cross the Gorbad at a narrow place five miles inland, and keeping the line about that distance from the sea, and to the north of your route, we strike down the isthmus into Ormara on the western side, in order to avoid the drift sand-hills. ..."

After continuing a description of the line up to Gwādar, Mr. Walton adds:—

"I need not tell you of the physical difficulties of the country we have come through. The want of water in many places has driven us to endure great hardships. A body of 25 Europeans, and 600 natives passing through this utterly barren country, must expect to meet with very great difficulties. Often I have been obliged to prohibit ablutions of any kind, and to place guards, with drawn swords, over dirty puddles .... From Karāchi the double line is completed, and working to Shor Kundi, and from Pasni to the Karwat Pass; it will be entirely finished by the end of this month. Both Europeans and natives have throughout behaved excellently, and by enforcing the strictest discipline, I have now nearly got through the enterprise without a grumble. Of course, all had to be fed from Karāchi; and the posts being all of iron, brought from England, were distributed eighteen to the mile, and required many camels, which were likewise almost entirely supplied with provender from Karāchi. We are all exhausted, and glad our labours are

near an end, as the hot weather has again set in, and many
deaths are occurring among the natives . . ."[1]

Six years had scarcely elapsed from the completion
of the line along the Makrān coast, from Karāchi to
Gwādar, when a second line was commenced in prolongation to the westward, the terminus of which was
Jask. Its length was estimated at 329½ miles.

Mr. Walker, the superintendent, on whom devolved
the main labour of personal and detailed supervision,
performed his task with zeal and ability. The country
to be traversed was, according to his report, in parts
composed of high and irregular hills, rivers which as a
rule were not to be readily spanned, deleterious saltpetre
marshes, and impracticable rocky ground; and on this
account it was no simple matter to mark out a suitable
course. The work of construction, however, once begun,
the first 115 miles to Charbar, the single intervening
station on the road from Gwādar to Jask, were covered
in twenty-six days, despite of thirty miles of rocky
ground and ten of puzzling hills. The remainder of
the distance, or nearly two-thirds of the whole way,
presented much level ground, but the necessity of
avoiding marsh and saltpetre forced the working parties towards harder soil, rock, and low hills. In some
cases it became imperative to blast holes and build up
the standards in masonry.[2] "The weather," wrote Mr.
Walker, "had become intensely hot, frequently ranging
as high as 156° on the work and 128° under canvas

[1] Vide Proceedings Royal Geographical Society, May 11, 1863, page 117;
extract of letter dated Gwādar, April 5, 1868, from Mr. Walton to Major
Goldsmid.

[2] The total of working days is given at 69, and shows a mean of 4 miles
1359 yards per day; of which the maximum was 10 miles 1060 yards, and
the minimum 500 yards.

The question of water supply for 400 men, which from the first was of great moment, assumed a serious and embarrassing shape. It was perplexing to move on four camps over parts where water was only to be had at distances of from twelve to twenty-four miles; whilst we could work at the most in the hard ground four miles per day." Delays in progress were mainly ascribed to the great mortality which occurred among the contractor's camels, and the want of others to replace them. The route from Charbar to Jask was reported strewn with the dead and dying animals engaged in the distribution of the telegraph material, and succumbing to the fierce heat. One gratifying circumstance was the maintenance of good relations with the natives, notwithstanding provocations on their part in the way of exactions and general troublesomeness. Mr. Walker, in concluding his report, spoke in the highest terms of the construction staff, and especially Messrs. Pressman, Scroggie, and Stranack, from whom he received zealous and efficient assistance.*

When Major Champain reached Paris on his way to Bombay, and not a month before the sad accident which befell the *Carnatic* in the Gulf of Suez, he was met there by Colonel Goldsmid, on his return from a visit to certain continental cities. The object of his new tour may be briefly explained.

---

* Superintendent's Report, No. 68 of August 26, 1869, to the Director Makran Coast and Submarine Telegraph; copy enclosed in the Director's Report to Secretary to Government, Bombay, No. 802 of the 31st idem. It was recommended to the favourable consideration of the British Government that "all who worked between Gwadar and Jask should receive one month's pay, and those engaged between Gwadar and Charbar half a month's, as gratuity," and the Bombay Government forwarded it, with their strong support, to the Government of India; but for reasons assigned the Governor-General in Council was unable to accede to the recommendation.

STATEMENTS OF EUROPEAN ADMINISTRATIONS.

While in Bombay at the commencement of 1859, the complaints of the mercantile community, and his own observations on the irregularity, delays, and inaccuracies still occurring in Anglo-Indian correspondence, had induced the Chief Director to move his representative at home formally to address the States concerned, parties to the International Congress of Vienna; and the latter officer had proceeded upon this information, to repeat a remonstrance which he had already put forward in a similar sense on his own responsibility. After some interchange of letters, the Director of the telegraph office at Berne, who had been nominated at the Vienna conference a kind of general referee or secretary in such matters, took action upon Major Champain's appeal, in a suitable manner; but Colonel Goldsmid, on revisiting Constantinople later in the year, finding the complaints of the Indian public more urgent than before, submitted a new memorandum on the subject to her Majesty's Ambassador at the Porte.

Later again, or in July 1869, the Berne office supplied fuller information on the proceedings taken. Seventeen administrations had been addressed by circular, of whom only three, namely, Roumania, Persia, and Servia, had failed to send replies. Of the fourteen communications received, those of Russia, France, Switzerland, Austria, and Turkey, alone require present notice.

Russia, while declaring that the necessary measures had been taken to remedy, as much as possible, the specified irregularities, brought to mind that " the construction on Russian territory of a special line with two wires, solely intended for Indian correspondence," was being successfully carried out.

France, Switzerland, Austria, and Turkey, made

mention of the arrangements concluded on the 22nd July, 1868, in Vienna, for the establishment of direct communication between London, Paris, Vienna, Constantinople, and India: the first to certify that they had executed all the engagements accepted by them on this behalf; and Turkey to announce that her contemplated lines were in course of construction and would be shortly completed.

Turkey, moreover, in asserting the reforms she had effected in her telegraph service, threw the blame of the defects complained of in many instances on other administrations than her own.

Austria notified that a conference of the delegates of the Austro-Hungarian, Servian, and Ottoman administrations was about assembling at Semlin " to open an inquiry into the progress of Indo-European telegraphic correspondence, and regulate the service on the international line in the countries represented at the conference."

Finally, Italy, noting the care with which she had established and organized her international lines, stated that " negotiations had been entered upon between the Italian, Turkish, and French Governments, to devote to the Indo-European service a special wire throughout the three States."

On the 13th August, Colonel Goldsmid left London, on a short and somewhat rapid tour, to bring personal inquiry and personal effort to bear upon the whole question. A year had passed since the Vienna conference, and there had been ample time afforded for the promised ameliorations of the service. He visited Brussels, the

---

Letter and Enclosure from Chief Director Government Indo-European Telegraph, No. 287 of September 6, 1869, to Under Secretary of State for India.

OLD OBSTACLES NOT REMOVED.

Hague, and Frankfort-on-the-Maine, conferring at each place with the director of the telegraph administration as to the course taken by Indian telegrams through their respective lines. From Frankfort he went on to Berne, the seat of the Secretariat of the Telegraph Congress, where he met with M. Curchod, the intelligent Director; and thence passed on to Florence, where the Italian Director-General showed him the draft convention resulting from the negotiations above mentioned, and to which his Government was a party. From Florence he returned *via* Paris to London, conferring with the French Inspector-General of telegraphs; and communicating on the subject with Lord Lyons, as he had done with Mr. Lumley at Brussels, Mr. Bonar at Berne, and Mr. Herries at Florence. He embodied in his report a record of his opinion that the "lines, though working more steadily than heretofore, were not fulfilling the reasonable expectations of her Majesty's Government and the Indian public;" and added, "at the risk of repeating an old story," a summary of the matter, an extract from which will throw a light on the position, diplomatically considered.

"Where our Indian telegraphic correspondence mainly fails is in the irregular means of intercommunication existing for England and Western Europe with the cable of her Majesty's Government in the Persian Gulf. To and from this cable are two principal connecting lines, which for mere distinction may be called the 'Russo-Persian' and 'Indo-Ottoman;' one through Constantinople and Turkey in Asia to the station at Fāo; one through Russia and Persia to the station at Bushahr. The opening of a second route by a private company under concessions from the Russian and Prussian Governments promises success, but it is still important to improve the communication through Turkey by all available means. Independently of the unanimously expressed desire of the States, parties to the Vienna Convention, to aid her Majesty's Government in this respect, France has signed a separate convention with Austria, Switzerland, Servia, and Turkey, and is now negotiating a second with Italy and Turkey for the same specific object. The first of these conventions was to have had effect from October last, but the Turkish Administration does not appear to have yet completed its part of the intended programme. The second is to have effect from the 1st May next. It is to be hoped that there will not then been like failure of fulfilment by one contracting party. Meanwhile our best line of communication appears to be through Belgium or Holland to Frankfort, Vienna, and Constantinople."

The report concluded with a proposal to address the foreign administrations through the ordinary diplomatic channels:

"In the Vienna Convention were laid down eight routes for Indo-European messages. Of these five passed through Western Europe and the 'Indo-Ottoman' lines; three through Russia, Persia, and the 'Russo-Persian' lines. The States directly concerned in the transmission of messages passing between England and India by these eight routes, are—France, Belgium, Holland, Prussia (comprising northern Germany), Russia, Switzerland, Austria, Italy, and Turkey.

"Russia alone is unconcerned in any traffic by the 'Indo-Ottoman' lines. As a rule, she would receive telegrams through Persia only."[1]

It was submitted that her Majesty's representatives at the courts here mentioned be made acquainted with the circumstances of the case, in order that, should occasion offer, diplomatic aid be afforded in certain practical ways indicated. And one point in the Chief Director's mind seemed to merit particular attention:

[1] Colonel Goldsmid to the Under Secretary of State for India.

"Mr. Siemens is shortly about to open his Russo-Persian line, and a cable is to be laid in the Red Sea. Unless the Ottoman Administration act up to the spirit of its convention, there is little doubt that Indian traffic will soon flow in another direction from that hitherto unwillingly but necessarily taken. Such results will at all events not have been brought about by any action on the part of her Majesty's Government, whose officers have ever been ready, and are now ready, to lend assistance towards perfecting the condition of the Ottoman lines of telegraph to India."

The remainder of the year 1869, and the first two months of 1870, were fully occupied with questions of economy and finance. Political preliminaries had been well nigh exhausted; the telegraph posts and wires from England to India had been put into a regular system, and section by section had an intelligible organization through two distinct lines ranging from London to Karáchi: as regards directing agencies no better course could be pursued than to rest awhile upon oars exercised without remission for some five years. The great object now in view, decrease of expenditure, was to be attained rather in watching the progress of reforms and innovations actually introduced, or about to spring into existence, than in devising new ones. Therefore had one of the Chief Director's first proposals been the abolition of his own appointment, and that his Assistant should undertake the whole charge single-handed. The proposal was to be experimental for a year, during which period the proposer would avail himself of the furlough regulations to enjoy relaxation from official work. Three months had not elapsed of this leave when Colonel Goldsmid was nominated to the charge of a political mission of twofold character, the duration of which might be for years;' and at Stockholm in September, while *en route* for Persia, he tendered resignation of his telegraph directorship. But there was another reason for watching progress and pausing in the work of active reform. The Red Sea cable was about to open traffic in opposition to the Turkish lines and recently constructed Indo-European telegraph of the Messrs. Siemens; and a very few months would prove whether competition was under the circumstances possible, or whether those writers in the press who passed a wholesale condemnation on the Government measures were true prophets.

It were an invidious, and happily a needless task to repeat the many statements so freely circulated to the detriment of the Persian Gulf and Makran coast lines, and the replies equally ready to be given, but more charily published, on the part of Government officers. Allusion is made especially to the period of the first promulgation of the prospectus of the British Indian submarine telegraph. Time has now sufficiently proved that the channels through which Government was endeavouring to "force telegraphic communication" were not "as difficult as the world can produce;" and that the measures which have resulted in the splendid lines now existing between England and India were not by any means apt illustrations of a virtual trial of "the impossible," followed by "matters-

---

¹ The settlement of the Turco-Persian frontier question was, for example, authoritatively commenced, it is believed, by H.M. Government, in conjunction with Russia, more than thirty years ago. As regards the actual demarcation of a boundary line, such may not yet have been carried out or accepted by the litigating Powers; but the labours of the mixed Commission have certainly produced admirable maps of the disputed territory.

of-course failure.' Yet this was the first of a series of charges brought against those who sanctioned both labour and expenditure on the objects we have sought, however feebly, to express in the present volume. For the remainder, reference is solicited to the columns of the daily papers throughout the year 1869 and up to March 1870, when the Viceroy and Governor of Bombay added their own personal felicitations to the congratulatory telegrams with which the chairman of the British India Submarine Company was greeted on the successful accomplishment of his work.¹

There are two points in these attacks upon Government work which may be briefly noticed. In so doing all intent is disclaimed at reviving an undesired discussion. The question is propounded in a general, rather than particular sense. Firstly, it is assuredly an illogical and an unsound theory to maintain that Government is fair game for depreciation and invective because it is more commonly pictured in a collective than an individual form. Some one person or some two or three persons must be responsible and should be held responsible for certain acts, whether they be shielded with the ægis of the State, or open to criticism and censure as an immoral play or a street obstruction. With ministers and high officials, this personal responsibility is more or less acknowledged; not so, however, with humbler

---

¹ The few strong expressions quoted from the public press in this paragraph will show that specific instances are not wanting in illustration of the feeling indicated; though these are mild indeed compared with some of the charges adduced. On the other hand, what better proof of impartial action could be found than the fact, that Government publicly congratulated the Companies on those submarine telegraph achievements which met with merited applause and honour in all quarters; while sea-cables were laid and landline obstacles surmounted by their own officers in comparative silence?

workmen. These are doomed to hear patiently their work vilified and run down, because they have neither the *status* to be publicly responsible, nor the liberty of speaking as they would wish to speak on behalf of those they serve. Surely, if Government cannot approve the exercise of greater license to their servants—and the wisdom of this course is in no way impugned—it is but just that those who publicly attack Government measures, and know the men who recommend and execute, should name the one as well as condemn the other. Fair play in these matters is not only desirable on the score of ordinary morality, but to hasten the time when individual work and individual efficiency shall be tested and certified in every department of Administration; when the question of cost shall no longer be the gravest consideration for parliamentary commissions, but the question of *return for cost*; when a vague desire for reduction of salary shall be substituted by a firm exaction of an equivalent to salary; in fine, when abstract ideas about Government offices and administration shall give place to definite truths.

Secondly, no reasoning can modify the application to Government of the code of honour which prevails between man and man. A contractor has no more right to saddle the State with an iniquitous money burthen than in the case of a private individual; nor has a tradesman any more moral warrant to sell bad wares to his country than to his countrymen, or than a Government servant has to submit an undue claim, because it can be compressed within the literal meaning of a regulation. Upon this principle, therefore, does it behove the officers of Government, individually, to be jealous of the interests as of the honour of their masters, and they are in duty bound to protect the one and the other to the utmost of their limited powers. If attacked in print, they should be attacked in a way to which they can readily respond, and as much facility is due to the circulation of their answers as to the charges which have rendered those responses necessary.

The summary of work performed since March 1870 to the close of 1873 will be an appropriate conclusion to the narrative of the telegraph.[1] The Siemens' line from London to Tehran, joining the Persian line at the latter city, under the supervision and management of British officers, as far as Bushahr where it meets the British Government cable, fairly opened on the 31st January, 1870. The Red Sea cable commenced work on the 26th March following; but the Falmouth-Gibraltar section, without which the Aden line is practically imperfect, was not completed till the 13th June. In merely chronicling this latter achievement according to the letter of our task, we have no desire to depreciate its importance. A great and successful undertaking of the kind, replete with personal as with public interests, cannot fail to command graphic description equally with a world-wide laudation; and in this particular instance all that had to be promulgated on the subject has long since become matter of record.

Later in the same year Major Champain again proceeded to Persia. His chief reasons were to inspect the line, to judge for himself of the necessity of replacing the old wooden poles by iron standards, and last, not

---

[1] For the official details contained in the remainder of this chapter, I am chiefly indebted to a memorandum kindly prepared for me by Major J. U. Bateman Champain, R.E., much of which has been extracted *verbatim*.

least, endeavour by every possible means to curtail the working and maintenance establishments. After a march with Captain St. John in the depth of winter from Tehran to Bushahr, he continued his journey to India, there to give in his report upon the Persian line, and recommendations for future action.

In June, 1871, he returned by the overland route, and in September, attended, in company with Colonel Robinson, R.E., the Indian Director-General, a meeting at Berne to consider the question of rival companies or organizations working the lines to India. The service had greatly improved, but the traffic proved too inelastic for three lines; and it seemed highly probable that, at the low rates then in force, the two companies would be obliged to withdraw, leaving the Turkish line, which was supported almost entirely by Imperial resources, to fall back, perhaps, to its old state of inefficiency. The result was an unavoidable increase in the charge from the 2*l*. 17*s*. fixed by the Congress of Vienna, to 4*l*. 10*s*., or about the original tariff. In November, Colonel Robinson and Major Champain were nominated by the Indian Government as delegates to the triennial Telegraph Conference of States interested, held this year in Rome. The latter officer was, moreover, authorized to represent Persia on the same occasion. Among other questions considered was that of tariff, and the 4*l*. 10*s*. message of twenty words was modified to 4*l*.

In June, 1872, Major Champain again repaired to Persia, *viâ* the Caspian, to renew the treaty which expired in the autumn. He was detained there until the 5th December, when he returned, by the Caucasus, with a new Convention to last for twenty-three years, or the full period of the Siemens' concession. This Convention was subsequently approved by her Majesty's Government, and ratifications were formally exchanged at Tehran on the 31st March, 1873. The articles are twenty in number, and definitively lay down the terms on which the international traffic is in future to be worked, the system on which accounts are to be settled, the duties and responsibilities of the English staff employed in the country, and the protection to be accorded them by the Persian authorities.

In March, 1873, the Chief Director started once more for India, to discuss and settle with the Indian Government many questions affecting the general administration of Persian and Persian Gulf lines. Returning to London in August, he proceeded the next month, with Mr. Cappel of the Indian Department, to Vienna, there to consider, with the Russian and Prussian Directors-General, the possibility of reducing the standard of twenty words for telegraphic messages. The result of this minor conference was a reduction, from the 15th November, 1873, of a standard of twenty words at 100 francs, to one of ten words at 50 francs, with regular gradations of prices for each word over ten. And the increase of traffic following the reduction proved, *i.e.* for the month succeeding its operation, most encouraging.

The speed and accuracy of working, both *viâ* Tehran and *viâ* Suez, are now acknowledged, and, as a rule, really leave little to be desired. But although matched in efficiency, the Company's cables have hitherto enjoyed the greater patronage of the public. And reasons for this preference seem readily to present themselves. Let us take two of the more palpable.

Imprimis, the different companies between England and India by the Mediterranean and Red Sea having amalgamated, are better able to advertise and bring their merits to notice than the Indo-European telegraph, which is half in the hands of a company, and half in those of Government. Secondly, the Eastern line, which works in connection with the trans-Indian Cable Companies, has a practical monopoly of the messages from Singapore, China, &c., which in former days had to be posted to Galle and were thence telegraphed by the Persian Gulf.

As it will be impracticable to prolong the present account a day longer than the close of the year 1873, we publish, in bringing this portion of our volume to an end, a table showing the yearly progress of the telegraph working by Turkey and Russia, both, from the first to the latest registries. It would manifestly be unfair to take the pace *viâ* Russia, from 1865 to 1869, as a sample of international working, because the line was not an organized one, and very few messages passed by it. Turkey had, on the other hand, been much encouraged, and yet—while showing by occasional flashes of improvement how well she *could* work—her average rate was nearly as bad in 1869 as when the wires were first laid. Since 1870, the improvement in the Turkish lines must be attributed to greater attention having at length been effectually given to the lines between London and Constantinople, and also to the comparatively trivial traffic in this direction; the bulk of the messages naturally being conveyed *viâ* Suez or *viâ* Tehran.

"Three hours, nine minutes," truly says Major Champain, "is a particularly good average rate of speed when one remembers what countries and seas are traversed by the Indo-European despatches, and how any important interruption affects the calculation. Of course many messages pass from end to end of the line in a few minutes."

TABLE *showing the average Speed of Telegraph working from England to India (Kurachi) in the years 1865 to 1873 inclusive.*

	Viâ Turkey.			*Viâ* Russia and Persia.		
	Days	Hrs	Min	Days	Hrs	Min
1865	6	8	44	17	5	5
1866	5	8	50	10	9	34
1867	5	3	37	7	5	19
1868	5	2	58	5	2	3
1869	5	14	13	9	10	39
1870	2	18	16	Jan. 11	23	55
				Feb. to Dec. 1	13	10
1871	1	17	57	—	8	37
1872	1	6	20	—	6	7
1873 Jan. to Oct.	—	19	12	—	3	9

For later working, we can only entreat those interested to judge for themselves on good evidence; such, for instance, as is supplied by the telegrams published in the daily papers, or the unerring experience of mercantile offices.

In the Introductory Chapter[1] we proposed to show a kind of profit and loss account for the Cis-India Telegraphs of Government. As regards political and commercial value, it may be permitted us, perhaps, to ask the reader of these pages to add the details herein contained to the more palpable and general data he must already possess, and the conclusions he may already have arrived at, before pronouncing a final judgment. In respect of cost, instead of discussing this question in the body of a work rather narratory than comprehensive, it has been thought better to procure an authentic statement comprising the latest information on record, and

[1] Page 3, *ante*.

attach it, for ready reference, as the last page of the Appendix and volume. The statement bears the signature of Mr. Alfred Brasher, a gentleman who has rendered long, steady, and intelligent service to the Direction of the Indo-European Government lines, and than whom no one should be more competent to deal with the practical fiscal results of the whole procedure by which this department of administration has been affected.

THE "TWEED," PAYING OUT PERSIAN GULF CABLE, IN TOW OF STEAMER.

PART II.

TRAVEL.

"The second part of the charade takes place. It is still an Eastern scene. . . . The Eastern voyagers go off dancing, like Papageno and the Moorish King in the Magic Flute."—VANITY FAIR.

CHAPTER VII.

BAGHDAD—HOW REACHED FROM THE PERSIAN GULF.—
BAGHDAD TO CONSTANTINOPLE VIÂ MOSUL AND MARDIN.

BAGHDAD, the City of the Khalifs, notwithstanding its pleasant associations for reading, romantic boyhood, is comparatively but little known to full-grown Englishmen in its reality. It may be that we liked the place as boys, owing to the kind of fairy inconceivableness with which it was invested; and that its khalifs, wazirs, princes, princesses, merchants, barbers, and many *dramatis personæ*, charmed us as much by their brilliant unsubstantiality as by their acts and words. Now that age has blunted our enjoyment of theatrical display and Oriental romance, we do not care to acquaint ourselves with an existent Baghdad; and we are just as indifferent in asking whether the favoured city of the "Arabian Nights" is really Baghdad at all, and not Cairo which it more resembles, as whether it is situated in Turkey or Persia. Here, for the benefit of the uninitiated, let the opportunity be taken to place on record the fact that Baghdad is not, and has not been Persian for more than two centuries. It is the capital of one of the finest dependencies of the Ottoman Empire, won for them by the young, but fierce and resolute Sultan Murad, or Amurath IV., in 1638, shortly before his death.[1]

In these matter-of-fact practical times, the simpler way for the European traveller to reach Baghdad is by embarking at Bombay in a steamer of the British India Company, and proceeding up the Persian Gulf to Basrah. Thence to Baghdad up the Tigris may be readily accomplished by Turkish or English river steamer in four or five days. The city of dates is rather nominal than real in this programme; for the coaling station off which lie the British boats, and where passengers land and loiter, is Margil, a very few miles higher up than the creek leading to Basrah from the Shatt-el-Arab.

A Vice-Consul, or Assistant British Resident, hoists his colours here, and is under the orders of her Majesty's Consul-General at Baghdad. His dwelling-house is pleasantly situated by the river-side. A brick, single-storied building, with tolerably thick walls and the usual Indian verandah, it is not ill adapted to the fierce heat of at least half the year; but it seems to want the appliances of the Indian bungalow, such as the punkah and thermantidotes. That part of the year is, fortunately, of a milder character, may be gathered from the existence in this house of a handsome English-looking fireplace, with mantelpiece complete, the effect of which is both refreshing and ornamental. There is something genial in a fireplace in the far East, though we may never chance to see a fire lighted in it. The kind host who received me on two distinct occasions at his Margil residence now rests for ever in those distant lands. He was one of those to make his presence felt in such manner that his absence would be, as it is, regretted. The neat

[1] Professor Creasy's "History of the Ottoman Turks," vol. i. p. 408.

sitting-room, with its smart coloured sketches by amateur artists, its well-framed "Peace and War," by Landseer, and "English Homestead" of Herring, and its few but ever welcome books, are reminiscences of a taste which has passed away in its early genuineness.

In this neighbourhood is a monument erected by Sir R. Grant, once Governor of Bombay, and others, to the memory of officers and men lost by the foundering of the *Tigris*, in Colonel Chesney's expedition in 1836. It did not strike me as kept in very good order, nor is it more than an ordinary tablet *in memoriam*: but the subject is worthy a respectable commemoration. Colonel Chesney and Captain Blosse Lynch were of those who survived: a brother of the latter, an officer in the Bombay army, was among those who perished.

The first object of interest, to the traveller moving up by boat from Margil to Baghdad, is the point of junction of the Tigris and Euphrates, just above which, on the latter river, is Korna, alleged to be the site of the Garden of Eden. Here are some scattered mat and mud hovels exceedingly dirty, trees and vegetation, a leaning minaret, and little else to attract attention. Somewhat higher up the river is a bank of gardens; and here I was fortunate enough to see realized a charming picture of Mesopotamian village life and scenery, the bright green produce of the soil forming an agreeable contrast to the brown, orange, and magenta dresses of the women moving through it. Higher still are the Marshes, a vast flat, many long miles in extent on either side, studded, however, with green wheat cultivation. Pig and pelican now pass within easy reach of the sportsman on the paddle-box. But these matters appertain to the diary, which may be taken up on board the *Comet* steamer, the day after leaving Margil. The year is 1864 :—

"*April* 15.—After a heavy storm of wind, lightning, and rain last night, during which we ran aground on the left bank of the Tigris, and owing to which we had to make fast until daylight, the morning was tolerably cool and pleasant. More pig shooting yesterday. One large sow was killed by R., a smaller animal by Captain S.; others may have fallen which were not recovered. Sport resumed this morning. River becomes very winding, and presents, moreover, many sharp angles and turnings. Villages occasionally seen; some of great length, but all apparently of a locomotive character. Population sparse, as also cultivation; and yet how rich must be the neglected soil! Cattle abundant, especially buffaloes; sheep also in plenty. The cows are not in good condition, a result attributed to the purging properties of new grass, rather than any normal imperfection; and last winter, in its severity, was injurious to the pasture. Observed many tents, and took special note of Professor Rawlinson's 'reed cabins, supported by the tall stems of the growing plants bent into arches, and walled with mats composed of flags or sedge.' An Arab chief came on board the steamer. He is said to be the son of a *celebrated* rebel of repute, who long resisted the Turkish authorities. He himself now professes great loyalty, and wears the European coat and trousers like the Osmanli. No dress, in my humble opinion, could be less becoming to the character, habits, and bearing of the well-born Arab. This chief's features are manly and good, but the expression is unsafe. Notwithstanding his body garments, he wears the native 'Akal,' or rope of camels' hair, on the head, twisted around the kerchief drooping over his shoulders. The general aspect of the river to-day was that of an extensive reed marsh: water high and nearly level with the banks, and yet the channel in some places so narrow as to resemble a canal. Passed last night the tomb of Ezra, the prophet, a handsome building with enamelled dome. Passed this day Abu-robà, literally 'Father of sour cream.'

"*April* 16.—On deck at dawn. Captain S. soon on the watch. After a time, get my double-barreled Baker and load with ball, arming myself, besides, with a ship's Enfield. No shot obtainable before breakfast; but aroused from an easy chair during the day by the familiar stirring sound. Five or six balls are despatched after one animal; still piggy does not fall. Colonel S. lends me his breech-loading carbine. Suddenly a new pig appears. One fires, then another; the beast looks

THE PROPHET EZRA'S TOMB, ON THE TIGRIS.

at us—is he wounded, or only bewildered? All hands are on deck; the *Comet* brings to, and Lieutenant B., Dr. A., Captain S., and I proceed to the shore. Our first beat fails to find, the second is more successful, and a huge sow faces us. Captain S. fires and hits, fires again and kills. The beast rolls over, to be secured by the Mosali sailors, who had brought their spears. One or two of a litter being then captured, we move on to track the boar, supposed to be in the vicinity, but it was not forthcoming. Our ranks were now swelled by additional comers, Colonel S., Lieutenant C., and Sir C. B.

"Our course to-day is through country much as that of yesterday, as regards want of population and cultivation. What are called the Marshes, however, ceased last evening on arrival at Amāra, where the land became less swampy and perhaps a little higher at the banks. This said Amāra is a new Turkish settlement formed at a point where the river, turning at a sharp angle to the left, is continued, as it were, to the right also, by an offshoot, called the 'Had,' which loses itself amid the marshes. Amāra is on the proper left bank, having the Tigris on one face and the Had on the other. We stopped for a moment there to drop our Arab Ottoman. It was quite interesting to see this rising Asiatic town, the house tops crowned with curious gazers, and the Osmanli Nizams and Irregulars crowded here and there on the quay. One remarkably characteristic figure, dressed out and exhibited on the wall of his house, recalled Byron's lines:—

"Begirt with many a gallant slave,
Apparell'd as becomes the brave,
Old Giaffir sate in his Divan."

There was a fair English-looking boy at his side; nor should the ladies of the *háram* be forgotten.

"*April* 17.—This morning, at about half-past seven, reached Kūt-al-Amāra, a wood station, with a Turkish detachment of 300 men under a Mir Alāi (Colonel). Strolled on shore, and conversed with soldiers and others. Regiments composed of Arabs as well as Turks, and the dresses are of several shades and varieties of slovenliness. The Sultan's representative here is not fond of pipe-clay at all events. Had just entered a courtyard or barrack-square, where some hundred men might have been huddled into eight or ten small pale-green tents, and was watching the soldiers at drill, when S. and A. joined me. We were invited to visit the Mir Alāi, and proceeded upstairs to a reception-room, not much better than that of a native pleader in India. It overlooked the drill-ground in the court of the whole building. We were ushered in and seated on a sofa. Soon came a portly Turk, probably a Binbāshi (Major), who talked fair Persian, and with whom we got on comfortably enough. Then appeared the great man himself; he could hardly speak any language but his own, and my Turkish was, perhaps, no better than his Arabic. However, we managed among us to keep up the conversation. We had two instalments of coffee, after which I proposed departure, but our friend begged we would inspect the troops in the ground outside the building. This we agreed to do, for there was no resisting the pressure used. There were the men on one side, leaping and performing certain antics meant to illustrate the new bayonet exercise—a strange operation at any time, and by soldiers of any nationality, but made particularly so by these quaint handlers of old flint muskets: on the other side, they were going through the manual and platoon exercise in small squads. Some of the old Turkish Colonel's sayings may be recorded. Though not very clean in person, he was pleasant in his hearty joviality, and his sentiments were of the most friendly description: 'The Dāolat [1] Ingliz (English Government) was all one with the Dāolat Osmanli (Turkish Government). All that he possessed was ours, and *vice versâ*.' Again: 'In ten years more, under Sultan Abdul Aziz, there must be a great change in Turkey. She will have progressed incredibly. At such time her civilization will be complete and of the first order; she will possess the best of shops, manufactories (fabricas), all.' Then, in special allusion, perhaps, to C., to whom he was vainly endeavouring to make himself intelligible: 'How good would it be if we could only but understand one another!' The place was foul and filthy, and the parade-ground in wretched order. Colonel S. pointed inquiringly to certain objects which seemed out of character in the latter; but no explanation was afforded. The station is, however, only of recent growth, and, all things considered, it may serve as a sign that Turkey has set to work in earnest to Europeanise the Arabs under her control, and bring them into the civilized subjection which Time has compelled

---

[1] Here pronounced "Devlet." This national difference of pronunciation it is which causes Arabic names, such as Ahmad, Muhammad, Rashid, Wali, &c., to be tortured into Achmet, Mehmet, Reschid, Vely, &c.

her to substitute for the harder servitude of her early institutions.

"*April* 18.—Passed a new-looking fort and village, called Güldeh, or Azizya, a station for a Kaimakam (Lieutenant-Colonel); but apparently uninhabited, owing to the high state of the river, which overflows its banks here as elsewhere. We might have walked over to the wood station, 'Homaniyah wall,' in, perhaps, ten minutes, from a point in the Tigris whence, owing to the most tortuous of courses, it took us about two hours to steam there. We landed when replenishing fuel; and C. and I inspected some mounds like *tumuli*. These are damp and soft, and the impress of feet upon them is whitened with saltpetre, while the lower ground is quite dry. They are covered, moreover, with broken pottery and bricks. The last showed an arrow-shaped mark, which Colonel S. thinks must have some meaning. Pretty wild birds and pretty wild flowers visible. More shooting to-day, the pig being varied with wild cats. Saw Baghdadya in the distance, said to be a favourite resort of lions. An Arab at the wood station assured S. that a lion was in the habit of paying nightly visits to his locality, and that he had fenced himself in for protection. These lions if worthy the name, must be small and inferior; for this country shows no forest or cover, in accordance with our notions of the residence of the king of beasts. I almost question whether some, perhaps all, are not lynxes. In any case great excitement prevails, and sport is contemplated on a future occasion. The Tigris presents banks to-day much as usual—that is, covered with little beside tamarisk and liquorice.

"*April* 19.—Another stick early this morning, then another, and another; the two first before dawn, and the last the most serious, so serious indeed as to require all hands to work the ship off. Ctesiphon full in sight: we had passed it during the darkness. As our worthy commander had anchored and let off steam, it was proposed that we should go on shore and attempt to reach the old ruin. It may reasonably be inferred that at this part of the river were the two cities (El Madaïn), Ctesiphon on the left, and Seleucia on the right bank, and that the ruin known as 'Tak-i-Kasr' is a vestige of the palace where, according to Gibbon, 'Chosroes Nushirwan gave audience to the ambassadors of the world.' Near it is a domed building called Sulman Pāk, supposed to be the tomb of the prophet's barber; but these Muhammadan legends are too common to be trusted, and are in most cases either perversions of ancient tradition, or applied to comparatively modern structures without historical interest. Owing to the overflow of the river and consequent intervention of a canal, our approach to Ctesiphon was interrupted, nor could we get within some 400 yards of this really beautiful and interesting relic of Parthian magnificence. Of Seleucia, on the opposite side of the Tigris, the remains are probably centered in two mounds known to the inhabitants as Tel Omar and Sirhan, the first of which was opened by Mr. John Taylor, her Majesty's Consul for Kurdistan.[1] On returning to the ship we were followed by a party of town Arabs who had been on a pilgrimage to the Sulman Pāk, and who were inclined to be communicative. There had also been a larger party of men and women from Baghdad whose tents were pitched near the tomb.

"On approaching Baghdad up the river, the country became more cultivated. Many fields of barley, many gardens, many enclosures with cattle, many Arab families, Shaikhs' tents of camel or goat hair, and other characteristic objects, render the

---

[1] The late Lieut. Bewsher, I.N., who commanded the *Comet*, and was one of the party visiting Ctesiphon with us on this occasion, thus wrote of the ruin, as it now stands, after closer inspection :—" A magnificent arch 86 feet high from the under part to the ground, and 82 feet broad at the foot. From this arch a vaulted room extends 153 feet to the rear. The roof of this has partially fallen in, and tradition says the place was struck by lightning in the year of the Prophet's birth. The building faces the winter sunrise, or east south-east, from which direction it has a most imposing appearance. The front walls of the two wings are alone standing, the rooms having fallen in. In the centre of the arch are marks of thousands of bullets that, report says, were fired at a huge ring which supported the curtain of the audience chamber. This ring had, doubtless, excited the cupidity of the Arabs during many centuries, and defied all attempts to remove it till gunpowder put a more formidable agent into the hands of its many enemies. Mr. Rich was told that this ring proved to be of gold." *Journal of Royal Geographical Society*, vol. xxxvii. paper viii. 1867.

panorama lively, varied and interesting. At length, amid a long row of trees, the houses and minarets of the city are visible. For eight years the river has not been known to have attained such a height. Eight years ago I am told there was a considerable overflow, flooding one or two villages. The golden domed mosque of the Kazimain and tomb of Zobeide no sooner appear in sight than we feel our river trip at its conclusion; the gardens and residences along the river become part of the city itself, the suburbs being left behind; and we quickly come to anchor near the British Residency. They say that the large house overlooking us contains the harem of a wealthy merchant. The ladies appear to find amusement at the windows; and no wonder. How monotonous must be the life within the walls of that blank edifice!"

Before continuing to extract from the pages of a diary, I will say a few words on a city in which I passed a month on the occasion of this my first visit. It had been agreed that I should undertake the land inspection of the telegraph line from Baghdad to Scutari; so that when Colonel Stewart and party left on the 28th April to return to India, I remained behind at the Residency, preparatory to moving in the opposite direction.

The streets are narrow, dirty, gloomy and irregular; there is nothing about the dwelling-houses, even the best, to make them desirable, except it be the position which, in some cases, combines the advantages of garden and river. Here and there is a prettily domed mosque, but painfully like a crockery "finján," or coffee cup, of blue flower pattern. Perhaps the most remarkable characteristic of the town is the large concourse of Muhammadans whether Persian, Turk, or Arab; and when to these are added the Syrian and Chaldean Christians, Jews and Armenians, it may well be conceived that the public thoroughfares are not wanting in picturesque groups and the echo of divers tongues. By far the least interesting living object is the male European, whose native dress, whatever its convenience, has not the most remote claim to grace or beauty.

The gardens, in spite of the exaggeration of Eastern poets who would lead the reader to imagine every garden a kind of terrestrial paradise, exhibit nothing in comparison to the highly-cared-for horticulture of Europe. There is a wildness and untidiness which may be very charming in their way, but which are not likely to meet with approval from the fastidious *habitués* of Chiswick, and like fashionable resorts, at home or abroad. Still there are flowers and shrubs meriting favourable notice, and the orange trees and pomegranates are not to be slighted.

The grounds known as "the gardens" *par excellence*, are traversed by a wide thoroughfare intersected by watercourses, roughly bridged over as in India. On either side long mud walls, with gates more or less rude or ornamented, mark the different allotments. Some are private property, some "Wakf" or religious bequests. But the term "garden" is here again not according to our English dictionary. These are rather date plantations, overgrown with grass and wild vegetation, and varied with irregularly planted trees. The wood used as fuel in the river steamers is mostly, I understand, tamarisk. Good coal, at the time of which I write, was procurable direct from home at a cost of £2 10s. per ton.

As regards interiors, I will describe my own room in the British Residency, which may be taken as a specimen of the style of architecture and adornment common to the better class of houses. Its front is about south-west, to the river, and the entrance door at the back is north-east, to the court. This court-yard is square, and marks the harem or retired part of the house. We are on the upper floor, and overlook the court from a kind of terrace or verandah. On one side of me is the Resident's apartment, on the other a spare room for a guest. My room is about eighteen feet long by twelve broad, and fourteen feet in height. It is built of brick, thickly coated with plaster. The wall is divided by a ledge, above and below which are recesses, the first reaching to about a foot from the ceiling, the second descending to a point about thirty inches from the floor. The lower recesses are quaintly fashioned in the upper interior, within a generally square frame. The higher ones are regular Moorish arches set in similar square outlines. The ground division of the wall is ornamented with neatly designed birds and flowers and other fancy mural patterns moulded in plaster, the white colour being relieved by the blue edging. This terminates, however, just under the recesses, so that the bottom of the walls is quite plain. The ceiling division of the wall, and ceiling itself, are profusely adorned with designs of flowers in various rather dingy colours, the centre of each Moorish arch being especially favoured by a large glass cone supported on a glass crescent with a middle horn apparently extemporised for the purpose. This figure occupies the whole length of the arch, and is very conspicuous. In the centre of the ceiling, also, is a large piece of glass, a projecting figure of many angular pieces like the bits of a Chinese puzzle. To the back or towards the court, however, instead of the conical figure within the arch, are three glass windows. There are windows also on the sides of the room for the use of ladies of the harem overlooking a kind of boudoir.[1]

The river of Baghdad is, no doubt, the main feature of the place. An eye accustomed to the monotonous waters flowing through Sind and the Punjáb; and to the clusters of houses near the banks, such as Haidarabad and Kotri, or Multan and Shir Shah; to scenic groups, such as Sakar-Bakhar-Rohri, and the general panorama of the Lower Indus, will see little novelty in the aspect of the Tigris at this particular stage. Muddy walls and muddy waters are too much the rule, and fresh green trees and bright edifices too much the exception, to make the *tout ensemble* attractive; while, even amid exceptions, there is perhaps nothing at Baghdad so unique and gem-like as Khwája Khidhr's island above Bakhar. But the stranger from Europe will not be so fastidious in appreciation of Oriental landscape. As already stated, the river was exceptionally high in the spring of 1864, and the houses on either bank looked most insecure from aqueous intrusion; so that a visit at that season was hardly well timed for favourable impressions. Then, walls of gardens came down occasionally with a crash; and I had reason to believe walls of houses also. The very heavy rain may have caused these accidents as well as the river overflow; but so it was, and so it is recorded.

[1] First impressions are recorded, when the zone, as here described, had not become so constantly recurring an object to the writer as it has been during the last ten years. The word 'harem' applies to the original native design.

Her Majesty's Consul-General in 1864, with that kind hospitality which has distinguished his whole tenure of office at Baghdad, kept very much open house, open stables, and to no small extent open purse for the entertainment of his frequent guests. Always ready to arrange participation in easy local ceremonial, pastime or relaxation of some kind, for such as were not burdened with daily routine of work, the order of the day would find variety in visiting, riding, shooting, sailing, and sight-seeing. My first visit to his Excellency Namik Pasha, governor of the province, recalls a stirring scene in the court yard of the Residency. Some eight horses richly caparisoned, and a few more of less ambitious externals, but all fine spirited Arabs, were on one side waiting the pleasure of their intended riders, each horse checked and watched by an attendant groom. On the other side was a plainly saddled bay, and a stout grey pony, equipped for work, waiting the coming of the Chevalier Romulus B. and Mr. P., both bound for a ride to Tehran, *viâ* Karmanshah, the former going thence on a mission of patriotism and philanthropy to Bukhara, the latter to take the Caspian and Russian route to England. Our progress through the streets on that day was productive of no small stir. Guards turned out to present arms; shopkeepers and passers by stared at each and all of us with apathetic amazement. We were ushered in, presented in due form, and got satisfactorily through the somewhat monotonous but rather interesting process of an official call.

Not many days after this formal visit we dined with the Pasha. The dinner was abundant in products of a mixed *cuisine* more French than Turkish; but it savoured of error to see the Turks ranged on one side of the table and the European guests on the other. The champagne was drinkable; the sherry bad: all wines were passed round at a hospitable but dangerous pace. The next day a return dinner was given at the British Residency. On that occasion I sat between the Commander-in-Chief of the Forces and the Commandant of Artillery, the former conversing much in Turkish and the latter in Italian. My impressions of these convivial reunions is, upon the whole, favourable. True that the talk they promote is mostly superficial, and the interchange of thought and sentiment they effect is rather weak and meaningless. But then they are necessary and more or less useful. Observance of social amenities keeps individuals on better behaviour than if they never met but on official business, and makes them feel that duty to their country is inseparably allied to duty towards each other. To judge from Namik Pasha, Turkish diplomatists would seem especially reserved and dignified; but such is not invariably the case. Nor is the Turkish Muslim regardless of distinction amid Faringis as the Indian Muslim, to whom the Englishman is the true European, and whose apprehension of every other country of Europe is of the vaguest kind. The former has a sufficient number of conflicting European elements to deal with to be compelled, in spite of general aversions, to prefer one to the other; and in this sense England had, in 1864, no reason to complain of his avowed predilections. The little artilleryman, beside whom I sat at dinner was, however, a Hungarian, his name and title being both of official adoption.

A picnic given by the hospitable Mr. and Mrs. L. afforded us more insight into the general society of Baghdad. Diplomacy, the telegraph, commerce, medicine, and the Missionaries were all represented in the persons of nine gentlemen, and five of these were accompanied by their wives. The feast was lavish; the table groaning with viands, among which was a whole lamb. Champagne and soda-water flowed abundantly together, while beer was broached *à discretion*. A stranger would be struck by the easy and not inharmonious blending of Oriental with European languages at these entertainments, and the fluency with which ladies speak the first, in the circles of this outlying city of a civilized world.

Among other visits paid, was one to the Persian Minister at the Sublime Porte, who stayed a few days at Baghdad on his way to Constantinople. In Mirza Husain Khan I had the pleasure to recognize a former acquaintance of Bombay, where he had been Persian Consul. His fluent French, polished manners, and lively talk, made him a really pleasant companion. He took advantage of his health and physical activity to ride off to Kerbela, the great place of Shia pilgrimage, which, though at some considerable distance, is readily attainable with good horses over a level country. In accordance with annual custom, the festival of the Kurbān or sacrifice, falling this year on the 16th May, the Resident made then his round of early morning calls upon the native dignitaries, commencing with the Pasha. Availing myself of the opportunity of accompanying him, I paid my respects to the Accountant-General, the Collector of Customs, the Municipal Commissioner, and the Military Accountant. Colonel K.'s tact and knowledge of languages enabled him to do the conversation on these occasions excellently. This sort of thing is quite an art in itself, aptness for which would appear constitutional; and indeed the repeated discussion, before breakfast, of sweetmeats and hot and cold beverages, independently of politics and popular topics, is not to be accomplished by everyone. It need scarcely be said that pipes, coffee, and *sharbat* are essential at Baghdad as elsewhere in the East, only the visitor may exercise his discretion in selecting the Turkish *chibouk* or Persian *kalian*. The man who resists both stimulants must have the moral courage to write himself down a tolerated Goth.

The mosque of the Kázimain or two Kázims; the tomb of Zobeide, of repute in the "Arabian Nights;" the madrasahs or colleges; the singular ruin of Aggarkuf; and the Bazar, should certainly be "done" by the sight-seeing traveller whose star has led him to Baghdad; and above all he should take advantage of the occasion to ride sixty miles south to Hillah, and visit the site of ancient Babylon. Were it not that other cares and occupations had as good right to my time, I should plead guilty to great, although qualified neglect in this respect. A large party of us steamed up the river and inspected the bright golden domes at the shrine of the Kázims: but, beyond a closer acquaintance with an object familiar in the distance; a short ride from the landing-place to the tomb and back again on a Rosinante with a deep red saddle-cover; and the honour of tea, coffee, sugar and water, pipes, and conversations with the Mutawali, or administrator of the sacred treasury, and some Arabs, whose fluent Hindustani was suspicious, I gained little from the excursion. The Bazar I passed and repassed as much perhaps on chance as on special occasions. Inferior to that of Constantinople, it is no doubt first class in Asia, and may be safely recommended to afford pleasant pastime to the Oriental *flâneur*.

The Church of England service in English was performed on Sundays in a small building capable of holding about fifty persons. Doctor E. at this time always officiated, for his brother missionary, Mr. B., was absent on a tour in Persia. These gentlemen are sent to the Jews only, and are themselves converts from Judaism. They reside here with their families, and are held in high esteem. Dr. E. is a good Arabic scholar, and showed me several versions of the Arabic Testament, one with the full punctuation which was, I think, in course of publication, and had been translated from the original Hebrew up to the book of Joshua. He informed me there were 15,000 Jews in Baghdad, but that only three Jewish children attended his school out of a total of forty-five. The instruction given was English and Arabic, geography, and moral lessons. It was difficult to secure the services of a good master and mistress, as well as meet all incidental expenses, on a limited allowance of £30 per annum.

From the number of coins and curiosities brought for my inspection, I should fear the market was open to the importation of fictitious antiques. Yet the eagerness evinced for excavating mounds and graves showed that the search for genuine relics was carried on with undiminished vigour. One man, I was informed, had recently been buried alive while digging into a *tumulus*. Colonel Kemball had found some handsome coins and earrings, and had despatched them homeward; but the post was robbed, and all the valuables had been lost or abstracted.

There were, and are probably still two posts between Baghdad and Europe: one *viâ* Damascus, Beyrout, and the Mediterranean; one *viâ* Diarbekir, Samsūn, and Constantinople. The former and speedier might be considered the English, and the latter the Turkish post. It is worthy of remark, that Damascus and Baghdad were in the old high road from Tangiers to China. Lelewel says: "une autre route continentale à travers toute l'habitable était moins connue aux Mahomédans. Elle passait de Tanger par Égypte, ensuite par Damask, Koufa, Bagdad, Bussora, elle pénètre dans Ahwaz, et par le Fars, Kirman, Sind, Hind, elle poussa jusqu'en Chine."¹ Makran might safely be interpolated after Kirman, but it should be with reference to the route through Bampur, Kéj, and Béla. The whole line might be commended to the notice of those who still believe in the undoubted merits of an unbroken railway from Constantinople to Karáchi.

The Baghdad boil, leaving a scar commonly called the date mark, attacks most Europeans at some period of their residence in the city. Dr. Wood told me that the Jews enjoy peculiar exemption from this disorder, which circumstance if well authenticated is at least noteworthy. In recording the ravages of disease, modern travellers lay great stress on the visitation of 1830-31; the horrors of which were increased by an inundation fearfully destructive to life and property. But even these dire calamities do not seem to have reached the figures representing the losses in 1773. In those days there were no railways, telegraphs, or other means of rapid locomotion to facilitate the check, as well as the spread of exaggerated rumour. So let us hope, even now, that the estimate of a quarter of million of deaths from one pestilence, recorded a century, or nearly a century ago, was a misapprehension.²

¹ "Géographie du Moyen Age." Brussels, 1852, p. 32.
² "Annual Register," 1773; "History of Europe," p. 29.

Having obtained all the requisite authority by telegraph from Constantinople, and by written orders from the Pasha of Baghdad, I made arrangements to start on the long journey to Scutari which lay before me. Mr. Superintendent Kersting, of the telegraph, was to be my companion for the whole way. Ahmad Efendi, an Egyptian engineer officer in the Pasha's employ, was to accompany me as far as Jazirah, or to the limit of the Baghdad jurisdiction. I had engaged for the occasion a Persian cook, a Baghdad Christian valet, and an Arab groom; had purchased three horses outright, and had hired mules as far as Mosul. I had invested in saddles, saddlebags, horsegear, provisions for man and beast, cooking pots, cooking and table utensils, candles, towels and every kind of necessary for the expedition; had held consultations and passed decisions on the nature and amount of baggage to be carried, and had fixed the day and hour of departure. On the 18th May, the vanguard of servants and encumbrances was to be got clear of the town gates for an early start in the morning; and I was to time my own movements so as to come up with the rest of the party in the evening of the 19th. Premising that the cook's name is Kurban Ali, and the valet's Shukūri, I will resume the journal:—

"*May* 19.—After breakfast this morning, leave cards, pay visits, return to the Residency and take leave of Colonel K. and other friends. The hot weather having fairly set in, the Baghdad people are just going in to their *sardābs*, or underground houses. We, who are turning to the plains, have at all events a prospect of cooler weather westward, and the excitement of travelling and change of scene will serve as antidote to

START FROM BAGHDAD.

the first few weeks of heat. Find Ahmad Efendi waiting for me, and after a few preliminaries we start together. The ride was all very well for a novelty, but my friend, though chatty and sociable, seemed little disposed to go out of a walk. This was wearying and unexpected. My object in starting after my companions had been to ride the first stage fast; and how to get through 24 miles at three miles and a half an hour I knew not. The sun was hot, the conversation monotonous, and night likely to set in before we reached our destination. Induced my friend to gallop a little now and then; but he evidently did not like it, and the horsemen who attended him were ill disposed to go out of their usual pace, whatever he did. Finally we separated. I overtook a stranger with horses; talked and rode on with him at a good pace for some distance; then came up with a telegraph official who took me in charge near Jadidah, the name of the first halting-place. For a long time, however, I could not trace the whereabouts of my party. My guide wished me to name a house on which to be quartered. Should it be the 'Batran's?' This question perplexed me; for who was he that I should so use him? Very tired, and night having set in, I at length reached a close, hot house, where our people had been bundled up, animals and all, in very tolerable proximity; and where fleas thrived largely. Dined roughly, and enjoyed some hock immensely. Country to-day flat and desert, bordering for the most part on the river.

"*May* 20.—From Jadidah to a place of the same name in Turkish, or Yenijeh; only 14 miles. The Arabic *jadid*, 'new,' is the Turkish *yeni*. There are three villages here similarly designated. Route through grain fields, with many traces of river overflow and recent rains. From Baghdad, for about 60 miles upwards, the Tigris is found to flow in a southerly direction, and nearly parallel to it is the Diāla; the distance between the two varying from 5, 10, to 30 miles. Again from the Diāla runs the Khālis, not marked upon the map. Across a country affected by these waters the telegraph line has to shape its course from Baghdad. This year a heavy overflow of the Tigris brought no less than sixty-five posts under water in the section of our attendant *chaush*, or sub-inspector, and thirty-five in that of a neighbour. These men appear hardworking and intelligent, and to do their best to repair the damage done. Our *khan* to-day is a dirty, though not ill-built room, with an opening through which I can see the horses picketed and cared for. Perfectly pestered with fleas, and something, whether gnat, fly, or mosquito, stings sharply through the stocking. Under the circumstances gladly take leave of pen, ink and paper, and close the journal.

"*May* 21.—Started at about 4.30 A.M., and follow the telegraph line for some distance towards Deli Abbas, the 'mad Abbas.' Halted at Dizhdeti on the post road, about 24 miles. It is a small village, so far as the habitable part is considered, but the ruins seem to have been extensive. Put up in Arab huts where we have a cool night and I get the first good sleep since departure. Old Q. dines with us and is evidently happy. His black costume, hanging coat and quasi-knickerbocker trousers; his nutcracker nose and chin, and thin visage; his gait and attitude, above all the sinister facial expression, give him the look of a second class Mephistopheles. These hair tents, or *buit-es-sha'ar* as they are called, are much to my liking. Dogs, sheep, cattle of all kinds, such companions are ever available to defeat all sense of loneliness.

"*May* 22.—Intended arrangements for the day obstructed by servants and circumstances, and instead of entering the Hamrin hills which lay before us, we accept the reception prepared for us at Ramlat, or the 'sand hills,' a cluster of Arab tents in the plain; after marching 10 miles.

"*May* 23.—Perhaps it is as well that our sober friend did not dine with us according to invitation yesterday. For his rigid notions of woman's proper sphere might not have approved or appreciated those laughing, curious faces of Arab girls looking over the partition between their part of the tent and ours; a *status* which might be precarious at home, but is little so in these parts. One had a joyous English countenance, not the only one I have seen of the type. Started about 5 A.M. to-day, an hour at least too late; and marched for an hour to the fort of the Hamrin. Took leave of our Arab host and family, presenting a China red silk handkerchief to the man for his sick child. That he or some of his company had one, I knew, because the poor thing cried bitterly and moaned long and painfully during the night. And on turning round to bid adieu to the good people, after mounting my horse, I saw a child in arms exhibited with the rosy present on its head. In saying *salam aleikum* to these poor Arabs, I mean more than an ordinary salutation. They gave me shelter when I needed it on my long journey; they cheered with merry, homely faces, when reminders of such things were pleasant. About 6.30 A.M. entered the hills. Day cloudy and windless, but not close; flies excessive. Hamrin range low and very rocky. Pass a small building called Aïn Tinat; a kind of miniature fort. Country for the most part a desert plain to the foot of the hills on either side, but near 'the black mound,' or Kāra Tēpeh (τάφος), are patches of refreshing cultivation. Six miles before this our stage, cross a tolerably good bridge over the Naring: brick, and having six arches some twenty feet high; above, roughly macadamized. Rode part of the way with a Baghdad Arab, travelling, as he explains, to collect money from certain villages. Put up at the *khan* at Kāra Tēpeh, but invited to dinner at the house of a wealthy Saiyid, whither K. and I proceed at 5.30 P.M.

"At these native banquets the number of the dishes is as many, I take it, as can be conveniently managed, so as to follow one another in rapid succession. The silence preserved during the meal is evidently a time-honoured custom of the country; pointing and signs are allowable, but the tongue has no occupation, except as a mute auxiliary to the organs of mastication. This silence in actual words is, however, most disagreeably broken at the end of the repast by the ceremony of rinsing out the mouth and washing the hands. Mine host at Kāra Tēpeh was, in this respect, positively horrible; and his after-dinner practices were such as almost to obliterate the pleasant appreciation of his hospitality. On rising to depart I thanked him for his kindness. 'Siz musāfir,'[1] was the curt and quiet reply,

---

[1] Turkish and Arabic. Literally, "traveller;" but commonly in Asiatic Turkey "a guest."

which, being fully interpreted, is simply this: 'It is the law of my religion that I should entertain travellers. You are one; consequently to that law you are indebted and not to me, in being made my guest.' I certainly had not accepted his invitation with the readiness which I might have exhibited; and even after dining with him was disposed to believe that he wanted me to serve a friend, relative, or dependant in the person of a chaush who was out of his chief's good looks. But later consideration renders clear to my mind that this little request was not the cause as much as the consequence of partaking of this man's hospitality. Returned to the dirty *khan*. Found Shukri the worse for liquor, and other disagreeables. March to-day 23 miles.

"*May* 24.—Early start. Rode through plains, and low, rocky hills. Kifri six hours, or 18 miles. Intermediate halt at the Chauan river, where the Efendi spread a small sheet and invited me to sit. The thoroughly Turkish-Asiatic town of Kifri looks picturesque in the distance, as descending from the low hills we first sight it. A mile of plain intervenes; one or two abrupt hillocks of pale colour are behind us; further back are giant mounds rather than hills, and behind them a long range of orthodox hills looking like a third line of the Hamrin. They tell me, however, that these ceased yesterday. Weather hot, and flies, as usual, abundant.

"*May* 25.—March to Baiat, or the huts of an Arab tribe so named; 5¾ hours, or about 19 miles. The sour milk (*shauwam*) is acceptable on arrival, and the fresh milk excellent. Locusts plentiful, damaging the few crops of the season. Vegetation scarce near the hills on the east; country stony and desert.

"*May* 26.—Zind, an encampment of Kurdish cultivators; 6¼ hours, or 20 miles. Reach telegraph line from Baiat through locust-eaten barley fields and cultivation. Follow the line over the *Chai* (river) of Tūz Khūrmati, a village which we leave to the eastward. One man tells me that it must contain 600 houses; another 200. I believe it to have possessed at one time the higher number, but to have suffered severely from plague. It may have revived in later years. Pass a second hut shallower river close by the same place, and the Kurn Chāi at some distance further. Alight at Dolankir, where there are huts and a running stream, and breakfast. Near Kurn Chāi is a hard, sandy plain, cracked in several places, and covered with short, dry, spare grass. Telegraph line carried along in excellent direction, but needs strengthening at the rivers with masonry pillars.

"*May* 27.—March to Tāza Khūrmati, the 'fresh date,' in opposition to Tūz Khūrmati, the 'salt' or probably 'dry date:' 7 hours, or 22 miles. Cross the Tāuk Kum Chāi, a broad river bed, of which the right bank is about 60 feet high. At two hours is Lasan, a small ruined village with shrine of Imam Hasan, frequented by pilgrims. Tāza Khūrmati reached through grain-fields and over an undulating country. May contain 200 houses. Put into roomy quarters, but full of flies.

"*May* 28.—March to Kerkūk: 3¼ hours, or 14 miles. Grain-fields and undulating country nearly the whole way. Pass Tissin to the left. Kerkuk looms out in the distance like the background of an oriental melodrama. It is just the sort of scene that would foreshadow the coming of a ferocious Pasha, Turks, Kurds, and so forth, men and women with scimitars, agitated choruses, and other conventional accompaniments. Proceeded to telegraph office, a tolerably extensive building, and evidently cared for. Met by the Mudir, or Superintendent, S. Bey, who received us politely in a cool, clear, airy upstairs room; and looked a friendly and comfortable Turk, without prejudices or bigotry sufficiently marked to stand in the way of his advancement at home or abroad. The face is decidedly handsome, and lights up continually with a good-humoured smile. Two assistant Mudirs joined our party. One of these was a young exquisite in a uniform composed of the telegraph dark cloth with pale blue facings, gold embroidery, and an ornament resembling a flash of forked lightning; red bagging trousers, and two pairs of shoes, into the inner of which passed his straps. His really delicate-looking hands were set off by an evidently pet turquoise on a pet finger. Had been in hopes we should have remained where we were, but our guide had provided for us otherwise. We were taken to a *konak* (house), a receptacle of fleas and flies, which overlooked a farmyard of considerable filth. However, Ali Chaosh had done his best, and as Ali Chaosh's father was the owner of our quarters, what was to be said? Restless night, as might have been expected.

"*May* 29.—Hait to-day. They say there are 2,500 houses in Kerkûk, or perhaps 10,000 inhabitants, including a tenth of the number in the citadel. My servant informs me there are two Chaldæan churches, or places of worship here. Talk with the Bey and others at telegraph office. Pasha clearly not popular. Among other stories told of him, one is to the effect that he puts hundreds of prisoners into the lower rooms of the telegraph building, thus converting it into a jail. This public mode of living is distressing. To-day, Sunday, nothing but visits, even among the flies and fleas of my own apartment. There is the Telegraph Mudir, a gallant Army-Major, and an assistant-superintendent. How many chibouks are got through I know not. Eventually we adjourn to a garden full of fruit and other good things, and feast on apricots and raki! One of my new acquaintances is a Frenchified Turk, and has acquired much in Paris, besides the language, which he mistakes for progress and civilization. One glass of raki in the morning, and four in the evening, this is his quantum; and he is sure it is necessary for his health. 'J'ai ma femme,' he says, 'ma petite fille de six mois, et mon nègre, voilà tout.' Young Turkey is represented by many such as this.

"*May* 30.—An embargo was laid on our mules yesterday. They were seized by order of the Pasha to be pressed into Government service, and, accompanied by two companies of infantry, ordered off to Sulimania, in Kurdistan. But we managed to get the mistake rectified. Marched this morning to Yurinja, 5 hours, or 16 miles; and passed a very hot day in a Kurdish tent afterwards. Country exhibits little cultivation, and that in the low ground generally undulating and stony, with more or less steep hills. Bash Chaosh says that Kurds used to make a mark of the porcelain insulators to fire at; but they now, as well as the Arabs, are beginning to be accustomed to the telegraph. At the fifth hour, wheat abundant, and many huts appear in sight.

"*May* 31.—March to Girdashina, a Kurdish village distant nearly an hour from the post road: 5¾ hours, or 19 miles. Pass through much fine cultivation, with occasional hilly and stony ground. In the third hour, Altun Kiupri, the Golden Bridge, a tolerably large village, with perhaps 200 houses, situated on the lesser Zāb. The inhabitants, however, call the river, at this particular point, by the name of the village. The bridge is a steep

ALTUN KIUPRI.

granite structure, and picturesque. Below it the waters pass with considerable force among detached rocks to the Tigris. When the traveller from Kerkūk first sights Altun Kiupri, the landscape presented is worthy the pencil of any artist. Some of the Kurdish women are handsome and attractive. Their rich, brown, gipsy complexions, and black or dark-blue dresses and turbans, have something of Egyptian character; but I should be inclined to award the palm of beauty to the Kurds.

"*June* 1.—March to Karamlik, a Kurdish village near the

line of telegraph, and distant about four miles from the large town of Arbeil, on the post road—6 hours, or 24 miles. Hilly and undulating country, with much cultivation. Nothing can well be more graceful and beautiful than the early morning dress of rural nature in these parts. The wheat-fields are variegated with many colours, but all are pale. The wild flowers do not contrast so much as blend with the standing crops of grain; pale pink, pale blue, pale yellow, millions of charming white flowers—all these are exquisite in company with the green and hay colour of the fields. Arbeil is undoubtedly the ancient Arbela of classical history. It is a town much resembling Kerkuk, from its position on a flat-topped hill. I am told that it contains 2,000 houses, an estimate which would comprise the lower as well as higher portion. Passed, to-day, Kush Tepeh and Gul Tepeh, procuring water from a Kurdish woman at a well, and *shonina* from a hut at the village of Timar beyond. The Efendi sent to Arbeil for ice, which we found a great luxury. Our chaosh of to-day was a Kurd named Kādari; he was attentive to our wants, and the tent allotted to us was pitched on a high, open, and eligible spot.

"*June* 2.—Karamlık to Zāb Su, 4½ hours, or 20 miles, but did not cross the river till the afternoon, putting up in a tent on the left bank for the earlier part of the day. Thermometer at midday, 107°.8. Average heat in the shade, 96°, as recorded for eight days at different periods between 7 in the morning and 12. Yesterday it was 102° as early as 8.30. Passed some magnificent wheat crops, and observed many wild grasses and flowers, suggestive of a *coiffure à la Cérès*, suitable to Perdita, or fair-haired beauties of the day. These were in the high ground before the descent to the Zāb. Ferry-boat most primitive; had to come back after the first ineffectual attempt to get over, the rudder rope breaking. The river comes down here with great force. Its deliciously cold waters are the melted snows of Kurd hills in the neighbourhood of Rovandiz. A second attempt to cross was more successful, but much time was taken up in the whole operation. The Efendi's horse was gallantly swam over by one of the men. It was quite exciting to watch the struggle across the rapid stream, which seemed to gain power on the right, or further bank.

"*June* 3.—After a night passed in a tent, over which the wind whistled and moaned, make an early start, and accomplish 19 miles. Country hilly, but showing much cultivation. Sunrise magnificent. Notwithstanding a clouded sky and appearance of rain to the north-east, day was inaugurated amid the Kurdistan hills with a grandeur defying the skill of the painter or poet to describe. The golden tints and edging, and bursting flood of light were worthy of the highest art; but what, after all, is this, when limited to man's pigmy powers of pourtrayal? Crossed the Khāzir Su, a smart, strong stream, whose waters, however, lacked the luxurious freshness of the Zāb. They state that the two join at about 9 miles below our crossing, and flow as one river into the Tigris at 18 miles lower still. This is quite a land of *tumuli* or *tepēs*, and some of them are covered to the very top with rich wheat. Hills less frequent from the Khāzir Su onwards. Put up at the village of Shah Kuli.

"*June* 4.—March to Mosul, right bank of the Tigris, leaving the mounds of Nineveh on the left bank, together with the village of Nabi Yunus; distance about 16 miles. On crossing the ferry, find a Kavās, who escorts us to the house of Mr. Rassam, the Vice-Consul. Hospitably received in his large, comfortable, oriental house, with its marble walls, *surdābs* and conveniences. Visit the Pasha and Kaim-makam commanding troops, also the telegraph office, which is a good roomy building, and the inmates of which are polite and attentive.

"*June* 5.—Halt at Mosul. After breakfast called on Chaldæan Patriarch, whom we found in company with the Chaldæan Metropolitan, a newly-made bishop, the Syrian bishop, and others. Sat down and conversed for some time in the Turkish fashion, or with chibouks. The scene was novel and interesting. The Chaldæan Patriarch is a handsome old man, with a benign countenance, but his manner in addressing us was to me not half so pleasing as that of his companions. Two of these spoke fair French; with the rest it was necessary to use Arabic or Turkish. It appears that these churches have communications with those of Malabar in India, and are a branch of the Romish Propaganda. Went into the church of the Miskinta (probably Arabic 'Miskinah'¹), who, the Syrian bishop explained to me, was supposed to be the poor widow of Saint Luke, xxi. 2; also believed, as I understood, to be a martyr. Her tomb is exhibited. The Syrian bishop took us to his church and cathedral, two edifices of recent construction, and by no means inelegant. They are built of marble, of which the cost is here comparatively trifling, much being procurable in the neighbourhood of the town. The interior of the cathedral has its two aisles and altars, and is well proportioned. The centre archway and altar-piece are remarkably attractive. We paid the bishop a short visit at his house, where he had a nice little civilized sitting-room and inner chamber, both fitted with book-cases furnished with books. I could not but notice with pleasure that among volumes of French, Italian, and Arabic, was an English Milton. We held a short conversation in Italian, and my mind reverted to Rome in 1848, at which time my new acquaintance was a student there; and I well remember attending a ceremony in that particular year at the Propaganda, in the presence of the late Cardinal Mezzofanti. Students were reciting in fifty-two different languages, and Syriac was probably one. The town of Mosul is dirty and irregular, but its Moorish doorways are agreeable, as are also, standing beside them, certain figures, with an English look of the fifteenth century. Some children have handsome faces. Long talk this evening with my host, whose intimate knowledge of the Semitic tongues enables him to impart much useful information to more ordinary Orientalists. He considers that Persian words may have crept into the Bible text and become misinterpreted from lack of punctuation; instancing that 'khamosh' may have been supposed a Hebrew word very similar in sound; though the meaning of one being 'silent,' and of the other 'harnessed,' the latter interpretation would be erroneously adopted. Speaking of the Muhammadan mosque at

---

¹ The actual word used in the latest Arabic version of the Testament in the verse noted, though not in verse 3, where, however, in English, "poor widow" is repeated.

Nabi Yunus, which we had visited yesterday before crossing the river, and of the subterraneous passages inspected there, Mr. R. was of opinion that the place must formerly have been a temple of fire worship, from the blackened appearance of the roof.

"*June* 6.—On going down to the breakfast-room this morning, found again the Syrian bishop. He was gentlemanly and agreeable as before, but his dress was particularly striking. I could not avoid a feeling that there was something studied and theatrical in its harmony: all was so neat and apparently so correct. Indeed, the violet garment, the black cowl with a gold cross admirably set off upon the dark ground above the forehead, and the well-dressed whiskers, beard and brows, all presented a picture not easily to be forgotten by a traveller recently from India. His brother came afterwards: a very different man, whose relationship destroyed much of the romance with which the first was invested. The Christians here are distinguishable by a dark turban or shawl of one colour tied round the head. Mrs. R. thinks there must be some 20,000. As the Roman Catholics call their followers Chaldæans, to separate them from the Nestorian Christians, so do they call Syrian Christians those whom they have gained over from the Jacobites. There are two kinds of wine at Mosul, white and red. The first is palatable, and has a smack of a German or Hungarian vintage. The second I do not care for.

"*June* 7.—In the middle of the Tigris at Mosul is a stone bridge, or the section of a stone bridge. On either side of it flows a rapid channel. The right bank, or that on which the town stands, is connected with this construction by a bridge of boats. They have lately been working at a new stone structure to complete the junction on the opposite, or Nineveh bank; but Ali Efendi, the Egyptian engineer employed on this duty, appears to have been unprovided with due materials, and the whole affair now consists of a set of incomplete arches unavailable for transit of passengers. Instead of keeping the main line of telegraph on the left bank, and running a wire across to Mosul for local purposes, the authorities have brought in all the wires, both from Baghdad and Constantinople, into the office at Mosul, and thus imperilled the whole communication, owing to the insecurity of the river crossing. This appears to me a grievous and unnecessary defect, and I understand that it has already been the cause of needless interruption to traffic by the wires. Start at 4.30 P.M., after an early dinner with Mr. and Mrs. R., to whom I am indebted for the hospitality so heartily tendered. March to Tel Keif, a Chaldæan village, 3¼ hours, or 10 miles. Slept at top of an old house, and passed a somewhat restless night, probably on account of the high wind and rain.

"*June* 8.—March to Fâyida, 6 hours, or 20 miles. Hilly and undulating country, fallow ploughed, and cultivated at intervals, very dry, and swarming with locusts and insect life. Ground at times stony and steep. Grain wants strength and substance. Took note of fallen or damaged poles and other faults on the telegraph line here evident. Put up in something very like a stable, where we were pestered by fleas and flies. Rain

"*June* 9.—March to Girk Osman, 7 hours, or 21 miles. Pass Gerishikurt, a Christian or 'Raya' village, situated in low ground at the foot of hills. Should be approached from the northward to be seen with advantage. Built near a running stream coming down from the green fields above, and brought artificially and, with unconscious beauty, into a miniature cascade, the Degirman, or mill, is charmingly romantic. In spite of the heat and length of the march, I could not but return to inspect the little scenic *bijou* in detail. From this place cross over hills with abundant pasture and ploughed fields, and grain in abundance. Pass several villages, and observe the Kurdistan ranges running from N.N.W. to S.E. Thunder-storm last night and rain to-day cool the temperature, and the change is delightful. Thermometer on arrival in Kurdish tents, 84°. The Kurdish ladies of Batil, a small village about half an hour before arrival, are fair for Asiatics, have an Italian look, and are undeniably handsome. The three perpendicular chin marks are characteristic, though hardly becoming.

"June 10.—Girk Osman to Karola: Kurd huts on the farther side of Khabūr river: 7 hours, or 22 miles: a long march, which gives us a good sunning. Country variable, from stony to pasture and cultivated ground. The post-road goes off through the hills on our right towards Zakhūr, while the telegraph line continues to run along their base, though not exactly parallel to them. Cross two difficult streams, the Mazra and Girkulderasi Su. Dismount and breakfast lightly, in a rustic bower of sticks and leaves, at the Kurdish village of Pāibuzan, the 'goat's foot,' on the further side of a gully. After passing Deirabun Tepeh and Deirabun, we descend into the valley of the Khabūr, and, following the telegraph posts through grassy, marshy, and ungenial lands, proceed up the bank for about three-quarters of an hour, when we reach the ferry. Do not admire the arrangements made here for the line. Fatiguing day for the horses, and the swim across the Khabūr was no poor item of the day's work for the tired brutes.

"June 11.—This morning the smart Kurdish lady in the hut, or rather her half of our hut, or tent, partitioned off by a mat about 3½ feet high, rose and yawned unreservedly, then buckled on her jewels to the neck, and from the neck to the headgear, according to the fashion of her country: while the dry old gentleman, whom I take to be her husband, looked less irritable than last evening, when the arrival of our escort disturbed his equanimity. I should have wished to photograph that face of the almost buxom wife with her dark disheveled hair; but my happiest remembrance of these Kurdish beauties is that of the fair plaited locks hanging down under the *fez*; and how much more elegant does that small red cap so look than when on the uncombed head of a Turkish official! March to Jazirah, 6½ hours, or 20 miles, a town on the right bank of the Tigris, over hilly and undulating country, occasionally rich in cultivation, and abounding in grasses and wild flowers of all kinds and colours. Rejoin the post-road long before the end of the day's journey. Cross the river on a *kelek*, or 'raft,' some kind passengers helping my people to swim the horses.

"June 12.—Jazirah, said to be the principal city of the

Chaldæans in the low country. Telegraph office here a barn, and an unsavoury one. The whole place is uninviting, hot, foul, and should be sickly. Went to inspect an ancient gate, but odour so offensive and dogs so unfriendly, that we did not achieve our purpose. Nor could I find time to go down to an old bridge which had attracted my attention on arrival, and which seemed to me a monument of a more classical age than that of the Baghdad Khalifs. The arch at the ferry looks, on the other hand, Moorish, and of the Muhammadan period. It has an Arabic inscription, which I did not decipher.

"*June* 13.—Glad to leave this town and rise to the heights overlooking the river. As I am following the telegraph posts, I leave the post-road to the south, and its principal stations, Dára and Nisibín. Move now in a westerly direction; and march to-day to Azukh, 6 hours, about 18 miles. This is apparently a Jacobite village, with some 150 houses. On our way pass through wheat-fields, a village called Hosel, with vines and mulberry trees, and a deep stony defile, to the Kurdish village of Deshtedar, where we refresh. The kind villagers cooked us a splendid omelette and brought it in a fryingpan, with other savoury ingredients of a travelling breakfast. In return gave two pretty little Kurdish children with red caps ornamented with silver-looking ornaments, a couple of half kirans. On the way from Deshtedar to the stage for the day, observe a cool spring under a rock. Rain is very naturally treasured in this rather dry and stony country, and there are both open and covered tanks for the reception of water. Occupy the house of Musa Chaosh at Azukh, and submit patiently to a succession of visits. The Matran (Metropolitan) I wished to see, but I could have dispensed with the old Turk of the scrubby beard, and perhaps, too, with the Chaldæan of Diarbekir, who spurt out their calls in an unconscionable degree. Still, both were characters, in their respective ways. Sleep in the open air to-night, and escape the torment of fleas ever ready to attend on the stranger here.

"*June* 14.—Azukh to Bar-saberin, 5½ hours, or 16 miles. A very stony, hilly march, though not so much so as yesterday.

My old horse down once on his knees. During the first hour pass the ruined Kurdish village of Geziris. The plateau on which we travel has a rich soil, but it is poorly cultivated. Grasses are abundant. In the third hour, reach the defile of Midda, and the village bearing that name, said to contain 100 houses. Make an incipient breakfast here much against my will. But the comical old Turk of yesterday, who is accompanying me to Mardin, says: 'Baghdad' (pointing to his stomach) 'is in ruins: we must rebuild her;' and such reasoning compels me to give in. Two huge bowls of prepared rice, milk, and *shanino*, are brought in for our acceptance. The old Turk and Musa Chaosh do more justice to the repast than K. or I, but this is not surprising. These Christian, or 'Raya' villages are curious. Huge irregular stones, piled one upon the other and fitting with great nicety, the larger crevices being filled with small stones; such are the walls. The roofs are of branches, sticks, beams, and leaves, on which is thrown a coating of mud; and while they enclose an apartment beneath, the same become floors to an outer sleeping site, whereof the canopy is heaven. The streets are most irregular, and the general plan of the town looks confused; but in such a wilderness of stones what order can be expected? It is as though they had been showered down in every direction. Approaches to the village are also lined with these, in walks rising on either side. Some of the women and children are remarkable: the first as interesting in appearance, the second for great beauty and attractiveness. On the whole, I should hope the places are thriving. Great visiting on arrival at Bar-saberin, the tower of which and adjoining house are almost church-like in the distance. Had to take to task my *zabtia*, or soldier, for his behaviour to the people at Midda, and told him he should come to me for his own as for his horse's food while in my service. A Turkish soldier's comprehension is not equal to this kind of teaching; and he would have to unlearn the simplest lessons of his childhood to grasp the meaning."

It is not that the Turkish articles of war have omitted provision for cases of this nature. They are, on the contrary, singularly comprehensive and minute for a people of Oriental tastes and habits. But many of those forming the complete code in 1855-6 have been, doubtless, mere formal entries disregarded in ordinary practice. The 35th applies to the present instance:

"Whoever, attached to the army, shall in any place snatch (steal) anything from the inhabitants (Ex.: in the street, or other place, he may snatch the *fez* from a child's head, or any person's clothes or money); if an officer, after reduction to the ranks, he shall suffer three years' mean employment in the dockyard; or if a private, he shall be put in irons and suffer three years' mean employment."

ARTILLERY SOLDIER, 1855-6.   INFANTRY SENTRY, 1855-6.

I take advantage of this brief digression to say a few passing words on the Turkish soldier, whom I have known for many years, and who, at the time of writing the diary under extract, was undergoing a change of much importance. The attention given to the outward appearance of the "nefer," or "full private," as he is more pleasantly than lucidly described in England, has been remarkably evinced since the Crimean War by the marvellous transformation of an ungainly figure, whether linesman, gunner or trooper, into a smart and well-equipped combatant. The

TURKISH INFANTRY, 1862.

"Zouave," traceable to an excellent hint derived from the French alliance, gives perhaps the best illustration of this result that could be found. Without, in this place, disputing or endorsing the assertions of those champions of Turkish progress who commend generally her practical civilization, whether exhibited in financial furbishing or in army re-organization, we may confidently affirm that if the same amount of labour has been bestowed on the officering, the regular paying, and moral disciplining of the soldier as on his clothing and setting up, the Sultan's army need not fear comparison with the better forces of Europe. This change, visible to me in the garrisons below Baghdad, naturally became more apparent at Constantinople; and in subsequent visits to the latter city it has become more remarkable still.

"*June* 15.—March to Middiat, 9 hours, or 21 miles; over very difficult country. There are stony hills covered with jungle, or dwarf scattered forests—and intersected with deep dales and gullies. Walked much on foot in order to examine more closely the telegraph line; and glad to rest and await my companions at Chaosh Ali's leaf house, and drink a cup of his *shanina*. Joined by K. there, and breakfasted on bread and eggs and more *shanina*. Hence we rode over to the monastery, called by the Kurds *Deir el Umr*, and by Christians *Mar Jibrail*, near the village of Kife Bey. Alighted, and went into the old church, said to have been built 1,500 years ago in the days of Constantine. It is a vaulted building, about 50 feet long by 26 broad, opening out in the centre to a chapel and altar. In the church is a long stone table, the single slab being about 11 feet by 5, on which rests a prized volume of the Syrian Scriptures. The slab shows a cleft across; which is explained to have been the act of Taimur Lang, or Tamerlane, who robbed the jewels of the altar. A ruffianly Kurd, one Yezdan Shah, is said to have done some damage here also but a few years ago. The mosaic on the roof of the chapel and the tesselated pavement are worth inspection. At one time the monastery is said to have contained 1,000 monks, while now there are only three. Altogether the visit was highly interesting. At Middiat I was lodged in a Jacobite house under the care of two old ladies. The Turks made a show of sending soldiers for my protection; as if a Jacobite town was not fully as safe as a Muslim one.

Middiat is moreover, so they say, the centre of 300 towns, and head-quarters of the Mudir, or District Governor.

"*June* 16.—March to Kharbat Tāo, called also Kharbat Jinglez and Kiir Ninek, an Arab and Kurd village: 6 hours, or 18 miles. An easy stage compared to that of yesterday and the day before, and the path has almost the appearance of a made road. The country, however, here and for miles on every side, may be described as hilly, stony, and wooded. It is continued ascent and descent, except where the turn of the valley, gully, dale, or defile, as it may chance to be called, leads in the direction of the traveller's path, at which time he commonly moves along low beds of cultivation, separated one from the other by stone walls of two or three feet in height. Nothing can be richer than the soil; and the water, wherever obtained, is excellent.

"*June* 17.—Mardin, 7 hours or 21 miles. Pass Kharbat-ul-Kelej, Maserte, Kharia Belik, and before the fifth hour, reach Reshmil, a village in a deep valley, with pleasant gardens. We are led into one of these by our chaosh, who gives us a capital breakfast of rice, sweet omelette, *yoghurt* (clotted cream), and bread. The gardener's children and the Kahia, or head man of the village, add mulberries, cherries, and apples, to all of which we do justice. The rich soil producing these gardens, with walnut, plum, and many more fruit trees, besides innumerable flowers, is at the foot of a basin amid hard, stony hills, offshoots of Mons Masius. From Reshmil the ascents are steeper, and valleys deeper and more marked; and on one of the most remarkable of the hilly series is Mardin. The town is picturesquely situated on the slope of a conical hill, the apex of which is crowned by a remarkable and very ancient fort, having the appearance of natural rock; however supplemented in its interior appliances and resources by artificial construction. There is a very singular rock on an adjoining eminence invested with a similar defensive character. Entered the gate of the town, and rode up a dirty, steep, stony street to the telegraph office. This was about 1 P.M.; and the sun was intensely hot and air oppressive. A cool breeze was felt as we opened out the southern aspect of the hill, and with it the magnificent view of the plains of Mesopotamia. The houses of the town are solid and comparatively good; but there is filth and misarrangement everywhere. The building appropriated to the telegraph is small; the instruments appeared in good order; the Mudir, or Superintendent, received us in his shirt sleeves, a costume which may have denoted a certain recklessness and independence of authority as much as a sense of climatic lassitude. This worthy was about to be removed to Khanikin, on the Turco-Persian frontier towards Baghdad, and evidently did not approve of the transfer. Doubtless it had a penal bearing; though, *primâ facie*, I could not admire the official wisdom which had provided a substitute at Mardin. The Efendi who had come to relieve the Bey would assuredly have found a place in Thackeray's 'Book,' had it treated of Turks as of Britons in the monosyllabic class.

"*June* 18.—Halt here to-day. Called on Mr. W., an American Missionary, who has been here for five years. He is full of information, and his amiable lady and attractive children enable him to carry on his labour of love and usefulness by a cheering, homely presence in the midst of exile. He reckons the population of Mardin to be about 22,000, of whom one-half are Christians, and two-thirds of these again Roman Catholics; we may roughly suppose 7,000 Romish to 3,500 non-Romish followers of the Chaldæan and Syrian churches. The sectarian designations of Nestorian and Jacobite, applied to distinguish dissenting branches, and insisted on by the Roman Catholics, are said to be giving way before a re-assumption of the original popular names. K. and I dine with Mr. W. and family, going up afterwards to the fort and citadel. I should revise my description of yesterday by saying that the Mardin hill is pyramidical in shape, with a flattened top, surmounted by natural rock artificially fitted into a fort, dating, it may be, from the time of the early khalifs, but I think *before*. The eastern, south-eastern, and southern sides are those of the town, whose houses rise to nearly the whole height of the rock, or some 400 feet. A hill passed on our route to this one, and which is

THE WOMAN'S FORT.

crowned by as remarkable a summit, is called Kāf Sanūnī. Another, quite close, and more like that of Mardin, is called Kalat-ul-Marra, or 'Woman's Fort.' Both have legends, but I can only recall the second, which is as follows. It was defended by a woman against Tamerlane for a long period, and until the garrison were on the point of starvation. Suddenly, a favourite bitch had a litter, and the idea was conceived of sending the milk in a basin as a present to the fierce besieger. Tamerlane, on seeing this, thinking the garrison well supplied with provisions, abandoned the siege as hopeless! Mr. W. thinks there are no Roman remains, certainly no Roman walls, in Mardin, though it is asserted by some that the walls of Meride, its ancient name, are in good preservation. The Yuzbāshi, or captain, of the fort guard, received us with much civility, and gave us the customary coffee at the gate. After enjoying a magnificent view, and looking at the surrounding lions, we returned to our quarters at the telegraph office, taking leave of our excellent host and guide, and his intelligent son."

PERSIAN SERVANT : TABRIZI.

CHAPTER VIII.

BAGHDAD TO CONSTANTINOPLE.—THE ROUTE CONTINUED THROUGH DIARBEKIR, SIVAS, ANGORA, AND BY STEAMER FROM ISMID.

As an embellishment to the story of Tamerlane and the 'Woman's Fort,' I was further informed that a fig-tree which the conqueror planted on commencing the siege had actually come to perfection before the said siege was raised. Here is another strange local tradition. A Pasha of Jazirah, in the good old time, or before chronologies were tested, sent for a celebrated architect to build him a bridge such as the world had never seen before. The mandate was obeyed: a magnificent unique structure was completed, and the promised sum duly paid. Everyone was struck with admiration at the performance; but one doubt was alive in and troubled the Pasha's breast, vitiating his satisfaction with alloy. He feared that the architect might build a second and a similar bridge for some other employer. He wished to be possessor of the choicest specimen of work by a genius who, in this final instance, had eclipsed himself. Accordingly he made up his mind to destroy him. But his plans were frustrated; and the intended victim forestalled his intention in a way little anticipated.

Coming to the Pasha, he informed him that the bridge, as now constructed, would not stand the assault of time, but that if he gave him a certain number of skins filled with vinegar and certain specified liquids, he would so secure the cement, that the work would never decay or fall to pieces. The Pasha complied; the experiment was made; the cement, instead of becoming stronger, melted; the bridge disappeared, and with it the architect, who escaped to lands far away.

"*June* 19.—March to Shaikhāna, 5 short hours, or 15 miles. For the first half, over difficult, hilly, and stony ground, to a kind of outpost in the hills at Amr Agha Powār, and over a tolerable road for the remainder of the way. Shaikhāna is a dreary spot in respect of house and village, but pleasant in its trees. An old woman, children, a *chaosh*, and a *zabchi* (soldier or policeman), give us a surfeit of their society, and no secret is made of the wish to draw the stranger's money. Amuse myself with losing piastres to children by making them guess the hand which contains them; but own to disappointment at being *asked* for a present in return for mulberries and milk. It is so much more pleasant, in the case of a supposed gift, to make a voluntary than a forced return. Sleep in the open air without search for better accommodation.

"*June* 20.—Ak Punghar, the 'White Fountain,' passing Abu Giaour and Khanik Ashāda, 9 hours, or 27 miles: a long march. Nature of the country, low hills covered with pasturage; track stony, but not difficult. Cross the Gok Su, a narrow bed of torrent. Our stage is rather a wretched place, out in the open, with no trees. Met the Turco-Hungarian Commandant of artillery from Baghdad, on his way to Constantinople. He dined with us, and my companion K. being a Hanoverian, the two enjoyed a German conversation with a kind of national gusto.

"*June* 21.—Diarbekir, 6 hours, or 18 miles. Country covered with grass and undulating; very fine, rich, brown soil, but stony. On our way into the town passed an old bridge across the Tigris, which is here comparatively small and shows very muddy waters. Under the arches of this bridge is a lower road in which the artillery Pasha's ladies placed themselves while we proceeded along the bank above. Passed the English Consul's country residence, but Mr. T. is now absent. Met and accosted two individuals on horseback with a strong resemblance to Frenchmen, and found that one was the French Consul. He informed me, moreover, that he was quite ready to transact any little business we might require in the absence of his British colleague, as indeed he had promised the latter to do. Rode with them through part of the town and took leave. Put up at the telegraph office, situated at the further end of Diarbekir from that at which we entered, and received with great cordiality and attention by the Mudir's Efendi. In the afternoon, called on the Pasha, a hearty, military-looking man, who talked pleasantly and was most polite. His band played like that of the Pasha of Mosul on a similar occasion, but the music was queer and national. M. Pasha is a Mushir, or full general officer, and has come from command of the army in Roumelia to take up joint civil and military rule in Kurdistan, of which Diarbekir is the head quarters. Bazar good. Astounded at the large blocks of ice exhibited for sale at a mere trifle.

June 24.—Halt. Have to receive many visits. Among others, a native of India was brought in and introduced by the Telegraph Bey as Haji Baba, an astrologer. I do not like his looks. He may be a refugee, a mutineer—I know not what. His face is that of a Lascar, or little better, but he has a strange smattering of knowledge. With a dash of the Fakir, there is something also in him of the ordinary Munshi, or teacher of Hindustani. The man has long, oiled, curved hair, combed down behind the ears; a dark and unmistakeably Indian complexion; a manner such as I have often seen among Indians desirous to dazzle by display of general knowledge. He took occasion to show off his handwriting, and to talk to me of officers whose names are well known in Western India. I asked myself, 'Who is this man, who appeared at Diarbekir from Mosul some three months ago; whence his fine clothes; and how long and on what errand is it that he has left his country?' His own story is that he lived in the Bendi Bazar at Bombay; that he quitted India about fifteen or sixteen years ago, before the annexation of the Punjab; that he is always travelling; and that he has visited Bukhara, Astrakhan, and many out-of-the-way places. He talks of Colonel Stoddart, but cannot know much, save by hearsay, of his personal history. His age may be thirty-five; but it is hard to say exactly. He practises as an astrologer, but takes no money, appearing to be independent both in respect of money and effects. He had seen and conversed with Mr. T. before his departure from Diarbekir. His Arabic is poor, but good *for an Indian*; his Persian is Indian and fluent: Hindustani is, of course, his native tongue. Visit also from the Pasha's Italian doctor, R., to whom I was glad to be able to offer a glass of English bottled beer, for he so thoroughly appreciated it. K. and I, under strong pressure, went to dine with this medico in the evening. The invitation was meant kindly, but gladly would I have escaped it. In the first place, we the guests found ourselves seated on the ground before a small table of olives and cherries, cheese and cucumbers, and such like. With these and conversation, cigarettes, and potations of peppermint and water, time passed till dark, and I was contemplating a means of escape. However, that which had transpired was a mere overture or prelude; and dinner, substantial dinner, followed in earnest. I cannot describe it, but it seemed interminable. The *cuisine* was the Pasha's, and the Pasha's secretary was with us to taste it. I believe the Pasha himself to have been the instigator of the whole scheme. We all ate out of the same dish, but were favoured with separate spoons. Dinner over, there was more to be done. I was to witness an entertainment such as the *beau monde* of Diarbekir was pleased to patronize. *Proh pudor*, it was not edifying or entertaining. They called in a blind piper, a half-starved, half-clothed boy with a tambourine, and a creature dressed as a woman, who danced to the music in the style of an Indian nautch. The dancer was clad in a short jacket, with Albanian petticoat; and whirled round and round to a slow tune, gesturing and contorting the limbs and body in the coarsest and most barbarous manner. Glad were we to get back to our lodging and prepare for a start in the morning.

"*June* 23.—I am told there are 20,000[1] inhabitants in the town of Diarbekir, of whom half are Christian, and these chiefly Armenian. There are about 600 Protestants who attend the American Mission chapel in the German Consulate. The city is well situated on the left bank of the Tigris, and, independently of its local advantages and handsome structures, is admirably adapted by geographical position to become a leading commercial capital of Asiatic Turkey. If the loss of its prosperity be attributable to faulty government and general insecurity, there is no reason why ancient glories should not revive with correction of such abuses; and progress in this respect certainly does mark the efforts made by modern Ottoman administrators. March to Dimika, encamping near Kurdish huts outside of village: 7 hours, or 20 miles. Diarbekir being a town of considerable size, with gates and walls, it takes time to get clear of it; and five o'clock is an early hour to stir up the inhabitants with the tramp of travellers. Road stony till we reach the open country, when we exchange the pavement for a fair track over green fields. Work begun on a high road projected hence to Samsun on the Black Sea—a good and civilized idea. Each Pasha is responsible for the share of his own Pashalic. The tents pitched near the scene of operations looked like business, but the labourers were few and seemed to want a system. Green fields and cultivation for four hours, up to a narrow stream called the 'Devagechi.' Passing Gath Tepeh, a small hill with ruined village, and leaving Bektash to the left, we reach our day's stage. Servant laid up with fever.

"*June* 24.—Arganeh, 4 hours, or about 15 miles. Road good,

---

[1] Mr. Southgate, in his instructive volumes of travels, does not give so large a number. His data show 2,700 families, of whom rather more than half are Muhammadan. Among the Christians, Armenians have the preponderance; but he makes no specification of Protestants. He includes some 50 Jewish families also at Diarbekir. This was, however, thirty-six years ago, since which period many changes may have occurred. Mr. Consul Taylor, in 1865, gives a total of 33,981 houses to the "sanjāk" or district of Diarbekir, of which 23,497 are Muslim and 8,740 Christian.

for the most part over pasture and cultivation. Cross one ridge of the mountains which threaten obstruction, but a low and unimportant one. It leads to a second valley nearly surrounded by hill and mountain, Argāneh forming a conspicuous object in front. Kurds here friendly and hospitable, yet not so interesting as those met with near Mosul. In the afternoon K. and I sally forth to reach the monastery up the hill. The ascent is steep, but the toil is repaid. As we rise we get a grand view of the town immediately below us, and its 700 houses, looking like part of the rock on which they are built. Above us towers the Mariam Ana in romantic beauty. K. somewhat exhausted, so I enter the building alone. Ushered in to the 'Papās,' but fearing intrusion upon him, plan an early departure. All, however, goes smoothly, and after visiting the chapel and one or two other places, I am again invited into the presence of the Superior, and this time escorted into his private room. What will I take, coffee or rāki? and a case is opened containing certain choice bottles of certain choice *liqueurs*. I decline the spirit, on the plea of abjuring such practices when the sun is high: whereupon the Papās, with an expression of approval, orders a 'finjān' of most excellent coffee, so good that another soon follows, my host remarking on the smallness of the vessel. It should be noted that, before the coffee, a mysterious box is brought to me, in which a spoon, placed in proximity to a kind of preserve, clearly indicates that I am to taste a mixture not unlike a compound of dates. Having taken leave of the Papās, the next in rank carries me off to *his* apartment, and will not let me go till he also has feasted me. The fare provided is a roll, not unlike our own in daily use, but soft to the touch, and quite black inside; and butter or cream, and cheese, with, perhaps, one or more accessories. This Armenian monastery of Mariam Ana occupies a frontage of about 100 yards, looking south-west, one end turning to the south. I counted ten windows in the upper row of the long central building, and nine in the lower. The difference might have been imaginary, and caused by the position taken up for inspection.

It is situated at the summit of the Argāneh hill, which may be 700 feet above the level of the village below. The chapel attached to it is said to be very old, founded by St. Thaddeus the Apostle in A.D. 47. Old Armenian copy of the New Testament here preserved is a valuable relic. Below the monastery, at a point of the rock, is a curious ruin, an arch and a gate, which is a Musalman place of pilgrimage, called Zul Kifli. Another Musalman *ziarat* is at the Ali Daghi, on a hill close by. There is a Mudir in Argāneh. One half the town is said to be Christian, chiefly, I believe, Armenian Catholic. We put up in a garden not far from the *khan*, and well away from the town.

"*June* 25.—Topalusāk, 6½ hours, or 19 miles, through the mountainous region of the Barman. Many ascents and descents over hills clothed with verdure, with occasional stony and difficult bits. They have established here six posts at intervals of one short hour each, two chaoshes in every hut, to keep up a special service of foot inspectors of the line of telegraph. For the hard work of winter, especially, the relief must be acceptable.

"*June* 26.—Kizin, an easy march of 4½ hours, or 14 miles, full of interest. In one hour sight Guljak, the 'Little Lake,' a charming sheet of water among the hills. Its length is, from east and by north to west and by south, about twelve miles in the longest part; its breadth is at most four miles. On its southern side and at the widest part is Kartun, a village containing about twenty Kurd houses; and on the same side Guljak, a Hāva village, with a boat and about fifty houses. Here was once a monastery, which was cut off by the waters and isolated. There is said to be a cluster of some ten houses on the north, and a village about six miles to the west; Kizin, our halting-place, is about 1¼ miles to the east. Except a small open space on the Kizin side, the lake is nearly shut in by hills coming down to its waters. These hills, which become green in appearance on near approach, look sufficiently barren in the distance to make the blue waters of Guljak a charming contrast. On the Kizin side I observed two fishermen sleepily waiting to catch their prey. A miniature channel, some two or three yards long, is scooped out on the sandy beach, at the end of which is placed an open basket resting on its side, and inviting fish to enter; about half of it may be in the water. When the fish enter, the neck of the channel is closed with a stone or two, and they are prevented from returning backward. Indeed, a big fish which might easily enough be drawn into the channel, would have difficulty in turning and getting out under almost any circumstances, and even if the channel were not blocked up at the neck at all.

"Before coming up to the Little Lake, we breakfasted at the romantically situated village of Malatu, which strikes pleasantly the eye of the traveller on first nearing the foot of the mountain he has traversed on journeying from the Diarbekir side. It overhangs a dell with a pretty clump of trees and rivulet in the foreground,—a combination often seen in these localities. On completing our descent we sight, and encamp under a second portion, as it were, of the village; not quite so wild in appearance as the first, but of the same brownish-red hue, and equally like the soil from which it rises. Some of its walls are of one solid coating; others present the usual division into sun-dried bricks. Halt, under 'erik,' or plum-trees, on a gentle slope just above the valley, and enjoy a quiet rest to the music of the never-tiring rill beneath us. Met party with caravan, conveying lead to Diarbekir; probably from Tokat, whither copper is taken for moulding from the Argäneh mines. Pass the night amid the trees.

"*June* 27.—Kharput; 7 hours, or 21 miles, on a moderate computation. During the first four hours, cross the 'Deva Boiun' mountain, nearly 5,000 feet above the Black Sea level. Sight on the march a snowy range to the far north, and a grand plain between, on the further side of which other high points intervene. The view is magnificent, and an idea of the extent of low country may be formed from the fact that the Murad Chai, one of the largest rivers of Asia Minor, a section indeed of the Euphrates itself, appears like a petty canal in the midst of the plain through which it runs. Breakfast at an

Armenian village in the plain, with gardens, and apparently flourishing. Its home-made wine was very respectable. The village of Tesh, through which we ride a few minutes before reaching Mazra (the cantonment of Kharput on the hill), is a large place, with a *soupçon* of European arrangement; but it is dirty. Mazra has a British-Indian look about it in the distance, and has a Pasha's house, *koshlok* or barracks, and a telegraph office. We put up in the latter.

"*June* 28.—Halt. Quite a luxury to find oneself in a large room, even without tables or chairs; but the climate here is not so fine and fresh as I had been led to expect. Went up the hill to call on the American Missionaries. Accosted by one of them whom we passed in the road; he pressed us to come to tea and spend the evening; accepted for to-morrow. On calling to-day, saw no less than five ladies, two unmarried. Visited the Kharput chapel and Bedestan. In the way of articles for purchase there is not much beyond the common oriental bazar display. Some children's faces here, as at Diarbekir and at Mosul, are to me most winning: brown, ruddy, with long, thickly-grown fair hair, like peasant children of two and a half centuries ago in England, or some limmerings of Murillo and Reynolds. There is a *Consulat de France* at Kharput.

"*June* 29.—Further halt. Some derive Kharput, or Harput, from the Armenian words for stone and castle: but Mr. Consul Taylor refers to a definition by a literary Defterdar, from the Persian *khar*, a donkey, and *bût* an idol. The same authority adds that this allusion to Pagan worship has caused the Porte to change the name altogether to 'Mamuriat-ul-Azizah.' The height of the town is estimated by Mr. Brant and Lieutenant Glasscott, R.N. at 4,832 feet, and Mazra to be 3,618 feet above the level of the Black Sea.

"Our fat, good-natured friend, the Mudir of the telegraph station, dined with us last night; an Indian bullock-trunk serving for a table. He had sherry, beer, and sparkling hock, and seemed to relish the mixture. Guns firing to-day, and great sensation caused by the arrival of the Persian Ambassador on his way to Constantinople.

"Went again to the American Missionaries. Messrs. B., W., and A., with their wives and children, and Messrs. W. and R., occupy two very good houses in the highest and most airy quarter of Kharput. Their church is a roomy, square building, with an upper storey containing the class-rooms of a collegiate institution, besides six bedrooms to accommodate eighteen boarders. One room, called Mr. Robinson's, was built at the sole cost of a gentleman of that name, who remitted the money from England. He seems to have rendered great assistance to the Mission generally, who otherwise acknowledge considerable English and local (or Constantinople) support. Their envoy at the Porte is not, they say, quite in the same position to influence the Sultan on their behalf as the British Ambassador; and it is, therefore, to the representative of her Majesty that they look for much. Lord S. was a firm friend to them. Of Sir H. B. they say little; more of Mr. E., to whom they are attached from acts evincing personal interest. The American Mission has been here for seven years. I hear that one of the Pashas is so attached to Mr. B., a Turkish scholar and superior man in every way, that he takes him gently by the beard and kisses his forehead! Their account of the modern Turks is very cheering. How different from the bigoted Muslim in other places! Can this be in any sense a fruit of our Anglo-Turkish policy?

"*June* 30.— Kharput still. Dine with Mr. and Mrs. B. Visit the girls' school and collegiate institution. Young Armenian women are interesting, and have very handsome dark eyes, but want elegance of contour. The head is the most attractive part of the picture, one tied with a jaunty kerchief, one encased in an ornamented *fez*; but this comely head is put upon an awkward body, either very square or broad-shouldered, or with very slouching gait. Some faces remind me of Italian peasantry, some of English village life: all have a lower-class aspect. Miss W. examines in Armenian: the subject is 'Conscience.' The behaviour of the girls is superior; the order and attention remarkable. Among them are a few married women, wives of the elder students. The singing of the Armenian version of 'There is a happy land' was really good, and struck sensibly home. The Armenian collegiate youths are a heavy, unyouthful-looking set, with few exceptions. Can say little of their capabilities; for the questions put in geography and arithmetic were of a more than commonly primitive nature.

"*July* 1.—Difficulty about mules, but manage to leave Kharput. March in the afternoon to Khankui, 5¼ hours, or 10 miles. Plain and cultivated country in a broad valley between hills. The women in these parts wear a long gown with opening below the hip on either side, an under short petticoat reaching to the knee, and trousers; head tied up, and sometimes the mouth covered with a kerchief. There is a kind of pinafore also worn up to the neck; slippers are on the feet, the hair is plaited, and a cloth is folded round the waist. Khankui is Turkish. We are snugly enough put up at the top of a house, and get our quiet dinner at nightfall. Have again to take to task the soldier sent with me, for extortion on the villagers under cloak of my service. The Bash Chaosh, or inspector of telegraph, who accompanies me, is soldierly-looking and handsome, but empty-pated and conceited; and has more regard for his person and pocket than his duty. An old man named Fodiche, who came with us from Diardekir, is a model Bash Chaosh, and has spoiled me for all others.

"*July* 2.—Iz Oghlu, 7½ hours, or 25 miles. After more than five hours passing through village, valley and ravine, we descend into the valley of the Upper Euphrates, close by the caravanserai of the Sultan Murad. This resting-house is very solidly built, and the arches in what appears to have been a stable, are worthy of special note. The mosque has a yellowish stone frontage, which may have been later constructed than the dark stone of the inner building, but I doubt it. The rooms want air and ventilation; and though they may be cool caverns in the intense heat, in winter they should be suffocating with fires such as Asiatics love to kindle. The Euphrates is here at times very narrow; but variable in breadth, and tortuous. Banks in some places shelving, in others abrupt and crumbling. Observed an arrow-headed inscription on a stone within the frame of a rock. The stone is about five feet long by five feet broad, and faces S.S.E. to the river. There are about forty divisions of lines. Iz Oghlu is a remarkably ugly village; and its name presents a suggestive and appropriate combination for English ears.

"*July 3.*—I might have almost said that Iz Oghlu was *the* ugliest village I had ever seen, but that there was one immediately opposite on the right bank of the Euphrates which was uglier still. 'What is the name of that?' said I. 'Iz Oghlu,' was the reply. Yes, and there appear to be one or two more villages which enjoy the same denomination.

"I cannot, however, leave this place without reverting to those who extended to the stranger travellers there the right hand of fellowship. We were put into a house at Iz Oghlu, occupied by a Kurdish family. The owner was a young married man, seemingly well enough to do in the world, with flocks and herds and so forth, and a pretty, interesting young wife. His look was simple and honest, with a slight alloy, perhaps, of self-esteem; he had a countenance which, if fairer, might have been German, rendered so more especially by a reddish-brown moustache. The only, and I presume first child of this young couple, was an immense pet. It was at one time carried about by an elderly lady, whom I take to be papa's mamma, but who, *I am sure*, was baby's grandmamma; at another time, placed in a little cradle outside the door of the inner room. The little thing was not a bad kind of baby of a few months old, would open its bright little eyes if spoken to, and laugh; would cry as all babies do, when something happened to make it sufficiently sad for tears. In an auspicious moment, I went up to grandmamma with this loved plaything in her arms—the doll of her second childhood—and gave her the last of the rosy silk kerchiefs to which I have before alluded, and a supply of which I should recommend to all travellers in these parts. Dear old soul, how pleased and proud she was at this. Very soon was it taken in and shown to mamma; very soon was it taken in and shown to papa; very soon had the neighbours and kinsfolk admired the fortunate gift. The next move was to make a turban of it for baby's head; the next to bring baby so attired outside for exhibition. I afterwards saw the child sleeping with the handkerchief round its little head; indeed, I do not think I saw that child again in any shape, without that handkerchief. How pleasant and grateful, that a gift, however small, should be appreciated! How different from the *pour-boire* extracted from one by some *commissionnaire*, *garçon*, or *valet de place* in addition to liberal payment for service! I hope my young Kurd had none of that feeling when he looked, as I thought, coldly on me at parting. Perhaps I should not have told *my servant* to give him his 'bakhshish.'

"March to Burma, 5½ hours, or 17 miles, crossing the noble river of old in about two hours, at the Hardargemi Su Ferry. The country struck me as comparatively barren about this part, and wearing a sad and dreary look in spite of bold scenery. Observe a Rhine-like mountain, with something of a tower or castle on the summit.

"*July* 4.—Hasan Badrik, a Kizilbash village, 5½ hours, or 16 miles; reckoned 24 hours, or 72 miles from Kharput. To judge from the opinions of my Turkish attendant, the Bash Chaosh, these Kizilbash are considered a bad lot, and an orthodox Muslim will not eat with them. They also call them 'Alawis.' But I do not trust my Bash Chaosh, or his opinions. His manner in the road, his perpetual umbrella, his atrocious politeness, all annoy me. Why was not this fine animal made an Imperial trooper, to forage and swagger at his pleasure, instead of a telegraph official? and yet the work upsets his weak nerves, as it is, and tires him, and he wants to become an indoor manipulator instead of an outdoor inspector! Crossed the Sultan Su, a section of the Tokma Su, over which is a bridge of twenty-two arches, an old *khan*, and a burial-ground with inscriptions of recent date. One stone looks curious, is about 4 feet by 1½, and has four lines of quaint Arabic or Turkish letters, barely legible, part of which seems to be: 'Atamiz daolat Sultan-ul-Ghalib,' or 'Our master, the victorious monarch.' A fight among

Kurds is said to have taken place here not many years ago; hence the graves. We are approaching the hills, and about to rise into mountainous tracts. This *kaza*, or 'district' of Argavan, consists of many *paras*, or villages, of which Hasan Badrik is about the chief. Akcha Dagh is a neighbouring district, peopled by many Kurds and Kizilbash.[1]

"*July* 5.—March to Hākim Khan; 6 hours, or 18 miles. After three-quarters of an hour the telegraph line leaves the road to plunge into gullies and over acclivities, and through most difficult country (more so than, I think, any we have hitherto traversed, not excepting the Batman Dagh, Deva Boiun, or country between Jazirah and Mardin); meets the road again in about an hour, and then skirts it, more or less, up to the point where it descends into the Kuru Chai, and keeps a good course near its bank. Halt and refresh on reaching this river. Find the ruins of an old bridge, in the shape of one whole arch and some remains of pillars. Below these is running a narrow, but rapid, stream towards the Euphrates. The water is delicious. Our horses are tied by one leg and turned out to graze on a fresh green bit of pasture. Near the bridge are the ruins of an old *khan*. Our own siesta was among rose-bushes, thorn and tamarisk trees, circled with beautiful wild flowers of mostly delicate hue—yellow, pale rose, pale blue, and white—at a stone's throw from the water still flowing in the bed of the mis-called *kuru*, or 'dry' river, a humble source of the great Euphrates. Descent to Hākim Khan, stony; the soil of a white colour, as between Reshmil and Mardin. Passed on our left, high, rocky table-land, said to be inhabited by Kurds of the Akcha Dagh. Hākim Khan, a singular and unattractive place, situated in a basin between high hills, and looking hot and feverish. Doctored a sick chaosh here, who should, however, be allowed a change of air in preference to other medicine. K. complains, and looks worn and weary.

"*July* 6.—Hasan Chelibi, 4 hours, or 12 miles. Almost

[1] Mr. Consul Taylor, in his capital paper No. XI. in the 38th vol. of the Royal Geographical Society's Journal (1868), gives interesting information on the Kizilbash, and shows where more is obtainable.

wholly near the bed of the Kuru Chai, along a path tolerably free from obstruction. Passed a Kabah on the way, with whom I exchange a few words in Persian. Our stage of the day is a village of about 100 houses of Kizilbash. Put up in a cool mud house full of flies, and am visited by the Mudir. Landlord tells me that when Sultan Murad was here, he was *entertained by a certain Hasan* in so gentlemanly a style, that the monarch named the village after him, with the affix of Chelibi, 'gentleman.' Viewed from the high ground above, this village, buried deep in the basin formed by surrounding hills, has a sombre and strange appearance. The flat roofs, from which mis-shapen chimney-pots arise, give the notion that there are no houses there at all, but that the land is sown, as it were, with chimneys. There are two rows, however, of these flat roofs, one rising upon the other; and a big gutter below, once a mountain streamlet, but perverted from its former origin. At night, transferred my cot and bedding to the house-top and vainly tried to sleep. Some watchmen, intended, as it proved, for my special protection, kept talking insufferably.

"*July 7.*—In the morning, when I was preparing for a start, a nest of extortioners opened out. Everyone wanted *bakhshish*. 'I was your *mosafir* [?] country,' said one. 'I also,' said another, 'watching over the horses.' Shukuri was called to explain, but could not. The applicants then said that there might be 'Kurds' about. 'Kurds!' said I, 'more likely they are afraid of you. *Sis dun kerkiar.* I have lived in Kurds' tents, and never been troubled by fear of robbery;'—or words to this effect. Then came a fellow, professedly with civil messages from the Mudir, his bland expressions culminating in a request for *bakhshish*. There was something rude and ungainly in this dirty village of Hasan Chelibi that made one rejoice to leave it; and when I found an exit from the pinched corner into comparative space, I seemed to breathe a freer atmosphere. Country more open and green. The hills continue, but are more cheery. Aliaja Khan, 7 hours, or 20 miles. Put up in a small *khan* like that of yesterday. Room about 22 by 15.

A space is poled off for travellers. There is one low door for an entrance, and a fireplace opposite. The windows are barely a foot square, and limited to two. To-day the walls are white-washed, so that the place does not feel quite dungeon-like. There is, however, a larger *khan* here, now used as a storeroom, built of very fine stone. Chaosh pointed out a cross on one of the stones of this building, which indicated Christian handicraft. A smash of liquor-case reported to-day. Memo.: bought six bottles of brandy for the journey at Baghdad, have not tasted one drop, yet not one of these bottles is now left.

I have seen many ill-looking telegraph chaoshes on this journey, but Ali Chaosh, whose beat is from Hasan Chelibi to the three-hour *khan*, beats all: in ughness and ungainliness he is 'first-class.' And I am sorry to add that nothing has occurred to lead me to believe his *morale* superior to his *physique*. A very long face, with a very long, loose nose, frowning eye and uncomfortable mouth, a forehead whose principal feature is a batch of cropped hair smoothed down its centre, and a sharp chin; such is a portrait which reminds me of James's Gallon the Fool, in 'Philip Augustus.' I doubt whether the Turkish official is anything of that stamp, and should be sorry to trust his honour in any way. As to his dress, such slovenliness, such huge holes at elbow and knee, such dirt, such disorder, are barely describable. While on this theme, I may here record that if I never remember to have seen a well-dressed Turkish soldier in the olden time, the same remark applies at the present hour to a Turkish telegraph chaosh. Even later improvements in military costume are more laudable in masses than individuals. But what can be expected of a taste which tolerates men and women in red and yellow boots far too large for the feet and legs which they cover? The chaosh who met us at the *khan* was an Armenian, and spoke English a little, and Italian a little better. We talked immensely. He and his brother, the chaosh on the next beat, had been employed (as firemen, I think) on board an English steamer in the Black Sea. March to Kangal, 5 hours or 15 miles. The dreary nature of the country traversed since, and just before crossing the Upper

Euphrates—at first exhibited in sparse and dry cultivation and desolate look of villages, and latterly in the absence of villages altogether, halting-stations excepted—was never more strongly impressed upon my mind than on this day's journey. At the same time, the openness, as it were, of desolation and depopulation, is less painful to the eye and sense than the dreary basin in the immediately surrounding hills, hiding a dismal village such as Hakim Khan or Hasan Chelibi. Put up at a *khan*. Kurdish tents near the town.

"*July* 9.—Delikli Tash, the 'stone with the hole,' 4 hours, or 12 miles. A small Turkish village of about sixty houses. Country undulating; hills not actually barren, but of pale hue and wanting in bright vegetation. Armenian chaosh relieved by a corpulent Turk whom we meet on the way, and who escorts us to the day's stage. His interest with the Mudir procures us an excellent room; but we are doomed to a series of visits, and the Mudir *will* feed us, which are inconvenient contingencies. Compromise the matter by accepting breakfast only, pleading the state of my companion's health as an excuse for the heavier meal.

"*July* 10.—Ulieb, a short 4 hours, or about 10 miles. Armenian village of some sixty houses, dirty and offering little worthy of note. Road through a pass in the hills, and over high hilly tract to plain country. The fat chaosh is a great character. His name is Aflâtun, 'Plato.' He talks of Europe with immense *gusto* of beer, champagne, and ladies. His description of a German hotel he had once visited was capital; and equally amusing are his quotations from Hafiz, and the sighs with which each is accompanied. His politics are ambitious, and embrace a variety of individuals and subjects, such, for instance as Garibaldi, the French Emperor, Spain, Portugal, the war between Denmark and Germany, the war in America; but there is more ambition than profundity in his speculations. The secret of the 'Delikli Tash' was solved this morning. We descended a really fine pass of this name, sighting a grand panorama of the lower country and distant hills. On our left was a circular rock, with a hole sufficiently large to admit the passage of a tall, stout man, when stooping; or a moderately fat man, without stooping or squeezing at all. To pass seven times through this is, my stout friend informs me, to attain the desire of one's heart, whatever that may be. I think he claimed to have gone through the ordeal. If so, the effort must have been considerable. Met a poor Circassian, who asked for bread. Thousands of these families have arrived of late years, from Anapa and other places, at Samsun and Trebizond; and have been flooding the Sivas district. A village about 12 hours distant is said to contain a colony. Met three the day before yesterday, armed, and dressed in their picturesque native costume. For breakfast to-day, have bread like a blacksmith's or cobbler's leather apron, eggs boiled hard and cut up into slices, excellent cow's milk, and hard but good cheese.

"*July* 11.—Sivas: 6½ hours, or 20 miles. Good road among the mountains, with descent into a high, broad plain, watered by the Kizil Irmak, or 'red river.' Met camels bringing hemp from Tokat, which Plato tells me is manufactured into ropes there prior to export, and grows abundantly in the neighbourhood. Less than half way, Tuzlu Punar, the 'salt spring,' where the Ottoman Government has posted two of its servants to make the most of the produce. Realization stated at 40,000 piastres, or 400*l.* per annum; but Sivas has much more salt than in this one spot. The aspect of the city from the distant heights is pleasing. Dotted here and there with trees, at times in large extended clusters, the houses and citadel cover a vast space, and appear much scattered. Met by the telegraph superintendent, M. Efendi, at several miles out of the town: a youngish but self-confident man of pleasing address, not unlike an Indian irregular horseman. White coat, waistcoat, and trousers, high polished boots—such was his attire; and he rode a smart white horse with a smart embroidered saddlecloth, military saddle, and holsters. His face is plain, pitted with small-pox, by which one eye has been sensibly affected; nor has he the advantage of hair on the cheek, upper lip, or chin, to conceal defects: but his manners promise well for an Asiatic, and I am favourably prepossessed in his behalf. After crossing the bridge at the Kizil Irmak (Sultan Murad's again), a body of horsemen under Tade Sirkardeh received us from the Pasha, and escorted us into the town. This was an honour for which I was not prepared. Put up at the Serai, where also is the telegraph office; and visited by Dr. W. and two of his Armenian pupils. Letters had preceded me to this gentleman from his fellow-countrymen, the American Missionaries of Kharput, and I had moreover sent a few lines to him myself on the subject of K.'s health, before entering Sivas.

"*July* 12.—Make up my mind to halt until the 14th, for two or three strong reasons. K. requires rest, and so do the horses. Call on Dr. W., whom I take to be a physician-missionary here. Meet a Mr. L. and another gentleman, and Mrs. W. and Mrs. L. Afterwards called on the Pasha, who gave me a cordial welcome, and with whom I did a chibouk or two and some coffee. He put me much in mind of the generally received portraits of one of our best known modern Indian heroes. The Efendi gave me about four hours of his society to-day, thereby showing a deplorable ignorance or recklessness of the value of time. He does not sport his chibouk, but cigarettes and *soap* may become equally impediments to progress. I have asked him to dine with us to-morrow. There would, I feel sure, like to come, but our habits will not admit of it, when, as they tell me, he was once a collector of customs on the Bosnian frontier, and that a certain Mudir of a district near Baghdad was his clerk! Dr. W. estimates the population of Sivas at 10,000 houses, or from 40,000 to 50,000 souls, of which more than a fifth are Armenians. Bought good woollen stockings made here, and tasted splendid tobacco of the country. Bread good, meat also. Wine of a pale straw colour, like bad sharp beer or flat cider; very different from the cheery red wine of Kharput. Cherry ice to-day—a great luxury. The view from our windows over the tops of houses and towards the hills, immediately above a little bit of quasi-garden, is certainly less Asiatic than we had been led to expect. But the English sky and climate have, perhaps, more to do with the feeling of nearness to one's fatherland than more tangible things. Thermometer in the heat of the day only 78°

There is a Liva Pasha, or Major-General, here, commanding the troops.

"*July* 13.—I feel quite sure that the electric telegraph in Turkey is abused by those who have the power of abusing it, inasmuch as a vast number of telegrams on the public service are intercommunicated without the faintest occasion, and for the mere sake of gratifying the vanity or whims of members of the Administration. This entails much extra labour which could be avoided, and converts a valuable State engine into a plaything.

"I learn that the district of Azizya has been made over to the immigrant Circassians, under the superintendence of a specially-appointed Kaimakám. Its *merkéz*, or 'head-quarters,' at Ponar Bagh, may be distant some 24 hours from this place in a southerly or south-westerly direction. The Emperor of Russia replies to the charge of forcing on the exodus by a statement that endeavours were made not to exterminate the population, but simply to keep them at a greater distance, or towards the Kouban. It is said that part of three important tribes, one of which boasts a population of 30,000, are now located on the right bank of that river. The Oubyhs turned a deaf ear to proposals of settlement, and preferred war to the limitations of the Kouban. The Grand Duke Michael has himself been down to the scene of distress, and endeavoured to relieve the sufferers, as well as facilitate the emigration. Our Ambassador at the Porte proposes to colonize with Circassians the space between the Black Sea and Erzerum, a proposal supported by France, by Ali and Fuad Pasha. A letter from Samsun of the 15th June states that 100,000 Circassians were then there, and typhus was raging among them. The numbers at Trebizond I have understood at no less a figure, and they are reported to have died there at the rate of 100 per diem. There is something very dreadful in all this. The Turks are a hospitable people, no doubt, and welcome readily, as brother Muhammadans, the sufferers from the encroachment of a foreign enemy; but this accession of a sickly, helpless, and otherwise undesirable population must be detrimental to healthy progress. The ac-

been the mosque, but this is a doubtful point. Met an Indian to-day, whom I take to be a suspicious character. What can these fellows be doing here? He professes to have been a wanderer for fifteen years.

"*July* 14.—Pasha kindly offers to cash a bill for us, about which there is some difficulty with the Bazar merchants. To use an expression of one of my Sivas friends, I surmise that a certain departmental official here 'stimulates.'

"*July* 15.—There have been great changes of late in the political distributions in Asia Minor, of which one of the most important is the creation of an Erzingan Pashalic. Erzerum takes in Moosh and Van; for there is no Pasha at Bitlis, which is still represented as comparatively insecure. Mr. B., a Missionary stationed there, tells me there may be 4,000 or 5,000 houses at Bitlis, of which 1,200 are Armenian. It is near the Lake Van, described as a pleasant enough residence in exchange for a town. The Sipan mountain runs down to the lake, and rises probably to 5,000 feet above it, being thus at least 9,000 feet above the sea level. Dine with Dr. and Mrs. W., Mr. and Mrs. B., a Missionary and lady from Constantinople, and some young children. The Armenian waiting-maid might from her appearance have been English. Mr. L. and lady were not with us, owing, it may be, to the sickness of their young folks, who seem susceptible to fever here. Plato is in attendance with a lanthorn to escort us home. People are apt to be taken up in the streets at night: but great privileges are allowed to Europeans, under which head Americans are naturally included at Sivas. The European, or it may be rather considered the Christian political shield, is largely protective among the modern Muslims of Asia Minor.

"*July* 16.—Sivas to Muntashir, 7 hours, or 21 miles, in the afternoon. Kind Dr. W. came to see us before starting; nor would he accept any remuneration for professional services rendered to K., a fact which speaks more for the goodness of his heart than his worldly wisdom. First twelve miles near the bank of the Kizil Irmak, which, notwithstanding the high hills on its left, is here but a magnified muddy stream, winding westward and southward. Leaving it, I strike into a track of the Tokat road, which leads to the Yeldiz Su, or 'Star-water,' a stream of some dimensions crossed by an old bridge. Thence to Muntashir about five miles. Find village deserted, except by two or three women and children; and our caravan, though despatched at an early hour from Sivas, had only just arrived. Cold enough to make me put on a thick overcoat, and resort to a thick double blanket.

"*July* 17.—Halt to-day. Weather lovely, air clear and fresh; nothing of India here. This little village, with its pears, plums, poplars, and tamarisk trees is not very pretty or picturesque, but so far as we can judge from the 17th July, it possesses a splendid climate. Hearing yesterday of its hot and cold springs, I got a guide to take me there. This guide is worthy a leaf in the notebook, for he is a type to be pleasantly remembered. Zuarna was quite the old Asia Minor Turk; his old, white-bearded, sharp-featured face, with its slight nose straight but peaked, and greyish indistinct eyes, was surmounted by an untasseled fez, round which was tied a green turban. His shoulders were bent by age and infirmity, and were not improved by the dingy blue striped vest, tied with an old dirty white cloth round the waist. His black Huchara-like unmentionables were notored and showed other colours; his toes were bound round with strips of worsted, tied with worsted thread, and stuffed, with the feet, into an old slipper or shoe; his were uncovered at the upper part of the calf below the knee. Patches many were visible in his exterior. He was about sixty, he said, but did not seem to know whether more or less; and he carried a stick with which he stumped along cavalierly. The best part of his outer man was his bare bit of leg, which looked sturdy and of healthy colour. We must have walked nearly four miles to the springs, and the same distance back, to say nothing of my own particular wanderings at the place itself. The old boy carried me over a brook, somewhat deep and wide. Two old women were sitting on the opposite side. They had their two donkeys awaiting their pleasure beside them, and seemed dames well enough to do in the world. One spoke across the brook to Zuarna, first about himself, then about *shu adam*, 'that man;' meaning my humble self. Who was I, and whence had I sprung? '*Shu adam*,' said I, in Turkish, 'has come from Baghdad, and is going to Constantinople.' After a little bit of talk we went on our way, I thinking that the old lady might have offered the loan of her animal to get me across the water. The springs are well worth the visit, and I may jot down some account of my hurried inspection of them. I had no compass with me, but should put them down to be about fifteen or sixteen miles west of Sivas—some on the very high ground, some nearer the valley of the Yeldiz Su. I only visited the first; the latter were, I was told, comparatively hot springs. To begin from the westernmost part, or that nearest to the village of Muntashir, whence I walked over: I ascended a hill for, it may be, 300 or 400 feet, when there arose a kind of basin formed by two ridges of sand-stone, semi-circular and semi-oval in shape, and of considerable length, not closed at either extremity. One ridge, that to the left, continued its course eastward, and this course I now follow. At about 500 yards from the point of separation from the opposite ridge we observe a series of springs—or I should call them, volcanicitos. At first there is nothing but a deep fissure in the backbone of the ridge, choked up for the most part with wild flowers and grasses; we then come to little pits and large pits, where once were living springs; then to two or three live springs themselves, more or less large; then a gap; then a further ascent with a tolerably large basin; a further ascent, with a basin at top, of oval shape, which we pause to describe. It may be 12 feet long, and is on sand-stone; the water is tepid, and trickles through a narrow cleft into a larger and lower basin of circular shape. This last is walled round with huge blocks of stone, say some 30 feet in circumference; the water is tepid and emits smoke: counted six springs working in it. Beside it is a small spring, whose water looks clearer than that of the large basin to which it is tributary. Further on is another, also tepid, in which I counted seven bubbles at work. We next have a grassy gap of say fifty yards, then a sand-stone ridge, again full of springs. The first contains very nearly cold water:

then comes a remarkable one on a high point, about 18 feet in circumference. Below the ridge are also two basins to be noted: one about 12 feet long, slightly oval, in which I counted five spouts and a minor one: water tepid; and one, the largest of all, perhaps 40 feet in circumference, coldish. Ascending the ridge again, which turns a little bit to the northward, we now have a long backbone in which may be counted more than forty-five springs, varying in size and power. Those not bubbling are not included, nor is one nearly cold. The ridges average perhaps 15 feet in height, slopes are gentle, backbone is sharp: in one place only, on the western side among the extinct springs, there was a broad trough of some extent. Where the springs were active, the water was trickling down in all directions. Those pointed out to me in the distance on crossing the Yeldiz Su showed like a cascade. The springs rise in little globules just above the surface of the basins, it is difficult to count them: one rises almost in the other, in appearance from under the water. The neighbouring ground is hard stone and sand. People bathe here, and the waters are considered healing; but I was advised not to stay too long in them. Some of the small springs made a grumbling, gurgling sound, as though eager to display themselves. All go by the general name of 'Chermik,' and I hear there are, besides those at the Yeldiz Su (called Kaïna Chermik) three others at no great distance, as follows:—

"1. At Kohneh, near Yuzgat, which we may yet manage to see.

"2. Near Amasia, called 'Kaeza Chermik' whence fresh water in the first instance, issues from the breast of a figure like a woman.

"3. At Kizilja Kui, called 'Sok Chermik,' where the water is cold also.

"*July* 18.—Kuwak, 4 hours, or 13 miles. In about two hours reach Yeni Khan, one of Sultan Murad's halts, where he left a specimen of sturdy architecture. Was walking into the village when a Turk met me and shewed me the house where K and the chaoush who had preceded me were to be found. 'What is that building?' said I, referring to a white structure on an eminence. 'A *kalisa*' (church), he replied. 'What,' said I, 'are there any Christians here?' He explained that there were two distinct divisions of the same village; the one half Muslim, the other Christian. We had entered by the former. 'And are you then,' continued I, inspecting him somewhat narrowly, 'a Christian?' 'No,' said he, 'I am a Muslim, but I am coming with you.' That is to say, he was coming with me over to the Christian side, to pick up any stray piastres we might have to distribute there. Hospitably received by the Armenian Kabia, who gave us a basin of excellent *yoghurt*, some aprons of bread (the bread in these parts is just like a leather apron), cheese, and a very greasy omelette. Proceeded on our journey to Kawak, a picturesque-lookish village, built, as it were, into and out of the sides of two high hills, and facing into a ravine between, down which flowed a mountain stream. The first house to which we were taken not pleasing our Sivas chaosh, we were transferred to a second, in an upper storey, clean enough in the woodwork, but whose cushions had fleas. Still, it was comparatively an eligible abode. Thermometer 63° at 2 P.M. Yeni Khan may have 120 houses, of which 60 are Armenian and 60 Turkish: Kawak 100, all Muhammadan. Met many carts and camels to-day, bringing wheat from Yuzgat, and wood from this neighbourhood. On the right of our road was a Circassian village.

"*July* 19.—Ekkaji, 5½ hours, or 16 miles, a prettily situated Turkish village, with a delicious climate. First part of road among ploughed fields and cultivation in comparatively low land. After three hours, and passing the two Kizilbash villages of Aghír Kaya and Kara Kaya,[1] country more undulating and hilly, till in five hours a mountainous range is approached, where, turning off to the left, we find our stage. Some Turkmans had just brought their tents to a neighbouring spot. Observed many locusts to-day, but of a smaller kind than in Mesopotamia. Good old people at village; and get snug open quarters, where we can, at least, breathe freely, and use a clean porch with a westerly aspect, if the house be too dark and close.

"*July* 20.—What can be expected, sleeping in so many

[1] "Heavy rock," "black rock."

strange houses; and, in the first part of almost every marching day, sitting or lying on so many strange couches, with pillows and all complete? I will not dilate on the horrors to which my companion and I have awakened. Suffice it to say, that last night at Lıkkatı was a night to be remembered. When morning came I was glad; but the gladness was that sort of unnatural sentiment which results from a state of mind highly to be deprecated. Mushallem Kalehsi, 6½ hours, or 20 miles; over high and wooded country, or difficult and intersected by a deep ravine, with gradual descent towards the completion of the stage. The place itself is an ordinary village with the 'Fort of Mushallem,' standing on a steep hill of perhaps 300 feet. It is about as difficult to get antiquarian information out of a Turk as out of an Indian peasant. My chaush told be that 'Mustallem was a Genoese, and built a fort.' The name sounds more Hebrew than Italian. A new chaush, at the village, stated that the place was built by Bahram Shah, and taken by Mushallem, a Muslim; a story which the old ex-Mudir, my landlord, so far confirmed as to admit the capture. The fort is, at the south-east corner and eastern face, a ruin, or beyond a ruin, but there is more of an old bastion. The south and south-western face may be 40 yards in length, with two towers. To the north, the ruined wall is looped for musketry, and being built up to the natural defences, which are round, presents an impregnable front. On the west is a gate, through which we entered, and over which are letters in Arabic or Turkish; but the side of the hill was too perpendicular to enable me to stand fronting and looking above it, with sufficient freedom to decypher the inscription, even supposing the words legible. Other remains here look interesting.

" *July* 21.— After a delightful night passed in my own particular greatcoat, on a small raised wooden platform in the verandah of a small house, away from all blankets, cushions, and borrowed bedding; march to Kara Maghara, the ' black cave'; 5 hours, but 18 miles. An Armenian complains of theft of his horse and gets me to take his deposition for communication to the authorities. To-day's march easy and pleasant. Pass many villages, and take note of abundance of sheep and poultry. The graveyards are dotted with large, sharp, upright stones, marking the respective places of burial. The women, who show their faces more than usual, are not bad looking, but scarcely attractive. The children are handsome and ruddy.

"*July 22.*—Kohineh, or Koyneh, a Turkish and Armenian village, with more than 100 houses. There is the constant earthy, sombre appearance about the place; but it has a certain element of life to make it remarkable. We are put into an Armenian ironsmith's abode, and have a tolerable look-out through two windows into a kitchen garden. The windows have no glasses, but are of respectable dimensions, about 4 feet by 2½, with four rows of fancy wooden bars running down them, crossed at right angles through a square figure common to both. Our march to-day was over a fine, high tract of country, part of this vast plateau of Asia Minor, which we have so keenly appreciated since reaching Sivas its natural capital. There was an occasional descent into a valley, or lower plain. Observed much cultivation, but also much apparent waste land, probably dependent on dews in the absence of rain. Wheat backward. Halted for refreshment at Burun Eurun, and imbibed milk in a gay, painted chamber, in the presence of the Imam, and a large party of serious, hospitable Muslims. We have entered the Yuzgat district, called here 'kasaba,' which again is divided into nine 'kazas.' A Mudir rules the kaza, and a Kaimmakám, or similar officer of rank, the kasaba.

"*July 23.*—Yuzgat: 6 hours, or 18 miles; over a fine but rather mountainous country, enlivened by villages and streams. These large hilly basins are not wanting in verdure, or barren of trees, or cultivation; but they have the mark of solitariness, and the traveller becomes impressed with a silence which feels unnatural as he wends his way through them. Even when a caravan passes, it seems to pass in quiet; and the fine air and climate, however delightful, fail to impart the cheeriness inspired by pleasant scenery. There is no looking from a distant height, upon a vast plain and its city, as at Sivas. Expectation is not raised that the oft-repeated and not very striking mountain amphitheatre will open out into the locality of a city at all; rather does it seem to lead the way to an undulating, half cultivated table-land. At length, Yuzgat shows itself, and artistically, though rather close. Are met by H. Efendi, and excellently quartered by the Kaimakam, or local governor. Mr. F., the American Missionary, kindly visits us in acknowledgment of a letter brought from Sivas. Tea at his house, and coffee with the old Kaimakam.

YUZAT

"*July* 24.—The day commenced well, and more like the Sabbath than most Sundays passed on our present journey. Went at 9 A. M. to the Missionary chapel, and found a congregation of about 160. Counted some 50 men and 50 boys, and took Mr. F.'s estimate of the women to reach a higher figure than required to complete the number assumed. These last are separated from the rest of the worshippers by a wooden trellised partition. They can be seen, and their little ones heard, but that is all. The arrangement appears good for an Eastern country. Mr. F. performed the whole service in Turkish. It opened with a hymn, which sounded familiar, and a prayer. 'Pir Punghar,' the title to guide the singers, is evidently the 'Punar,' 'well,' or 'fount,' and I believe myself correct in associating the words with the well-known —

"There is a fountain filled with blood;"

or one, at least, of its versions adopted in our hymnals. An exposition of Scripture followed, then another hymn, then a discourse and the final prayer. The preacher was fluent and fervent. The singing, though not superior, was effective enough to produce that home thrill, that breath of retrospect, which many must have experienced, though few can describe its mysterious charm. There were three or four good faces among the boys; but, with notable exceptions here and there, the congregation looked poor and unwashed. Some half dozen very respectable-looking men came up spontaneously after the service, to shake me by the hand as a new comer. Many boys were drowsy, some unsteady; but as a whole, the congregation was orderly and attentive. May this good work prosper; and all honour to these excellent single-hearted Missionaries, who humbly, unobtrusively, but very meaningly, devote their lives to its furtherance!¹ They hold an annual meeting at Constantinople, to which a representative is sent from each Turkish station. Visited by the Kaimakám and suite.

"*July* 25.—Yuzgat is a town of no ancient repute, having been founded a little more than a century ago by Paswan Oghlu, otherwise known as Chouban Oghlu, or Ahmad Pasha. The population has been estimated at 5,000 or 6,000 only, but I should consider this to be too low a computation. March to Gūdak, a short 6 hours, or 18 miles. Have taken leave of Mr. F. and his bright partner. He speaks excellent Turkish, and has therefore great advantage over those members of the

---

¹ In recalling the pleasure derived from this chance acquaintance with our Transatlantic brethren in Asiatic Turkey, I seem to forget all physical fatigues and inconveniences of a long journey; and it is with sincerity that I add a weak testimony of respect to the many they must have already received from passing travellers.

man village, with some forty houses. These Turkmans profess to be of the same family as those of Samarkand and Bukhara, the terror of the Persians, and to have settled here about 150 years ago. At the Deliji Su, cotton is growing in abundance on the left bank. I am told that 250 okas (687¼ lbs.) are sold this year. At about halfway is the village of Karlangusht, at which no male inhabitants were visible, and the females did not seem disposed to be communicative. Shukuri failed in getting *yoghoort*, and said he was taken for a Circassian, a statement which in some sense explains why we should be avoided. After passing Husain Bey Ohbasi, find our way to Hasan Bey Ohbasi, our stage, where we are put up in Hasain Bey's own house, which we are informed, and soon prove on experience, is thrown open to travellers by the hospitable owner.

"*July* 28.—Yakhshi Khan, or Yakhshan, 5½ hours, or 16 miles. The muleteers' bells were heard at a very early hour; in fact, it was moonlight, and not a streak of dawn was visible. Yet we failed to start as early as intended, nor was there any chaosh in attendance. A youth, dignified by the title of 'Wakil,' or Agent, presented himself as substitute for his father, the absentee, and was admitted to guide and enlighten us in the matter of the telegraph line. He was a pretty boy; and his wild, flowing black hair burst forth bushily from beneath a very common fez, over shoulders covered by the loose red jacket of Asia Minor, on the back of which was a black embroidery in shape like a cross, and the sleeves of which were hanging down in hussar fashion. A fanciful red and spotted waistcloth was wound across his under-gown of yellow ground and many-coloured stripes. His bare leg was visible over his boots and leggings. Spear in hand, and mounted on a flea-bitten grey horse, he looked rollicking, jaunty, stupid and unimpressible, if such a combination can be rendered intelligible. Left the road to follow the telegraph line, which takes its course over undulating country and among luxuriant cultivated and ploughed fields. Cross to the right bank of the Kizil Irmak, before reaching our stage. Observed many fields of yellow wheat under the reaping process, as we moved along to-day. Men and women rode donkeys to the work. The first sate heavily back and looked ungainly. The second, wearing white shift and unmentionables, and on the head a red cap bound round with a light kerchief, their long hair falling in plaits behind, looked well and Ruth-like, as they tapped with their sickles the necks of the patient animals to increase their speed. An old chaosh with a shaved head, and otherwise Quixotic spear, as thoroughly comical and characteristic a figure as I had seen in Asia Minor, accompanied us into the station; and well he did so, for we had dismissed our handsome but utterly useless boy attendant.

"*July* 29.—Hason Oghlu, 6½ hours, or 19 miles. Re-crossed the Kizil Irmak, finding it up to the horses' girths. Traversed a rocky and mountainous tract to the descent to Kilinjer, a pretty picturesque village of some fifty houses, with a solid and regular look, and amid trees and cultivation. Observe two high mountains, W.S.W. Inna Dagh, and N. and by W. Idris Dagh. Hills again, and after another smart ascent and descent, sight in the gully to our right the villages of Yenikshik, 60, and a minor Yuzgat, above 100 houses. Halt at the fountain and horse-trough in the latter; but both these villages have a hideous and sickly garb, and we quit them readily for large fertile grain-fields, not yet under the sickle though availing the operation. This continued fertility is refreshing. The amber poppy and magenta thistle have lost their old colour and richness, but are seen as of old on this march. Part from old Bekir, the comical chaosh.

"*July* 30.—Angora, or Engureh, 6½ hours, or 20 miles. Move along a charming road through a valley between long ranges of hills. Pass a *khan*, water-mills, and rows of trees by the side of a brook. The cultivation becomes more and more luxuriant as we advance. We enter a new valley literally choked with corn, as well as trees in groves, lines, and clusters; sparkling with running water; replete with villages and cheer-ful agricultural life. Scarcely turning away from this, we sight Angora rock and castle. About half way I had come upon a burial-ground where was a broken pillar, with a seemingly Kufic inscription, nearly opposite which, across the path, was an unmistakeable lion, sorely disfigured, but perfect enough to possess great value. I questioned an old labourer on the spot about these monuments. 'Baba,' said he, 'they are old: no one can read, no one can know anything about them.' The next time the old fellow addressed me, he applied the pilgrim's affix, Haji, and said 'Haji Baba:' but though full of friendliness, he was not full of information. Met by a large cavalcade which the Pasha very kindly sent out to meet and escort us in. Most hospitably and honourably received, excellently housed; and the Pasha's servants deputed to attend us at all hours.

"*July* 31.—Had intended to halt: but summoned by telegram to Constantinople with all speed. Determine thereupon to leave this morning after breakfast, and post at all events to Ismid, on the Sea of Marmora, about 210 miles. K. and the horses and servants can follow at leisure.

"The Turkish pronunciation of Angora would induce me to write 'Engureh.' In leaving it in its better known etymology I must premise that the accent is *never* thrown on the second syllable. Murray estimates the population at 20,000, a third of whom are Armenians. This certainly does not appear an over-statement.[1] What a mass of houses is there over that fort-crowned hill! It must be the southern aspect that we so much admired on riding round last evening, when the fort was divested as it were of the town, and stood out in real grandeur. The striking effect was not unlike that produced by one of the many beautiful views of the Castle in Edinburgh presented to the lounger in the neighbourhood, and on the level of Princes-street. Endeavour to get a short ramble among the local curiosities; and an old Italian doctor, whose acquaintance I made yesterday on arrival, sends his son to attend me. Just saw enough of an old Roman ruin with Latin inscriptions, for which objects modern Ancyra is renowned, to wish to learn more about it; but have no time for a closer inspection.

---

[1] M. Perrot, estimating the population within the last ten years, gives to Angora 45,000 inhabitants, of whom 25,000 are Turks, 12,000 Armenian Catholics, 4,000 Armenian non-Catholics, 3,000 Greeks, and 1,000 Jews.— (*Souvenirs d'un Voyage en Asie Mineure.* Paris, 1864.)

"But the classical or beautiful inanimate is not all that is here calculated to arrest the inquirer's attention. Angora has what may be called a determinate reputation for goats, and an indeterminate reputation for cats. To the truth of the first I can testify from the sight of the most lovely of their species—exquisite little capricioling quadrupeds of drooping silky coats, admiration of which even the fatigue of a weary march could not restrain. As regards the cats, my experience of them is confined to specimens shown in Europe; for not one could I find in Angora, where they told me I must be looking for the 'Van köhsi,' or cat of the Lake Van.

"The famous goats, producing a wool renowned over the world, abound in the vicinity of the town from which they derive their name. It is said that they are only found within certain circumscribed limits, which may be defined as between the left bank of the Kizil Irmak and Sevri Hisar, the latter place marking the most southerly point, and the Black Sea being the northern boundary. A space of 500 geographical square miles may here be assigned, from which removal would cause deterioration. It is represented to be a known fact that if transferred to the east bank of the Kizil Irmak, they suffer from the *mal de pays*. Many are lost from exposure, but the losses are made up for by breeding with common goats, and as it is supposed to be recovered in the third generation. The Angora goat gives, I have learnt,[1] one oka, or 44 ounces avoirdupois, of wool; and the quantity supplied throughout the wool region is estimated at from 350,000 to 400,000 okas, *i.e.* 962,500 lbs. to 1,100,000 lbs. From the same authority it appears that 40,000 okas (110,000 lbs.) are expended in thread manufacture in Asia Minor itself, of which more than half is sent to Holland, and

---

[1] These particulars are the same as reported by me to the Government of India nine or ten years ago, and were obtained from the *Journal de Constantinople* of September 5, 1864. It is well, however, to note that Mr. Consul Taylor says the Angora goats thrive "wonderfully in the neighbourhood of Jazirah" on the Tigris; and that the mohair obtained from them was bought up there in 1863 by native traders from Kaisaria and Constantinople to the amount of 25,000*l*.

8,000 to 10,000 okas (17,500 lbs.) are converted into home-made shawls and stuffs.

"Take leave of all friends and start. The Pasha insists on sending four mounted soldiers with me on my journey, but after getting out a mile or two, I manage to dismiss them and find myself alone with the *suraji*, or groom, who is judged indispensable by the custom of the country. Reach Amir Yaman in about two hours, and Ayash in less than three hours afterwards. Large town in a mountainous tract, where I get a fresh horse and *suraji*. Between Ayash and Bei Bazar, grow wearied of the repeated stoppages of my companion, and push on independently. Soon find myself quite alone; night sets in before I reach the stage; I lose the track, and, *me voilà*, fairly bewildered. At length I make for a light at some distance off, and discover a party of people sitting round a fire. Doubtless my solar *topee* and general costume are strange to them, but they hear my story and respond to the appeal with which it closes. I offer a small silver piece (beshlik) for a guide to Bei Bazar, and a young lad is mounted on a steed and sent with me. The place is about a couple of miles further. On the way the boy turns round and says: 'This *beshlik* is for me; what are you going to give the horse?' The appeal was irresistible; and I was glad to give two more beshliks before dismissing my guide, after he had safely lodged me at the posthouse for the night. Half-a-crown, under the circumstances, was not a heavy payment. Dined off grape soap and bread, and endeavoured to sleep in the posthouse verandah; but disturbed by the arrival of the dawdling *suraji*. Gave him his *bokhshish*, though far from pleased with his behaviour. Under fifty miles to-day.

"*August* 1.—Great delay in making a start, and have to get through eleven hours with dubious change of horses. Road partly over heavy sand and among high hills. Brief halt at a coffee-shop in Chair Kui, where I was not over hospitably entertained while paying my footing. One hour after leaving Nullakhan, the post station, came upon rich grain-fields; in two hours, pass a halfway house; in three hours is a water saw-mill; in four hours I make a considerable and very winding ascent to the heights overlooking the Mudurli valley. Leave my *suruji*, whose horse is done up, and push forward. Reaching the summit of the wooded mountain, commence the long descent on the other side, and manage to make the post-town just before nightfall. Find the posthouse, a small building in a narrow street, but can nowhere procure a dinner! Somewhat faint from want of food, proceed to telegraph office, but return to hunt up any kind of refreshment at a shop, and with the aid of a chaush. A greasy dish of eggs is offered, of which I partake sparingly, adding bread; and then turn in to sleep in an open frontage looking into the street. I must not forget to record that after leaving Bei Bazar this morning I discovered that the *suruji* of the previous evening had taken advantage of my absence to help himself to the few eatables and drinkables that were to be found in the saddle-bags he was carrying on my particular account, and had especially disposed of every drop in my single bottle of sherry! More than 60 miles to-day.

"*August* 2.—Start from Mudurli at an early hour, about 3 or 3.30, certainly before dawn. A cup of hot milk and a slice of bread is brought to me ere starting, and is most acceptable. This attention must be attributed to a little display of vexation on my part last night, when contrasting the good treatment I invariably received among Kurds and Arabs with that experienced from the more civilised Turks of Asia Minor. It is not much I ask for—a bit of cheese or an egg to relieve the dryness of the bread about dinner time; and a loaf, or dry bread or biscuit, to eat on horseback for breakfast as we jog along. The nine hours' stage to Torbalu we manage to accomplish in about six hours, getting in at 10 A.M. The scenery from Mudurli to this place is beautiful; the road along a magnificent valley flanked by forest-clad mountains. The wood is mostly fir. Fields and forests emit a delicious perfume. Here and there are hedges such as those in dear old England. Get through two more stages, namely, Torbalu to Terekli, and Terekli to Gaiveh, each of six hours, making up twenty-one hours, or a good sixty-three miles for the day. So tired, that I am tolerably indifferent to the information that horses are not at once procurable at Gaiveh. Besides, it is night when I arrive. This posting in

Asia Minor has its disagreeables, especially as regards the seat on horseback. They put one's British saddle on a thick native quilting, and not on the back of the horse; consequently, the rider is immensely and most unpleasantly exalted. Galloping is painful; trotting is painful; the horse is uneasy, and the rider also, under the circumstances. On one occasion to-day, I had to dismount and get the whole affair re-arranged, the *suraji* returning nearly a mile into Terekli to get what was required. Loss of time and temper ensue on these *contretemps*, and are all the more distressing if one is in a hurry. I had intended pushing on all night to catch the morning steamer leaving Ismid for Constantinople; but wearied nature and exhausted patience disposed me to sleep at the Gaiveh coffee-shop, leaving instructions for an early start.

"*August* 3.—My night's rest at the coffee-shop, however, was not a long one, for several of its *habitués* persisted in sitting with me to discuss the American war, the late Chinese war, cotton, and electric telegraphs. One old man declared that were peace restored to America, Asia Minor cotton would no longer be sought after by England, but would drop from 26 to 6 or 10 piastres the oka (2¾ lbs.) To some extent he is right. The value is sure to deteriorate when a poor market becomes an abundant one. But there may be room for both products; and if the Asia Minor cotton be good and susceptible of improvement, there is no knowing for how long a period it may be purchased by English manufacturers. Gaiveh, where our discussion was held, is a great cotton-growing locality; and our little parliament showed no small intelligence, especially in the person of one of its members. Before reaching Angora, I had been informed that in Kalaja Kirkin, a district in the pashalic or *kasaba* of Angora, near which I passed, no less a yield than 13,750 lbs. had been obtained—I presume this last year. The impetus lately given to the cultivation had been most effective. Start early this morning, but are a long time about the six hours' march to Sabanja, a village with a fine lake, the view of which from the high ground on the Gaiveh side is very fine. From this place, after a short friendly chat, make a fresh start and got upon a broad dusty road well indented with ruts. Soon spy out the position of Ismid, and the hills forming the sides of its long gulf. Stop at a coffee-house about three-quarters of a mile out of the town, and hold a little talk with a lounger there. These roads, it should be mentioned, are sprinkled with *derevens*, or halting barns, where pipes and coffee are procurable, far away from towns or even villages. At Ismid, found a café and *locanda*, kept by a quasi-English Vice-Consul with a kind of Polish-Greek name. His son did the civil to me, and I put up there. Visited telegraph station. Sent over to the cook's shop and got chopped meat and vegetables, bread and wine; and thoroughly enjoyed the first approach to a dinner I had had since leaving Angora on the 31st ultimo, together with a quiet airy room in which to eat and sleep. About 40 miles to-day.

"*August* 4.—Ismid, the original Olbia, and subsequent Nicomedia, the capital of Nicomedes, king of Bithynia. Mr. Walsh speaks of it in 1825 as having stood for 2,400 years on the same spot. The situation is certainly well chosen, and the *coup d'œil* from the sea charming. As usual in Turkish fashionable resorts near the capital, the Sultan's *kiosk* is the conspicuous object; and to make it exclusive, his Imperial Majesty seems to have cleared himself an amount of eligible ground in the heart of a populous town, after a fashion which would elsewhere severely try the loyalty of the sufferers. Steamers run to and fro between Ismid and Constantinople almost daily; and the Sultan makes frequent visits here in one of his yachts or tenders."

I will now pause; for too much on Ismid and its history would be out of place at the close of a long and desultory chapter. Suffice it to say that I was thankful to have arrived so far on my journey; thankful to exchange the rough routine of marching and posting in Asia for an eight hours' pleasure trip in a steamer leaving this morning for the City of the Sultan;

and thankful to find myself this evening at Misseri's hotel, which from long association and kind attentions has become for me more than an ordinary halting-place.

PERSIAN SERVANT (BAGHDADI).

CHAPTER IX.

LONDON TO KARACHI, VIÂ ST. PETERSBURG, MOSCOW, AND
NIJNI NOVGOROD. — AN EPISODE OF THE EASTERN
CRIMEA.

UNDER instructions from the Right Honourable the Secretary of State for India, I returned from Constantinople to London in May 1865; whence, after assuming a general superintendence of the Persian Gulf cable and Anglo-Persian land-line, so far as her Majesty's Government was represented in the latter, I again set forth on the 23rd June, charged with a special mission to Tehran. A Convention was to be concluded with the Shah, in supersession of existing provisional arrangements for the conduct of the telegraph; and I was to impart and be responsible for all details which her Majesty's Minister at the court of Persia might require to be put before him pending negotiations.

Four days in Paris enabled me to confer with the Director-General of Ottoman telegraphs, Agathon Efendi, then on a special mission from Constantinople connected with the resilient question of Turkish finance; as well as to accomplish work incidental to my charge, and proposed journey. *Au reste*, the time was not one to choose for sight-seeing in this *galère*. The *beau monde* had fled; the *bourgeoisie* were in the ascendant. Monceaux and St. Cloud were all very well in the way of crowds, of grottos and waterworks; but what they had to show, animate or inanimate, was of a most familiar kind. The Académie was open, and Marie Saxe and Faure were drawing fair houses to the "Africaine," with its impossible Brahmins and other *dramatis personæ*; but the weather was too hot, and there was too little attraction, to make theatres generally desirable to passers-by. That huge caravanserai, the Grand Hotel, so largely patronized by American travellers, was as full and unlike a home as usual; but the cafés, the restaurants, the boulevards, in fact all recognized Paris, wanted the *verve* which makes it so pleasant a reminiscence to the many.

When looking at this beautiful city as it *is*,[1] I cannot avoid contrasting it with what it *was*, not half a century ago; when the Champs Elysées were a kind of out-of-town garden or promenade. There was a Beaujon there, or minor Vauxhall, where fireworks were exhibited at night, and the *Montagnes Russes* amused loungers in the day. And the streets, how wonderfully improved, not only in width and architectural display, but in order and cleanliness! The shops are brilliant in the extreme: the crowds of passengers on foot, and of vehicles, are increasing: the pavement of the busiest thoroughfares is exquisitely smooth and still. If Baron Haussmann has failed to please the Parisian, he has surely merited a statue from the cosmopolite. Much has been done of late years to beautify and improve London; but we have not connected our principal railway stations one with the other, above-ground and through the metropolis, as they have

[1] In 1865, before the war and its disastrous consequences.

done across the Channel, to the convenience of the million, if only to the taste of the hundred. The mind which designed the Rue Lafayette, and similar main streets, might have continued the few suggestive yards opened out by the North-Western Railway at Euston in one grand line of thoroughfare to Waterloo Bridge. This *en passant*, and irrespective of money or property considerations.

On the 28th June, I left Paris for St. Petersburg, and breakfasted the next morning at Berlin. The next morning I crossed the Russian frontier, and at four o'clock on the following afternoon I was dining at the Russian capital; thus accomplishing, in round numbers, some 1,750 miles in less than 80 hours, or 3½ days and 3 nights.[1]

There was little worthy of record on the journey. Between Paris and Cologne, I found myself in a carriage with two smoking merchants, a lady and gentleman who might have been father and daughter, and a Hamburgher, who, not content with asking me many substantial questions, answered others of an imaginary nature; for I am not aware of having put them to him, and his replies were addressed with painful directness to myself. He told me of his family, his travels, that he was on his way home, and that there would be great joy on his return; subjects which one perverse nature is apt to put to another perverse nature at unfortunate seasons, when an appeal to sympathy is, at the least, ill-timed. Passing through Berlin, in the omnibus, it was my chance to hear a warm discussion between two fellow-passengers divided

---

[1] In 1871, I made the journey from St. Petersburg to London in much the same time; and in 1872 the improved railway communication in Russia enabled me to reach London from Persia in 13 days.

in opinion on France and Germany, both as to towns and inhabitants. One was loud for French, and one for German soldiers. In considering Prussia as a military nation, it was questioned whether the military spirit had free action under the influence of pipe-clay, and whether over-attention was not paid to the dress and *tenue* of the soldier. All the railway stations, for instance, turn out soldierly-looking officials, many admirably dressed men, and the duties are performed with great military precision and discipline; but was this the class of heroes for war? and had they the *élan* of the rough, ready, and slipshod Zouave or Turco? On the other hand, France was criticized for her want of solidity and inordinate love of display. To me it seemed that there might be some reason and truth on each side of the question; but I little dreamt of the practical solution to be publicly proclaimed, a few years later, to at least one phase of the discussion.

The Prussian first-class carriages on this line are exceedingly comfortable, and seldom, I take it, at ordinary seasons full. Refreshment is fairly provided, and time given to partake of it. I plead guilty to utter ignorance of Königsberg, or when we arrived there; but its hour by the Livret Chaix is 3.47 A.M., and we were all up and stirring at the frontier, four hours further. In the first place it is the Prussian station of Eydtkuhnen; and five minutes afterwards the Russian one of Wirzboloff. At the latter was an inspection of passports and baggage; and realizing here the very disagreeable position of hearing unintelligible words and wanting some to give in exchange, I took a gloomy view of travelling in general, and was disposed to convict every man of a surreptitious act who came to a country without knowledge of its language. The mood, however cynical, was evanescent, and did not prevent me from regarding with interest the new picture before me. We were waiting in the refreshment room the signal to re-enter the carriages. Among other characters on which attention could not fail to rest, the typical idler of the continental *buffet* was not wanting. Here it was illustrated in the person of a military dandy, whose local status was probably derived from a garrison at or near the frontier. He was talking affable French to a lady behind the counter, who should nevertheless be a countrywoman of his own; and every now and then he turned to twist his particularly long whiskers *à la Dundreary* before the looking-glass in the most self-satisfied manner. His light-coloured cloak was opened at the throat just sufficiently to display a small star and medals of brilliant hue. He seemed to know everybody, and to take a kind of superintendence of everybody he knew, and all that belonged to them. A huge dog alarmed an old lady who was talking long and earnestly in French to a pale, gentlemanly boy about ten or eleven years old. Here it must be recorded in favour of the smart officer, that, although evidently disposed to regard the circumstance jocosely, a sense of propriety prevailed, and he turned the offender out of the room.

As we passed through Wilkowitchki and Pilwitchki on the way to the larger towns of Kovno and Wilna, I was struck with the scant population. At Dünaburg a pleasant companion, a Russian officer, left me to proceed to Riga. The Russian first-class carriages, as those in Prussia, are very good, and the lavatories and conveniences added to the sleeping arrangements deserve notice; but I do not prefer them unreservedly to our own. To learn the

Russian alphabet, the railway traveller may be recommended to practise on the names of stations. They are well supplied with letters, as for instance Debenskaya and Preobrejenskaya, and may be checked with a continental Bradshaw. At this said Preobrejenskaya the only object that attracted my attention was a very plain, Tartar-faced lad with fine large roses wreathed round his shabby hat, which seemed, moreover, to have a broad plume sticking out of it. Another pleasant companion, who spoke English and French as well as his native Russian, left me at Gachina between the Lake Pskoff and St. Petersburg. The whole country up to the capital is monotonous and *triste* to a degree.

On the recommendation of the fellow-traveller last alluded to, I drove to Miss Benson's on the English Quay, whither I was conveyed under the particular instructions of a polite old warrior at the railway station, whose breast carried a full battery of medals. The abode in question is of the nature of a private hotel or boarding-house, and, though not in any way pretentious, better suits the taste of an English traveller passing through the Russian capital than do the larger and more orthodox establishments, which are at best second-class compared to those of Paris and Western Europe. At all events I had a tolerably large bedroom wherein to wash and dress in peace, fitting myself before long to enter a droschky and drive to her Majesty's Embassy. Here a sedate German-speaking porter informed me that the Ambassador was absent from St. Petersburg; it was too late in the day to expect the further attendance of any secretary; so leaving a few lines for the *Chargé d'affaires* I returned to my quarters, joining a *table d'hôte* with our hostess at one end, her sister at the other, and some three or four lodgers sitting sparsely here and there.

The day following that of arrival was Sunday, and I attended divine service in a very well-arranged building. It contained a vivid "Descent from the Cross" as an altar picture, and other appropriate accessories to church ornament. The congregation was not numerous or, perhaps, aristocratic. Many of its members had a semi-Russian appearance, and reminded me of the Levantine element observable in the Embassy chapel at Constantinople; but the fashion of St. Petersburg was out of town, and it is presumed that British Protestantism had representatives in that particular sphere who were doomed or pleased to follow suit. The chaplain was a good reader, and preached a good sermon on the words "The sword of the Lord and of Gideon," showing that man must use his own efforts as well as look "to the hills" for help.

On Monday, agreeably to appointment, I accompanied her Majesty's *Chargé d'affaires* to the house of the Russian Minister for Foreign Affairs. Mr. L. had very kindly and promptly procured me the honour of an interview, and had taken the trouble to discuss with me previously the question of the overland telegraph to India, in which he expressed much interest. This gentleman's reports and investigations on the important subject of Central Asian traffic were such that for personal apprehension of the objects of the Indo-European telegraph, I could not well have addressed myself to a more fitting medium. The Minister received me with cordiality, conversed freely on ordinary topics, both in French and English, and referred me to a secretary for any detailed information I might require.

Prince G. is rather tall, somewhat inclined to stoutness, has a high forehead, grey hair, and ruddy complexion. The features are rather square than flat or angular, and the eye, though light in colour, is full of meaning. He spoke of Lord Palmerston's age, remarking that he himself, who was twenty years younger, had had enough of public life. He did not envy me my journey to Persia, facetiously requesting that if I fell sick, it should be beyond Russian territory, or out of the range of his responsibility.

On Tuesday I called on the Director-General of Imperial telegraphs, and broke ground on the departmental details of international traffic. Without putting forward any definite proposals, or even suggesting a definitive understanding, I thought it well to generate, as it were, free and friendly interchange of ideas on a matter of mutual interest and universal benefit, in which political mistrust or jealousy had necessarily no part whatever. Indeed, I could not reasonably have done more, even if authorized. Some facts, such as the tariff and state of the line, it was imperative to ascertain, unless we were to ignore the Russian route altogether, which the bad working of the Turkish wires alone rendered inexpedient. General G. is a dark, middle-aged, wiry-looking man of fair height and build; inclined to be lean rather than stout, and of an Italian middle-class physiognomy. He is very go-ahead, wants telegraphs all over the world, and all at a cheap rate. He told me they were hard at work at the line connecting the Amoor with Russian America, and that when the Americans joined on, they hoped to encircle the world. This was their part: ours the Indian and Atlantic cables; all grand efforts, under Providence. This interview completed the little incidental public business I had to transact at St. Petersburg; so that on Wednesday the 5th July I resumed my journey at mid-day, taking a ticket by rail to Moscow.

St. Petersburg on this first visit did not charm me. It gave me the notion of a mass of houses set down in a wilderness, and ranged along a river and its canals, rather than a leading city of Europe. It seemed as though we had entered it without the usual preparation, such as suburbs and paved approaches; and when in it, I missed the civilized finish which might have been anticipated. Perhaps it was this feeling of disappointment which blinded me to many beauties, and caused me to exaggerate defects rather than find cause for imperfection. But my first impressions of St. Petersburg were certainly not so favourable as those obtained from after visits. It put me in mind of New York, in the driving of its coachmen, the passage of its tramway cars, and in other outward tokens; but for the stranger traveller a Fifth Avenue Hotel was wanting in the picture. The shops struck me as inferior to those of London, Paris, or Vienna; nor did I admire the Navsky Prospect for any architectural design so much as for mere length and *coup d'œil*. Some buildings and monuments, however, appeared to be noble exceptions, and worthy of any place. The cathedral of St. Isaac stood out simple and grand; the statue of Peter the Great looked full of life and beauty; the palaces had architectural elegance as well as solidity. It was the perpetual stucco, which was too profuse and palpable; and the streets and squares were disproportionately wide, while the pavement was really wretched. A delicate person, at the mercy of a fiery droschky-driver, would have been jolted into irrecoverable ailments; a stout person in similar circumstances would have undergone a change in constitution; the only person to whom the ordeal could have been recommended was the sufferer from moral rather than physical ills. Then again, in the droschky there was only just room for one, and this one should have been able to hold on by both hands at any time; but the denizens of St. Petersburg seemed fond of driving in couples. A man and his *chère amie*, he holding her with deft firmness round the waist; this was no unusual national picture. I might say more, but the city has been described by those who have lived there and are acquainted with its interior as well as exterior aspect; and these first impressions were derived from a four days' imperfect consideration of the latter.

The Petersburg-Moscow Railway Station is a large, handsome building; and luggage is weighed and tickets are given by the Imperial army much in the style adopted by civilians elsewhere, except that the military are perhaps more alive to what are commonly called "tips." I found myself in a carriage with two men, who might be Russian or Hungarian. Not entering into any conversation with them, I tried to read a "Petit Manuel de la Langue Russe," but soon fell off to sleep. The heat was intense, as it had been during my short stay at the capital, where, by the way, the very brief nights at this season of the year cannot fail to surprise the stranger to extreme northern latitudes. Had it not been for the frequent stoppages, and inducements to get out and refresh on our road, of which the natives are not slow to avail themselves, I should probably have slept longer than I did. Our route lay through the provinces or "governments" of Novgorod and Twer. The country was green and wooded; there were rivers and bridges, and highly respectable railway stations. The *tables d'hôte* were better than I expected to find, and the time given to profit by them was ample; but I could not keep pace with my companions in feeding and liquoring, and my ten o'clock supper consisted of a cigar and a lump of eating chocolate. At 8 A.M. the next day we reached Moscow.

I had intended not to remain here more than a few hours, but a slight attack of indisposition, and intimation that the Astrakhan boat would not leave Nijni for two or three days, led me to defer my departure till the afternoon of Friday the 7th July. I had been recommended to the Hôtel Billet, and went there accordingly. It is conducted, like Miss Benson's, on the private hotel or boarding-house principle, and Madame Billet is an Englishwoman. On the opposite side of the street is a rival house, strangely alike in designation, for it is kept by M. Billot, whose name it bears.

A solitary stroll in the afternoon of the day enabled me to inspect the exterior of the palace and the surrounding gardens of the Kremlin; to admire a speaking bronze statue of Menin and Pojarsky within the walls, and specially note a singular Tartar-looking structure explained to be the Church of St. Basil, built by Ivan the Cruel. The miniature domes and blue tints of this last are very striking, and the *coup d'œil* of the whole is charming. The next day, accompanied by an unavoidable *commissionnaire*, I visited the interior of the Kremlin. Some of the apartments are gorgeously fitted up; the throne room being prominent and unique. The pictures are well worth inspection, and boast originals of first-rate artists. I lighted on one said to be a

Rembrandt, but which I myself might have innocently
accepted as the work of a British artist; for it looked
Hogarthian. The Polish historical pictures brought from
Warsaw are very attractive. In the large hall are four
fine paintings illustrative of the life of Alexander Nevsky,

GREAT BELL OF MOSCOW.

and a grand specimen of quite recent art, representing
a severe battle between the Russians and Tartars. The
hall of St. George is interesting from the rolls of knights
inscribed on its walls. Pillars and ornaments of mala-
chite and verd-antique add much to the splendour of

the apartments in the Kremlin; but perhaps the Tartar orientalism is the most memorable feature of the place. Concentrating attention in a corner full of quaint and tasteful designs, it would be easy to imagine oneself in a pavilion of the Great Khan. There is a fine view from the terrace, especially in the direction of the Warsaw road with the intervening gold-domed Church of the Saviour. The rooms in the palace were filled with old soldiers wearing gold chevrons, each of which indicated five years' service. One man had nine medals on his breast, inclusive of stars and crosses. The ribbons explanatory of these are seemingly drawn across a plate of metal, secured by a long pin; or the plate itself, if such it be, is coloured to represent the ribbons. I should have liked to "tip" all these veterans, but there were too many; so a rouble for the principal conductor was held sufficient. In the Emperor's bedroom was a small altar, most elaborately filled with paintings and ornaments.

The "government" of Moscow, though one of the smallest of the provinces of Great Russia in actual area, has perhaps the largest population. More than ten years ago it was estimated at above a million and a half. No doubt the city accounts for a vast number of inhabitants. I was informed that it contained no less than 400 churches, and that the rule was to allot a church or chapel to every Government building. There are also some monasteries and convents. The English Protestant church is a quiet edifice, capable of accommodating at least a hundred: it has one small altar-painting of the Saviour. The chaplain had left on the very day of my visit, and the churchwardens knew nothing of the appointment of a successor. Judging from the streets and highways in Russia, the visitor whose wanderings have heretofore been confined to the western half of Europe may be pardoned for recording a strong impression of the plainness of the inhabitants. Certainly the men and women observed here in outside life and society are, as a rule, not handsome; and the general appearance of the *mujjiks* and drivers of public vehicles, who abound in the two cities of St. Petersburg and Moscow, is primitive and graceless. A hat like a chimney-pot or inverted flower-pot with invisible brim, exemplifies a very prevailing fashion in Moscow; the shabbier, the more characteristic it is. One of broad brim and lower crown often adorns the hirsute visage of the togated, upper-class coachman, who, but for his boots and head-gear, would exhibit a get-up resembling the liveries of the Presidency grandees of India. His state robe is encircled at the waist by a shawl or belt similar to theirs, and he is not wanting in the air of solemn vacancy so befitting the aristocratic "Gāriwāla." As for the females, I believe that the Muscovites themselves would acquit me of undue national prejudice in awarding the palm to a countrywoman of my own. Among those whom I saw in the town, my hostess was assuredly the belle. It will be contended that, as regards men and women, I am only speaking of those who show themselves abroad at the most unfashionable of seasons; consequently of the lower, and, in physical parlance, less-favoured classes. The observer's experience of the "upper ten thousand" would, clearly, give a very different result.

At the "Billet" *table d'hôte*, I made the acquaintance of a pleasant Dutch gentleman, who was to be accompanied on his travels, at least as far as Baku on the

Caspian, by a second gentleman from Riga. A third whom I also met might have been German or Italian. We conversed on Baghdad and on Muhammadan ruins; and a conviction clung to me that we had foregathered elsewhere, more than a thousand miles from Moscow, perhaps in India. Bidding farewell to my host and hostess I started at 5 P.M. on the 8th July for Nijni Novgorod, which place I reached by rail at about eight the next morning.

But a word on the journey. I was put into a good first-class carriage on the German and French system. Shortly after, a strange-looking old man of Jewish physiognomy, and with a long white beard, was brought in by a young man of the poorer class, who spread his bed and waited on him. They had between them a large amount of dirty, loose luggage, much of it in bundles. The old man lay mumbling, and I thought was an invalid; but a Russian officer sitting opposite me seemed to read my thoughts, and informed me he was drunk! Other passengers entered the carriage, and one of them, regarding the aged Enochonian as an intruder, protested against his retention, and obtained his removal—a measure achieved with some difficulty by the military and railway staff. Some conversation with the officer followed. He was an engineer of high standing, bound to Astrakhan, short, jovial, cigar-smoking, German by birth, and able to talk English and French tolerably. A clean-shaved, comfortable Russian, also in our carriage, spoke French with great fluency, and asked me many questions on India, and our ways and customs there; to all of which I replied with as much frankness and little diplomacy as I thought compatible with common sense. This same gentleman was most kind in aiding me at the railway station at Nijni Novgorod, where he procured a droschky, arranging with the driver to take me to Niquita's hostelry for 1 rouble and 25 kopecks (about four shillings English)—not a heavy charge for a very long drive, involving a ferry across the water. I must not forget the Orékhovskaia cotton-mills passed between Moscow and Vladimir, to which the attention of travellers, whose time is their own, might be turned with advantage. The place has a working and busy appearance.

Nijni Novgorod is situated on a high promontory marking the junction of the Oka and Volga, and on the right bank of either river. To reach the town, the traveller from St. Petersburg crosses the Oka, and its breadth at this point can be but little less than that of the better known stream in which its own identity becomes thenceforward absorbed. The quay, a comparatively modern construction, devised, according to M. de Custine, to remedy the mistake of the founders of Nijni in building a town upon, or rather behind, the high ground, was in the roughest of states when I was conducted along it. A rapid rush through Dublin, with unsteady luggage, in an outside car, to catch a train, would be a joke to the drive I then had with my poor wild droschky man. We had, both of us, to hold on by the portmanteaux at times, and once we might have rolled over the bank into the river without any difficulty. Before us was a restive team, aggravating the ordinary danger; but neither did the vehicle it drew or its passengers come to grief.

Niquita's was more of a cabaret or tavern than a hotel: but I got fairly treated there. Despite of greasy soup—a plate of capital fish with *sauce piquante*, a wild

duck, an ice, and a pint of Château Lafitte, made up a
satisfactory dinner; and though the sleeping-berth looked
rather queer, it was neither lively nor uncomfortable.
Some restless party in the room adjoining was heard as if
rolling about in bed, or constantly getting out of it and
in again; but I am not aware that we met face to face.
In the morning I was visited by an Italian, who offered
his services. Liking his looks, I gave him employment
for an hour or so as guide, in default of a more lasting
engagement. Early in the afternoon, I found myself on
board the Volga steamer. The remainder of the journey
to Tehran will perhaps be better described by extracts
from a rough diary; but reserving these for a separate
chapter, I venture upon a brief digression which it is
hoped will be found excusable in illustration of Russian
hospitality and courtesy to strangers. I have already
instanced one or more cases of travelling politeness, and
may have yet a stronger instance or so to place on record
in the course of the current narration. Opportunity is
now taken to bring forward a personal reminiscence of the
Crimean War, which, although once embodied in print,[1]
may not have been generally read or known. Such an
episode appears more appropriate to the present chapter
than the relation of any special experiences of Russia or
of Russian life and character acquired in recent years.
For of three passages through Russia, including two
visits to St. Petersburg and Moscow, effected since the
journey now described, I shall have occasion to make
some general use as the volume progresses.

It was about the middle of December 1855. We

[1] See a paper in *Colburn's United Service Magazine* for November and
December 1857 and January 1858, entitled "A Visit to the Tchernomorsky
Cossacks."

were at Kertch, in the Eastern Crimea, holding the town chiefly with a Turkish garrison. A few miles from us, at Yenikale, was her Majesty's 71st Regiment; at a less distance in the opposite direction was a detachment of our French allies:—

"Rumours of the enemy's presence in the neighbourhood became rife, and the report of a patrol having made its appearance a few miles to the southward was ere long verified by the French Chasseurs, who discovered a body of supposed Russian hussars at the village of Shorabash, distant about fifteen versts, or twelve miles, south-west, from our head-quarters. No harm was done beyond the exchange of a few shots, the respective parties keeping at a respectable distance from each other. This naturally put everyone on the *qui vive*, especially as we had at this time just sent out more than a hundred Turkish cavalry with a hundred infantry, to cover foragers at a place called the 'Spanish Farm,' situated six miles west of Kertch. The said farm contained a large supply of hay, which, after coquetting about for some days, we at length found necessary to appropriate on certain war terms made with the owner (Spanish consul at Odessa), through his Crimean agent. *A la guerre comme à la guerre*: it was not of the best description for our purpose, but would prove at all events useful during the existing and impending scarcity. Owing to the apparition at Shorabash, which is little more than six miles south of the farm, the detachment was further strengthened by 200 infantry. Though the enemy were not visible in any strength to the videttes, intelligence was brought to the officer commanding at the farm, that the Russians were combining troops preparatory to some forward movement; and names of places were mentioned where the men were collecting. Our *chef-de-police* told a different story, but it was resolved to keep on the alert, on the principle of never slumbering at our posts before the enemy.

"On Sunday the 16th December (the Cossacks were partial to disturbing us on Sundays), a Tartar came in and reported that our cavalry had at length met the foe in earnest. His tale was a confused one—he was panting and frightened. All the particulars that could be gathered were that a party of Turkish horsemen had left the farm in the morning to reconnoitre, and had fallen in, at some distance off, with a large body of Cossacks, with whom they were, at the time he left, hotly engaged. The Tartars, he said, had fought valiantly in support of their Turkish brethren. He and a comrade had been sent to give notice of what had happened. His comrade's horse had fallen on the way, and he had returned alone. On that same evening more than one of us rode out to the detachment and learned the particulars from the gallant officer who had commanded the handful of cavalry in question, and of whom nearly half were still missing. They had gone out to reconnoitre, had successfully skirmished with a body of Cossacks whom they had encountered on the way, and were eventually overpowered by a vastly superior number who had been concentrated in the vicinity; and some two score, under the commandant, had cut their way through the ranks of their opponents, effecting an orderly retirement to the farm. The British leader had been slightly wounded in the neck, but his belt bore the mark of more than one lance-thrust. His brave young subaltern had been severely wounded, and was in the hands of the enemy. A Turkish Yusbashi (or captain) had been killed on the field. Beyond a certain number of missing, little else of actual loss was known. Several of the enemy were reported killed and wounded.

"The day following it was arranged that a flag of truce should be sent to the enemy's camp, in order that the number of killed, wounded, and prisoners on our side should be correctly ascertained. It was my fortune to be named for this duty. In the afternoon I set out for the Spanish farm, and joined the officers of the detachment at mess, as my instructions were to start from thence in the morning.

"The four companions with whom I shared the sleeping-apartment that night will acquit me of indulging in a mere *façon de parler* in talking of the rats and mice, or both, by fifties or hundreds. Over the body, in at the boots, into pockets of pantaloons and pantaloons themselves, in the hair of the head,—skipping, singing, screeching—scarce are the lights put out, than these inmates of the Spanish farm seek all the nooks of sleeping humanity within reach, and treat their possessors with no more respect than if they were cheese or candles. In vain is the stick at work—in vain are the arms and legs set in active motion—in vain does one holloa with stentorian power: they will no more 'move on' than the street-singer or organ-grinder, except to return at the shortest notice. The dawn of day was grateful. I jumped up, hastily added such few essential articles of equipment as were not already on, and proceeded to muster my retinue. We were twelve in all, viz.:— six Turkish troopers, a French servant of the wounded officer, my own Arab groom, a Tartar guide, a young German who spoke Russian, an Assistant-Surgeon of the force, and myself. A spare pony accompanied to bring up stray baggage, and in case of need.

"It was a cold, frosty morning. I allowed my escort swords and pistols only as weapons, and one lance to carry the flag of truce. The Turk does not sling his carbine on the back, the more convenient and soldierly method for long marches. A Cossack was observed on one of the small hills overlooking the farm. He appeared to be watching our movements, but did not wait the approach of the Turkish day vidette, whose usual post he was occupying.

"We started at about 8.30 A.M., at a slow pace, taking the path below, and following the hills which incline W. and S.W. After proceeding for about a mile or more, we turned to the higher ground near a ruined village, and struck off in a due southerly direction towards the plain country, to meet the post-road from Kertch to Kaffa. This was in accordance with the orders given, but contrary to the suggestions of the guide, who wished me to adopt a more direct route to Akkoz, or Sultan Ovka, the fifteen-mile posthouse. As it was, we did not reach this point for three or four hours. Here we watered our horses, and questioned some Tartar horsemen on the probability of falling in with the Cossacks up the high road. They were not so communicative as might have been wished, but we determined to push on and take our chance. It must have been at about one in the afternoon that we first sighted the enemy's outposts. There was a long embankment from the high ground on either side the road, running at right angles to the road itself, where it crossed, and left a clear space for traffic and travellers. This embankment, about the height of a tall man, resembled an ordinary Indian 'band,' defining a canal, tank, or field; and more than one of the same character, and of considerable antiquity, might be traced in the environs of Kertch. It seemed to imply territorial division, and may have been used in ancient times for defensive purposes. On the hillock to the right, I observed a cluster of horsemen which I conjectured might be a cavalry picket. Some two or three descended to the level ground on the inner side of the embankment, and hastily crossed the road. There was a long, low, level ridge to the left, parallel to the road. Upon this it struck me that there might be a chain of posts, for one man started off apparently to communicate with some party or parties in the interior, and on the same line. I proceeded slowly to the passage between the two embankments, where I halted. It seemed as though we had arrived at the acknowledged boundary, and that this was the proper place for parley; but no herald appeared, and so we passed through. The horsemen became now more scattered, and crossed or approached the road one at a time, or by twos or threes, but all at a respectful distance, quite out of hail. On the inner side of the embankment was a ditch sufficiently broad and deep to shelter cavalry, who would be able to raise themselves in the stirrup and fire over the earthy parapet at an advancing foe.

"It was evident that we were among the Cossacks, and had not only reached, but passed one of their outposts. That they saw us there could be no doubt. We were especially conspicuous in our varied costumes. Save the six *sowars* (Turkish cavalry), no two but were almost wholly unlike, while none could be said to wear the actual dress of his country. For instance, the poor Frenchman was made up in the shreds and patches of a reckless Levantine; the Arab's garments were as much Frank as Turkish, but had nothing of Syria, Egypt, or Mecca; the interpreter had something the appearance of the foreign Ambassador in the 'Horse of the Cavern' at Astley's; the Tartar would have been orthodox had we not taken him into British clothing as well as pay; the doctor wore his 'Contingent' uniform, which is saying enough for its singularity; and I myself, in addition to uniform, had a French capote and high fur boots, which would have been remarkable under any circumstances. We were moreover doubly conspicuous from our position in an open road, the only objects there discernible.

"We may have gone on about a furlong when I pulled up again. There were two Cossacks to our right front whose attention I determined to attract if possible. Accordingly, halting the party in the road, I took the flag-bearer and interpreter with me and gave chase across country. The horsemen crossed me and made for the road. Thither, with a corresponding movement, I returned, inclining towards the point which they themselves seemed bent upon reaching. Perseverance gained the desired end. On coming to the road they paused in their course and watched us. I held out signals of parley, response was made, and we were motioned to advance. In another five minutes we were on the most friendly terms with our new acquaintance; in ten, our whole party were moving together, under their escort, towards the village where we were to await a reply to the request made in the letters of which I was bearer.

"The principal spokesman was a tall, stalwart man, under the middle age, with a pleasing expression of countenance. He entered into earnest conversation with the interpreter on the subject of the recent skirmish, asked many questions regarding the Turks and ourselves, and replied to the numerous interrogatories put to him on our side. Chiefly was I desirous to ascertain the fate of the British officer and the surviving prisoners. They were all at Arginn, the second post-station, about thirty miles from Kertch, and, from what we could gather, doing well. Three troopers had died of their wounds.

"These were the Tcherna-Morsky, or Black Sea Cossacks. They wore the long grey coat and trousers, with red facings and shoulder cords, the latter showing the number of the regiment as well as the button. The cap was red at the skull, bordered with deep fur, not unlike the 'kalpak' in use with the Tartars. Indeed, in the distance it is difficult to distinguish the mounted Tartar from the mounted Cossack, owing to the similarity of head-gear. The belt contains pistols and knives, and the firelock is slung across the back. The officer's curved sword has no guard at the hilt. The horses are sturdy, but small, and the rude high saddles are as primitive as oriental. As we proceeded onward, our party was every now and then strengthened by a stray cavalier. The new arrivals were inquisitive, but never impertinent. One of our Turks was recognized as having taken a part in the affair of the 16th. This circumstance showed us that our escort had been recently our immediate and actual enemy.

"After a desultory ride of some six or seven miles, never forsaking the highway, we arrived at the Tartar village of 'Karmitch xelitchi' (the Russian orthography). Like most Tartar villages of any pretensions, it had one or two buildings of a better order, but the greater part of the habitations were little better than huts of boso, irregular stone walls, and substantial rooms. On the right, and immediately behind the houses, were two abrupt hillocks, between which was a narrow pass. The Frenchman called my attention to a number of Cossacks discernible, as he said, through this opening. 'Regardez-y un peu, Monsieur; on les voit bien là derrière.' There might have been an army there to garrison

<blockquote>
'the glen
At once with full five hundred men.'
</blockquote>

but I doubted the fact. It would have been a bleak encampment, and with no conceivable object.

"We were told to dismount, and that an answer would soon

arrive from Arginn regarding our further progress. A heavy snowstorm was threatening, and we were glad to get shelter for our cattle as well as ourselves. In about half an hour, or between three and four P.M., a cavalcade was seen approaching. At their head rode a lieutenant-colonel of the 2nd regiment of Tcherna-Morskys, dressed much in the same way as his men, the cartridges arranged *à la Circassienne*, that is, obliquely across his breast, on either side, not unlike a double set of Pandean pipes. With him was a medical officer in a dark blue uniform, with the usual long Russian uniform coat and stiff forage-cap, the only relief to which was a narrow red binding. They both received us with kindness and civility; but it was evident that we were to go no further until 'further orders.' This, to say the least, was somewhat disheartening, for the prisoners were only five miles off, if indeed so much; and the accounts of my poor friend, the officer, were anything but satisfactory.

"We were taken to a small Tartar lodging. Entering at a kind of kitchen or wash-house, from thence we passed into a side room on the left hand. This contained a plain sofa, about eight feet in length, a table, a few chairs or stools, and a sort of 'buffet,' and was evidently the reception-room of strangers. Here we all sat down and proceeded to business. I delivered my letters in due form, one for the commandant of the outposts (opened by the lieutenant-colonel himself), one for the general commanding the Russian troops in the Eastern Crimea. Both documents set forth the object of my visit, namely, to learn the fate of the missing officer and men, and their wants, if any, which could be supplied by us: a medical officer had accompanied the flag of truce, in case his services should be available for the wounded. I added my own request for permission to proceed to Arginn, as I was so close at hand, to be the better able to make a satisfactory reply to my superiors. The lieutenant-colonel protested that, for his part, he had not the power to let me continue my route so far, but informed me that if I would wait until the following morning, he would doubtless be enabled not only to obtain an answer to the letter for his general, but also a definite permission or refusal to proceed myself to Argun. Though not instructed to remain for a reply to the letter in question, it seemed that my own request involved the success of so material a part of my mission, that I could not well do otherwise than await its result. The evening was too far advanced to admit of my taking back at once the whole party, weary and hungry withal, from a long ride, with unrefreshed cattle, and through a snowstorm. I should not omit to mention that, as regards accepting any extraneous medical aid for the wounded, it seemed a point of honour not to entertain the notion.

"After the lieutenant-colonel had completed and forwarded his despatches, he insisted on undertaking the duties of host. He had taken particular account of the number of my horses and followers, and given orders for their subsistence; and he now wished to do the honours of hospitality to the inmates of the Tartar domicile. We were three strangers: the interpreter, the assistant-surgeon, and myself. The two last sat on the long sofa, the first on a seat facing it; a low table, somewhat larger than a garden stool and less than an Indian 'teapoy,' being placed between us. It just contained the dish of the course, and the bottle for general circulation. I speak in the singular number, for we all ate and drank in common; that is, soup out of the same bowl, meats or sweets out of the same dish, and wine or spirits out of the same glass. Our host and the Russian doctor occupied places close beside us, but excused themselves from joining in the repast, as they had either already dined or were to dine at Argun. The latter spoke very good French and we managed to get on famously. The worthy Cossack could barely recall a few words in that tongue; but his good-looking rotund face, burly person, and merry twinkling eye, told me that we only required a common language to be on equally excellent terms. They left us at an early hour, promising to supply the required intelligence in the morning, and with many apologies for the poorness of our accommodation.

"It is to be feared that, in spite of Cossack civility, an absurd idea of comfort caused me to congratulate myself on having the room for the rest of the night to our three selves. If indeed so

I must have experienced a little disappointment on finding a new character appear on the scene in the person of a lieutenant of the 2nd Tcherna Morskys. This was to be our permanent host, and he introduced himself accordingly, through the medium of our interpreter. Tall, upright, cropped, clean-shaved, save in the moustache, dressed in the plain uniform of his regiment, he was the true impersonation of the Russian subaltern of Cossacks. The face was that of the bronzed campaigner; he need scarcely have told us that his better years had been passed in Circassian warfare. He breathed of the Caucasus, of Crimean and Circassian outposts. But he was withal a jovial, well-meaning soul, and played the part of entertainer with the most military exactitude. 'He was not of the noblesse,' he took care to inform us; 'nothing but a plain, blunt soldier, fond of his glass and his meal. Though accustomed to night-work out of doors, he had no objections to a pipe and a fire within; and he was rather thankful to us than otherwise that our presence had procured him the exchange of a comfortable seat by a stove for the back of a horse in the snow. But he feared we should find him an unpolished host, in spite of the best and most hospitable intentions.'

"Notwithstanding pressing requisitions to eat and drink up to any amount, we turned in at an early hour. My companion, the assistant-surgeon (who took greatly with the Cossacks), and I shared the long sofa, each claiming an end, and inclining our legs right or left at the place of meeting, according to circumstances. The lieutenant and interpreter made up comfortable enough beds on the ground; two or three Cossacks and the Tartar owners of the house filled up the blank spaces. We must have held as many as any respectable 'licence to contain' would admit of, on such state occasions.

"I slept much better that night than on the previous one at the farm. There were no rats to disturb one; and the day's work had made us all tolerably sleepy. In the morning the one small window was opened, and we performed our respective ablutions. There was but one basin, brought first to mine host, by way of example, it is supposed, to the guests. Holding his hands over it, palm upward, while an attendant Cossack poured water into them, he bathed his face and neck with great gusto; and I was not long in imitating his proceedings. After this, could I refuse the proffered comb, with a valet supporting the looking-glass, as he had done the basin? These arrangements completed, there was little else than to buckle on a stock, pull on a pair of boots, and imbibe a morning glass of *raki*, to make us ready for breakfast.

"After the morning's meal, I began to grow impatient for the arrival of a messenger from Arginn. My Cossack friend of the day previous was to return himself; but this step would almost appear needless were I allowed to continue my route at once. Towards midday, intelligence arrived that an officer of rank (a prince) was on his way to visit me, and would bear the general's instructions for my after guidance. It was contrary to my intention to lose time thus, but there now appeared to be no remedy; for, had I returned to Kertch, I had no list of prisoners, and no actual knowledge of their condition or wants, to take back with me, whereas a half-hour would bring me to the spot where all were now stationed. I could then ascertain from my brother officer's own lips what were his wishes and requirements; and they might allow me a few minutes' conversation to the same effect with the Turkish troopers. I resolved, therefore, to await the arrangements of the delegate from Kaffa. The lieutenant redoubled his attentions, and did all he could to kill my time in the manner most agreeable to myself. In some way or other—what with a little talk in one's own language between the assistant-surgeon and myself (the only two Englishmen of the party); interpreted dialogues with our host; an unlimited supply of tea and other creature comforts (so frequent as to endanger the truth of their appellation)—the day *did* pass until a French note reached me from the Russian doctor, begging me not to wait dinner for the lieutenant-colonel, who was detained at Arginn owing to the non-receipt of a reply to his communication on my behalf. He did not mention his wounded British patient. I could only hope that he was no worse.

"Daylight was excluded, and our shutters were closed at an

early hour. We dined, as we had breakfasted, four at the small table, and on the principle of community acknowledged on the former occasion. But there was a visible improvement in the fare. The cutlets showed signs of culinary skill, and there was a cold confection of cream, tempting as a Nesselrode or an English ice-pudding. The Crimean wine of which we partook was palatable, and a by no means unpleasant change from indifferent sherry. It should be noted that, notwithstanding frequent libations of *raki*, or spirit, tea (without milk) is in very general request among the Russians. In the present case, the usual spacious urn smoked on the side-table from morning till night, and was in constant requisition. We drank the refreshing beverage in tumblers. It was too sweet to suit my taste; but being in Rome one must do as the Romans. I used to drink it with my good friends the Chinese, without sugar or milk at all, during the campaign against the Celestial Empire.

"Night fairly set in, and no lieutenant-colonel or prince appeared. The worthy host seemed at a loss how to amuse us and while away our time. He had insisted on our unbuttoning our coats, and had made his Cossack pull off our boots. He had given us meat and drink and tobacco to the top of our bent; yet we continued to smoke our meerschaums or clays, and he his 'trapca,' in silent expectation of an arrival. An idea seemed to strike him. Would we object to singing? By no means. So the concert began.

"A young sergeant was introduced, and sat down in a further corner of the room. The lieutenant took pains to inform us that he was of gentle blood, as though in explanation of his admitting the social companionship of a *sous-officier*. There was something very prepossessing in this man's appearance. Tall, handsome, and of commanding figure, there was a simple modesty in his demeanour which could not fail to carry its own recommendation to the stranger. This was especially remarkable in the short account which he rendered of his own share in the late skirmish.

"The Tartar landlord was another of the audience. He was an old man with well-defined features, partaking little of the

Kalmuck or Mongol contour; and his dress was of better material than usually worn by his fellow-countrymen at Kertch. 'Murad' was a constant butt for the lieutenant, who joked him on his wealth and his wife, how he buried one and shut up the other; and Murad wisely returned good for evil by snuffing the candles and performing sundry ministering offices for the society at large. I was inclined to believe the wealth and wife both fictitious, but there seems to be truth in the story; and, from what I since heard, Murad has perhaps little reason to complain of his Russian masters after all. I had already ingratiated myself in the day-time with the old man, by reading to him the first chapter (Fátiha) of an Arabic Koran, discovered upon a shelf in his house. So remarkably clear was the type, and so well got up the whole volume, that I made a point of securing one from the same press, on my return to Kertch. It is a credit to the printing establishment of the distinguished city of Kazan, and might be imitated with advantage in Egypt and India.

"The singers were three in number, and favoured us with some pleasing national airs, much in the style of glees. One of the three was a mimic, and partly a ventriloquist, and amused the audience by his imitations of old women, children, and cats. We came gradually to a 'health' song; that is, as each one of the party drank, separately in the one glass, to his neighbour's health (using the words '*kazaska snarova*'), the singers broke out into a brief accompaniment in support of the toast. On seeing that this performance had been received with approbation, the lieutenant proposed, through the interpreter, that we should drink the health of her Majesty Queen Victoria. What loyal subject could refuse the invitation? The proposal was met with enthusiasm, and while each raised the glass and drained its contents, the Cossack voices rose as before in melodious strain, to do the toast honour.

"It was growing late. Suddenly a noise was heard outside, and visitors were announced. I hastily buttoned up my uniform coat, and pulled on my boots. Scarcely had I done so when the door opened, and an officer, in a green-and-gold hussar uniform, appeared, in company with the lieutenant-colonel of

Cossacks. He came up and addressed me in English. There were no objections to my proposed visit; but, alas! it would now be of no avail. The British officer had died, that very afternoon, of his wounds, and the Turkish prisoners had been removed. The latter had been indeed met with by my informant on his way from Kaffa to Argiun! This was a melancholy piece of intelligence; and any further delay on my part would now appear useless. But an inclination to avail myself of the permission accorded, to proceed as far as Argiun, got the better of all other considerations. It was so close at hand, and the visit there would render my mission so much the more complete. I should, at least, see my poor friend's body. I put the matter in this light to the Prince. He acquiesced without a moment's hesitation; and his carriage was ordered to be in readiness to receive us.

"The ground was one vast sheet of snow, and the cold outside was intense. I jumped into the conveyance—a kind of single-bodied chariot, drawn by six horses, two and two abreast—and was placed between the Prince and the lieutenant-colonel. We moved along at a brisk pace, and were not so much jolted as might have been expected. After having accomplished about a couple of miles, or more, of our journey, a white handkerchief was handed to me, with a request that I would bandage my eyes. This I did; though, from the front leathers of the carriage being strapped down, I could see nothing, before this, save one or two faint snowy lines. Two miles more brought us to our destination.

"I descended from the carriage, led by the hand like a blind man. After proceeding one or two paces in what I imagined to be the entrance of a house, I heard a voice chanting. This grew louder and more distinct as I advanced. When they told me to take off the bandage it was to realise just what I had pictured. I stood by the bedside of the dead young soldier, and the voice that I had heard was that of one chanting a requiem. The chanter was a Cossack. He stood in the corner of a large, low room, an open book and a candle on a table before him. He was officiating, it was stated, in the temporary absence of the priest, who had probably retired to rest. The corpse was arrayed in the whitest of linen. The handsome face wore a placid and serene expression. A bandage on the arm showed the mark of a sword-cut. The death wound was not outwardly visible: it had been caused by a ball which, after grazing the hip, had lodged in and been extracted from the body. I had now received ocular demonstration, had such been required, that all due attention had been paid to the dead, and I felt an inward conviction that the same care had been shown to the living.

"I stayed in a side room in conversation with the Prince for about a quarter or half an hour, while the Russian doctor whom I now again saw, wrote for me the names of the surviving Turkish prisoners. I then rose to bid the two farewell. My eyes were again bandaged, and I was led back into the carriage, this time to be accompanied by an officer with whose rank I was unacquainted. The Prince shook hands with me warmly when seated, apologizing for not returning himself. He could not at first find my hand, nor could I, blindfolded, see that he was leaning over into the vehicle, offering his; but his *Dozsvidanié eietse razne* enabled me to respond to the appeal. What strange anomalies in war!

"It must have been long after midnight when I turned in to the quarters allotted me in at the Tartar village. The assistant-surgeon was fast asleep at his end, and the Cossacks and Tartars looked happy enough in their respective nooks. Giving notice of an early start, I willingly accepted such sleep as could be invoked at a short notice.

"After sunrise... the lieutenant insisted on giving us breakfast and riding with us to the entrenchment. Healths were exchanged again and again in the never-failing *raki*. We pushed on at a smart pace, for it was bitter cold, and we had about twenty-six miles of snow-covered ground before us. On reaching the outpost there was an interval of dismounting and embracing to be performed, not, however, of any long duration. The shabby whip which I obtained from my worthy host as a parting token, though it excites little admiration among friends at home, has to me a value more than meets the eye.

ASTRAKHAN FISH TOI-CART.

CHAPTER X.

LONDON TO KARACHI.—THE ROUTE CONTINUED FROM NIJNI NOVGOROD BY THE VOLGA TO ASTRAKHAN, AND THENCE, BY THE CASPIAN, TO TEHRAN.

THOSE who have visited Nijni in later years may think that before taking leave of the place I should have said a word in favour of a more known establishment than Niquita's, the great resort in fair time, Soboloff's Hotel. Well : I certainly became acquainted with such a refuge in September 1870, and was one of those who put up there on that occasion in the small dressing-room of a steamy bath-room, owing to the prior occupation by more fortunate travellers of the usual sleeping apartments. To say that we were driven, for the one night of our sojourn at Sokoloff's, to pass time at the Nijni theatre in witnessing Offenbach's "Orfée," so disfigured as to be barely recognizable in the abstract, is no testimony to the comforts of our home; but we can vouch that the hotel was inhabited by as many as it could hold, and should therefore be popular, or at least a recognized institution. Now to take up the diary of 1865:—

"*July* 9.—I have a snug cabin in which to sit and write, but the boat is a small one. The saloon is comfortable, and a *restaurateur* on board caters for the wants of the passengers. Meet a former travelling companion, a Russian officer, going to Tiflis *viâ* Astrakhan and Petrovsk. The rest of the first-class diners are a stout person, said to be travelling for amusement, and of well-to-do appearance; a well-shaved man, who introduces himself to me as an inspector of schools; and a third who looks much more like the ordinary Englishman than an inhabitant of this overgrown country. We have also a lady passenger, and there are both male and female in the second class. The Volga scenery is not unlike that of the Lower Danube, though its villages are now and then sufficiently pretty to remind one of Stenia or other nooks of the Bosphorus. I see nothing to warrant a comparison with the Rhine, which one or two of my fellow-travellers put forward. The dwellings are chiefly wooden cottages in long rows, or partly detached and scattered, with an occasional brick and mortar building. The churches or convents, with globular steeples or tower tops, each one surmounted by a cross, and coloured blue, or gilt, or silvered, are conspicuous and familiar objects. The right bank is high, and has, I think, the greater number of dwelling-places. The left is low, and resembles the crumbling banks of the Indus. Population is scant. A rose, or brick-coloured shirt, worn outside the blouse, is in common use with the men, and is usually accompanied with cap and boots—sometimes the flower-pot hat instead of the cap. Long, white, straight hair is also a frequent appendage to the headgear. We leave Nijni at 3, and touch at Isádd at 8 P.M.

"*July* 10.—Passing Vasal Silska at 3 A.M., Kosara Damaiska at 8, Cheboksa at 10, and Sandéri at noon, we reached Kazan at about 4 in the afternoon. The hospitality and friendliness of Russians to strangers is remarkably shown in the manner in which my fellow-passengers by steamer ply me with good wine at dinner, and drink my health and success in the Persian expedition. We are six at table, inclusive of a lady of agreeable address and mien. I would wish to join the general conversation, instead of confining myself to the French *entr'actes*, but my Slavonic is at fault. We have a grand leave-taking after dinner; for all but M. de P., the Russian officer, and I, are to *remain* at Kazan, where the lady has a daughter at school. There is a delay here of several hours, so I join De P. in a droschky, and we drive up to the town, a distance of about five miles from the landing-place.

"The Marquis de Custines was prevented by ill-health from prolonging his tour eastward to Kazan, and consoled himself by looking at drawings of the town shown to him by the Governor of Nijni Novgorod. There is much truth in his remark: 'C'est toujours la même ville d'un bout de la Russie à l'autre: la caserne, les cathédrales en manière de temples, rien n'y manquait; je sentais que tout ce rabâchage d'architecture ne valait guère la peine d'allonger mon voyage de deux cents lieues.' But I certainly had thought otherwise of Kazan, judging that if exceptions to 'rabâchage' be allowed, it should be in favour of that town. I was somewhat disappointed in the solution of the question. Upon the whole, Kazan *is* a Russian-looking town, with little genuine Tartarism. It has its Kremlin, its wide, straight streets, up and down hill, bad pavement and so forth. The approach to it, by a river suburb and wretchedly made road, rather sets it off as a picture. We pass on our left a pyramidical tomb, marking a burial-place of Russians killed some centuries back in a fight with the Tartars. There is a Tartar and Chinese look about some of the people, but the Russian element is gaining ground. Kazan has probably from 40,000 to 50,000 inhabitants. We strolled in its gardens, prettily arranged along a shabby and little watered canal, and went into one or two of its shops, which make a respectable outward show. Purchased a small box of tea for three roubles; and drank tea, moreover at a restaurant, where a long, covered table gave note of a *table d'hôte*; but the dirty yard, almost on a level with the window sills, was enough to destroy the appetite of the diner. Visited the printing office, a place of considerable attraction to me since buying a Koran printed there from a Tartar in the Crimea, shortly before close of the campaign in 1855-56.[1] Here I found the whole establishment Russian, though Tartar workmen are employed in setting up the Arabic and Turkish types. What would have been said of the Honourable East India Company had they printed and sold the Koran to the money profit of the State? The type is excellent, and the carefully punctuated volume would supply an infinite number of valuable reading lessons to the Arabic student: but what Propaganda would sanction the principle involved in the result? One Tartar publication was called the 'Alti Permak' or 'six fingers.'

"*July* 11.—Our passengers from Kazan this morning included the renowned General T. and the Civil Governor of Simbirsk. The first is a little above the middle height, rather stout in build, of swarthy brown complexion, with grey hair and moustache, probably under 50 years of age. The expression of face is good, not stern, and the features are somewhat irregular. His appearance is that of a thorough soldier, and his uniform is a part of himself. He addressed me in French, and we talked on various subjects, among others his visit to England last November. The great increase of traffic on the Volga during the last twenty years, which he pointed out to me, was quite borne out by the statement of Mr. M., a Director of the Volga Company, in one of whose steamers we were then moving. I had seen Mr. M. and his partner, Mr. G., at Nijni, and the latter had kindly given me letters for Astrakhan. Mr. M.

---

[1] See page 562, *ante*.

is a fellow-passenger, and proceeds to Saratoff on a tour of inspection. He appears to be just the man for his position, speaks Russian, French and German with fluency, and has full information on all matters connected with his work. There are, I believe, four English Directors in the Volga Company, and only one Russian Director; but it is not the only company owning passenger steamers on the river. Its two principal rivals are the Samalot, and Caucas and Metcūr. It was, however, the first in the field, and had two tugs afloat twenty years ago. One boat, the *Czarina*, had been brought out by Mr. M. from England. He had steamed in her to St. Petersburg, taken her to pieces for canal conveyance, and towed her to the Volga, where she was again put together. Our saloons are about 24 feet by 14, and have twelve berths in four divisions of three berths each. There is also an upper saloon, small, but airy. I have a private cabin, and next me is the ladies' saloon, or 'Dámeskáya.' There is a second class; and on deck is the captain's cabin, 'Capitanskáya.' Our captain is a Courlander, or German Russian, and was taken prisoner by the English in a merchant ship during the late war. A year in London made him proficient in the language. They say there are 400 steamers on the river; that as much as 500,000 'pouds' weight (nearly 8,000 tons) may be towed up in barges; and that the Volga Company's boats can tow two-fifths of that amount. From ocular demonstration at this season, I should not demur to these statistics. The governor of Simbirsk, Mr. B., is, I understand, of German extraction. Like many Russians, especially German Russians, he is almost English in dress and manner. He leaves us at Simbirsk, a large town of about 23,000 inhabitants, on arrival in the evening. This place was nearly burnt down in August last.

"*July* 12.—Reach Samara before mid-day. This is a rising town, marking a point of the Volga where the river, having run its extreme course eastward, and approached nearest to Orenburg, turns sharply to the west. Its government is quite of recent institution, having only been added to the nine divisions of Eastern Russia in 1860. Among the projects about to be put in execution, or the execution of which has already been commenced, by the progressive spirit of the age, influencing Russia as other great countries of Europe, is that of a railway from Moscow to Saratoff. I learn that it is either finished, or nearly finished up to Riazan; but that want of funds will stop it for a time at that place.[1] The *Grande Société des Chemins de Fer*, whose are the Warsaw, and Moscow to Nijni lines, was to have undertaken the work, and the Odessa lines also; but it has been supplanted. Rumour is rife of excessive demands on the part of some railway contractors; yet rumour may be wrong, and there may be no foundation for supposing that in this case the various and continuously-proffered claims took at one time the shape of a needless luxury, such as 'gloves for coachmen.' My own impression is that a line from Moscow to Saratoff would be well chosen, as would also be one from Nijni to Simbirsk, or from Simbirsk to Sizran, independently of the river. A glance at the map explains at once the object of these connections. All the large Russian towns on the banks of the Volga seem built upon the same principle. They have long, wide streets parallel with the river and quay, and other long, wide streets at right angles. Here and there is a market-place. A great many churches, with dome or tower, relieve the monotony of the low white houses. There is either no pavement at all, or the irregular stones irregularly put together present a state of things worse than the plain earth itself. The next town of importance to Samarra, on the left bank, is Sizran on the right bank of the river, which we reach in the evening. It is said to contain 12,000 inhabitants. At about 11 P.M., or a little earlier, we were at Khvalin or Khvalinsk, also on the right bank, with a reputed population of some 12,500. Here a party of us took a night stroll through the dreary sandy streets; but notwithstanding the thirst for adventure which influenced one or two of my companions, we returned to our boat without an incident worthy of record.

---

[1] Since the period of my visit, the said railway—at first prolonged from Riazan to Voronesch, as though in abandonment of the Moscow-Saratoff project—has been completed. In 1874, the proposal is to extend the line from Saratoff to Termez on the Oxus, Indiaward. Such is progress in Russia!

"*July* 13.—Lieutenant-Colonel T. of the Engineers, is a cheery Russian officer whose acquaintance I have made on board the Volga steamer. He served against us in the Crimean campaign, but is on that account none the less friendly and well disposed. Passed Volsk in the morning, and reach Saratoff about mid-day. The first is said to have some 23,500 inhabitants, the second must boast at least 35,000. Here we stayed till 5 P.M.; spending most of our time on shore. Dined at the Voxall, after an excursion to the gardens, three miles away, amid excessive heat and dust. The restaurant overlooked the Volga, and was close by the landing-place of the steamers. Our fare was varied, if not gastronomically harmonious. We had soup, fish, fowl, cutlets, raspberries and cream, and beer. The soups have hard names, but they are good, especially those with vegetables. I cannot share the general admiration for the smaller kind of sturgeon, called 'sterlet,' so celebrated on the Volga. The word 'borch' may be found useful in ordering a pleasant soup; and 'kwás' is a remarkably nice drink, not unlike cider, but professedly obtained from barley. I recommend both monosyllables to the attention of young travellers in Russia. Close to where we sat, three ladies of vocal powers and evident local celebrity were singing to an orchestral accompaniment. One, a quiet, pensive-looking girl, spoke German to a young Courlander of our party, whose father, a respectable and well-known Lutheran pastor, was also passenger in the *Czarina*. Had he been present, I doubt whether he would have encouraged the conversation, which, however, was soon interrupted. The old gentleman is doing tourist as well as engaged on a pastoral visit. I am told that this day (the 1st of June by Russian computation) is the hundredth anniversary of the foundation of the German colony of Ekaterinestadt, which we passed this morning on the left bank of the Volga, and that these colonies of Catherine II. extend along the river from above the latter place to Sarepta, which we do not reach until late in the day to-morrow. They are said to furnish an agricultural population to the Steppes, a tract commencing on the left bank of the Volga at Samara, touching the Caspian southward, and extending on the east far beyond the Oural river. Weather intensely hot, and not improving as we descend the river. At night we touch at Kamutchin, a large village on the high ground, right bank. By the aid of a misty moon on the wane, and a fine array of stars, some of us who venture on shore climb the rough ascent, and find ourselves on the road to the huts and

KAIMUCK OF THE STEPPES NEAR ASTRAKHAN.

houses. One or two of my more volatile companions insist on entering a *cabaret*, where a man is playing the old and universally-known 'Lancers,' on a barrel-organ. De P. takes the handle of a second instrument, and performs also, while the waiter lights a candle for his guests. Notwithstanding the musical inducements, we resume our walk towards the open country. Soon we are saluted with the cries and howls of dogs, which are pronounced significant of wolves in the neighbourhood. The hour and evident desolation are not favourable to prolonged ambulation. We stroll back to the boat, just as a second steamer arrives. It is from Astrakhan, and I have some talk with a Persian passenger on board.

"*July* 14.—Late hours at night cause late rising in the morning. Did not leave my cabin till the day had grown old and hot. Arrive at about 3.30 P.M., at Czaritzin, a tolerably large town on the right bank, which Jonas Hanway puts down as 688 miles distant from Moscow. Young R. asked me to come on shore, and so I did, for we had proposed to ourselves an excursion to the spot where are exhibited the hat and walking-stick of Peter the Great. Not succeeding in finding a droschky, we took to a cart, covered over with a bit of felt or blanket, and evidently designed for the transport of goods. Just, however, as we were starting, my companion remembered that a train was to leave that same afternoon for Chirskaya, or that part of the Don to which the Czaritzin Railway proceeds, and he and his father, the pastor, as also the engineer colonel, were to avail themselves of it. Consequently, it was important to certify the time at his disposal. He would make inquiries at the station close at hand. We jumped off, not *out* of our conveyance, and entered the house. Here also was a restaurant. What was my surprise to find seated in the public room, at a table, discussing red wine, cigars, and something perhaps more substantial, some acquaintances whom I had met a few months before at Constantinople, and with whom I should have proceeded thence to Tiflis, but for Colonel Stewart's sad and fatal illness. After a few words of cordial greeting, Lord C. H. and Mr. E. determined to join the search for the imperial hat and stick, and accompany us on the primitive vehicle we had engaged. Off we go, four on a cart, and rattle along at fair speed till our progress is arrested by a river, apparently an inlet of the Volga. Failing to catch the ferry-boat, we secure a rowing-boat, and effect the crossing; but alas, when on the other side, the distance to the supposed relics was too great to attempt the full excursion, so we returned, balked of purpose, to the steamer. Introduced my companions to the Russian colonel, and the day was most inviting for a parting cup at separation. Move into Sarepta, where the pastor, his son, and Colonel P. leave us, the last embracing me in the fashion of his country, and I becoming a Russian for the nonce. Young E., though intelligent and agreeable, has imbibed certain material notions strangely dissonant with his father's profession. Much as these results of modern education are to be regretted, I do not consider them evidences of any more serious internal conviction than the propriety of donning, morally or physically, the gown of some particular college of thought adventitious to the student. Sarepta is a clean and cheery-looking German colony, taking its name probably from the city of Sidon, so called in the fourth chapter of St. Luke—the 'Zarephath' of the Old Testament.[1]

"*July* 15.—This morning I can say with Clarence, 'Oh! I have passed a miserable night.' Fresh arrivals among the passengers had created excitement on board the steamer; but the life and excitement was not confined to mere humanity. Something on the velvet cushions of my own particular cabin had alarmed me yesterday before nightfall, and certain small insects which moved like the tiniest of cockroaches had kept me sensitive to the possibility of disturbance. I shook out and beat the useless finery, and lay down. Notwithstanding this preliminary movement, the precaution proved utterly futile. The onslaught was indescribable. Such parts of the body as were not tightly encased fell easily before the enemy. Sleep was out of the question. It was as far away from reach as a clean English bedroom. Lazily moved on the cruel hours. The past and the future seemed nowhere; all was present, and the present was wearisome indeed. Once—it might have been 3 A.M.—we

---

[1] I do not know how the spelling is regulated in the English reading of the two passages noted. In the latest Arabic version of the Scriptures I find the word written "Sirfati" and "Sarfati," the vowel change being only in the accentuation. The Latin Vulgate has Sarephta (iii. Regum 17-9) and Sarepta (Lucas iv. 26); an apparent difference only, as the *p* and *ph* correspond with the *f*.

THE GNAT OF THE STEPPES.

stopped. The heat became excessive; the wind ceased; in came the gnat of the steppes. A gnat, indeed! a sort of giant mosquito! The cabin was alive with these savage insects, buzzing lustily for blood. Never shall I forget my introduction to this unforeseen and most undesirable acquaintance. About 6 A.M. I bethought me of a vigorous movement which, if successful, would procure me a short sleep. It was broad daylight, and we had started on our course. Such of the insects as had not taken the hint to leave, and there were many of these, were settled on the walls and in dark corners. I rose and attacked them as they reposed, smiting in all directions, and occasionally with evident success. After a long and vigorous pursuit, accompanied with much slaughter, I hoped to have achieved my object, and lay down. Shortly, the buzz was again audible; and this time the intruders seemed concentrated towards myself instead of scattering and colonizing as before. In fine, I could scarcely get one wink of sleep, and rose in anything but lively mood to wash and drink coffee. De P. came in and sat with me; he also had suffered from the visitation, but had slept until the gnats had supplemented the more sluggish insects. Indeed, however hidden and impalpable the physical effects of the later operations, there was clear evidence of the damage done by the first assailants to the whole body of passengers. The second class had turned out on deck in hopeless misery. A Greek family furnished a notable illustration of the ravage committed. The paterfamilias of this group was, by the way, a strange old gentleman. According to his own admission, he was travelling with his wife, daughter, and female companion, from Vienna to Astrakhan in search of a son-in-law. I was not aware that such articles abounded on the northern steppes of the Caspian; but we live and learn. We are on shore at Astrakhan about 3.30 P.M.; and I make my way to a hotel near the landing-place, late Bremsel's.

"*July* 16.—Awake this morning at Astrakhan, and experience a heat like one's old enemy in India. It is doubtful whether the mat blinds should be furled or let down at an early hour. From my window I see the cathedral in the Kremlin. It is the prominent and characteristic building of the place, said to have been erected by the Metropolitan, Samson, at his own cost in 1696.[1]

"There is a house to the left of red brick, and at the corner of a street. Looking out of one of its lower windows is a female with a red kerchief over her head, perhaps observing me at my open casement. There is a huge signboard and inscription on the front side of her house, and a small piece overlaps on which I can read ЛЕБЕДЬ which I make out to be, in Roman letters, 'lebed,' a swan. On the house to the right is the continual ПРОДАЖА or intimation such as 'Here is sold.' The small upper domes on the church and tower are green, surmounted with gold. In the little arches are paintings. The houses at Astrakhan have usually one story, and are of wood or brick, red, white and of other hues. The small unpretending quays on the outlet of the Volga are rather pretty, and the view of the wooden bridges across this small river is pleasant enough. Dined to-day with M. Victor de P., my fellow-traveller's brother, who is a merchant of Astrakhan; and a sumptuous repast it was they gave me, inaugurated with *caviare* and shellfish, and crowned with ice in profusion. The amiable hostess could speak English, but general conversation was carried on in French. We were quite en *famille*, six in all, of whom two were ladies, Madame P. and her husband's sister; and a third lady joined us after dinner. Among other topics was discussed the literature of the day, and I was astonished to find not only Morier, whose Persian romance is equally adapted to the continental as English taste, but Dickens and Thackeray appreciated in Astrakhan. 'Vanity Fair' and 'Pickwick' are said to be capital in Russian! As regards Russian original literature, I noted down rather the substance than the actual exposition of the views expressed. They do not consider themselves sufficiently advanced in social civilization to present a gallery of finished portraits to the satirist. 'It is all very right and proper,' said V.

---

[1] "Histoire des Découvertes faites par divers Savans Voyageurs." Lausanne, 1784. Tome ii.

'for you in England to criticise and ridicule various members of your society who deserve the treatment; but what can our Russian authors do in this respect, when all society is, as it were, in transition? Any such proceeding would be productive of ill-feeling and could do no good. Nay, it would fall flat and unintelligible.' Whatever amount of roubles is realised by the local municipality—and money seems plentiful in Astrakhan—the body corporate is unable to spend more than eighty at a time (about £12), but the governor may authorize an outlay up to 600. Great complaint is made of centralization as an obstacle to progress, and the wish is evident to develop local resources independently of St. Petersburg. I have remarked this on more than one occasion during my few days' experience in Russia, and in the language of apparently sensible and well-informed men. Called on the Persian consul this morning, and, at the time previously arranged, was ushered into a respectable apartment terminating in a smaller one with the usual chairs and sofa. Took a seat on the last, looking stately and serious, while a secretary in spectacles sat on the arm-chair at the further side. We had exchanged a few words in Persian, when the consul himself appeared. He was a mild, thin, middle-aged man, of polite manners and address, and we had a long talk. I am more sure of his figures than his currency; but he certainly represented the Persian imports to Astrakhan as four times the amount of Russian exports to Persia. Cotton, he informed me, was imported in large quantities both from Mazanderan and Khurasan. He knew several British officers connected with his country, and spoke of them by name. His inner room was hung closely with portraits, amongst others her most gracious Majesty; and in the larger one was a prominent picture of the Emperor Alexander. There was also the Shah, as natural, and there were several officers in blue uniform whom I took to be Russian. He wrote something diffuse in Russian on my passport, affixing his seal, and promised to send me a letter for the *wali*, or governor of Resht. Three or four whiffs at his *kalian* formed a necessary interlude in our proceedings. Dined again to-day at the Russian merchant's, resuming acquaintance with Russian cookery, in which the fish, soup, and cakes, and the *caviare* are important elements.

"*July* 18.— Again on board the *Czarita*, with English letters for consignment to Captain S., who kindly promises to get them stamped at Kazan. Strange that no postage-stamps should be procurable at Astrakhan, a place of much the same comparative commercial note in Russia as Leith or Hull, if not Glasgow or Liverpool, in our island home; and it would be remarkable indeed were no stamps to be got in those flourishing ports. The double commerce of the Volga and Caspian is its portion. Its quays and wharves abound with traffic; its boats are assuredly to be reckoned by thousands; its inhabitants are mixed and various, and strictly commercial or working. Yet my host avers they could not get me three stamps of 30 kopecks each! Went last evening, and again this morning, to see the barge which is to convey us to the Caspian steamer; but could not obtain a passage-ticket, as my passport had been given up and retained. Mr. O., for whom—as well as the more celebrated Mr. S.—I had received letters from Mr. G., is an apothecary; and the whereabouts 'in which he dwells' having been discovered, I had referred to him on the subject of rats. He politely asked me to dinner and tea, and undertook to do the needful with my passport. Accepting the latter offer, I had left the paper with him, and he certainly kept it a tolerably long time. However, all went well at last. The dust of this place is a great nuisance, and its prevalence forced me to close to-day the windows of my apartment. It really is a good room of its kind; 17 feet by 9, and about 18 feet high, with a well-boarded floor of good, polish-taking wood; and it has two fine large windows. Furniture—sofa with dark glazed cover, the worse for wear; *in situ*, five chairs, and two small tables, of which one is very rickety and like an Indian *tipoi*, or 'teapoy.' There is a looking-glass, a suspended double lamp, and there are brass fixtures for a stove, and lights. At night I lie down on the sofa, or divan, putting my saddle under my head, filling up the hollow with a railway rug, and covering it with a towel for precaution against insects. No sheets, coverlets, or superfluous luxuries are provided in the Astrakhan hotels, at least to my knowledge. Dine again with my Russian friends preparatory to taking final departure from Russia.

"*July* 19.—In truth these De P.'s have been very attentive to me, and I have reason to remember gratefully their attention and hospitality. The sister's husband is in England. Another sister, whom I did not see, is married to a high functionary in the Caucasus. Our parting dinner yesterday was agreeable in its friendliness. I returned from it to the hotel, and got my baggage weighed and put into the barge bound for the Caspian. Another night on the sofa, and this morning early I came on board. Felix de P. my old travelling companion, and a young lady whom I had met at his brother's, had arrived before me, having made a midnight embarkation. Mademoiselle —— has just come down from St. Petersburg to take up the post of governess at Lenkoran, on the Caspian, in the family of the commandant. She has a pleasing manner, and leaves a favourable impression. We start about 7 A.M., in presence of assembled crowds, amid which the high Persian hat is very conspicuous. Indeed we have on board a great many Persians, who spread carpets and smoke *kaliuns* after the little-changing customs of their country. But all are not Persians; for I am addressed at breakfast, in French, by a portly dame in a dressing-gown, with a semi-Dutch and a semi-Jewish appearance, whose whereabout and whatabout perplex me. I begin to think that queer characters of either sex abound as much on the water as on land. The Danube steamer is a case in point; and I am not sure that the Scheldt and Rhine boats might not be trusted to supply further examples, together with the Volga 'Parachod' and Astrakhan barge. Madame B.'s history savours of the 'fast,' but contains enough romance and incident for a sensational novel. Mistress of a hotel, but not of herself and fancies, she wanders the world strangely, hovering near the steppes and the Caspian; a curiosity in her own particular way, but little known to those who have never visited these parts. At night we reach the sea, and find the *Archduke Michael* waiting to receive us, in about eight feet of water

Manage to get ourselves and our luggage on board, amid much confusion and a certain amount of mismanagement.

"*July* 20.—By some strange process, inexplicable, but certainly undergone, we got settled last night in our sea-boat, leaving Chitterilingore, or the four hills, at about 2 A.M. In the saloon were De P., a Teutonic Russian, and a Dutch tourist; perhaps one or two more. Talked much with our captain, who had accompanied us in the barge from Astrakhan—a tall, big-boned, German Russ, who speaks English well, and has an English name. His engineer is a thorough Englishman from Newcastle, whose acquaintance I am glad to make. At about 10 at night we reached Petrovsk, on the western shores of the Caspian, where De P. leaves us: during the day we had touched also at Chundrakoffsky, or a place rejoicing in some such name. De P. is a companion whom I shall miss; nor am I the only one on board to regret his departure, though the captain and he are not on the best of terms. He committed to my charge the lady traveller, whose Caspian voyage wanted yet some days of completion. The Caucasus and Mercury Company have three passenger steamers, two English and one Swedish built. We are now in the last, the *Grand Duke Michael*, the others being the *Prince Bariatinsky* and the *Tsarevitch Constantine*. They have also six trading steamers, exclusively perhaps of a smaller class of boat. The Russians have stations east as well as west of the Caspian, namely, at Tiouk Karagan and mouth of the Oural river north, and at Ashurada to the south-east.¹ A steamer runs from Astrakhan to Tiouk once a month, thence proceeds north to the Oural, and returns to Tiouk and Astrakhan. This appears to be a commercial, if not postal arrangement. The harbour at Tiouk is said to be an admirable one, but the station is not popular, owing to the barrenness inland. It occurs to me that a position might be selected lower down, to correspond with the railway, when completed, from Poti to Baku, and carry on traffic still further eastward, and, *vice versâ*, open out for the markets

---

¹ Those who have become interested in the Central Asia question, and followed its mazes during the last two years, will add more names to the list.

of Europe the bazars of Central Asia. What a grand development of national resources would such a line prove![1] Stay off Petrovsk for the night, and in not very comfortable condition. We are as unsteady at anchor as in progress, and the ship is not built for the comfort of passengers.

"*July* 21.—They are building a pier, or making a harbour at Petrovsk:[2] at all events, Government is not asleep, and attends to progress there as elsewhere. From this place we move out, with the irregular coast, seaward, and then in again and along the shores of Daghistan, until we stop at Derbent, a picturesque town on the slope of a hill, with a line of walls running down to the sea front. For passengers to whom moments are precious, there is much time lost in waiting so long at these ports. A run from Astrakhan to Enzeli might, otherwise, be accomplished in three or four days. From Petrovsk there is a road of about 500 versts (332 miles), through the mountains, to Tiflis; but from Derbent, a nearer point as the crow flies, I understand that the journey would be difficult. Failing in a convenient opportunity, I do not land;[3] but the place is of considerable interest, not alone on account of its romantic position, but of associations which belong to the days of Alexander. I hear mention of

---

[1] Krasnovodski, occupied by 3,000 Russians in 1869, would represent an occupation such as here contemplated four years before realization. But however complacently the question be regarded in a geographical and cosmopolitan sense, the purely political aspect cannot be set aside. There is very much to be said and very much to be conjectured on these matters generally, as treated in recent Blue Books. And when this diary was written, the spontaneous speculations of the press and the forced discussions of diplomacy had not peopled the wastes immediately east of the Caspian with armies of the future, nor raised up in the heart of their sterility both military depôts and strategical points. Home-thrusts like the Oxus boundary question, and stubborn facts like the Khiva expedition, have a hothouse power in ripening theories about Central Asia; nor is it a bad result of such contingencies that the full-grown taxpayer of Great Britain should know more of Oriental actuality, to say nothing of mere orthography, than is to be learnt from the Aladdins and Sindbads of our boyhood.

[2] Since completed; and I can bear personal testimony to its great use, and the skilful solidity of its construction.

[3] I did so, however, on a subsequent occasion, having touched at Derbent again in 1870, 1871, and 1872.

ancient remains, which may be worth the inspection. Our messing on board the *Michael* is not bad, and every meal is charged at a fixed rate. I attend all upon principle, though appetite is not always to be commanded. Our captain tells wonderful stories of Turkmans, one of which is to the effect, that a smaller skipper on the Caspian was in chase of a Turkman craft guilty of piracy, failed in an attempt to destroy her with cannon shot, but succeeded in running into her, breaking her in half, and thus sinking the wreck and whole crew! With the exception of six Russians employed in the engine-room, the captain, first officer, engineer and saloon servants, I understand that the crew of the *Michael* are Tartars. They are preferred to Russian sailors, owing to the imbibing propensities of the latter. Many Persians are among the deck passengers, and miserable enough they look in the midst of their bundles on deck. They are not, as a rule, allowed access to the poop, nor should I suppose they were treated with more consideration than are native passengers in a British boat on the Indian seas. Though information of all sorts is procurable on board, I cannot admit that a sea passage on the Caspian has intellectual charms or much mental profit, especially with uneasy waters such as these.

"*July 22.*—Reach Baku in the afternoon, passing island with gas factory and lighthouse on the main land. Baku is an old Tartar town, and shows signs of former note and consideration. It is now being moulded into fashion suitable to the present age and the progressive ideas of its present masters, and promises further improvement. Built on the slope of a hill, and partly inclosed by a wall similar to that of Derbent and other Caucasian towns, its houses are of mud, brick and stone, and there are but few trees to relieve the monotony of Asiatic dust. There is something very familiar to me in the contemplation of its long lines of bazar, which strike me as mere reproduction of a common Oriental picture. The shopkeepers are mostly Caucasian, Tartar and Persian; the true Russian being scarce among them. With the Persians I felt at home, and could get on famously; with the others I could manage to attain intelligibility by the use of Osmanli Turkish. Mademoiselle E, the

Dutch chevalier and friend, and I, soon find our way to the shore, and proceed to examine the place; commencing with a few small purchases, such as fruit, cigarettes and a hat turband, and continuing with the more luxurious *passetemps* of a drive. The lady and I occupy one droschky, and our companions another, and the respective coachmen obey instructions to show us the town and its lions. The hired vehicles of Baku are driven by Tartars at a smart pace, and are not bad of their kind, notwithstanding a shakiness and brittle exterior. Observed a handsome Armenian church under construction, and many stone houses rising near the water; but the quays, which are so susceptible of development, are comparatively neglected. Probably the municipality is fettered here as at Astrakhan, and probably such results as malversation and maladministration of funds, when realised, may not be unknown at Baku. The prominent building in Baku, towards the sea and lighthouse, is called 'The Maiden's Tower,' and it has a local legend somewhat of a Cenci character. The story goes that a Tartar princess was proposed for in marriage by her own father, and that she naturally declined the offer; that he became fierce and pressing, and she ostensibly submissive and yielding; that she made her consent conditional on his building her a tower, *the* tower, *par excellence*, of Baku; that he agreed to the terms laid down, made over to her the completed building, and that her first act on obtaining possession was to throw herself from its highest point and perish! I had no notion that Baku had ever boasted a Beatrice; but I cannot say that the legend has altogether convinced me of the fact. There are several baths here, notably those of the club, arsenal, and custom-house; admission to which may be procured by visitors with friends, interest, or a little coin of the realm. Return to steamer, all the better for our trip and relief from cabin life, and with the resolution to make exploration of the volcanoes and volcanic fires which have given such celebrity to this port. Many visitors to our captain to-day, a circumstance which seems to corroborate his own claims to notoriety. Did not see the caravanserai, but there is, it is believed, a good one for the use of stray travellers.

"*July* 23.—Went in the evening to look at the wonderful fires, distant about twenty-one miles from the town in an easterly direction; for at Baku a wide tongue of land projects to seaward considerably in advance of the general line of coast west of the Caspian. Amid the fires is a large factory, and thither Mr. H. our English engineer, who acted as guide to Mademoiselle E. and myself, directed the coachman to drive. On arrival we saw the German assistant superintendent and his family, who received us with civility and hospitality combined, thanks, doubtless, to the presence of a mutual acquaintance, in the person of an introducer. To say that these fires are curious, or worth seeing, is to say nothing. They are marvellous, and worthy of classification among natural wonders. There is a large tract of ground near the sea, on the peninsula of Absharan,[1] out of which gas issues in profusion. The whole soil appears to be impregnated here with naphtha, and the application of fire to the vaporous region will cause a flame to arise, extinguishable only by water or smothering. Many flames are aroused and kept alive, for use in various ways. In the kitchen of our host, for instance, they played a conspicuous part, cooked his meat, boiled his water, warmed such things as had need of warming, and served to economise domestic labour. The aspect of the fires at night gives the notion of a watchful camp. Many are built upon; that is, the fire is carried through a conductor raised upon it. Each of the two stone pillars at the factory gate is thus surmounted with a high, bright flame. A photograph would convey no notion of these phenomena, and to represent them with any approach to truth or correctness would tax the powers of a consummate artist. Attached to, and perhaps a little higher than, the large factory wall inclosing the several buildings of the establishment, is an inclosure of a castellated kind. It has a rampart, and on the rampart is a little house like that above the gateway of an Oriental fort. Beside this house the steps lead down to the lower court, a space of about ten yards square, in the centre of which is a Hindu temple,

---

[1] I take the etymology which looks the most likely.

Near the foot of these steps is shown a large dark stain, marking the spot where the last Hindu fakir perished, the last who had made a pilgrimage to Baku. I am told that there have been as many as forty at a time here; and, to judge from the numerous rooms or cells, this might well have been the case. I entered one cell, that of the last hermit, and about it was the unmistakable architecture of the Indian domicile; the earthen threshold, and cooking-place, and seat; a broken ewer of earthenware made the recollection even more vivid. And why

HINDU PILGRIM.

was this wretched man murdered? All that the factory people knew on the subject was that there were two Hindus there. One went back with intent to return to his own country, and the other remained, already then a resident of many years. One day the family of the factory went to Baku, leaving the *fakir*, as they supposed, well and safe. On their return, he was found murdered, and his idols and little property had been stolen. Suspicion fell on the Tartars, but I have not heard that any Tartar was tried or questioned on the matter. The papers of the deceased were retained by the Russian police. They say that the land, as well as a monastery built upon it, was bought by the Hindus, and dates from a very old period. Hanway, travelling more than 120 years ago, talks of the Indians' worship at Baku, and of the number of devotees there being generally forty or fifty.¹

'*July 21.*—A river steamer came in with damaged engines this morning. Up early in search of a bath, obtaining one with little difficulty in the custom department. Although they are reported to be private, a tall Caucasian official, who speaks Persian, admits me as a special favour, in consideration of a *small douceur*. I am inclined to the belief that he has authority and instructions to admit strangers to the privilege. At all events, two Russ bathers came out when I was holding a position before the door, and said nothing. The Dutch chevalier and his companion are seriously purposing a start inland to-day. They have hired an Italian servant, and he is to get them a carriage, so that Baku is not without its civilized resources. The said servant may do very well, notwithstanding that he has been picked up at random. In fact, all Italians from Suez to Constantinople, and from Constantinople to Baku, generally expressed lines which include considerable circuits seem to me picked up in this way, and some prove very good acquisitions. They go through strange adventures; and their histories, if reported in detail, would possess many startling and sensational incidents. I had a Francesco in the Crimea, an invaluable scamp, whose roguish tricks have not effaced the memory of his good services. This Baku Italian has amusing acquaintances, one of whom I chance to meet; he is the keeper of the Hôtel d'Italie, a shabby kind of restaurant. Mine host, a Piedmontese, with rings in his ears, was formerly joint owner of eighteen dogs and monkeys. The monkeys had arrived at Astrakhan *en route* to Tiflis, *via* Baku, when by some sad accident, of flood or field, they all perished. The travelling establishment, which had acquired a high repute, was brought to an untimely end;

---

¹ Life of Jonas Hanway, 1785.

and the *entrepreneur* had to make his own way on as well as he could. He found himself at Baku, and started a restaurant there. I have not ascertained what became of the dogs, but some might deem too close an inquiry, under the circumstances, undesirable. The Hôtel d'Italie is said to be very indifferent; but what can one expect at such a place, if comparisons be allowed? A second steamer comes in this afternoon, almost exactly resembling that of the morning. She is from Astrakhan; whereas the other was working up from the opposite direction, and broke down, as I learn, near Lenkoran. Another drive to-day through the town and environs. The same sights present themselves as before; there are the same monotonous lines of Tartar, and Circassian, and Persian caps and faces—the same monotonous forms of male bathers. We were to have gone to-day to see the wonders of naphtha exhibited in the water as on land, for there are marine gas fountains on the sea side of Baku, said to be worthy the traveller's notice; but the weather was unfavourable, and our design abandoned. I am told that the gas rises in a disturbed circle of about fourteen inches diameter, and may be set on fire in the midst of the salt sea waters. Many of these circles are formed at short distances one from the other."

The fires of Baku have attracted so much attention from Caspian and Caucasian travellers, and are really so well worthy of more general discussion and intimate acquaintance by the scientific world, that I here venture to make a short pause, and add a few fresh words on the subject. It seems to me that although very much may have been written about these ignitible vapours, whether in a scientific or whether in a historical point of view, very much more remains to be recorded. The two newest accounts now before me are by foreign explorers. There may be others of later date by Englishmen, which I have overlooked or of which I know nothing; but neither Mr. Mounsey nor Sir Arthur Cunynghame include any such notices in their Caucasian travels. I now refer to Professor de Filippi's visit in September 1862, and one made four years previously by M. Moynet, a fellow-traveller with Alexandre Dumas, narratives of which were published in 1865 and 1863 respectively. Both, concisely related, are interesting; and M. Moynet supplements his literary matter, or *vice versâ*, with accurate drawings of Astrakhan, Derbent, Baku, and the Fire Temple. In detailed description, however, both fall short of M. Gmelin's report, for which we are indebted to the last century.[1]

M. de Filippi gives the yield of the naphtha wells in the Absharan peninsula at a mean of 300,000 puds yearly, or nearly 4,700 tons English. He states that there are several kinds, of which the most remarkable are the solid and pitchy, found at Chelekan Island in the south-east corner of the Caspian, exported to Russia, Persia, and Bokhara, for much the same uses as asphalte in France and Italy; and the viscous and liquid, like the petroleum of Baku. The product is, in his estimation, inseparable from the inflammable gas with which the whole soil is more or less impregnated. Whether the combination is natural, fortuitous, or caused by volcanic agency, he leaves to further inquiry. Professor Stoppani of Milan, and Signor Abich, are those to whose theories he refers in elucidation of these singular phenomena; but he is not prepared to subscribe fully to their conclusions.[2]

[1] "Histoire des Découvertes faites par divers Savans Voyageurs," &c. Tome ii. Lausanne, 1784.

[2] "Mi pare che la cosa non sia per anco sufficientemente dimostrata, sebbene i fatti addotti dal Prof. Stoppani siano di molto peso, e ricevano l'appoggio dell' incontestabile autorità del Sig. Abich, il quale ha trovato nella disposizione de' vulcani di fango e delle sorgenti bituminose della penisola di Apscheron uno stretto rapporto colle linee di dislocazione dovesta alle emersioni trachitiche." ("Viaggio in Persia." Milano, G. Daelli e Cia., 1865. Note p. 329.)

As regards the marine gas, he writes: "About an hour's distance south of the city, near the shelving banks of the shore, there are strong gaseous fountains, gurgling, and throwing out a certain amount of petroleum, which spreads itself, in the finest of veils, on the surface of the water. The contact of a lighted torch causes to be aroused from within whirlwinds of fire . . . and my comrades revelled in steering their boat amidst them, guided by the powerful arm of Captain Muller, the hairs of whose head and beard were exposed to the scattered flames." M. Moynet's account is fuller still. He is in a boat with others. A sailor throws lighted tow into the sea, where the waters appear fermented. In an instant the whole surface is in flames to the extent of some forty metres (forty-five yards). The experiment is repeated; the fire spreads; and they move about in the midst. On leaving the spot our author looks back upon the still bright flames, remarking that they will continue to burn until put out by a high wind, "which may, perhaps, not come for a fortnight or even a month."[1]

It is by no means improbable that the natural wonders of Baku were known to Zoroastrians before the Muhammadan era; moreover, that the same importance was attached to them by the fire-worshippers of old. But it is a very great mistake to make the modern Hindu pilgrim to the west shores of the Caspian a Parsi, or a descendant of Parsis. He has really no affinity with the Bombay *millionnaire* and his sect, as inferred by M. Moynet. The Italian professor seems also to have fallen into a like error when he calls the officiating Hindu "an

[1] "D'Astrakhan à Bakou," Octobre 1858. See "Le Tour du Monde," 1863. Hachette, London and Paris.

Indiano spiccato della metropoli Ghebra di Bombay." The term "Gabr" could now hardly apply to any than the Parsi, according to Oriental usage and parlance; and he leads us to infer that his pilgrim is of this class.

July 27.—Start at about 3 A.M. The night had been fine, but heavy rain preceded actual weighing of the anchor. Reach Salian at 10.30 A.M., and take in a solitary letter sent out from shore by boat. Land here very low; a strip of green grass is just discernible, but there are half a-dozen small craft to mark the place. Pass the mouth of the Kur, where the water is shallow and there is a reputed resort of flamingoes. We are at Lenkoran about 3.30 A.M. This is a small Russian station near the sea-shore, much wooded but otherwise not remarkable. See another steamer at anchor near us, one of the commercial class, not intended for passengers. Her English engineer, brother of our own of the *Michael*, pays us a visit. The two give me the impression of being worthy members of a steady, honest family, right well and honourably disposed. The governess takes leave and goes to the shore, in company with her new mistress, who had come to fetch her in a large boat. I augur nothing from appearances, for appearances may be as deceitful on the Caspian as elsewhere; but I sincerely hope that her lot has fallen in a pleasant place. Madame is a dark-complexioned, plain personage, of middle age, clearly self-reliant in matters of dress and outward bearing. She is apparently much wearied and put out by the effort of boating and boarding the steamer, begs for water, indulges in conventional byplay, sits down languidly, calls for and operates upon a long brown paper cigarette, asks questions, and makes references. Her attendants consist of a stout, wild-looking man of martial aspect, with hair floating wildly from under his forage cap, military dark coat, and white trousers, possessing, withal, a smiling and facetious manner and address; a second stout person in white military uniform, looking very sleek and pleasant; and a shabby, common soldier orderly, who answers readily, but loudly and familiarly, to all his mistress' requisitions. Poor Mademoiselle! You look half afraid of your new career; and there is no wonder. The position is on few occasions void of painful anticipations; and there is a kind of severe isolation in these parts which needs counteraction from extra human kindness. The captain pointed out to me to-day, on his map, the course of the high hills visible near Lenkoran. It appears that the valley of the Kūr is flat and extensive. From a little below Baku to near Lenkoran the country bordering on the sea is mountainless; but in the neighbourhood of the last-named port, the mountains of the Talysa mix with those of the Kara Dagh, and the long lofty line is formed which belts in the provinces of Ghilan and Mazanderan, and only fails towards Khurasan and the east. Weigh anchor for the island of Sāri, and get on shore there before dark. Join the captain, engineer and a third, in quest of pheasants, and accompanied by dogs. Find little, however, but mosquitoes, and are caught in heavy rain. Return wet to supper.

"*July* 26.—A thunderstorm last night is succeeded to-day by very heavy rain and bad weather. The captain and engineer take advantage of a break to go again to the island on a shooting excursion. By the way, a sad story is told in connection with Sāri, and the circumstance narrated is said to have happened only about six weeks ago. An old man, Persian or Tartar, had been left in charge of the wood there. He, a son, and two daughters, were the sole inhabitants, the girls being young, of some fourteen years and twelve respectively. Not long ago he thought it incumbent on him to undertake a pilgrimage, and setting forth left his children at Sāri. During his absence certain ruffians took advantage of the occasion to land and murder the young occupants of the island, after outraging the girls. Suspicion fell on a boat's crew now under trial; but it appears doubtful whether justice will ever overtake the miscreants in the ordinary course. The island is about ten miles in length by only 1 or 1½ mile broad, is covered with grass and brushwood, has good well-water, and could afford excellent pasture for cattle. In consideration of the comparative vicinity of Baku, and its likelihood of becoming a place of great local, if not general importance, I think that Sāri might be turned to good account.

At Baku there is no grazing for flocks and herds, and though good grapes grow there, I do not think it has much fruit or vegetables of its own. The vine is far from being a stranger in volcanic soil; and certainly the Caucasian wines are not to be despised. We had to-day some white 'Derbent,' a drink not unlike Sauterne; and the red Derbent is already an old and approved acquaintance. The captain and engineer return to the steamer at about 1 P.M. drenched with rain, and with no larger trophy than three pheasants. There may be some truth in the charge brought by the former against his dog, that he is too fat and well-fed from a ship life to do his duty in the field. Weigh anchor again, and steam to Astara, touching first at Lenkoran again for letters. This latter place has a feverish look.[1] A small sturdy tower is pointed out as its fortification, and near it the Lenkoran river runs into the sea. Astara marks the Persian frontier on the seaboard. It is a small place situated in the wooded belt of low land at foot of the mountains, and between them and the Caspian. One of our fellow-passengers, the superintendent of customs, landed here. If carrying a gun gives claim to the title, he must be a sportsman.

"*July* 27.—Sight Enzeli soon after breakfast, and I make preparations accordingly. This repetition of matter-of-fact incidents, such as packing luggage and paying bills, is a disagreeable feature in travelling. It is so necessary and yet so harassing. Make the best of my way to the shore, and present myself to the Russian Consul, Mr. E., a short, busy man, somewhat past middle age. Nothing can be more gracious and hospitable than his reception. He places at my disposal the traveller's room in his house, an apartment about 14 feet by 6, with pictures of flowers and females. A *décolletée* beauty on the ceiling is rouged up to the eyes, and surrounded with miniatures of attendants in all kinds of impossible positions and attitudes, to say nothing of the flying charmers supporting her. The *niches* in the wall remind me of Baghdad, and I now feel in Asia in earnest—a sensation of sorrow mingled with hope. It is sad to have to complain of hospitality; but it is of its signs and effects in certain places,

---

[1] It has, I believe, been abandoned as a station, by Imperial decree.

not of the virtue itself that complaint is made. Oh, Mr. P., kind Mr. P., why did you put rum in my tea? why make me drink absinthe? why insist on my pouring down my throat wine for breakfast? and why call on me to take a parting glass, when my head was aching and my spirits could derive no strength from such vulgar stimulants? Yet all was meant in kindness, and your little friend, the dragoman of the Russian legation at Tehran, played his part right well in the conversation. Finally the Consul gave me his *ghulam*[1] and letters of introduction, and off I started under most favourable auspices. But the sun was hot, and the sight of Persian boatmen recalled past years which I cared not to revert to; and the head was very painful and heart somewhat sick; and I had four long hours to accomplish in working up the Enzeli lake and quasi-river. The acacia and other trees were very pretty in the narrow water passage; and the boatmen were not so coarse and savage as many I have known. But my energies failed me to profit from the passing hour, and I dozed and dreamt disquietedly. After a wearisome water journey we reached the Pir's halting-place, from which one *farsakh*, or less than four miles, remains to Resht. Horses were prepared, and we mounted. Three only were put in requisition: one for myself, one for the *ghulam*, one for the baggage; and what a road! it was a continual rut or puddle. My portmanteaux were bespattered in merciless style, and looked as if they would come down at any moment. On the way, the Jilwadar, or attendant groom, dismounted, then remounted the heavily-laden beast, performing the second part of the feat with a dexterity savouring of the circus. At length we reached Resht, first going, under the *ghulam*'s guidance, to the Russian Consul's, but afterwards fairly bringing to at the most hospitable house of Messrs. V. and M., of the well-known firm of Ralli and Co. Here I was provided with a comfortable bed and bedroom, and felt myself quite well off again. I had not only a bed, but sheets, and could actually undress; had it not been for sand-flies and mosquitoes, I should have slept splendidly.

"*July* 28.—Mine hosts persuade me to stay the day and not

---

[1] *Ghulam*; a mounted attendant, or special retainer.

start until to-morrow; but I do not quite approve the arrangement, owing to the loss of so much time already. However there is much to do in the way of preparing for a journey, and we set about arrangements this morning in earnest. Get out new saddle and have it put in order, presenting the extra bit and bridle to M. Buy saddle-bags, felt and necessaries, and out with revolver. Initiate myself, moreover, into the current coin of the country, obtain 50 Persian tomans—in short do much useful work with intent to leave to-morrow morning. Look at some beautiful Resht embroidery, which is very tempting. Messrs. Ralli and Co. are building a very snug house for their representatives here, and in supersession of their present quarters, which are by no means bad. Resht is the chief town of Ghilan and the S.W. of the Caspian, corresponding, as it were, to Asterabad on the S.E. It is a quiet sort of place, but, as the emporium of the silk of the province, it has become the residence of English, French and Russian Consuls or Vice-consuls, and of European merchants more or less in number. I hear that the Russian Consul has a hundred Russian subjects to look after at Enzeli alone. Some if not all of these are probably Armenians, said to be the great exporters of cotton from Persia to Russia. Resht is a thoroughly Persian town, with dirty and close streets, the houses of Europeans being its only decent buildings. Report current of a row at Tiflis, checked, however, by prompt and vigorous government action. Obnoxious taxes are the commonly-reported cause, and Armenians are supposed to be implicated. How graceful and elegant is the Persian 'Abresham' or silk tree, with its fine indented leaf, and pale, delicately-scenting flower! To understand Persian paintings, it is essential to see Persian gardens and vegetation. The soil here is rich and fertile. Met the French Consul, a genial, merry man, and good Eastern scholar. Bedroom walls present appearances which lead me to call in aid. Perhaps it was the determined assault made upon the reposing sand-flies which enabled me to pass a tolerably satisfactory night.

"*July* 29.—My first day's 'chaparing.' *Chapar* is a word which becomes so familiar to the ear after a short residence in these parts, that an explanation of its meaning seems to be an almost incomprehensible exigency to those who are not outsiders in Persian experiences. In plain English it means riding post; and the *chapar* horses are horses engaged or kept up especially for postal service, consequently only to be found on certain roads where are regular postal stations. There is a *chapar* from Resht to Tehran, the first stage of which is Kadum, the second Rustamabad, and the third Manjil, which three, making a rough total of 60 miles, sufficed for my first day's journey. We started, probably after 5 A.M., as we were delayed by the non-arrival of our horses. I had my own especial animal, and the *ghulam* his; while two more horses, one of which was mounted by the 'shagird chapar,' or attendant groom, carried the baggage. All my traps accompanied me, and my kind hosts had had the portmanteaux carefully strapped and covered with many layers of protective stuff. The country was, for the first 15 or 20 miles, through thick forest, along a good road, almost entirely shaded from the sun by the many and various trees on either side, none growing to any great height, but affording admirable shelter. It was that kind of country which brings to the *habitué* of the Indian jungle a vivid recollection of spots where jungle fowl start up and cross the path at every step; such as I have seen near Berhampore, in the Northern Circars, only more European. The sky here is not so thoroughly Asiatic as in India, and something around savours of home and English lanes and byways. We reached the first 'chaparkhāna,' or post-house, sooner than I expected and indulged in tea and cold water; perhaps more, but I forget. It strikes me we had the eggs and 'chūrek,' or country bread, at Rustamabad. Between this last station and Manjil, we left the woods; and got among the hot hills, crossing a bridge over the 'Safid Rud,' or 'white river,' a mile or two before the post-house. Our route had been for some time along the left bank of the river, which has much the character of a large mountain torrent. I was tired on reaching the third *chaparkhāna*, but had not much of an appetite. Got through some broth, and laid down to rest on anything but the most comfortable of beds.

The *ghulam* is attentive and useful, and the people at the post-house are as civil as may be expected. Mosquitoes, fleas, or some strange stinging insects make me shift my position. The sound of drawing the *kalians* is continual outside the room, and though sufficiently hushed and monotonous to induce sleep, is not actually provocative of that often-sighed-for result. Night comparatively cool, quite as much so as I could have expected at this season and in such latitudes.

"*July* 30.—Manjil to Kazvin: two long, weary, dreary stages of about fifty miles or more; first to Kharzan, which place it seemed as if we were never to reach, and then a still heavier stage to Kazvin. There was no mistake to-day about the heat. We had left the shaded lowlands of Ghilan, and passed into the bare mountainous country dividing them from Azarbaijan and the Kazvin district; and we had now descended into the plains at the south side of the Elburz. To me there is little attractive in the views of to-day: I have seen so much of the same kind, enough to be surfeited. Mountain scenery is always, in some way, pleasant in itself; but the view, from high ground, of distant, hot, wide-spreading plains, with black streaks indicating cities or gardens, is the contrary. Kazvin lies before us, a dark mark, long, long before we near it, nor does it invite the approaching traveller from Europe with anything genial or *sympathique*. It has certain associations, this city; but they are too local to bear much general interest. I was thoroughly tired when I reached the post-house, and soon resolved to go no further for the day. Walked over to the telegraph office, which I found situated in what resembled the square of a mosque; the head officials discussing *kalians* outside, while seated on the stones. An Armenian came up to me, and as he was evidently anxious to shake hands, I accommodated him. He addressed me in good French. He was specially employed to teach the use of the Morse instrument. Sent a telegram in Persian to Captain S at Tehran. Coming into Kazvin to-day, I was an involuntary witness to the painful administration of a punishment called the 'felek.' It is a bastinado confined to the soles of the feet, which are inverted for the purpose,

KAZVIN TO MIAN-JŪ.

But it has been described over and over again by competent pens.

"*July* 31.—Kazvin to Mian-jū, about 70 miles. We did our first short stage to Adilabad in capital time. The next, a somewhat longer one, to Safar Khwajah, was fairly accomplished. Here I attempted breakfast, but with little or no appetite. Drink, drink, drink; this was the chief requirement, and there

THE "FELEK," OR BASTINADO.

was plenty of good water on the road to satisfy my longing. The next stage was a long one indeed, nor was the fourth to Mian-jū less heavy. So much depends on the kind of cattle one gets in these *chaparings*, whether the journey is tedious or easy. A hundred miles on good fast horses may be easier than half the distance on impracticable beasts. We were now drawing close up to the foot of the mountains on our left, and passed

Kirij, where is one of the royal palaces. But for the most part the country is dreary and desolate. There is but little vegetation, and all has a dried-up appearance. A bunch of grapes presented from time to time, is to the travelling horseman about the most cheery product of the soil. The post-house at Mian-jū is a rude sort of building on the approved principle. An orthodox *chupar khana* is composed of a square court, three sides of which are stables; the fourth side being the front, with a central gate and room to right and left. Above the gate is an upper room which, with a lower side room, is usually at the choice of the traveller. You may sleep on the roof of the stables, if you do not mind risking a fall into the court-yard—upon a horse, possibly, or mule picketed outside; or on the roof of your lawful room near the gateway, according to the time of year and state of the thermometer. On reaching Mian-jū, I found the travellers' room occupied, so remained outside. Not being able to get even bread to eat, I opened a tin labelled 'fried sole,' which I had picked up at St. Petersburg, and attacked it. Some small boys watched intently the operation; but I did not long gratify their curiosity. It was dry fare and wanted relief, which I could not procure. Contenting myself with consuming half the shreds of the fish (for such they really were) I gave the balance to the *gluttons*, who did not, however, show signs of rapture at the meal in prospect. The occupant of the upper room was an Italian lady, widow of a telegraph *employé* of Tehran. Her little daughter was a pretty child, and peered at me from the upper story. They were travelling towards Europe in a *kajawah* or 'litter,' and started afresh soon after my arrival.

"*August 1.*—Move a little earlier than I had proposed, but do not regret having done so, as we have a tough and hot ride in. My horse lumbered heavily along, and required constant urging, even to fall into his short, jerky steps; and the road, though tolerably level, was stony. Keep along the foot of the hills, and at last sight Tehran, situated in the low ground. Glad enough to arrive and dismount at the British legation, from which I walk over to Captain S.'s house, close at hand. Here I breakfast, and rest from a three days' posting. The house is neat and comfortable, and contains good furniture. Find books and papers which, though not of the newest, amuse me, especially *Punch* and G.'s book on Persia. M. G. was secretary to one French mission, and Minister in another. He is rather severe in some of his remarks on our Indian navy, and his views of English men and manners in general. Joined by Captains St. J., P., Mr. D., and others during the day; and am taken out to the summer quarters of the British officials. The mission-house at Gulahak has been recently built, and is agreeably situated in a good, large garden. Am received and hospitably entertained by Mr. A. Dine at the legation, and find myself, like a true wanderer alighting on a resting-place, devouring rather than eating the contents of passing dishes, drinking cool drinks with indescribable *gusto*, and crowning the day's luxuries by a delicious repose between clean sheets, with a soft winsome pillow for the head, actually covered with a clean pillow-case! If on the completion of an ordinary journey, how much more, after a weary 'chapar' in Persia, does the jaded traveller say with Molière:—

"J'aime fort le repos, la paix, et la douceur."

TIFLIS WINE-SELLER.

DEMAVEND.

CHAPTER XI.

TEHRAN. THE ROUTE TO KARACHI CONTINUED THROUGH
ISFAHAN AND YEZD, TO KARMAN.

TEHRAN, the modern capital of Persia, though not of
recent origin, cannot be said to have been a place of
much repute before Agha Muhammad, the first of the
Kajar kings, made it his royal residence in about 1788.
At this period, a little known but intelligent English traveller, Ensign Franklin, arrived at Bushahr from India and
moved into the interior. It is unfortunate that opportunity was not afforded him to prosecute his journey,
for he does not appear to have gone much further north
than Shiraz, between the neighbourhood of which city
and the sea his personal experience of the country

was limited. Even the names of Jonas Hanway, and John Bell, of Antermony, scarcely suffice to make the eighteenth other than a barren century in enlightening Europe on Persia, compared to the seventeenth and nineteenth.

The great want of Tehran is a river, the feature of all others in the landscape which should be indispensable to the site of a capital. Otherwise it is perhaps little more open to objection than Ispahan or Kūm, which possess, at least, something of the kind. But after all, Shiraz the lauded, Tabriz, Kāshān, Yezd, Mashhad, and Karman, are much in the same case; all built on riverless plains and all at the foot or in a basin of hills, and mostly having pleasant "yalāks," or summer resorts, easy of access, which are preferred by the higher orders to the towns themselves during the prevalence of the hot season.

My notes of Tehran in 1865 made it a kind of six-doored polygon, having two gates to the north called Dāolat and Shamiran, two to the south, called Shah Abdul Azim and Nāo, the Dulab or east gate, and the Kazvin, or west gate. The "shahr panah," or wall, looked mean, as all such defences usually are; the ditch was clumsy and uneven: the whole thing was ill calculated to resist determination if provided with a pop-gun. But the city has greatly encroached on the surrounding space during the last ten years. Formerly some four miles in circumference, it is now being extended to an outer ditch and wall, thrown out on each side far beyond that limit. To mould it, however, into a respectable capital will be difficult, unless a Persian Haussmann can be found to take the matter in hand, with money to build and license to destroy. At present it is a confused mass of narrow and miserably paved streets, with outlying passages and byways of more promise, such as here and there an embryo boulevard or a carefully-lined road. The bazar is good of its kind, and has its architectural merits; the caravanserais also deserve honourable mention, and the telegraph and arsenal might pass muster as Oriental institutions. There are, moreover, a few respectable houses, occupied by European legations, or Persians of distinction; but the palace and its adornments are not such as the Shah-in-Shah can be very proud of after his visit to Europe and acquaintance with the abodes of European monarchs. Morier supposes Tehran to be the Tahors of the Theodosian tables, and recognizes it in its integrity of nomenclature in the fourteenth century, when reading about the journey of the Castilian ambassadors to Taimur. Pietro della Valle visited it in the seventeenth century; also an English traveller, Sir Thomas Herbert, who spells it "Tyroan." As the latter interprets Ispahan by "Spawhawn," and "Larijan" by "Larry john," the actual orthography used to represent sounds is not so material as the sound itself, and in this respect we need not cavil even at a superfluous letter. It is by the same quaint writer not incorrectly described to be "situate in the midst of a faire large Plaine, which although invironed in some parts with Hils of stupendious height, yet some ways affoords an ample Horizon." But there is evidence that it was a royal resort, if not an actual residence, in Herbert's statement that "the Towne is most beautified by a vast garden of the kings, succinct with a great towred mud-wall larger than the circuit of the Citie." He reckons it has 3,000 dwelling houses, "in few of which are fewer than a dozen people," an estimate which would certainly give 30,000 inhabitants. Tehran may now possess 100,000. Had there been no famine or consequent sickness of late, the figures might have been rated certainly a fifth higher.

Since riding into Tehran on the 1st August, 1865, it has been my lot to revisit the place no less than four times—that is, in 1867, 1870, 1871, and 1872; and my residence there, within or without the walls, is nearly that of a twelvemonth. While speaking then of a first acquaintance, more than four months in duration, I naturally take advantage of experience obtained in subsequent sojourns.

Mr. Alison gave me a courteous and hospitable reception; invited me to be his guest during my stay, and placed a saddle-horse and two mounted "ghulams," or special servants, at my disposal. Escorts in Persia, much as peons in India, cannot well be avoided by those who have positions to keep up in the regard of the outer world. Whatever personal inclination one may acknowledge, the flattering infliction is compulsory. My own tastes bid me thoroughly subscribe to the sentiment so well expressed by our keenest of modern humourists: "If I were a duchess of the present day, I would say to the duke, my noble husband, 'My dearest grace, I think when I travel alone in my chariot from Hammersmith to London, I will not care for the outriders.'" But her Majesty's Minister at the Court of Persia could not say as much to his secretary or steward when preparing for his drive in the suburbs of Tehran. Or if he did, he would show, to the world without, symptoms of official incapacity; perhaps, in the sight of his *entourage*, of disordered intellect.

Having so much work to do with the telegraph officers,

I thought it better to make arrangements for messing with them, but availed myself of the envoy's kind offer to the extent of occupying a tent, and subsequently an empty bungalow, in the mission grounds. It was the

KHEITS, OR IRREGULAR CAVALRY.

summer season, and the legations had moved out to their hot-weather retreats upon the slope of the mountain range north of Tehran, other Europeans following, as much as possible, their example. The spot to which British residents repair at these times is the village of Gulahak, distant about seven miles from the city, whence it is reached by a really good road, the greater part of which, as it leads to royal summer quarters, was constructed by royal command. On this road, to the right of the traveller proceeding from Tehran, is the "Kasr-i-Kajar," or palace of the Kajar, a building now seldom occupied by the Shah himself, and attracting attention rather from its imposing site and grounds than any architectural beauty. I have heard that some Persians have compared it with the palace and gardens at Versailles. With all respect for its favourable position, I cannot see the force of the comparison. It has, however, been fully described by Morier and more recent writers.

About the middle of October the legations move into the city again, greatly to the joy of the native establishments, who begin to look cold and unsettled when the first and warmer month of autumn has passed away. So was it in 1865. The British mission was then by the Nāo gate, or between the Nāo and Shah Abdul Azim. The Russian was in the "Ark," or citadel, near the Daolat. The French was by the Kazvin gate; and the Turks were located in the heart of the town. A change has come over this state of things; and better provision has been made, at least for England and Russia, the representatives of which powers boast highly respectable abodes in the Persian capital. The British flag now marks a handsome and commodious building, or set of buildings, outside the old wall and a little within the projected barriers, rendered by the taste and skill of the architect worthy the residence of the envoy and staff of Persia's truest friend among the states of Europe. Captain

Pierson, R.E., has devoted his time and energies to the accomplishment of this work; and its successful completion must be to him a source of legitimate pride and satisfaction. The new Russian legation has been constructed near the Shamiran gate within the old walls, and is a comparatively massive building, without much attempt at novelty of design. While expressing approval of the new diplomatic residences, however, we should not fail to mention that for Tehran, a purely Oriental city, isolated by custom and distance from the favoured cities of western civilisation, the old and abandoned abode of the Sheils, Rawlinsons, MacNeills, and other diplomatists of Anglo-Persian history, was by no means a bad mansion, and its gardens were superior in their way.

As regards the official business on which I had been despatched, it may be said that the whole month of August, as well as one half of September, was taken up with ceremonial preliminaries to discussion, with visits and introductions. But I was able also to confirm, by personal proof, the impressions of Persian character derived from books, and that kind of chance intercourse with natives of Persia available to many officers in India. The language should have a charm for all students, its grammar is so plain and intelligible, and its words are so musical. But its authors are untranslateable; and Sir William Jones himself has verified this assertion by bringing his own exquisite taste and talent to bear on English interpretations with but faint success. And the mysticism of books, the want of plain fact and plain phraseology in popular literature, the sacrifice of sense to style in the most ordinary writings of the day; all these things are significant of national character.

Education starts on the falsest of false principles, and all study is of show and sound. Appearances are everything; realities nothing. In the abstract, politeness is rather a virtue than perfidy a vice, and good faith and honesty have little weight in the moral scale: nevertheless, circumstances may make it otherwise under the doctrine of expediency. Hence a vague mode of verbal expression and avoidance of matter of fact. Hence concealment of self and suspicion of others. And as diplomacy is supposed to comprise every form of astuteness and craft, hence needless but conventional prolongation of negotiations with European powers, and the intervention of delays and difficulties on the most trivial of pretences. Added to this must be taken into consideration a perverse but perhaps fading habit, in the East, of vaguely associating Englishmen with unlimited means and money, which has, in the present age, to say the least, a retarding tendency in concluding Anglo-Persian treaties or conventions.

During the month and a half in question I was presented to his Majesty the Shah by Mr. Alison, who further took me to call on the Sipah Salar, or virtual Premier; on the Minister of Foreign Affairs, Mirza Said Khan; and on the Minister of Science, better known as Ali Kuli Mirza, the Itizād-es-Saltaneh, or "Right Arm of the State." A second visit to the Minister of Foreign Affairs enabled me to broach the question of business, but the progress made, if entitled to be called progress at all, was hardly material: for the statesman, quaintly oblivious of my seven weeks' sojourn at Tehran and introduction to himself a full month before, asked the nature of my employment, and when duly re-advised, remarked, not on the gist of the proposed convention, but on the fewness of its articles. The Russo-Persian Telegraph Treaty, it was observed, contained thirty-eight, and this had barely a third of that number. I called also on the Sartip, or Director-General of the Telegraph, Ali Kuli Khan, a Persian of above average intelligence, and with strong reasoning powers, wanting direction.

But visiting was not exhausted in a Persian social atmosphere. Two dinners with Monsieur de Giers, the Russian Minister at Zergandah, close to Gulahak, the second in honour of the Emperor's *fête* day; one dinner with the new-coming Turkish Minister, Khair Ullah Efendi, at his halting-place, twenty-five miles out of Tehran, and before entrance to the capital; frequent guests at our home mess; and a dinner every two or three days at the British legation; besides one or two "outings" of a friendly character, represented, moreover, a status which placed me tolerably *au courant* with the local European society and gossip. So that when, on the 19th September, I was placed for the first time in real business communication with the Persian Government, and broke ground in earnest with the Persian Foreign Minister, I knew tolerably well the people with whom I should have to deal directly, and what support or opposition, if any, might be expected from those who could only exercise either in an indirect manner. Not the least encouraging result of our interview on this occasion was the understanding on which we parted company, that I was to return to resume discussion on the day following. My experience at Constantinople would not have led me to expect this continuous exertion on the part of the Turkish authorities.

Oriental diplomacy is proverbially slow, and those who

hope to find Persian statesmen faster than their neighbours, will be mistaken, unless prepared to cut the knot by extraneous agency. Being myself naturally bound by civilized orthodoxies, and not accredited to negotiate on personal responsibility, I soon realised the mistake of excessive hopefulness, and of faith in brisk beginnings: for the vigour of the prelude meant no more than a movement in *adagio*. Two more months passed, and we had failed to complete. But the verge of completion had then been attained, and my seventh visit to the Foreign Minister on the 15th November promised to be the last. So, happily it proved. Business was prolonged until a late hour, and when daylight was exhausted we had recourse to candles. The convention was signed and sealed by her Majesty's Minister, and the Persian Minister for Foreign Affairs, on the 23rd December, and in less than a fortnight from that date, I was well on my travels again.

Certainly, if hospitality and mental and physical diversion could compensate for official *contretemps* and annoyances, they were not wanting at any period of my sojourn on this occasion. Tehran was unusually favoured by European strangers at the close of the year. French and English travellers of distinction glided in from the West; British-Indian homeward-bound visitors laboured up from the East. The Russian legation entertained occasionally and on a large scale; the French *chargé-d'affaires* received friends in a small but sociable way; and as for the British mission, it was exceptionally festive: for my own part I almost seemed to live there. After the arrival at Tehran of Khair Ullah Efendi, the Turkish envoy, dinners, or rather banquets of welcome were given by England and Russia both. The British gathering was remarkable not only for the fusion of Persian and European society which it displayed, but for the ready manner in which the Ottoman diplomatist and Persian statesman descended from their conventional pedestals to join the mixed multitude assembled, in the ordinary and very unceremonious game of Fool.

Hunting and coursing—"*la chasse*," as the thing was comprehensively interpreted to a mixed and polyglot society—consisted in riding about, for two or three hours, with two or three hawks, two or three dogs, and a train of galloping Persian attendants, looking for hares and partridges. If we saw any unfortunate one of the first, off we went, following the dogs either steadily and determinedly, or in fits and starts, according to the nature of country traversed. Always stony, it is at times a succession of pits and hillocks, difficult to cross with speed, steep and injurious to cattle; and the hound, scenting and tracking the hare, has been known to pass clean away from his masters, to be missed for the best part of an hour, and to be discovered in a ditch, exhausted and showing signs of unbecoming degluttition. But its deeds are, in such case, at best obscure and doubtful. If we saw a partridge, the hawk was slipped, and the poor bird victimized or not, just as its flying served. This description of sport applies to the hare also, to deer and larger game; and it was no rare occurrence on the plains north of Tehran to fall in with antelope, or find horsemen to pursue them. Persians declare that the hawk will even kill an eagle by pouncing on the back of its neck, and thence directing its fierce onslaught upon the eyes and head. Although these people take apparently more delight in sport, the vigour of which is, as it were, impaired by the introduction of a feathered assistant, than in the uncompromising hunting of Europe, there is no lack of bold riders among them. Their caracolling is of a fierce and frantic kind, and often merges into hard and continuous running, with a clear indifference as to whether they are being carried across country or along flat roads.

THE SHAH.

Visits to the Shah at his capital will no longer possess the interest they did before his Majesty came to England; but as the ceremonies observed on these occasions in Persia were not reacted in Buckingham Palace, I may revert to the second interview with which I was honoured in 1865, a month before my actual departure from Tehran. The first had been a mere presentation in common with some brother officers, and at one of the king's country seats near Gulahak. This one was ostensibly for leave-taking, though in reality, with the hope that it might promote haste in concluding the work on which I was awaiting the royal decision; and it was held in town. The palace has an element of the picturesque in exterior, and is distinguished by comparatively high towers rising behind the wide square, with its low buildings, tank and gardens. On first arrival, her Majesty's Minister, the Oriental secretary, and I, were shown into a waiting-room, at the top of which we found three vacant chairs as it were inviting us; two placed lower down the apartment, were already filled by Persians in respectable drab " abas," or long cloaks. After seating ourselves, we remained for some time in silent contemplation of odd old portraits and pictures with which the walls were covered. The first resembled the short-haired beauties of the reign of Charles II., or the Sylvias and Perditas of later reigns. The second were varied, European or Asiatic. Among them was a group, in which the Virgin and infant Saviour were conspicuous. There was also a banquet reminding one of the Don Quixote and Dulcinea period. When we had made a fair inspection of the subjects generally, the Master of the Ceremonies came in and took his seat next Mr. Alison; offering an explanation for his previous absence, by the statement that the Russian Minister was still in conference with the Shah. In about half an hour more we were summoned to the royal presence, and immediately put ourselves in movement. On our way we met the Russian Imperial envoy in full diplomatic uniform, attended by an *attaché* similarly attired. We walked through courts, flowers, water-courses, tanks and so forth, till we came to the royal *locale*. Here we took the cue from our Persian fugleman for the first mark of acknowledgment, or performance of the old regulation military salute. It was given on the first sight of the king sitting in his sitting-room, as on a stage, with the curtain drawn aside. On we went a few paces: then salute the second. The regard which met us was, perhaps, more instructive than encouraging for *débutants*. We next entered a doorway and ascended a few steps, turned to the left, came into a small room with a curtain, which we lifted and passed on into another room, where salute the third was made in the royal presence. Her Majesty's Minister sat down as provided by treaty, and the secretary proceeded to interpret the brief conversation which ensued. His Excellency soon took occasion to bring me forward, and after I had replied to the questions put to me by his Majesty, chiefly relating to my proposed journey eastward, and evincing somewhat of kindness as of courtesy, leave was asked and taken, and the withdrawal salute closed the stricter ceremonial observances of the day.

The privilege accorded at this time of an inspection of the crown jewels, which I enjoyed in common with four other European sight-seers, needs little more than bare mention in these pages, as it has already supplied material for printed narrative.[1] Magnificent pearls: a special pearl watch-chain: diamonds of wondrous size and beauty in the shape of rings and pins: tray after tray of bewildering valuables of all sorts: the "Daria-i-Nur," or "sea of light," a diamond brought from Delhi by Nadir Shah, said to have depreciated the value of a million

[1] Lord Pollington's "Half Round the Old World," pages 228-233. Moxon, 1867.

from the simple scratching on it of the name of Fath Ali Shah; the Aurangzeb ruby in the crown, massive but murksome; coats of poor cloth lavishly bedecked with the costliest jewels; such were among the facts to which I can bear testimony. But last year the jewels, or many of them, were exhibited at Buckingham Palace.

In speaking of the festive gatherings at Tehran, I must not forget an invitation from the "Sipah Salar," a title corresponding with Commander-in-Chief, or leader of the army; a high Minister of State, who though not exercising the concentrating functions of a Grand Wazir, approached the nearest in position to the holder of that often-suspended office. Before the close of our telegraph proceedings, he asked her Majesty's Minister and a large number of European officials, to a banquet; and it was with much regret I found myself unable to attend from indisposition. That it was a grand affair was clear to me from the reports of the guests, as well as from a choice bill of fare replete with French gastronomic technicalities, and headed by a lion and sun of the approved national pattern. There was a quiet, courteous geniality about this nobleman which attracted me greatly towards him. I had gone to him one day when telegraph negotiations had entered an unpromising phase, thinking his aid and influence might avail me. A swelling in the foot, very probably gout, kept him to his bed, which was spread out in true Persian fashion on the floor. He made me draw my chair towards him, and we talked for a long time. The business portion of the conversation was hardly satisfactory; but it was not a tissue of promises and set phrases. These I could not have believed: whereas I *did* believe in his personal good wishes, and predictions of an eventual solution of our difficulties which would, more or less, be mutually agreeable. But he was more at home in generalities, and especially questioned me on Lord Palmerston, and the Houses of Lords and Commons. I called on him again before leaving Tehran, when he received me in the palace. This was a short visit, and almost wholly on business; but it seemed to me to have had a beneficial result. I never saw the Sipah Salar afterwards. He had his enemies among men of power; and intrigue and conspiracy are ever busy in Persia. Removed from head-quarters, there is a mystery about his further career. Whether he died in honour at Mashhad, or under what circumstances, historians will have something to say. The court chronicler may have said it already. Let us hope it has been, or will be recorded with the fairness that is the very essence of history.

A Minister of Foreign Affairs at Tehran cannot well be what is called a popular man with foreign legations; and if those known to us by the more recent annals have not usually been so regarded, their shortcomings in this respect must be laid to the system as much as to the individual. Persian jealousy could not brook the notion that the representative of Government—in this case of the Shah himself—should be officially lost sight of as it were by the intervention of personal regard; and that esteem or friendship for the man should be mingled with any consideration of the measure it is his duty to discuss. The old school, with its ingrained suspicion and narrow conservatism, is therefore not uncommonly resorted to for the selection of those who are to regulate the exterior relations of the State: and though it is not by any means to the more bigoted members of this class of politicians that power is thus offered and entrusted, yet are the chosen few quite wanting in the show of geniality—the *empressé* manner—by which the travelled Persian or the pupil of *la jeune Perse* is distinguished. In their stead is found the old Persian phase of Oriental breeding; pleasing in its courtesy and polite address, but too artistic to be credited, and *minus* the majestic freedom from condescension and conventionality of the Arab host, and the stately ease with which self is forgotten by the Shaikh in the religious performance of a social duty. The incumbent on the occasion of my present mission, had been for many years in the post, and was there until very recently, when replaced by the ex-Grand Wazir. Among Orientals, he would be considered a man of much reading and general knowledge, and the mode in which his own appreciation of position and reputation is exhibited, would pass as the most consummate statesmanship. Among Europeans, opinion on such points may always be of different shades; but few, if any, could be expected to paint him in the colours used by a native limner. For my part, I met with courtesy and fair personal treatment at his hands; and was enabled to certify to the Minister's possession of a keen insight, *savoir-faire*, and other qualities which to my mind, rendered his original appointment as intelligible as the duration of his responsibilities. His demeanour, without being morose or especially grave, was to some extent affected by palpable bodily infirmity, less of age than accidental sickness; and he was not reserved in describing or dwelling on his physical complaints; but he could bear up vigorously against such outward assailants if his loyalty demanded the effort, and the Shah could not have had a more anxiously devoted or submissive servant. There were times when a French sentence, studiedly and smilingly uttered, would escape him, and on such occasions, the working of an under current of humour would appear on the surface.

But it is high time to bid farewell to Tehran. Ere doing so, let us take a parting look at Demavend, the noblest and most graceful of Persian mountains, and the most beautiful feature in any landscape comprehending it, of which the Tehran *entourage* may form part. Fully clad in wintry white, heavily or lightly streaked, or only tipped with snow, according to the season and the circumstances of the year, it presents a spectacle in which the most *blasé* and fastidious of beholders can find no flaw. Young and impressible travellers will, on their side, regard it with enthusiastic admiration.

On the 4th December, Major Murdoch Smith and I left Tehran for Ispahan, resolved to perform this part of the journey by "chapar," a process of locomotion already mentioned. Some kindly members of the Russian legation rode with us for a short distance from the town; but our fellow-countrymen had official indoor business to detain them. The get-up for these occasions must be regulated more or less by the season, but warm clothing is indispensable in winter, and a great-coat should never be forgotten, though not always worn. High boots, cords, coats with multifarious and readily-accessible pockets, and a solar hat, may be considered fitting requisites for every temperature. It is usual for the European traveller to stow what baggage he cannot allot to his own horse on that of his personal attendant, and failing the sufficiency of this provision, to load therewith the groom of the post-house, whose presence, or payment for whose supposed presence, is insisted on. Beer and books, preserved meats and wearing apparel, and essentials of the toilet, are commonly part of the contents of the saddle-bags; and a pistol and flask are almost always in the holsters. I take this opportunity of recommending my latest practice as worthy of imitation; that is, to furnish the holsters as a dressing-case and pistol-case respectively, filling in the spare places with small articles of constant requirement. A Government order for horses at the postal stations is procurable at Tehran, and should be provided; but where the traveller is known, or where his purse is freely opened, it is not exacted after the first change. Moreover, it may be taken for granted that incoming post-horses have been obtained under authority; therefore the same authority warrants the relief. Touching the quality of the cattle themselves it is to be borne in mind, "that the horses are not necessarily fast because used for posting. Some move along heavily and lazily from first to last; some require great tact and effort to be brought into action at all; and some have actually no go in them. Nor is it uncommon for the 'chapar' horseman to get a cropper. He should avoid all sudden rises in the road, because the descent is dangerous to the 'chapar' horse in motion; and this course, difficult at all times, is at night impossible."

The distance from Tehran to Ispahan may be roughly estimated at 250 miles of country easily recalled to memory. The first twenty-five miles are over comparatively fertile plains, ending with an ascent of barren, dreary hills, and a descent into a cluster of villages amid cultivation. The next sixty miles, leading to the sacred city of Kûm, at the foot of a mountain range, are for the most part over sheer desert and unmitigated desolation.

[1] The quotation is from my own "Notes on Eastern Persia and Western Baluchistan," read at the British Association in 1866.

The caravanserai and post-house of Hauz-i-Sultan; the caravanserai at Sadrabad; and the small post-house and bridge at Pul-i-Dalák, present the main features in the retrospect: away from these landmarks, carcases and skeletons would perhaps be the more notable symbols in the landscape. Well has part of this melancholy tract been called the plain of the Angel of Death. Local traditions make it a resort of *ghouls*, fairies, or spirits of some kind. We should imagine that they must be messengers of gloom, whom the wayfarer, seeking cheer and encouragement, would rather shun than welcome. Another sixty miles from Kúm, brings the traveller, turning eastward from an otherwise southerly course, and skirting the line of mountains on his right, to the city of Kashan. This section of plain can boast of villages and cultivation; and at Nasarpur, where the fine caravanserai provokingly invites to an extra halt, are melons as delicious, perhaps, as the world can produce. From Kashan the resigned and weary post-horse is urged, by his fretful and weary rider, across a plain of some extent, and for twenty-seven miles altogether, to the charming village of Kohrud, situated in the mountainous district whose name it bears. After a descent into the plains on the southern side of the range, and accomplishment of another short twenty miles, the post station of Bideshk, or caravanserai of São, is next reached: and hence a further short sixty miles of country remain to be traversed before reaching Ispahan. By rising early, and converting the morning into the midday meal which it is commonly made in Persia, my comrade and I disposed of this distance before breakfast.

Kúm is held in high repute as a sacred city, second in importance to Mashhad only. It contains the tomb of Fatima, and the bones of thousands of Muhammadans bequeathed to its honoured soil by the superstition of sorrowing friends and relatives. It is a large, straggling, ill-kept, uninviting place; and on any occasion that duty has taken me there, I have been glad to leave it behind. Kashan has not much more attraction as a residence; but it is deservedly famous for its silks and potteries.

BRIDGE AT ISPAHAN.

Ispahan has been so frequently and so well described that I will not venture to linger in that city. Any notice of its monuments, bazars, piazzas and streets, would be superfluous; any lamentations over its ancient glories and modern decadence would be platitudes. We visited the Chahal Situn and Sadri palaces, climbed the high staircase overlooking the Shah Maidan, experienced the reality of the shaking minarets, and "did" many things which the reader would not care to re-do with us in these pages. The general impression of the place was that it must have fitly represented the regal state and grandeur of modern Persia. Independently of noble, though dilapidated exteriors, there was an attraction in the taste of the rooms and fittings, especially the ceilings and windows of palace interiors, non-existent at Tehran. As for the semi-barbarous paintings—the most notable figure in which is Fath Ali Shah, usually on horseback—I was impressed by their unmistakable individuality; but the stolid way in which the *dramatis personæ* stick wild boar or destroy lions, looking all the time to the front, is ludicrous in the extreme. The costume of a period ranging from Charles II. to George I. seems to be popular; and the "pretty pages," with ruffs and knee-breeches, or Louis XIV. coats and continuations, are quite numerous.

Julfa is the head-quarters of the orthodox Armenian Church; the Archbishop here being supreme both in Persia and India. In 1865 I was informed that of their four schools (of which one is for girls) one boys' school was kept up by the subscriptions of a Calcutta merchant. The number of pupils in each was given at seventy. As a rule the Julfa clergy appeared very friendly and well disposed towards the British residents; and readily joined in their social gatherings. A day or two after arrival I had the pleasure of meeting, at the house of M. Stephen Agenor, the Archbishop, a monk, and two priests; and of joining my kind host in welcoming the Archbishop, the monk and M. Agenor at our own lodging the day following. A Christian Baghdad merchant formed on each occasion a pleasant addition to the dinner party.

Many Europeans who have died in Persia have been buried in Julfa beside the Armenian Christians, and a visit to the burial-ground and perusal of the several inscriptions on the tombs will well repay the traveller for the little cost entailed in time and trouble. Two may be found sufficiently interesting for extract :—

"Gulielmus Bell Joan. F. Northambriæ apud regem Abbas, pro Angliæ agens (sic). Año Dñi 1624, æt: suæ 33. Mensis Feb: die 24, Ispahani defunctus. Ad patem peregrinum—

Hexastichon

"Vive domi sed vive Deo, sic sero Senectus
Colliget ad charos membra soluta Patres.
Longinquis vitam dum conor quærere regnis
Heu! juvenem incautum mors inopina peremit.
Sed Christo vivens colui morienseque vocavi
Ed vixi quantum vixerat ille sat est."

The next is headed :

"Memento mori :

"Hic jacet insignis Doctor R^{us} Edwardus Puget Ang^{lus}
S.S. Trinitatis Collegii apud Cantabrigiam Socius
Theologus et Mathematicus læ talal artem (or ?)
Ut Divina cognosceret et mundana
Sed mundum vere reputans ut punctum
Extendebat lineas ultra tempus
Ut pulcram in æternitate oxyedron formaret.
Tand^{em} quinquagenarius ultimo puncto vitam clausit
In Patriam perennem redeundo sistebat mors
Obyt enim Ispahani die 21 Janr. A°. 1702-3 sec^{dm} styl. vet
Abi viator et ab insigni Doctore
Disce in tempore Æternitatem."

"Thus, with all diffidence, rendered :

"Live in thy home, yet live to God ; that so
    Mature old age may set thy members, freed,
Beside thy fathers ; I, resolved to go
    Forth to far lands, a vagrant life to lead,
Perish beneath the unexpected blow
    Of Death. Since living I have learnt to heed
My Saviour's worship ; dying, this will be
Comfort enough to feel I've lived as long as He."

There are, moreover, tombstones with Dutch and French inscriptions of the seventeenth century. Among the last, I was struck by the words "Cy gît Rodolfe" on a long, wide slab. They are said to mark the resting place of a traveller or settler, who had killed a Muhammadan and was sentenced by the mullas to death. An offer of pardon was made to the accused, but accompanied by the condition that he should renounce his own faith and become a Musalman. He declined the conditions, together with many inducements, and preferred to die in honour. The tomb, it is said, was at one time much visited by strangers.

The diary is now resumed from the date of quitting Ispahan; or on the 18th December, 1865:

"Left at about 1 P.M. Passed, or sighted, the three bridges Aliverdi Khan, Kaju, and Jin; crossed another. Passed also the ruins of palaces, and a building on which was the inscription 'Banda Shah Walaiat Thamasp Sāni 1144.'[1] Nags very bad. Mine showed a frightful raw sore on the haunch, and S.'s stumbled. B. and the Wakil ride out with us part of the way and we agree to purchase B.'s pony and A.'s hack. Make the exchange on the road, and just as well we did so, for when the saddle and cloth were taken off the back of my steed, he showed a mass of sores and cicatrices such as had I known of, I could not have ridden on. Here must have been the secret why the poor beast went tolerably well. March about fifteen miles—but had we gone by the right road, we might have saved two; at first over a country intersected with *kanāts* and water-courses, most of them dry; and fields under recent cultivation, amid swarms of pigeon-towers; then on a tolerably good road, leaving hills to our near right, one or two of the higher order having a snow-covered peak to the far left. Reach the old Gulnabad caravanserai soon after sunset. Find a *kāfila* of camels there.

---

[1] A.D. 1731.

Muhammad Khan says they bring tobacco, *bark*,[1] and cotton from Yezd. Road tolerably level; population decidedly sparse. We have now twelve beasts in all, eight mules and four horses. S. has three and I have two servants. Besides our two selves, the party further consists of the *charwadar* and five men.

"*December* 19.—Turn out after tea, about 8 A.M., and take observations on roof of caravanserai; S. with prismatic, I with common pocket compass. Gulnabad was formerly a large town, but was destroyed by the Afghans under Mahmud, in the days of Shah Husain Safavi. It was the scene of a great fight, and is a place of many graves as of ruins. March at about 10 A.M. and arrive at Sagzi at about 1.30 P.M., 3½ hours, say fourteen miles. Part of the road white with salt efflorescence, part with frost. The country is almost a desert, although there are occasional patches of past cultivation. The caravanserai is a good one, but has been deserted by its guardians. Its architecture and solidity corroborate the truth of the statement that it was built by Shah Abbas. My informant says his father remembers the Afghan invasion; but as this was about 145 years ago, I am inclined to doubt his accuracy. We are further informed that they have had no snow here for long though it has fallen in the hills; that there are about 70, 80, or 100 houses in the village, which is south of the caravanserai, and within walls; that there is a *hamam* here, built by Shah Abbas, still used, in the morning by men, in the daytime by women; finally that there is no tobacco or cotton received from Yezd, but sugar.

"*December* 20.—March to Kupa, 21 miles, 5 hours. Hills on our left running from N.W. to S.E., on our right in much the same direction from the Ispahan plain. Soil good, gravelly, and in parts strong, has an iron and slaty appearance. Strong mirage. Passed some *hauzes*[2] inclosed for receiving rain water; also many *kanats*. The pits dug at intervals for these had a strange appearance in the mirage. The caravanserai, west of the village, is very solid and well built. There appear to be the usual number of rooms—*i.e.* twenty-four, with stables at the back, and upper and lower rooms for hot weather. There are tombs outside, and an

---

[1] Cloth of camel's hair. [2] Tanks.

inclosed tank. A caravan of pilgrims, which was at the last stage, has accompanied us here. They had just reached Ispahan from Kerbela, and are now on their way back to Yezd. Take note of one or two small villages among the hills to our left. The last have been whitened by a fall of snow mingled with rain during the night. The general aspect this morning was very beautiful; and we had a sunny and almost cloudless day. The wind blew strongly from the westward on our arrival. We have here apples, pomegranates and other fruit.

"*December* 21, 1865.—Lāghara, 29 miles: 7 hours and 20 minutes, riding and walking. A bitter cold march. At eleven miles, Mushkinūn, a large village with gardens, but comparatively deserted; pass at two miles to right, Imam Zadah Kasim, the gilt dome of which was visible. The road gradually rises to the hills, amid which our course evidently lies. Enter them at about fifteen miles, having met the snow at Mushkinūn. Fourteen miles further, Lāghara, a village in a hollow, with poor accommodation. We are put up in the *katkhuda's* house, and our servants soon find fire. No one is forthcoming but a small boy, and he is made to show us our lodging. On the whole it was a very good one, and better than we were warranted to expect on arrival at a late hour, after passing the *manzil* (stage) which had been named to us, namely Mazra-i-Yezdi. Servants get great beams of wood, and an old door, and burn them in the room next ours, on account of the intense cold. They open also the *katkhuda's* stores of firewood and chopped straw. I object to the whole proceeding, but they assure me all will be well, and the man will receive his money. At present he is *non inventus*. S. orders three kirans to be given to the only man we can find, as a retaining-fee, and this seems to have a good effect. In the hills we passed several *abādis*, here called *mazras*, which consist generally of a few walled-in fruit gardens, a fort, apparently for the reception of inhabitants in case of attack, and often built on a mound, and one or two mud houses. From the leafless appearance of the trees, and sparseness of population, these *mazras* are not, however, very cheery to the traveller. What sad, habitual story-tellers are these people! Either they are unable to reply to the questions put to them, or they accept any suggestion of the questioner, and confirm it with the never-failing *bali*.[1] There is about six feet of snow on the ground. The sunset on these low hills is very grand. The highest points are perhaps 1,500 to 2,000 feet. Our caravan of pilgrims had halted also at Lāghara.

"*December 22.*—Villagers turn out, and get presents or payment for goods, both men and women. I like to see this done. The system of plundering on the arrival of a 'gentleman' is not simply Persian, but Oriental, and the servants here do not seem to me worse than their Indian brethren. 'The king's servants take everything they find,' said one, thinking me very soft for questioning his proceedings. So it is, no doubt; but the custom is un-English, and unpalatable to Englishmen. Start at about 10 A.M., and reach our stage soon after 2 P.M., sixteen miles. Although we are well out of the snow and hills, bitter cold is Beinbiz, where we meet with a most hospitable reception. Old Haji Husain gives us a capital, clean room—the best, by far, we have had on the road since leaving Tehran; and his little girls come and look at us through the trellised windows. Our march to-day was tortuous to some extent in the hills, but the general direction as we descended was east; a large plain was observed to the N.E., bounded by a range of hills, some of considerable height. In fact the whole country is very hilly, and many of these hills are solid rock, with abundant quartz and limestone. Pass a *kāfila* of camels with wheat, bound for Yezd, and with henna and clothes *from* Yezd. The last is expected from Minab and Karman. Had ocular demonstration to-day of the common custom of using a donkey to lead camels. With such aid, it is much easier for the driver to change his line of direction than in trusting to camels only. When requisite, he seizes the donkey, almost like a child, turns him the way he likes, and the camels follow. On the whole, we find civility as we progress. The road salute is often tendered us, and I invariably make a point of returning it.

"*December 23.*—Nāogümbaz, 12 miles. Fine road the whole way; a gentle descent from the hills into an open country, along which a carriage might be driven with ease. The march was

[1] 'Yes,' which affirmative is, however, expressed in many indirect ways.

cold, but the weather magnificent. Our course was easterly, over a plain bounded by high, rugged hills with sharp angular tops. There is a fine caravanserai here, and close beside it a *chaparkhana*; for the post road at Kashan is met at this point. Choose the latter. We had been gazed at last night at Bambiz as though we were wild animals, and the curtains had been drawn aside in the morning to exhibit us gratis at breakfast. But as our spectators were mostly children, the process was bearable; and S. appropriately remarked on the inevitable sensation which would attend the appearance of two Persians, with a retinue such as ours, in an English village. Now and then, it is true, the older folks were detected looking through the crevices of doors, and adopting similar stealthy devices; but I firmly believe the main object was to gather that we were comfortable. No doubt we are the first, or nearly the first Europeans whose visit is recorded at Bambiz. From inscriptions on the wall we learnt that our landlord, his father, wife, and sister, had all performed the pilgrimage to the *haramein*, or sacred cities of Mecca and Medina. The first, however pious and strict a Muslim, was assuredly no bigot in his behaviour to Faringis.[1] When offered his toman, as a natural present for kindness and civility, he seemed loth to accept it, because our supplies had been paid for; a reasoning the application of which at such a time is no less gratifying in its rarity than warranted by its logic.

"*December* 24.—Akda, 26 miles, thus divided: twelve to an *ab ambar*, or inclosed reservoir, built by Hasan Akdāi quite in the present day, where we breakfast; three more to a second reservoir and new caravanserai and fort, built by some munificent Reshti; eight to the village of Shahrabad, and three to station. The snow came gradually on us from the hills to our right, and lasted for some four miles; but it was not so cold as yesterday. Akda was once apparently a large village, though it is now deserted. Its houses are for the most part inclosed by a wall,

---

[1] In December 1870, I again passed by Bambiz, and my old host, Hāji Muhammad Husain, came to see me in tents. He greeted me with a warmth which astonished one of the members of the mission present on the occasion.

We put up in a good post-house; with the option of using, if necessary, a handsome caravanserai, especially distinguished by its cupola or minaret-looking *badgir*.[1] We had given our servants orders to provide a Christmas dinner for to-morrow; but by some perversity or misapprehension the special meal was brought in to-day.

"*December* 25.—It had already been my fate to spend a Christmas at little known localities, as for instance, in 1854 at Brahmanabad, and in 1861 at Hūki (which I leave to be discovered on the map). This year the scene was to be Māībat, perhaps equally inconspicuous.[2] This last-named station we reach after a march of some thirty miles, or ten leagues as accurately estimated by M. Rabie, about half a century ago. For the most part the road is dreary and wanting in villages. Jatta, the dilapidated caravanserai station at which we breakfast, barely deserves mention. But as we near our halting-place and look around, large villages are observed at various distances, telling of population and cultivation in spite of a certain monotonous lifelessness and want of relief in their clay and mud colours. There is a rugged, untidy appearance in the environs of Māībat. The soil is in great vogue for building and pottery. Consequently it has been indented and cut up to an enormous extent, and after the most approved style of Oriental irregularity. But the most notable objects are the hills on either side. Those on our right approached to within a few miles of our march of to-day, and a new and picturesque range opens out as we advance. On our left the hills are distant, being divided from our road by a desert plain some forty miles in breadth, sloping down to a low valley like the bed of a river, and gradually rising on the further side, into regions of snow. Seldom have I beheld anything more enchanting than the higher of these mountains for an hour or two before sunset. The clouds had dispersed from its crest, and left it to stand in exquisite relief against a delicious Persian blue sky; but below the crest was a belt of dark cloud like Saturn's ring. The base of the

---

[1] A kind of tower open at the sides, erected for the purpose of ventilation.
[2] I may now add Kalā-i-Kāzī, for the Christmas of 1871.

whole range was more or less filled up with mist and snow. The general effect was grand; and, as the sun got lower, a lurid red glare fell upon the scene and varied it most agreeably. S. and I dismount at the *chaparkhana*, where our *numads* (felt carpets) had been spread. It was well that we had anticipated our Christmas dinner; for to-day there was but humble fare. Our old muleteer, or assistant *charvadar*, started off this morning from Akda before ourselves. Snow had already come down freely and covered the ordinary road, and still continued to fall, so that all tracks of travellers were in parts wholly obliterated. The man had lost his way, and we had lost our dinner; for with him in his difficulty was the bulk of our commissariat. He is still missing at nightfall.

"*December* 26.—A Saiyid brought some specimens of pottery, four (*kūzas*) jugs, which were stated to be *pishkash*, or presents. But it was not easy to carry them to Yezd and Karman. March about fifteen miles to Himatabad, passing many farms and a surprising amount of cultivation; but inhabitants are sadly scarce. Much cotton grows here. The cypress and fir give pleasant shade to the landscape. The mountains, however, are the main scenic attraction. To-day our right-hand view is the finer. S. considers the range on a par with the Elburz, and I agree with him. They are more varied in character, if the average height be not so great; and one or two points must reach 7,000 feet. *Chaparkhana* at Himatabad.

"*December* 27.—After devouring an unexpected batch of English letters brought by special messenger from Tehran, we march over a sandy soil, first amid gardens, then over a plain, through the widely-spread village of Eskizar to Yezd. We are escorted into the city by the *istikbāl*, or cavalcade of reception, shown to a comfortable lodging in the *ark* (citadel), near the governor's own quarters, and treated with much courtesy and hospitality.

"*December* 28.—There are no less than twenty-three plates of sweetmeats displayed on the ground in our outer apartment, and perhaps a thousand apples, oranges, pears and pomegranates. We receive visits from a Mirza, who, together with our Mihmandar, stays with us during breakfast; also from an intelligent and travelled Darvish, professedly a Turk, who sits for a considerable time; from the heads of the Parsi community; and from Hindus. The Parsis, of whom there are probably some 3,500 in Yezd, retain throughout Persia the designation of 'Gabr;' they are distinguished from the ordinary inhabitants by a uniform turban of a drab or dust colour, which aptly harmonises with the sober and not undignified character of their features, garb, and demeanour; and whatever their ways and customs, or however backward their worldly civilisation, they present here an outer type far more picturesque and interesting than to be noted among their brethren of Bombay and India. The Hindus are from fifteen to twenty in number; the literal account rendered is fifteen traders and two servants. All, or almost all, are Shikarpūris. I recognised one or two faces among them. Some profess to remember me, and a practical instance in support of such profession is given by recalling a visit which I am stated to have paid, in company with the lieutenant of police, to a particular house in their native city. They wear the Persian hat, and are otherwise outwardly denationalised, but look what they really are, through all disguise of costume. No Jews called; but I am told there are as many as a thousand, including women and children. Truth is not always attainable in official statistics. When these are incidentally obtained from hearsay, and in the less known parts of Persia, they must be put to the arbitration of probability and common sense. I should roughly estimate the whole population of Yezd at 40,000, an eighth being allowed as a maximum for Parsis and non-Muhammadans. Called on the governor, known, moreover, as the 'general adjutant,' who received us in a friendly manner. He is short, sallow-complexioned, round-faced and of barely middle age; had been in London, Paris, and St. Petersburg, and speaks tolerable French, with the hesitation natural to one living far away from European centres. Tea, cigarettes, and the *kalian*, combined with conversation to temper the formalities of a first interview. Our friend the Darvish was present, and took his seat on the ground; the 'Nāzim-ul-Tujjār,'[1] a commercial dignitary, and withal a fine-looking Tehrani Persian, also came.

"*December* 29.—Visit the town, after breakfast, on foot, accompanied by Hindus, who look on us as their special patrons. Return and receive visits from the Wazir, an elderly gentleman of common Persian type. The Hindus call again in a body. Visited also by the Malik-ul-Tujjār, or head of the merchants of Yezd, who looked so well in his native turban that we could not but inwardly congratulate him on the fortune which saved him from his native hat. Spoke to him about the Hindus, and commended them to his care.

"*December* 30.—Yezd is situated in a sandy plain, high and open, between two ranges of mountains, running, in a general direction, from north-west to south-east. On the west is the open country from Kāshan; on the east an apparent desert dividing the province from Sistan, and little traversed by man and beast. The mountains north of Yezd are fine, and in certain lights picturesque; those to the south are, however, the more remarkable, and boast one or two peaks of great height, bold, rugged, and fantastic; presenting at all times a beautiful view, and worthy of more notice than a faint line or blank in our best maps.[2] Silk is here manufactured, the raw material being obtained in the neighbouring villages; but it is probably inferior to that of Ghilan. It is included among articles of export, as are also hennas,[3] dyes, cottons, and felt carpets.[4] Wheat is imported; for the patches of cultivation around the town, and neighbouring towns or villages, afford an insufficient supply to the inhabitants. The streets are wretched and blank like those of most Persian towns, but not especially dirty. There must be about fifty mosques, of which the Jama Masjid has a fine, high frontage, overlaid with the pretty blue tiles so

---

[1] The Arabic article "al" or "ul" takes the sound of the initial consonant of the next word, and is pronounced "ut."

[2] This deficiency is now being remedied, and the surveys of Major Murdoch Smith, R.E., in 1866-7, and Quartermaster-Sergeant David Bower, R.E., in 1871, will, it is hoped, be turned to good account.

[3] Chiefly from Khabis, near Karman.

[4] From Taft near Yezd.

common at Tehran. There are other mosques, as also caravanserais worthy of note; and of the 'maidans,' or piazzas, the Shahi Mardan, the Maidan-i-Khan, and the Chakmak may find a corner in the traveller's diary; the first, because it is the scene of the great annual festival of the Muhammadans, or 'Place du Muharam;' the second from its bustle and traffic; the third from some local associations which have given it its name. Yezd is supplied with water according to the season. If snow or rain be plentiful, it is well for the inhabitants; otherwise there is an inevitable scarcity. This year the snow seems to ensure a good supply. Call on the governor again to-day, and take leave; also on the 'Sarhang,' to whom we owe a visit, the Wazir, and the Malik-ul Tujjár; and look in upon the Hindus at the caravanserai, before returning to our quarters. The principal Hindu now here is one Sahib Rao, *gumáshta*, or agent of Jairam Das, a wealthy trader of Shikarpur; but the names of Nandaram and Daiaram, other Shikarpuris whose agents are also in the place, are more familiar to me. It is a matter of wonder how these men venture so far from their own native country, as to Yezd, Bukhára, and other cities of Persia, central Asia, or Afghanistan, to exercise a narrow traffic and precarious usury among men of a totally different creed and iconoclasts of the strongest type. But the Shikarpur Hindu is proverbial for his wandering propensities. We visited the shawl manufactory, and greatly admired the striped and flowered patterns.

'The governor gave us, as before, a cordial and courteous reception. He spoke much of the pottery for which the country from Kashan to Yezd is famous, and showed us certain specimens of blue and white delf, which would have been more pleasing, had the designs been Persian instead of weak imitations of Chinese drawings. The chief manufactory is at Naïn, on the north-west frontier of Yezd; but Káshan itself, Máibut, and doubtless other places in the neighbourhood possess their skilled artizans. I remember the story being current at Tehran, that one out of forty young Persians, who had been sent to Europe to undergo a course of training in various branches of science and manufacture, returned to his native land skilled, as he thought, in pottery, and was deputed to Nain to impart a new knowledge to its workmen. The result was that he could teach them nothing, but rather found that he had much to learn from his own countrymen. His Excellency to-day was attired in a shawl-coat, bordered with lace; wore a satin spotted neck-tie, passed through a ring, with turned-down collars; and otherwise showed his independence of any set national costume. He broke through, in our honour, the usual tea, coffee and *kalian* routine, by insisting on opening a bottle of pale ale, an article we did not expect to recognise in longitude 54, and latitude 31. In sober seriousness, our whole treatment at Yezd was unexceptionable, and will ever be cited by me as one out of many examples of Persian friendliness and hospitality, gleaned in personal experience. The following is a strange story, illustrative of Oriental men and manners:—

"In the later days of Fath Ali Shah, a royal prince was governor of Yezd. Called away to Tehran for a time, he left his government in the hands of a trusted minister. This last, in lieu of honourably fulfilling his trust, played 'fantastic tricks,' like Angelo; and when his master returned, refused him admittance into the town. A siege ensued, and the riddling of the fort walls with balls. Finally, law prevailed, and the graceless Wazir fled towards Sistan, turning to seek refuge (*bast*) in Mashhad. Hence arts and promises prevailed on him to emerge, and come to Tehran. Once in the capital, he was handed over to the harem of his outraged master, and stabbed and hacked to death with scissors!

"*December* 31.—The fruits of Yezd are delicious and plentiful; but would not suffice to tempt Europeans to a prolonged residence in this remote city. Yesterday, a fine buck was brought in. We have been presented with venison and feathered game, with cigarettes, and wine, said to be sherry but very like brandy; in fact, we have been surfeited with good things. To-day we were visited by the brother of the merchant chief, who had been to Bombay and Mecca; by relatives of the Imam Juma, whose title corresponds in some way to that of bishop of the diocese; by the head Parsi, and a companion; and one or two more. March out in the afternoon to Muhammadabad, a short ride of little more than two hours, passing on the way some gardens and other cultivated land. This village seems to consist of one long street, with a row of mulberry trees on either side, and many water-courses. Judging from the show of spectators of our entry, it should have a tolerably large population. As every available man, woman, and child must have been turned out, we might venture an estimate of 600 or 700. Our host was the son of the Nazim-ul-Tujjar, and performed his part with courtesy and credit. We were located in a long room with skylights, and ornamented with transparent marble slabs, much in use here, and obtained from the neighbouring quarries. Our *menu* of the day was as follows:—rice in profusion and well boiled; fowl stewed with prunes; meat, minced and fried into flat cakes; pigeons and game birds swimming in grease; chickens roasted to chips, salt and dry; scraps of good cheese, with herbs and excellent fruit. Few large towns of Persia that cannot produce wine of some description: that of Yezd is thick, and not superior.

"*January* 1, 1866.—New Year's Day. March to Sar-i-Yezd, the 'boundary of Yezd,' 16 miles. It has a *chaparkhana*, with small snug rooms and a good caravanserai. The ruins, with a background of hills, are picturesque. Our Mihmandar left us this morning, receiving a suitable present, and selling his horse to me for 40 tomans (£16) and A.'s hack, which I had purchased on leaving Ispahan. Course rather S.S.E. than S.E. The 'Shir-kuh,' rising majestically out of clouds on our right hand, or somewhat north of west, is here considered, with pardonable inaccuracy, the highest mountain in Persia. What studies for artists are to be found in these sharp Persian hills and beautiful skies! The stately stillness cannot but strike the beholder who is alive to these impressions; but the light veil thrown over the whole colour of the landscape is to me always the greatest charm, as it is one of the special peculiarities of Persian scenery. The Shir-kuh is reckoned at 36 miles from Sar-i-Yezd. Yesterday we opened out the valley beneath it. The whole snow-tipped range is marvellously fine. Met many camels going into Yezd. Road here and there slightly rising, but for the greater part level; sandy or stony, and barren and desert in character and surroundings.

"*January* 2.—March to Zain-u-din, 19 miles. Road for the most part hard and good, occasionally sandy and undulating. We follow the range of snow hills on our right, and find our halting-place near a spur from these running eastward. The hills on our left run eastward from the Yezd plain; and a branch from them, taking a southerly and south-westerly direction, forms to our front a kind of amphitheatre with a space of some miles between, through which passes the Karman road. Zain-u-din has a caravanserai of solid burnt brick, built with luxurious completeness by Shah Abbas; a circular hexagon, of which the gate forms, as it were, a side. Five good travellers' rooms face a similar number in the inner court; and there are stables and other rooms at the back. Above, the rampart and casements tell a tale of local insecurity and anarchy; and the partial *délabrement* looks more the result of violence than of age; but the assailants, whoever they may have been, Baluchis or Bakhtiaris, could not effect actual demolition. The position is as isolated as can be imagined. All in the immediate neighbourhood is a blank; there are no provisions, the water is salt, and wood is scarce indeed. An old custodian is living here, and may have lived here for years. Should there be no passing caravans, his physical subsistence would seem precarious: otherwise, his being stagnates rather than vegetates in retrospection. As for current events he neither knows or asks anything; he cannot say who is governor of the province in which he resides or who is his minister.

"*January* 3.—Karmanshahān, 16 miles. Road over plains, with slight ascent, between snow-tinged rocky hills, averaging 800 feet, on the right, and a low range on the left. There is a good, new, casemated caravanserai here, just built by the present Wazir of Karman, in whose praises the wall-distaining poets are profusely eloquent. Matchlock men are stationed in the place to guard the few ruined houses, fort, and road generally. Country very barren. Firewood scarce; but there is a kind of brushwood called 'bota,' which is abundant, especially near the hills.

"*January* 4.—Shams; a caravanserai of Shah Abbas, and post-house; 17 miles. The road for five miles rises gradually to a low spur of hills forming a semicircle from N.W. to S.E.; among

KASHKAI, MEMBER OF A LARGE ILIAT TRIBE.

which we pass over a broad, stony road, into a plain country. The door of the *chaperkâna* having been recently demolished by Bakhtiaris, according to the information given us by a Persian official, who stated he had been sent in pursuit of the marauders, we put up in a smoky room of the caravanserai. This also had been damaged by hostile hands; but fastidiousness in such matters was out of the question."

For a minute I will break off from the diary to venture upon a separate retrospect of Shams, in the caravanserai of which little-known locality I woke on the morning after arrival. It is early. The daylight penetrating a hole in the dark, vaulted roof, enables me to inspect the room in which my comrade and I have spread our bedding. Its height may be reckoned 22 feet; its length and breadth 18 by 12. On my side, the right, facing the single door—it will be understood there are no windows—are three large recesses in the wall (*takchahs*) of about four inches in depth; and below these are two of smaller outline but twice as deep, useful to us for depositing articles of apparel or daily requirement. The centre upper recess has a corresponding one on the opposite side, flanked by blocked-up, or nearly blocked-up arches. Two archways below these have been utilized as cupboards. The one nearest to Major Murdoch Smith has been covered to keep out the wind by a curtain on which a lion and sun, together with other lions, red deer, and peacocks, supply a characteristic, if not always a cheerful subject of contemplation. The walls and floor are of solid burnt brick, the walls, roof, recesses, and archways being quite black with smoke and age. So solid and massive are its large brick squares, that the floor appears to be of cut, quarried stone. Our fireplace consists of a central hole in the ground, whence the blaze from the brushwood, cheering in itself, but blinding in its attendant smoke, ascends towards the perforated roof. Light is visible through the cracks of a reduced and rickety door, opening in two divisions from the centre; but does not pour in so generously as from above. The whole scene is suggestive of a stage dungeon; and an *aria* from the "Trovatore" by my companion seems to intensify the resemblance. On the other hand, the native inhabitant is rather an Adelphi than an opera figure. Our guardian is a sharp, hungry-featured, wizen old man, attired in a felt, sugar-loaf cap, blue shirt, and drawers with waistband; having an old *postin*, or wool-lined cloak, thrown over his square, spare shoulders; whose grey beard bears the mark of dye long unrenewed; and whose cold feet and ankles find but scant cover and warmth in slippers. He is clearly out of sorts, and not by any means enchanted at our visit. It is possible, however, that the room we occupy may have been his own. His fine black cat seems to point to such a conclusion; for she comes in and out at pleasure, drinks the stranger's drinking water, sleeps on the stranger's bed, eats bones or similar perquisites, and purrs constantly in clear approval of her treatment.

January 5.—Anar, 23 miles. For the greater part over a desert plain, sandy or stony, and with scarcely even a bit of brookwood. On our left a fine mountain range, with Kuh-i-Bawar and Kuh-i-Zarand far away. The rocky range to right looks rather like the upper section of a high range than complete in itself; and is bold and rugged, showing great variety of shape and size, though generally low. Anar from the distance is picturesque, and an oasis in respect of cultivation and the rough necessaries of life. Before entering the town we pass an Imamzadah on a hillock, and new caravanserai. There are said to be 400 houses here. Much soil about the place is of a whitish colour, rocky, and yielding arable crops. There is the usual *chupurkhana*.

January 6.—Baiaz, 18 miles. Road tolerably good and

level, with some cultivation and a fair amount of cotton. Stony where it turns to our post-house. They are building here a new caravanserai. The village may boast about thirty houses.

"*January* 7.—Kûshkûh, 18 miles; over gravel and a good sandy road, amid much cultivation and many villages. The snug *chaparkhana* at this place is in charge of an old woman, and the bread and water provided are simply delicious. Fall in with gipsies. Some of the women have handsome faces; and are importunate as usual. They go by the name of *Kulba-band*, or *Ghurbati*,[1] of which the first may signify the necessity imposed on them of manual labour, and the second the nomadic nature of their lives. The caravanserai has been lately built by a Yezd merchant.

"*January* 8.—Bahramabad, 25 miles, over a road of which the first half, or nearly two-thirds, is not so good as on the previous days. Pass the villages of Husainabad, Hormuzabad, Dehanabad, and Mahdiabad. We have now reached a very flourishing and rising town, situated in the head-quarters of the Karman cotton districts, of quite recent institution; and owing its immediate success to the inundations which ruined the neighbouring 'Kaleh Agha,' together with its selection as a postal station by the Amír Nizam, or former Prime Minister in Persia. Besides cotton there is much wheat grown, and castor oil abounds; mulberry trees are also to be found. Visited by the local governor and resident agent of the Karman Minister. We were treated with much courtesy and civility, and leave Bahramabad with a most favourable impression of men and manners in this part of Persia.

"*January* 9.—Kabutar Khan, probably *Khana*, or 'pigeon house,' from a tower beside the village, 26 miles. Road good; near cultivation; then among water-courses; then over a waste tract for nine miles, and finally over heavy sand till close to station. Before starting we had been provided with a breakfast by the kindly governor, consisting of (*chilāo*) plain boiled rice, (*pilao*) rice prepared with lemon peel and condiments, a fowl with prunes, and a meat hash; orange and lime sherbet, con-

[1] "Tied to the plough" and "wanderer."

fection of quince and pomegranate, excellent pickles, tolerable bread, and last, not least, tea with milk; altogether, very palatable fare. The caravanserai here was built by the Beglerbeg of Karman twenty-two years ago. Noticed lately a curious method of digging and throwing up earth embankments in small fields. Two men work together; and while one digs, the other holds the arm of the spade by a cloth tied round it, pulling it to him as his fellow turns the earth. This arrangement is primitive, but believed to be common hereabouts. Kuh-i-Darawan is among the hills to the left of our road.

"*January* 10.—Baghin, 30 miles; a march broken by a halt and breakfast at the midway 'Rabat,' or caravanserai. The road is between low ranges of mountains, across a high alluvial plain, stony or with gravel, and much strewed with wild vegetation, as yesterday. The more productive soil seems to be at the immediate foot of the hills where flocks and herds are seen collected. Rabat is near the hills, on our left. In the neighbourhood is much cultivation, and there are one or two villages. The caravanserai is a splendid structure, built by the present Minister of Karman about two years ago, a functionary who is quite the Marquis de Carabas in these localities. Baghin has a caravanserai, and is a village of about seventy houses, mostly inclosed within a mud wall. Those outside present a ruined appearance. There is not much cultivation visible around; but there are signs of agricultural activity, and oxen ploughs are working until sunset. The hills to E.S.E. and S.E. loom out largely, and are covered with snow.

"*January* 11.—March into Karman, the capital of the province, about 19 miles, over a fair road, rising at first, and then gradually sloping down into the plain country. Met about 2½ miles from the gates by a large cavalcade, headed by a fine-looking Persian with a long, black beard. A prominent figure in his immediate train is the Parsi agent, who is a kind of representative of his co-religionists in Eastern Persia. Pass into the citadel, which has a handsome mud wall—if mud can be so qualified—and are shown to our quarters. We have two good though small rooms in the house of the *sarhang*, or lieutenant-colonel; and, as we move into the house, are saluted by a body of soldiers in red uniform, drawn up in parade order with presented arms. Eight copper dishes, of a diameter exceeding two feet, are laid out in our honour, with the following contents: two with Khabis oranges; two with Khabis pomegranates; one with Karman water melons; one with musk melons; one with ten loaves of sugar, and one with five boxes holding cakes and sweetmeats."

The last detail is trivial, but may afford some notion of the ways of those among whom my companions and I had been thrown in the course of duty.

SENTRY.

NATIVE OF MAKRAN.

CHAPTER XII.

KARMAN TO CHARBAR AND KARACHI; THENCE TO THE THREE INDIAN PRESIDENCIES AND SIMLA. SOMETHING ALSO ABOUT KARACHI TO GWÁDAR AND CHAHBAR; WITH A FINAL GLANCE AT OTHER OVERLAND ROUTES AND CITIES FOUND IN THEM.

KARMAN, capital of a homonymous province clearly to be identified with the Carmania of Arrian and Pliny, is a large town of between 30,000 and 40,000 inhabitants; distinguished not so much for site or buildings,[1] as for a certain commercial and manufacturing industry, which

[1] The streets are mean and narrow for the capital of a province; and there are few monuments of interest. Perhaps the most remarkable of these is a very old "Kubbah" or domed sepulchre, of great height, and embellished with some handsome blue tiles, the remains of what must have been a truly elegant exterior. No one seemed to know to whom it was dedicated, or whose tomb it covered.

finds practical illustration in its possession of many Hindu residents, and in the justly admired shawls and carpets turned out from its stores. The difficulty in reaching it from its nearest sea-port, Bandar Abbas, is great, owing to the mountainous nature of the intervening country; and the distance is so considerable that it behoves all those who seek a *rapprochement* between Persia and British India to give attention to the best means of intercommunication by land. Karachi seems to be the natural point of meeting; and although the roads now joining that port to Karman city make the aggregate of miles to be traversed verge on a thousand, I cannot but think that were there a good safe connecting highway through Bampur, either by the sea-coast and Gwādar, or the Kej valley, impetus would at once be given to a most desirable traffic. Moreover, a great obstacle would be removed to immediate action, and a practical course laid down, in the matter of a railway to India; whether such inevitable mark be attained by Government, by private enterprise, or individual philanthropy. At least, political preliminaries have, in this instance, been disposed of by recent definitions of territorial boundary.

We remained four days at Karman, most hospitably and honourably cared for by the late Muhammad Ismail Khan, Wakil-ul-Mulk, then Minister of the nominal governor Prince Kāiomars, son of Kahraman Mirza,[1] and afterwards governor himself. My kind host, a remarkable man, and of original character, though belonging to the old Persian school, forms naturally the prominent figure in the diary now again laid under contribution:

[1] Third son of Abbas Mirza; therefore, uncle to the present king.

"*January* 11.—Our *Mihmandar*, whose face beams with good humour and quasi *bonhomie*, does not insist on inspecting us at meals; but a less fastidious individual, for whom I entertain no pleasing recollections, has appeared on the scene, determined to renew an acquaintance formed in India. He accompanied the cavalcade sent out in our honour to-day, and though mounted on a donkey, while all others were on horses, he lacked the merest semblance of humility, and his conversation was incessant.

"*January* 12.—The Minister is to come into town this evening; and to-morrow our formal visits are to be paid. Attempts are being made to dissuade me from going to India by Bampur, owing to the inconvenience (*zahmat*) entailed; but for this I was prepared, and answer accordingly. The Minister's son, the *Serhang* Ali Murtaza, has gone with a force of cavalry, infantry and guns, into Balachistan, apparently to collect the yearly revenue. Yesterday we were favoured with *raki*; but to-day a Parsi brings us two bottles of country wine, which is agreeable to the taste, but not equal to the description given by the *Mihmandar*, who pronounces it the finest wine in the country, warranted free from all ingredients of headache. The latter, somewhat illogically, asserts he has never tasted it himself; but fortifies his judgment upon it by a story to the effect that a former Karman ruler, Khan Baba Khan, tasted every local wine procurable, and gave the preference to Karman produce. Kinnier makes Khabis fifteen days' journey from this place, and the maps follow his data. Here they tell me it is a flourishing town at a distance of 14 *farsakhs* only, or about 70 miles.

"*January* 13.—Call on the Wakil-ul-Mulk to-day at 8.30 A.M.; our interview lasting for an hour or more. He is short, very stout, has a large nose and generally prominent features, with an eye sufficiently sharp to make itself appreciated through a pair of monster spectacles which impart no little character to the portrait. He was dressed in a very clean and neat Persian costume, wearing a drab coat of beautifully fine texture and red nether garments like those of Indian Parsis. He received us with a brisk cordiality for which I was hardly prepared; and we had scarcely sat down at his invitation, when he poured out a volley of compliments and pleasant preambles to conversation such as I had been little used to hear even from his talkative countrymen. The English were his *beau-idéal* of strangers: 'he had known them,' he said, 'from childhood; his father had been Sir John Malcolm's *Mihmandar*. There never was such a man as "Malcolm Sahib." Not only was he generous on the part of his Government, but with his own money also.' Mr. Ellis had also been his great ally; and he gave us an amusing and intelligent version of this gentleman's own account of his Mission to China. Of Sir J. M'Neill he spoke in terms of high praise; Fath Ali Shah admitted him to his private apartments, and treated him as one of his nearest friends and acquaintances. On other British Ministers in Persia he discoursed in a like kindly strain, from personal knowledge or repute; then turned the subject to Afghanistan, news of which country he received from the native paper published at Karáchi. From this and Central Asian politics he came to the object of our journey, and here some difficulties presented themselves to his mind. Evidently he did not care to have the telegraph at his head-quarters; he suggested that a better road might be found for it from Yezd to the sea-coast than through Karman. As it was, S., who wished to reach Bandar Abbas, could not proceed by the direct route, which was impassable from the snow. He would have to accompany me four marches towards Bam. With regard to my once projected course, he could answer for me to Bampur; but how to proceed thence to Gwādar was not so simple. He himself had had to send his engineer to that part of the coast in disguise; and he strongly advised me to assume the Baluch costume for the second part of the journey, having donned the Persian hat for the first. Our servants were summoned, and subjected to a cross-examination on their qualifications and antecedents. Muhammad Rahím looked alarmed; but Hassan, the *pahlawān* (or 'athlete') stood the test well, smiling at his discreet inquisitor's caution to avoid practising his professional tricks on the Baluchis. Trusty guides would be provided; one for each of us respectively. Letters would be given to us for the chiefs of Bam and Bampur, but the Minister would not recommend a match along the coast, where his control was hardly recognized. Every now and then our energetic host would rise from his seat and, *more suo*, not *more Persico*, bustle about the room. He had things to show us; and not caring to have servants always about him, he fetched his own boxes, opened them with his own hand, stooped to pick up any fallen articles—in short, proved himself a most agreeable rarity. Among coins produced was an English dragon sovereign of George IV., stated to have come in with other gold and silver prizes as an instalment on a robbery from M. The Wazir, or, as he is commonly called, the 'Khan,' has abjured smoking; but snuffs like a genuine snuffer. Return home to breakfast; and after breakfast are escorted to the bazaar; a goodly collection of shops, the new section of which is on a large and solid scale. Visit two shawl *karkhánas* (manufactories), and one for carpets.¹

---

¹ Major Murdoch Smith says:—"In making the carpets, the threads (all of one colour) forming the length of the web are stretched on an upright loom consisting of two horizontal rollers. The cross-coloured threads that form the pattern are worked in by as many small boys as the breadth of the web will allow to squat in front of the loom. As the work progresses, the web is gradually rolled up on the lower roller. After every two or three rows have been worked, wide-toothed combs are inserted in the woof, and hammered down with a mallet, to keep the carpet close and firm. The master-weaver draws and colours the designs on paper, ruled to represent the different threads; after which he teaches the pattern to the pupils, who commit it to memory. The shawls are woven in a similar manner, almost the only difference being that the looms, or rather frames, are horizontal instead of upright. The memory of the workmen cannot possibly be assisted by seeing the pattern develop itself, as they always work with the reverse side of the web upwards. The *karkhanahs*, or workshops, in which the weaving is carried on, are such low, dark, miserable rooms, that one cannot but wonder that they should produce such beautiful manufactures. The shawls vary in price from 5 to 50 tománs (20l.), and fine carpets cost as much as from 4 to 10 tománs the square yard. Very few of the finer sort are made for sale in the bazaars, almost all being made to order for grandees in all parts of the kingdom. The spinning and dyeing of the wool for the carpets, and the *kork* for the shawls, are also carried on in Karman, which thus produces the raw material and completes its manufacture." ("Official Report to the Director Indo-European Telegraph," dated Bombay, March 7, 1874, par. 44.) *Kork* is the goat's fine, short wool nearest the skin. Precisely

The former are highly interesting; all is hand, and there is no shuttle work. Boys are generally employed, of an age varying from 10 to 14, and they learn the design to be followed, by heart, doing a certain allotted portion per diem. The occupation, carried on in a wretchedly confined room, cannot be said to be a healthy one or likely to promote physical vigour and development. How an English lad of the same age and under similar circumstances would sigh for out-door pleasures; and for him, whence would arise the contentment visible in the sickly countenance of the young Karmanis?

"Our progress through the town to-day was the cause of much excitement and curiosity on the part of both sexes. The Minister has announced a visit for to-morrow morning, an hour after sunrise! The active old gentleman has clearly no sympathy with sleepy travellers. The Prince sent us two large trays of sweetmeats. We are to make our call on him to-morrow.

"*January 14th.*—Visit from the Wazir before breakfast. He was blithe and fatherly, and full of anecdotes. He talked much of Dr B., like whom, he declared, he had never seen a doctor in Persia; giving force to the assertion by adding that he who said to the contrary lied! Had he not foretold that Kahraman Mirza would die in five years, if he did not take care; and had not the prediction been fulfilled, almost at the time specified? Called on the Prince, whom we found a good-looking young man of about two- or three-and-twenty; and by whom we were received in a neat apartment, in a gentlemanly and unostentatious manner. The shape of his face and its rich brown complexion were well suited to the custom of young Persia, which scrupulously removes all debateable hair save that on the upper lip; his fine eye, though somewhat reddened, was not yet dimmed by dissipation; and the toilet would have been quite passable in a European sense, notwithstanding the trimmed Karman shawl-cloak and striped military trousers, but for the loud pattern of the under garment with its many flowers. If conversation,

---

the same word is used in Turkish to mean the "pelisse" commonly worn by Osmanlis and other Muhammadans. It is one of the chief exports from Karman to India.

rambling on railways, balloons, and telegraphs, did not flow freely from paucity of known subjects of mutual interest, there was no disagreeable hitch or halting to mar satisfactory accomplishment of the visit, with its accompanying *kaliuns* and liquids. We were made to sit on two chairs while our entertainer preferred to retain his more natural position on a handsome rug apparently of Western manufacture. Called also on the Mujtahid, or High Doctor of Divinity. We found him sitting with a small party, among whom was the Imam Juma, and the Wazir's young son, a smart boy of about fifteen. The reception was cordial, and conversation pleasant and unconstrained. I am inclined to write down this *mujtahid* as good a Mussulman as can be imagined, and as liberal and free from prejudice as can be looked for among any in his position. The Hindus at Karman seem less demonstrative than their brethren at Yezd: in number there are about fifteen. Our presents to-day from the Khan consisted of large game, fruit, and four kinds of ice—lemon, cinnamon, saffron, and peppermint water. We learn that the old fort here, called by some Kaleh-i-Dokhtar (virgin fort) or Kaleh-i-Ardashir (fort of Ardashir), was built by Ardashir Babegan, son of Babak, and conqueror of Karman, according to Persian history in an English dress; but son of a shepherd, and born at Shahr Babak (the town of Babak), as I am told here.

"*January 15th.*—Visited the Khan at an early hour to take leave, and thank him sincerely for his great civilities. He had before told us that the requirements of his position, one of which was the yearly supply of a considerable sum [1] to the royal coffers, made him a merchant as well as minister; and, not unexpectedly, we found him deeply engaged in business. Much of his time, indeed, must have been passed among his bales and papers. But just as he could turn, in an instant, from personal cares to the details of provincial administration, so was he always ready to give attention to the cases and claims of individuals. He had the character of knowing the history of every resident in

[1] Mr. Markham ("History of Persia") says 200,000 tomans (£80,000). The same figure was given to me in 1866.

Karman; and, judging from ourselves, he took little time in learning the wants of strangers. Our last interview gave us no cause to change the high estimate before formed of his friendly consideration. I wished him to name some article of English or Indian manufacture he would allow me to forward from Bombay, as the merest *souvenir* of a short but pleasant acquaintance. Reiterating an assertion that he needed nothing but reciprocity of kindly feelings, he said, if I insisted on sending something, let it be a translation of the history of Persia, which he had understood the friend of his boyhood, Sir John Malcolm, had written. On his part, he would give me a written account of Karman.[1] Like all his countrymen, he had quaint superstitious notions. One was that, until arrived at forty, no man's judgment was to be trusted. Up to that age he held all acts committed to be more or less of the nature of mistakes! Another was in the infallibility of 'mumia,' a kind of resin exuding from rock, to serve as a cure and prophylactic in physical emergencies. The tiny box which was placed in my hands this morning, though its contents had the semblance of ordinary salve or ointment, was to my mind a signal proof of regard, and valued accordingly. At the same time, I fear that had I needed the virtues it was assumed to possess, I should have been at a loss for the means of practically eliciting them. The specific would nerve the system to meet danger, or restore it when the danger had passed, besides exercising a more palpable medicinal power; but I was not quite clear on the mode of application, or whether internal or external, or both.[2] A further token of the Khan's especial favour towards

---

[1] Both promises have been fulfilled. But while the "History of Karman" duly reached its destination, the translation of Malcolm's "History of Persia," commenced under sanction of Sir Bartle Frere, and completed under authority of Sir Seymour Fitzgerald, respectively Governors of Bombay in Council, has been necessarily presented to the son and successor of Muhammad Ismail Khan, first Minister, but afterwards sole responsible Governor of Karman.

[2] As the word signifies, even to an English ear—for "mummy" is the Persian, Spanish, and Italian *mumia*, *momia*, or *mummia*—the material effecting the corporeal preservation of man's frame after death, is evidently considered to possess properties available for the sustentation of a living body.

me was exhibited in the spontaneous offer of an order to visit the frontier fort of Bam.[1]

"In bidding us farewell, which he did in evident sincerity, the Khan commended us to the protection of the Universal Father—of Him who is Omnipotent, without respect of places or persons.

"Our special guides appear proper and trustworthy men, and S. and I start from Karman prepared for a speedy separation and more adventurous travel than heretofore. March this day about 25 miles to Mahūn, a large and populous village with many gardens, well situated on high land at the foot of hills, and proud in the shrine of Shah Niāmat Ullah, of prophetic renown among the holy men of Islam. The locusts are reported to have done much damage during the past hot weather. At Mahūn I am informed that 500 are produced from one only: but the Khan's more definite and less extreme statement was to the effect that for one locust, dying within the earth it penetrated, 84 (or 92) succeeded, in the first instance crawling, then gradually rising to pursue, in airy flight, a career of active destruction.

"*January* 16.—A mischievous story about one of our attendants related to me by Mirza M. to exalt his own character and prove his disinterested devotion to our service, put me to the inconvenience of being my own Munshi and addressing a letter of some length to the Wazir. Despatching the same to Karman without acquainting the Mirza, I received a letter in reply confirming me in my impressions of double-dealing on the part of this Indo-Persian, whom I dismissed in no agreeable mood. We are located in an outer court, as it were, of the shrine of Niāmat Ullah, where the building seems intended to afford accommodation to pilgrims. The rooms are compact and solidly constructed of baked bricks, quite in keeping with the durable caravanserais already noted in this province. We are taken

---

[1] When the Mission under my orders was at Bam on its way to Makran in 1871, and again on its way to Sistan in 1872, no plea would suffice to procure admission to this fort for any of the officers composing it. The local Governor expressed himself powerless in the matter.

over to the shrine, and received there by a septuagenarian darvish, whose son, a fine, well-looking man, below middle age, attends us in our quarters. The old man's story reminds me of the three last vicars of my home parish, who had between them occupied the post a full century and a half. His father had lived till ninety years or more, and he himself bids fair to follow the paternal example. The family had been custodians of the shrine for twelve generations. We ascend to the outer roof, and as our guide proposes a visit to the interior, under the blue dome, we turn to continue our inspection. But having descended and approached the entrance, we are stopped by a request to take off our boots; and equipped as we are for travelling, it becomes a question whether curiosity shall be satisfied at the cost. Declining to press the matter, I was about beating a polite retreat, when the old darvish invited us in, all booted and spurred. Contenting myself with an inspection from the threshold, I saw the handsome tomb of Yezd-like marble, and a beautiful carpet worked by Ustâd Husain, the head craftsman of Karman. The shrine was covered with books, and overhung with large dark eggs, in size like those of the ostrich. Ride from Mahûn in a S.S.E. direction, keeping the Jufar mountain on our right and Jûgh Karman range on our left, for some fourteen miles; when we reach the snow elevation and follow a wet and slippery winding path turning from S. to S.E. for about four miles, till we perceive three rock caves and soon afterwards the caravanserai of Hanaka, built by the Khan. The ice and snow had been quite recent; weather moderately cold; but scenery most desolate. It is said that both copper and coal are to be traced in the neighbourhood. My *ghulam*, or guide, is a great sportsman, and brings in two fine *kabaks* (partridges) and the smaller *tihu*, all acceptable additions to our table. His tall hat (*kulla*) and spectacles give him a strange appearance; and he has a strange way of attaching the last to the first, dropping them to the bridge of his nose when required. The reigning Shah must be credited with the sensible reduction of the *kulla* which had attained, and threatened among certain classes to attain still more, preposterous dimensions. The story goes that, so strictly had the regulations on the subject been carried out in Tehran, that the sentry posted at the public entrance leading to the royal palace had instructions to measure any hat of suspicious size whose wearer ventured to pass his beat, and if the prescribed length were found to be transgressed, the knife or scissors came into instant requisition.

"*January* 17.—March to Räinn, about twenty-six miles; of which the first ten are over snow-covered hills to the caravanserai of Kaleh-i-Shor. Into this, if the traveller feel disposed to enter, he finds a low room in the centre of the building open to the front. Should such accommodation be insufficient, he creeps under a small archway, visible on either side, through a mere hole, to resume a standing position only when under the vaulted roof within. Here he has a room divided by domes and arches into four separate sections; and each dome is provided with a central orifice for the passage of light and air. I should not recommend halting at this caravanserai, which is the reverse of cheerful. Two miles further, and we commence a descent from the hills; the last eight or ten miles being over a stony plain through which a road has been to some extent marked out and cleared. Our *istikbal* is headed by the *zabit*, a well-dressed smart village officer, attended by two cavaliers and a donkey rider. As we pass among the houses, walls, and gardens, a goodly number of villagers turn out to meet us. We are shown into capital quarters, and treated as guests of the Karman governor.

"*January* 18.—Detained all day at Räinn, the snow falling heavily; but we are well enough cared for, and have fair quarters in a spacious court which seems to have served the purpose of a caravanserai. The *chinar* (plane) grows here to a remarkable size, and there are walnut-trees. Opium is cultivated here and at Mahun; the latter having much repute.

"*January* 19.—Strong wind during the night. Morning being fine, we resume our journey and march about thirty-three miles to Tahrud, the 'bottom of the mountain stream;' rather a mud caravanserai than a village, and the temporary abode of a few cultivators. After two miles' riding we reach a *kharaba* or rain; and then, up to our station, there is scarcely visible a building of any description. We follow a high road, in general direction S.E. by E., for about fourteen miles, over a large, open, and slightly undulating plain. Muleteers then turn off to the left and take a north-easterly course over heavy ground, and a *kavir*, or salt marsh. After some four miles we reach and follow, first east and then south, another road, for the most part in the bed of a *rud-khana*, or mountain-fed river, and eventually come upon Tahrud at the foot of a tolerably high range of hills, just where this torrent seems to have expended itself. The prospect here is very desolate, notwithstanding cultivated patches. How Pottinger calls this a a town, I can only explain from the false replies commonly given to a stranger's questions, or from some misapprehension.

"*January* 20.—March to Sabristan, or Sarvistan, twelve miles, first in the unlooked-for direction of S.S.W. and afterwards, eastward of south, to a steady course of S.S.E. From broken ground and torrent beds we come to a tolerable track, and eventually meet the road we had followed for fourteen miles on leaving Raïnn yesterday. Three miles out of Tahrud we passed a fine, picturesque fort and ruins on our left. Might not this be the town of Pottinger, laid down in maps? or is the latter Awar, a village of 200 houses, fourteen miles N.N.W. of Sabristan and seven from Tahrud? Put up in caravanserai, and prepare for separation from S. to-morrow. He moves to Bandar Abbas over the high pass to the southward; whilst I seek a road through the plain country on our east, leading to Bam and Baluchistan.

"*January* 21.—It is not pleasant to lose an agreeable travelling companion, even when one's lot is to be passing through the civilized countries of Europe: but in a waste and weary land, where the step of an European is not traceable for half a century, to lose a fellow-countryman with whom one has just accomplished more than 800 miles of Persian snow and desert with the full consciousness that some hundreds of miles more of similar country have to be traversed in comparative loneliness, is rather a serious matter. To be stared at on arrival at every stage, or on encountering stray wayfarers; to be watched in one's every movement if the assigned particular corner of the halting-place be quitted; to pass eighteen out of twenty-four hours in a sort of prison routine; all this is bearable enough in company with an honest, truth-telling, English associate; but alone, it is wearisome, and especially at an age when young enthusiasm has been supplanted by something more sombre and matter-of-fact. Major S. quitted me after breakfast this morning. We parted with mutual good wishes, and hopes of speedy re-union on the coast of Makran."

My instructions to Major Murdoch Smith, dated the day before we separated, contained the following passages:—

"So much will depend on your own discretion and judgment, you are also so well acquainted with what are our present objects in ascertaining the several routes from one line of land telegraph to another; and how essential it is to keep clear of all political questions in our intercourse with the inhabitants of the coast; that I will abstain from hampering your movements by any further or more definite proposals hereon.

"It is probable that I may reach Charbar about the 12th or 14th proximo, when it would give me great pleasure to meet you again. But I can neither ask you to detain the steamer, nor to guide your plans by mine, as it is impossible for me to anticipate my movements beyond Bampur, which I am led to expect may be reached on the 3rd February. Besides, if it were practicable to proceed from the latter place to Gwâdar direct, I should prefer adopting that route, as one hitherto untravelled by Europeans."

The official results of the double journey have been already stated.* And, independently of submission to Government, my diary from Sabzistan to the coast has

* Chapter V. pages 280 *seq*.

long ago been before the public.¹ In relating, therefore, a fresh story on the subject, I will endeavour to avoid undue repetition and prolixity.

Long sight and a pocket compass were sufficient aids to get a fair notion of the country we were traversing; and it became very evident we had made two marches instead of one. After leaving Raium, had we not turned off to Tahrud, we might have pushed on at once to Sabristan; or having turned off to Tahrud, my comrade and I might have parted there, and one march thence by direct road would have taken me to Darzin. As it was, I had about eighteen miles to accomplish to reach the latter place from Sabristan. But remedy there was none. The arrangement had probably been made in pure consideration to ourselves, and to keep us together to a point held mutually convenient for dividing camps. Remonstrance, therefore, having become vain, we had nothing left but to start each according to the way chalked out for us, and this we did. My suite consisted of the guide, Hashim Beg; two personal servants, one of whom, Hassan the athlete, had at least a commanding *physique*; the muleteer; and a small boy, who sat, in elevated position, on a well-packed white pony. On our right was the noble

---

¹ Journal of Royal Geographical Society, vol. xxxvii., pages 284 to 297 inclusive. But another cause for brevity in these records of Eastern Persian travel is to be found in the fact that a volume is now under preparation, by Government authority, giving the scientific as well as political results of my later missions to Persia and adjacent countries. As the road measurements of the Survey officers will therein be recorded with precision, as well as other observations notified, any lists of officially reported *routes*, more particularly those traversed in the present volume, would be here superfluous. Under the circumstances stated, the reader will understand that the publication of this and similar information has only been reserved, not indefinitely put on the shelf.

snow-covered range we had first observed in passing down to the plain below Raiun; and I am well inclined to accept the theory which makes the Deh Bakri pass, whither Major Smith had proceeded, the same as intended by Marco Polo in the "mountain whence there is a considerable descent," reached after a seven days' journey from Karman. On our left was a low, rocky range of irregular hills; and before us, as we moved eastward, was a vast open space into which we were steadily advancing. Two uneventful marches over a sparsely-cultivated and poorly-peopled tract brought us to Bam. The stage intervening has its historical associations of the age of Rustam; but, in its bare modern reality, is little more than a caravanserai.

Bam—properly Bahm, if it really take its name from Bahman, the supposed founder—is a large town of, it may be, five or six thousand inhabitants, situated on a high plain, between a mountain range to the south and low rocky hills north, amid gardens and cultivation. Before the formal annexation of large tracts east of Narmashir, it had a political as well as strategical importance from its position as the frontier town of South-eastern Persia. Now it is better known as the capital of the Bam-Narmashir district, conveniently situated in a highway leading to Karman, Sistan, and Bampur respectively.[1] The reported slaughter of prisoners and erection of a pile of heads there, by Agha Muhammad Khan, after his defeat of the gallant Lutf Ali Zand, and the rebellious resistance offered forty years later within its

[1] One of the names of Bam is said to have been "Arba," which in Arabic means "four," and supposes a fourth road to Khūrasan. This last would appear to be, however, much the same as the Sistan highway, even though it branch through Khabis and west of the Sistan Lake.

walls by Agha Khan Mahlati, of our own day, have rendered the place historically eminent in modern times; and its fort and citadel enjoy a more than local reputation. To say, however, that the fortifications were accounted, in Pottinger's time, "beyond any comparison the most defensible in Persia," means nothing, unless we remember, how armed and provided were the probable besiegers. During my stay here, which extended one day over that of arrival, I took occasion to inspect the stronghold, drinking a cup of the commandant's tea *en passant*; and to receive visits from any persons disposed to call. Among these were the garrison doctor, a sallow-faced, intelligent Karmāni, dressed in a red cloak and shawl turban; the local governor's brother-in-law, and my acting host, owing to the governor's absence; and an individual who remembered me at Karāchi. The doctor said the *mūmia* I possessed was greatly prized, and only procurable from a hill or rock at or near Babahan, between Shuster and Shiraz, in the south-west of Persia.

From Bam to Regan, a distance of about sixty miles, the road runs through the district of Narmashir; and for two-thirds of the way among farms and forts promoting or protecting cultivation. The population, too scant for the fertile soil, is essentially pastoral and agricultural: and villages such as Kruk, Naimabad, Azizabad, and, quite recently, Wakilabad, give speaking testimony to the industry and resources of their inhabitants. But in this country, as in Russia before the serf emancipation, the want of a wealthy farming, or independent rural community is fatal to real progress. Industry does not go ahead and thrive on its own account: labour is the peasant's; but its produce, save the sorry hire, is that of the man in power. Here and there may be found a well-to-do trader who has a comfortable dwelling and brings up his family in comparative comfort; but such cases are certainly not the rule, and depend more on adventitious advantages than industrial efforts. If Persia would only try the experiment of encouraging agricultural travail in Narmashir by timely relief instead of habitual exactions; by rewarding proved honest labour with land

giants; and above all by ensuring security and freedom from molestation to poor as well as rich; I think she would soon welcome the result in a population doubled in number and many more miles of grain-fields. The first march out of Bam, I put up at a kind of fort, with court and buildings full of poor cultivators or tenders of cattle of all ages and both sexes. Though water there was abundant, cultivation had not spread. The next march brought us to the populous village of Naïmabad, the walls of which too closely confined its numerous inhabitants. Our arrival here was productive of a slight disturbance; for the man on whom we were billeted seemed at first unwilling to give us the asked-for accommodation; and no sooner had he been talked over by my Persian *attachés*, than his ladies appeared at the door of the room required, and stormed loudly. Seeing Hassan quietly appropriating the quarters at this particular juncture, I felt bound to censure his proceedings; but no harm had been done. The billet was accorded, and complete pacification ensued. The third march from Bam was to Regan, when we left the more fertile lands and gradually descended to a vast, open, hard plain, with scattered, wild vegetation. As the plants and bushes thickened, the ground became less level and more sandy. Regan itself was barely visible among the low jungle until we had just reached it.

Murtaza Kuli Khan, the *sarhang*, eldest son of the Wazir of Karman, was at the time of our arrival at this station, halting there on his way to Bampur, with a detachment of *sarbaz* and guns. With him also in camp was Ibrahim Khan, governor of Bampur. The former had been prepared by his father for my arrival, and anticipated any movement I should make towards acquaintance by a message asking which of us should call upon the other first? Pahluwān Hassan answered that I was tired with travelling: so the *sarhang* himself came to see me, and was soon joined by Farj Ullah Khan, governor of Bam, and a smart officer of engineers. We had a lively and pleasant meeting; and my satisfaction would have been complete but for the disappointment experienced on learning that, for some forgotten reason, I must halt a day at Regan. The *sarhang* was to start a day before me and proceed to Bampur by the upper route, through Sarhad. In the evening I returned the visit paid me, and after a warm reception, I was perched on a chair, *nolens volens*, like the compulsory president of a promiscuous debating society; while seated on the ground were the *sarhang*, the engineer officers, and a third, unknown, on one side of me; and an elder of Regan, Ibrahim Khan, and a *naib* (lieutenant), on the other. The *sarhang* I found a stout, cheery and good-looking young man of winning address. The Bampur chief was sturdy and thick-set, beyond middle age, with a round and not very expressive face, set off by a well-dyed beard; and his Persian was hard to understand. The bustle and noise of camp were quite grateful in these parts; and the drums were especially welcome. Later in the day a message or two passed between Ibrahim Khan and myself about my proposed journey; and by his suggesting a direct move to Bandar Abbas, I inferred that he would have wished to dissuade me from prosecuting it. But my mind had been made up on the subject; and I saw no cause to retreat from my resolve. On the day following, the brave army marched out of Regan, and I was left to get through twenty-four hours in that very unattractive collocation of a hundred mud houses. My abode was within a large quadrilateral inclosure; and as if the outer wall were insufficient protection, Hasan must needs bolt me in at night.

From Regan to Bampur, a distance roughly computed at 180 miles, we made out a nine days' journey exclusive of one halt. The first half to Khosrin led through a barren, dry tract, for the most part sand-hills of various shapes and sizes—some forming fantastic, unmistakable landmarks, some bearing names which served to distinguish normally dim localities. This region, however distasteful to the ordinary traveller, would be found an interesting field for geologists, from the western entrance of the rocks at the hot springs of Abigarm, to the south-easterly exit near the torrent of Khosrin; but its dreariness is indescribable: and the heat in summer must be terrific. Yet here and there is pasture; and water is, at certain seasons, abundant in the midst of this desolation. It was with a sensation of relief that we emerged from the hills upon the slopes which led to the vast Bampur plain. This tract was of a different character to that we had passed through; but the rugged outlines of the scenery behind us remained long visible as we continued our easterly course. In using the term "Bampur plain," I seek to express the whole high land bounded on the west by the desolation just described; on the north by extensive desert as well as hill chains or detached irregular ranges, amid which the snow-covered Basman mountain rises in surpassing height and beauty; south and east by a barrier of continuous rock, through which the passes into Makran and Kalāt, respectively, are limited, by vulgar and perhaps truthful tradition, to seven in number. The character of this plain, more than 100 miles in length, is that of central fertility with a ring or belt of desert near the bordering hills. Actually touching the hills again, there is, in some spots, a show of verdure. The grain and vegetable-yielding land is interspersed with trees, and these, though generally low, are not without a certain importance: notably the babul, tamarisk, and wild caper, of which the last presents occasionally a very graceful appearance.

Our camping-ground, between Khosrín and Bampur, was at Laddi, Kalanzao, Chahi Shor, and Kuch Girdan: names which mark no precise locality, but signify that the wayfarer's great essential, water, is procurable. If one well be choked, there will doubtless be a second in the vicinity to supply its place. But an experienced guide is invaluable, because these wells are hard to find, even for the initiated, and shepherds and goatherds are not always on the spot. At Kuch Girdan there is the Bampur river. Our guide, Hashim Beg, though he actually accompanied me further, had been ostensibly relieved at Bam by an artillery *naib* called by my facetious athlete, "the voiceless." He was truly a solemn and silent individual, who hovered about me phantom-like at unexpected moments, and looked, as he rode along at my side, not unlike the *Commendatore* in "Don Giovanni." He again had been replaced at Regan by one Thamasp Kuli, of aspect smart but sinister. A cast in the eye was perhaps, after all, the only true drawback to his good looks. He proved himself, at all events, a vigilant and intelligent *ticerone*; and though, availing himself of the occasion, he had agreed to escort some people and quadrupeds to Bampur on his own account, he did his duty to myself honestly and well. He wore a medal for gallantry in action with the Baluchis at Erofshan. Before reaching Bampur, my own two personal attendants had both shown signs of languor and despondency, especially Pahluwán Hassan, whose *morale* was in truth far behind his *physique*. Neither of them was exactly comfortable on a camel, the animal selected for their conveyance in Baluchistan; but the athlete prided himself in having achieved a superiority in this respect over his fellow-servant. One day on the march he seized the opportunity of Rahim's camel falling with its rider, to tell me a story to the poor man's prejudice, when just as he was reaching the climax, down came his own camel. His dismay and discomfiture were ludicrous. I never heard and never asked for the conclusion of his narrative.

Kuch Girdan, the last stage on the march from Narmashir to Bampur, is not exactly the place to choose for halting; but as at Regan, so here also, the step was a necessity. I reached this place on the afternoon of the 4th February, after a hot and weary march, during which I had walked some three or four miles, in consideration of my steed's sore back, a contingency that had begun to assume grave proportions; and on the following morning, after a night *al fresco*, there I still was among the tamarisk bushes, not preparing a start, but awaiting camels which had failed to appear. Thamasp Kuli had written to Ibrahim Khan to announce my approach, and intention to ride in to Bampur on that same afternoon; adding an expression of hope on my part that he would dispatch me to the sea-coast as early as possible; and a return messenger had brought intelligence of the safe arrival of all whom I had left at Regan, with an intimation that I could come in as intended, or wait until the next morning. The state of affairs, however, decided me to adopt the latter course; so I remained another day at Kuch Girdan, almost buried in the sand, which a strong and incessant east wind, originating in a cold mist before dawn, cast over us from hillocks not many hundred yards away. The diminutive tent I had provided myself with came up, it is true, in the course of the evening; but something more substantial was required for cleanliness, exclusive of convenience or comfort. The camels did not all arrive; one poor beast was reported to have died on the road; and the drivers were out all night.

On the morning of the 6th February we moved to Kasimabad, a small village of Baluchis, with a farm-fort, where the inhabitants, generally, looked poor and savage; the children being half naked, the men ill-clothed, and the women dirty and disheveled. The black complexions and ill-favoured countenances, together with the squalor and wretchedness everywhere apparent, gave me a painful impression of the population in these parts. African types I had already observed; and their recurrence at Kasimabad led me to suppose that, irrespectively of the practice of keeping private slaves, a system of slave colonizing had been pursued, and might be still in force in Persian Baluchistan. The hut in which I was installed was formed of tamarisk trunks and branches, a few sun-dried bricks, mud, and other odds and ends, procured from the jungle.

Our entrance into Bampur was according to the approved Persian custom in such matters. I had been provided with a good riding camel in place of my sore-backed horse for the first part of the march; and I subsequently dismounted and exchanged the seat for one on a Persian charger, saddled and caparisoned in the native fashion. As we drew near, Suliman Khan, deputy-governor of Bampur, came out to meet me. Baluch cavaliers, paraded on the road-side, fell in with the retinue. Persian horsemen, eager for display, started to the front, and skirmished, firing at full speed to their front, flanks and rear, with skill and effect; the variety of colours and costumes observable in the mixed cavalcade served to vivify and light up the picture. On arrival, discarding ceremony, I went straight to the tent of the *sarhang*, and met with a warm and friendly reception. Suliman Khan accompanied me, and Ibrahim Khan came in while we were conversing together. However true might be the rumours of his hostility and misdoings, I had no personal objection to the short, squat, bluff, plain-spoken Bampur chief; and preferred his open opposition, if such were purposed, to the sleek looks and expressions of the conventional Oriental host. To his objections to my move to the coast direct, or at Gwädar, I proposed that he should simply pass me to the limits of his own territory, where it touched that of Kalat, and I would get Fakir Muhammad, the local governor on the other side of the frontier, to escort me thence to the sea. Eventually, this project fell to the ground. He was not on good terms with the chief named, nor could he be answerable for me farther than Sarbaz. But Ibrahim Khan showed me, in his rough way, real civility. He promised to send me to Tenk, a small fishing village, whence a boat might be procured for passage to Maskat, or elsewhere. The *sarhang* took comparatively little part in the discussion; but his behaviour would have done no discredit to the polished gentleman of Europe.

The next morning the governor of Bampur and his deputy brought over my appointed guide, one Mashhadi Abbas, an old collector of revenue, whose Persian *kulla* and dyed beard were no doubt more familiar than pleasing objects to the Baluchis. To my surprise and satisfaction he agreed to take me at once to Charbar, and guaranteed that the journey should be performed in seven days. Our bargain was instantly struck, and in another twenty-four hours we were on the move again.

Bampur,[1] at the period of my first visit was a village of some 400 habitations. That belonging to the governor best deserved the name of house. It was not only distinguished by size, but in the possession of a *badgir* rising, tower-like, from the roof. The fort, visible for a considerable distance, from whatever side approached, had been built on a long, irregular mound, the higher or northern side of which supported the citadel, whence the walls had been carried down in a north to south direction. There were soldiers and guns inside; but the *sarhang's* detachment was encamped on the plain below. My quarters were in a small house in a fine, large, walled-in garden of recent formation, possessing date-trees, the *kunar* and the *sipistán* close beside the tents, and within easy hearing of drum, bugle, and word of command. Had I myself been governor and detachment commandant, I could not have asked for better fare or better treatment than was freely bestowed upon me by the civil and military authorities; the parting from whom was effected in the same cordial spirit as had rendered memorable our original meeting at Regan. And here let it be understood that the *quid pro quo* principle, prevailing all over the East and rampant in Persia, was not the motive for hospitality in the instance rendered. If presents were made at all, they were comparatively valueless. The *sarhang* positively, but in the most courteous manner, declined a *souvenir* from me representing any worth in money, but solicited in

---

[1] Literally, 'Bahmanpúr,' so called, if the late Wakíl-ul-Mulk's authority be unassailed, from the son of Bahman, founder of Pahm, a monarch commonly identified with Artaxerxes Longimanus, but whom to fit into Karman history, we should rather seek to recognise in Ardashír Babagan.

lieu a pair of ordinary wire spectacles. If the friendliness exhibited was not spontaneous, it must have been exercised in deference to the wishes of the Wakil-ul-Mulk, minister of Karman; and even this view of the case is by no means barren of honour or credit to the Persian character.

On the morning of the 8th February, I mounted my camel—for horses had been discarded—and turned my face to the coast. We were but a small party. I had the two Persians, now much subdued; while Abbas, the guide, was accompanied by two armed Baluch cavaliers, and an old man who stumped his way on foot. Revisiting Kasimabad, where we breakfasted, then turning to the south, we crossed a desert country, and, after about twenty-seven miles, dismounted near a well and sand-hills to rest and pass the night. On the next day we marched nearly the same distance to Maskotu, breakfasting on the way beside the huts of Lashāri Baluchis, who supplied us with delicious *māst* (the Turkish *yoghurt*), fresh butter and dates. The country traversed was still desert, but the heavy sand gave place to harder ground as we neared the hills. Men, women, or children were seldom encountered. One woman was observed dyeing clothes, the dye, almost black in colour, being made of the bark of the date-tree, mixed with clay and water. Maskotu we found to be a village of few inhabitants, shortly before visited by cholera, succeeding small-pox. It consisted of the usual huts and two castellated buildings in more or less preservation, and there were many date-palms there on the south bank of a large, broad and dry river bed. Our third march was to Fanoch, about twenty-five miles; over a road, hard or sandy, stony or gravelly, intersected with many beds of streams and small ravines, and passing, at intervals, among small black hillocks. In this village were grouped a large number of huts, and among them rose the customary fort; there were numerous palms, and patches of cultivation—wheat, beans, and barley; but were it not for the pleasant contrast afforded by its life and colours to the surrounding monotonous waste, Fanoch would merit little notice from passing travellers. One of our Baluchis left us to-day, and I did not regret his departure, for he was grumbling and discontented. What I like in these men is their thorough nationality, and pride of nationality. What I dislike, is the way they have of showing it.

The chief of Fanoch, Chakar Khan, was absent when we were at his village; but his son, a handsome and well-mannered little boy, came out and kissed my hand. I presented him with a *kamarband*, or waist-cloth, which might, if necessary, serve the purpose of a turban. I was told there were about 100 houses at this place; but could hardly believe it had 500 inhabitants. My old guide informed me he had five wives here, and five at Bampur. I must not forget the explanation which he gave to-day of some large, pale, circular patches, almost circles, standing out distinctly from the darker soil around them. They were the "Pāyi-duldul-i-Ali," the feet, or rather the prints of the feet of the mare of Ali,[1] so venerated by all Shias. That these marks may have been four feet in circumference or more, did not seem to necessitate objection on my part so much as the fact that they were in a single line and at uneven distances one from the other, and I therefore asked what had become of the second foot, hind or fore. The guide's answer was

[1] "Nomen mulı sibi qui Muhammedis erat," is, on the other hand, Freytag's interpretation.

to the effect that his version of the legend was given as he had received it; but he was not prepared to criticise or discuss its merits.

From Fanoch, we pursued a zigzag course to the south for about sixteen miles, when our small party entered the "tang," or pass—in the present instance, a very narrow and rough defile between steep rocky hills, links of the long Makran chain. This confined passage shortly widened to an open space, with a view of distant elevations; again did the route close in and expand as before. Leaving the village of Dehan to the left and Benth to the right, we halted a mile or two below the second. Of the one we saw nothing but date-palms; of the other some few huts appeared among the trees. Abbas informed me that so severe had been a recent visitation of cholera, that Dehan had been almost depopulated, and if the 500 deaths reported at Benth were correctly estimated, there also much the same result must have been experienced. A fine old Baluch to whom I addressed myself said that the sickness had quite ceased. On the march to-day I witnessed an extraordinary scene. The Baluchis of Fanoch, of all ages and both sexes, were out in large numbers, locust-hunting; and the vigour with which the sport was carried on, was not more remarkable than the abundance of game at their disposal. As we rode among the scattered insect legions, it seemed as though each stroke of hand, cap, or kerchief, was a capture, and yet did not the swarms perceptibly diminish. The statement made to me at the time, that these locusts were boiled and salted for eating, does not in my opinion admit of the least doubt; and if any evidence were wanted in support of the literal meaning of the word in Scripture (St. Matthew iii. 4), the practice of Makran

Baluchis might be cited in addition to that of the Arabs detailed by Hasselquist.

The next day's march, our fifth from Bampur, was a stiff one to myself and servants: how much more so to a stray follower or two who accompanied us a great part of the way on foot, and the camels! I rose before three A.M., and while looking about me, was asked the time by Ablas. Hearing my reply, he gave the signal to start. There were no tents to strike or bedsteads to pack; and we moved in as light marching order as the prospective requirements of Indian Presidencies would permit; but it was about 3.40 when we broke ground. After nearly seven hours on camelback, we pulled up for a short hour, resuming work before 11.30. At 4.40 we selected a resting-place for the night, and called it Gunz, the name of the district generally, as of the cape stretching from it seaward. Since our entry within the Makran barrier, and for more than twenty miles to-day, we had followed or guided ourselves by the bed of a river called at its rise above Fanoch the "Annito," and afterwards the Bonth. To-day we had left it where its waters, joined by the tributary Nasferan, flow down to the sea under the name, first of Korandab, then of Kalig, the fishing hamlet at its mouth; and our course lay in an easterly direction towards the Tenk river. After a surfeit of stones and hills, we debouched upon a plain, hard but sandy, with much low jungle and wild vegetation, the last similar to that of the Sind outlying wastes, which might be classified, for distinction, into products eaten and products rejected by camels. We had passed during the day a block of whitish stone scooped out at the top like an apothecary's mortar. This was explained to us to be a frequent resort of the

Makranis, because the powder obtained there was an infallible remedy for toothache. I believed it in some way associated with other marvellous tokens of the presence of the Prophet's son-in-law, such as the Pir Ali, the cleft in which rock is attributed to a blow from his sword. Legends of Ali abound throughout Makran; and the marks of his foot are pointed out, or tangible evidences of his physical prowess adduced, in all parts of the country. Amid a normal population of Suni Baluchis, the fact may be thought to tell of old Persian occupation; but it is open to question whether the assumed associations are genuine, or imported by annexation of the last few years. The morning after bivouac at Gunz, having re-rolled our bedding spread there on the sand, we started at four A.M., and after fair camel-marching for about an hour and a half, lost our way in a kind of defile or deep bed of a torrent. We had taken a low and narrow passage among rocks instead of an upper path unknown; and had got so perplexed in the darkness, that we had to await the broader light of day. After resuming our march, we came upon a *dowāra*, or encampment of nomads, among whom our Persian guide had acquaintances who helped to put us on the right road. We found the Tenk *rudkhana* very wide, and the water, as usual, confined to particular shallow channels, or a pool here and there. At nine A.M. I congratulated myself on getting clear of the river; but after a short progress to the east, we fell in with it again, and were detained between its high banks for long. Rain had set in before mid-day; and up to nearly three P.M. we worked on under difficulties. Camels do not affect mud, and mud is quickly produced in these parts by heavy showers: but our poor beasts did their work right well, and slipped and struggled bravely on our behalf. We made an attempt to reach the Khaur-i-Kir,¹ which brings down the waters from Gaíh, but failed; for when we had come within five miles of its right bank, our course was impeded by a rapid stream which had suddenly risen into importance, and forced its way violently through the yielding sand. So we encamped near some inhospitable rocks, awaiting a more favourable opportunity. The rain came down in torrents, and drenched us all. Hassan rigged up a temporary tent for me with an india-rubber covering; but, independently of holes filled with bits of stick or left open to chance, unless I could double up snail-like under its limited shelter, it was only available down to the waist. So I sat holding an umbrella, smoking, and spasmodically endeavouring to dry my inner garments at a poor fire, until a star appeared, then another and another, and a break in the N.W. caused my spirits to rise with the conviction that a good time was at hand. I turned in and tried to sleep near some half-burning sticks, but woke at one A.M. cold and comfortless, and amused myself with the fire again, and so on until break of day. How to name our halting-place was difficult; but I jotted down "East of Bir rocks, and made the distance marched twenty-eight miles. In this day's march, one of those many instances of popular superstition peculiar to the Baluchis passed under my observation. We were passing the shrine of Shai, or Saiyid Harun in the bed of the Tenk river, and two Baluch guides had accompanied us from the *douaro*,

¹ From Karáchi westward, all along the Makran coast, and up to the mouth of the Shatt-el-Arab, the word Akaur is applied to the river mouth, or to that part of the river which is near, and receives the salt waters of the sea. I counted no less than twenty-seven of these creeks between Sonmíaní and dusk.

to point out a bye-path avoiding a deep water passage likely to cause detention. Suddenly the guides stopped their camels and dismounted. One took in his hand a biscuit, turned to the right, and reverently placed his offering on the ground: the other advanced a few paces in the same direction, and made a solemn bow. Closely watching the quarter indicated by these movements, I saw a tree which, though a tamarisk, looked Druidical and picturesque; but Mashhadi Abbas assured me the real shrine was a well. He further informed me that no Baluch ever passed this place without laying there his offering, or would think of reclaiming any money or property accidentally dropped there: that if a traveller halting for the night burnt the wood and gave his cattle the fodder procurable on the spot, it would be well with him; but that if he took the wood to burn elsewhere, it would be impossible to light it; or if he cut or carried away the grass for consumption elsewhere, it would kill the animal it was intended to nourish.

On the next day we succeeded only in reaching the Khaur-i-Kir. Nor did we accomplish this five miles without an intervening halt at a Baluch *dowāra*. On arriving at the bank, we found the ground so soft and untenable for camels, and the current so strong, that we gave up all hope of immediate crossing, and put up where we were for the night, choosing the higher ground among tamarisk and *kirir* (wild caper) bushes. The next morning we passed over the stream, which had much decreased, and pushed on for eighteen miles to Khaur Sangam, which was crossed with comparative ease. Halting to breakfast and rest our camels on the left or further bank, we made a fresh start soon after mid-day. The country had been rendered somewhat difficult owing to the heavy rain and consequent floods; but we managed to work our way amid low hills and rocky ground, varied with sandy and alluvial soil and dwarf scattered jungle. At sunset we reached a large salt-water *khaur*, and were in the close neighbourhood of the sea. I descried the smoke of a steamer in the bay of Charbar; but the village itself could not be reached until we had ascended and descended the intervening hill of Tiz. We contrived to attain the top of this eminence; but as it was too dark to discover the downward path, we spread our bedding, as had now become a habit, under the open canopy of heaven. The ground was hard and interspersed with rock, and the dews fell heavily; but we could estimate our day's march at the respectable figure of forty-three miles, and the familiar sound of a ship's gun told us there were friends to meet in the morning. So the night was really a pleasant one.

The descent was steep, but only three miles remained to Charbar; and we were not long in getting over those on the morning of the 10th February. Here we were met and welcomed by the Arab governor and his minister; by Lieutenant Stiffe and Mr. Johnstone; and last not least by my good friend Murdoch Smith, with whom I had thus again foregathered only two days later than the date anticipated in my official letter addressed to him on parting. He had made his way to Bandar Abbas by a mountainous route little frequented by modern travellers, but not wholly unknown to a reading public, reaching the sea coast on the 3rd February, when I was yet two marches from Bampur. Here he was joined by Vice-Consul Johnstone, who had arrived, under instructions, from Bastah; and on the 7th of the month both officers had embarked on board the *Amberwitch*, for disembarkation at Henjām, Masandam, and Jask respectively. From the last place they had proceeded by land for about sixty-seven miles to Sooraf, whence, taking to the steamer again, they had continued their route by sea to Charbar.

It was the smoke of the *Amberwitch* bringing Major Smith and his companions into port which I had noticed on the previous evening. Most thankful was I that our plans had been blessed with successful execution; and that a kind Providence had preserved us to meet in health and safety through a rough and unusual journey.

Setting aside all political considerations, and looking at Western Baluchistan as a region to be revisited, if only to compare its geographical and ethnological status with what it was in Pottinger's time more than half a century before, a journey such as I have imperfectly sketched could hardly be void of interest. And even had the travels of Pottinger and Grant been of sufficiently recent date to render superfluous any following in their footsteps, I believe myself correct in stating that no English, and very possibly no European traveller of whom anything is known, had ever penetrated the Fanoch pass at all. As regards the question of personal risk, I am not prepared to say that there is none whatever, especially at times when resistance is exercised by petty chiefs against the local authorities; nor do I for a moment dispute the wisdom of proceeding with tact and caution on all occasions; but I can honestly assert that on no occasion was any molestation offered to myself, nor can I subscribe to the opinion of even so excellent an authority as the late Muhammad Ismail Khan, minister and governor of Karman, that either Persian or Baluch disguise was essential to the safe conduct of an English officer, as enjoined on me for the roads west and south of Bampur respectively. Of course, had I persisted in going by Gaih or Kasrkand, it is impossible to say what would have been the result; but the danger, to my mind, would rather have been from enforced association with Persians than the mere dress of the Faringi. My two attendants, moreover, were most conspicuous in their attire. Hassan the *pohlywān* was in a loud and incongruous mixture of green and brown; and Rahim Beg had boots more becoming Dirk Hatterick than a Persian *pesh-khidmat* (valet). These men were not improved by their journey into Baluchistan. It was not judged advisable to encourage intercourse on their part with the natives; there was no necessity to employ them as caterers, for the guides were better fitted to the work; nor did they seem to care to meddle with matters in which the way to *mudakhil* was not clear. One, the man of physical strength, fell into despondency, and was perpetually groaning over the *inakun* (desert) into which he had been led; the other seemed to have lost both common sense and energy. The lament over the solitude was intelligible, if not excusable. Without exaggeration, the traveller might ride for twenty miles together, and not see even so much as a beast or a bird, much less a human being.

Our onward progress from Chadar was not by land. We remained but a few hours among our Arab friends, and were conveyed by the *Amberwitch* to Gwadar, where we passed the next day at the Resident's quarters, re-embarking at night for Karachi, which was reached on the 20th February. Here I experienced the never-tiring hospitality of the chief engineer of the Sind Railway and his lady; and making their house my head-quarters for five days, or until departure of the Bombay steamer, renewed friendships in a province which I had long known, geographically in its length and breadth, politically in its native population, and generally in its past and present customs and resources; and whose welfare could not but command my deep interest at all times. We landed at Bombay on the morning of the 8th February, and remained there until the 17th March, when we re-

BALUCH WOMAN (COAST OF MAKRAN).

embarked to steam down the coast to Baipur. Crossing Southern India by rail, inclusive of a deviation from Coimbator to Utakamand, and remaining three short days at Madras, we took steamer again on the 28th idem over the still irrepressible surf, and reached Calcutta on the 2nd April. As the seat of government had been transferred for the time to Simla, four days were sufficient for our work at the City of Palaces; and after a long railway journey to Delhi, broken by a night's adventurous dâking to Lucknow and speedy return to Cawnpore, we found ourselves riding up on the 15th April, to Kasauli, whence we passed on, over the high mountain roads, to the grateful *rhododendra* of the splendid sanitarium, so wisely selected for retaining and recruiting energies which belong essentially to distant latitudes, and without which the administrative reins would fall irrecoverably slack. On the fifth day after arrival we returned to Kalka and the hot plains, thankful for a kindly reception in every sense, and most promising, as regarded our official plans, on the part of the highest authorities; bearing away, moreover, pleasant recollections of renewed intercourse with acquaintances, some of whom I had known as cadets when orderly officer at Addiscombe, and for one of whom, at least, I felt that, if life were spared, a career of useful distinction might be safely predicted.

Dâk carriages and railway brought us through Lûdhiana, Jalandar, Amritsar and Lahor to Multan, where we caught the river steamer on the 25th April. Both Amritsar and Lahor are well known to merit the traveller's attention. The Sikh temple, at the first, is one of those picturesque *bijoux* for which Indian scenery is noted. At the latter city, the courtesy of the Lieutenant-governor[1] provided us with ready means for inspection of the principal objects of interest; and elephants were brought into requisition for the streets and public places.

A passage up or down the Indus is a wearisome affair at almost any time, and we had the misfortune to get what is called "snagged" on the eighth day after embarkation. Whether river conservancy has effected

[1] The late much-lamented and respected Sir Donald Macleod.

or will effect a full remedy for this highly probable contingency, is a question on which there may be conflicting opinions; but the present age of Indian progress cannot dispense with those railway links still required to join Calcutta to Karáchi. On the 5th May we reached Kotri, whence the railway soon carried us to the seaboard; and after five more days passed in the modern capital of Sind, we returned to Bombay. Before the close of May, Major Smith had returned to Persia, and I, having paid my respects at Mahableshwar, was on my homeward way in a steamer of the P. and O. S. N. Company. Constant journeying of a different kind had made me look upon reaching the deck of these vessels as almost equivalent to arrival in England. It seemed as if all trouble and responsibility for the rest of the journey had at such time virtually ceased. The traveller—handed over to stewards, innkeepers, *valets de place*, and the rest of that *genus* who, without any especial philanthropy or self-sacrifice, make administration to the wants of their fellows the business of their lives—has really no need of exercising his own independent judgment.

To spare my readers, upon whom these travels must have already somewhat palled, I will not dwell on the land journey from Karáchi to Charbar still wanting to complete a real overland route home, and performed by me in two separate sections. It shall be touched on with the brevity becoming the modicum of space assigned at the conclusion of a long story.

In December 1861, under orders of Government, I moved, with an escort of Sind horse, from Karáchi along the Makran coast, into the supposed land of the ancient fish and turtle-eaters ($ἰχθυοφάγοι$ and $χελωνοφάγοι$). During that seven weeks' march of 392 miles I had an excellent opportunity not only of examining a little-known country, but of studying and forming acquaintances with an interesting people. For, strange to say, notwithstanding proximity to Makran (rendered our immediate neighbourhood by the conquest of Sindh), Englishmen as a rule neither cared to penetrate into that country, nor to know its history and polities. Of the few individual exceptions, the most notable, perhaps, was the late Mr. John MacLeod, collector of customs at Karachi, who proceeded by land to Gwadar as a simple traveller in 1853, and who collected much valuable information on the trade and inhabitants of the coast. My object was to make arrangements with local chiefs for the protection of a contemplated line of telegraph; and as the Khan of Kalat, who held suzerain authority in Eastern Makran, gave his countenance to the procedure by sending an agent to accompany me, the difficulties in the way had been in some degree removed. The aspect of the country traversed was desolate, and the inhabitants were few. Yet were there gems of wild, romantic scenery to be discerned among the Hinglaj mountains, especially in the approach to the shrine of the Hindu pilgrims. Population was almost entirely concentrated, as a rule, in the fishing villages, such as Sonmiáni, Ormara, Pasni, and Gwádar. The nomads were found occasionally in small bodies, where there was cultivation, water or other life-sustaining attraction, and their presence was invariably signified by the use of the word "halk." If this be, as I believe, the Arabic "khalk," the meaning is simply "human creatures"—a group or collection of human beings. Cultivation, however, except at the villages or in their immediate precincts, could hardly be said to exist. Fodder for cattle was chiefly grazing for camels, and even this was not always procurable. We laid in a stock at Karāchi for the horses, replenishing as best we could. Water was, upon the whole, sufficient for the wants of our party, and we numbered more than sixty, inclusive of Europeans.[1] Gwādar was estimated by far the most populous of the fishing villages, and could boast of more than 1,000 houses, while Sonmiāni and Ormara had barely a third of that number, and Pasni had not 100. The inhabitants of Gwādar were mostly Mēds, or boatmen and fishers; in a lesser ratio, Baluchis, Hindus, Khwojas, Arabs and slaves. Of these the Arabs formed the smallest, but at the same time the ruling section. Perhaps the governor and staff, with attendant soldiers, were the sole representatives of the race, inclusive, in some cases, of households. The slaves were proportionally few, according to the statement given; but the principle of slavery was fully acknowledged, and the slave possessor clung tenaciously to his privilege. We have already shown the fort and huts thrown together on the neck of a sandy isthmus beneath a low promontory. This last is long, rocky and flat-topped, and though singular in shape has its *pendant* at Ormara. The most picturesque object in the vicinity of the port was a hill to the north, but the landscape, with the sea to the front and high mountains in the background, as a whole, was worthy the artist's attention.

Recalled from Gwādar in 1862, owing to circumstances which rendered further negotiations at this particular period premature, it was not until seven years

---

[1] I was accompanied by Lieut. Campbell and Dr. Lalor, of the Sind Horse; also Mr. Henry Ryland, a meritorious member of the Uncovenanted Service. The first alone survives.

later that I made the short land journey from Gwādar to Charbar. On the 14th February, 1869, Captain Ross, Mr. Superintendent Walker of the telegraph and I, attended by two or three personal servants and some Baluchis, moved out of the former place together. We made no show in cattle, retinue, numbers, or equipage; but the political agent, who did the catering, was able to supply tents and all requisite for our purpose. Our first march was a short one of twelve miles, of which ten were along a fine beach, the bottom of the west bay of Gwādar; our second led, from the creek by which we had encamped, over an undulating sandy tract, sparsely dotted with wild vegetation, for fourteen miles, to the Enteri Khaur, supposed to mark territorial boundary; our third, also fourteen miles, brought us through much the same description of country to a large river called the Dasht, where we halted a day for the transaction of business with the Baluchis, who put in an appearance soon after our arrival. Their visit took us by surprise, from the manner in which it was effected. Suddenly the announcement was made that a cavalcade was approaching from the bank of the river opposite to that of our encampment. We went out to reconnoitre, and returned with the conviction that the new-comers were the chiefs of the district whom we had expected to see, and made preparation for their reception accordingly. Whether from the repeated matchlock-shots, or the time taken by the party in crossing the river, or the disturbed state of the neighbouring tracts, or other cause unknown, we were unable to determine; but the rumour spread that the visitors were strangers and might have come with aggressive objects. Emerging from the tents a second time we witnessed a strange scene. The notion that a raid was imminent seemed to have possessed the natives in camp. Our party, all included, must have been under thirty; but the sensation was like that of a multitude. Women and children, of whose existence we had not been aware, came rushing in we knew not whence, and buried themselves hurriedly in the near tamarisk bushes; flocks appearing as if by magic, and stray cattle of kinds, were hurriedly driven in close beside our tents; men armed themselves and loaded their firearms. At least half an hour elapsed before it was certified that all was well, and that the looked-for chiefs were indeed the arrivals. When this result was generally apprehended, women, children, and quadrupeds re-appeared from their hiding-places, and moved away as purposely though not as briskly as they had come in. Our fourth march was a short one of about eleven miles; first across the river, which was waded with some little difficulty, and afterwards over an open country much as before, but with a soil of a whitish hue, like hard, broken clay. As we had salt water at this last stage, it was a satisfaction to push on another twelve miles to Sikari, our fifth march. On the way we passed two white hillocks, the further and higher one being of graceful shape, like a miniature Demavend. These are classined in the language of the coast among the "Daria Cham," or mud volcanoes, and my inspection of the nearer one proved to my mind its affinity to those between Sonmiáni and Ormara.[1] Our sixth march to Rodi, fifteen miles, was for the most part over a plain with a white clay surface, sometimes smooth as ice, sometimes broken

---

[1] Lieut. Stiffe attributes the outflow of those which have been observed in their active state to hydrostatic pressure rather than volcanic agency. See paper in Quarterly Journal of Geological Society for February 1874.

and rugged. The vegetation was sparse but continuous, consisting chiefly of the wild caper and a succulent plant called "kuni," much affected by camels. Near Rodi we discovered a Baluch settlement with flocks and herds and cultivation. The milk and buttermilk here obtained were most acceptable. Leaving a conspicuous landmark, the Khaki Kuh, or "earth hill," to our right, we turned to some clay hills with sharp, angular tops, and came upon clusters of mat huts, by the occupants of which we were visited. The women and children were black enough to be slaves. We made our seventh march, of fifteen miles, to Kachāo, riding the first half through a vast mass of small white hills covering the wide space between Khaki Kuh and the sea. While we overlooked these singular excrescences at one time from a high pathway, at another we had to wend our way through a bed below. Tired of slow moving, Captain Ross and I galloped away independently of guides, and after a time emerged from the pale hillocks upon a bright yellow sandy elevation, whence we got a fine view of the deep blue sea beneath. The contrast was charming, and I could not but feel that despised and avoided Makran had wonderful and varied effects of light and shade, of sunrise and sunset, of hill and plain, of seashore, well worthy of record. Nothing in its way could well be finer than these yellow sands and this blue water. We had to turn inland again to find our encampment on a white hard plain, divided from the sea by a rugged hill range. Our eighth and last march brought us into Charbar. We were able to gallop the greater part of the first nine miles to Tizcopan; the valley bearing which name, with its grateful banian tree and abundant green grass, was a truly refreshing sight.

Then came eight hilly miles, for the march was seventeen, and our 110 miles were completed. To Captain Ross the fact was comparatively unimportant. He had accomplished this little journey before. But for me it was otherwise. In carrying out on this occasion the wishes of Government, I was enabled to gratify at the same

GEORGIAN MINSTRELS, FROM A TIFLIS PHOTOGRAPH.

time a long-entertained ambition to "do" the full overland route from Karáchi to the Caspian.

In the first sketched-out programme of the present volume, I had proposed to tell of a journey from Constantinople to Tehran by the Black Sea, Poti, Kutais, Tiflis, and Tabriz, rendered memorable to a fellow-traveller and myself by the intense cold experienced; and of the prolongation of the same journey to India by Hamadan, the west of Persia, Khanikin and Baghdad. And the pleasant but better-known European routes leading to and from Constantinople, and particularly those including Vienna and the Danube, had reverted to my mind as affording, possibly, fit material for its lighter pages. But it seems to me that enough has already been recorded to tax the reader's patience, and that the publication of these further notes, if needed at all, may well await a fitter season. In the meanwhile, I take the opportunity of putting in a word of strong recommendation for the costume photographs of our countryman, Mr. Westly, at Tiflis; of advising any amateur traveller proceeding from Tehran to the Turco-Persian frontier near Karman-shah to visit the rock inscriptions at Besitun; and of placing a passing personal memorial, as it were, on the tomb of an old, faithful, and stout-hearted Tabrizi servant, whom I lost from sunstroke, haply combined with less immediate causes, at a caravanserai within twenty miles of Baghdad, just as we had completed a hot and hard ride from the Persian capital.

Nor can I miss the occasion of thanking most warmly the many kind hosts who helped me on this latest-mentioned as on other sections of my travels. Some have gone to the pilgrim's common bourn. Of these last, the name of one reverts instantly to mind, who, whether discharging his official duties in Northern Persia or on the shores of the Black Sea, could shed the light of his modest labours even upon Western Europe, and make his allotted corner, however remote, a centre of general and extensive usefulness.

Beyond the natural request for indulgent consideration of an imperfect performance, little more remains to be said. It may be thought that too much has been told of the difficulties in establishing an extraordinary line of land telegraph, and not enough of the friendly action of those through whose territories it runs. Such has been far from the writer's intention. He readily acknowledges the goodwill and co-operation without which the wires at this moment and daily conveying Anglo-Indian messages to and fro could assuredly have had no existence.

"CHAPARING."

APPENDIX.

CHAPTER I.

MEMOIR OF COLONEL PATRICK STEWART.

READERS of the memoir will kindly bear in mind that in sketching out a real character it has not been intended to place on record simply its most attractive points. In like manner, if running a mile in six minutes be held of no account when public schoolboys commonly do it in five; or if the incident of the bears (page 28) be thought trivial by experienced sportsmen, and indicative of rashness by the uninitiated, allowance will doubtless be made for the production of a faithful portrait.

The following letter addressed by the late Dr. Livingstone to Mr. MacLeod Stewart, Colonel Patrick Stewart's brother, cannot fail to be read with interest. Its receipt while this volume was in the press will explain why it is found in the Appendix:—

"NEWSTEAD ABBEY, MANSFIELD, NOTTS,
11th February, 1865.

"MY DEAR STEWART,
"It is with no feigned words I say that I was deeply moved when I read the sad news of your dear brother's death. I noticed the tear in his brotherly eye when he parted with you on the ship's deck at Bombay and loved him for it, and I liked him still more when in the voyage I came to know him better. One of the notices of his departure uses the word 'love-compelling.' That he truly was: I never liked one more in so short a time. He was exceedingly loveable, and I feel sure has gone to the regions of love where his qualities of mind and heart will have full development in a higher and nobler sphere. You must excuse my writing thus. It is out of

the fulness of my heart; and I am sure I wish I could comfort you in this heavy loss.

"We once conversed on the subject of the possibility of spirits returning to their former haunts, and I in joke said, 'Well, if they do come, they may be expected to speak good English.' This was in reference to the spirit-rapping nonsense. He replied that he often thought deeply on that subject, and seriously too, on the possibility of friends returning, as the idea is expressed in the 'May Queen,' in Tennyson, which you will remember:

'I shall listen what you say,
When you think I'm far away.'[1]

I enjoyed his company vastly and parted at Cairo. He wished me to stop a week, and we were to meet in Galloway. . . . You must please excuse this effusion. It springs from the heart of your sympathising friend.

(Signed)   "DAVID LIVINGSTONE."

CHAPTER II.

Last lines of page 84.

IN an interesting series of articles on the Province of Kurdistan, published in the *Levant Herald*, the following passage attracted my attention when at Constantinople:—

POLES AND RAFTERS.

"A large portion of the export of these articles takes place from the Diarbekir *sanjak*, but three times its amount and value is exported from the northern districts of the Saert *sanjak* to Mosul and Baghdad by the Bohtan-Su and its head waters, which irrigate large plantations of the poplar used for building purposes. They are divided for sale into three kinds, called 'Qadr,' 'Mirdinjak,' and 'Shugel,' which vary in thickness and length, the first being one foot in diameter, and about fourteen feet long, the second six inches and less in diameter, and ten feet long, and the third thin pieces used for filling in the roofs of houses and rooms. At the place of their growth the two first are sold respectively for thirty piastres (5s. 5d.) and four piastres (9d.) each, and the latter for one piastre (2d.) for fifteen pieces. The first pays a duty at Mosul of five piastres (10½d.) on each stick, and the

---

[1] "New Year's Eve," 16th Stanza:

"Though I cannot speak a word, I shall hearken what you say,
And be often, often with you when you think I'm far away."

APPENDIX.   631

other two 10 per cent. in kind. The people engaged in this traffic
are mostly from Mosul, and—though in a small way—like the
lumber trade in Canada, experience and skill are required to evade
accident, and to float these timbers through the intricate, rapid and
confined streams of the tributaries that lead into the Buhtan Su and
Tigris. Once arrived at the latter river, all the pieces are collected
and joined into a raft, which then pursues its downward course
without any more difficulty or detention."

The native terms have been rendered in the newspaper etymology.
"Qadr" is probably the Arabic word "Kadr," signifying power or
quantity. The "jak" in the next word may be used to show a substance of lesser degree; and "Shugel" is doubtless the Turkish-
Arabic word "Shukaln," meaning split or cleft.

An additional extract from the same authority should have sufficient
value to warrant insertion. We must premise that it is dated some
few years ago:—

"INTERNAL TRADE OF THE PROVINCE.

"The whole value of the trade confined to the pashalik itself is,
approximately, about £800,000 sterling, based principally upon the
money value of the vegetable yield of the province. For as it must
always happen in these countries, where the price of grain, no matter
the amount of the yield, is yearly subject, owing to the destitution
and encumbered position of the raisers, to fluctuations varying from
50 to 100 per cent. at stated periods, the principal domestic trade
will be in those articles of universal consumption offering such fixed
and solid profits to the capitalist; here then, too, as elsewhere, the
chief branch of that trade is in cereals, or money advanced on crops,
absorbing a sum of £250,000. Money so advanced is either the
property of capitalists, or men of small means, who run the risk so
as to ensure their supply of grain for the year at moderate prices.
In forming the estimate of this trade I have taken into consideration
the totals of the animal and vegetable produce of this pashalik, and
deducted from each item the money value of the amount actually
exported (£179,800), and that consumed by the peasant and producer
amounting to £338,400. A sum of £50,000 is employed in loans at
interest, and in the petty transactions and trades incidental to an
eastern province. Excepting the manufactures—silks, cottons, and
leathers, and shallee, to be mentioned further on—already noticed,
none of them is important or interesting enough to call for any
special notice. The transit trade of Diarbekir consisting of British
goods, fancy foreign goods from Constantinople, cotton goods from
Erzeroom, and British manufactures, colonials, and French and Swiss
goods from Aleppo, for Baghdad, amounts to £200,000; but beyond
some trifling commission, it does not benefit the commerce of this

place, although giving good employment to the people engaged in the raft business and to local muleteers.

"In spring a raft takes five days between Diarbekir and Mosul, and from fifteen to twenty-five in autumn. Each one carries fifteen cantars of goods, and is composed of 150 skins at five piastres (10¾d.) each. Small wood for the flooring, and six light poles for the frame work cost 80 piastres (14s. 6d.), and the wages of the man conducting it another 60, making a total of 840¹ piastres—equal to 7l. 12s. 8d. But as the skins are serviceable for several trips, and the wood is saleable at Mosul, the real cost of a raft, to the trade, is really very trifling. It is a strict monopoly, the exclusive right of making and working them being annually sold by government for about 100l. On an average, 300 of these *keleks* (rafts) go to Jazireh, 600 to Mosul, and 200 to Baghdad, annually, from Diarbekir."

CHAPTER III.

CONCLUDING EXTRACTS FROM THE "TIMES," p. 128.

The question of difficulty in telegraphing through an unbroken circuit of 1,200 miles has long since been set at rest by successful working through much longer distances. And arguments used in October, 1862, for laying cables in short sections were found not only obsolete in 1873, but they had actually become so in 1866, or in less than three years after they were promulgated. Well might Colonel George Chesney say, in reference to our imitative rather than original military organizations, that in *some matters*, "England led the way. Witness our aptitude for commerce and colonisation, our railways, telegraphs, and manufactures."² As regards telegraphs, the progress of late years has indeed been marvellous. How little could those of our countrymen, who wondered at Edgeworth's mechanical ingenuity displayed about the dawn of the present century, in imparting distant intelligence, have foreseen the telegraphic feats of the days in which we live. Lord March once expressed his regret to Sir Francis Delaval that he could not hear the result of the Newmarket racing of the day until about nine in the evening. The latter offered to bet £500 that Edgeworth would obtain it for him by five in the afternoon. He had a system on which he could quite rely. Hampstead and Great Russell

¹ 80 in orig.; the real total would, however, be 840.
² Address delivered at the Royal United Service Institution on the 27th March, 1874.

APPENDIX. 633

Street were successfully connected by his method; but, we are told, "it was too expensive for common use."[1]

THE ARABS AT MASANDAM, p. 142.

Patrick Stewart thus wrote from Maskat on the 23rd February, 1864, to Sir Bartle Frere, then Governor of Bombay :—

"I am very anxious indeed to give a correct account of all that has taken place since we had the great satisfaction of anchoring the cable-ship in the magnificent land-locked harbour at the head of Malcolm's inlet. But I fear this is no very easy task, especially as I am still scarcely fit for work, though very much better than when I last wrote.

"In the first place I must explain that, from the state of the weather at the time we first approached the Arabian shore, we were obliged, as a precaution, to retain the *Victoria* till the cable-ship had anchored, and we were therefore unable to send down for Colonel Disbrowe so soon as I had wished.

"It was not till the night of the 14th that he arrived, and although his presence would have been very valuable to us in the earlier period of our stay, he had no means whatever of joining us till he did. On his arrival he aided us in every way in his power, and has continued to do so ever since, making over for our use his own tents and a portion of the material intended for his own residence.

"I should also mention that it was not till the 12th that Colonel Goldsmid and Mr. Walton overtook us in the gun-boat, which had remained at Gwādar to bring on the staff and apparatus required there during the preliminary tests.

"As regards our actual experience at the new station, and the important subject of its security, I wish to say that (though I hope and trust I shall never become an alarmist) I think it would be wrong in me to abstain from expressing my opinion.

"For the first week after our arrival I was almost constantly on shore, striving with more or less success to conciliate the people who came to us, and to induce them to assist us, and during this time I could not but notice many little incidents calculated to cause uneasiness. For the first day or two all seemed to go well. It is true that excessively little work was done, but as yet there was nothing to make us suppose that the Arab inhabitants were other than the miserably poor, inoffensive race they had been represented. Gradually, however, things changed. Shaikhs and their followers came crowding in from neighbouring villages, each more impudently importunate for presents than his predecessor. While almost demanding these, they would occasionally make the pretence of offering to help us with

[1] Extracts from Edgeworth's "Memoirs of Himself," in Annual Register, 1820.

workmen. But, when questioned as to terms, the most unheard of claims would follow: sometimes as much as ten rupees per man for a day's work that was to cease at 2 p.m.! On one occasion, men who had consented to undertake something for us at a moderate rate were attacked in rather a savage manner by those of another village. On this a strangely exciting scene arose: every man arming himself with a tent peg, or anything else that came to hand, and joining in the *mêlée a outrance*. Goldsmid and I were alone and unarmed in the centre of them, and, for a few moments, the affair looked really awkward, though it was eventually settled by the Arabs themselves, no one molesting us in the slightest degree. At this time our temporary office was still on board ship, and we were only endeavouring to prepare for the reception of the people on shore.

"Before we had long been thus employed we became aware of a regular system of scarcely concealed pilfering which threatened to become a really serious annoyance. Beyond expostulating with the shaikhs, who (though themselves the worst of all) had promised to prevent all this, we could do nothing without risk of widening the breach it was our great object to close. Altogether, at the time I speak of, our dealings with the Arabs were far from satisfactory. I believe these extraordinary inland lakes were at one time almost the head quarters of the Gulf pirates, and I have no doubt that many of our friends at Maklab (the isthmus), if they do not now practise it, would gladly take to the trade again if opportunity offered. They are false, cunning, and greedy to a degree; under no sort of authority, and strangely ignorant of English power. In fact, from all I have seen, I am most strongly of opinion that it would be most imprudent to leave our station (whether while temporarily located at Maklab, or when removed to Khasab to a more permanent footing) without the protection of such an armed vessel as will, by her mere presence, overawe the Arabs, and deter them from mischief. I do not know which of the vessels of the Royal Navy might best be spared, or whether your Excellency will think it advisable to send any one of them, but I really believe that it will be true economy to act as I venture to suggest, and I am very glad I am enabled to say that Colonel Goldsmid *entirely* concurs in this opinion. Colonel Disbrowe has, I know, written officially on the same subject.

"When obliged to send the gun-boat to Khasab for water or for other purposes, I was often reminded of the old puzzle of the fox, geese, and corn, in trying to arrange that the camp should not be left unguarded.

"I am sure Disbrowe was wise in not landing the Imam's guards at our temporary station. We could not have done this without serious risk of provoking a collision; and it was, I think, much more prudent to employ them (as we have done) in guarding the building materials and stores at Khasab.

"As a proof that these Arabs can go beyond the limits of such ignorant mischief as we complain of, I may mention a fact of which

Disbrowe is preparing an official account), viz., that the village, from which we must look for our main supply of water at present, was burnt to the ground and nine of the people murdered a very few weeks ago, by those of another village lying on the opposite side of our camp.

"As my latest telegrams from our new station must have led your Excellency to expect to hear of me next from the head of the Gulf, the fact of this letter being written from Maskat must require explanation.

"Knowing how much must be pre-arranged at Bushahr and Fão if our English *employés* are to be properly housed and cared for before next hot weather, I was most anxious to go on to those places at this time. But although the state of things at our new station began to improve very much about the time Colonel Disbrowe arrived, and are now, I hope, in a still more satisfactory condition, I do not think I would have been justified in withdrawing a steamer, and in leaving the neighbourhood of Masandam for more than a very few days, unless our relations with the Arabs had been on a much better footing than they are.

"By coming to Maskat to meet the mail steamer on her way up the Gulf, I was enabled to receive letters from, and to write to, Bushahr, Basrah, and Baghdad; also to obtain materials and supplies we stand in need of for the station; while Colonel Disbrowe has succeeded in transacting some important business with the Imám, and is now ready to return for a prolonged stay at the station. Colonel Goldsmid and Mr. Walton remained behind, with the gun-boat on one side of the isthmus, and the *Victoria* on the other. Our people are all under shelter; and matters, when we left, were looking much more promising than they had done for some time before.

"We shall return at once to the spot, and I shall be able to report by telegraph if anything important occurs. If all goes well we shall open the station at Bushahr about 15th March and at Fão ten days later.

"I have written to Captain Young explaining what we most require in the way of assistance from him.

"Pray forgive my writing to yourself demi-officially on the subject of our difficulties. I thought it was in some respects better to do so, as the 'political' part of the work is not properly mine."

COLONEL STEWART'S REPORT OF 11TH JUNE, 1864, TO BOMBAY GOVERNMENT, p. 169.

As there are so many names mentioned in the paragraph immediately following that last quoted in this page, after-consideration has led me to insert it in the Appendix:

"In thus attempting to give a general description of the operations in the neighbourhood of Fão, I feel that I have not sufficiently explained either the nature or extent of the difficulties that were experienced, nor done justice to the energy and courage of the officers and men who volunteered for and successfully completed the work. I consider it would have been simply impossible to ensure success had it not been that English gentlemen were found willing to toil on cheerfully day after day, in sun and mud, everywhere setting an example that excited even the apathetic Arabs to enthusiasm. In landing the end of the cable from boats on the 5th April, Sir Charles Bright and Messrs. Laws, Webb, Lambert, Woods, and Alexander (members of his staff), effected what was perhaps the most difficult individual operation of the whole, involving, from the nature of the ground to be traversed, not merely hardships and exposure, but direct and not inconsiderable danger. In this work, Colonel Goldsmid and Captain Bradshaw also took part, and on them, more, perhaps, than any others, fell the burden of continued labour and exposure during the whole of the protracted operations at Fáo. Working parties of officers and men from the *Coromandel* were also constantly employed; and it gives me great pleasure to record the obligations I am under to Captain Carew for the cordial assistance which, though always rendered, was never more prized than on the occasions I now refer to. I have already spoken of the manner in which the river steamer *Comet* was employed, but not of the very valuable assistance received from Captain Bewsher, both in his own vessel and on shore; and I hope I may be allowed to take this opportunity of recording his services as well as those of the Government Telegraph Staff (Mr. Brasher's especially, and Messrs. Kersting, Gregory, Patten, and Gaulburn), who volunteered for duty on shore.]

CHAPTER IV.

KÚM AND KASHAN, p. 199.

HERBERT's description of these places is very quaint and worth extracting :—

"Coom is a Citie placed in the halfe way betwixt the two Royall Cities, *Casbeen* and *Spawhawn*; it is scituate in a faire and sensible Horizon, and in Front of both Kingdomes, *Media* and *Parthia*.

"It was in ages past call *Goriana*, and afore that *Arbacta*, perhaps built by *Arbaces*, who in the yeare from *Adam* 3146, gaue end to the Assyrian Monarchy (rapt from effeminate *Sardanapalus*, the sixe and thirtieth from *Ninus*, first Emperour and Monarch of the World), and by which, a beginning to the *Median* Dynastie.

"The new ruines about her, may gaine beliefe to the Inhabitants, who say it was once comparable in pride and greatnesse to mightie

Babylon, but what euer it has beene, tis now a pleasant, fruitfull and healthy City and the people curteous.

"By some tis called *Coim*, and by others *Com*, vnfitly, for they pronounce it *Coom*. The Citie has two thousand Houses in her, welbuilt, sweet and wel-furnished, her streets are wide, her *Bazar* faire, and her *Mosque* of most honourable esteeme among them, therein is richly entombed *Fatima*, daughter and heire of their greatest Prophet *Mahomet*, and married to *Mortis Haly*, the king and much reuerenced prophet of the *Persian*. Her Tombe is round like other *Mosques*, the Ascent three or foure steps of silver.

"This City is watered with a sweet but small River, which deriues her spring out of the Coronian Mountaines, the aire here is second to none for freshnesse, nor wants this Towne any fruit requirable for the Zone tis placed in it, it has Grapes good and great store. Melons of both sorts, Cowcumbers, Pomegranads, Pome-citrons, Apricocks, Peaches, Plums, Pistachoes, Peares, Apples, Quinces, Almonds, Figs, Walnuts, Cherries, Berries, and the best wheat bread in *Persia* (*Gombazellello* excepted).

"Neere abouts was that great and terrible combat of *Hismael* and thirty thousand *Persians*, against *Selymus* the First and three hundred thousand *Turks*, where the victor *Turks* lost more then the vanquisht *Persians*, and had been defeated, had not the great Ordnance terrified the *Persian* horse; this battaile was fought *Anno Domini* 1514, begun at *Coy* in *Armenia* and ended here, and by the *Turkes* is cald the *Day of Doome*."

Khoi, near which the battle was fought between the Sūfī king Ismail and the Sultan Selim I., must be some 600 miles, as the crow flies, from Kum; and much further still by any routes through which troops could pass. Nor am I aware that there is extant any authority in support of the statement that the conflict "ended here." Professor Creasy, in his history of the Ottoman Turks (vol. i. p. 224–5) says the victory was complete, and that Selim, putting the male adult prisoners to death, *marched upon Tabriz*, then the Shah's capital. He levied, moreover, on the conquered city, a contribution of a thousand artizans, transferring them to Constantinople. The struggle took place, it is believed, as stated by Malcolm, "on the frontiers of Azarbaijan," or in that vicinity; but the scene was, in all probability, west of Tabriz. Of Kashan, we are told that it is "a famous citie in *Parthia*, whose *metropolis* is *Spawhawn*, whence she is distant sixtie miles and odde." He continues:—

"The antiquitie of it is not much, in this name, either taking beginning from *Cazan Mirzey*, sonne to *Hocem*, or from *Cassan*, who in the yeare 1202 was utterly ruined by the Great Cham, the rule

APPENDIX.

SERVICES OF DIRECTOR AND SUPERINTENDENTS OF PERSIAN TELEGRAPH,
p. 230.

1. Major John Underwood Bateman Champain, Royal Engineers (Bengal), was appointed to the distinguished corps of which he is a member in June 1853. Less than four years from that date the Indian Mutiny had broken out; and his services in the cause of its suppression and restoration of order are such as to warrant detailed narration.

Early on the 12th May, 1857, a sowar rode into Rurki bringing the news of the outbreak at Meerut. Captain Fraser, commanding the Sappers and Miners there, that very day marched his regiment to the scene of disturbance; and Lieutenant Champain, then acting for Lieutenant Chesney as Assistant Principal of the Thomason College, with his Principal's approval, volunteered, and was permitted to accompany.

On the 16th May, at Meerut, a large proportion of these very Sappers mutinied, and Captain Fraser was shot dead at his own encampment. Champain assisted in carrying him to hospital, and the next day was appointed adjutant of the corps, vice Lieutenant Maunsell, who assumed command. Most of the men present in the lines when the mutiny took place ran off to Delhi; but from working parties absent at the time, and a few individuals who remained faithful in the midst of temptation, a body of some 300 sepoys was formed, which nucleus was afterwards reinforced from Rurki. The carbines of these men were taken from them; but when ten days afterwards General Wilson determined to march on Delhi, the native sappers were re-armed, and Lieutenant Champain testifies that during his adjutancy their conduct was most exemplary, nor was there one deserter among them throughout the campaign.

Lieutenant Champain was present at both actions on the Hindun river under General Wilson, and at Badli ke Sarai and the capture of the heights before Delhi under General Barnard. Regimental adjutant during the whole siege, he took also the duties of field and assistant-field engineer, not having had probably, for three months, one whole night in bed. He was specially thanked in orders by General Barnard for rapidly constructing an urgently required battery, afterwards designated "Champain's" by written instructions of Colonel Baird Smith. Never absent for one hour from duty through sickness or any other cause, he was employed either to superintend or assist in the construction of, without exception, every single battery thrown up during the whole siege. On the 15th September he was wounded, but while on the sick list, owing to the number of engineer officers incapacitated, he volunteered for duty and was present at the capture of the Palace.

Lieutenant Maunsell's wounds having necessitated his departure to the hills, Lieutenant Champain succeeded to the command of the Sappers, and was in that position on the march to Agra and seven or eight minor expeditions in the vicinity, including the capture of Fathpur Sikri. He further commanded a small force of nearly 2,000 men, including Sappers, 21st Panjab Infantry, two guns, and a detachment of Hodson's Horse and 9th Lancers, on the march from Agra to Fathgarh, where he joined the Commander-in-Chief in November or December 1857. He continued to command the Sappers, numbering some 500, on the march to Cawnpore and the Alambagh, returning to his post of adjutant on the return of Lieutenant Maunsell in March 1858. He was present at the final capture of Lucknow, twice acting as Sir Robert Napier's orderly officer, with Lieutenant Elliot Brownlow who was killed when associated with him in this duty.

Major Champain was thanked specially in orders by Sir Robert Napier for having, with Captain Medley and 100 sappers, held for a night the Shah Najif, an advanced post of great strength, abandoned by eight companies of the 93rd on account of its remoteness from the army. Assisting to prepare the plan of the siege for submission to the Commander-in-Chief, he was ordered by Sir Colin Campbell, after the capture of Lucknow, to erect fortified posts for outlying detachments of police and regular infantry. Of these he completed about twenty. He was present at fourteen or fifteen minor engagements under Colonel Walter and others, and was thanked in a despatch by Captain MacMullin for services rendered in a rather severe affair near Balia. He was the only engineer officer employed at the capture of Jagdispur, where probably more than 16,000 troops were engaged under Sir John Douglas; and he was particularly recommended by that officer in his final despatch. He joined in pursuit of the rebels to the Kaimur hills, and when matters looked more quiet, he was appointed Executive Engineer of Gondah. Hence he was transferred to Lucknow, of which station he was Executive Engineer till ordered to Persia with Major Patrick Stewart in 1862.

He is now Chief Director of the Government Indo-European Telegraph, a department in which he has done continuous good service in Europe and Asia for some fourteen years.

2. Major Robert Murdoch Smith, of the Royal Engineers, a first lieutenant of September 1855, and second captain of June 1864, had been employed, before joining the Persian telegraph in 1863, in conducting excavations and researches at Halicarnassus and on the African coast; and is joint author, with Captain Porcher, R.N., of an interesting and admirably-illustrated volume on Cyrene. He is now director of the Indo-European telegraph in Persia, having succeeded Major Champain in the appointment more than nine years ago.

3. Major Oliver B. St. John, of the Royal Engineers (Bengal), is an officer of seventeen years' service. After employment for more than four years in the Public Works Department, in the north-west provinces of India, he volunteered and was chosen for service in Persia. On arrival at Bushahr in January 1864, he took charge of the fifth and last of the telegraph divisions, considered by Colonel Stewart the most important and difficult of all. From December 1865 till June 1866 he had charge of the Director's office, and from March 1866 till January 1867 his own immediate superintendence extended over the whole line from Tehran to Bushahr. During this period the second wire was erected. Proceeding home in May 1867, he was thence despatched to Abyssinia to take charge of the field telegraph and army signals, organised for service during the war. The telegraph was carried 200 miles from the coast under great difficulties; Lieut. St. John was mentioned in Lord Napier's despatches, received the thanks of the Government of India, and was further recommended to the Commander-in-Chief for a brevet majority on attaining the rank of captain. At the close of 1868 he returned to Persia, where he remained for three years, rendering services to which the Chief Director attributed much of the success attending the Russo-Persian line of telegraph. In October 1871, Captain St. John was ordered to Baluchistan, with local rank of major, to complete the survey of the Perso-Kalat frontier, as provided for under Sir F. Goldsmid's settlement. He returned to England on completion of this work in October 1872, since which he has been employed in the India Office preparing maps of Persia and the Baluchistan frontier. The former will be based on longitudes of the principal Persian telegraph stations fixed by Major St. John in co-operation with Colonel Walker

of the Indian Trigonometrical Survey, Captain Pierson, R.E., and Lieutenant Stiffe, I.N., by whom time signals were exchanged between Greenwich and Karachi on the one hand, and the stations in Persia on the other.

4. Captain William Henry Pierson, of the Royal Engineers (Bengal), is an officer of more than fifteen years' service. He served with the field force under Lieutenant-Colonel Gawler in Sikhim, as assistant field engineer, from 24th January to 30th April, 1861; was mentioned on that occasion in despatches, and received the thanks of the Government of India. Employed in India under the Public Works Department, and as assistant to Chief Engineer of Oudh up to September 1863, at which date he was transferred to Persia to assist in the construction of the telegraph. Services placed at disposal of Lords Commissioners of H.M. Treasury to superintend building of British Legation in Tehran; and so detached from telegraph duty from May 1864 to October 1871. Acted as director, Persian telegraph, from 19th October, 1871, to 4th October, 1873.

5. Captain (Local Major) Beresford Lovett, C.S.I., is a second lieutenant of June, and first lieutenant of Royal Engineers (Bengal), of August 1858. He had rendered good service on the north-west frontier of India, when appointed to Persia for the telegraph in 1866. After arrival in that country, he officiated, from January 1867 to October 1868, in the place of absent superintendents, and was favourably noticed for the part he took in bringing about the settlement of a serious disturbance which had occurred at the Abádeh station in June 1870. A very large number of men had been collected on that occasion to threaten the telegraph office, their leader's object being to visit his wrath upon a fellow countryman, one of the line guards employed by the British officers. Acts of aggression and gross violation of duty and propriety had followed, contrary to the spirit of the Anglo-Persian convention; and Lovett was despatched to investigate matters on the spot. Aided by the chief local authorities, and acting with judgment and energy, he was able to fulfil his mission successfully; and it was one which illustrated, in a remarkable manner, the peculiar position of British telegraph-signallers in Persia, and what semi-magisterial duties had to be discharged by the superintendents. In the same year, Captain Lovett was appointed engineer officer to the Perso-Makran and Perso-Afghan Boundary Commission; on completion of which duty, and return to England, he has been employed

in the map department of the India Office, turning to practical account the geographical information acquired in his recent surveys.

6. Mr. Henry Valentine Walton was appointed Inspector in the Indian Telegraph Department on 17th December, 1856. Proceeded at once to India, where he served with zeal and efficiency during the Mutiny as a volunteer at Agra. He was also present at, and took part in, the battle at Neemuch, for which services he received the Mutiny medal. This gentleman subsequently joined the Telegraph Department in Persia, and was one of the first superintendents on the lines under construction in 1863–64. He remained in this appointment until his death at Shiraz in May 1871. Mr. Walton's zeal and ability had been long recognized in the Persian telegraph, to the success of which he had contributed by hard and unusual services. And he held certificates giving testimony to the fulfilment of prior special duties, such as do not fall to the lot of Indian *employés* in ordinary times. He had saved his instruments at the critical period of the Mutiny; and had suffered exposure, want, and sickness, in the capacity of sergeant of the Agra Militia, and one or the other in some degree when in charge of the Fort Electrical Telegraph Office.

It is not unworthy of remark that Major Champain and Captain Pierson were highly distinguished cadets at the Military College, Addiscombe. The first came out at the head of his term, a position he had maintained uninterruptedly from the day of entrance. The second came out first in *three* terms, four being the usual number. Both were Cheltenham boys.

CHAPTER V.

CHIEF DIRECTOR'S REPORTS OF PROCEEDINGS, p. 295.

The reports referred to are those made at uncertain intervals to the Government of Bombay, which for some years exercised immediate control over the Indo-European telegraph. One dated Tehran, 4th November, 1865, was reprinted by order of Parliament, and will be found (p. 436 to 442) in the Appendix to the report on East India Communications, dated 26th July, 1866. From the other, bearing date Panab, 22nd June, 1867, the following are full extracts:—

"I take advantage of the present occasion of my return to Bombay, to submit for the information of Government a brief report in continuation of No. 90 of 4th November, 1865, showing how far the proposals made nearly twenty months ago for the better conduct of the Indo-European telegraph have been carried out or otherwise, and to what extent the views then expressed have been confirmed, or anticipations realised.

"2. There can be but little question that the Turkish line has improved, and will continue to improve. Reference to the daily press will suffice to show that messages come and go through Constantinople with a regularity of speed hitherto unknown; and I have reason to believe that the just complaints on the score of unintelligibility are becoming less numerous and important. The anticipation in my former report of messages passing 'to and fro between London and Karachi in 5½ hours' has been already so far realised that Mr. Walton's statement of the 31st ultimo shows 6h. 24m. as the minimum time of transit in May 1866, 3h. 13m. in July, and 3h. 54m. in October. Allowance must be made this year for extraordinary inundations in Turkish Arabia.

"3. But by the 'Turkish line,' it must not be understood that the whole link between London and Fao is supplied, or that a message reaching Constantinople from India can necessarily find its way thence in a few minutes, or even hours, to the west of Europe. Last autumn especially the detention of telegrams at Constantinople before one of the European lines would receive them, had become notorious; and the causes to which this discouraging circumstance was traced were productive of similar delay with regard to messages passing eastward to the Turkish capital.

"4. In giving attention, therefore, to the perfection of the Turkish Asiatic correspondence, it has also been essential to bear in mind that this section has proved by no means the least efficacious on the whole Indo-European line; and the Continental war of the past year has afforded additional proof of the necessity of having more than one independent wire through Europe, which can be depended on for the transmission of Indian telegrams.

"5. I am of opinion that, as a general basis of security, we should rely on not less than two routes between England, or Western Europe, and Constantinople. Present experience points for this purpose to the one through Paris, Basle and Vienna, found the best available during the war; and another through Italy and the Adriatic cable, viâ Valona and Salonica. The Russo-Prussian route, leading to Persia, should, no doubt, be the general alternative; to be used at the discretion of the public, either on the ground of efficient working or economy, or in the event of interruption on what may perhaps be appropriately termed the main line.

"6. And in this view I may state that considerable progress has already been made. Under the authority of the Right Hon. the Secretary of State for India (Viscount Cranborne), I have been enabled during the past year to confer officially, on the matter of East India telegraph communications, with the chief directors of the telegraph both in Paris and Vienna; and Major Champain has been employed on like missions at Berlin and St. Petersburg. The result of these semi-diplomatic discussions has been in every way successful. It has shown the readiness of foreign governments to assist in advancing telegraphic communication with Asia, as a mere question of benefit and progress. It has also produced more substantial fruit. Our commissioner at Constantinople, Mr. Courtenay, has just reported the satisfactory information that the Foreign Office had authorized Lord Lyons to accept 'two special direct wires between Vienna and Constantinople, one *viâ* Bosnia, the other *viâ* Servia, with absolute priority for Indo-European messages on whichever is best for the time being.' And I learn by Major Champain's own telegram and letter from our accountant in London, that the Prussian and Russian Governments have made over to Messrs. Siemens and Co., of London and Berlin, the exclusive working of two distinct wires which are to be constructed with special regard to Indo-European traffic. Russia is said to have even gone so far as to allow the firm to construct and own the line in her dominions. I am awaiting Major Champain's report of the particulars of this negotiation, he having been present on the occasion at St. Petersburg under official sanction. It should perhaps be mentioned that this scheme contemplates junction with the Persian, and not the Turkish wires.

"7. If we can now secure the same facility of working between Turin and Constantinople, as between the latter city and Vienna, we may trust to ordinary arrangements for the use of any other line having London and the Bosphorus for its terminal points. The Ottoman Government is pledged to perform its share of the undertaking, and I think it would be well to commence at once discussion of the subject with the Italian Administration of Telegraphy.

"8. For the use of Turkish-Asiatic as well as Russian-Asiatic, and Persian wires, the Indian Government has the advantage of being able to treat on her own immediate interests, and independently of private telegraph companies. It has been difficult hitherto to fix a uniform rate of payment for any but messages passing to and fro through Turkey; but if the conventions already concluded by her Majesty's ambassador at the Porte and her Majesty's minister at Tehran be supplemented by a quadrupartite agreement reconciling certain discrepancies of tariff arising out of separate conventions now existing between Russia and Persia, and Persia and Turkey, I see no reason to apprehend further complications or obstruction to traffic in Asia generally, whatever the route taken.

"9. Hitherto, as an alternative, or indeed in any other sense, the Russo-Persian line has not answered so well as expected. The cause is not to be attributed, in any important degree, to the Caucasian or Russian wires running north of the Persian frontier at the Arras (Julfa), but mainly to the inefficient state of the Persian line between the frontier and Tehran. When travelling in February last, I found the wire broken, and the ends far apart, amid the snow hills between

Marand and Sufian, north of Tabriz; and recent residence at Tehran has shown me how imperfect is the communication between Tabriz and the capital. This section of the line is about 450 miles in length, and is to be furnished with a second wire for our special benefit; but its management is not in our hands. The Russians have already sent telegraph officers, and, as I understand from them, have also supplied wire and insulators. At all events, the latter materials are not wanting; but the Persians are depended on for posts, and until those now in use are strengthened or replaced, the line cannot be considered trustworthy. I have strongly urged that if this section be included in the Siemens scheme above mentioned, it should be the first to which attention is given.

"10. It may not be superfluous to repeat that the line in Persia, on which the British Government possesses an exclusive wire worked by her own officers under the five years' treaty of November 1865, extends for about 1,100 miles, or from Bushahr to Tehran on the one side, and Tehran to Khanikin on the other. It should, moreover, be clearly understood that, north of Tehran, we have no control whatever. The second, or English wire, has been put up from Bushahr to Tehran, by far the larger division; and on its completion to the Turkish frontier, the treaty will be declared to have effect. I very lately came down the whole western line from Tehran to Khanikin, and can bear personal testimony to the fact that the sole cause of delay in carrying out the convention is the conduct of the Persians themselves. Orders for the supply of posts are issued by the higher authorities of Government, and those orders are disobeyed or ignored. Contracts are made, and, as a matter of course, broken by the contractors. The united influence of British officers and friendly pressure on prominent contractors eventually bring about the desired result; but only in the tardiest manner, and after loss of much time. Indeed time has no recognised value in Persia.

"11. Full explanations have been submitted to Government why the Persian line has not worked so well during the past eighteen months as at the first. A general renewal of posts and great difficulty in procuring these may perhaps be put down as the principal reason. But there has also been wilful damage to contend with, and it is not easy to detect, or always punish, when detected, the perpetrators. My former published report was not, however, silent on the likelihood of interruptions, and a very severe winter (1865, 1866) added to the contingencies then described. I have now great hopes of successful working, and would refer to the rapid communication between Tehran and Bombay during the past month or six weeks, in proof of the efficacy of the second wire so far as completed. It would be injustice to the officers employed were I to limit acknowledgment of their exertions and usefulness to mere allusion in a report like the present.

"12. The question of extending the Persian land-line to Gwadar, so as to form a complete alternative to the Gulf cable, will best be illustrated by a short account of my own movements since the date of my last general report. On the 4th December, 1865, under sanction of the Bombay Government and her Majesty's minister in Persia, I proceeded from Tehran to Ispahan, and thence turned off eastward to Yezd and Karman, with a view of ascertaining what advantages that part of the country offered, either politically or physically, to the erection of a line of telegraph. Major Smith, R.E., accompanied me to Bahristan, about a hundred miles east of Karman, and there we separated, he to make his way directly to the coast at Bandar Abbas, and I to work through western Baluchistan or Charbar near Gwadar. Our two journeys were successfully accomplished. We met again at Charbar, and leaving that port, went by sea to Karachi and Bombay. Thence we proceeded on a tour of duty to the other presidencies of India, returning to Sind by Delhi and the hills. At Simla I had the honour of submitting to the supreme Government the heads of a proposed convention with Persia based on the reports which we had just sent in to the Bombay Government; and, as the scheme met with general approval and support, I was authorized to supply all essential data for a full Foreign Office treaty. Embarking from Bombay in May, I arrived in England on the 18th June, 1866, and after many official references and communications, besides giving evidence on the subject before the parliamentary Committee on East India Telegraphs, I received final instructions on the 18th October following. These were to proceed to Persia at once to offer the terms proposed, and negotiate under the authority of her Majesty's minister at the Shah's court. I set out on the same date from London, but did not reach Tehran till the middle of February of the present year, having been directed by telegram from Lord Cranborne to remain at Constantinople so long as required by her Majesty's ambassador, who considered a temporary detention there important. My stay in Tehran, though prolonged to three months, did not, as in the previous case, result in successful negotiation; but I do not consider the labour expended to have been in vain, nor the discussion commenced, to be finally closed. The occasion was perhaps unfortunate. So rare a circumstance as the Shah's journey to Mashhad absorbed all ministerial as well as popular attention, and a new telegraph convention could hardly be admitted to interfere with the state programme. There is good reason to believe that the whole question can be re-opened within the year, and with fair prospect of success. Government will however be enabled to draw its own conclusions, as my reports on this matter have been many and in detail.

"13. In the concluding paragraph of the report of which this is a continuation, I stated my intention to submit 'what are the prospects of a new direct communication between Constantinople and Tehran by the junction of the wires from Erzrum to Tabriz.' It appears that a line has already been completed, from Sivas, a station in Asia Minor on the direct Baghdad line, to Erzrum and Kars; and from Alexandropol, on the Russo-Turkish frontier, to Erivan; leaving a distance of but a few miles between Kars and Alexandrapol, to open out a new direct communication between Constantinople and Tehran. The use of such an alternative line would be of great importance to the Indian public in the event of interruptions between Sivas and the Persian Gulf, and I have received authority from the India Office to negotiate, and also had some communication with the Turkish Director-General on the subject. I know of no better or likelier means of bringing the line into the Indo-European system than by settling a tariff for it, among other rates to be put before the proposed conference mentioned in paragraph 8.

"14. There is, moreover, now in progress a junction of the Turkish Asiatic line at Kifri, above Baghdad, with Khanikin, by a short cross wire; and this, when completed, will materially add to the security of our traffic. In the event of interruption below Kifri, the Indian telegram can at once pass into the Persian lines.

"15. The matters above noted will doubtless interest the commercial public. The record may serve at least to show what means appear calculated to render telegraphic communication between Europe and India more rapid, more regular, and more secure, and to what extent these means are made available. But it should also be stated, that while the present report embraces merely a general system of semi-political organization, the scientific officers of the department do not lose sight of the professional minutiæ of telegraphy, and are ready to avail themselves of, or advocate any innovations in code or apparatus which may be found desirable.

"16. The introduction of the Paris convention, under certain modifications, has been notified by the Secretary of State as applicable to Indo-European messages from the 1st proximo. I have to thank Major Champain for his attention to this important arrangement as well as for his continued and unremitting exertions to advance in every way the interests of the telegraph.

"17. A system of account has been introduced for telegrams passing from England to India viâ Constantinople, by which the London companies pay at once to the India Office such part of the cost of a telegram as would cover the transit through the cable and India, continental administrations only receiving and accounting for the charge up to Fao, or to the extreme end of the Ottoman territory. I was desirous of introducing the same system for the Russo-Persian line, assimilating the charges from Tehran to India to those from Fao to India, for simple facilitation of account. The proposal, when made through her Majesty's ambassador at Constantinople, was at once accepted by Turkey, and communicated to the neighbouring administrations; but for the Russo-Persian line, though Persia agreed on her part, Russia withheld consent. To prevent misunderstanding, I addressed a long explanatory memorandum to M. de Giers, the Russian minister at Tehran, and forwarded it through Mr. Alison just before leaving Persia. But I can hardly anticipate that it will obtain the end required, for Major Champain was at St. Petersburg at the time

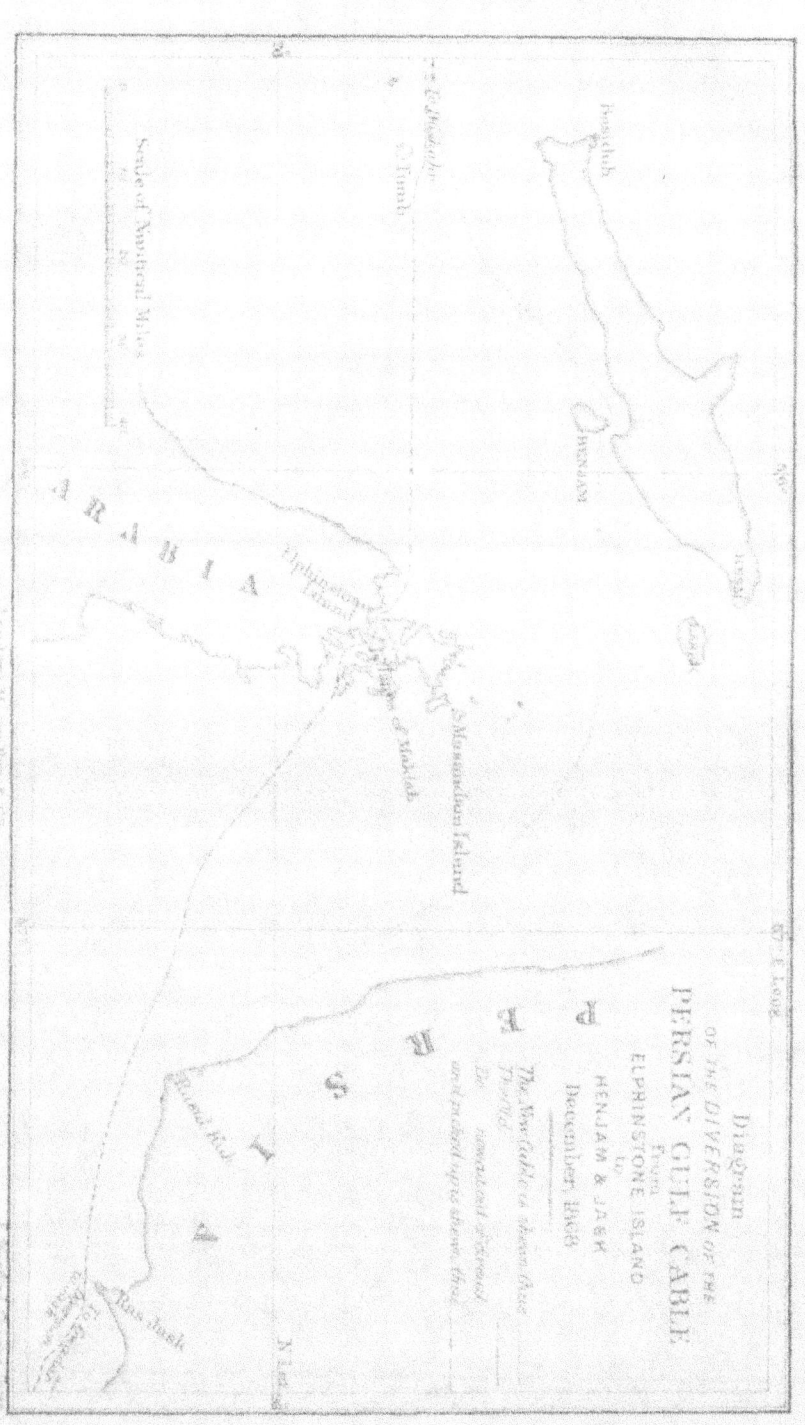

that the refusal of the Russian administration to accept our proposals was made known to the Persian Director-General, and he was consequently able to combat personally any ordinary objections offered. Under the circumstances the sole conclusion to be drawn is, that Russia, having in a convention with Persia, fixed a certain tariff on *all messages* passing from her frontier to Bushahr, declines to modify that tariff on Indo-European messages, although we, by a separate convention with Persia, have laid down a tariff equally high (and even higher) for about two-thirds of the same distance.

"18. Having last year visited the stations of Gwādar and Karāchi, I was glad to have the opportunity of visiting, this year, Fāo, Bushahr and Masandam. I certainly am of opinion that, in a purely sanitary point of view, it would be desirable to move the establishment at the last named to a less confined locality. The heat may not be very much greater than at Bushahr, but the high encircling rocks and limited view to seaward must have a depressing effect upon Europeans, especially during the hot season. On this subject, as well as on certain other questions of telegraph organization and detail not here noticed, I propose doing myself the honour of separately addressing government."

CHANGE IN THE COURSE OF CABLE, p. 301.

On the 6th February, 1869, Col. Goldsmid thus addressed the Bombay Government:—

"Referring to my letter on which was published Government Resolution No. 15 of the 14th ultimo, I have the honour to forward the engineer's report, and an accompanying diagram, in illustration of the change effected in the course of the cable in the Persian Gulf. These were only received yesterday.

"2. I would respectfully suggest that Mr. Walton's and Lieutenant Stiffe's reports, if printed with the forwarding letters, would form an appropriate continuation to the late Colonel Stewart's report of laying the cable between Gwādar and Masandam, and Masandam and Bushahr. The importance of the latter operation renders all the more important the modification now effected in the original project."

The engineer's letter was dated the 11th January, and may be given nearly *in extenso*:—

"I beg to report the completion of the two diversions of the Persian Gulf cable from Masandam to Jask and Henjām, there remaining now only the picking up of fifty miles of the cable, cut out of circuit from Masandam to the eastward, which will be done next trip. Altogether 153·3 nautical miles new cable have been laid, and 120 miles of the original cable cut out of circuit, besides about five miles picked up and relaid in the course of the work.

"The new cable was laid from the *Amberwitch* in the two trips made since the 1st October, half of the cable being taken from Kurāchi the first time, laid, and the ends buoyed; and the rest laid and work completed during the trip just concluded.

"The time actually occupied in coiling this cable on board at Karāchi has been five days for each trip, or an average of fifteen miles *per diem*. The cable has been paid out at an average rate of five and half knots per hour, and the amount of slack paid out about two per cent.

"The cable laid on the first trip was left buoyed, to facilitate picking up the ends to splice on the remaining cable, and the whole of the cable was safely laid without any hitch or accident.

"On the 1st December the smaller diversion of the cable through the new station at Jask was commenced. This was facilitated by the original line of the cable passing within two miles of that point. The operations were commenced by landing two shore ends, taking the ends into the temporary office, and laying them to seaward towards the line of cable; four miles were thus laid, and the ends buoyed. The cable was then cut on the morning of the 3rd December, each end successively picked up a short distance, and coiled towards the buoys, when the surplus was cut off and the ends spliced to the shore ends, completing the work the same evening. The amount cut out of circuit was two and quarter miles, so that the line was permanently lengthened by one and three-quarter miles. The interruption for the Jask-Gwādar section was seven hours, and for both sections only twelve hours.

"The accompanying diagram¹ will give an idea of the considerable amount of work involved in the great diversion from Mussendam to Henjam. The whole of the new cable was first laid and the ends buoyed; buoys were put on the old cable at the two points where it was intended to cut it, and the ends which had been landed at Henjam were coiled up across the island direct, until the establishment of the office there.

"A *minimum interruption of the traffic* was of the greatest importance, and by taking every care to avoid delay, it amounted only to fifty-two and half hours for both ends, of which twenty-one were occupied in the passage from one end to the other.

"On the 9th December the cable was grappled, in thirty-five fathoms to the eastward of Tumb Island, after considerable trouble, as owing to the very rocky and uneven nature of the bottom it could not be got hold of nearer than twelve miles to the place where it was intended to cut it. The cable was hove up and cut at 3.20 P.M., and as all this length had to be picked up, the final splice on this side (the Henjam-Bushair section) was not completed till noon on the following day. The section was then completed in twenty-one hours after first interruption.

"The ship arrived at the end of Ras al Kuh at 9 A.M. on the 11th December, when the cable, which had been previously grappled and

¹ See copy attached.

buoyed, was hove up in sixty-two fathoms, cut, and the Jask end wound in and then paid out to the buoy on the new cable, which was got on board, and the final splice finished, the same evening by night, and the bight finally shipped, thus completing the diversion. The good condition of the old cable is sufficiently shown by its standing the enormous span strain of being hove up to the surface in such deep water as sixty-two fathoms without parting. It required all the mechanical power available in the ship to get it to the surface, and I estimate that the cable was then lifted off the bottom of the sea for at least a mile on each side.

"I then proceeded to Bushahr to repair the Fáö cable, after which I returned to Karáchi, having on the way picked up and brought down altogether nearly seventy miles of the old cable, all of which is in good order.

"After all the new cable was laid, tests taken through the whole 150 miles, before communication was made with the old cable, showed that the insulation was very high."

CHAPTER VIII.

THE MURAD CHAI SEEN FROM THE DEVA-BOYUN MOUNTAIN, p. 441.

ACCORDING to Mr. Brant's Map, the Euphrates rises as the Murad Chai, among the mountains north, and eastward of Lake Van, in the Pashalik of Bayazid. It commences by running to the north, turns sharply to the westward, and after being fed by the Sherian Sû and one or two small streams, it passes to the south, S.S.W., S.W., west and by south, and again west, till, meeting a new feeder in the Charbchar Sû, it makes a fresh zigzag to the south, and then commences its long, irregular passage to the west, where it takes the classical name of Euphrates. The source of the Tigris should be near the Giuljak Lake, and still nearer to Argana Madan. According to Mr. Brant we should have crossed it, on issuing from the Batman, on our way to Kizin and Kharput. But both these great rivers have many sources, if every feeder be admitted to claim a right to partnership. We passed one source of the actual Euphrates, that is of the Murad Chai before it becomes the Euphrates, on our road to Hasan Chelibi and the Kizilbash mountain homes: it was undignified by the title of Kuru Chai, or the "dry river."

CHAPTER XI.

PROFESSOR de Filippi, in his "Viaggio in Persia," gives a graphic account of an ascent of Demavend, to accomplish which he left

Tajrish, one of the summer resorts of European diplomatists, on the 9th August, 1862. He was accompanied by MM. Lessona, Orio, Ferrati, Clemencich, Doria, Centurione and (Major) Champain. They entered the Elburz mountains by Sinak and a branch of the Jajrud; and passing near the village of Kubad almost hidden by the trees, they arrived at Hafiebeh, where quarters were assigned them in the Sadr Azim's castle. Continuing their journey on the day following into the valley of the Lar, they found the river of that name abounding in trout, and were charmed with the scenery and climate. Tents were pitched at Haular Khan. On the 11th they were guided by the course of the river, and pursued their way among the tents of the Kurd Iliats, who migrate in summer from Veramin to the cooler mountain pastures. It was not until the 13th that the summit of Demavend was attained. Although the first to set foot there was Signor Orio, who patriotically signalised his achievement by waving his handkerchief affixed to a stick with a loud-sounding "Viva Italia," he was immediately followed by Champain; whom, moreover, Professor de Filippi associates with Professor Lessona in the performance of another and more perilous feat,—viz., the intricate passage of a deep, snow-filled chasm without the aid of a guide.

The narrator himself could not share the honour with the rest. After accomplishing four-fifths of the ascent, he was compelled by nausea, vertigo, and other natural physical results of the rarity of the atmosphere, to abandon his intentions. Nor was he the only sufferer. Others also had equally expended their efforts in vain. We are led to infer that only four of the party, Orio, Ferrati, Lessona and Champain were successful. The two last heard, at the same moment, when just below the crater, a loud noise above them, and saw a thick vapour arise, the air being filled with sulphurous exhalations. The original may here be quoted (p. 267):—

"Il Prof. Lessona ed il Capitano Champain furono i soli che, governando prudentemente il bastone, escirono da questo passo senza ajuto della guide, mentre altri due non furono salvi che per la prontezza onde furono soccorsi. Al di là di questo passo l'erta riprende faticosissima su di una cresta rocciosa, poi di nuovo su di un'erta di lapilli più ripida delle precedenti. Da questo punto si vede già l'orlo del cratere tutto giallo di solfo. Succede un nuovo avvallamento occupato da una gran massa di neve meno erta della precedente, ma non meno pericolosa in altra ora ed in altra stagione, quando, solidificata dal freddo, non ceda sotto il passo. Qui il Prof. Lessona ed il Capitano Champain sentirono contemporaneamente uno scoppio dalla cima del monte, e videro sollevarsi un denso getto di vapore: l'aria d'ogni intorno era piena di esalazioni solfuree. Si compie l'ultimo tratto della salita nella neve cosparsa di polvero di solfo, o nella roccia incrostata di solfo. Primo a toccar la sommità (eran le 2 pomeridiane) fu Orio, che fece sventolar il fazzoletto sulla punta del bastone, gridando *viva Italia*. Fu immediatamente raggiunto dal capitano inglese, poi dagli altri."

Professor de Filippi reports the several ascents of Demavend accomplished or attempted from 1837 to 1862 inclusive. He also states the result of surveys and observations at different periods. The truest computation of height is believed to be that of the Russian Chronometrical Survey in 1861-62, determining it at 5,670 metres, about 18,000 English feet.

STATEMENT

REFERRED TO AT THE CONCLUSION OF THE FIRST PART, pp. 389, 390.

The Indo-European Telegraph Department had, so far as its lines extended, the monopoly of traffic between Europe and the East, from the commencement of 1865 to the commencement of 1870. Its earnings during that period averaged in round numbers £92,000 per annum, and its expenditure £87,000. A slight profit was thus realised.

From March 1870 to the present time, the department has had to compete with the powerful opposition of the Eastern Telegraph Company, owing principally to which, its earnings for the three years, ending March 1873, fell to an average of £53,000 per annum; but its expenditure was on the other hand reduced to an average of £75,000. In 1873-74 the earnings rallied and increased to about £61,000, and the expenditure, though not yet finally ascertained, is estimated not to have exceeded £68,000. A further improvement is continuing, the result for the present year, anticipated by the writer, being earnings £65,000 and expenditure £65,000; or the attainment of a point at which the revenue and expense will be again equal, preparatory it is hoped, to the gain once more of a slight profit.

Besides the competition of the Red Sea line, other causes have however materially affected the financial position of the department. The first was, the bad working on the foreign lines, between the head of the Persian Gulf and England, which continued the whole of the five years the department possessed the monopoly of communication, and prevented the realisation of a fair return on its capital.

A portion of the bad working no doubt occurred in Europe; but by far the chief part took place in Turkey, where, notwithstanding the permanent presence of a British Commissioner at head-quarters; frequent visits of the chief directors of the department; and reiterated remonstrances and complaints; nearly all messages were subjected to enormous delays, and transmitted in the greatest disorder; the common stoppage of traffic at the central office of Pera alone being on the average upwards of eighteen hours per message.

The tariff in force between England and India from 1865 to the end of 1868 was £5 for a message of twenty words. On 1st January, 1869, it was reduced to £2 17s., the reduction being made partly in consequence of public complaints of dearness, and partly in deference to the views of the chief continental telegraph authorities assembled in conference at Vienna in 1868, who, while officially promising to interest themselves in the improvement of Indo-European communication, then for the first time brought prominently into international notice, strongly urged that the rates beyond Europe should be made less costly. The experiment, however, was unsuccessful. The bad working west of the Persian Gulf continued, and proved an insuperable obstacle to a sufficient increase in the number of messages to compensate for the reduction in tariff. The result was that in 1869 the department sustained a loss in revenue of nearly £20,000.

In 1870, the aspect of Eastern telegraphy entirely changed. The Indo-European Telegraph Company, projected in 1868, with a name closely assimilated to that of the Government Department, and with the object of establishing a solid line from London through Prussia and Russia to Tehran, where the wires managed by the department terminate, completed its work of construction on the 30th January, and on the 31st, the new through route was opened. In a month or two it became thoroughly organized, and messages were transmitted by it in fewer hours than they had taken days before, and with an accuracy of reproduction and precision of order, to which no semblance of an approach had ever previously been made. Traffic at once began to increase, and the £2 17s. rate would doubtless now have yielded a satisfactory profit to both the Indo-European Company and the Indo-European Department; but the Red Sea line, projected in 1869, was at this time also opened, and a great proportion of the messages at once diverted to it. Considerably as the total traffic continued to increase, yet being now divided among three routes, it proved insufficient to pay either; the rates *via* Tehran and *via* the Red Sea were therefore raised to £4 10s. in February 1871. But this tariff still proving inadequate to produce a fair remuneration, the Indo-European and Red Sea Companies complained that their lines, paid for and maintained by private capital, and furnishing for the first time efficient communication with India, should be undersold by the Turkish line, which, supported by state revenues, continued to work, at a dead loss, at the old £2 17s. tariff. A sub-international conference was held at Berne to consider the question. The importance of maintaining the incomparably improved means of communication furnished by the companies was fully recognised; and, as the only means of effecting it, the Turkish administration was persuaded to raise its rates to £4 10s. also. In July 1872, however, the rates were again somewhat lowered, and made £3 15s. *via* Turkey, and £4 *via* Tehran, or the Red Sea, which figures have continued in force for Anglo-Indian messages up to the present time. But for Australian, China, and other far east messages, reductions have been made on the Cis-Indian lines, equalling a discount of from 20 to 30 per cent. from the rates named, in order that the total through charges should not be considered prohibitory.

The tariff hitherto spoken of has been for a message of twenty words, increasing by one-half for every additional ten, or fraction of ten, words above twenty. This is the European international system, and has been so for upwards of thirty years. Upon the comparatively short and inexpensive lines of the Continent and the United Kingdom it has answered very well; but upon very long and costly lines it is unsuitable. Eastern and European merchants have, from the first, made considerable use of language of preconcerted meaning in their messages, accomplishing thus the double object of ensuring additional secresy and economizing words. Within the last few years, they have so elaborated and perfected this mode of telegraphy, that a single word generally represents a whole sentence. They therefore frequently require to send only five or six words in a message. As under the international rules no proportionate reduction of charge can be made for this description of traffic, the want has been met by *packing*, a business which has been organized since 1872, and has yielded great profits to the organizers, from the capital expended in establishing the telegraph lines. A packer collects, for instance, four messages of five words each, at say 5s. per word, puts them into one message of twenty words, and sends the latter to his agent for £4, thus clearing by the transaction £1, less his working expenses.

But effective measures have for some time been in progress to check this business. The representatives of the Indian Government at the International Telegraph Conference of 1871, foreseeing that the twenty word standard could not be permanently upheld, obtained from the European Administrations the best agreement then possible for a lower standard, and caused to be inserted in the International Convention a provision for ten-word messages, with a subsequent charge for each single word on the lines east of Europe. It being impossible, however, at the time to arrange for any reduction of the European transit charge, the provision was temporarily kept in abeyance. But it has, at some little pecuniary sacrifice, been lately brought into force where most needed, and ten-word messages at half rates, with subsequent gradation per single word, have been introduced between England and India with marked success, inflicting a heavy blow upon the packing business. Steps are being further taken to introduce a word tariff, pure and simple, for all Indo-European messages. When this is effected, the ground, for the most part, will be cut from under the packers' feet, and the business will die away, or nearly so.

The improvement in the means of communication with India since 1870, and the subsequent extension of the telegraphic system to China, Japan, Australia, &c., have increased the traffic on the Cis-Indian lines to about three times what it was in the days of monopoly vid Turkey, with postal service only beyond India. About 40,000 rates of twenty words each now represent the traffic per mensem through the Cis-Indian lines. Of the total, the Turkish line obtains about 4 per cent., the Tehran line about 32 per cent., and the Red Sea line the remainder, or about 64 per cent.

One reason why the Eastern line obtains the bulk of the traffic is, that being in the hands of a single company, its actions are freer, and its interests can be better pushed than those of the other lines, which, belonging partly to a company, and partly to different governments, cannot move in any matter without previous consultation of the directorates, and consequent loss of time. But the chief reason of the advantage possessed by the Eastern Company undoubtedly is, that it is intimately associated with the Extension companies beyond India, and this association secures to it a virtual monopoly of the Trans-Indian messages. These, although less remunerative than Indian ones, yet make a considerable show in point of numbers.

As the messages vid Turkey and vid Tehran both necessarily pass over the lines of this department, the latter transmits rather more than one-third of the entire traffic exchanged between Europe on one side, and India and the far East on the other, and this third represents really a greater number of rates than the department dealt with when it possessed the monopoly of Eastern communication. The reduction of tariff, however, and the passage of nearly all its present share of the messages, over a shorter length of its cables, render the receipts now of less value than formerly.

Briefly, the main reasons why the department has not hitherto been more financially successful are, first, that when it had the monopoly of communication, the bad working of the foreign lines, west of the Persian Gulf, prevented all development of traffic; and secondly, that immediately a friendly and excellent route connected its lines with England and traffic began to become remunerative, an opposition line opened, and at once shared the messages.

The earnings of the department shown in the Revenue Account are made up of the entire net receipts of the Persian Gulf cables and land lines, and a portion of the Persian receipts, obtained as follows. The entire *transit* receipts between Bushahr and Tehran (the Persian length worked by officers of the department), are subject to a first charge of about £4,800 per annum for Persian royalty. Half the balance is received by the department as earnings, and half is due to the Indo-European Company in return for the risk incurred by it in guaranteeing the royalty, and for the obligation contracted by it of being the medium for the payment of the Persian debt, shown in the capital account. The Company's half is, however, sequestrated by the department, till the debt is liquidated.

A. BRASHER.

APPENDIX.

Note to foregoing.—Mr. Alfred Brasher was appointed traffic manager of the Indo-European telegraph in 1865, and was the first officer who held any appointment of this nature under the Indian Government. He drew up the whole of the numerous forms required for the department, organized a check and account office at Karáchi, prepared the large tariff books (then showing separate rates for towns as well as countries) used throughout India from 1864 to 1869, and translated the different conventions whose rules prevailed in India during the same period. Independently of these indoor duties, he had taken part in the Persian Gulf Cable Expedition of 1864, and lent active aid, by superintendence and otherwise, in the work of connecting the Turkish land wires below Basrah to the cable at Fáo. Mr. Brasher's forms were borrowed and his check and account system was adopted by the Indian telegraph department on re-organization, and a similar appointment to his own was created under the title of Traffic Director.

In 1867 he was promoted to his present post in London, the work of which comprises settlement and revision of international and departmental accounts, preparation of budget estimates and capital and revenue accounts for parliamentary reference, translation of Berne circulars, and fulfilment of the duties of the Chief Director on any occasion of that officer's absence from England.

F. J. G.

MIAN KOTHAL. (*See p.* 395.)

INDEX.

N.B.—Oriental terms, and names of ships, are printed in italics.

A

Abádeh, 305
abas, 552
Abdui, Valley of, 186
Abdullah, 151
Abdul Aziz, 339
Abol, 147
Abich, Signor, 528
aberism, 531
Abru Efendi, 263
Absheron, 524; naphtha wells at, 525
Abul Fath Mirza, 597
Abu Ginom, 435
Abyssinia, 441
Adair, Dr. Ponsonby, 131
Addiscombe, Military College at, 9
Aden, 88
Afghanistan, 73
Agamemnon, H.M.S., 50, 118
Agathon Efendi, 263
Aganur, Mr. Stephen, 230
Agha Muhammad Hasan Khan, the Nawab, 180
Agha Muhammad, 540
Agha Khan Mahlati, 597
Agra, 22, 32, 52
Agram, 342
Agreements, 208, 216, 233, 335
Ahmad Efendi, 413
Aimini, R., 610
Ain Tinat, 415
Aix, 50
'*Akai*,' 396
Akcha Dagh, 447
Akda, 567
Akkoz, 493
Ak Punghar, 435
Alambagh, The, 38, 40, 41, 46, 47, 49
Alawis, 446
Albania, 75
Aleppo, 85
Alexandrés, 122
Alexandretta, 221
Alexander Nevsky, 485
Alexander, Mr., 636
Algiers, 122

Alipur, 19
Ahson, Mr., 210, 552
Ali Chaosh, 418
Ali Daghi, 440
Ali Efendi, 423
Ali Kuli Khan, 518
Ali Khan Beg, 254
Ali Murtaza, 554
Alishated, 32, 33, 38, 43, 44, &c.
Allaga Khan, 418
Alti Permak, 503
Altun Kupri, 419
Amára, 398
Amasia, 81
Amisdah, 28, 52
Amberwitch, 125
American Missionaries in Armenia, 442
Amir Yaman, 469
Amoor, 481
Amphía, 20
Amr Agha Powár, 485
Amritsar, 52
Anar, 578
Anarkullee, 28
Ancyra, 467
Andrew, Mr., 64
'Angel of Death,' Plain of the, 559
Anglo-Indian telegraph, 62; telegraphic messages, table showing average speed of, 589; telegraphs, financial statement of Mr. Brasher, 653
Anglo-Ottoman Convention, 109; protocol, 102
Angora, 71, 81, 466; goats, 468
Arab, curious story of an, 171
Arab workmen, 173
Arabic Koran, 502
Arabs, 81, 85, 95
Arabs at Massadam, 633
Araxes, R., 270
Arba, 596
Arbaeta and Arbaces, 199
Arbeil, 430
Archduke Michael, 519
Ardashir Babagan, 558
Argana Madan, 654

Brabant, Duc de, 247
Bradshaw, Captain, 152
Brahminabad, 568
Brant, Mr., 142, 651
Brasher, Mr., 390; financial statement of, 653
Breussel's Hotel, 515
Bright, Sir Charles, 113, 119, 124, 131, 162, 166, &c.
Brindisi, 63
Bristol, 17
British India Steam Navigation Company, 383
Broomlow, Lieutenant Elliot, 640
Bruges, 56
Brunel, Mr., 17
Brunner, M., 341
Brussels, 378
Bucharest, 75
Bukhara, 487, 528
Bulwer, Sir H., 79, 213
Burana, 496
Bushahr, 53, 85, 89, 91, 116, 127, 131, 250
Bushahr-Tehran route, Colonel Stewart's report on, 94; telegraph, Lieutenant St. John's report on, 304
Bushahr-Shiraz survey, 183
Bushahr-Fâo submarine cable, 165, 178

C.

Cairnsmore, 9
Calcutta, 17, 19, 22, 32, 40, 125, &c.
Calcutta, 362
Campbell, Sir Colin, 38, 39, 41, 44, &c.
Canning, Lord, 32, 42
Capitanskaya, 509
Capper, Mr., 387
Cardiff, 17
Carew, Lieutenant, 131, 636
Carmania, 582
Carmichael, Sir James, 340
Carnatic, wreck of the, 365
Caroline, 363
Carpendale, Captain, 160, 301
Carthew, Mr., 68
Catherine II., 511
Caucus and Mercer Company, 509
Caucasus, 329
Cautley, 19
Cawnpore, monument at, 35; destruction of telegraph wire at, 32; telegraph office near, 46
Centurione, Signor, 652
Ceylon, 31
Chahal Sitou Palace, 560
Chahgodak, 183
Chahi Shor, 502
Chahkutah, chief of, destroys wire, 255
Chair Kuf, 469
Chakar Khan, 507
Chakmak, 572
Chaldæa, 67
Chaldæan bishop, 421

Champain, Major, 182, 206-388; services of, 639; ascends Demavend, 652
Chaosh at Hasan Chellbi, 119
chapar, 193
chaparkhana, 535
Charbar, 134; and Jask, proposed new stations, 288, 594, 614
Charbehar 89, 651
Chasseur-à-cheval, Persia, 324
Chattin, Colour-Sergeant, 313
Chatterton's compound, 123
Chatham, 15
Chauncey, Lieutenant, 29, &c.
Chauvin, Colonel von, 325
Chebeksa, 507
Chelekan Island, 528
Χελώσοφάγοι, 619
Chepstow, 17
Chesney, Colonel, 395; Lieutenant, 639
China, 411, 656
Chinar, 305, 369
Chizkaya, 513
Cholera in India, 53
Chosroes Nurshirwan, 401
Chunar, 27
Church, 535
Circassian Exodus of 1864, 453
Clarendon, Lord, 61
Clark, Mr. Latimer, 113, 114, 116, 122, 125, 358, 364, 366, 368, 371, &c.
Clemenrich, M., 652
Clifton, 17
Clyde gunboat, 160
Coimbator, 617
Colburn's United Service Magazine, 496
Comet, Diary on board of the, 171
Constable, Captain, 116
Constance, 108
Constantine, 420
Constantinople, 53, 56, 61, 69, 72, 80, &c.
Continental railways, 477
Conventions, Turco-Persian, 243; Anglo-Persian, 273, 294, 321, 387; Anglo-Ottoman, 109; Paris, 648; Revision of last at Vienna, 353
Coromandel, 131
Corpatrick, 124
Courtenay, Mr., 261
Cranborne, Lord, 329, 644
Creasy, Professor, 637
Ctesiphon, 400
Cunynghame, Sir A., 527
Curchod, M., 379
Custines, Marquis de, 507
Cyrene, 641
Cyrus, tomb of, 369
Czarina, 511
Czaritzin, 513

D.

Dacca, 366
Daghistan, 527
Damram, 572
Dair-el-Kmr, 439
Dâk station, 38

INDEX.

Forster, Rev. Charles, 143
Fowles, Corporal, 315
France, 377, 477
Frankfort-on-the-Maine, 379
Frazer, Captain, 639
Frederick William, Prince, 50
Frere, Sir Bartle, 279
'Friend of India,' 24
Fuad Pacha, 73
Fury, 189

G.

Gabler, Captain, 372
Gaev, 530
Gachion, 479
Gali, 612, 616
Gan Island, 368, 371
Galoch, 471
Galata, 54
Galle, 32
Ganges, R., destruction of a rebel stronghold on the, 36; destruction of temples on the, 44; fortification between the Ganges and Jumna, 44
Garhwála, 487
Garoosh, 192
Garstin, Colonel, 19
Gastinger, Captain, 224
Gawler, Lieutenant Colonel, 642
Gemgeen minstrels, 425
Gurishkurt, 424
Gezires, 427
Ghanam, 143
Ghases, 143
Ghazireh, 430
Ghiláu, 531, 571
Ghoorkas, 46
Ghulka, 143
Ghublash Ghazireh, 142
Ghulam, Persian, 168, 551
Ghurbati, 572
Gibbon, 491
Gibraltar and England submarine cable, 52
Giera, M. de, 618
Girdashna, 619
Girk Osman, 424
Girkuddarost Su, R., 425
Gisborne, Mr. Jacquel, 91
Glasscott, Lieutenant, 412
Gmelin, M., 528
Gok Su, 405
Golden Horn, 259
Gomish, 640
Goodfarn, Mr., 636
Gopargunj, 34
Gorbad, R., 374
Government House, Calcutta, 42
Grand Trunk Road, 28
Grand Hotel, Paris, 475
Grande Société des Chemins de Fer, 510
Grant, Sir Patrick, 37
Grant, Sir H., 305
Graves, Corporal, 396

Great trigonometrical survey of India, 36
Green, Sir H., 86
Green, Major Malcolm, 92
Greener, Mr., 79, 83
Gregory, Mr., 636
Gubba, 400
Gulabak, 539
Gulnabad, 563
Gui Tepeh, 420
Gunjak, 440, 651
Gutlak, 404
Gutta-Percha Company, 123
Gwádár, 53, 56, 59, 112, 120, 131, 583, 594, 616, 620; and Fáo submarine cable, 112, 621; and Musandam submarine cable, 131, 133; rendezvous of Persian Gulf cable ships and steamers at, 133
Gwalior forces, defeat of, 42
Gwattar, 282

H.

Hab Hill, 573
Habaláin, 137
Had, R., 398
Hafichab, 662
Hague, The, 379
Hamar Efendi, 215
Hyderabad, 158
Haji Iatis, an astrologer, 436
Haji Mahmud, 156
Hail, a hospitable, 567
Hian, 454
Hakim Khan, 147
Halicarnassus, 641
halk, 620
Hamadán, 315
Hamilton, Corporal, 230
'Hamilton' poles, 367
Hamrin, 415
Hanaka, caravanserai of, 591
Hanlar Khan, 652
Hanway, Jonas, 513
Hardargemi Su Ferry, 416
Harris, Lord, 32
Hasan Ali Khan, Nawab, 236
Hasan Akdai, 567
Hasan Balrik, 446
Hasan Bey, 405
Hasan Bey Ohbasi, 465
Hasan Chelibi, 447; extortionate natives at, 448
Hasan Oghlu, 466
Hashim Bey, 395
Hassi ipiiki, 610
Hasunga, 303
Hauz-i-Sultan, 199
Havelock, General, 34
Hawes, Lieutenant, 65
Henjam, 238, &c.
Henley and Co., 117
Herbert, Sir Thomas, 542, 636
Harries, Mr., 379
Hillah, 409
Himatabad, 569

INDEX

Montefika, 54
Moore, Mr., murder of, 34
Morgan, Lieutenant, 568
Morier, 549
Mosaic sailors, 597
Moscow, 484
Mosul, 61; proposal for a subdivisional between, and Bagdad, 75
Mounsey, Mr., 537
Mornet, 528
Mushkhil, 239, 616
Mudir, 417
Mudurli Valley, 470
Muhammad Ismail Khan, 583
Muhammad Rahim, 583
Muharram festival, 238, 572
Mujtahid, 558
Mukalaa, 141, 147
Muller, Captain, 529
Multan, 613
Mulvie, 83
Mussia, 559, 597
Muntashir, 455; springs near, 457
Murad Chai, R., 441, 651
Murillo, 342
Murtaza Kuli Khan, 599
Musa, 146
Musa Chauck, 126
Muscovite Mujuk, 487
Mushkhan, 565
Mustashir, 203

N

Nabi Yunus, 421
Nagpur, 296
naib, 609
Nafinabad, 597
Nain, 572
Nakshab-i-Taimur, 184
Nakshab-i-Rustam, 191
Narnik Pasha, 231
Naudaran, 572
Nao Gate, 245
Nacodimus, 566
Napier of Magdala, Lord, 25
Napier, Sir Robert, 540
Narmashir, 597
Nasteran, 610
Nathienz, 232
Nushatri, 448
Navargu, 283
Naring, R., 415
Neemuch, battle at, 643
Neill, Colonel, 33, 39
Nestorians, 432
Nevsky Prospect, 482
New Holland, 80
New Testament, old Armenian copy of, 440
Nicomedes, 472
Nicomedia, 472
Nijni Novgorod, 489
Nile boat, 8
Nil Gauj, 19

Nineveh, 67; modern, 421
Niquita's hostelry, 489
Nishin, 426
Nissa, 265, 312
Noberan, 319
Norman, Corporal, 224, 396
Northcote, Sir Stafford, 298
North Woolwich, 123
Novgorod, 483
Nullahan, 469

O

Oberhausen, 50
Odessa, 329
Oka, R., 489
Olbia, 472
Oman, 136
Omar Pasha, 71
Omar Faizi Efendi, 206
Orekhovskaia cotton mills, 489
Oriental diplomacy, 547
Oriental statesmen, 231
Orio, Signor, 652
Ormara, 374, 620
Orontes, R., 63
O'Shaughnessy, Sir W., 21, 65-72
Osrnadi, 396, 398
Ostend, 50
Ottoman Government, 67; negotiations with the, 96
Ottoman telegraph administration, 71
Oudh, 643
Oudit, M., 258
Oural, R., 512
Outram, Sir James, 39
Owen, Captain, 362
Ozna, R., 519

P

Palmerston, Lord, 481, 555
Palmyra, 63
Panjab, 28
Papas, 459
paras, 447
Paris, 341; past and present, 475; Exhibition of 1855, 29
Parsis, 529
Pasargadae, ruins of, 399
Pasni, 374, 620
Paswan Oghlu, 463
Peattie, Corporal, 213
Peek, Mr., 311
Peel, Sir Robert, 60
Pelly, Lieutenant-Colonel, 162
Penang, 52
Pera, 54
Perceval, Mr. Joyce, 246
Perrot, M., 467
Persepolis, 191
Peshawar, 21
Peter the Great, 513
Petrovsk, 506; pier at, 521

Sayid Harun, 612
Sayid Khan, Mírza, 210
Saiyid Muhammad, 147
Sakar, 155
Salian, 550
Salonica, 346
Salt Desert, 189
Samalot Company, 539
Samara, 511
Samarkand, 405
Samsun, 221
Sandoway, 23
Sankey, Colonel, 85
Saratoff, 509
Sarhas, 182
Saridots, 413
Sarepta, 511, 514
'Sarhad,' 192
'Sarhang,' 254, 524, 580
Sárí, Island of, 531
Sar-i-Yezd, 574
Sarvistan, 189
Saxe, Marie, 475
Scroggie, Mr., 376
Scutari, Stewart's tomb, 59; connection with Constantinople, 80; telegraph office at, 81; Diarbekir survey, 82
Seleucia, 62, 460; Syrian ports below, 63
Selim I., Sultan, 637
Semaphore, 40, 47
Semi-vowels, 134
Semlin, conference of delegates at, 378
Servia, 341
Severn, R., 17
Sevri Hisar, 468
Shabar, R., 185
Shalms, 143
Shadwan Island, 366
Shagird chapar, 505
Shah of Persia, H.M. the, 255, 551
Shah, Abbas, 564
Shah, Abdul Azim, 545
Shahi Mardan, 572
Shah Husain Safavi, 584
Shah Kuli, 420
Shah Maidan, 569
Shah Najif, 39, 640
Shah Niamat Ullah, 590
Shahr Babak, 588
Shahr-panah, 541
Shahrabad, 567
Shahzadah, 226
Shaikh Suliman, 346
Shakhana, 433
Shamiran, 546
Shammer Bedouins, 86
Shams, 578
Shamsabad, 192
Shanina, 430
Sharrat, Mr., 229
Shash Deh, 189
Shatt el-Arab, R., 54
Sheerness, 118
Sheil, 546
Sherían Su, 651
Shiaz, 608

Shikar, 27
Shikarpur, 184
Shikarpuris, 576
Shilwar, 161
Shiraz, 96; Wazir of, 241; and Bandar Abbas, most direct route between, 189; difficulties at, 225; Ispahan route, 190
Shir-kuh, 574
Shir Shah, 405
Shusa, 143
Shorabash, 491
Shor Kandi, 374
Shukuri, 412, 448
Shum Valley, 374
Shuster, 597
Sibi, 143
Siddons, Mr., 21
Siemens, Dr., 325
Siemens and Halske, 117, 334
'Siemens,' standards, 307; proposal, 331; concession, 337
Sikandar-bagh, the, 39
Sikkim, 642
Shobirak, the civil governor of, 568
Simla, 31
Sinak, 652
Sind, 89; railway, chief engineer of, 616
Singapore, 52, &c.
Sin-sin, 198
Sipah, 151
Sipah Salar, 547
Sirhan, 491
Sistan, 571
Sistan Mission, 195
Sivas, 64, 451, 617
Sizran, 510
Skene, consul, 85
Smith, Colonel Baird, 639
Smith, Major Murdoch, 221, 641
Smythe, Major Carmichael, 10
Soboloff's Hotel, 505
Sohar, 138
Sonmiani, 620
Southgate, Mr., 438
souars, 494
Spanish farm, 492
Speed of Anglo-Indian messages, 380
Stanley, Lord, 234
Stena, 506
Steppe, 511, 515
Sterlet, 511
Stewart, Colonel Patrick, memoir of, 9-59; otherwise mentioned, 69, 78, 93, 105, 115, 131, 140, 169, 178, 203, 206, 213, 218, 220, 221, 247, 249, 256, 258, 265, 323, 339
Stewart, Mr. McLeod, 629; Capt. Colvin, 131
Stiffe, Lieutenant, 116
Stockholm, 382; tar, 122
Stoddart, Colonel, 437
Stoppani, Professor, 528
Stranoch, Mr., 376
Stuart, Hon. Mr., 229
Stuart, Captain, 572

672   INDEX.

Suaidah, 62
Subduvzi cable, 73, 74, 87, 90
Submarine cable, 61, 112, 114, 122, 128, 134, 131, 161, 165, 178
Submarine Telegraph Committee, 113
Suez, 365
Sufian, 636
Suliman Khan, 604
Sulimanieh, 418
Sumach Pils, 461
Sutton Bar Segar, 141
Sultan Murad Caravanserai, 444
Sutton Ovks, 183
Sutton Su, R., 496
sword Star, 171
Sonderi, 507
Suraf, 282
sword, 469
Swindon, 17
Switzerland, 577
Syrian bishop, 422

T.

Tabatabi Kabir, 117
Table Bay, 18
Tabriz, 200
Tabrizi, 633
Tabors, 642
Tahrud, 592
Takour, 542
Taimur Lang, 460
Tajbat, 189
Tajin (Juna?), 191
Tak-i Kasr, 400
Tauerkus, 639
Tsagi Karun, 149
Tarsh, 271, 35, 637
Task Aman-Sul-R, 427
Taylor, Mr. H., 277
Taylor, Mr. John, 104, 127
Tazi Khorasan, 117
Toberan Martyr Cemetery, 491, 492, &c.
Tehran, 53, 207, 541, 545, 540; Table route to, 625
Tepriah, 602
Telegraphs, Calcutta-Lahore, 12; Prome-Sandoway, 29; Agra-Calcutta, 32; Madras, Ceylon, and Calcutta, 32; Cawnpore the Allanbagh, 38; Karachi-Constantinople, 66; Seatan-Baghdad, 71, 72, 73; Mosul-Baghdad, 85; Karachi-Bassrah 88; Karachi-Gwadar, 114; Baghdad-Bandar Abbas 201, 203; Special Line to Nissa, 241; Isphan-Sweder, 268 Yerd, 272; Bushahr-Tehran, 304; Tehran-Kirman shah, 354 Hamadan, 358; London-Tehran, 381; Basso-Persian, 527
Telegraphs during the Indian Mutiny, 47
Tel Keif, 424
Tel Omar, 461
Tenk, R., 282
Terekh, 479

Termok, 540
Terrible, H.M.S., 203
Teali, 442
Thackeray, W. M., 10, 432
Theckioos, St., 440
Thunarp Kull, 407
Thermia, 54
Thibet, 31
Thorn, 329
Thomson, Mr. Donald, 216, 218
Thomson, Professor, 312
Tiflis, 215
Tigress, perilous adventure with 4, 26
Tigris R., 62; quest on the, 392; rise of the, 407
tepid, 518
Tinak Karagan, 539
Tissin, 417
Tischopen, 624
T-kat, 64. 131
Tokma-su, 456
Tolport, Captain, 300
tombirok, 460
Torkish, 479
Trebizond, 451
tsepar, 504
Tubera, 829
Tunb Island, 130
Tunis, 342
Turkey, 66; special wire for Indian messages through, 76; singular statistics, 246; and Russia, proposal for a new telegraph line between, 235
Turkish Arabia, 54; English interior in, 275
Turkish officers, 55
Turkish soldiers, 428
Turkish treatment of, 71
Turco-Russian frontier, 76
Turco-Persian frontier, 196
Turkomans, 465
Turakhan, 543
Tuzen Punar, 454
Tyara, 424

U.

Ujain, 108
Ujain Rao water, Colonel Stewart's report, 110
Ustad Husain, 501
Utakamand, 617

V.

Vada, Pietro della, 212
Valans, 545
Van, 455
Van, Lake, 654
Van-kedm, 468
Vassil Sitzka, 307
Vermain, 655
Victoria, 165, 632
Vienna, International Congress at, 377

INDEX

Vigilant, 171
Vladimir, 489
Volga, R., 489, 596; traffic on the, 509; "Paroebod," 519
Volsk, 511
Vornesch, 510
Vougy, M. de, 340
Voxall, The, 511

W.

Wakf, 465
Wakilabad, 597
Wakil-ul-Mulk, 282, 607
Walker, Mr., 117, 374, 622
Wali, 317
Walsh, Mr., 472
Walter, Colonel, 640
Walton, Mr., 98, 144, 250, 268, 543
Waring, Mr. Scott, 184
Warsaw, 329
Webb, Mr., 179, 626
Westly, Mr., 626
Wheatstone, Professor, 748
Whittingham, Corporal, 257
Witkowitchki, 478
Wills, M.B., Mr. Charles, 289
Wilna, 478
Wilson, Schatz, 321
Wilson, General, 639
Windham, General, 38, 50
Windsor Castle, 50
Wirzboloff, 477
'Woman's Fort,' The, 435
Wood, Sir Charles, 209
Woods, Mr., 639
Wulkersdorff, M., 341
Wye, R., 17

Y.

Yakhshi Khan for Yakhshant, 465
Yarinja, 478
Yáwar, 244
Yenikale, 491
Yenikshik, 466
Yenijeh, 413
Yezd, 571; proposed telegraph line through, 279; Chief Director's report thereon, 281; opinion of Indian Government, 285; a Yezd story, 573
Yezdikhast, 192; view of, 226
Young, Mr. A. P., 180
Yoghurt, 465
Yuzgat, 71, 461; view of, 462; Sunday at, 463
Yuzbashi Omar Faizi Efendi, 246

Z.

Zab, R., 420
Zab, Great, 86
Zab, Lesser, 419
Zabeln, 435
Zab Su, 420
Zain-ed-din, 575
Zanguiabad, 192
Zanzan, 191
Zerobia, 132
Zergunduli, 548
Zerra, 314
Ziarat, 449
Zind, 416
Zobeide, tomb of, 77, 102
Zoroastrians, 629
Zouave, 430
Zul Kifl, 440

THE END.

LONDON: R. CLAY, SONS, AND TAYLOR, PRINTERS, BREAD STREET HILL.

In 8vo, cloth, price 10s. 6d.

ESSAYS ON EASTERN QUESTIONS.

BY

WILLIAM GIFFORD PALGRAVE.

AUTHOR OF "CENTRAL AND EASTERN ARABIA."

CONTENTS.

CHAP.
I.—Mahometanism in the Levant.

II.—Mahometanism in the Levant (continued).

III.—Mahometanism in the Levant (concluded).

IV.—The Mahometan "Revival."

V.—The Turkomans and other Tribes of the North-east Turkish Frontier.

VI.—Eastern Christians.

VII.—The Monastery of Sumelas.

VIII.—The Abkhasian Insurrection.

IX.—The Poet 'Omar.

X.—The Brigand, Ta'abbet Shurran.

The *Saturday Review* says:—"The book is decidedly a valuable addition to the stock of literature on which men must base their opinions of the difficult social and political problems suggested by the designs of Russia, the capacity of Mahometans for sovereignty, and the good government and retention of India."

MACMILLAN & CO., LONDON.

TRAVELS.

AT LAST: A CHRISTMAS IN THE WEST INDIES. By the Rev. Charles Kingsley, Canon of Westminster. With Numerous Illustrations. New and Cheaper Edition. Crown 8vo. Price 6s.

THE NILE TRIBUTARIES OF ABYSSINIA, AND THE SWORD HUNTERS OF THE HAMRAN ARABS. With Maps and numerous Illustrations. By Sir Samuel Baker. Fifth Edition. Crown 8vo. cloth extra. 6s.

THE ALBERT N'YANZA GREAT BASIN OF THE NILE, AND EXPLORATION OF THE NILE SOURCES. With Maps and numerous Illustrations. By Sir Samuel Baker. Fourth Edition. Crown 8vo. cloth extra. 6s.

A YEAR'S JOURNEY THROUGH CENTRAL AND EASTERN ARABIA, 1862-63. By W. G. Palgrave. With Map and Plans. Sixth Edition. Crown 8vo. 6s.

THE MALAY ARCHIPELAGO: THE LAND OF THE ORANG-UTAN AND THE BIRD OF PARADISE. A Narrative of Travel. By Alfred R. Wallace. With numerous Illustrations. Third and Cheaper Edition. Crown 8vo. 7s. 6d.

GREATER BRITAIN: A RECORD OF TRAVEL THROUGH ENGLISH-SPEAKING COUNTRIES DURING 1866-67. By Sir Charles W. Dilke, M.P. Sixth Edition. Crown 8vo. 6s.

SIX WEEKS IN THE SADDLE: A PAINTER'S JOURNAL IN ICELAND. By S. E. Waller. With Illustrations by the Author. Crown 8vo. 6s.

BY SEA AND BY LAND: A TRIP THROUGH EGYPT, INDIA, CEYLON, AUSTRALIA, NEW ZEALAND, AMERICA—ALL ROUND THE WORLD. By Henry A. Merewether, one of Her Majesty's Counsel. Crown 8vo. 8s. 6d.

MACMILLAN & CO., LONDON.

BEDFORD STREET, COVENT GARDEN, LONDON
July 1874.

MACMILLAN & CO.'S CATALOGUE *of Works in the Departments of History, Biography, Travels, Critical and Literary Essays, Politics, Political and Social Economy, Law, etc.; and Works connected with Language. With some short Account or Critical Notice concerning each Book.*

HISTORY, BIOGRAPHY, and TRAVELS.

Arnold.—ESSAYS IN CRITICISM. By MATTHEW ARNOLD. New Edition, with Additions. Extra fcap. 8vo. 6s.

The Essays in this Volume are—"The Function of Criticism at the Present Time;" "The Literary Influence of Academies;" "Maurice de Guérin;" "Eugénie de Guérin;" "Heinrich Heine;" "Pagan and Mediæval;" "Religious Sentiment;" "Joubert;" "Spinoza and the Bible;" "Marcus Aurelius." Both from the subjects dealt with and mode of treatment, few books are more calculated to delight, inform, and stimulate than these charming Essays.

Baker (Sir Samuel W.)—Works by Sir SAMUEL BAKER, M.A., F.R.G.S.:—

THE ALBERT N'YANZA Great Basin of the Nile, and Exploration of the Nile Sources. Third and Cheaper Edition. Maps and Illustrations. Crown 8vo. 6s.

"Bruce won the source of the Blue Nile; Speke and Grant won the Victoria source of the great White Nile; and I have been permitted to

Baker—*continued.*

succeed in completing the Nile Sources by the discovery of the great reservoir of the equatorial waters, the Albert N'yanza, from which the river issues as the entire White Nile."—PREFACE. *"As a Macaulay arose among the historians,"* says the READER, *"so a Baker has arisen among the explorers." "Charmingly written,"* says the SPECTATOR, *"full, as might be expected, of incident, and free from that wearisome reiteration of useless facts which is the drawback to almost all books of African travel."*

THE NILE TRIBUTARIES OF ABYSSINIA, and the Sword Hunters of the Hamran Arabs. With Maps and Illustrations. Fourth and Cheaper Edition. Crown 8vo. 6s.

Sir Samuel Baker here describes twelve months' exploration, during which he examined the rivers that are tributary to the Nile from Abyssinia, including the Atbara, Settite, Royan, Salaam, Angrab, Rahad, Dinder, and the Blue Nile. The interest attached to these portions of Africa differs entirely from that of the White Nile regions, as the whole of Upper Egypt and Abyssinia is capable of development, and is inhabited by races having some degree of civilization; while Central Africa is peopled by a race of savages, whose future is more problematical. The TIMES *says: "It solves finally a geographical riddle which hitherto had been extremely perplexing, and it adds much to our information respecting Egyptian Abyssinia and the different races that people over it. It contains, moreover, some notable instances of English daring and enterprising skill; it abounds in anecdotal tales of exploits dear to the heart of the British sportsman; and it will attract even the least studious reader, as the author tells a story well, and can describe nature with uncommon power."*

Baring-Gould (Rev. S., M.A.)—LEGENDS OF OLD TESTAMENT CHARACTERS, from the Talmud and other sources. By the Rev. S. BARING-GOULD, M.A., Author of "Curious Myths of the Middle Ages," "The Origin and Development of Religious Belief," "In Exitu Israel," &c. In Two Vols. Crown 8vo. 16s. Vol. I. Adam to Abraham. Vol. II. Melchizedek to Zechariah.

Mr. Baring-Gould's previous contributions to the History of Mythology and the formation of a science of comparative religion are admitted to be of high importance; the present work, it is believed, will be found to be of equal value. He has collected from the Talmud and other sources,

HISTORY, BIOGRAPHY, & TRAVELS.

Jewish and Mohammedan, a large number of curious and interesting legends concerning the principal characters of the Old Testament, comparing these frequently with similar legends current among many of the peoples, savage and civilised, all over the world. "These volumes contain much that is very strange, and, to the ordinary English reader, very novel."—DAILY NEWS.

Barker (Lady).—*See also* BELLES LETTRES CATALOGUE.

STATION LIFE IN NEW ZEALAND. By LADY BARKER. Second and Cheaper Edition. Globe 8vo. 3s. 6d.

These letters are the exact account of a lady's experience of the brighter and less practical side of colonization. They record the expeditions, adventures, and emergencies diversifying the daily life of the wife of a New Zealand sheep-farmer; and, as each was written while the novelty and excitement of the scenes it describes were fresh upon her, they may succeed in giving here in England an adequate impression of the delight and freedom of an existence so far removed from our own highly-wrought civilization. "We have never read a more truthful or a pleasanter little book."—ATHENÆUM.

Blanford (W. T.)—GEOLOGY AND ZOOLOGY OF ABYSSINIA. By W. T. BLANFORD. 8vo. 21s.

This work contains an account of the Geological and Zoological Observations made by the author in Abyssinia, when accompanying the British Army on its march to Magdala and back in 1868, and during a short journey in Northern Abyssinia, after the departure of the troops. Part I. Personal Narrative; Part II. Geology; Part III. Zoology. With Coloured Illustrations and Geological Map. "The result of his labours," the ACADEMY *says, "is an important contribution to the natural history of the country."*

Brimley.—ESSAYS BY THE LATE GEORGE BRIMLEY, M.A. Edited by the Rev. W. G. CLARK, M.A. With Portrait. Cheaper Edition. Fcap. 8vo. 2s. 6d.

George Brimley was regarded by those who knew him as "one of the finest critics of the day." The Essays contained in this volume are all more or less critical, and were contributed by the author to some of the leading periodicals of the day. The subjects are, "Tennyson's

4   MACMILLAN'S CATALOGUE OF WORKS IN

Poems," "Wordsworth's Poems," "Poetry and Criticism," "The Angel in the House," Coventry Patmore's "Life of Sterling," "Firmilian," "My Novel," "Guesses," "Westward Ho!" Warren's "Now and Then," Comte's "Positive Philosophy,"—*It will,* JOHN BULL *says,* "*be a satisfaction to the advocates of sound criticism and painstaking erudition some to find that the Essays of the late George Brimley have reappeared in a new and popular form. They will give a healthy stimulus to that spirit of enquiry and liberal order of our literary taste which cannot be too often revived without sufficient investigation.*"

Bryce.—THE HOLY ROMAN EMPIRE. By JAMES BRYCE, D.C.L., Regius Professor of Civil Law, Oxford. Fourth Edition, Revised and Enlarged. Crown 8vo. 7s. 6d.

The object of this volume is not so much to give a narrative history of the countries included in the Romano-Germanic Empire—Italy during the Middle Ages, Germany from the ninth century to the nineteenth—as to describe the Holy Empire itself as an institution or system, the wonderful offspring of a body of beliefs and traditions which have almost wholly passed away from the world. To make such a description intelligible it has appeared best to give the book the form rather of a historical than of a dissertation; and to combine with an exposition of what may be called the theory of the Empire an outline of the political history of Germany, as just as some limits of enquiry of a volume of this kind. "*Mr. Bryce has sketched the history of an astonishing institution in a style of singular force, clearness, and vivacity. On every page there is the stamp of a sure hand, conversant, indeed with the subject and the sources that gave it power, but also possessed with a definite idea.*" "*It would,* supply *a want; it offers a key to much which men read of in their books as isolated facts, but of which they have hitherto had no connected exposition set before them. We know of no writer who has so thoroughly grasped the real nature of the mediaeval Empire, and its relations alike to earlier and to later forms.*"—SATURDAY REVIEW.

Burke.—EDMUND BURKE, a Historical Study. By JOHN MORLEY, B.A., Oxon. Crown 8vo. 7s. 6d.

"*The style is terse and lucid, and bristles with epigram and point. Its method gives it permanent, in such force of description and reflection it should stand alone, and what may, there, it as a work of high thought.*"—SATURDAY REVIEW. "*A model of compact con-*

HISTORY, BIOGRAPHY, & TRAVELS.

demnation. We have seldom met with a book in which so much matter was compressed into so limited a space."—PALL MALL GAZETTE. "An essay of unusual effect."—WESTMINSTER REVIEW.

Chatterton: A BIOGRAPHICAL STUDY. By DANIEL WILSON, LL.D., Professor of History and English Literature in University College, Toronto. Crown 8vo. 6s. 6d.

The author here regards Chatterton as a Poet, not as a "mere rustler and defacer of stolen literary treasures." Reviewed in this light, he has found much in the old materials capable of being turned to new account; and to this material research in various directions has enabled him to make some additions. He believes that the boy-poet has been misjudged, and that the biographies hitherto written of him are not only imperfect but untrue. While dealing tenderly, the author has sought to deal truthfully with the failings as well as the virtues of the boy; having always in remembrance, what has been too frequently lost sight of, that he was not a boy—a boy, and yet a poet of rare power. The EXAMINER *thinks this "the most complete and the purest biography of the poet which has yet appeared."*

Cooper.—ATHENÆ CANTABRIGIENSES. By CHARLES HENRY COOPER, F.S.A., and THOMPSON COOPER, F.S.A. Vol. I. 8vo., 1500–85, 18s.; Vol. II., 1586–1609, 18s.

This elaborate work, which is dedicated by permission to Lord Macaulay, contains lives of the eminent men sent forth by Cambridge, after the fashion of Anthony à Wood, in his famous "Athenæ Oxonienses."

Cox (G. V., M.A.)—RECOLLECTIONS OF OXFORD. By G. V. Cox, M.A., New College, late Esquire Bedel and Coroner in the University of Oxford. *Cheaper Edition.* Crown 8vo. 6s.

"An amusing farrago of anecdote, and will pleasantly recall in many a country parsonage the memory of youthful days."—TIMES. *"Those who wish to make acquaintance with the Oxford of their grandfathers, and to keep up the acquaintance with Alma Mater during their father's time, even to the latest novelties in fashion or learning of the present day, will do well to procure this pleasant, unpretending little volume."*—ATLAS.

"Daily News."—THE DAILY NEWS CORRESPONDENCE of the War between Germany and France, 1870—1. Edited with Notes and Comments. New Edition. Complete in One Volume. With Maps and Plans. Crown 8vo. 6s.

This Correspondence has been translated into German. In a Preface the Editor says:—

"*Among the various pictures, recitals, and descriptions which have appeared, both of our gloriously ended national war as a whole, and of its several episodes, we think that in laying before the German public, through a translation, the following War Letters which appeared first in the* DAILY NEWS, *and were afterwards published collectively, we are offering them a picture of the events of the war of a quite peculiar character. These communications have the advantage of being at once entertaining and instructive, free from every romantic embellishment, and nevertheless written in a vein intelligible and not fatiguing to the general reader. The writers linger over events, and do not disdain to surround the great and heroic war-pictures with arabesques, gay and grave, taken from camp-life and the life of the inhabitants of the occupied territory. A feature which distinguishes these Letters from all other delineations of the war is that they do not proceed from a single pen, but were written from the camps of both belligerents.*" "*Their notes and comments,*" *according to the* SATURDAY REVIEW, "*are in reality a very well executed and continuous history.*"

Dilke.—GREATER BRITAIN. A Record of Travel in English-speaking Countries during 1866-7. (America, Australia, India.) By Sir CHARLES WENTWORTH DILKE, M.P. Sixth Edition. Crown 8vo. 6s.

"*Mr. Dilke,*" *says the* SATURDAY REVIEW, "*has written a book which is probably as well worth reading as any book of the same aims and character that ever was written. Its merits are that it is written in a lively and agreeable style, that it implies a great deal of physical pluck, that no page of it fails to show an acute and highly intelligent observer, that it stimulates the imagination as well as the judgment of the reader, and that it is on perhaps the most interesting subject that can attract an Englishman who cares about his country.*" "*Many of the subjects discussed in these pages,*" *says the* DAILY NEWS, "*are of the widest interest, and such as no man who cares for the future of his race and of the world can afford to treat with indifference.*"

Drummond of Hawthornden: THE STORY OF HIS LIFE AND WRITINGS. By PROFESSOR MASSON. With Portrait and Vignette engraved by C. H. JEENS. Crown 8vo. 10s. 6d.

Dürer (Albrecht).—HISTORY OF THE LIFE OF ALBRECHT DÜRER, of Nürnberg. With a Translation of his Letters and Journal, and some account of his Works. By Mrs. CHARLES HEATON. Royal 8vo. bevelled boards, extra gilt. 31s. 6d.

This work contains about Thirty Illustrations, ten of which are productions by the Autotype (Carbon) process, and are printed in permanent tints by Messrs. Cundall and Fleming, under licence from the Autotype Company, Limited; the rest are Photographs and Woodcuts.

Elliott.—LIFE OF HENRY VENN ELLIOTT, of Brighton. By JOSIAH BATEMAN, M.A., Author of "Life of Daniel Wilson, Bishop of Calcutta," &c. With Portrait, engraved by JEENS. Extra fcap. 8vo. Third and Cheaper Edition, with Appendix. 6s.

"A very charming piece of religious biography; no one can read it without both pleasure and profit."—BRITISH QUARTERLY REVIEW.

European History, Narrated in a Series of Historical Selections from the best Authorities. Edited and arranged by E. M. SEWELL and C. M. YONGE. First Series, crown 8vo. 6s.; Second Series, 1088-1228, crown 8vo. 6s. Third Edition.

When young children have acquired the outlines of history from abridgments and catechisms, and it becomes desirable to give a more enlarged view of the subject, in order to render it really useful and interesting, a difficulty often arises as to the choice of books. Two courses are open, either to take a general and consequently dry history of facts, such as Russell's Modern Europe, or to choose some work treating of a particular period or subject, such as the works of Macaulay and Froude. The former course usually renders history uninteresting; the latter is unsatisfactory, because it is not sufficiently comprehensive. To remedy this difficulty, selections, continuous and chronological, have in the present volume been taken from the larger works of Freeman, Milman, Palgrave, Lingard, Hume, and others, which may serve as distinct landmarks of historical reading. "We know of scarcely anything," says the GUARDIAN, of this volume, "which is so likely to raise to a higher level the average standard of English education."

Fairfax (Lord).—A LIFE OF THE GREAT LORD FAIRFAX, Commander-in-Chief of the Army of the Parliament of England. By CLEMENTS R. MARKHAM, F.S.A. With Portraits, Maps, Plans, and Illustrations. Demy 8vo. 16s.

No full Life of the great Parliamentary Commander has appeared; and it is here sought to produce one—based upon careful research in contemporary records and upon family and other documents. "Highly useful to the careful student of the History of the Civil Wars... Probably as a military chronicle Mr. Markham's book is one of the most full and accurate that we possess about the Civil War."—FORTNIGHTLY REVIEW.

Faraday.—MICHAEL FARADAY. By J. H. GLADSTONE, Ph.D., F.R.S. Second Edition, with Portrait engraved by JEENS from a photograph by J. WATKINS. Crown 8vo. 4s. 6d.

PORTRAIT. Artist's Proof. 5s.

CONTENTS:—I. *The Story of his Life.* II. *Study of his Character.* III. *Fruits of his Experience.* IV. *His Method of Working.* V. *The Value of his Discoveries.*—*Supplementary Portraits. Appendix.—List of Honorary Fellowships, &c.*

"Faraday needed a popular biography. It were as simple and as pure, as well as as strong, in outline, to do justice indeed to do justice for future generations, as is wholly indifferent to works and such instruction, as have to do appreciation of the hard lines of operation, and even conveyed with a sense of the mere nature of the spiritual, ought to be widely and familiarly known to a herald at large; and Dr. Gladstone's book is excellently adapted to that end."—GUARDIAN.

Field (E. W.)—EDWIN WILKINS FIELD. A Memorial Sketch. By THOMAS SADLER, Ph.D. With a Portrait. Crown 8vo. 4s. 6d.

Mr. Field was well known during his lifetime not only as an eminent lawyer and a strenuous and successful advocate of law reform, but, both in England and America, as a man of wide and thorough culture, varied tastes, large benevolence, and lofty aims. The present sketch was locked upon as a private lots, and it is expected that this brief Memoir will be acceptable to a large number besides the many friends at whose request it has been written.

Forbes.—LIFE AND LETTERS OF JAMES DAVID FORBES, F.R.S., late Principal of the United College in the University of St. Andrews. By J. C. SHAIRP, LL.D., Principal of the United College in the University of St. Andrews; P. G. TAIT, M.A., Professor of Natural Philosophy in the University of Edinburgh; and A. ADAMS-REILLY, F.R.G.S. 8vo. with Portraits, Map, and Illustrations, 16s.

"*Not only a biography that all should read, but a scientific treatise, without which the shelves of no physicist's library can be deemed complete.*"—STANDARD.

Freeman.—Works by EDWARD A. FREEMAN, M.A., D.C.L.:—

"*That special power over a subject which conscientious and patient research can only achieve, a strong grasp of facts, a true mastery over detail, with a clear and manly style—all these qualities join to make the Historian of the Conquest conspicuous in the intellectual arena.*"—ACADEMY.

HISTORICAL ESSAYS. By EDWARD FREEMAN, M.A., Hon. D.C.L., late Fellow of Trinity College, Oxford. Second Edition. 8vo. 10s. 6d.

This volume contains twelve Essays selected from the author's contributions to various Reviews. The principle on which they were chosen was that of selecting papers which referred to comparatively modern times, or, at least, to the existing states and nations of Europe. By a sort of accident a number of the pieces chosen have thrown themselves into something like a continuous series bearing on the historical causes of the great events of 1870–71. Notes have been added whenever they seemed to be called for; and whenever he could gain in accuracy of statement or in force or clearness of expression, the author has freely changed, added to, or left out, what he originally wrote. To many of the Essays has been added a short note of the circumstances under which they were written. It is needless to say that any product of Mr. Freeman's pen is worthy of attentive perusal; and it is believed that the contents of this volume will throw light on several subjects of great historical importance and the widest interest. The following is a list of the subjects:—I. "The Mythical and Romantic Elements in Early English History;" II. "The Continuity of English History;" III. "The Relations between the Crowns of England and Scotland;" IV. "St. Thomas of Canter-

16   MACMILLAN'S CATALOGUE OF WORKS IN

Freeman (E. A.)—*continued.*

bury and his Biographers;" V. "The Reign of Edward the Third;" VI. "The Holy Roman Empire;" VII. "The Franks and the Gauls;" VIII. "The Early Sieges of Paris;" IX. "Frederick the First, King of Italy;" X. "The Emperor Frederick the Second;" XI. "Charles the Bold;" XII. "Presidential Government."—"*All of them are well worth reading, and very agreeable to read. He never touches a question without adding to our comprehension of it, without leaving the impression of an ample knowledge, a righteous purpose, a clear and powerful understanding.*"—SATURDAY REVIEW.

A SECOND SERIES OF HISTORICAL ESSAYS. 8vo. 10s. 6d.

These Essays chiefly relate to earlier periods of history than those which were dealt with in the former volume—to the times commonly known as "Ancient" or "Classical." All the papers have been carefully revised, and the author has found himself able to do very much in the way of improving and simplifying the style. The principal Essays are:— "Ancient Greece and Mediæval Italy;" "Mr. Gladstone's Homer and the Homeric Ages;" "The Historians of Athens;" "The Athenian Democracy;" "Alexander the Great;" "Greece during the Macedonian Period;" "Mommsen's History of Rome;" "Lucius Cornelius Sulla;" "The Flavian Cæsars."—SATURDAY REVIEW.

HISTORY OF FEDERAL GOVERNMENT, from the Foundation of the Achaian League to the Disruption of the United States. Vol. I. General Introduction. History of the Greek Federations. 8vo. 21s.

Mr. Freeman's aim, in this elaborate and valuable work, is not so much to discuss the abstract nature of Federal Government, as to exhibit its actual working in ages and countries widely removed from one another. Four Federal Commonwealths stand out, in four different ages of the world, as commanding above all others the attention of students of political history, viz., the Achaian League, the Swiss Cantons, the United Provinces, the United States. The first volume, besides containing a General Introduction, treats of the first of these. In writing this volume the author has endeavoured to combine a text which may be instructive and interesting to any thoughtful reader, whether specially learned or not, with notes which may satisfy the requirements of the most exacting scholar. "The task Mr. Freeman has undertaken," *the* SATURDAY REVIEW *says,* "is one

Freeman (E. A.)—continued.

of great magnitude and importance. It is also a task of an almost entirely novel character. No other work professing to give the history of a political principle occurs to us, except the slight contributions to the history of representative government that is contained in a course of M. Guizot's lectures. . . . The history of the development of a principle is at least as important as the history of a dynasty, or of a race."

OLD ENGLISH HISTORY. With *Five Coloured Maps*. Second Edition. Extra fcap. 8vo., half-bound. 6s.

"Its object," the Preface says, "is to show that clear, accurate, and scientific views of history, or indeed of any subject, may be easily given to children from the very first. . . . I have throughout striven to connect the history of England with the general history of civilized Europe, and I have especially tried to make the book serve as an incentive to a more accurate study of historic geography." The rapid sale of the first edition and the universal approval with which the work has been received prove the correctness of the author's notions, and show that for such a book there was ample room. The work is suited not only for children, but will serve as an excellent text-book for elder students, a clear and faithful summary of the history of the period for those who wish to revive their historical knowledge, and a book full of charms for the general reader. The work is preceded by a complete chronological Table, and appended is an exhaustive and useful Index. In the present edition the whole has been carefully revised, and such improvements as suggested themselves have been introduced. "The book indeed is full of instruction and interest to students of all ages, and he must be a well-informed man indeed who will not rise from its perusal with clearer and more accurate ideas of a too much neglected portion of English history."—SPECTATOR.

HISTORY OF THE CATHEDRAL CHURCH OF WELLS, as illustrating the History of the Cathedral Churches of the Old Foundation. Crown 8vo. 3s. 6d.

"I have here," the author says, "tried to treat the history of the Church of Wells as a contribution to the general history of the Church and Kingdom of England, and specially to the history of Cathedral Churches of the Old Foundation. . . . I wish to point out the general principles of the original founders as the model to which the Old Foundations should be brought back, and the New Foundations reformed after their pattern." "The history assumes in Mr. Freeman's hands a signi-

HISTORY, BIOGRAPHY, & TRAVELS. 13

book consists of seventeen moderately sized chapters, each chapter being divided into a number of short numbered paragraphs, each with a title prefixed clearly indicative of the subject of the paragraph. "It supplies the great want of a good foundation for historical teaching. The scheme is an excellent one, and this instalment has been executed in a way that promises much for the volumes that are yet to appear."—EDUCATIONAL TIMES.

Galileo.—THE PRIVATE LIFE OF GALILEO. Compiled principally from his Correspondence and that of his eldest daughter, Sister Maria Celeste, Nun in the Franciscan Convent of S. Matthew in Arcetri. With Portrait. Crown 8vo. 7s. 6d.

It has been the endeavour of the compiler to place before the reader a plain, unvarnished statement of facts; and, as a means to this end, to allow Galileo, his friends, and his judges to speak for themselves as far as possible. All the best authorities have been made use of, and all the materials which exist for a biography have been in this volume put into a symmetrical form. The result is a most touching picture skilfully arranged of the great heroic man of science and his devoted daughter, whose letters are full of the deepest reverential love and trust, simply copied by the noble soul. The SATURDAY REVIEW says of the book, "It is not so much the philosopher as the man who is seen in this simple and lifelike sketch, and the hand which pourtrays the features and actions is mainly that of one who had studied the subject the closest and the most intimately. This little volume has done much within its slender compass to prove the depth and tenderness of Galileo's heart."

Gladstone (Right Hon. W. E., M.P.)—JUVENTUS MUNDI. The Gods and Men of the Heroic Age. Crown 8vo. cloth. With Map. 10s. 6d. Second Edition.

This work of Mr. Gladstone deals especially with the historic element in Homer, expounding that element and furnishing by its aid a full account of the Homeric view and the Homeric religion. It starts, after the introductory chapter, with a discussion of the several races then existing in Hellas, including the influence of the Phœnicians and Egyptians. It contains chapters on the Olympian system, with its several deities; on the Ethics and the Polity of the Heroic age; on the Geography of Homer; on the characters of the Poems; presenting, in fine, a view of primitive life and primitive society as found in the poems of Homer. To this New

Edition various additions have been made. "Seldom," says the ATHENÆUM, "out of the great poems themselves, have these Divinities looked so majestic and respectable. To read these brilliant details is like standing on the Olympian threshold and gazing at the ineffable brightness within." "There is," according to the WESTMINSTER REVIEW," probably no other writer now living who could have done the work of this book. . . It would be difficult to point out a book that contains so much fulness of knowledge along with so much freshness of perception and clearness of presentation."

Goethe and Mendelssohn (1821—1831). From the German of Dr. KARL MENDELSSOHN, Son of the Composer, by M. E. VON GLEHN. From the Private Diaries and Home-Letters of Mendelssohn, with Poems and Letters of Goethe never before printed. Also with two New and Original Portraits, Facsimiles, and Appendix of Twenty Letters hitherto unpublished. Crown 8vo. 5s. Second Edition, enlarged.

This little volume is full of interesting details about Mendelssohn from his twelfth year onwards, and especially of his intimate and frequent intercourse with Goethe. It is an episode of Weimar's golden days which we see before us—old age and fame hand in hand with youth in its aspiring efforts; the aged poet fondling the curls of the little musician and calling to him in playful and endearing accents "to make a little noise for him, and awaken the wearied spirits that have so long lain slumbering." Here will be found letters and reports of conversations between the two, touching on all subjects, human and divine—Music, Æsthetics, Art, Poetry, Science, Morals, and "the profound and ancient problem of human life," as well as reminiscences of celebrated men with whom the great composer came in contact. The Diary appended gives, among other matters, some interesting glimpses into the private life of Her Majesty Queen Victoria and the late Prince Albert. The two well-executed engravings show Mendelssohn as a beautiful boy of twelve years.

Green.—A HISTORY OF THE ENGLISH PEOPLE. By the Rev. J. R. GREEN, M.A. For the use of Colleges and Schools. Crown 8vo. 8s. 6d.

Guizot.—M. DE BARANTE, a Memoir, Biographical and Autobiographical. By M. GUIZOT. Translated by the Author of "JOHN HALIFAX, GENTLEMAN." Crown 8vo. 6s. 6d.

HISTORY, BIOGRAPHY, & TRAVELS. 15

"It is scarcely necessary to write a preface to this book. Its lifelike portrait of a true and great man, painted unconsciously by himself in his letters and autobiography, and retouched and completed by the tender hand of his surviving friend—the friend of a lifetime—is sure, I think, to be appreciated in England as it was in France, where it appeared in the Revue de Deux Mondes. Also, I believe every thoughtful mind will enjoy its clear reflections of French and European politics and history for the last seventy years, and the curious light thus thrown upon many present events and combinations of circumstances."—PREFACE. "The highest purposes of both history and biography are answered by a memoir so lifelike, so faithful, and so philosophical."—BRITISH QUARTERLY REVIEW. "This eloquent memoir, which for tenderness, gracefulness, and vigour, might be placed on the same shelf with Tacitus' Life of Agricola. . . . Mrs. Craik has rendered the language of Guizot in her own sweet translucent English."—DAILY NEWS.

Hamerton.—THE INTELLECTUAL LIFE. By P. G. HAMERTON. With a Portrait of Leonardo da Vinci, etched by LEOPOLD FLAMENG. Crown 8vo. 10s. 6d.

"We have read the whole book with great pleasure, and we can recommend it strongly to all who can appreciate grave reflections on a very important subject, excellently illustrated from the resources of a mind stored with much reading and much keen observation of real life."—SATURDAY REVIEW.

THOUGHTS ABOUT ART. New Edition, revised, with an Introduction. Crown 8vo. 8s. 6d.

Hole.—A GENEALOGICAL STEMMA OF THE KINGS OF ENGLAND AND FRANCE. By the Rev. C. HOLE, M.A., Trinity College, Cambridge. On Sheet, 1s.

The different families are printed in distinguishing colours, thus facilitating reference.

Hozier (H. M.)—Works by CAPTAIN HENRY M. HOZIER, late Assistant Military Secretary to Lord Napier of Magdala.

THE SEVEN WEEKS' WAR; Its Antecedents and Incidents. *New and Cheaper Edition.* With New Preface, Maps, and Plans. Crown 8vo. 6s.

16   MACMILLAN'S CATALOGUE OF WORKS IN

Hozier (H. M.)—continued.

This account of the brief but momentous Austro-Prussian War of 1866 claims consideration as being the product of an eyewitness of some of its most interesting incidents. The author has attempted to ascertain and to advance facts. Two maps are given, one illustrating the operations of the Army of the Maine, and the other the operations from Königgrätz. In the Prefatory Chapter to this edition, events resulting from the war of 1866 are set forth, and the current of European history traced down to the recent Franco-Prussian war, a natural consequence of the war whose history is narrated in this volume. "Mr. Hozier added to the knowledge of military operations and of languages, which he had proved himself to possess, a ready and skilful pen, and excellent faculties of observation and description. . . . All that Mr. Hozier saw of the great events of the war—and he saw a large share of them—he describes in clear and vivid language."—SATURDAY REVIEW. "Mr. Hozier's volumes deserve to take a permanent place in the literature of the Seven Weeks' War."—PALL MALL GAZETTE.

THE BRITISH EXPEDITION TO ABYSSINIA. Compiled from Authentic Documents. 8vo. 9s.

Several accounts of the British Expedition have been published. They have, however, been written by those who have not had access to those authentic documents, which come thereof and are fit only for the termination of a campaign. The endeavour of the author of this work has been to present to readers a correct and impartial account of an enterprise which has rarely been equalled in the annals of war. "This," says the SPECTATOR, "will be the account of the Abyssinian Expedition for professional reference, if not for professional reading. Its literary merits are really very great."

Hughes.—MEMOIR OF A BROTHER. By THOMAS HUGHES, M.P., Author of "Tom Brown's School Days." With Portrait of GEORGE HUGHES, after WATTS. Engraved by JEENS. Crown 8vo. 5s. Fifth Edition.

"The boy who can read this book without deriving from it some additional impulse towards honourable, manly, and independent conduct, has no good stuff in him. . . . While boys at school may be heartened by

HISTORY, BIOGRAPHY, & TRAVELS. 17

various conflicting theories of the characters of the great Englishmen whom they have been taught to admire or to hate, here, in the guise of the simplest and the most modest of country gentlemen, they may find an exemplar which they cannot do better than copy."—DAILY NEWS.

"We have read it with the deepest gratification and with real admiration."—STANDARD.

"The biography throughout is replete with interest."—MORNING POST.

Huyshe (Captain G. L.)—THE RED RIVER EXPEDITION. By Captain G. L. HUYSHE, Rifle Brigade, late on the Staff of Colonel Sir GARNET WOLSELEY. With Maps. Cheaper Edition. Crown 8vo. 6s.

This account has been written in the hope of directing attention to the successful accomplishment of an expedition which was attended with more than ordinary difficulties. The author has had access to the official documents of the Expedition, and has also availed himself of the reports on the line of route published by Mr. Dawson, C.E., and by the Topographical Department of the War Office. The statements made may therefore be relied on as accurate and impartial. The endeavour has been made to avoid tiring the general reader with dry details of military movements, and yet not to sacrifice the character of the work as an account of a military expedition. The volume contains a portrait of President Louis Riel, and Maps of the route. The ATHENÆUM calls it "*an enduring authentic record of one of the most creditable achievements ever accomplished by the British Army.*"

Irving.—THE ANNALS OF OUR TIME. A Diurnal of Events, Social and Political, Home and Foreign, from the Accession of Queen Victoria to the Peace of Versailles. By JOSEPH IRVING. Third Edition. 8vo. half-bound. 16s.

Every occurrence, metropolitan or provincial, home or foreign, which gave rise to public excitement or discussion, or became the starting point for new trains of thought affecting our social life, has been judged proper matter for this volume. In the proceedings of Parliament, an endeavour has been made to notice all those Debates which were either remarkable as affecting the fate of parties, or led to important changes in our relations with Foreign Powers. Brief notices have been given of the death of all noteworthy persons. Though the events are set down day by day in their

18   MACMILLAN'S CATALOGUE OF WORKS IN

order of occurrence, the book is, in its way, the history of an important and well-defined historic cycle. In these "Annals," the ordinary reader may make himself acquainted with the history of his own time in a way that has at least the merit of simplicity and readiness; the more cultivated student will doubtless be thankful for the opportunity given him of passing down the historic stream undisturbed by any other theoretical or partizan feeling than what he himself has at hand to explain the philosophy of our national story. A complete and useful Index is appended. The Table of Administrations is designed to assist the reader in following the various political changes noticed in their chronological order in the "Annals."— In the new edition all errors and omissions have been rectified, 300 pages been added, and as many as 36 occupied by an impartial exhibition of the wonderful series of events rendering the latter half of 1870. "We have before us a trusty and ready guide to the events of the past thirty years, available equally for the statesman, the politician, the public writer, and the general reader. If Mr. Irving's object has been to bring before the reader all the most noteworthy occurrences which have happened since the beginning of her Majesty's reign, he may justly claim the credit of having done so most briefly, succinctly, and simply, and in such a manner, too, as to furnish him with the details necessary in each case to comprehend the event of which he is in search in an intelligent manner." —TIMES.

Jebb.—THE CHARACTERS OF THEOPHRASTUS. An English Translation from a Revised Text. With Introduction and Notes. By R. C. JEBB, M.A., Fellow and Assistant Tutor of Trinity College, Cambridge, and Public Orator of the University. Extra fcap. 8vo. 6s. 6d.

The first object of this book is to make those lively pictures of old Greek manners better known to English readers. But as the Editor and Translator has been at considerable pains to procure a reliable text, and has recorded the results of his critical labours in a lengthy Introduction, in Notes and Appendices, it is hoped that the work will prove of value even to the scholar. "We must not omit to give due honour to Mr. Jebb's translation, which is as good as translation can be. . . . Not less commendable are the execution of the Notes and the critical handling of the text."—SPECTATOR. "Mr. Jebb's little volume is more easily taken up than laid down."— GUARDIAN.

Kingsley (Charles).—Works by the Rev. CHARLES KINGSLEY, M.A., Rector of Eversley and Canon of Westminster. (For other Works by the same Author, see THEOLOGICAL and BELLES LETTRES Catalogues.)

ON THE ANCIEN RÉGIME as it existed on the Continent before the FRENCH REVOLUTION. Three Lectures delivered at the Royal Institution. Crown 8vo. 6s.

These three lectures discuss severally (1) Caste, (2) Centralization, (3) The Explosive Forces by which the Revolution was superinduced. The Preface deals at some length with certain political questions of the present day.

AT LAST: A CHRISTMAS in the WEST INDIES. With nearly Fifty Illustrations. Third and Cheaper Edition. Crown 8vo. 6s.

Mr. Kingsley's dream of forty years was at last fulfilled, when he started on a Christmas expedition to the West Indies, for the purpose of becoming personally acquainted with the scenes which he has so vividly described in "Westward Ho!" These two volumes are the journal of his voyage. Records of natural history, sketches of tropical landscape, chapters on education, views of society, all find their place in a work written, so to say, under the inspiration of Sir Walter Raleigh and the other adventurous men who three hundred years ago disputed against Philip II. the possession of the Spanish Main. "We can only say that Mr. Kingsley's account of a 'Christmas in the West Indies' is in every way worthy to be classed among his happiest productions."—STANDARD.

THE ROMAN AND THE TEUTON. A Series of Lectures delivered before the University of Cambridge. 8vo. 12s.

CONTENTS:—*Inaugural Lecture; The Forest Children; The Dying Empire; The Human Deluge; The Gothic Civiliser; Dietrich's End; The Nemesis of the Goths; Paulus Diaconus; The Clergy and the Heathen; The Monk a Civiliser; The Lombard Laws; The Popes and the Lombards; The Strategy of Providence.* "*He has rendered,*" *says the* NONCONFORMIST, "*good service and shed a new lustre on the chair of Modern History at Cambridge. . . . He has thrown a charm around the work by the marvellous fascinations of his own genius, brought out in strong relief those great principles of which all history is a revelation, lighted up many dark and almost unknown spots, and stimulated the desire to understand more thoroughly one of the greatest movements in the story of humanity.*"

20 MACMILLAN'S CATALOGUE OF WORKS IN

Kingsley (Charles)—continued.

PLAYS AND PURITANS, and other Historical Essays. With Portrait of Sir WALTER RALEIGH. Crown 8vo. 6s.

In addition to the Essay mentioned in the title, this volume contains other two—one on "Sir Walter Raleigh and his Time," and one on Froude's "History of England,"—all three contributed to the NORTH BRITISH REVIEW. Mr. Kingsley has already shown how intimate is his knowledge of the times in which all three essays touch.

Kingsley (Henry, F.R.G.S.)—For other Works by same Author, see BELLES LETTRES CATALOGUE.

TALES OF OLD TRAVEL. Re-narrated by HENRY KINGSLEY, F.R.G.S. With *Eight Illustrations* by HUARD. Fourth Edition. Crown 8vo. 6s.

In this volume Mr. Henry Kingsley re-narrates, at the same time preserving much of the quaintness of the original, some of the most fascinating tales of travel contained in the collections of Hakluyt and others. The CONTENTS *are—Marco Polo; The Shipwreck of Pelsart; The Wonderful Adventures of Andrew Battel; The Wanderings of a Capuchin; Peter Carder; The Preservation of the "Terra Nova;" Spitzbergen; D'Ermenonville's Acclimatization Adventure; The Old Slave Trade; Miles Philips; The Sufferings of Robert Everard; John Fox; Alvaro Nunez; The Foundation of an Empire.* "We know no better book for those who want knowledge or seek to refresh it. As for the 'sensational,' most novels are tame compared with these narratives."—ATHENÆUM. "Exactly the book to interest and to do good to intelligent and high-spirited boys."—LITERARY CHURCHMAN.

Labouchere.—DIARY OF THE BESIEGED RESIDENT IN PARIS. Reprinted from the *Daily News*, with several New Letters and Preface. By HENRY LABOUCHERE. Third Edition. Crown 8vo. 6s.

"The 'Diary of a Besieged Resident in Paris' will certainly form one of the most remarkable records of a momentous episode in history."—SPECTATOR. *"There is an entire absence of affectation in this writer which richly commends him to us."*—PALL MALL GAZETTE. *"On the whole, it does not seem likely that the 'Besieged' will be superseded in his self-assumed function by any subsequent chronicler."*—BRITISH QUARTERLY REVIEW. *"Very smartly written."*—VANITY FAIR.

Leonardo Da Vinci and his Works.—Consisting of a Life of Leonardo Da Vinci, by MRS. CHARLES W. HEATON, Author of "Albrecht Dürer of Nürnberg," &c., an Essay on his Scientific and Literary Works by CHARLES CHRISTOPHER BLACK, M.A., and an account of his more important Paintings and Drawings. Illustrated with Permanent Photographs. Royal 8vo. 31s. 6d.

Liechtenstein.—HOLLAND HOUSE. By Princess MARIE LIECHTENSTEIN. With numerous Woodcuts and Five Steel Plates. 2 vols. 8vo. 32s.
Also an Edition in 4to. half-morocco, with Permanent Photographs, Woodcuts, and India Proofs of Steel Plates. £4 4s.

Macmillan (Rev. Hugh).—For other Works by same Author, see THEOLOGICAL and SCIENTIFIC CATALOGUES.

HOLIDAYS ON HIGH LANDS; or, Rambles and Incidents in search of Alpine Plants. Second Edition, revised and enlarged. Globe 8vo. cloth. 6s.

The aim of this book is to impart a general idea of the origin, character, and distribution of those rare and beautiful Alpine plants which occur on the British hills, and which are found almost everywhere on the lofty mountain chains of Europe, Asia, Africa, and America. The information the author has to give is conveyed in untechnical language, in a setting of personal adventure, and associated with descriptions of the natural scenery and the peculiarities of the human life in the midst of which the plants were found. By this method the subject is made interesting to a very large class of readers. "Botanical knowledge is blended with a love of nature, a pious enthusiasm, and a rich felicity of diction not to be met with in any works of kindred character, if we except those of Hugh Miller."—TELEGRAPH. "Mr. M.'s glowing pictures of Scandinavian scenery."—SATURDAY REVIEW.

Martineau.—BIOGRAPHICAL SKETCHES, 1852—1868. By HARRIET MARTINEAU. Third and Cheaper Edition, with New Preface. Crown 8vo. 6s.

A Collection of Memoirs under these several sections:—(1) Royal, (2) Politicians, (3) Professional, (4) Scientific, (5) Social, (6) Literary. These

Memoirs appeared originally in the columns of the DAILY NEWS. *"Miss Martineau's large literary powers and her fine intellectual training make these little sketches more instructive, and constitute them more genuinely works of art, than many more ambitious and diffuse biographies."—* FORTNIGHTLY REVIEW. *"Each memoir is a complete digest of a celebrated life, illuminated by the flood of anti-clerical light which streams from the gaze of an acute but liberal mind."—* MORNING STAR.

Masson (David). For other Works by same Author, see PHILOSOPHICAL and BELLES LETTRES CATALOGUES.

LIFE OF JOHN MILTON. Narrated in connection with the Political, Ecclesiastical, and Literary History of his Time. By DAVID MASSON, M.A., LL.D., Professor of Rhetoric and English Literature in the University of Edinburgh. Vols. I. to III. with Portraits. £2 12s. Vol. II., 1638—1643. 8vo. 16s. Vol. III. 1643—1649. 8vo. 18s.

This work is not only a Biography, but also a continuous Political, Ecclesiastical, and Literary History of England through Milton's whole time. In order to understand Milton, his position, his motives, his thoughts by himself, his public words to his countrymen, and the probable effect of those words, it was necessary to refer largely to the History of his Time, not only as it is presented in well known books, but as it had to be ascertained by express and laborious investigation in original and forgotten records; thus, of the Biography, a History grew; not a mere popular compilation, but a work of independent search and method from first to last, which has cost more labour by far than the Biography. The second volume is so arranged that the reader may select or omit either the History or Biography. The NORTH BRITISH REVIEW, *speaking of the first volume of this work said, "The Life of Milton is here written once for all." The* NONCONFORMIST, *in noticing the second volume, says, "Its literary excellence entitles it to take its place in the first ranks of our literature, while the whole style of its execution marks it as the only book that has done anything like adequate justice to one of the great masters of our language, and one of our truest patriots, as well as our greatest epic poet."*

Maurice.—THE FRIENDSHIP OF BOOKS; AND OTHER LECTURES. By the REV. F. D. MAURICE. Edited with Preface, by THOMAS HUGHES, M.P. Crown 8vo. 10s. 6d.

HISTORY, BIOGRAPHY, & TRAVELS.

Mayor (J. E. B.)—WORKS Edited By JOHN E. B. MAYOR, M.A., Kennedy Professor of Latin at Cambridge:—

CAMBRIDGE IN THE SEVENTEENTH CENTURY. Part II. Autobiography of Matthew Robinson. Fcap. 8vo. 5s. 6d.

This is the second of the Memoirs illustrative of "Cambridge in the Seventeenth Century," that of Nicholas Farrar having preceded it. It gives a lively picture of England during the Civil Wars, the most important crisis of our national life; it supplies materials for the history of the University and our Endowed Schools, and gives us a view of country clergy at a time when they are supposed to have been, with scarce an exception, scurrilous sots. Mr. Mayor has added a collection of extracts and documents relating to the history of several other Cambridge men of note belonging to the same period, all, like Robinson, of Nonconformist leanings.

LIFE OF BISHOP BEDELL. By his SON. Fcap. 8vo. 3s. 6d.

This is the third of the Memoirs illustrative of "Cambridge in the 17th Century." The life of the Bishop of Kilmore here printed for the first time is preserved in the Tanner MSS., and is preliminary to a larger one to be issued shortly.

Mitford (A. B.)—TALES OF OLD JAPAN. By A. B. MITFORD, Second Secretary to the British Legation in Japan. With upwards of 30 Illustrations, drawn and cut on Wood by Japanese Artists. Two Vols. crown 8vo. 21s.

Under the influence of more enlightened ideas and of a liberal system of policy, the old Japanese civilisation is fast disappearing, and will, in a few years, be completely extinct. It was important, therefore, to preserve as far as possible trustworthy records of a state of society which, although venerable from its antiquity, has for Europeans the dawn of novelty; hence the series of narratives and legends translated by Mr. Mitford, and in which the Japanese are very judiciously left to tell their own tale. The two volumes comprise not only stories and episodes illustrative of Asiatic superstitions, but also three sermons. The preface, appendices, and notes explain a number of local peculiarities; the thirty-one woodcuts are the genuine work of a native artist, who, unconsciously of course, has adopted the process first introduced by the early German masters. "These very original volumes will always be interesting as memorials of a most exceptional society, while regarded simply as tales, they are sparkling, sensational, and dramatic, and the originality of their ideas and the quaintness

24 MACMILLAN'S CATALOGUE OF WORKS IN

of their language give them a most captivating piquancy. The illustrations are extremely interesting, and for the curious in such matters have a special and peculiar value."—PALL MALL GAZETTE.

Morley (John).—EDMUND BURKE, a Historical Study. By JOHN MORLEY, B.A. Oxon. Crown 8vo. 7s. 6d.

"The style is terse and incisive, and brilliant with epigram and point. It contains pithy aphoristic sentences which Burke himself would not have disowned. Its sustained power of reasoning, its wide sweep of observation and reflection, its decided ethical and social tone, stamp it as a work of high excellence."—SATURDAY REVIEW. "A model of compact condensation. We have seldom met with a book in which so much matter was compressed into so limited a space."—PALL MALL GAZETTE. "An essay of unusual effort."—WESTMINSTER REVIEW.

Morison.—THE LIFE AND TIMES OF SAINT BERNARD, Abbot of Clairvaux. By JAMES COTTER MORISON, M.A. Cheaper Edition. Crown 8vo. 4s. 6d.

The PALL MALL GAZETTE calls this "one of the best contributions in our literature towards a vivid, intelligent, and worthy knowledge of European interests and thoughts and feelings during the twelfth century. A delightful and instructive volume, and one of the best products of the modern historic spirit." "A work," says the NONCONFORMIST, "of great worth and value, dealing most thoroughly with one of the most interesting characters, and one of the most interesting periods, in the Church History of the Middle Ages. Mr. Morison is thoroughly master of his subject, and writes with great discrimination and fairness, and in a chaste and elegant style." The SPECTATOR says it is "not only distinguished by research and candour, it has also the great merit of never being dull."

Napoleon.—THE HISTORY OF NAPOLEON I. By P. LANFREY. A Translation with the sanction of the Author. Vols. I. and II. 8vo. price 12s. each.

The PALL MALL GAZETTE says it is "one of the most striking pieces of historical composition of which France has to boast," and the SATURDAY REVIEW calls it "an excellent translation of a work on every ground deserving to be translated. It is unquestionably and immeasurably the best that has been produced. It is in fact the only work to which we can turn for an accurate and trustworthy narrative of that extraordinary career. . . . The book is the best and indeed the only trustworthy history of Napoleon which has been written."

HISTORY, BIOGRAPHY, & TRAVELS.

Palgrave (Sir F.)—HISTORY OF NORMANDY AND OF ENGLAND. By Sir FRANCIS PALGRAVE, Deputy Keeper of Her Majesty's Public Records. Completing the History to the Death of William Rufus. Vols. II.—IV. 21s. each.

Volume I. General Relations of Mediæval Europe—The Carlovingian Empire—The Danish Expeditions in the Gauls—And the Establishment of Rollo. Volume II. The Three First Dukes of Normandy; Rollo, Guillaume Longue Épée, and Richard Sans-Peur—The Carlovingian line supplanted by the Capets. Volume III. Richard Sans-Peur—Richard Le-Bon—Richard III.—Robert Le Diable—William the Conqueror. Volume IV. William Rufus—Accession of Henry Beauclerc. It is needless to say anything to recommend this work of a lifetime to all students of history; it is, as the SPECTATOR *says, "perhaps the greatest single contribution yet made to the authentic annals of this country," and "must," says the* NONCONFORMIST, *"always rank among our standard authorities."*

Palgrave (W. G.)—A NARRATIVE OF A YEAR'S JOURNEY THROUGH CENTRAL AND EASTERN ARABIA, 1862-3. By WILLIAM GIFFORD PALGRAVE, late of the Eighth Regiment Bombay N. I. Sixth Edition. With Maps, Plans, and Portrait of Author, engraved on steel by Jeens. Crown 8vo. 6s.

"The work is a model of what its class should be; the style restrained, the narrative clear, telling us all we wish to know of the country and people visited, and enough of the author and his feelings to enable us to trust ourselves to his guidance in a tract hitherto untrodden, and dangerous in more senses than one. . . . He has not only written one of the best books on the Arabs and one of the best books on Arabia, but he has done so in a manner that must command the respect no less than the admiration of his fellow-countrymen."—FORTNIGHTLY REVIEW. *"Considering the extent of our previous ignorance, the amount of his achievements, and the importance of his contributions to our knowledge, we cannot say less of him than was once said of a far greater discoverer—Mr. Palgrave has indeed given a new world to Europe."*—PALL MALL GAZETTE.

ESSAYS ON EASTERN QUESTIONS. By W. GIFFORD PALGRAVE. 8vo. 10s. 6d.

Palgrave (W. G.)—continued.

CONTENTS:—*Mahometanism in the Levant—The Mahometan Revival—The Turkomans and other Tribes of the North-East Turkish Frontier—Eastern Christians—The Monastery of Sumelas—The Abkhasian Insurrection—The Poet Omar—The Brigand Tū Abbet Shurran.*

"These essays are full of anecdote and interest. The book is decidedly a valuable addition to the stock of literature on which men must base their opinion of the difficult social and political problems suggested by the designs of Russia, the capacity of Mahometans for sovereignty, and the good government and retention of India."—SATURDAY REVIEW.

ESSAYS ON ART. Extra fcap. 8vo. 6s.

Mulready—Dyce—Holman Hunt—Herbert—Poetry, Prose, and Sensationalism in Art—Sculpture in England—The Albert Cross, &c. Most of these Essays have appeared in the SATURDAY REVIEW and elsewhere: but they have been minutely revised, and in some cases almost re-written, with the aim mainly of excluding matters of temporary interest, and softening down all asperities of censure. The main object of the book is, by examples taken chiefly from the works of contemporaries, to illustrate the verdict, that art has fixed principles, of which any one may attain the knowledge who is not wanting in natural taste. Art, like poetry, is addressed to the world at large, not to a special jury of professional masters. "In many respects the truest critic we have."—LITERARY CHURCHMAN.

Pater.—STUDIES IN THE HISTORY OF THE RENAISSANCE. By WALTER H. PATER, M.A., Fellow of Brasenose College, Oxford. Crown 8vo. 7s. 6d.

The subjects of the studies contained in this volume are taken from the history of the Renaissance, and touch what the author thinks the chief points in that complex, many-sided movement. The PALL MALL GAZETTE says:—"The book is very remarkable among contemporary books, not only for the finish and care with which its essays are severally written, but for the air of deliberate and polished form upon the whole."

HISTORY, BIOGRAPHY, & TRAVELS.

Patteson.—LIFE AND LETTERS OF JOHN COLERIDGE PATTESON, D.D., Missionary Bishop. By CHARLOTTE M. YONGE, Author of "The Heir of Redclyffe." With Portraits after RICHMOND and from Photograph, engraved by JEENS. With Map. Two Vols. 8vo. 30s.

Prichard.—THE ADMINISTRATION OF INDIA. From 1859 to 1868. The First Ten Years of Administration under the Crown. By ILTUDUS THOMAS PRICHARD, Barrister-at-Law. Two Vols. Demy 8vo. With Map. 21s.

In these volumes the author has aimed to supply a full, impartial, and independent account of British India between 1859 and 1868—which is in many respects the most important epoch in the history of that country that the present century has seen. "It has the great merit that it is not exclusively devoted, as are too many histories, to military and political details, but enters thoroughly into the more important questions of social history. We find in these volumes a well-arranged and compendious reference to almost all that has been done in India during the last ten years; and the most important official documents and historical pieces are well selected and duly set forth."—SCOTSMAN. *"It is a work which every Englishman in India ought to add to his library."*—STAR OF INDIA.

Raphael.—RAPHAEL OF URBINO AND HIS FATHER GIOVANNI SANTI. By J. D. PASSAVANT, formerly Director of the Museum at Frankfort. With Twenty Permanent Photographs. Royal 8vo. Handsomely bound. 31s. 6d.

To the enlarged French edition of Passavant's Life of Raphael, that painter's admirers have turned whenever they have sought information, and it will doubtless remain for many years the best book of reference on all questions pertaining to the great painter. The present work consists of a translation of those parts of Passavant's volumes which are most likely to interest the general reader. Besides a complete life of Raphael, it contains the valuable descriptions of all his known paintings, and the Chronological Index, which is of so much service to amateurs who wish to study the progressive character of his works. The Illustrations by Woodbury's new permanent process of photography, are taken from the finest engravings that could be procured, and have been chosen with the intention of giving examples of Raphael's various styles of painting. The SATURDAY REVIEW *says of them, "We have seen not a few elegant specimens of Mr. Woodbury's new process, but we have seen none that equal these."*

Reynolds.—SIR JOSHUA REYNOLDS AS A PORTRAIT PAINTER. AN ESSAY. By J. CHURTON COLLINS, B.A. Balliol College, Oxford. Illustrated by a Series of Portraits of distinguished Beauties of the Court of George III.; reproduced in Autotype from Proof Impressions of the celebrated Engravings, by VALENTINE GREEN, THOMAS WATSON, E. R. SMITH, E. FISHER, and others. Folio half-morocco. £5 5s.

Robinson (H. Crabb).—THE DIARY, REMINISCENCES, AND CORRESPONDENCE, OF HENRY CRABB ROBINSON, Barrister-at-Law. Selected and Edited by THOMAS SADLER, Ph.D. With Portrait. Third and Cheaper Edition. Two Vols. Crown 8vo. 16s.

The DAILY NEWS *says:* "*The two books which are most likely to survive change of literary taste, and to charm while instructing generation after generation, are the 'Diary' of Pepys and Boswell's 'Life of Johnson.' The day will come when to these many will add the 'Diary of Henry Crabb Robinson.' Excellences like those which render the personal revelations of Pepys and the observations of Boswell such pleasant reading abound in this work. . . . In it is to be found something to suit every taste and inform every mind. For the general reader it contains much light and amusing matter. To the lover of literature it conveys information which he will prize highly on account of its accuracy and verity. The student of social life will gather from it many valuable hints whereon to base theories as to the effect on English society of the progress of civilization. For these and other reasons this 'Diary' is a work to which a hearty welcome should be accorded.*"

Rogers (James E. Thorold).—HISTORICAL GLEANINGS: A Series of Sketches. Montague, Walpole, Adam Smith, Cobbett. By Prof. ROGERS. Crown 8vo. 4s. 6d. Second Series. Wiklif, Laud, Wilkes, and Horne Tooke. Crown 8vo. 6s.

Professor Rogers's object in these sketches, which are in the form of Lectures, is to present a set of historical facts, grouped round a principal figure. The author has aimed to state the social facts of the time in which the individual whose history is handled took part in public business. It is from sketches like these of the great men who took a prominent and influential part in the affairs of their time that a clear conception of the social and economical condition of our ancestors can be obtained.

History learned in this way is both instructive and agreeable. "His Essays," the PALL MALL GAZETTE says, "are full of interest, pregnant, thoughtful, and readable." "They rank far above the average of similar performances," says the WESTMINSTER REVIEW.

Seeley (Professor).—LECTURES AND ESSAYS. By J. R. SEELEY, M.A. Professor of Modern History in the University of Cambridge. 8vo. 10s. 6d.

CONTENTS:—*Roman Imperialism*: 1. *The Great Roman Revolution*; 2. *The Proximate Cause of the Fall of the Roman Empire*; 3. *The Later Empire.*—*Milton's Political Opinions*—*Milton's Poetry*—*Elementary Principles in Art*—*Liberal Education in Universities*—*English in Schools*—*The Church as a Teacher of Morality*—*The Teaching of Politics: an Inaugural Lecture delivered at Cambridge.*

"He is the master of a clear and pleasant style, great facility of expression, and a considerable range of illustration. . . . The criticism is always acute, the description always graphic and continuous, and the matter of each essay is carefully arranged with a view to unity of effect."—SPECTATOR. "His book will be full of interest to all thoughtful readers."—PALL MALL GAZETTE.

Somers (Robert).—THE SOUTHERN STATES SINCE THE WAR. By ROBERT SOMERS. With Map. 8vo. 9s.

This work is the result of inquiries made by the author, of all authorities competent to afford him information, and of his own observation during a lengthened sojourn in the Southern States, to which writers on America so seldom direct their steps. The author's object is to give some account of the condition of the Southern States under the new social and political system introduced by the civil war. He has here collected such notes of the progress of their cotton plantations, of the state of their labouring population and of their industrial enterprises, as may help the reader to a safe opinion of their means and prospects of development. He also gives such information of their natural resources, railways, and other public works, as may tend to show to what extent they are fitted to become a profitable field of enlarged immigration, settlement, and foreign trade. The volume contains many valuable and reliable details as to the condition of the Negro population, the state of Education and Religion, of Cotton, Sugar, and Tobacco Cultivation, of Agriculture generally, of Coal and Iron Mining, Manu-

30 MACMILLAN'S CATALOGUE OF WORKS IN

tures, Trade, Means of Locomotion, and the condition of Towns and of Society. A large map of the Southern States by Messrs. W. and A. K. Johnston is appended, which shows with great clearness the Cotton, Coal, and Iron districts, the railways completed and projected, the State boundaries, and other important details. "Full of interesting and valuable information."—SATURDAY REVIEW.

Tacitus.—THE HISTORY OF TACITUS, translated into English. By A. J. CHURCH, M.A. and W. J. BRODRIBB, M.A. With a Map and Notes. New and Cheaper Edition, revised, crown 8vo. 6s.

The translators have endeavoured to adhere as closely to the original as was thought consistent with a proper observance of English idiom. At the same time it has been their aim to reproduce the precise expressions of the author. This work is characterised by the SPECTATOR *as " a scholarly and faithful translation." Several improvements have been made in this Edition, and the Notes have been enlarged, with the view of rendering the work more intelligible and useful to the general reader.*

THE AGRICOLA AND GERMANIA. Translated into English by A. J. CHURCH, M.A. and W. J. BRODRIBB, M.A. With Maps and Notes. Extra fcap. 8vo. 2s. 6d.

The translators have sought to produce such a version as may satisfy scholars who demand a faithful rendering of the original, and English readers who are offended by the baldness and frigidity which commonly disfigure translations. The treatises are accompanied by Introductions, Notes, Maps, and a chronological Summary. The ATHENÆUM *says of this work that it is " a version at once readable and exact, which may be perused with pleasure by all, and consulted with advantage by the classical student;" and the* PALL MALL GAZETTE *says, " What the editors have attempted to do, it is not, we think probable, that any living scholars could have done better."*

Thomas.—THE LIFE OF JOHN THOMAS, Surgeon of the "Earl of Oxford" East Indiaman, and First Baptist Missionary to Bengal. By C. B. LEWIS, Baptist Missionary. 8vo. 10s. 6d.

This biography, founded on the most trustworthy materials attainable, will be found interesting, not only to all who take an interest in mission work and the spread of Christianity, but to all who care to read the life of an earnest man striving to benefit others.

Todhunter.—THE CONFLICT OF STUDIES; AND OTHER ESSAYS ON SUBJECTS CONNECTED WITH EDUCATION. By ISAAC TODHUNTER, M.A., F.R.S., late Fellow and Principal Mathematical Lecturer of St. John's College, Cambridge. 8vo. 10s. 6d.

Mr. Todhunter has enjoyed favourable opportunities for becoming practically acquainted with the matters on which he treats. A long residence at Cambridge, continued occupation in lecturing, much experience in examinations, both in the University and elsewhere, and a share in the deliberations of several important Syndicates which have been employed in the reconstruction of official courses of study have induced and enabled him to form definite opinions on many points connected with the general subject of education. The names of the several Essays are:— I. The Conflict of Studies. II. Competitive Examinations. III. Private Study of Mathematics. IV. Academical Reform. V. Elementary Geometry. VI. The Mathematical Tripos.

Trench (Archbishop).—For other Works by the same Author, see THEOLOGICAL and BELLES LETTRES CATALOGUES, and p. 51 of this Catalogue.

GUSTAVUS ADOLPHUS IN GERMANY, and other Lectures on the Thirty Years' War. By R. CHENEVIX TRENCH, D.D., Archbishop of Dublin. Second Edition, revised and enlarged. Fcap. 8vo. 4s.

The lectures contained in this volume form rather a new book than a new edition, for on the two lectures published by the Author several years ago, so many changes and additions have been made, as to make the work virtually a new one. Besides three lectures of the career of Gustavus in Germany and during the Thirty Years' War, there are other two, one on "Germany during the Thirty Years' War," and another on Germany after that War. The work will be found not only interesting and instructive in itself, but will be found to have some bearing on events connected with the recent European War.

PLUTARCH, HIS LIFE, HIS LIVES, AND HIS MORALS. Four Lectures by RICHARD CHENEVIX TRENCH, D.D., Archbishop of Dublin. Fcap. 8vo. 3s. 6d.

32 MACMILLAN'S CATALOGUE OF WORKS IN

These Lectures will be found to contain an account of nearly all that is known of Plutarch, and of his works, especially his celebrated "Lives," with conjectures as to the influence of the latter upon men who lived after Plutarch's time.

Trench (Mrs. R.)—REMAINS OF THE LATE MRS. RICHARD TRENCH. Being Selections from her Journals, Letters, and other Papers. Edited by ARCHBISHOP TRENCH. New and Cheaper Issue, with Portrait. 8vo. 6s.

Contains Notices and Anecdotes illustrating the social life of the period—extending over a quarter of a century (1799—1827). It includes also Poems and other miscellaneous pieces by Mrs. Trench.

Wallace.—Works by ALFRED RUSSEL WALLACE. For other Works by same Author, see SCIENTIFIC CATALOGUE.

Dr. Hooker, in his address to the British Association, spoke thus of the author:—"Of Mr. Wallace and his many contributions to philosophical biology it is not easy to speak without enthusiasm; for, putting aside their great merits, he, throughout his writings, with a modesty as rare as I believe it to be unconscious, forgets his own unquestioned claim to the honour of having originated, independently of Mr. Darwin, the theories which he so ably defends."

A NARRATIVE OF TRAVELS ON THE AMAZON AND RIO NEGRO, with an Account of the Native Tribes, and Observations on the Climate, Geology, and Natural History of the Amazon Valley. With a Map and Illustrations. 8vo. 12s.

Mr. Wallace is acknowledged as one of the first of modern travellers and naturalists. This, his earliest work, will be found to possess many charms for the general reader, and to be full of interest to the student of natural history.

THE MALAY ARCHIPELAGO: the Land of the Orang Utan and the Bird of Paradise. A Narrative of Travel with Studies of Man and Nature. With Maps and Illustrations. Third and Cheaper Edition. Crown 8vo. 7s. 6d.

"*The result is a vivid picture of tropical life, which may be read with unflagging interest, and a sufficient account of his scientific conclusions to stimulate our appetite without wearying us by detail. In short, we may*

safely say that we have never read a more agreeable book of its kind."—
SATURDAY REVIEW. "His descriptions of scenery, of the people and
their manners and customs, enlivened by occasional amusing anecdotes,
constitute the most interesting reading we have taken up for some time."—
STANDARD.

Waller.—SIX WEEKS IN THE SADDLE: A PAINTER'S
JOURNAL IN ICELAND. By S. E. WALLER. With Illustrations by the Author. Crown 8vo. 6s.

Ward (Professor).—THE HOUSE OF AUSTRIA IN THE
THIRTY YEARS' WAR. Two Lectures, with Notes and Illustrations. By ADOLPHUS W. WARD, M.A., Professor of History
in Owens College, Manchester. Extra fcap. 8vo. 2s. 6d.

*These two Lectures were delivered in February, 1869, at the Philosophical
Institution, Edinburgh, and are now published with Notes and Illustrations.
"We have never read," says the* SATURDAY REVIEW, *" any lectures which
bear more thoroughly the impress of one who has a true and vigorous grasp
of the subject in hand." " They are," the* SCOTSMAN *says, " the fruit of
much labour and learning, and it would be difficult to compress into a
hundred pages more information."*

Ward (J.)—EXPERIENCES OF A DIPLOMATIST. Being
recollections of Germany founded on Diaries kept during the years
1840–1870. By JOHN WARD, C.B., late H.M. Minister-
Resident to the Hanse Towns. 8vo. 10s. 6d.

*Mr. Ward's recollections extend back even to 1830. From his official
position as well as from other circumstances he had many opportunities of
coming in contact with eminent men of all ranks and all professions on the
Continent. His book, while it contains much that throws light on the
history of the long and important period with which it is concerned, is full
of reminiscences of such men as Arrivabene, King Leopold, Frederick
William IV., his Court and Ministers, Humboldt, Bunsen, Raumer,
Ranke, Grimm, Palmerston, Sir de Lacy Evans, Cobden, Mendelssohn,
Cardinal Wiseman, Prince Albert, the Prince and Princess of Wales,
Lord Russell, Bismarck, Mdlle. Tietjens, and many other eminent Englishmen and foreigners.*

Warren.—AN ESSAY ON GREEK FEDERAL COINAGE.
By the Hon. J. LEICESTER WARREN, M.A. 8vo. 2s. 6d.

The present essay is an attempt to illustrate Mr. Freeman's Federal Government by evidence deduced from the coinage of the times and countries therein treated of.

Wedgwood.—JOHN WESLEY AND THE EVANGELICAL REACTION of the Eighteenth Century. By JULIA WEDGWOOD. Crown 8vo. 8s. 6d.

This book is an attempt to delineate the influence of a particular man upon his age. The background to the central figure is treated with considerable minuteness, the object of representation being not the vicissitude of a particular life, but that element in the life which expressed itself on the life of a nation,—an element which cannot be understood without a study of aspects of national thought which on a superficial view might appear wholly unconnected with it. "In style and individual power, in breadth of view and clearness of insight, Miss Wedgwood's book far surpasses all rivals."—ATHENÆUM. "As a short account of the most remarkable movement in the eighteenth century, it must fairly be described as excellent."—PALL MALL GAZETTE.

Wilson.—A MEMOIR OF GEORGE WILSON, M.D., F.R.S.E., Regius Professor of Technology in the University of Edinburgh. By his SISTER. New Edition. Crown 8vo. 6s.

"An exquisite and touching picture of a rare and thoughtful spirit."—GUARDIAN. "No more than any book of which we have lately read deserved a minute and careful biography, and by such alone could he be understood, and become loveable and influential to his fellowmen. Such a biography his sister has written, in which labor reach almost to the charm of a complete autobiography, with all the additional charm of being unconsciously such. We revere and admire the heart, and earnestly praise the patient tender hand, by which such a worthy record of the earth-story of one of God's true angelmen has been constructed for our delight and credit."—NONCONFORMIST.

Wilson (Daniel, LL.D.)—Works by DANIEL WILSON, LL.D., Professor of History and English Literature in University College, Toronto:—

PREHISTORIC ANNALS OF SCOTLAND. New Edition, with numerous Illustrations. Two Vols. demy 8vo. 36s.

Wilson (Daniel, LL.D.)—continued.

One object aimed at when the book first appeared was to rescue archæological research from that limited range to which a too exclusive devotion to classical studies had given rise; and, especially in relation to Scotland, to prove how greatly more comprehensive and important are its native antiquities than all the traces of intruded art. The aim has been to a large extent effectually accomplished, and such an impulse given to archæological research, that in this new edition the whole of the work has had to be remodelled. Fully a third of it has been entirely re-written; and the remaining portions have undergone so minute a revision as to render it in many respects a new work. The number of pictorial illustrations has been greatly increased, and several of the former plates and woodcuts have been re-engraved from new drawings. This is divided into four Parts. Part I. deals with The Primeval or Stone Period: Aboriginal Traces, Sepulchral Memorials, Dwellings, and Catacombs, Temples, Weapons, &c. &c.; Part II. The Bronze Period: The Metallurgic Transition, Primitive Bronze, Personal Ornaments, Religion, Arts, and Domestic Habits, with other topics; Part III. The Iron Period: The Introduction of Iron, The Roman Invasion, Strongholds, &c. &c.; Part IV. The Christian Period: Historical Data, the Norse's Last Relics, Primitive and Mediæval Ecclesiology, Ecclesiastical and Miscellaneous Antiquities. The work is furnished with an elaborate Index. "One of the most interesting, learned, and elegant works we have seen for a long time."—Westminster Review. *"The interest connected with this beautiful volume is not limited to that part of the kingdom to which it is chiefly devoted; it will be consulted with advantage and gratification by all who have a regard for National Antiquities and for the advancement of scientific Archæology."*—Archæological Journal.

PREHISTORIC MAN. New Edition, revised and partly re-written, with numerous Illustrations. One vol. 8vo. 21*s.*

This work, which carries out the principle of the preceding one, but with a wider scope, aims to "view Man, as far as possible, unaffected by those modifying influences which accompany the development of nations and the maturity of a true historic period, in order thereby to ascertain the sources from whence such development and maturity proceed. These researches into the origin of civilization have accordingly been pursued under the belief which influenced the author in previous inquiries that the investigations of the archæologist, when carried on in an enlightened spirit, are replete

Wilson (Daniel LL.D.)—continued.

with interest in relation to some of the most important problems of modern science. To reject the aid of archæology in the progress of science, and especially of ethnological science, is to extinguish the lamp of the student when most dependent on its borrowed rays." A prolonged residence on some of the recent sites of the New World has afforded the author many opportunities of investigating the antiquities of the American Aborigines, and of bringing to light many facts of high importance in reference to primeval man. The changes in the new edition, necessitated by the great advance in Archæology since the first, include both reconstruction and condensation, along with considerable additions alike in illustration and in argument. "We find," says the ATHENÆUM, "the main idea of his treatise to be a pre-eminently scientific one,—namely, by archæological records to obtain a definite conception of the origin and nature of man's earliest efforts at civilisation in the New World, and to endeavour to discover, as if by analogy, the necessary conditions, phases, and epochs through which man in the prehistoric stage in the Old World also must necessarily have passed." The NORTH BRITISH REVIEW calls it "a mature and mellow work of an able man; free alike from crotchets and from dogmatism, and exhibiting on every page the caution and moderation of a well-balanced judgment."

CHATTERTON: A Biographical Study. By DANIEL WILSON, LL.D., Professor of History and English Literature in University College, Toronto. Crown 8vo. 6s. 6d.

The author here regards Chatterton as a poet, not as a "mere vulgar forger of other men's literary treasures." Reviewed in this light, he has found much in the old materials capable of being turned to new account; and to these materials research in various directions has enabled him to make some additions. He believes that the life-poet has been misjudged, and that the biographies hitherto written of him are not only imperfect, but untrue. While doing full justice, the author has striven to deal truthfully with the failings as well as the virtues of the boy, bearing always in remembrance, what has been too frequently lost sight of, that he was but a boy—a boy, and yet a poet of rare power. The EXAMINER thinks this "the most complete and the purest biography of the poet which has yet appeared." The LITERARY CHURCHMAN calls it "a most charming literary biography."

HISTORY, BIOGRAPHY, & TRAVELS.

Wyatt (Sir M. Digby).—FINE ART: a Sketch of its History, Theory, Practice, and application to Industry. A Course of Lectures delivered before the University of Cambridge. By Sir M. DIGBY WYATT, M.A. Slade Professor of Fine Art. 8vo. 10s. 6d.

"*An excellent handbook for the student of art.*"—GRAPHIC. "*The book abounds in valuable matter, and will therefore be read with pleasure and profit by lovers of art.*"—DAILY NEWS.

Yonge (Charlotte M.)—Works by CHARLOTTE M. YONGE, Author of "The Heir of Redclyffe," &c. &c. :—

A PARALLEL HISTORY OF FRANCE AND ENGLAND; consisting of Outlines and Dates. Oblong 4to. 3s. 6d.

This tabular History has been drawn up to supply a want felt by many teachers of some means of making their pupils realize what events in the two countries were contemporary. A skeleton narrative has been constructed of the chief transactions in either country, placing a column between for what affected both alike, by which means it is hoped that young people may be assisted in grasping the mutual relation of events.

CAMEOS FROM ENGLISH HISTORY. From Rollo to Edward II. Extra fcap. 8vo. Second Edition, enlarged. 5s.

A SECOND SERIES, THE WARS IN FRANCE. Extra fcap. 8vo. 5s. Second Edition.

The endeavour has not been to chronicle facts, but to put together a series of pictures of persons and events, so as to arrest the attention, and give some individuality and distinctness to the recollection, by gathering together details of the most memorable moments. The "Cameos" are intended as a book for young people just beyond the elementary histories of England, and able to enter in some degree into the real spirit of events, and to be struck with characters and scenes presented in some relief. "*Instead of dry details,*" *says the* NONCONFORMIST, "*we have living pictures, faithful, vivid, and striking.*"

Young (Julian Charles, M.A.)—A MEMOIR OF CHARLES MAYNE YOUNG, Tragedian, with Extracts from his Son's Journal. By JULIAN CHARLES YOUNG, M.A. Rector of Ilmington. With Portraits and Sketches. *New and Cheaper Edition.* Crown 8vo. 7s. 6d.

Round this memoir of one who held no mean place in public estimation as a tragedian, and who, as a man, by the unobtrusive simplicity and moral purity of his private life, won golden opinions from all sorts of men, are clustered extracts from the author's Journals, containing many curious and interesting reminiscences of his father's and his own eminent and famous contemporaries and acquaintances, somewhat after the manner of H. Crabb Robinson's Diary. Every page will be found full both of entertainment and instruction. It contains four portraits of the tragedian, and a few other curious sketches. "In this budget of anecdotes, jokes, and gossip, old and new, relative to Scott, Moore, Chalmers, Coleridge, Wordsworth, Croker, Mathews, the third and fourth Georges, Bowles, Beckford, Lockhart, Wellington, Peel, Louis Napoleon, D'Orsay, Dickens, Thackeray, Louis Blanc, Gibson, Constable, and Stanfield, etc. etc., the reader must be hard indeed to please who cannot find entertainment."—PALL MALL GAZETTE.

POLITICS, POLITICAL AND SOCIAL ECONOMY, LAW, AND KINDRED SUBJECTS.

Baxter.—NATIONAL INCOME: The United Kingdom. By R. DUDLEY BAXTER, M.A. 8vo. 3s. 6d.

The present work endeavours to answer systematically such questions as the following:— What are the means and aggregate wages of our labouring population; what are the numbers and aggregate profits of the middle classes; what the revenues of our great proprietors and capitalists; and what the pecuniary strength of the nation to bear the burdens annually falling upon us? What capital in land and goods and money is stored up for our subsistence, and for carrying out our enterprises? The author has collected his facts from every quarter and tested them in various ways, in order to make his statements and deductions valuable and trustworthy. Part I. of the work deals with the Classification of the Population into—Chap. I. The Income Classes; Chap. II. The Upper and Middle and Manual Labour Classes. Part II. treats of the Income of the United Kingdom, divided into—Chap. III. Upper and Middle Incomes; Chap. IV. Wages of the Manual Labour Classes—England and Wales; Chap. V. Income of Scotland; Chap. VI. Income of Ireland; Chap. VII. Income of the United Kingdom. In the Appendix will be found many valuable and carefully compiled tables, illustrating in detail the subjects discussed in the text.

Bernard.—FOUR LECTURES ON SUBJECTS CONNECTED WITH DIPLOMACY. By MONTAGUE BERNARD, M.A., Chichele Professor of International Law and Diplomacy, Oxford. 8vo. 9s.

These four Lectures deal with—I. "The Congress of Westphalia;" II. "Systems of Policy;" III. "Diplomacy, Past and Present;" IV. "The Obligations of Treaties."—"Singularly interesting lectures, so able, clear, and attractive."—SPECTATOR. "The author of these lectures is full of the knowledge which belongs to his subject, and has that power of clear and vigorous expression which results from clear and vigorous thought."—SCOTSMAN.

Bright (John, M.P.)—SPEECHES ON QUESTIONS OF PUBLIC POLICY. By the Right Hon. JOHN BRIGHT, M.P. Edited by Professor THOROLD ROGERS. Author's Popular Edition. Globe 8vo. 3s. 6d.

The speeches which have been selected for publication in these volumes possess a value, as examples of the art of public speaking, which no person will be likely to underrate. The speeches have been selected with a view of supplying the public with the evidence on which Mr. Bright's friends assert his right to a place in the front rank of English statesmen. They are divided into groups, according to their subjects. The editor has naturally given prominence to those subjects with which Mr. Bright has been specially identified, as, for example, India, America, Ireland, and Parliamentary Reform. But nearly every topic of great public interest on which Mr. Bright has spoken is represented in these volumes. "Mr. Bright's speeches will always deserve to be read by one who cares for the history of our time, and many brilliant passages, perhaps a few entire speeches, will really become a part of the living literature of England."—DAILY NEWS.

LIBRARY EDITION. Two Vols. 8vo. With Portrait. 25s.

Cairnes.—Works by J. E. CAIRNES, Emeritus Professor of Political Economy in University College, London.

ESSAYS IN POLITICAL ECONOMY, THEORETICAL AND APPLIED. By J. E. CAIRNES, M.A., Professor of Political Economy in University College, London. 8vo. 10s. 6d.

CONTENTS.—*Essays towards a Solution of the Gold Question—The Australian Episode—The Course of Depreciation—International Results—Summary of the Movement—M. Chevalier's Views—Co-Operation in the Slate Quarries of North Wales—Political*

Cairnes—*continued.*

Economy and Land—Political Economy and Laissez-Faire—M. Comte and Political Economy—Bastiat.

"*The production of one of the ablest of living economists.*"—ATHENÆUM.

POLITICAL ESSAYS. 8vo. 10s. 6d.

The following are the Titles of the Essays in this volume:—I. Colonisation and Colonial Government. II. The Revolution in America. III. International Law. IV. Fragments on Ireland,—1. The Agricultural Revolution—Protection and Free Trade. 2. The Emigration. 3. The Irish Cottier. 4. Irish Landlordism. V. Our Defences: A National or a Standing Army. VI. Thoughts on University Reform à propos of the Irish Educational Crisis of 1865—66. VII. The Present Position of the Irish University Question—1873.

The SATURDAY REVIEW *says, "We recently expressed our high admiration of the former volume; and the present one is no less remarkable for the qualities of clear statement, sound logic, and candid treatment of opponents which were conspicuous in its predecessor. . . . We may safely say that none of Mr. Mill's many disciples is a worthier representative of the best qualities of their master than Professor Cairnes."*

Christie.—THE BALLOT AND CORRUPTION AND EXPENDITURE AT ELECTIONS, a Collection of Essays and Addresses of different dates. By W. D. CHRISTIE, C.B., formerly Her Majesty's Minister to the Argentine Confederation and to Brazil; Author of "Life of the First Earl of Shaftesbury." Crown 8vo. 4s. 6d.

Mr. Christie has been well known for upwards of thirty years as a strenuous and able advocate for the Ballot, both in his place in Parliament and elsewhere. The papers and speeches here collected are six in number, exclusive of the Preface and Dedication to Professor Maurice, which contain many interesting historical details concerning the Ballot. "You have thought to greater purpose on the means of preventing electoral corruption, and are likely to be of more service in passing measures for that highly important end, than any other person that I could name."—J. S. MILL, in a published letter to the Author, May 1868.

Clarke.—EARLY ROMAN LAW. THE REGAL PERIOD. By E. C. CLARKE, M.A., of Lincoln's Inn, Barrister-at-Law, Lecturer in Law and Regius Professor of Civil Law at Cambridge.

The beginnings of Roman Law are only noticed incidentally by Gaius or his paraphrasers under Justinian. They are, however, so important, that this attempt to set forth what is known or may be inferred about them, it is expected, will be found of much value. The method adopted by the author has been to furnish in the text of each section a continuous account of the subject in hand, ample quotations and references being appended in the form of notes. Most of the passages cited have been arrived at by independent reading of the original authority, the few others having been carefully verified. "Mr. Clarke has brought together a great mass of valuable matter in an accessible form."—SATURDAY REVIEW.

Corfield (Professor W. H.)—A DIGEST OF FACTS RELATING TO THE TREATMENT AND UTILIZATION OF SEWAGE. By W. H. CORFIELD, M.A., B.A., Professor of Hygiene and Public Health at University College, London. 8vo. 10s. 6d. Second Edition, corrected and enlarged.

In this edition the author has revised and carefully re-cast his work, and rendered any index unnecessary by a fuller table of contents. The headings of the eleven chapters are as follow:—I. "Early Sewerage: Roman Heaps and Cesspits." II. "Pails and Trenches: Cess and Dust." III. "Improved Midden-Pits and Cesspools: Midden-Closets, Pail-Closets, etc." IV. "The Dry-Closet System." V. "Water-Closets." VI. "Sewerage." VII. "Sanitary Aspects of the Water-Carrying System." VIII. "Value of Sewage: Injury to Rivers." IX. "Town Sewage: Attempts at Utilization." X. "Filtration and Irrigation." XI. "Influence of Sewage Farming on the Public Health." An abridged account of the more recently published researches on the subject will be found in the Appendix; while the Summary contains a concise statement of the views which the author himself has decided to adopt; references have been inserted throughout to show from what sources the numerous quotations have been derived, and an index has been added. "Mr. Corfield's work is entitled to rank as a standard authority, no less than a convenient handbook, in all matters relating to sewage."—ATHENÆUM.

Fawcett.—Works by HENRY FAWCETT, M.A., M.P., Fellow of Trinity Hall, and Professor of Political Economy in the University of Cambridge :—

THE ECONOMIC POSITION OF THE BRITISH LABOURER. Extra fcp. 8vo. 5s.

This work formed a portion of a course of Lectures delivered by the author in the University of Cambridge, and he has deemed it advisable to retain many of the expositions of the elementary principles of Economic Science. In the Introductory Chapter the author points out the scope of the work and shows the vast importance of the subject in relation to the commercial prosperity and even the national existence of Britain. Then follow five chapters on "The Land Tenure of England," "Co-operation," "The Causes which regulate Wages," "Trade Unions and Strikes," and "Emigration." The EXAMINER *calls the work "a very scholarly exposition on some of the most essential questions of Political Economy;" and the* NONCONFORMIST *says "it is written with charming freshness, ease, and lucidity."*

MANUAL OF POLITICAL ECONOMY. Third and Cheaper Edition, with Two New Chapters. Crown 8vo. 10s. 6d.

In this treatise no important branch of the subject has been omitted, and the author believes that the principles which are therein explained will enable the reader to obtain a tolerably complete view of the whole science. Mr. Fawcett has endeavoured to show how intimately Political Economy is connected with the practical questions of life. For the convenience of the ordinary reader, and especially for those who may use the book to prepare themselves for examinations, he has prefixed a very detailed summary of Contents, which may be regarded as an analysis of the work. The new edition has been so carefully revised that there is scarcely a page in which some improvement has not been introduced. The DAILY NEWS *says: "It forms one of the best introductions to the principles of the science, and to its practical applications in the problems of modern, and especially of English, government and society." "The book is written throughout," says the* EXAMINER, *"with admirable force, clearness, and brevity, every important part of the subject being duly considered."*

Fawcett (H.)—continued.

PAUPERISM: ITS CAUSES AND REMEDIES. Crown 8vo. 5s. 6d.

In its number for March 11th, 1871, the SPECTATOR *said: "We wish Professor Fawcett would devote a little more of his time and energy to the practical consideration of that monster problem of Pauperism, for the treatment of which his economic knowledge and popular sympathies so eminently fit him." The volume now published may be regarded as an answer to the above challenge. The seven chapters it comprises discuss the following subjects:—I. "Pauperism and the old Poor Law." II. "The present Poor Law System." III. "The Increase of Population." IV. "National Education; its Economic and Social Effects." V. "Co-partnership and Co-operation." VI. "The English System of Land Tenure." VII. "The Inclosure of Commons." The* ATHENÆUM *calls the work "a repertory of interesting and well-digested information."*

SPEECHES ON SOME CURRENT POLITICAL QUESTIONS. 8vo. 10s. 6d.

ESSAYS ON POLITICAL AND SOCIAL SUBJECTS. By PROFESSOR FAWCETT, M.P., and MILLICENT GARRETT FAWCETT. 8vo. 10s. 6d.

*This volume contains fourteen papers, some of which have appeared in various journals and periodicals; others have not before been published... They are all on subjects of great importance and universal interest, and the names of the two authors are a sufficient guarantee that each task is discussed with full knowledge, great ability, clearness, and earnestness. The following are some of the titles:—"Modern Socialism;" "Free Education in its Economic Aspect;" "Pauperism, Charity, and the Poor Law;" "National Debts and National Prosperity;" "What can be done for the Agricultural Labourer;" "The Education of Women;" "The Electoral Disabilities of Women;" "The House of Lords." Each article is signed with the initials of its author. "In every respect a work of note and value.... They will all repay the perusal of the thinking reader."—*DAILY NEWS.

WORKS IN POLITICS, ETC.

Fawcett (Mrs.)—POLITICAL ECONOMY FOR BEGINNERS. WITH QUESTIONS. By MILLICENT GARRETT FAWCETT. New Edition. 18mo. 2s. 6d.

In this little work are explained as briefly as possible the most important principles of Political Economy, in the hope that it will be useful to beginners, and perhaps be an assistance to those who are desirous of introducing the study of Political Economy to schools. In order to adapt the book especially for school use, questions have been added at the end of each chapter. In the new edition each page has been carefully revised, and at the end of each chapter, after the questions, a few little puzzles have been added, which will give interest to the book, and teach the learner to think for himself. The DAILY NEWS *calls it "clear, compact, and comprehensive;" and the* SPECTATOR *says, "Mrs. Fawcett's treatise is perfectly suited to its purpose."*

Freeman (E. A., M.A., D.C.L.)—COMPARATIVE POLITICS. Lectures at the Royal Institution, to which is added "The Unity of History," being the Rede Lecture delivered at Cambridge in 1872. 8vo. 14s.

Godkin (James).—THE LAND WAR IN IRELAND. A History for the Times. By JAMES GODKIN, Author of "Ireland and her Churches," late Irish Correspondent of the *Times*. 8vo. 12s.

A History of the Irish Land Question. "There is probably no other account so compendious and so complete."—FORTNIGHTLY REVIEW.

Goschen.—REPORTS AND SPEECHES ON LOCAL TAXATION. By GEORGE J. GOSCHEN, M.P. Royal 8vo. 5s.

Mr. Goschen, from the position he has held and the attention he has given to the subject of Local Taxation, is well qualified to deal with it. "The volume contains a vast mass of information of the highest value."—ATHENÆUM.

Guide to the Unprotected, in Every Day Matters Relating to Property and Income. By a BANKER'S DAUGHTER. Third Edition. Extra fcap. 8vo. 3s. 6d.

Many widows and single ladies, and all young people, on first possessing money of their own, are in want of advice when they have commonplace business matters to transact. The author of this work writes for those who know nothing. She aims throughout to avoid all technicalities; to give plain and practical directions, not only as to what ought to be done, but how to do it. "Many an unprotected female will bless the head which planned and the hand which compiled this admirable little manual. ... *The book was very much wanted, and it could not have been better done."*—MORNING STAR.

Hill.—CHILDREN OF THE STATE. THE TRAINING OF JUVENILE PAUPERS. By FLORENCE HILL. Extra fcap. 8vo. cloth. 5s.

In this work the author discusses the various systems adopted in this and other countries in the treatment of pauper children. The BIRMINGHAM DAILY GAZETTE *calls it "a valuable contribution to the great and important social question which is so ably and thoroughly discussed; and it must materially aid in producing a wise method of dealing with the Children of the State."*

Historicus.—LETTERS ON SOME QUESTIONS OF INTERNATIONAL LAW. Reprinted from the *Times*, with considerable Additions. 8vo. 7s. 6d. Also, ADDITIONAL LETTERS. 8vo. 2s. 6d.

The author's intention in these Letters was to illustrate in a popular form clearly-established principles of law, or to refute, as occasion required, errors which had obtained a mischievous currency. He has endeavoured to establish, by sufficient authority, propositions which have been too suddenly impugned, and to point out the various methods of reasoning which have led some modern writers to erroneous conclusions. The volume contains: Letters on "Recognition;" "On the Perils of Intervention;" "The Rights and Duties of Neutral Nations;" "On the Law of Blockade;" "On Neutral Trade in Contraband of War;" "On Belligerent Violation of Neutral Rights;" "The Foreign Enlistment Act;" "The Right of Search;" extracts from letters on the Affair of the Trent; *and a paper on the "Territoriality of the Merchant Vessel."—"It is seldom that the doctrines of International Law on debatable points have been stated with more vigour, precision, and certainty."*—SATURDAY REVIEW.

Jevons.—Works by W. STANLEY JEVONS, M.A., Professor of Logic and Political Economy in Owens College, Manchester. (For other Works by the same Author, see EDUCATIONAL and PHILOSOPHICAL CATALOGUES.)

THE COAL QUESTION: An Inquiry Concerning the Progress of the Nation, and the Probable Exhaustion of our Coal Mines. Second Edition, revised. 8vo. 10s. 6d.

"*Day by day,*" *the author says, "it becomes more evident that the coal we happily possess in excellent quality and abundance is the mainspring of modern material civilisation." Geologists and other competent authorities have of late been hinting that the supply of coal is by no means inexhaustible, and as it is of vast importance to the country and the world generally to know the real state of the case, Professor Jevons in this work has endeavoured to solve the question as far as the data at command admit. He believes that should the consumption multiply for rather more than a century at its present rate, the average depth of our coal mines would be so reduced that we could not long continue our present rate of progress. "We have to make the momentous choice," he believes, "between brief greatness and long-continued prosperity."—"The question of our supply of coal," says the* PALL MALL GAZETTE, "*becomes a question obviously of life or death. . . . The whole case is stated with admirable clearness and cogency. . . . We may regard his statements as unanswered and practically established.*"

THE THEORY OF POLITICAL ECONOMY. 8vo. 9s.

In this work Professor Jevons endeavours to construct a theory of Political Economy on a mathematical or quantitative basis, believing that many of the commonly received theories in this science are perniciously erroneous. The author here attempts to treat Economy as the Calculus of Pleasure and Pain, and has sketched out, almost irrespective of previous opinions, the form which the science, as it seems to him, must ultimately take. The theory consists in applying the differential calculus to the familiar notions of Wealth, Utility, Value, Demand, Supply, Capital, Interest, Labour, and all the other notions belonging to the daily operations of industry. As the complete theory of almost every other science involves the use of that calculus, so, the author thinks, we cannot have a true theory of Political Economy without its aid. "Professor Jevons has done invaluable service by courageously claiming political economy to be strictly a branch of Applied Mathematics."—WESTMINSTER REVIEW.

Macdonell.—THE LAND QUESTION, WITH SPECIAL REFERENCE TO ENGLAND AND SCOTLAND. By JOHN MACDONELL, Barrister-at-Law. 8vo. 10s. 6d.

"His book ought to be on the table of every land reformer, and will be found to contain many interesting facts. Mr. Macdonell may be congratulated on having made a most valuable contribution to the study of a question that cannot be examined from too many points."—EXAMINER.

Martin.—THE STATESMAN'S YEAR-BOOK: A Statistical and Historical Annual of the States of the Civilized World. Handbook for Politicians and Merchants for the year 1874. By FREDERICK MARTIN. Eleventh Annual Publication. Revised after Official Returns. Crown 8vo. 10s. 6d.

The Statesman's Year-Book is the only work in the English language which furnishes a clear and concise account of the actual condition of all the States of Europe, the civilized countries of America, Asia, and Africa, and the British Colonies and Dependencies in all parts of the world. The new issue of the work has been revised and corrected, on the basis of official reports received direct from the heads of the leading Governments of the world, in reply to letters sent to them by the Editor. Through the valuable assistance thus given, it has been possible to collect an amount of information, political, statistical, and commercial, of the latest date, and of unimpeachable trustworthiness, such as no publication of the same kind has ever been able to furnish. "As indispensable as Bradshaw."—TIMES.

Phillimore.—PRIVATE LAW AMONG THE ROMANS, from the Pandects. By JOHN GEORGE PHILLIMORE, Q.C. 8vo. 16s.

The author's belief that some knowledge of the Roman System of Municipal Law will contribute to improve our own, has induced him to prepare the present work. His endeavour has been to select those parts of the Digest which would best shew the grand manner in which the Roman jurist dealt with his subject, as well as those which must illustrate the principles by which he was guided in establishing the great lines and propositions of jurisprudence, which every lawyer must have frequent occasion to employ. "Mr. Phillimore has done good service towards the study of jurisprudence in this country by the production of this volume. The work is one which should be in the hands of every student."—ATHENÆUM.

Rogers.—COBDEN AND POLITICAL OPINION. By J. E. THOROLD ROGERS. 8vo. 10s. 6d.

Smith.—Works by Professor GOLDWIN SMITH:—

A LETTER TO A WHIG MEMBER OF THE SOUTHERN INDEPENDENCE ASSOCIATION. Extra fcap. 8vo. 2s.

This is a Letter, written in 1864, to a member of an Association formed in this country, the purpose of which was "to lend assistance to the Slave owners of the Southern States in their attempt to effect a disruption of the American Commonwealth, and to establish an independent Power, having, as they declare, Slavery for its corner-stone." Mr. Smith endeavours to show that in doing so they would have committed a great folly and a still greater crime. Throughout the Letter many points of general and permanent importance are discussed.

THREE ENGLISH STATESMEN: PYM, CROMWELL, PITT. A Course of Lectures on the Political History of England. Extra fcap. 8vo. New and Cheaper Edition. 5s.

"*A work which neither historian nor politician can safely afford to neglect.*"—SATURDAY REVIEW. "*There are outlines, clearly and boldly sketched, if mere outlines, of the three Statesmen who give the hints to his lectures, which have well deserving of study.*"—SPECTATOR.

Social Duties Considered with Reference to the ORGANIZATION OF EFFORT IN WORKS OF BE-NEVOLENCE AND PUBLIC UTILITY. By a MAN OF BUSINESS. (WILLIAM RATHBONE.) Fcap. 8vo. 4s. 6d.

The contents of this valuable little book are—I. "Social Disintegration." II. "Our Charities—Done and Undone." III. "Organization and Individual Benevolence—their Achievements and Short-comings." IV. "Organization and Individuation—their Co-

50 MACMILLAN'S CATALOGUE OF

operation indispensable." V. "Instances and Experiments." VI. "The Sphere of Government." "Conclusion." The views urged are no sentimental theories, but have grown out of the practical experience acquired in actual work. "Mr. Rathbone's earnest and large-hearted little book will help to generate both a larger and wiser charity."—BRITISH QUARTERLY.

Stephen (C. E.)—THE SERVICE OF THE POOR; Being an Inquiry into the Reasons for and against the Establishment of Religious Sisterhoods for Charitable Purposes. By CAROLINE EMILIA STEPHEN. Crown 8vo. 6s. 6d.

Miss Stephen defines Religious Sisterhoods as "associations, the organisation of which is based upon the assumption that works of charity are either acts of worship in themselves, or means to an end, that end being the spiritual welfare of the agents or the performers of those works." Arguing from that point of view, she devotes the first part of her volume to a brief history of religious associations, taking as specimens—I. The Deaconesses of the Primitive Church. II. The Béguines. III. The Third Order of S. Francis. IV. The Sisters of Charity of S. Vincent de Paul. V. The Deaconesses of Modern Germany. In the second part, Miss Stephen attempts to show what are the real wants met by Sisterhoods, to what extent the same wants may be efficiently met by the organisation of corresponding institutions on a secular basis, and what are the reasons for endeavouring to do so. "The ablest advocate of a better line of work in this direction than we have ever seen." EXAMINER.

Stephen (J. F.)—Works by JAMES FITZJAMES STEPHEN, Q.C.:—

A GENERAL VIEW OF THE CRIMINAL LAW OF ENGLAND. 8vo. 18s.

The object of this work is to give an account of the general scope, tendency, and design of an important part of our institutions, of which hardly any one can have a greater moral significance, or be more closely connected with broad principles of morality and politics, than those by which men rightfully, deliberately, and in cold blood, kill, enslave, and otherwise torment their fellow-creatures. The author makes it possible to explain the principles of such a system in a manner both intelligible and interesting.

Stephen (J. F.)—continued.

The Contents are—I. "The Province of the Criminal Law." II. "Historical Sketch of English Criminal Law." III. "Definition of Crime in General." IV. "Classification and Definition of Particular Crimes." V. "Criminal Procedure in General." VI. "English Criminal Procedure." VII. "The Principles of Evidence in Relation to the Criminal Law." VIII. "English Rules of Evidence." IX. "English Criminal Legislation." The last 150 pages are occupied with the discussion of a number of important cases. "Readers feel in his book the confidence which attaches to the writings of a man who has a great practical acquaintance with the matter of which he writes, and lawyers will agree that it fully satisfies the standard of professional accuracy."—SATURDAY REVIEW. "His style is forcible and perspicuous, and singularly free from the unnecessary use of professional terms."—SPECTATOR.

THE INDIAN EVIDENCE ACT (I. of 1872). With an Introduction on the Principles of Judicial Evidence. 8vo. 12s. 6d.

No one is more competent than Mr. Fitzjames Stephen to write on the subject of which he here treats. The Introduction, indeed, may be regarded as a short treatise on the theory of evidence, and, in connection with the appended Act of 1872, the author hopes it may prove useful to civil servants who are preparing in England for their Indian career, and to the law students in Indian Universities. The subject is one which reaches far beyond law. The law of evidence is nothing unless it is founded upon a rational conception of the manner in which truth as to all matters of fact whatever ought to be investigated. The four Chapters of the Introduction are—I. General Distribution of the Subject; II. A Statement of the Principles of Induction and Deduction, and a Comparison of their Application to Scientific and Judicial Inquiries; III. The Theory of Relevancy, with Illustration; IV. General Observations on the Indian Evidence Act.

Thornton.—ON LABOUR: Its Wrongful Claims and Rightful Dues; Its Actual Present State and Possible Future. By WILLIAM THOMAS THORNTON, C.B., Author of "A Plea for Peasant Proprietors," etc. Second Edition, revised. 8vo. 14s.

The object of this volume is to endeavour to find "a cure for human destitution," the search after which has been the passion and the work of the author's life. The work is divided into four books, and each book into a number of chapters. Book I. "Labour's Causes of Discontent." II. "Labour and Capital in Peace." III. "Labour and Capital in Antagonism." IV. "Labour and Capital in Alliance." All the highly important problems in Social and Political Economy connected with Labour and Capital are here discussed with knowledge, vigour, and originality, and for a noble purpose. The new edition has been thoroughly revised and considerably enlarged. "We cannot fail to recognise in his work the result of independent thought, high moral aim, and generous impartiality in a noble cause. . . . A really valuable contribution. The manner of facts accumulated, both historical and statistical, make an especially valuable portion of the work."—WESTMINSTER REVIEW.

WORKS CONNECTED WITH THE SCIENCE OR THE HISTORY OF LANGUAGE.

(*For Editions of Greek and Latin Classical Authors, Grammars, and other School works, see* EDUCATIONAL CATALOGUE.)

Abbott.—A SHAKESPERIAN GRAMMAR: An Attempt to illustrate some of the Differences between Elizabethan and Modern English. By the Rev. E. A. ABBOTT, M.A., Head Master of the City of London School. For the Use of Schools. New and Enlarged Edition. Extra fcap. 8vo. 6s.

The object of this work is to furnish students of Shakespeare and Bacon with a short systematic account of some points of difference between Elizabethan Syntax and our own. The demand for a third edition within a year of the publication of the first, has encouraged the author to endeavour to make the work somewhat more useful, and to render it, as far as possible, a complete book of reference for all difficulties of Shakesperian Syntax or Prosody. For this purpose the whole of Shakespeare has been re-read, and an attempt has been made to include within this edition the explanation of every idiomatic difficulty (where the text is not confessedly corrupt) that comes within the province of a grammar as distinct from a glossary. The great object being to make a useful book of reference for students and for classes in schools, several Plays have been indexed so fully, that with the aid of a glossary and historical notes the references will serve for a complete commentary. "*A critical inquiry, conducted with great skill and knowledge, and with all the appliances of modern philology.*"—PALL MALL GAZETTE. "*Valuable not only as an aid to the critical study of Shakespeare, but as tending to familiarize the reader with Elizabethan English in general.*"—ATHENÆUM.

Besant.—STUDIES IN EARLY FRENCH POETRY. By WALTER BESANT, M.A. Crown 8vo. 8s. 6d.

A sort of impression rests on most minds that French literature begins with the "siècle de Louis Quatorze;" any previous literature being for the most part unknown or ignored. Few knew anything of the enormous literary activity that began in the thirteenth century, was carried on by Rutebeuf, Marie de France, Gaston de Foix, Thibault de Champagne, and Lorris; was fostered by Charles of Orleans, by Margaret of Valois, by Francis the First; that gave a troop of versifiers to France, enriched, strengthened, developed, and fixed the French language, and prepared the way for Corneille and for Racine. The present work aims to offer information and direction touching these early sports of France in poetical literature. "In one masterly sized volume he has contrived to introduce us to the very best, if not to all of the early French poets."—ATHENÆUM. *"Industry, the insight of a scholar, and a genuine enthusiasm for his subject, combine to make it of very considerable value."*—SPECTATOR.

Hadley.—ESSAYS PHILOLOGICAL AND CRITICAL. Selected from the Papers of JAMES HADLEY, LL.D., Professor of Greek in Yale College, &c. 8vo. 16s.

Hales.—LONGER ENGLISH POEMS. With Notes, Philological and Explanatory, and an Introduction on the Teaching of English. Chiefly for use in Schools. Edited by J. W. HALES, M.A., late Fellow and Assistant Tutor of Christ's College, Cambridge; Lecturer in English Literature and Classical Composition at King's College School, London; &c. &c. Extra fcap. 8vo. 4s. 6d.

This work has been in preparation for some years, and part of it has been used as a class-book by the Editor for the last two years. It is intended as an aid to the Critical study of English Literature, and contains one or more of the larger poems, each complete, of prominent English Authors from Spenser to Shelley, including Burns' Saturday Night and Twa Dogs. In all cases the original spelling and the text of the best editions have been given; only in one or two poems has it been deemed necessary to make slight omissions and changes, that the "reverence due to boys might be well observed." The latter half of the volume is occupied with copious notes, critical, etymological, and explanatory, calculated to give the learner much insight in the structure and connection of the English tongue. An Index to the notes is appended.

Hare.—FRAGMENTS OF TWO ESSAYS IN ENGLISH PHILOLOGY. By the late JULIUS CHARLES HARE, M.A., Archdeacon of Lewes. 8vo. 3s. 6d.

Helfenstein (James).—A COMPARATIVE GRAMMAR OF THE TEUTONIC LANGUAGES: Being at the same time a Historical Grammar of the English Language, and comprising Gothic, Anglo-Saxon, Early English, Modern English, Icelandic (Old Norse), Danish, Swedish, Old High German, Middle High German, Modern German, Old Saxon, Old Frisian, and Dutch. By JAMES HELFENSTEIN, Ph.D. 8vo. 18s.

This work traces the different stages of development through which the various Teutonic languages have passed, and the laws which have regulated their growth. The reader is thus enabled to study the relation which these languages bear to one another, and to the English language in particular, to which special attention is devoted throughout. In the chapters on Ancient and Middle Teutonic languages no grammatical form is omitted the knowledge of which is required for the study of ancient literature, whether Gothic or Anglo-Saxon or Early English. To each chapter is prefixed a sketch showing the relation of the Teutonic to the cognate languages, Greek, Latin, and Sanskrit. Those who have mastered the book will be in a position to proceed with intelligence to the more elaborate works of Grimm, Bopp, Pott, Schleicher, and others.

Morris.—HISTORICAL OUTLINES OF ENGLISH ACCIDENCE, comprising Chapters on the History and Development of the Language, and on Word-formation. By the Rev. RICHARD MORRIS, LL.D., Member of the Council of the Philol. Soc., Lecturer on English Language and Literature in King's College School, Editor of "Specimens of Early English," etc., etc. Third Edition. Fcap. 8vo. 6s.

Dr. Morris has endeavoured to write a work which can be profitably used by students and by the upper forms in our public schools. His almost unequalled knowledge of early English Literature renders him peculiarly qualified to produce a work of this kind; and English Grammar, he believes, without a reference to the older forms, must appear altogether anomalous, disjointed, and unintelligible. In the writing of this volume, moreover, he has taken advantage of the researches into our language made by all the most eminent scholars in England, America, and on the Continent. The author shows the place of English among the languages of the world, expounds shortly and with great minuteness "Grimm's Law," gives a brief history of the English language and an account of the various dialects, investigates the history and principles of Phonology, Orthography, Accent, and Etymology, and devotes several chapters to the consideration of the various Parts of Speech, and the final one to Derivation and Word-formation.

Peile (John, M.A.)—AN INTRODUCTION TO GREEK AND LATIN ETYMOLOGY. By JOHN PEILE, M.A., Fellow and Assistant Tutor of Christ's College, Cambridge, formerly Teacher of Sanskrit in the University of Cambridge. New and revised Edition. Crown 8vo. 10s. 6d.

These Philological Lectures are the result of Notes made during the author's reading for some years previous to their publication. Their subject-matter put into the shape of lectures delivered at Christ's College, is one set to the "Independent" day. They have been printed with some additions and modifications, but substantially as they were delivered. "The book may be accepted as a very valuable contribution to the science of language."—SATURDAY REVIEW.

Philology.—THE JOURNAL OF SACRED AND CLASSICAL PHILOLOGY. Four Vols. 8vo. 12s. 6d.

THE JOURNAL OF PHILOLOGY. New Series. Edited by W. G. CLARK, M.A., JOHN E. B. MAYOR, M.A., and W. ALDIS WRIGHT, M.A. Nos. I., II., III., and IV. 8vo. 4s. 6d. each. (Half-yearly.)

Roby (H. J.)—A GRAMMAR OF THE LATIN LANGUAGE, FROM PLAUTUS TO SUETONIUS. By HENRY JOHN ROBY, M.A., late Fellow of St. John's College, Cambridge,

Part I. containing:—Book I. Sounds. Book II. Inflexions. Book III. Word Formation. Appendices. Second Edition. Crown 8vo. 8s. 6d.

This work is the result of an independent and careful study of the writers of the strictly Classical period, the period embraced between the time of Plautus and that of Suetonius. The author's aim has been to give the facts of the language in as few words as possible. It will be found that the arrangement of the book and the treatment of the various divisions differ in many respects from those of previous grammars. Mr. Roby has given special prominence to the treatment of Sounds and Word-formation; and in the First Book he has done much towards settling a discussion which is at present largely engaging the attention of scholars, viz., the Pronunciation of the Classical languages. In the full Appendices will be found various valuable details still further illustrating the subjects discussed in the text. The author's reputation as a scholar and critic is already well known, and the publishers are encouraged to believe that his present work will take its place as perhaps the most original, exhaustive, and scientific grammar of the Latin language that has ever issued from the British press. "The book is marked by the clear and practical insight of a master in his art. It is a book which would do honour to any country."—ATHENÆUM. *"Brings before the student in a methodical form the best results of modern philology bearing on the Latin language."*—SCOTSMAN.

Taylor (Rev. Isaac).—WORDS AND PLACES; or, Etymological Illustrations of History, Ethnology, and Geography. By the Rev. ISAAC TAYLOR. Third Edition, revised and compressed. With Maps. Globe 8vo. 6s.

"In this edition the work has been recast with the intention of fitting it for the use of students and general readers, rather than, as before, to appeal to the judgment of philologers. The book has already been adopted by many teachers, and is prescribed as a text-book in the Cambridge Higher Examinations for Women: and it is hoped that the reduced size and price, and the other changes now introduced, may make it more generally useful than heretofore for Educational purposes.

Trench.—Works by R. CHENEVIX TRENCH, D.D., Archbishop of Dublin. (For other Works by the same Author, see THEOLOGICAL CATALOGUE.)

Archbishop Trench has done much to spread an interest in the history of our English tongue. He is acknowledged to possess an uncommon power of presenting, in a clear, instructive, and interesting manner, the fruit of his own extensive research, as well as the results of the labours of other scientific and historical students of language; while, as the ATHENÆUM says, "his sober judgment and sound sense are barriers against the misleading influence of arbitrary hypothesis."

SYNONYMS OF THE NEW TESTAMENT. New Edition, enlarged. 8vo. cloth. 12s.

The study of synonyms in any language is valuable as a discipline for training the mind to close and accurate habits of thought; more especially is this the case in Greek—"a language spoken by a people of the finest and subtlest intellect; who saw distinctions where others saw none, who divided out to different words what others often were content to huddle confusedly under a common term." This work is recognised as a valuable companion to every student of the New Testament in the original. This, the Seventh Edition, has been carefully revised, and a considerable number of new synonyms added. Appended is an Index to the synonyms, and an Index to many other words alluded to or explained throughout the work. "It is," the ATHENÆUM *says, "a guide in this department of knowledge to whom his readers may entrust themselves with confidence."*

ON THE STUDY OF WORDS. Lectures Addressed (originally) to the Pupils at the Diocesan Training School, Winchester. Fourteenth Edition, revised and enlarged. Fcap. 8vo. 4s. 6d.

This, it is believed, was probably the first work which drew general attention in this country to the importance and interest of the critical and historical study of English. It still retains its place as one of the most successful if not the only exponent of those aspects of Words of which it treats. The subjects of the several Lectures are—I. "Introductory." II. "On the Poetry of Words." III. "On the Morality of Words." IV. "On the History of Words." V. "On the Rise of New Words." VI. "On the Distinction of Words." VII. "The Schoolmaster's Use of Words."

Trench (R. C.)—*continued.*

ENGLISH PAST AND PRESENT. Eighth Edition, revised and improved. Fcap. 8vo. 4s. 6d.

> This is a series of eight Lectures, in the first of which Archbishop Trench considers the English language as it now is, decomposes some specimens of it, and thus discovers of what elements it is compact. In the second Lecture he considers what the language might have been if the Norman Conquest had never taken place. In the following six Lectures he institutes from various points of view a comparison between the present language and the past, points out gains which it has made, losses which it has endured, and generally calls attention to some of the more important changes through which it has passed, or is at present passing.

A SELECT GLOSSARY OF ENGLISH WORDS USED FORMERLY IN SENSES DIFFERENT FROM THEIR PRESENT. Fourth Edition, Enlarged. Fcap. 8vo. 4s.

> This alphabetically arranged Glossary contains many of the most important of those English words which in the course of time have gradually changed their meanings. The author's object is to point out some of these changes, to suggest how many more there may be, to show how slight and subtle, while, yet most real, these changes have often been, to trace here and there the progressive steps by which the old meaning has been put off and the new put on—the exact road which a word has travelled. The author thus hopes to render some assistance to those who regard this as a serviceable discipline in the training of their own minds or the minds of others. Although the book is in the form of a Glossary, it will be found as interesting as a series of brief well-told biographies.

ON SOME DEFICIENCIES IN OUR ENGLISH DICTIONARIES: Being the substance of Two Papers read before the Philological Society. Second Edition, revised and enlarged. 8vo. 3s.

Wood.—Works by H. T. W. WOOD, B.A., Clare College, Cambridge:—

THE RECIPROCAL INFLUENCE OF ENGLISH AND FRENCH LITERATURE IN THE EIGHTEENTH CENTURY. Crown 8vo. 2s. 6d.

Trench (R. C.)—continued.

CHANGES IN THE ENGLISH LANGUAGE BETWEEN THE PUBLICATION OF WICLIF'S BIBLE AND THAT OF THE AUTHORIZED VERSION; A.D. 1400 to A.D. 1600. Crown 8vo. 2s. 6d.

This Essay gained the Le Bas Prize for the year 1870. Beside the Introductory Section explaining the aim and scope of the Essay, there are other three Sections and three Appendices. Section II. treats of "English before Chaucer." III. "Chaucer to Caxton." IV. "From Caxton to the Authorized Version."—Appendix: I. "Table of English Literature," A.D. 1300—A.D. 1611. II. "Early English Bible." III. "Inflexional Changes of the Verb." This will be found a most valuable help to the study of our language during the period embraced in the Essay. "As we go with him," the ATHENÆUM *says, "we learn something new at every step."*

Yonge.—HISTORY OF CHRISTIAN NAMES. By CHARLOTTE M. YONGE, Author of "The Heir of Redclyffe." Two Vols. Crown 8vo. 1l. 1s.

*Miss Yonge's work is acknowledged to be the authority on the interesting subject of which it treats. Until she wrote on the subject, the history of names—especially Christian Names—as distinguished from Surnames—had been but little examined; why one should be popular and another forgotten—why one should flourish throughout Europe, another in one country alone, another around some petty district. In each case she has tried to find out whence the name came, whether it had a patron, and whether the patron took it from the myths or heroes of his own country, or from the meaning of the words. She has then tried to classify the names, as to treat them merely alphabetically would destroy all their interest and connexion. They are classified first by language, beginning with Hebrew and coming down through Greek and Latin to Celtic, Teutonic, Slavonic, and other sources, ancient and modern; then by meaning or spirit. "An almost exhaustive treatment of the subject . . . The painstaking toil of a thoughtful and cultured mind on a most interesting theme."—*LONDON QUARTERLY.

R. CLAY, SONS, AND TAYLOR, PRINTERS, LONDON.

www.ingramcontent.com/pod-product-compliance
Lightning Source LLC
Chambersburg PA
CBHW080416230426
43662CB00015B/2123